Romanian Literature as World Literature

Literatures as World Literature

Literatures as World Literature takes a novel approach to world literature by analyzing specific constellations—according to language, nation, form, or theme—of literary texts and authors in their world-literary dimensions. World literature has been mapped and theorized in the abstract, but the majority of critical work, the filling in of what has been traced, lies ahead of us. *Literatures as World Literature* begins the task of filling in the devilish details by allowing scholars to move outward from their own area of specialization. The hope is to foster scholarly writing that approaches more closely the polyphonic, multiperspectival nature of the world literature we wish to explore.

Series Editor:
Thomas O. Beebee

Editorial Board:
Eduardo Coutinho, Federal University of Rio de Janeiro, Brazil
Hsinya Huang, National Sun-yat Sen University, Taiwan
Meg Samuelson, University of Cape Town, South Africa
Ken Seigneurie, Simon Fraser University, Canada
Mads Rosendahl Thomsen, Aarhus University, Denmark

Volumes in the Series

German Literature as World Literature
Edited by Thomas O. Beebee

Roberto Bolaño as World Literature
Edited by Nicholas Birns and Juan E. De Castro

Crime Fiction as World Literature
Edited by David Damrosch, Theo D'haen, and Louise Nilsson

Danish Literature as World Literature
Edited by Dan Ringgaard and Mads Rosendahl Thomsen

From Paris to Tlön: Surrealism as World Literature
By Delia Ungureanu

American Literature as World Literature
Edited by Jeffrey R. Di Leo

Romanian Literature as World Literature
Edited by Mircea Martin, Christian Moraru, and Andrei Terian

Brazilian Literature as World Literature (forthcoming)
By Eduardo F. Coutinho

Modern Indian Literature as World Literature (forthcoming)
By Bhavya Tiwari

Romanian Literature as World Literature

Edited by
Mircea Martin, Christian Moraru, and Andrei Terian

BLOOMSBURY ACADEMIC
NEW YORK • LONDON • OXFORD • NEW DELHI • SYDNEY

BLOOMSBURY ACADEMIC
Bloomsbury Publishing Inc
1385 Broadway, New York, NY 10018, USA
50 Bedford Square, London, WC1B 3DP, UK

BLOOMSBURY, BLOOMSBURY ACADEMIC and the Diana logo
are trademarks of Bloomsbury Publishing Plc

First published 2018
Paperback edition first published 2019

Cover design: Simon Levy

Library of Congress Cataloging-in-Publication Data
Names: Martin, Mircea, 1940- editor. | Moraru, Christian editor. | Terian,
Andrei, 1979- editor.
Title: Romanian literature as world literature / edited by Mircea Martin,
Christian Moraru, and Andrei Terian.
Description: New York : Bloomsbury Academic, 2017. | Series: Literatures as
world literature | Includes bibliographical references and index.
Identifiers: LCCN 2017025596 (print) | LCCN 2017039206 (ebook) |
ISBN 9781501327926 (ePub) | ISBN 9781501327933 (ePDF) | ISBN 9781501327919
(hardcover : alk. paper)
Subjects: LCSH: Romanian literature–Appreciation. | Romanian
literature–20th century–History and criticism.
Classification: LCC PC808 (ebook) | LCC PC808 .R58 2017 (print) | DDC 859/.09–dc23
LC record available at https://lccn.loc.gov/2017025596

ISBN: HB: 978-1-5013-2791-9
PB: 978-1-5013-5464-9
ePDF: 978-1-5013-2793-3
eBook: 978-1-5013-2792-6

Series: Literatures as World Literature

Typeset by Integra Software Services Pvt. Ltd.

To find out more about our authors and books visit
www.bloomsbury.com and sign up for our newsletters.

More than just an annex of cultural discourse, the question of identity fashions this discourse effectively ... Therefore, an adequate analysis of East European cultures should look into how the rhetoric of nationhood has infiltrated our time's concepts and paradigms. Romanian literary history ... teems with projects and vocabularies that cover up their substantial identitarian payload even though they have been developed in the field of literary ideas and claim, more often than not, to work on behalf of literary "universalization." ... An archaeology of national allegory likely to uncover and debunk the identitarian messages implicit in East and Central European literatures would have less to do with an ethical indictment of nationalism and more with an epistemological intervention meant to make clear how emerging literatures' values come about and relate to each other within various hierarchies, as well as how, similarly, certain terms and paradigms make a stronger impact than other concepts and cultural models. This kind of archaeology would go a long way toward helping us locate those literatures on the map of international values more accurately.

—Alex Goldiş, "'Alegoria naţională' în discursul identitar românesc"
("'National Allegory' in Romanian Identitarian Discourse")

Contents

Contributors

Imre József Balázs is an associate professor in the Department of Hungarian Literature of Babeş-Bolyai University of Cluj-Napoca, Romania, and editor of the Hungarian-language *Korunk* monthly. His primary research interests cover post-1900 Hungarian literature, intercultural communication in modern Transylvanian literatures, minority cultures, the avant-garde, and Socialist Realism. He is a member of the European Network for Avant-Garde and Modernism Studies. In 2006, he was awarded the Arany János Prize for Young Scholars by the Hungarian Academy of Sciences. His major publications include *The Avant-Garde in Transylvanian Hungarian Literature* (2006; Romanian translation, 2009), *The Avant-Garde and Representations of Communism in Hungarian Literature from Romania* (2009), and *The New Center: Tendencies in Contemporary Literature* (2012). He is currently completing a book on the international networks of Surrealism.[1]

Paul Cernat is an associate professor of Romanian literature in the Department of Literary Studies of University of Bucharest's Faculty of Letters. His research focuses on nineteenth- and twentieth-century literature, intellectual history, cultural studies and theory, and the relationships between literature and ideology. Besides numerous book reviews, articles, and collaborative volumes on modern literature and culture, he has published monographs such as Contimporanul: *A History of a Romanian Avant-Garde Magazine* (2007), *The Romanian Avant-Garde and the Peripheral Complex: The First "Wave"* (2007), and *Retromodernism in the Romanian Novel between World War I and World War II* (2009). He is at work on a book on radical modern culture and the young Romanian generation of writers and thinkers of the 1930s.

Bogdan Creţu is an associate professor of Romanian literature at Alexandru Ioan Cuza University of Iaşi, Romania, and Director of the Alexandru Philippide Romanian Philology Institute of the Romanian Academy. His scholarly interests are eighteenth- and nineteenth-century Romanian literature, the history of modern literary criticism, autobiographical writing, and contemporary Romanian literature. His books include *The Negative Utopia in Romanian Literature* (2008) and the two-volume *The Unicorn at the Eastern World's Gates: D. Cantemir's Bestiary—A Comparative Study* (2013), for which he received the Romanian Academy's "Titu Maiorescu" Prize for Literary Criticism.

Mircea A. Diaconu is a professor of Romanian literature in the Department of Romanian Language and Literature and Communication Sciences of Ştefan cel Mare University of Suceava, Romania. He has worked on the literature from the historical province of Bukovina between the First and the Second World Wars, as well as on modern and postmodern poetry. He is the author of *The Poetry of the Gândirea Group* (1997), *The Life and Works of Mircea Streinul* (1998), *The Iconar Movement: Literature and Politics in 1930s Bukovina* (1999), *The Faces of Poetry* (1999), *Cezar Baltag: A Monograph* (2000), *Ion Creangă: Non-Conformism and Frivolity* (2001), *South of God: Exercises of Lucidity* (2005), *Poetry Workshops* (2005), *Calistrat Hogaș: A Monograph* (2007), *Who's Afraid of Emil Cioran?* (2008), *I. L. Caragiale: Ironic Fatalism* (2011), and *Post-World War II Romanian Poetry: Poetic Experiments and Lives* (2016).

Caius Dobrescu is a professor of literary and cultural theory in University of Bucharest's Department of Literary Studies. He is a comparatist whose scholarship focuses on the development of the literary, social, and political imagination in the late global era and on literature's complex involvement in radicalism and counterculture in Western and Eastern Europe. He has contributed articles to journals such as *East European Politics and Societies, The Information Society, Journal of Global Initiatives, CLCWeb,* and *East-Central Europe.* He is the author of *The Radial Revolution* (2008) and *The Pleasure of Thinking: Romanian Literary Criticism between 1960 and 1989 and Its Intellectual Legacy—An Identitarian Scene on the Global Stage of Critical Culture* (2013), among other books. His current teaching and research explore the connections among literature, terrorism, secularization, and cultural tourism.

Teodora Dumitru has earned her PhD from University of Bucharest and is a senior researcher with the G. Călinescu Institute of Literary History and Theory of the Romanian Academy. Her work focuses on the relationships among literary criticism, theory, and science in the post-1900 period, as well as on literary epistemology, modernity and modernism, and postmodernism. Her publications include books such as *The Evolutionary Syndrome* (2013), *Literary and Political Modernity in Eugen Lovinescu* (2016), and *The Web of Modernities: Paul de Man—Matei Călinescu—Antoine Compagnon* (2016).

Alex Goldiș is an assistant professor in the Department of Romanian Literature and Literary Theory of Babeș-Bolyai University of Cluj-Napoca, Romania, and an associate researcher with Lucian Blaga University of Sibiu, Romania. His work deals mostly with twentieth- and twenty-first-century Romanian literature, the digital humanities, and quantitative cultural history. His articles have appeared in journals and essay collections published in Romania, Spain, Slovakia, and the Czech Republic. He is the author of two monographs: *The Entrenchments of Literary Criticism: From Socialist Realism to Aesthetic Autonomy* (2011) and *Methodological Updates in the Romanian Criticism of the 1970s and 1980s: Theories, Methods, Critics* (2012).

Mihai Iovănel earned his PhD from University of Bucharest and is currently a senior researcher with the G. Călinescu Institute of Literary History and Theory of the Romanian Academy. He has contributed a large number of entries to the seven-volume *General Dictionary of Romanian Literature* (2004–2009) and is one of the editors of the two-volume *Dictionary of Romanian Literature* (2012). He has also co-authored the ten-volume *Chronology of Romanian Literary Life: 1944–1964* (2010–2013) and is the author of two books of criticism: *The Improbable Jew—Mihail Sebastian: An Ideological Monograph* (2012) and *The Detective Novel* (2015).

Mircea Martin is a prominent figure of post–Second World War East European literary criticism, theory, and comparative studies. Loosely associated with the Geneva school of phenomenological literary analysis, he has taught for half a century in University of Bucharest's Department of Literary Studies and is currently professor emeritus. A corresponding member of the Romanian Academy, he is also Editor-in-Chief of *Euresis: Romanian Journal of Literary and Cultural Studies* and President of the Romanian Association of General and Comparative Literature. He has done extensive research in fields such as literary theory—particularly on the Geneva and Yale schools—history of Romanian cultural ideologies, and twentieth-century Romanian and European literatures. He has published numerous volumes and hundreds of articles in Romanian, French, and English. His latest books include monographs such as *Geometry and Finesse* (2004) and *Radicalism and Nuance* (2015), as well as the edited collections *Exploring the Past and the Present of Romanian Literary Theory* (2006) and *Universitas: Once upon a Time, There Was a Literary Circle …* (2008).

Doris Mironescu is an associate professor in the Department of Romanian Studies, Journalism, Communication Sciences, and Comparative Literature of Alexandru Ioan Cuza University of Iași, and a researcher with the Alexandru Philippide Institute of the Romanian Academy. His scholarship has focused on modern Romanian literature, nineteenth-century nationalism, life writing, the avant-garde, and contemporary Romanian poetry and fiction. In 2011, he published *Life of M. Blecher: Against Biography* (2011), for which he received the Romanian Academy's "Titu Maiorescu" Prize for Literary Criticism. He is currently preparing a critical edition of Max Blecher's works.

Ovidiu Morar is an associate professor in the Department of Romanian Language and Literature and Communication Sciences at Ştefan cel Mare University of Suceava. His interests include literary theory, modern poetry, the avant-garde, and Jewish literature. He is the author of monographs such as *Avatars of Romanian Surrealism* (2003), *The Romanian Avant-Garde* (2005), *Jewish Writers from Romania* (2005, 2nd ed., 2014), *Romanian Surrealism* (2014), and *Literature in the Service of the Revolution* (2016).

Christian Moraru is Class of 1949 Distinguished Professor in the Humanities and Professor of English at University of North Carolina, Greensboro. He specializes in contemporary American fiction, critical theory, as well as comparative literature with emphasis on history of ideas, postmodernism, and the relations between globalism and culture. He is the author and editor of a number of books. His recent publications are the monographs *Cosmodernism: American Narrative, Late Globalization, and the New Cultural Imaginary* (University of Michigan Press, 2011) and *Reading for the*

Planet: Toward a Geomethodology (University of Michigan Press, 2015) and essay collections such as *Postcommunism, Postmodernism, and the Global Imagination* (Columbia University Press/EEM Series, 2009) and *The Planetary Turn: Relationality and Geoaesthetics in the Twenty-First Century* (Northwestern University Press, 2015, with Amy J. Elias).

Carmen Muşat is a professor of literary theory and cultural studies in University of Bucharest's Department of Literary Studies. Her primary research areas are the interplay of literature and culture, modernism, postmodernism, narrative, intellectual history, and critical and political theory. She has authored several books, including *The Romanian Novel between the Two World Wars* (2nd ed., 2004) and *Strategies of Subversion: Description and Narrative in Postmodern Romanian Fiction* (2002). She is the Editor-in-Chief of the most influential literary-cultural magazine of postcommunist Romania, *Observator cultural*. She is currently at work on a book-length study of the literature of waiting and expectation.

Bogdan Ştefănescu is a professor in the English Department of University of Bucharest's Faculty of Foreign Languages and Literatures. His teaching covers British literature, critical theory, the rhetoric of nationalism, and the comparative study of postcolonialism and postcommunism. His latest books are *Postcommunism/ Postcolonialism: Siblings of Subalternity* (2012) and *Romanticism between Forma Mentis and Historical Profile* (2013). He has coauthored *Postcolonialism/Postcommunism: Dictionary of Key Cultural Terms* (2011) and coedited *Postcolonialism/Postcommunism: Intersections and Overlaps* (2011). He has contributed articles and book reviews to *Slavic and East European Journal, The Literary Encyclopedia, The James Joyce Literary Supplement, The Bloomsbury Review, Krytyka, Miscellanea Posttotaliariana Wratislaviensia* and chapters to collective volumes that have appeared in various countries. His translations, mostly from Romanian into English, have appeared in fifteen books published in Romania and the United States. A founding member of the Romanian Society for British and American Studies, he has served as Associate Director of the Romanian Cultural Institute in New York. He is currently Associate Dean of the Faculty of Foreign Languages and Literatures of the University of Bucharest and Editor-in-Chief of *University of Bucharest Review*.

Andrei Terian is Dean of Faculty of Letters and Arts and a professor of Romanian literature in the Department of Romance Studies of Lucian Blaga University of Sibiu. He is also a senior researcher with the G. Călinescu Institute of Literary History and Theory of the Romanian Academy. His specialties are twentieth- and twenty-first-century Romanian literature, cultural theory, the history of modern criticism, and comparative and world literature. He has published numerous essays in Romania and in international journals such as *Slovo, CLCWeb—Comparative Literature and Culture, World Literature Studies, Interlitteraria, ALEA: Estudos Neolatinos, Primerjalna književnost,* and *Transilvania*. His latest books include the monographs *G. Călinescu:*

The Fifth Essence (2009) and *Exporting Criticism: Theories, Contexts, Ideologies* (2013), as well as the coauthored reference series *General Dictionary of Romanian Literature* (7 volumes, 2004–2009) and *Chronology of Romanian Literary Life: 1944–1964* (10 volumes, 2010–2013).

Mihaela Ursa is an associate professor in the Comparative Literature Department of the Faculty of Letters of Babeş-Bolyai University of Cluj-Napoca. She has published widely in comparative literature, critical theory, gender studies, as well as on the erotic imagination and on fictionality and the problematics of authorship. She is the author of hundreds of articles and reviews, of several pieces in essay collections, and of award-wining books such as *The "Eighties" Movement and Postmodernism's Promises* (1999), *Gheorghe Crăciun: A Monograph* (2000), *Scriptopia, or the Fictionalization of the Authorial Subject in Theoretical Discourse* (2nd ed., 2010), *Eroticon: On a Lover's Fiction* (2012), and *Identity and Excentricity: Romanian Comparatism between Local Specificity and Globalization* (2013).

Notes

1   All titles of works by our contributors in languages other than English are given in translation.

Preface and Acknowledgments

Is Romanian literature a world literature? Are all literatures world literatures? Directly and indirectly, these are the pivotal twin questions our book is asking throughout. As the reader will discover, they are part of a whole range of concerns, conundrums, and interrogations that apply, today more than ever, to Romanian and, we argue, to *all* other literatures as well. We recognize that only some of these problems can be addressed comprehensively in these essays. We acknowledge, too, that many of these matters are thorny, contentious, and likely to remain so. In fact, the questions above are particularly loaded. They raise additional issues such as the nature of the world itself, of being of, in, and for it, of taking it in and of being present in it in *certain ways* that render literatures such as Romanian—entirely or in some of their authors or works— no less "worldly," of the world, than presumably "major" literatures such as French or British.

We do answer, then, the two questions in affirmative, with the proviso that we have italicized the phrase in the previous sentence advisedly. For, in the twenty-first century, the ways in which a literature participates in, and actually fosters, a world and acquires a presence and stature in it are no longer a foregone conclusion, a given, or a function of that literature's historically privileged or underprivileged position in a hierarchically organized and economically-politically constituted literary world-system. Loose as it may be, the system does exist. We do attend to it extensively and in a fashion implying a certain take on the system's workings. But we think we have reached a moment in the history of the world, world literature, and literary criticism where the case for the place, value, and interpretation traditionally assigned to various aspects and segments of world literary practices in the world *qua* world can be remade, whether we talk about individual writers or about a set of works, styles, genres, movements, or literary units known as "national"—be they Romanian, German, or U.S.

In what follows, we propose one way of making this case for Romanian literature and one way of mapping Romanian literature so as to enter our case persuasively. This is not another history of the country's literature even though our contributors have a lot to say about the urgency of rethinking the discipline. Instead, we take an inevitably selective look at the geo-historically constituted Romanian literary network and at the forms, venues, and connecting mechanisms in and through which Romanian texts come along and function as literary and cultural crossroads, relays, and hubs of aesthetic production, reproduction, and innovation while linking up with world "centers" of creativity. To that effect, we work, indeed, our way to the world of literatures "outwards," from specific Romanian literary-cultural examples, sites, and phenomena. We do so not only to align ourselves with the profile of Bloomsbury's "Literature as World Literature" series but also because this is how the Romanian writers themselves discussed in our collection operate. Furthermore, we have decided that our critical procedure should be apposite to its object. With that in mind, while our contributors theorize their interventions rigorously, they make a point of engaging concretely with material and contexts that go beyond a few exemplars—the usual suspects or "exceptional personalities" of Romanian cultural history. As the reader will also notice, these high-profile, internationally established figures have not been ignored either. But, generally speaking, the overall procedure and the critical-theoretical manifesto of sorts embedded in our project are *anti-exceptionalist*: much like we are weary of the a priori "centrality" of certain literatures and cultural models, we decline to trace Romanian literature's world itineraries by hopping from one isolated literary "peak" to another. Instead, the map we are drawing affords travels and explorations across richer, genuinely relational topographies complete with their transnational webs, routes, interchanges, and affiliating processes that give, we think, a better sense of how writers, works, styles, trends, movements, and formal-cultural categories can be said to be in, and to make, the world.

There is another map unfolding underneath all the others in *Romanian Literature as World Literature* and without which this book would not exist. Palimpsest-like, this map is less visible. It is our great pleasure here to peel off the rest and bring to light, albeit imperfectly, this hidden map, this thick latticework of inter-institutional and transatlantic fellowship, cooperation, exchanges, shared readings and writings, generous sponsorships, encouragement, and sheer hard work that, together, have made this book possible. We want to recognize first, at Bloomsbury, Senior Publisher David Avital, who first encouraged us to pursue our undertaking, and Editorial Director Haaris Naqvi, whose expert guidance and patience have been superb. Editorial Assistant Katherine De Chant has been very effective and uniquely responsive. We want to thank our colleagues from marketing and production, as well as to Bloomsbury's anonymous outside readers of our manuscript. We are also very grateful to distinguished Germanist, comparatist, and World Literature theorist Thomas Oliver Beebee, the Series Editor, whose interest in the book and generosity have been crucial and unflagging throughout.

This work was also supported by a grant awarded by the Romanian National Council of Research (CNCS—UEFISCDI, project PN-II-RU-TE-2012-3-0411). Logistically, institutionally, and otherwise, our endeavors can be described, to a significant degree, as a collaboration between University of North Carolina, Greensboro, and Romania's Lucian Blaga University and University of Bucharest, an undertaking that bears witness to these institutions' visions of the fast-globalizing international world, its themes and problems, and the need to tackle them by working together. The CNCS grant also provided funding for the "Romanian Literature, Literature of the World" symposium organized up in the Carpathians at Păltiniș, outside Sibiu, between September 17 and 19, 2015, which set the stage for all the work leading to *Romanian Literature as World Literature*. We also thank the LBUS Rector, Professor Ioan Bondrea, for his support of the Păltiniș project. Eleven out of our book's fifteen essays were initially presentations delivered at this gathering. UNCG has contributed mostly at the manuscript stage. Besides one of the book editors, the UNCG team included Laura Savu Walker of Columbia College, SC, an alumna of UNCG's English PhD program, and Beth Miller, who is completing her PhD degree in UNCG's Department of English. Savu Walker has been our associate editor, and she has put together the bibliography as well. Miller has served as our associate copyeditor. She is also the author of the Index. Initial translations of the Romanian texts submitted to our collection were done by Eva-Nicoleta Burduşel, Monica Cojocaru, and Andreea Teodorescu (all from LBUS), for Andrei Terian's essay; Florin Leonte, with the author, for Bogdan Creţu's contribution; Nicoleta-Loredana Moroşan (for Mircea A. Diaconu's piece); Adriana Copaciu (for Imre József Balázs's text); Alistair Ian Blyth (for the essay by Carmen Muşat); Carmen Borbély (for Paul Cernat's contribution). The Romanian originals provided by Ovidiu Morar, Mihai Iovănel, Mircea Martin, and Teodora Dumitru have been translated into English by Laura Savu Walker. The rest of the contributors have supplied material written in English. Along with all translations, the latter has been thoroughly revised, edited, and formatted by the UNCG team.

Christian Moraru would like to recognize the following institutions, programs, and individuals who have provided funding, guidance, and other forms of assistance: UNCG's Class of 1949 Distinguished Professor in the Humanities Endowment; the Fulbright Foreign Scholarship Board for a 2015 grant; the Alexander von Humboldt Foundation for a 2016 fellowship at Freiburg University, Germany; at UNCG, Chancellor Franklin D. Gilliam, Jr., and Provost Dana Dunn, for their enthusiastic support of advanced research bringing faculty and students, UNCG and the world together; the University for a Summer 2016 Faculty First Fellowship, as well as for a 2017 publication subsidy that has helped defray costs associated with the production of this volume; the College of Arts and Sciences for travel grants awarded by former and current Deans, Timothy Johnston and John Z. Kiss, respectively; UNCG's Atlantic World Research Network and its Director, Professor Christopher Hodgkins; UNCG's Office of Research and Economic Development and its Vice Chancellor, Dr. Terri L. Shelton, for much-needed funding throughout; UNCG's International Programs Center, for several recent travel awards, and the University's Walter Clinton Jackson Library staff for all their amazing work; the UNCG English Department's Head, Professor Scott Romine, for his unparalleled leadership, and the entire English faculty, for their collegiality. Gratefully acknowledged is also the support, kindness, and friendship of the following individuals: Henry Sussman, Wai Chee Dimock, Marjorie Perloff, David Cowart, Brian McHale, Ursula Heise, Paul Maltby, Bertrand Westphal, Sean Cotter, Andrei Codrescu, Mircea Cărtărescu, Jerome Klinkowitz, John Frow, Vincent B. Leitch, Zahi Zalloua, Nicole Simek, Keith Cushman, Karen Kilcup, Stephen Yarbrough, Monika Fludernik, Jan Alber, Jean-Michel Rabaté, Marcel Cornis-Pope, Ştefan Borbely, Corin Braga, Adrian Lăcătuş, Iulian Boldea, Alexandra Mitrea, and Radu Ţurcanu. Jeffrey R. Di Leo, distinguished theorist, critic, and editor of *American Literature as World Literatures*, has been of great help. Camelia has done her vitally important part, too, now as ever.

Romanian Literature as World Literature features only original work. Also, we would like to thank Mircea Cărtărescu, Marius Ianuş, and Florin Iaru for allowing Teodora Dumitru to quote from their poems in her essay. We are grateful to Ştefania Coşovei as well, for giving Dumitru permission to reproduce, in the same text, fragments of poems by Traian T. Coşovei, to Adrian George Sahlean for letting Andrie Terian use two stanzas of the English version of Mihai Eminescu's poem "Luceafărul" included in *Poezii alese-Selected Poems* (translation by Adrian George Sahlean [Bucharest: Univers, 2000, 55–95]), and to Andrei Codrescu for permitting Doris Mironescu to cite in his contribution eleven lines from the poem "Not a Pot to Piss In."

The Editors

Introduction:
The Worlds of Romanian Literature and the Geopolitics of Reading

Christian Moraru and Andrei Terian

Since "visual aids" rarely hurt a critical argument, we considered initially annexing an illustration, perhaps even a poster of sorts to an earlier draft of this introduction. We did, actually, toy for a while with the idea of using Diego Rivera's 1938 homonymous homage to André Breton's *Les vases communicants*. Then, we discussed putting together something similar to Kurt Schwitters and Theo van Doesburg's 1922 *Kleine Dada Soirée*.[1] Like the famous print, ours, we imagined, would be largely a textual collage and a multiply suggestive one at that. For not only does our essay collection dwell on the collage and collision of words and worlds, on the contaminating juxtaposition of literary works and the culture-spawning interfolding of geoaesthetic systems, but it also forefronts this worldedness and its wordings, this world-heavy "intersectionality," as process, location, focus, and method, all in one. That is to say, much like the communicating vessels trope, the multifaceted intersectional epitomizes, we argue, the genesis, positioning, and makeup of national literature, our subject, as well as an apposite way of tackling it. Indeed, alongside the crossroads, the nodal, the interstitial, and other figures in this series and within the more encompassing tropo-topology of world-systemic interconnectedness, networks, webs, and the like, the intersectional allegorizes a host of entwined, parallel, or homologous operations, procedures, techniques, stylistic arrangements, and venues: how national literature, and literature in general, comes about historically; where it lies or, better yet, the kind of physical, political, and emotional geography it *covers*; how it looks and what it is structurally; and how one might read it today so as to do justice to its history, spatiality, circulation, and cultural texture.

To drive home more explicitly this revealing and manifold isomorphism of literature's form, development, environs, and understanding, our poster would scour, we thought, for material recent book and article titles in new world literature and comparative literature studies. We would pick out key terms and phrases, but we would often reproduce whole titles also. Thus, scurrying in all directions, crisscrossing wildly, and forming obscure combinations not unlike on the dust jacket and title pages of Pascale Casanova's English translation of *The World Republic of Letters* would be word chains like "the world republic of letters" itself, then "the space of the world," "what is a world? On world literature as world-making activity," "sense of place and sense of planet," "planetary modernisms," "the planetary turn," "reading for the planet," "the long space," and, befittingly tucked away in a corner, "distant reading." True, our poster would advertise "the global remapping of American literature," "through other continents: American literature across deep time," "thinking literature across continents," "the worlding of American literature," "American literature in the world," and, with a wink at a forthcoming book in the same Bloomsbury series as ours, "American literature as world literature." We would not leave out the July/August 2015 special-focus issue of *American Book Review* entitled "American world literature," either, and we would squeeze in the ever-ominous "writing outside the nation" as well. We would find room also for "Is Australian literature a world literature?," "German literature as world literature," "Comparative Cultural Studies and the new *Weltliteratur*," "où est la littérature mondiale?," "French global: a new approach to literary history," not to mention "modern Britain and world literature." And, finally, uncoiling across the entire poster would be, less distinct in some places and more visible elsewhere, the final subheading of a 2015 article: "Romanian literature of the world."[2]

1. National Literature at the Crossroads

Under these and similar titles, critics such as Wai Chee Dimock, Thomas Oliver Beebee, Ursula K. Heise, Emily Apter, Marcel Cornis-Pope, John Neubauer, Adam Barrows, Amy J. Elias, Franco Moretti, Bruce Robbins, Pheng Cheah, David Damrosch, Caren Irr, Bertrand Westphal, Jérôme David, Paul Giles, Paul Jay, Gayatri Chakravorty Spivak, Eric Hayot, Elke Sturm-Trigonakis, Azade Seyhan, Rebecca L. Walkowitz, Rachel Adams, Susan Stanford Friedman, Peter Hitchcock, Ranjan Ghosh, J. Hillis Miller, and others provide the links of another chain that gets longer every day: they are those who have put out over the past decade or so books and articles that have changed the face of the humanities, of the study of national literatures and cultures in particular. They have reoriented the humanities in and for the post–Cold War-era geocultural landscape, and, even though this effort is at once relatively new and fueled by Johann Wolfgang von Goethe's early-nineteenth-century-*Weltliteratur* pronouncements, its upshots seem to be nothing short of epochal already. Oftentimes *post*national, inevitably *trans*national and therefore comparative one way or the other, these critical and theoretical interventions have brought about what Amy Elias and Christian Moraru have determined as a paradigm "turn."[3] Very basically, this shift has pressured the humanists to see and read *with the world* no matter what and where they are reading. The world-as-world, the world as system, as we say nowadays usually with a nod in the general direction of Immanuel Wallerstein's work, is becoming—has become—a prime *epistemological framework* of literary and cultural analysis. Thinking through the implications of this development for the study of national literatures—of *all* literatures—is, we believe, a pressing task for critics and theorists. In this book, we do our part by pursuing a worldly revisiting of Romanian literature. That is, what we seek to accomplish is a rereading of this literature as world literature. Reaching this goal is premised, with some notable provisos across the collection, on several defining and correlated interpretive routines, theoretical notions, choices, and claims. All of these are comparative in nature, and some of them are inflected politically, ethically, and epistemologically more than others.

To begin with, and to put it as plainly as possible, the body of work under scrutiny in our book is *read as world* and *with the world,* given that, as specified earlier, this reading is predicated on its object's worldedness, on its intersectional position in the network-world. The latter consists in a whole panoply of literary, cultural, and material geophenomena that render what is commonly designated as "Romanian literature" and its historical, national–territorial perimeter sectors of larger systems of sites and junction points where and through which such macrounits (zones, spheres, trans- and intercontinental corridors, global passageways) overlap, link up, run, and mark their presence. This means that this worldedness sometimes plays out as this literature's affiliations—plural, shifting, litigious—with bigger geoaesthetic flows, aggregates, and mentalities: regional systems and "subsystems" such as Eastern Europe and the Balkans, sub- and supranational cosmopolitan movements like the Enlightenment and the avant-garde, ethnolinguistic communalities and communities such as the Romance world, then wider, "Western," or even worldwide circulation of genres, themes, styles, fashions, epistemes. Or, conversely, this implies that worldedness translates into these ensembles' telescoped, scaled down, condensed, or encrypted presence inside the literature's and the country's own idioms, traditions, and space— the small, presumably "peripheral" world of Romania in the bigger world and vice versa, or, more likely, *both at once,* in proportions that fluctuate historically. This copresence of the national and the worldly, their mutual and multilayered imbrication, is the very matrix of intersectionality and, by the same token, an adequate modality of mapping out national identity, its much-debated uniqueness, and literature as a reliable vehicle for this distinctiveness. Make no mistake: while we insist, as we do repeatedly, on the crisis of the nation-state and its analytic paradigm, in no way does dealing with Romanian literature as world literature along these "nodal" lines assume the complete obsolescence or irrelevance, in Romania or elsewhere, of the nation-state, nationhood, national literature, and of their "smaller," precisely circumscribed places and local histories. Furthermore, the previous sentence is not a tactical concession to the recent nationalisms and populisms rearing of late their ugly heads in referenda and Presidential elections on both sides of the Atlantic either. For such developments, which remain anachronistic and hardly indicative of where the world as a whole is going or should be going, speak, we believe, not so much to the meaning of the *national* as to our continuing vulnerability to its visceral *nationalist* rhetoric inside and outside literature. We are, of course, aware of the distinction to be made here, but we do reject a certain simplifying understanding of the former also because the latter has been its rhetorical byproduct. Thus, alongside scholars working in other literatures, "in focusing on world literature as a critique of the nationalist organization of culture in the form of literary studies circumscribed by, and limited to, a nationalist politico-historiographical project," we too refute the "insularism" and "narrow-mindedness" of a project that is *not limited* to literary studies.[4] In this sense, the essays in *Romanian Literature as World Literature* should be read as an argument against today's Brexits as serviceable models or solutions for literature, literary criticism, culture, as well as for the world at large in the twenty-first century.[5] The world genie is out, but then it has been out all along; coaxing it back in the bottle will not work because, as we hope to demonstrate apropos of Romanian literature, there has never been *a* bottle in the first place, but many and interlinked—indeed, a system of communicating vessels. As Cornis-Pope comments on the "multicultural literary history" he has practiced for more than two decades now, the nodal or intercommunicational approach of this kind of undertaking does not "erase ... national histories [but] reconceptualize[s] them."[6]

Nor are we dismissive of individual and collective identities, or of their aspirations to a recognizable, characteristic, often "singular," and at times simply "incommensurable" expression that defies coming to grips with even when it is situated in worldly contexts. It seems to us, though, that we have reached a moment in geopolitical and intellectual history when we need to consider this kind of contextualization as an antidote to the epistemological "tunnel vision" that, as Stephen Greenblatt rightly contends, has made it difficult to get a handle precisely on what and where national literatures and identities and, once more, literature and identity broadly are, how they obtain, what they mean, how they do so, and how they evolve a "profile" susceptible of differentiating them from other literatures and identities entirely or partly.[7] Far from discounting such matters, the systemic, intersectional approach takes them seriously, "for real," because, critically speaking, it is *realistic* about them, about their ontology, about how this comes to be what it is, and about how this becoming is hardly a deployment of stable and cut-and-dried essences, monistic cultural morphologies, one-of-a-kind ethno-racial "character," unwavering teleologies, and other fictions of this sort.

Pushing back against such ideological constructs is the ethical thrust of this epistemological realism's investigative "optics." For, insofar as it accounts for the many worlds woven into the fabric of Romanian literature, our intersectional take on things acknowledges and honors the woof of the geocultural otherness in whose absence that literature would look rather threadbare. On the one hand, this ethics of the critical gaze, this discerning keenness on other places and others' place in the DNAs of national traditions, befits the study of most if not all literatures, and this is one reason our book's audience is by no means limited to specialists in Romanian, Romance, or East European studies. Working from a well-circumscribed corpus outwards, we engage with situations, propose analyses, reach conclusions, and bring forth theorizations of interest to critics, literary historians, and comparatists irrespective of residence and specialty—we challenge our colleagues, in fact, to put to test our hypotheses and findings in their fields, literatures, and contexts; and, in this provocatively metacritical sense too, our inquiry is, as suggested before, deeply world-minded. On the other hand—and with this we get more emphatically into the world-systems politics of our project—our sense is that, in treating national literature as "a particular nodal point"[8] in a larger unit, the intersectional tack stands a good chance to bust wide open the still dominant model of geocultural systems, whose nuanced understanding has been marred by a set of foregone conclusions derived essentially from a rather simplistic view of the cultural mechanics regulating centers and margins, "First," "Second," and "Third Worlds," and so on. In actuality, such a model usually features *one* center (Paris, London, New York, or Moscow) and a host of subordinate entities occupying, according to Casanova, the system's "outlying spaces."[9] The concentric circles on which these spaces are distributed horizontally make up, on the vertical axis of cultural power and symbolic authority, a hierarchy. Inside it, the historical production of "peripheries" boils down to a quasi-mimetic, aesthetically inferior reproduction of the core—hence the kindred *complexes* of "marginality," "provinciality," "backwardness," "derivativeness," "belatedness," and "inferiority" plaguing writers and literary historians who, as Mircea Martin has shown at length, have bought into or rejected this worldview.[10] What critics such as Cornis-Pope and Mario J. Valdés have proposed, though, and what we reiterate here is that a "nodal" epistemology may yield a description that would be not only more plausible but also more ethical and more empowering politically. "The concept of node," Valdés insists, "is a rich metaphorical alternative to the traditional metaphors of organicism ... [the node] is the starting point for multiple derivations; it can also be taken as a point in a network at which the multiple lines of development come together, or, to put it in broader terms, the point that is the hub of the network."[11] We might add that, according to the less "top-down," "centrist," and "organicist" system model underwritten by this epistemology, centers do not melt into thin air. That would be, we believe, wishful thinking. However, as Arjun Appadurai cogently stresses in *Modernity at Large*, there no longer is just one core dispensing culture, fashion, and prestige centrifugally and sanctioning "peripheral" values benevolently, but more[12]—more hubs and nuclei, more numerous, *softer* centers that would be both less aggressively centripetal and world-richer. These are nodal points in geographically and economically less pivotal and correspondingly less marginal locations that inject a multidirectional, multicultural, and pluralist ethos into geocultural systems that have been or have been described as one-dimensional, hegemonic, and where, as a result, traffics of innovation ("progress" issuing out of the center) and catching up ("imitation" of the same central West by the system's Rest) roughly follow parallel one-way streets.

What we witness in "marginocentric" nodes such as Romania's southwestern province of Banat[13] or even in Romania as a whole, then, is not so much a complete collapse of the rigid center–margin (Western–Eastern) binary but its "loosening." In turn, this allows for a stretching out of the cultural-historic fabric that, in a particular knot or node (Banat's main city of Timişoara, Banat itself, or Romania), "blows up" almost photographically and thus brings into view a complexity of texture, shape, and color, a worldedness that, back at the "strong" artistic and academic center (Vienna, Austria, Paris, or France), may be elusive, invisible, and, in extreme situations, inexistent. Bearing out a hypothesis advanced by world-systems scholars from Moretti to Nirvana Tanoukhi, the Romanian case study goes to show that, when reframed intersectionally, as nodal subsystems of a vaster, ever-fluid continuum, so-called "marginal," "minor," or "small" literatures acquire an unforeseen and unorthodox centrality. Counterintuitive because obtaining liminally, on the margins, and contrary to the misconceptions tied into the cliché of "provincialism," this position, we propose, affords some of its writers uniquely perceptive prismatic refractions of the wider world-as-world and these writers' critics insightful problematizations of some of the most defining aspects of world literature as a cultural-aesthetic phenomenon and discipline alike. Needless to say, this is hardly an argument for a Romanian "exceptionalism." But—and quite the opposite—it is one *from* a "marginalism" that we credit, however, with the ability to effectively focalize issues and raise questions pivotal to all literary-cultural systems: discourse, genre, theme, *mode*, and the role of their "deep-time"/"long-space" dissemination in the fostering and modernization of traditions all over the world; cultural movements such as Romanticism, Symbolism, and modernism, and their travel routes, expansion, and morphing across systems; the very problem of timelines, periodizations, categories, and designations (such as the "isms" listed above) in use, their Western-Eurocentric genealogies, and the applicability of this loaded nomenclature in "world" contexts today; the genetic *and* pluralizing function of the dynamic of land, language, and citizenship in the building up, refinement, and diversification of a certain national literary patrimony; ethnicities, minorities, minor languages and literatures, plurilingualism, diasporas, and the national–regional and world stages on which they assert themselves according to historically shifting scripts of birthplace, habitat, border, statality, jurisdiction, and the like; empire, colonization, modernization, and decolonization, old and new; cultural-stylistic mimicry and innovation; migration and translation; nativism and internationalism, isolationism and cosmopolitan resistance to it; national and nationalist allegiances, multiple, intra, extra-, sub- and transnational or transterritorial affiliations of a nation-state's writers, communities, and "provinces"; national membership and "world citizenship"; the "inside"–"outside," "we"–"they," and related dualisms, their "worldly" construction, and the world-intersectional deconstructions warranted by it.

2. Methodological Nationalism and After

Now, if you remember Schwitters and van Doesburg's work, you will probably agree that their "Soirée" would not be very different from ours. This is because, as Casanova's own "poster" clues us in while also deceiving us a little, what with its unmarked radiant globe crossed by word flows hinting at literary meridians and spaces unhindered by political borders and geographical coordinates, two interrelated things become more apparent at the dawn of the twenty-first century than ever before. First, the most defining and recognizable moments, quotations, and passages of various national epics and literary archives are just that: passages, movements, drifts (*dérives*) and derivations, affinities and associations with other textual and thematic networks where the passing, the movement from node A to node B along with whatever compounds this flux along the way are tantamount to and supersede the static and hemmed-in spatiality of traditional literary history. Second but related to this fluid reconceptualization of where and how literature occurs and is, the nation-state, in its possessive and "jealous" territorialism, is less and less—if it ever really was—a sufficient and effective aggregation and analysis unit for this semiotic mobility, that is, for literature's modality of coming along, of being, and of being somewhere, of obtaining in, and of occupying, a space, and of lending itself to critical description as well.

So what we are talking about is a twofold crisis, to which our book reacts in a number of ways. This crisis affects nation-states actually existing in the "real world" but also how we make sense of literature and of culture more broadly, how we place aesthetic production and reception on the map of the world and of the critical mind. But, we submit, like any crises, this one also presents us, and perhaps especially those of us working in self-perceived "minor" or "marginal" literatures, with unprecedented opportunities. Very basically, what we have noticed apropos of the nodal overhaul of traditional supranational systems occurs on the smaller, national scale: the more one opens up the classical—and classically territorialist— nation-state model, that is, the more one decenters it critically and pursues the textual and intertextual trajectories running through its ethnolinguistic and geo-administrative nodes, the more one is forced to reckon with literature's worldly presence, with literatures' and their authors' home in the world, be they presumably "major" or "minor," "central" or "peripheral," "capitalized" or (supposedly) lacking, as Casanova says, "cultural capital." A different currency system and axiological geography, a *counter*geography of alternative assessments and arrangements become possible at this point, a cartographic cure for various misperceptions, presumptions, and anxieties—incidentally, this is not what Casanova orders, for her critical prescription, as has been pointed out, is deceptively national, moreover, a Gallocentric placebo of sorts.

The reader may have also noticed that we are partial to a certain terminology, and that this is quintessentially spatial. That is because space itself, territory, is the key issue here, although time is surely impossible to ignore, as are the intricate and often contradictory and asynchronous histories embedded in territoriality and in its ebbs and flows across the ages. At any rate, what we are primarily talking about is the overhaul of the traditional dynamic of place and culture. More precisely still, at issue is the weakening of the "umbilical cord" between determinate locations, on one side, and, on the other, cultural formations such as discourse, identity, and community, which have been customarily viewed as "stemming," "coming from," and even "limited to" a particular, well-contoured, and largely stable territory whose political, economic, and epistemological sovereignty has been institutionally enforced. Some critics have gone so far as to maintain that holding sway after 1989 is a less bounded model of cultural origination, in which—with a rapidly aging pun—indigenous roots become rerouted first cross-regionally, trans- and intercontinentally, and then globally, and where inherited filiation yields to voluntary affiliation and "vertical" origination to horizontal contagion and dissemination. To be sure, there is little doubt that the path, makeup, functioning, and understanding of the locus-culture nexus have been shifting, faster and faster, across countries, cultures, as well as disciplines, where, consequently, we are running into problems testing the effectiveness of our approaches. But underpinning all this de-linking is the growing decoupling of nation-state territoriality and discourse location—literary discourse in our case—a disjoining complete with various de- and re-territorializations.

Simply put, the spaces of the nation and of literature, with everything they imply, no longer coincide. They never quite did, of course. But it was a top ideological priority throughout modernity to premise critical analysis, literary history, and even cultural studies a bit later on the strategic overlay of nation-states and literatures, chiefly on the overlap of national territoriality *and* national literature, and subsequently of ethnicity or "race," as wrote Romanian literary historian George Călinescu, *and* native statal turf, language *and* soil or land (land as native ground), all of them beholden to the same monist rhetoric of one language, *the* national idiom, which in turn bore out the assumed homogeneity of a single, dominant, and all-defining ethnic group inhabiting one geographically stable homeland. This mythical oneness is in play not only in Călinescu's field-shaping 1941 *History of Romanian Literature from Its Origins to the Present*, which, in its last pages, all but grounds originality in an ethnic essence and this anthropological monolith in "autochtony," in the mystique of ground itself, one whose authenticating authority is hardly available to the "allogeneic" (writers of Greek, Jewish, and other backgrounds). One way or the other, *all* Romanian literary histories and most national literary histories rest, to this very day, on the coterminality of the nation-state and literature, for they all have been harnessed to a vaster, more urgent, and arguably higher-stake enterprise: nation-building, modernity's defining priority. Accordingly, the nation, in its nation-state political embodiment, has been not only the overarching agenda for political leaders but also the master episteme for historians and literary historians in the post-Westphalian era and more markedly so between the 1848 European revolutions and the 1992 breakup of the Soviet Union. Throughout modernity, late colonialism, and the post-imperial epoch, in Europe and all over the world, the study of literature within and without nations' accredited institutions has been authorized by the nation-state because it served as a vehicle for the nation-state's self-founding. For the nation-state founds itself as it puts itself on the map but also as it funds, fashions, and enforces its founding stories, since they fundamentally—"foundamentally," we are tempted to write—narrate and sanction aesthetically its founding, its right to be where it is, and its uniqueness or at least "specificity" of being as it lies where it does. This is the "feedback loop," as Walkowitz has called it, through which the nation-state arises politically *and* narratively, making, narrating, and legitimizing itself into being, à la Bendict Anderson, drawing and policing its borders on the ground and on bookshelves, in scholarship about the life and cultural history inside those borders, all the more so when those borders are under threat.[14] This is, as Martin reminds us, precisely the case of Călinescu's *History*, which, in a gesture comparable to T. S. Eliot's intertextual nostalgia in "The Waste Land," shores the fragments of Romanian literary corpus against the ruins of the territorial body that made Romania into "Greater Romania" after 1918. Quite explicitly, Călinescu's book draws his country's literary map in direct and polemical response to the political map Nazi Germany and the Soviet Union had violently redrawn the year before his book appeared.[15]

Whether or not this context counts as epistemologically extenuating circumstances, it is not the only one of this sort. The disciplinary background should not be overlooked either. Dominant before and after Călinescu, the great tradition of European historiography accounts, at least in part, for the "hysterical" Herderianism of which Călinescu's mystique of oneness is conspicuously redolent. In all fairness, the Romanian critic only ups the ante—dramatically and deliberately so—of an episteme methodically fleshed out by Johann Gottfried von

Herder in his 1774 *This Too a Philosophy of History for the Formation of Humanity.*[16] Herder's book laid down a series of theses and tenets that would be embraced by all nineteenth-century literary historians: the indissoluble connections among language, literature, and nation; each nation's individual identity as materialized in its own national "soul" or "genius"; the importance of culture, of literature in particular, as receptacle and expression of the nation's "spirit"; the paramount role of folk and "old" literature in the articulation and preservation of this national specificity; literary history as a testimony, itself monumental, size- and rhetoric-wise, of this collective, heroic, and "one-of-a-kind" ethno-cultural formation; and literary historians as chroniclers, defenders, and exemplars of the tradition aesthetic and intellectual representations of this uniqueness have forged over the centuries.

Following the Herderian revolution in the understanding and writing of history and despite the incremental strengthening of aesthetic autonomism with and after Romanticism, all nineteenth-century European literary histories had a clearly marked, political and identitarian agenda. They strove, accordingly, to set up or reinforce the one language-one nation-one literature "organic" correspondence as described above, to legitimate claims to national territory, to prove, also by way of literary analysis, the existence and significance, inside that space, of a specificity "typical" of the national spirit and, more generally, to argue, from the latter, for the greatness of their nations. Thus, in the very first pages of his three-volume 1844 *History of French Literature*, Désiré Nisard postulated said correspondence: "Literary history begins," he proclaimed, "with the nation itself, with the language. It ceases only the day the nation is gone, when the nation's language becomes a dead language ... The literary history of France began the day the first word of the French language was written."[17] This post-Herderian, most intimate, originating and originality-begetting equivalence of the nation, language, and literature renders the latter a living archive of national affect, a trustworthy, multi-generational reflection of "the national sentiment." As José Amador de los Rios claimed in his seven-volume *Critical History of Spanish Literature* (1861–1865) two decades later,

> Made out of the most diverse elements, Spanish poetry, although subordinated to a unity concept that characterizes the goal and permanent principle of all its productions, cannot be for us just an object of artistic research. Identified with the national character and sentiment, this poetry stands in close harmony with the customs, beliefs, needs, and the triumphs of the Castilian people: it reveals their joys and sorrows, their happiness and misfortunes. Its wealth, although all-embracing as far as its external forms go, is its own with respect to the ideas that feed it, which ideas are deeply rooted in the hearts of a hundred generations.[18]

For nineteenth-century literary historians, a common language justifies and affords not only a nation and its literature, but also, and no less significantly, a territory organized into a national state. This explains both the critics' reluctance to deal with the various forms of extraterritorial (extra-statal) literatures and their tendency to play down or overlook entirely the diversity of languages and dialects inside national borders. For instance, in the final ("illustrated") version of Gustave Lanson's 1923 two-volume *History of French Literature*, a milestone in European literary historiography, "Occitan poetry," written as it was in *langue d'oc* and on French soil, is treated as a "foreign language literature" and thus simply ignored.[19] Instead, Lanson celebrates the territorial expansionism of the French crown, a process he sees parallel to and bound up with the military encroachments of the French language on neighboring idioms' turfs. "From all sides, on all borders" he comments, "as [French] kings were attaching new territories to their possessions, the French language was also making its conquests, by laying, with varying degrees of success, claims to territories where the language spoken was sometimes Celtic, sometimes German, sometimes Italian, sometimes Basque: from an official and administrative language, French displayed the tendency of becoming everywhere the language of literature and of the educated classes."[20]

Rooted in each other and mutually supportive, language and territory lay the nurturing foundation of the nation-state, which in turn reinforces them not only politically but also culturally, by sponsoring certain ways of understanding their history and material and aesthetic configurations. Literary critics and historians have acknowledged the sponsorship openly, and Călinescu himself is no exception. It is highly instructive that he formulates his acknowledgment in the same sentence in which he avers to be drawing an "unbiased" map of literature. As he writes about his *History* in the transported end of its preface,

> During these times of national suffering, such an unbiased book must reassure everyone that we do have a brilliant literature, which, on the other hand, despite the passing vicissitudes [of history], is produced on the territory of Greater Romania, one and undividable, a literature that serves *as the most accurate map of the Romanian people*. Eminescu in Bukovina, Hașdeu in Bessarabia, Bolintineanu in Macedonia, Slavici on the western border, Coșbuc and Rebreanu around Năsăud, Maiorescu and Goga along the Transylvanian [river] Olt are for us the eternal guardians of our everlasting soil. And now, putting an end to a self-deprecating attitude in which we have indulged for too long, it is time to proudly proclaim, after Miron Costin:
> "GREAT MEN ARE BORN IN MOLDOVA, TOO!"[21] (emphasis added)

The whole *History* is, in fact, a pep talk to a country that, by 1941, had lost more than one-third of its territory to neighboring Hungary, Bulgaria, and the Soviet Union. But the language of the preface as well as of the *History*'s famous coda, "National Specificity," is suffused with the rhetoric of the "vicissitudes" Călinescu deplores. Shot through with fantasies of "racial" purity and indigeneity and apprehensive of aliens' interpolations of the national epos, the book's postscriptum unabashedly predicates literary originality and representativeness on Romanian ethnicity, which is in turn literally territorialized and thus equaled with autochthony.[22] This is not only unfortunate but also ironic, and the irony has been compounded by history. Călinescu presses into service anthropological clichés of immutable racial exceptionalism, explicit or implied ethno-racial superiority, and barely veiled anti-Semitism, all of which were mainstream in National Socialism and would be so again in Romania's Socialist nationalism of the 1980s. By then, his work would become the uncontested gold standard of Romanian criticism. Moreover—and this is the darkest side of his legacy by far—his example would be obsessively invoked by the proponents of so-called "protochronism," a quasi-official, autochtonist, and ethno-supremacist doctrine of Romanian cultural, historical, and territorial "precedences."

Interestingly enough, Călinescu's authority would outlast the Communist regime. Alas, the "vicissitudes" would not go away either. In his 2008 *Critical History of Romanian Literature: Five Centuries of Literature*, Nicolae Manolescu, post–Second World War Romania's most influential critic, sets about a similarly compensatory cartography, and he does so still on behalf of the ever-besieged nation-state. The latter's existence, presumably borne out by its representation in traditional historiography, is now threatened by globalization, to wit, by "Americanization," academic and otherwise, and its fifth columnists. These are the "millennials" (*Generația 2000*) broadly, and, in particular, the critics belonging to this generation, some of whom contribute to *Romanian Literature as World Literature*. Manolescu makes his objectives and targets abundantly clear in his book's "Afterword" and "Epilogue." His enthusiasm for Călinescu's mapping is no less conspicuous. On a tone similar to his master's and also in the final paragraph of his own preface to the *Critical History*, he confesses that

> If, on the other hand, it is true (and how beautifully said by Călinescu in the end of the preface to his *History*) that literature "can serve [sic] as the most accurate map of the Romanian people," then, as far as I am concerned, I am no more than just one cartographer among dozens like me, hardworking and dedicated as I am to the notion that each writer deserves to be judged by his accomplishments, no matter how different his map might be from the *ideal map* literature lovers, in their naïveté, deem possible.[23] (emphasis added)

Like Manolescu's, Călinescu's *is* an "ideal map," not to say an imaginary one. But even a cursory reading of "National Specificity" is bound to show that, ossified and homogenous, more schematic, more overtly "centralized," and more ethnocentric than Manolescu's map, racialist and even racist at times, blatantly essentialist all around, Călinescu's literary-historical atlas is not a disembodied, immaterial ideal, some scheme concocted outside history and politics. Quite the contrary: it is a palpable construct, a philological-ideological assemblage endorsed by a national and, at times, nationalist epistemology.

We have argued on various occasions and repeat here that, as products *of* this endorsement, culture *and* cultural analysis are cover-up operations. As "streamlined" in schools, textbooks, and standard readings, culture in general and national culture in particular conceal, disregard, or short-shrift the many, the others, and the other places, geographies, and itineraries that have gone into the building of the one, of the same, of the "we," of the "here," and ultimately of the nation, complete with its collective mythology, solipsist fantasies, and institutionalized territorialism. Countercultural *because* cross-cultural or culturally intersectional, a reading of national literature with the wider world exposes, first, the compilation itself, the outsourcing of nativist allegories, the heteroclite underbelly of the putatively all-of-a-piece, the palimpsest quality of the nation's textual patrimony; second, the worldliness of the *bricolage*, the nomadic, peripatetic archive fixed into, and temporarily settled as, national literatures; and third, the historically produced and oftentimes epistemologically counterproductive "state-centrism," which, in aggressively territorializing—in limiting to statal territoriality—the genetic-interpretive play and overall domain of literary-cultural and humanistic discourse, jars with actual cross-cultural and cross-territorial scenarios through which this discourse comes into being, evolves, and spreads. As Neil Brenner maintains, the epistemological impasse one faces here has to do with institutions as much as with political cartography and space. "The epistemology of state-centrism," he says, can be understood in terms of a number of several "geographical assumptions," including the postulate "that social relations are organized at a national scale or are undergoing a process of nationalization," which in turn has "generate[d] a *methodical nationalism* in which the national scale is treated as the ontologically primary locus of social relations."[24]

Oddly enough, Brenner does not credit, if not Anthony Giddens and Herminio Martins, then at least Ulrich Beck. Since 2002, the German repeatedly used and refined the "methodological nationalism" concept and its critique, "methodological cosmopolitanism."[25] "Methodological nationalism," Beck expounds,

> assumes that the nation, state and society are the "natural" social and political forms of the modern world. It assumes that humanity is naturally divided into a limited number of nations, which on the inside, organize themselves as nation-states, and on the outside, set boundaries to distinguish themselves from other nation-states. It goes even further: this outer delimitation, as well as the competition between nation-states, presents the most fundamental category of political organization. Indeed, the social science stance is rooted in the concept of the nation-state. It is a nation-state outlook on society and politics, law, justice and history, that governs the sociological imagination.[26]

This outlook, Beck concludes, "prevents the social sciences from understanding and analysing the dynamics of the human condition in the twenty-first century."[27] Even though the state is well and alive rather than a "zombie categor[y]" sociologically speaking, the nation-state as an analysis unit across disciplines and, organized around it, state-backed epistemology have arguably become overbearing in their territorialism and increasingly inadequate as knowledge tools, as Giles, Dimock, Robbins, Spivak, and many others have insisted.[28] Appadurai is convinced, in effect, that nation-states "make sense" only if we think of them as elements of a system.[29] In the same vein, Australian critic Nikos Papastergiadis contends that "[a]rt cannot be explained"—or comprehensively explained any more—"as a social activity that fulfills the stated goals of a national ... agenda" and that "[t]he specific place of art is now increasingly located in networks that are both above and below the reach of the nation-state."[30] Breaking the epistemological mold of methodological nationalism and thus marking, in Romania as well, a new stage in literary and intellectual historiography, young critics such as Caius Dobrescu, Oana Strugaru, Alex Goldiș, Adrian Lăcătuș, Paul Cernat, Teodora Dumitru, Carmen Mușat, Alexandru Matei, Andrei Bodiu, Mihaela Ursa, Crina Bud, Mihai Iovănel, and Andrei Terian canvas more and more systematically these networks and their geoaesthetic nodes. One of Terian's aims in his 2013 book *Exporting Criticism* and elsewhere is, in fact, to set up such supra-, extra-, and transnational sites of expression, commerce, and interchange as foci of a "new history of Romanian literature."[31] After drawing a detailed comparison between Romanian and Western literary historiography, the critic concludes that the lingering allegiance of domestic historiography to the ethno-territorial and nationalist paradigm hinders progress in a discipline largely stuck in nineteenth-century methodologies and ideologies. He argues that a twenty-first-century history of Romanian literature should deal with medieval literature in idioms other than Romanian, with translations, with Romanian literary works produced in the Republic of Moldova, with Romania's "minority" literatures, and with the writings of Romanian exiles and emigrants irrespective of the languages they have used in their new countries.

3. Mind Maps and National Literature as World Eminent Domain: Scale, Territory, and Reading in the Twenty-First Century

The critical imaginary that subtends the endeavors of a growing contingent of Romanian scholars rests on an intersectional knowledge model that cuts across traditionally territorialized—territorially bounded or so pictured—societies and socioformations such as race, ethnicity, class, and so on. For "literature," they realize, is not just "written as a defense of the dignity of the strange," as Julia Kristeva famously suggests.[32] Literature *is* strangeness. It "defamiliarizes" things also, as we know too well. But, to actually do so, its making resorts most fundamentally to a sort of un-making spatially speaking, namely, to what has been called, after Gilles Deleuze and Félix Guattari, de- and re-territorialization. Such territorial dislocations translate the strange, the afar, the "other"—in sum, the world—to and into the throbbing heart of culture, rendering the latter's putatively egocentric, autochthonous hearth a paradoxically yet genetically necessary *allocentric* zone, a geocultural intersectionality.[33] In the process, cultural *poiēsis* denaturalizes the "national" in "national culture" and thereby helps cultural understanding, and ultimately culture itself, shed its national-*étatiste* epistemological straightjacket. Critics keen on this zone disclose culturally "classified" information about the recycled material's worldly provenance or, conversely, about the worldly affiliations of presumably discrete traditions and autonomous identities by laying bare the worldly relationality the cultural imaginary, old and new, threads into descriptions of allegedly self-subsistent entities. What these commentators promote, then, is a reading protocol driven by a posttraditional logic according to which cultural space's nationally legislated ("named") *nomos* is remapped heteronomously. In this space or intersection of spaces, this remapping relies on two intertwined, critical and geopolitical rearrangements.

The first operation has to do with the Ur-category of space itself. It concerns classical statal spatiality, impacting as it does the topocultural and political "centers" of world geography. Typically imagined as (rather than truly instantiating) an "organic" or "vertical" model of growing, such hubs are not surrounded, at least to the degree they used to be, by peripheries, semi-peripheries, circumferences, borders, and other "quilting points" or knots through which centers link up with other centers of power and administration.[34] The center itself now is, as specified above, a "soft" one, a node, and thereby, as Jacques Derrida already theorized it at length in the late 1960s, a collection of quilting points. A "literature for the planet"—that is, not "for the nation" alone—is, as Dimock similarly posits, an "off-center set of vibrations, chaotic and tangential," a field of energies, a flow.[35] The "crisis of territoriality" is thus not solely one of national frontiers, of "political sovereignty" and self-determination understood primarily as "peripheral" issues (pertaining to boundaries, margins, and so forth), but of centers themselves and of their very systems of stabilization, centralization, and control, of *state cultural apparatuses* and their aggressive *overdetermination* of culture's and cultural identity's meanings.[36] This overdetermination works as disguised self-determination or self-referentiality in that, regardless of what these meanings convey, at the end of our reading day they would index one thing: the state. This is because, as critics of methodological nationalism would insist, the state, in its self-perceived, ethno-linguistically, territorially, and institutionally homogenous configuration, has set itself up as the post-Wesphalian era's default aggregation unit and "scalar variety" of aesthetic production and analysis.[37] This arrogance, complete with the cultural-epistemological servitudes required of those buying into its premises, was already evident to Friedrich Nietzsche. In *Untimely Meditations*, he paints a famously disenchanted yet characteristically prescient picture of Western modernity and its fundamental institutions. "We live," writes the philosopher,

> in the age of atoms, of atomistic chaos. In the Middle Ages the hostile forces were held together by the [C]hurch and, through the strong pressure it exerted, to some extent assimilated with one another. When the bond broke, the pressure relaxed, [and] they rebelled against one another. The Reformation declared many things to be *adiaphora*, domains where religion was not to hold sway; this was the price at which it purchased its existence: just as Christianity has already had to pay a similar price in face of the much more religiously inclined world of antiquity. From there on the division spread wider and wider. Nowadays the crudest and most evil forces, the egoism of the money-makers and the military despots, hold sway over almost everything on earth. In the hands of these despots and money-makers, the state certainly makes an attempt to organize everything anew out of itself to bind and constrain all those mutually hostile forces: that is to say, it wants men to render it the same idolatry they formerly rendered the church. With what success? We have still to learn; we are, in any case, even now still in the ice-filled stream of

the Middle-Ages; it has thawed and is rushing on with devastating power. Ice-floe piles on ice-floe, all the banks have been inundated and are in danger of collapse. The revolution is absolutely unavoidable, and it will be the atomistic revolution: but what are the smallest individualistic basic constituents of human society?[38]

What the philosopher critiques here is a certain mental map of the world and the cultural, hermeneutic, and geopolitical imaginary behind it. This critique is as urgent today, after Nietzsche's "atomistic revolutions" have broken out and when, in a sense, they are still ongoing, as it was in 1874. Its main relevance is twofold. On one side, it speaks to the systematic efforts by various geoinstitutional apparatuses of modernity to aggregate the human domain into intelligible and manageable structures. The earlier Church, the Reformed Church after that, what with its partial "withdrawal" from the social, then capital, and, in the late post-Westphalian era, the nation-state have all scrambled, observes Nietzsche, to "organize" the human. Organize: read territorialize. Further, read: shape, contain, rule, and define—de-fine, that is, de-limit and set limits, boundaries, political and intellectual coordinates. This territorialization—which some equal with modernity itself—poses a meaning for something, that is, for human spatiality, for the social, and ultimately for the human itself. This positing implies the rather intellectually impatient decisional violence of paradigm setting: this is *the* model, *the* paradigm for the human; this is what human society and the human mean. On the other side, and thus tying into the second relevance of the passage, what humankind, the social, and the cultural signify—*what* they are—is a function of *where* they are. Here, territorialization gets quite literal. That is to say, *ontology becomes topology*, and topology becomes semiotics, which renders interpretation of a geopositioning protocol in a literal-statal sort of way. In other words, the positing of meaning goes hand in hand with position, with the human's place, which is also paradigmatic; linguistically, ethnically, politically, culturally, and so forth, the human is locational, assumed to play out *within* various "units." It is inside them, we are told, that the human makes sense, can be researched and described—inside them or, more accurately, inside *it*, the nation-state geoapparatus of discourse-making and discourse-processing. In modern history overall and surely in Nietzsche's time, the latest and by far most enduring installment in this hegemonic narrative of political, cultural, and epistemological scalarity has been the nation-state, through which the human, in its cultural expression, and the human world become intelligible to humanists for almost 200 years. One founding assumption of modern Western humanism at least since Julien Benda's *trahison de clercs* antinationalist argument is that one sees culture, and, with it, humankind and the world, through the nation-state—that the intelligibility model of the world is self-evidently and unassailably statal.[39] To go back to Nietzsche's liquid metaphor, culture is presumed to flow "paradigmatically"—and thus to be inevitably streamlined—within the "banks" of the nation-state, to be contained by it, so much so that it cannot but "internalize" the container itself, take it in but also take it up as its content or referent and have national historiography sanction the process in the bargain.

Of course, modern culture has greatly overflown its statal-territorialist riverbanks worldwide. Furthermore, as Romanian political scientist Adrian Florea notes, new data shows that "nonstate territorial units" are more numerous than "sovereign states with often disputed, but fairly stable, borders." Under these circumstances, the "anachronistic view" of "authority" (political, cultural, etc.) "being monopolized by clearly demarcated states that exercise full control over their territory" has become a true "stumbling block" in political science as well as in cultural analysis and other humanities in which epistemological mapping of human expression is still dependent on traditional, state-centered world cartographies.[40] As with the post-Reformation church, whatever spills over, whatever flows or falls outside the nation-state's jurisdiction, risks to be ignored or downgraded culturally, that is, to be treated as less typical, less representative, with paradigmatic condescendence, if you will. To be representative, and therefore canonical, is to be representative *of* certain aggregation units privileged by modernity, of nation-state territorialism first and foremost, and of classical identity formations such as race, ethnicity, and linguistic indigeneity, which have been usually associated with and situated within the master communal framework of the nation-state. What is not "representative" along these lines—the wealth of actual or presumed less "paradigmatic" phenomena we have been missing in our readings— tends to register and have registered much less on our radar screens: in our anthologies, in our sense of history, tradition, community, group membership, and the like. Because of this, a more world-oriented, nodal, and liquid epistemology is prompting us today to view national literature and literature at large as a less compartmental, nationally territorialized reality and more in terms of a world eminent domain of sorts. This shift in perspective would entail reconsidering the "one-on-one correspondence between the geographic and ethno-linguistic origins of a text and its evolving radius of literary action." "We need," as Dimock further argues, "to stop thinking of national literatures as the linguistic equivalents of territorial maps .... [H]andily outliv[ing] the finite scope of the nation, [literature] brings into plays a different set of temporal and spatial coordinates. It urges on us the entire planet as a unit of analysis."[41]

The second geopolitical and geocultural rearrangement promoted by critics indebted to this epistemology speaks to the intellectual energy of the "quilting-point" allocentric model of nodes, nodal cultural spaces, and the currents of culture forming them, transforming them, and sometimes dissolving them and carrying them around. This model does not simply "open up" the local to the global, thereby "resolving," in its "glocalizing" fervor, the local-global (or national-global) aporia, as many critics purport to do by following Roland Robertson's lead.[42] No "glocal" synthesis gels here. Nor should it, because it would still be a recipe for globalist homogeneity and for its implicit universalism. What takes hold instead is, as suggested earlier, a "compression" of the worlding world, which lies curled up inside the local, within which "here" and "there" remain distinct and yet intimately co-present, *with* one another. Detached from themselves in order to reattach themselves to others according to novel, posttraditional and "postethnic" attachments, allegiances, and affiliations, they *are* thus a discontinuity, a self-displaced continuum that exists in a self-other interface mode that neither obscures the other's cultural configuration nor obviates the need, indeed, the duty to figure it out.[43]

Thus reterritorialized as "nested territorial units"[44] of space, culture, and subjectivity—all of them qualified in terms of gender, sexuality, race, ethnicity, class, and faith and, reciprocally, serving themselves as qualifiers of such identitarian parameters—cultural territory calls for a new cultural studies approach attuned to the reciprocal articulations and imbrications of self and other, of the national writ large in the world and of the worldly writ small in the national. For this is what twenty-first-century literary cartographers draw, oftentimes against internationally recognized, mental and territorial delineations of statehood, national borders, and statal sovereignty: a world map tracing the world's mosaic-like flotsam and jetsam of many worlds. Yet again, the greater world nests compacted inside the national and the subnational, inside the allegedly peripheral, anonymous, isolated, and tiny. The map makers take this world apart, look into it, and put it back together into a critical narrative that does not redramatize the global nomos but reveals, under the magnifying glass of critical autopsy—etymologically, "eye-witnessing"— the worldly anatomy of elsewheres, multitudes, habits, and ways. The world of the nation is the world in a nutshell, they argue, as we also do here. To them, as to us, the nation and its idiomatic here and there make, in reality, for a culturally-historically *trivial* site—from the Latin *trivium*, "intersection of three roads" and more generally "crossroads"—a "pointillist" point in space and time where the world's other ways, routes, places, and histories cross, and so concurrently a colorful and pulsing cross-section of everything meeting, touching, classifying, mixing, and passing in and through it. Thus, what obtains is an "endless," non-kind type of "kinship" that is, as Dimock allows, neither fully genetic nor, as we stress, formally mimetic, if by this we mean intentionally (and submissively) reproductive of world-systems' putative centers of political, cultural, and economic power. "The infinite," the critic explains, "is embedded in the [finite], coiled in the former, and can be released only when the former is broken down into fractional units. For it is only when the scale is smaller and the details get finer that previously hidden dimensions can come swirling out." "Scalar opposites," Dimock argues, "here generate a dialectic that makes the global an effect of the grainy," which, we hasten to remark, is what no longer makes the "grainy," the trivial, and the micro a docile repository and mimesis of the global but the fine print in which the inscriptions and prescriptions of uniform globality are unwritten and reinscribed critically.[45] Either "over here" or "over there," the world's own footprint on "local" representations—the flipside of our ecological marks on the planet itself—becomes visible and thus lends itself to reading in those representations' fine print. Usually crystalizing at a deep level, that fine print is couched in the elusive language (allusions, connections, references, parallels, borrowings, puns, and cognate playful associations) where the *relation with the geocultural other*—other texts, histories, places, and people—turns out to be so instrumental to the meaning-making process at the writer's as well as the critic's end.

Because the object of this new geopolitical mapping of national literature is intersectional and unstable in structure, a comparative kind of optics is required. What makes this "looking art" a comparative endeavor is, for one thing, the very makeup of the national. If comparison involves, according to the Latin *comparō*, "placing" the world's pieces "together," then comparatism is an intellectual operation apposite to the nation's and the whole world's coming into being, to the juxtapositions (*comparationes*) the nation's and, on another scale, the world's coming together sets off. Today's critics realize that we are living, inside and outside our countries, in an increasingly "comparative" or "(con-)pairing" world that demands a congruously comparative reading. For another thing, a "comparative" ontology is not one in which said pieces run or flow on or within separate tracks, "riverbeds," etc. The tracks are redirected across other tracks and itineraries of commerce, exchange, influence, and derivation. And so, far from sounding the death knell of a "discipline" (Spivak's comparative studies), the new critical paradigm marks its rebirth. For, to unpack a text's worldliness is to read that text at the, and qua, crossroads, as a bundle of relations with other texts, people, and places.

Not only does the unraveling of this intersectionality come down to a comparative undertaking; it is also a mapping of sorts. Tracing all these relations entails painting a world, doing a geographer's job, uncovering the fluid, supra- and para-statal *continuum* in which literature aggregates. It is topo-poietic; it projects—*makes*—a space. As we have said, this space does not coincide with the physical expanse of the nation; it did not for Călinescu either, but he thought his *History* would convince its readers that, only months before his book's publication, the two were coterminous, and deep down he may have hoped that his work would hold its audience over until they would become so, or at least appear so, again. Further, this space is not set up according to a hierarchy of centers and margins. Nor does it look anything like the territories of those countries that put up walls and fences to keep immigrants, refugees, and other undesirables out. In fact, this space and the literature thriving in it are very much *like* those migrants and refugees, like the shifty and turbulent geography their nomadic lives collectively conjure up, and surely *unlike* the border patrol agents in whose role Călinescu casts his country's writers.[46] With an irony of which the critic does not seem to be aware, he is, at best, right for the wrong reason: these authors matter apropos of the national territory and space generally not because they *protect* already existing borders and the worlds inside them, but, again, because they *project*— because they write the frontiers into being, because they foster them discursively, because, in an important sense, they *invent* them. For this zone, this atypical terrain, is in, and simply is, what the work of late-nineteenth- and early-twentieth-century dramatist and short-fiction author Ion Luca Caragiale does for Bucharest and Berlin, for them together and in transit between them; it is what the same oeuvre does on the world stage, for Paris and its vaudeville tradition, and for a Romantic playwright like Romania's Vasile Alecsandri before them all, through Eugène Ionesco; it is—and it is where—Eastern Romania's small market towns, Bucharest, Zurich, and Paris, and then Romanian, French, German, and Yiddish intersect, courtesy of the European and Romanian–French avant-garde and Surrealism, wave after wave; it is where Bukovina borders on France, Italy, and Germany with Paul Celan and Gregor von Rezzori, and where Romanian writers have already won the Nobel Prize with Elie Wiesel and Herta Müller, before Mircea Cărtărescu or Norman Manea might. It is where the Banat region extends Central Europe eastwards across the Hungarian–Romanian border and where Julian Rubinstein's witty 2004 "docu-novel" *Ballad of the Whiskey Robber: A True Story of Bank Heists, Ice Hockey, Transylvanian Pelt Smuggling, Moonlighting Detectives, and Broken Hearts* tells a story in which Transylvania weaves Hungary and

Romania together inside the same geofictional map. It is where Benjamin Fundoianu is born, and where Benjamin Fondane is murdered in the Holocaust, and in the lives they all spend in between. It is where Max Blecher converses with Franz Kafka and Jonathan Safran Foer via Bruno Schulz. It is where literature is written in Romanian in Romania and by Romanians, but also outside Romania by Romanians in their ethnic diasporas, and outside Romania, or outside today's Romania, by anybody, regardless of ethno-racial origin, in Romanian or in any other language inside past and present frontiers—and pretty much any other combination of these topo-identitarian parameters. It is where E. M. Cioran and Matei Vișniec are when they give up their mother tongue—and where Manea does not—and it runs along the way Marcel Proust and André Gide took to become Camil Petrescu, Anton Holban, and Hortensia Papadat Bengescu. It is where world literature luminaries like Cărtărescu is when he makes us go back to his peers, Thomas Pynchon and Roberto Bolaño.

As the reader with a modicum of knowledge of Romanian literature has noticed, the majority of our references are to modern writers. Likewise, the pieces gathered in *Romanian Literature as World Literature* predominantly cover modern Romanian literature. This should come as little surprise. For one thing, this is what most of our contributors specialize in. For another, there is something to be said about the particular, perhaps paradoxical challenge cultural modernity mounts to contemporary critics and theorists, especially to those advocating, after Greenblatt, an explanatory "return to world literature and, more broadly, to world culture."[47] Where others see a radical and unprecedented "turn," as noted earlier, the Renaissance scholar talks about a comeback. His preference makes sense to the extent that the "vital global cultural discourse" so seminal to the dawn of national literatures is "quite ancient." "[O]nly the increasingly settled and bureaucratized nature of academic institutions in the nineteenth and early twentieth centuries, conjoined with an ugly intensifications of ethnocentrism, racism, and nationalism," the critic maintains, "produced the temporary illusion of sedentary, indigenous literary cultures making sporadic and half-hearted ventures toward the margins. The reality, for most of the past as once again for the present, is more about nomads than natives."[48]

Indeed, at the end of the day, what literature is not nomadic? What literature is not "immigrant"? What literature does not depend on—and sometimes is even "born"—in translation? What literature is not constituted on the go, in a "circulation" that no longer "trails production"? And what literary production is not transcultural and transterritorial? What literature does not "start as world literature"?[49] Having asked these rhetorical questions, it bears acknowledging, however, that what Greenblatt calls, in his "manifesto," "cultural mobility" demonstrably increases its speed and scope, and thus its proportions become truly global, with modernity and chiefly after modernity's aesthetic phase known as modernism. But he is right to observe that, concurrently, and at odds with this worldwide and worldly intersectional trend, modernity's rising nationalism circles the epistemological wagons around national literatures. This move brings about a widening incongruence between the nationally "ingrown" historiographies and their evermore "worlded" object. As in premodern times if not more, these literatures do capture and emulate thematically–formally processes and circuitries of communication, representation, and material–cultural values during the modern epoch as well. It is just that, under the pressure of nationalist ideologies, the discrepancy between object and method deepens in modernity. Closing this epistemological gap by opening up the concentric ramparts of Călinescu's national diagram—and by opening them onto the world—strikes us therefore as a matter of urgency in Romanian criticism as well. Again, as the reader minimally familiar with the history of Romanian letters will recall, ever since their early medieval rebirth more than a millennium after Dacia's Roman colonization, written culture and literature in Romania have been nurtured by and actively participated in regional, trans-regional, and even intercontinental communities, systems, and routes of learning, mentality, discourse, and style. From the religious literature in Old Church Slavonic to Romania's belated Renaissance and its erudite authors such as Dimitrie Cantemir to the thinkers and activists of the early-nineteenth-century Transylvanian School (*Şcoala ardeleană*) to the revolutionaries of the "1848 Generation," who spearheaded modernization in Romanian territories, examples abound. Far less numerous are critical works attuned to them, to their modern avatars, and to their worldly drive. Our book seeks to understand and correct this situation.

4. Romanian Studies for the Twenty-First Century: Method, Structure, Foci

"In the end," writes Terian in the article mentioned earlier, "the thing that has defined world literature since Goethe is the fact that it ceases to be a national asset that needs protection from Others' desires and indiscreet gazes, and turns into a shared asset, available to the whole world .... Therefore, in order to become a true literature *for* the world, Romanian literature should first learn to see itself as a literature *of* the world, as a cultural asset to which all the world's readers and critics, no matter their native culture, have equal ownership rights."[50] The emphasis in Terian's article and in this book as well falls not so much on literature as on its reading. In fact, one core tenet of the essays in *Romanian Literature as World Literature* holds that, in some of its most defining moments and works, this literature has come about by asserting its planetary belonging, its being in the world, for it, and of it.

But this literature's interpretation is another story. This is why our contributors' primary objective is taking steps toward telling this story—the very history of Romanian literature—otherwise. That is, in arguing for a "worlded" Romanian literature or a Romanian literature "of-the-world," our volume advocates, to paraphrase the title of a recent article by Rachel Adams, a cultural-epistemological "worlding of Romanian studies."[51] The perspective shift we propose is one away from the usually unfavorable and superficial juxtapositions allowed for by classical, nationalist, and sometimes imperialist comparatism (reading Romanian literature with other literatures), which keeps the objects of comparison separate and hierarchically organized, to a geo-intersectional analysis that "finds" its object *in* the world and *as* world, part and parcel of a "flat" world ontology of aesthetic objects and events. Keyed to recent developments in domestic and international criticism and theory, this analysis enacts, accordingly, a reading of Romanian literature *in* the bigger planetary networks and as literary-cultural router directing the symbolic traffics of these webs and redirecting their discursive energies through and into its own, stylistic and representational wiring.[52] Deliberately, the tenor of the previous sentence is both structural and kinetic. For, as world literature, Romanian literature has to have, and historically has had, a certain constitution and a *modality* to it, with the latter ascertainable as fluidity, as nomadism, and as an overall mobility enabling this literature to plug itself into world networks, to feed into them and to be nurtured by them, as well as to call, befittingly, for a reading inside and across them. Our book, we think, echoes and amplifies this call.

In that, *Romanian Literature as World Literature* is both a scholarly argument and a manifesto. The argument is actually a set of interrelated arguments, and the manifesto is critical–theoretical as much as it is political and geopolitical. The program or polemical agenda aspect of our intervention concerns how literatures such as Romanian have been read by old-fashioned comparatists occasionally deigning to register what happens when Madame de Staël is read in Romania but also how Romanian literature has been and is still being read at home within an ingrown critical culture stuck in an outdated Herderian mode and its "aestheticist" corollary. This explains our essays' reiterated references to Romanian critics of the exceedingly "long" nineteenth century. These critics remain relevant historically, for and within certain moments in Romanian literary and cultural history. We acknowledge their work, and sometimes even build on it, but we want to move forward so as to leave behind its epistemological paradigm and its heavily ideological and political baggage. Ordinarily overlooked in domestic debates, this payload must be weighed in terms of its bearings on Romanian literature and its international reception. Uncritical nostalgias for a mythical period between the First and Second World Wars, which account for Călinescu's protracted influence among literary historians and contributors to publications such as *România literară* as they do for the conservative and right-wing political op-eds carried by magazines such as *Revista 22*; ill-informed rejections of cultural studies of gender, sexuality, ethnicity, class, and other identity parameters of both human and nonhuman agents; cognate and equally self-disqualifying charges of "political correctness"; an antiquated formalism and the fetish of "aesthetic criteria" applied in self-sufficient close readings and in disregard of contextual factors so as to police the boundaries of a narrow and ahistorical canon; the notion that a work's value can be adjudicated within an exclusive group of critical "authorities"; relatedly, a flawed notion of what intellectual elites are and do—all these will only reinforce a parochialism that precludes, we insist, a reading and an appreciation of Romanian literature for what it is *urbi et orbi*.

Naturally, what a body of literary work does and means in the world and as world is hardly a single thing. Inevitably, our book offers one way or set of interrelated ways of bringing to light how the worldedness of Romanian literature has emerged at particular junctures in its history. No doubt, summarizing the entire story of this genetic process would take more than one book, and so our treatment of the problem at hand could not be and is not exhaustive. All we could do here in our attempt to rewrite this narrative was to try and supply a sufficiently functional theoretical model for this rewriting and activate it selectively, in relation to some chapters and characters of this story while balancing our desire to break new ground interpretively and the need to provide necessary background information to world audiences unfamiliar with Romanian literature—hence the element of survey, overview, and historical sketch in some of our essays. We did not steer clear of detailed textual analyses of "major writers" either, but, once more, we had to make some choices in terms of primary sources, coverage, and the like, and, as explained earlier, these choices do speak to a certain agenda. Much as we do not feel wedded to a literary-historiographical approach already outmoded in 1941, when Călinescu's magnus opus came out, we also think it is high time for a thorough revision and expansion of the nation's literary canon, and some of our foci reflect this urgency. Yet again, we can imagine an extension of our project in all sorts of directions across and outside Romania's modern literary culture. Pursuing those trajectories would bring into the conversation established "classics" who are not discussed here at length, from nineteenth-century prose author Ion Creangă to twentieth-century figures like Mateiu Caragiale, Hortensia Papadat-Bengescu, Lucian Blaga, or Nichita Stănescu, but also more peripheral figures; entire trends and movements such as the fascinating cluster of early Romanian postmoderns known as the "Târgoviște School"—Radu Petrescu, Mircea Horia Simionescu, Costache Olăreanu, and Tudor Țopa—and the "2000 Generation" of poets and novelists; male and female authors, already established or waiting to be discovered or rediscovered; writers residing in Romania or elsewhere; "world texts" that address world audiences deliberately but also more "world-shy" voices; high-brow and popular literature; works that do and do not take up explicitly "international" and "planetary" issues (the environment, geopolitical conflicts, etc.), and so on.[53] To quote Thomas Oliver Beebee, for each of these writers, trends, and groups a "world literary network" can be and, we believe, should be urgently reconstituted.[54] Sometimes, that network is not one either, but many, given that it can be recreated in all kinds of directions and ways, synchronically or diachronically, in proximity or at distance, and with a variety of network models in mind. While most of the critics in this book pursue the regional and world weft pulled by geo-historical currents through the warp yarns of Romanian literary and cultural fabric, one could envisage a plethora of comparative projects where a node or knot of this texture would be analytically untied "with"—so that its threads could be tied into—similarly "unknotted" texts, discourse, and cultural forms, near or remote. Apropos of such pairings, we have already mentioned Ion Luca Caragiale and ("with") Ionesco, but Caragiale's short fiction too could be set alongside modern and even postmodern humor (did anybody say *Seinfeld*?), and Caragiale's son Mateiu would definitely enjoy Oscar Wilde's company. These would be illuminating matchups, but, once one gets into the structural weeds of a particular network, the pairs could be further refined, shuffled, and broken down into trios, and so on and so forth. If a text is a cluster of texts drawn through and to each other by a worldly law of cultural attractions, then the "hairball of links" pursuable by the patient and informed reader becomes daunting—overwhelming and fascinating at once.[55]

In a way, then, because the possibilities are endless, the particular authors and texts under discussion are less important than their handling. At the same time, the specific material chosen by our contributors does help articulate our project's world literature argument in three key areas. The first is literary-cultural history as process and scholarly discipline. This is the focus of part I, the most emphatically "metacritical" in our book. We lead off with Andrei Terian's essay "Mihai Eminescu: From National Mythology to the World Pantheon," which traces the journey of Romania's "national poet" from a narrowly conceived ethno-cultural and mythopoetic project to a different, world-oriented literary vision and practice. This shift, Terian explains, occurs when the Romanian author discovers Hindu mythology and philosophy. Once this fundamental revelation has sunk in, the critic concludes, Eminescu reads world literature as Romanian literature and, vice versa, writes Romanian literature as world literature. Terian's reading of Eminescu's "exceptionalism" engages critically with an entire tradition of Romanian literary history. This kind of dialogue is also one of the main objectives of the other essays featured in this part. Specifically, these contributions revisit traditional Romanian literary historiography along with some of its favorite foci, with an eye to critiquing, retrofitting, and opening it up to broader geocultural meanings and implications, which the nationalist-philological paradigm is poorly equipped to flesh out despite—or perhaps because?—its exalted "universalist" rhetoric. Thus, the second chapter of this part, Bogdan Crețu's "*Aux portes de l'Orient*, and Through: Nicolae Milescu, Dimitrie Cantemir, and the 'Oriental' Legacy of Early Romanian Literature," sets out to lay bare the ideological infrastructure of Romania's literary history in conjunction with dominant readings of early and premodern authors such as Milescu and Cantemir. As Crețu points out after a brief theoretical detour through the problematic of scalarity, these were distinctly *trans*national and cosmopolitan figures, which did not deter those readings, however, from casting them in nationalist scenarios well before the advent of the nationhood concept and its militant discourses. The two scholars and writers' worldly pathos, Crețu shows, takes them, often physically, across continents and pulls a sometimes surprisingly "non-Orientalist" Orient into the fold of a national imaginary in which the East would remain a lasting if controversial presence. Caius Dobrescu's "'Soft' Commerce and the Thinning of Empires: Four Steps toward Modernity," this section's third piece, also touches on Milescu and Cantemir (here presented as "cultural brokers"), alongside later figures such as Ion Budai-Deleanu, Nicolae Bălcescu, Titu Maiorescu, and Ion Luca Caragiale, in a refreshingly brisk and thought-provoking "crash course" in Romanian cultural history recapitulated as a sequence of culturally opportunistic and long-headed negotiations of multiple imperial proximities and pressures. Skeptical of any teleology, Dobrescu nonetheless sees the "transmetropolitan" moment marked by the Junimea (Young Generation) Society toward the end of the nineteenth century as virtually solidifying the principal structures and discourses of Romanian modernity and its "planetary" aspirations. Like Crețu, he turns nationalism's self-bestowed *primum movens* prerogatives on their head by explaining how "originality"—a true obsession for Romanian critics—stems not from autarchic self-contemplation but from a variety of encounters with empires close and faraway and with their worlds. A more pointed dismantling of nationalist epistemology supplies, along similar lines, Alex Goldiş's chapter "Beyond Nation Building: Literary History as Transnational

Geolocation," which draws from Itamar Even-Zohar's polysystems theory and several historiographic traditions to unearth the "generative pattern" of historical descriptions of national literary systems in the European Southeast, especially in Romania. This pattern, Goldiș argues, is shaped by "structural correspondence," which, he also contends, renders literary history a closed system. Instead, the critic proposes an effectively interactional model allowing Romanian literary history to rebuild itself around a capability to "geolocate" its subject in the world in ways likely to neutralize deeply rooted "complexes" of "marginality," "derivativeness," "belatedness," and the like. These issues are central to the closing chapter of this section, Carmen Mușat's "After 'Imitation': Aesthetic Intersections, Geocultural Networks, and the Rise of Modern Romanian Literature." In a fashion similar to Dobrescu's take on Romanian cultural poetics, Mușat turns to "the principle of imitation," as Romanian cultural critics and historians have called it after Eugen Lovinescu. As she demonstrates, the imitative drive of Romanian literature and culture accounts not only for their modernization and ability to produce singular works but also for the built-in multiplicity—for the "many," for the *literatures*—of the national literary patrimony.

A second major thematics extensively examined by our book, this plurality is pursued in part II across ethnic, linguistic, literary, territorial, and political domains. The previous section largely concentrates on the pre–First World War rise of modern Romanian literature and literary-cultural ideology in the tug-of-war between empires and bourgeoning local sovereignty, imitation and autochthonous creativity, and the medieval and early modern past, on one side, and, on the other, the post-mid-nineteenth-century present in which Romania would tie up the loose ends of its various inheritances into a streamlined self-representation as a modern Romance-language culture of Eastern Europe. The onset of Romanticism brought about, as our contributors explain in part I, an acceleration of modernization understood and practiced as Westernization, with France as *the* European model. But this "internationalization" was not incompatible with the consolidation of nationalism, which would have decisive repercussions on said self-representation in literature and its studies—primarily on how modern Romanian critics, historians, and ideologues would perceive the literary production of their country. Dwelling on the literature written since 1918, when the Romanian nation-state ("Greater Romania") as we know it today was born, the four essays featured in part II suggest that this perception is reductive with respect to abovementioned plurality, and that it is high time the latter should be freed from the constructions of Romantic historiography and criticism. Mircea A. Diaconu makes this goal explicit in his chapter, "Reading Microliterature: Language, Ethnicity, Polyterritoriality." Here, he looks at the culturo-genetic and historically evolving asymmetries of idiom, political borders, and ethnic identity in the Romanian zone of Central and Southeastern Europe to disentangle the complex affiliations of ethnic minority writers, whether they are "intraterritorial" Hungarian- and German-language authors residing in Romania or "extraterritorial" ethnic Romanian novelists and poets publishing in their mother tongue or in other idioms and living in Serbia, the Republic of Moldova, Ukraine, and other neighboring countries. Herta Müller, Ioan Miloș, and Ion Druță supply the evidence in Diaconu's highly informative and persuasive effort to enlist his Deleuze and Guattari-inspired "microliterature" in the service of a geocultural, cross-systemic revisiting of "territorialist" notions of national literature and literary history. The French thinkers and their reflections on Kafka, minority literature, and the de- and re-territorializations operated by discursive, political, and institutional apparatuses also take front and center in Imre József Balázs's and Ovidiu Morar's contributions. In "Trees, Waves, Whirlpools: Nation, Region, and the Reterritorialization of Romania's Hungarian Literature," Balázs works out *histoire croisée*-inspired readings of contemporary, Transylvanian-born Hungarian novelists Ádám Bodor, Zsolt Láng, and István Szilágyi to lay out the motifs and stylistic stratagems to which they resort to mark their writings' insertions into world spaces and patrimonies vaster or just different than those of nation-states, their territorial turfs, and regional surroundings. Diving into the writers' literary "whirlpool," Balázs's central critical metaphor, the essayist brings to the surface, with a Moretti assist, worldly engagements and insights of which neither "methodological nationalism" nor "methodological regionalism" has been aware. In a similar fashion, in "Cosmopolites, Deracinated, *étranjuifs*: Romanian Jews in the International Avant-Garde" Morar offers up the fast-expanding literary experimentalism of early-twentieth-century Romania as a cosmopolitan intervention in a sociocultural landscape about to be taken over by extreme forms of nationalism and anti-Semitism. In a line of scholarship that runs through Tom Sandqvist's landmark 2006 *Dada East: The Romanians of Cabaret Voltaire*, Morar combines archival research, textual analyses, and Guy Scarpetta's cosmopolitan theory to help us see how Tristan Tzara, Gherasim Luca, and other Jewish–Romanian–French members of the European avant-garde "deracinate" themselves so as to open up Romanian literature and redistribute its energies across vast geographies of language, ethno-cultural and national membership, and aesthetic creativity. This section of *Romanian Literature as World Literature* closes with an essay that expands Morar's discussion by zooming in on the ambivalences of radicalism in the literature and politics of the same period. This is Paul Cernat's "Communicating Vessels: The Avant-Garde, Antimodernity, and Radical Culture in Romania between the First and the Second World Wars," which plays on the metaphor in his title's first part to describe the circulation of odd yet typical juxtapositions of progressivism and reactionarism, and modernism and antimodernism in the works of avant-garde artists and of the disciples of Nae Ionescu, an influential right-wing ideologue of the Romanian 1930s and early 1940s.

The communicating vessels through which Romanian literature gushes and merges with other currents of world literature enable flows "over deep time and across long space," as the title of our book's Part III suggests with a nod at Hitchcock, Dimock, and other recent postcolonial and World Literature theorists. Encapsulating the third key area of inquiry of our book, the phrase and its conceptual ramifications are visible in the opening chapter of this part, Mihai Iovănel's "Temporal Webs of World Literature: Rebranding Games and Global Relevance after the Second World War—Mircea Eliade, E. M. Cioran, Eugène Ionesco." Iovănel's essay proposes a geosociology of world success with applications to authors also central to Cernat's argument: Eliade, Cioran, and Ionesco. As Iovănel demonstrates in critical dialogue with Casanova, Moretti, and other critics, these three well-known Romanian writers achieve world fame by playing smart games of cultural self-positioning and self-repositioning across several literary-intellectual systems of variable geopolitical scope. "A Geoliterary *Ecumene* of the East: Socialist Realism—The Romanian Case," Mircea Martin's contribution, moves along similar lines by situating the Romanian Socialist Realism of the late 1940s, 1950s, and early mid-1960s in the context of the pseudo-ecumene enforced by the Soviet political–ideological hegemony of the time. If, as late as in 1984, Slovakian critic Dionýz Durišin was pointing to the "community of socialist literature" as an illustration of his supranational "interliterary community" concept, Martin's presentation makes it abundantly clear why this community was not one and why the whole Realist Socialist project was bound to go nowhere.[56] "Sovietization" is also at the core of Bogdan Ștefănescu's chapter, "Romanian Modernity and the Rhetoric of Vacuity: Toward a Comparative Postcolonialism." The critic tackles this process as a form of colonization and discusses the shaking off of the Soviet yoke as a postcolonial moment in contemporary Romanian history. Setting side by side discrete geopolitical subsystems formerly known as the "Second" and "Third" World, his postcolonial comparatism parses out the charged symbolism of the "void" in the literatures of the ex-colonies of Western empires and in the former Soviet republics and satellites. Emptiness, lack, and the discourses belaboring such themes, Ștefănescu maintains, attest to a "nodal convergence" of colonial projects, to their drawn-out traumatic fallout across the world, and to Romania's participation in this world during and after the Cold War. In the next essay, "Gaming the World-System: Creativity, Politics, and Beat Influence in the Poetry of the 1980s Generation," Teodora Dumitru goes back to the pre-1989 epoch, more precisely to the era's last decade, when, due to the post-mid-1960s nationalist resurgence, Romanian Communism no longer was the Soviet aftershock of the decades immediately following the Second World War; on the other hand, she notes, the "liberalization" of the late 1960s was a thing of the past. Nevertheless, the young poets of the 1980s and Romanian postmodernism more broadly came to the fore in overtly intertextual conversation with the Beat poets and American literature generally. Cornis-Pope has already observed that "in articulating the paradigm of international postmodernism primarily around Western experiences, Western theorists ignore the historical experience of the former [C]ommunist countries or exhibit a simplistic understanding of the fate of culture under totalitarian [C]ommunism."[57] Conversant with several literary and critical–theoretical traditions, Dumitru assesses the effectiveness with which poets such as Cărtărescu, Florin Iaru, and Mariana Marin negotiate, across literary, political, and national systems, a creative position allowing them to assimilate the Beats' lesson *and* remain original, as well as to publish *and* resist co-option by the regime's aesthetic-ideological apparatus. This part's fourth chapter, "How Does Exile Make Space? Contemporary Romanian Émigré Literature and the Worldedness of Place: Herta Müller, Andrei Codrescu, Norman Manea" by Doris Mironescu, addresses more direct reactions to the pressure this apparatus applied on Romania's writers: defection, exile, and other forms of bailing out and writing from physical locations presumably impervious to threats, compromises, and so forth. Mironescu's comments on Müller, Codrescu, and Manea engage with critics like Thomas Bender, Brenner, and Dimock to erode the "state-centric epistemology" that, in these and other cases, would make harder to appreciate the "worlded" spatiality the three Romanian-born expatriate writers foster in their works. In a sense, authors such as these, much like the Romanian–American comparatists of the 1970s and 1980s (Matei Călinescu and other academic exiles of the time) and Ionesco's generation before them, are Romania's literary and intellectual outposts in a steadily expanding world. But entire literatures can travel across and into other literatures without any change in writers' residence. This is what happens in translation, a phenomenon to which Mihaela Ursa attends in her essay "Made in Translation: A National Poetics for the Transnational World." Quite befittingly, Ursa's chapter rounds off our project by circling back to Part I's thorny issue of the "making" of a national literary culture. The twofold dialogue she proposes involves translation studies theorists—including scholars and translators like Sean Cotter, who has written authoritatively on the multicultural morphing Romanian nationhood undergoes in translation—and Romanian critics who have argued that "translations do not make a literature."[58] In disagreeing with the latter category, Ursa traces the evolving meaning and impact of translation as the translational content of various cultural programs echo more and more the transnational logic of post–Cold War redistributions of priorities, audiences, and markets.

Notes

1 Reproductions of Diego Rivera's *The Communicating Vessels* and Kurt Schwitters and Theo van Doesburg's *Kleine Dada Soirée* are, as one may imagine, widely available on the Internet. To get a general idea of what we are talking about, the reader in a hurry can check them out at http://www.moma.org/collection /works/63368?locale=en (accessed May 26, 2016) and http://www.moma.org /-collection/works/5533?locale=en, respectively (accessed May 26, 2016).

2 Andrei Terian, "Romanian Literature for the World: A Matter of Property," *World Literature Studies* 7, no.2 (2015): 3–14.

3 Amy J. Elias and Christian Moraru, "Introduction: The Planetary Condition," in *The Planetary Turn: Relationality and Geoaesthetics in the Twenty-First Century*, ed. Amy J. Elias and Christian Moraru (Evanston, IL: Northwestern University Press, 2015), xi–xxi.

4 Robert T. Tally, Jr., "World Literature and Its Discontents," *English Language and Literature* 60, no.3 (2014): 404. In the same vein, a prominent figure of Romania's new wave of critics, Mihai Iovănel, writes that "While Romanian historiography had played a positive role internationally by reinforcing the distinct image of the nation-state, domestically the discipline has worked as a brake on modernity through historians' elegiac lament of Romania's waning feudal society, more exactly, of that society's idealized image, a concoction for whose fabrication the same historians are responsible. To this very day, mainstream historiography produced in Romania is nationalist, hence the conclusion that the best Romanian histories have been written by foreigners. The concept of tradition undergirding all scholarship until the end of World War II is a fiction created by nineteenth-century historians" (*Evreul improbabil*

. *Mihail Sebastian: o monografie ideologică* [Bucharest: Cartea Românească, 2012], 146). Iovănel reiterates this critique of modern Romanian historiography in *Ideologiile literaturii în postcomunismul românesc* (Bucharest: Editura Muzeului Literaturii Române, 2017), 94–95. His 2017 monograph is the best discussion of literary ideology in post-1989 Romania.

5   On how late globalization forces Romanian critics to rethink literary history, see Oana Elena Strugaru's article, "Globalization and Literature: What Is Left of Literary History?" *Euresis* (2013): 140–146.

6   Marcel Cornis-Pope, "On Writing Multicultural Literary History Focused on the Novel and Other Genres," *Euphorion* 27, no.1 (2016): 29.

7   Stephen Greenblatt, "Cultural Mobility: An Introduction," in *Cultural Mobility: A Manifesto*, ed. Stephen Greenblatt, with Ines G. Županov, Reinhard Meyer-Kalkus, Heike Paul, Pál Nyíri, and Friederike Pannewick (Cambridge: Cambridge University Press, 2010), 3.

8   Thomas O. Beebee, "Introduction: Departures, Emanations, Intersections," in *German Literature as World Literature*, ed. Thomas O. Beebee (New York: Bloomsbury, 2014), 2.

9   Pascale Casanova, *The World Republic of Letters*, trans. M. B. DeBevoise (Cambridge, MA: Harvard University Press, 2004), 205.

10 Mircea Martin, *G. Călinescu și "complexele" literaturii române*, 2nd ed., with an *Argument* by the Author and an Afterword by Nicolae Manolescu (Pitești: Paralela 45, 2002), 10.

11 Mario J. Valdés, "Preface by the General Editor of the Literary History Project," in *History of the Literary Cultures of East-Central Europe: Junctures and Disjunctures in the 19th and 20th Centuries*, vol.1, ed. Marcel Cornis-Pope and John Neubauer (Amsterdam: John Benjamins, 2004–2010), xiv.

12 Arjun Appadurai, *Modernity at Large: Cultural Dimensions of Globalization* (Minneapolis: University of Minnesota Press, 1999), 19.

13 Marcel Cornis-Pope, John Neubauer, and Nicolae Harsanyi, "Literary Production in Marginocentric Cultural Nodes: The Case of Timișoara," in *History of the Literary Cultures of East-Central Europe: Junctures and Disjunctures in the 19th and 20th Centuries* (vol.II), ed. Marcel Cornis-Pope and John Neubauer (Amsterdam: John Benjamins, 2004), 105–124.

14 Rebecca L. Walkowitz, *Born Translated: The Contemporary Novel in an Age of World Literature* (New York: Columbia University Press, 2015), 26. Walkowitz also discusses Benedict Anderson's *Imagined Communities* in a World Literature context.

15 Mircea Martin, *Radicalitate și nuanță* (Bucharest: TracusArte, 2015), 13.

16 Johann Gottfried von Herder, *This Too a Philosophy of History for the Formation of Humanity*, in *Philosophical Writings*, trans. and ed. Michael N. Forster (Cambridge: Cambridge University Press, 2002), 272–360.

17 Désiré Nisard, *Histoire de la littérature française*, vol.1, 2nd ed. (Paris: Firmin Didot, 1854), 2. "L'histoire littéraire commence … avec la nation elle-même, avec la langue. Elle ne cesse que le jour où la nation a disparu, où sa langue est devenue une langue morte …. L'histoire littéraire de la France commence le jour où le premier mot de la langue française a été écrit."

18 José Amador de los Ríos, *Historia crítica de la literatura Española*, vol.1 (Madrid: José Rodriguez, 1861), xcv–xcvi: "La poesía española, formada con los más diversos elementos, bien que subordinados á un pensamiento de unidad que caracteriza al

cabo y es ley constante de todas sus producciones, no puede ya ser para nosotros objeto de mera investigación artística. Identificada con el carácter y el sentimiento nacional, se halla en estrecha armonía con las costumbres, con las creencias, con las necesidades, con los triunfos del pueblo castellano: revela sus alegrías y sus amarguras, sus felicidades y sus infortunios. Su riqueza, aunque allegadiza respecto de las formas exteriores, es propia respecto de las ideas que la alimentan, ideas profundamente arraigadas en el corazón de cien generaciones."

19 Gustave Lanson, *Histoire illustrée de la littérature française (An Illustrated History of French Literature)*, vol.1 (Paris: Hachette, 1923), 6.

20 Lanson, *Histoire*, 8: "De tous les côtés, sur toutes les frontières, à mesure que les rois rattachaient de nouveaux territoires à leur couronne, la langue française faisait, elle aussi, des conquêtes, disputant leur territoire avec plus ou moins de succès tantôt au celtique, tantôt à l'allemand, tantôt à l'italien, et tantôt au basque: de langue officielle et administrative, tendant partout à être langue de la littérature et des classes cultivées."

21 "În aceste timpuri de suferinţă naţională, o astfel de carte nepărtinitoare trebuie să dea oricui încrederea că avem o strălucită literatură, care, pe de altă parte, în ciuda efemerelor vicisitudini, se produce pe teritoriul României Mari, una şi indivizibilă, slujind drept cea mai clară hartă a poporului român. Eminescu in Bucovina, Haşdeu in Basarabia, Bolintineanu in Macedonia, Slavici la graniţa de vest, Coşbuc şi Rebreanu în preajma Năsăudului, Maiorescu şi Goga pe linga Oltul ardelean sînt eternii noştri păzitori ai solului veşnic. Şi după toate, după o prea lungă desconsiderare de noi înşine, e timpul de a striga cu mîndrie, împreuna cu Miron Costin: 'NASC ŞI ÎN MOLDOVA OAMENI!'" (G. Călinescu, *Istoria literaturii române de la origini pînă în prezent*, 2nd revised ed., pref. and ed. Alexandru Piru [Bucharest: Minerva, 1982], 6).

22 Călinescu, *Istoria literaturii române*, 974.

23 "Dacă, pe de altă parte, e adevărat, şi cât de frumos spus de către Călinescu în finalul prefeţei la *Istoria* lui, că literatura 'poate sluji [*sic*] drept cea mai clară hartă a poporului român,' nu mă consider, în ce mă priveşte, decît unul dintre zecile de cartografi, silitor şi modest benedictin al ideii că fiecare se cuvine judecat după ce a realizat, oricăt de mare ar fi depărtarea la care se află harta lui de *harta ideală* pe care, în naivitatea lor, iubitorii de literatură o cred posibilă" (Nicolae Manolescu, *Istoria critică a literaturii române: 5 secole de literatură* [Piteşti: Paralela 45, 2008], 18).

24 Neil Brenner, "The Space of the World: Beyond State-Centrism?" in *Immanuel Wallerstein and the Problem of the World: System, Scale, Culture*, ed. David Palumbo-Liu, Bruce Robbins, and Nirvana Tanoukhi (Durham, NC: Duke University Press, 2011), 109.

25 As Robert Fine shows in *Cosmopolitanism* (New York: Routledge, 2007), 7, Ulrich Beck formulated his famous critique of "methodological nationalism" probably for the first time in a 2002 article, then he reformulated it in "Toward a New Critical Theory with a Cosmopolitan Intent," *Constellations* 10, no.4 (2003), 453–468. After several more elaborations on the same subject, he takes it up again in "Cosmopolitan Sociology: Outline of a Paradigm Shift," a piece included in *The Ashgate Research Companion to Cosmopolitanism*, ed. Maria Rovisco and Magdalena Nowicka (Farnham: Ashgate, 2011), 17–32. On Giddens, Beck, Martins, "methodological cosmopolitanism," and its "equivocations" (including Beck's "post-universalism"), see Fine's excellent discussion in *Cosmopolitanism*, 1–14.

26 Beck, "Cosmopolitan Sociology," 18.

27   Beck, "Cosmopolitan Sociology," 29.

28   On Beck and the state as a "zombie category," see Fine, *Cosmopolitanism*, 6–7. Paul Giles has commented on territorialism, terrorism, and the "homeland security" approach to literature in his essay "The Deterritorialization of American Literature," in *Shades of the Planet: American Literature as World Literature*, ed. Wai Chee Dimock and Lawrence Buell (Princeton, NJ: Princeton University Press, 2007), 39–61.

29   Appadurai, *Modernity at Large*, 19.

30   Nikos Papastergiadis, "Spatial Aesthetics: Rethinking the Contemporary," in *Antinomies of Art and Culture: Modernity, Postmodernity, Contemporaneity*, ed. Terry Smith, Okwui Enwezor, Nancy Condee (Durham, NC: Duke University Press, 2009), 373.

31   Andrei Terian, *Critica de export: teorii, contexte, ideologii* (Bucharest: Muzeul Literaturii Române, 2013), 291.

32   Julia Kristeva, *Nations without Nationalism*, trans. Leon S.Roudiez (New York: Columbia University Press, 1993), 51.

33   Regarding a dynamic of "hearth" and "cosmos" close to planetary interplay of "here" and "there," see Yi-Fu Tuan, *Cosmos and Hearth: A Cosmopolite's Viewpoint* (Minneapolis: University of Minnesota Press, 1996), 187–188. On "egocentric" versus "allocentric space," see J. E. Malpas, *Place and Experience: A Philosophical Topography* (Cambridge: Cambridge University Press, 1999), 44–55.

34   On borders as "quilting points," see Anthony Cooper and Chris Rumford, "Cosmopolitan Borders: Bordering as Connectivity," in Rovisco and Nowicka, *The Ashgate Research Companion to Cosmopolitanism*, 273.

35   Dimock, *Literature for the Planet*, 178.

36   Daniel Levy and Natan Sznaider, "Cosmopolitan Memory and Human Rights," in Rovisco and Nowicka, *The Ashgate Research Companion to Cosmopolitanism*, 197.

37   Dimock, *Scales of Aggregation*, 219, 226.

38   Friedrich Nietzsche, *Untimely Meditations*, ed. Daniel Breazeale, trans. R. J. Hollingdale (Cambridge: Cambridge University Press, 2003), 149–150.

39   Julien Benda, *The Treason of the Intellectuals*, with a new introduction by Roger Kinball, trans. Richard Aldington (New Brunswick, NJ: Transaction, 2007).

40   Adrian Florea, "De Facto States in International Politics (1945–2011): A New Data Set," *International Interactions: Empirical and Theoretical Research in International Relations* (October 2014), http://dx.doi.org/10.1080/03050629.2014.915543 (accessed May 26, 2016).

41   Dimock, *Literature for the Planet*, 175.

42   Among critics for whom "novel assemblages of territory, authority[,] and rights" would deal successfully with the local (national)-global conundrum, I list here only Saskia Sassen with her article "Neither global nor national: novel assemblages of territory, authority and rights" (*Ethics & Global Politics* 1, no.1–2 [2008]: 61–79), Jahan Ramazani with "Poetry, Modernity, and Globalization," in Wollaeger with Eatough, *The Oxford Handbook of Global Modernisms* (New York: Oxford University Press, 2012), 301, and Beck, with *Cosmopolitan Sociology* (28–29).

43   Quoting Robbins in "Poetry, Modernity, and Globalization," Ramazani points to the "multiple attachments" following "detachments" from local bonds. Under planetarity, such detachments are not a prerequisite of with-being. On postethnic affiliation, voluntary rather than inherited by background, see David A. Hollinger, *Postethnic America: Beyond Multiculturalism* (New York: Basic Books/HarperCollins, 1995), and *Cosmopolitanism and Solidarity*. Delanty discusses the cosmopolitan local–global and

self–other interface in "The Idea of Critical Cosmopolitanism," in *Routledge Handbook of Cosmopolitanism Studies*, ed. Gerard Delanty (Abingdon: Routledge, 2012), 41.

44 On "nested territorial units," see Thomas Pogge, "Cosmopolitanism and Sovereignty," in *The Cosmopolitanism Reader*, ed. Garrett Wallace Brown and David Held (Cambridge: Polity, 2010), 114.

45 Dimock, *Genre as World System*, 89.

46 On Călinescu's *History* and Romanian writers as border guards or customs officials, see also Martin's *Radicalitate și nuanță*, 14.

47 Greenblatt, *Cultural Mobility*, 5.

48 Greenblatt, *Cultural Mobility*, 6.

49 Walkowitz, *Born Translated* 2, 31, 45, 47.

50 Terian, "Romanian Literature for the World," 11. Terian also addresses this problem in *Critica de export* and in a slew of articles published in recent years.

51 Rachel Adams, "The Worlding of American Studies," *American Quarterly* 53, no.4 (December 2001): 720–732. A few years after Adams, Susan Gillman, Kirsten Silva Greusz, and Rob Wilson published a piece titled "Worlding American Studies," in *Comparative American Studies* 2, no.3 (2004): 259–270.

52 The network has become a major epistemological trope over the past decade in world and Romanian literary-cultural scholarship. Recent additions to the vast bibliography accumulated around this discursive-analytic model include Patrick Jagoda's *Network Aesthetics* (Chicago: The University of Chicago Press, 2016) and, on the Romanian side, Teodora Dumitru's *Rețeaua modernității. Paul de Man—Matei Călinescu—Antoine Compagnon* (Bucharest: Editura Muzeului Literaturii Române, 2016) and Grațiela Benga's *Rețeaua. Poezia românească a anilor 2000* (Timișoara: Editura Universității de Vest, 2016).

53 According to Caren Irr, a book's identity or "citizenship" is a function of the audience that work targets. See her *Toward the Geopolitical Novel: U.S. Fiction in the Twenty-First Century* (New York: Columbia University Press, 2014), 11.

54 Thomas Oliver Beebee, "The World Literary Network of Lessing," presentation on the "Lessing and World Literature" panel, Modern Language Association Convention, Philadelphia, PA, January 6, 2017.

55 Beebee, "The World Literary Network of Lessing."

56 Dionýz Durišin, *Theory of Literary Comparatistics*, trans. Jessie Kocmanová, (Bratislava: Veda, 1984), 9.

57 Marcel Cornis-Pope, "Shifting Paradigms: East European Literatures at the Turn of the Millennium," in *Postcommunism, Postmodernism, and the Global Imagination*, ed. Christian Moraru, introduction by Aaron Chandler (Boulder, CO: East European Monographs/Columbia University Press, 2009), 27.

58 See Sean Cotter, *Literary Translation and the Idea of a Minor Romania* (Rochester, NY: University of Rochester Press, 2014).

Part I

The Making and Remaking of a World Literature: Revisiting Romanian Literary and Cultural History

Romanian nationalism was further discredited in the last decades of Communism, when it joined the hollow official rhetoric of Romanian exceptionalism. During the 1970s and 1980s, the nationalist monomania of imaginary local "precursors" of major breakthroughs in the modern arts and sciences—so-called *protochronism*—carried on and worsened the excesses and anxieties of pre–Second World War ethnocentrism, which, in turn, had only followed in the line of nineteenth-century Romantic tendencies …. Leaving behind the Communist project in 1989, Romania turns its sights to Europe and pins its hopes on it, for the country feels that it belongs to Europe. Going to show that European cultural integration is as arduous a process as sociopolitical integration, the extensive postcommunist-era debates on "Romanian literature's 'Europeanism'" bespeak the resilience of older cultural complexes, as the latter usually come into play alongside cognate obsessions of being too "Balkan" or not "enough" European, as well as alongside a lack of interest in "too peripheral" neighbors such as Hungary and Bulgaria. Turning such obsessions into viable cultural form is a major urgency that has been shaping postcommunist Romania and the positions taken up by an entire spectrum of voices, from the most stick-in-the-mud nationalists to the pro-European intellectual elites.

—Mihai Iovănel, *Ideologiile literaturii în postcomunismul românesc*
(Literary Ideologies in Romanian Postcommunism)

1

Mihai Eminescu: From National Mythology to the World Pantheon

Andrei Terian

"National poets"—what else could be more remote from world literature? Let us think about it for a moment, and perhaps ask ourselves also: If a poet belongs to a nation, then in what sense can he or she be said to belong to the entire world too? It is true that the nation is a world in and of itself. Yet, at least in the Romantic sense largely prevailing in the nineteenth century, the golden age of national poets, this world is or is seen, by itself and other national worlds, as a homogenous space, and this homogeneity—again, actual or imaginary—is not only linguistic but also ethnic and territorial. Borrowing Christian Moraru's terminological dyad here, the nation-world tends to emerge as a "globe" rather than as a "planet," that is, as a world actively limiting or even lacking "worldedness."[1] And, from the standpoint of this effective or putative worldly "scarcity," do not national poets come about and establish themselves—nationally—by turning their backs to the wide and diverse world of others, to the very domain of worldedness? Are they not, in other words, living proof that what is national and belongs to it, from collective imaginaries to sacrosanct territory, has an exclusive dimension, indeed, a nationally endemic aspect to it, and so it cannot, by its very nature, be transnational and participate in world dynamics, interchanges, and circuitries?[2] Further, if the answer here is "yes," then to what extent are the same poets capable of playing in arenas larger than the nation by the rules of the game called world literature? Are they not tempted under such handicapping circumstances to throw the game or perhaps sit it out? On the other hand, if the poets themselves, whom various nations have acknowledged as their cultural pinnacles, are not represented on the world literature stage, then what else could be representative and should be there for those communities? According to Mads Rosendahl Thomsen, when national champions enter the world literature contest on behalf of their respective nations, the contestants are not automatically excluded from the game. They only have to play by other rules, for the international literary canon is not the sum of national literary canons but arguably a different and complex network, which sometimes reproduces national hierarchies and other times upsets them.[3] And, given this reality, the poets' case seems closed. After all, in the transnational sphere where the world rankings, reputations, and success obtain, nations, their promotion apparatuses, and nationally minded critics can only do so much.

In what follows, I propose to reopen the case at the other end—not the end of national critics and literatures, but that of world literature. In so doing, I am not interested in evoking, as an alternative to the agonal metaphor above, the cheerily democratic *tableau vivant* of a World Parliament where each national literature dreams to be sending its envoys one day. What I want to do, instead, is to show how, in certain situations, national poets, *in order to become and be acknowledged as such*, take the longer, international and even intercontinental road home, to national recognition and, in our case, idolatry. As we will see, their glorious homecoming by the same token involves and, I would suggest, *calls for* a detour through the world archive, for deliberate and systematic formal and thematic protocols by which the poets expand their intercultural and intertextual network way beyond the nation's geoaesthetic perimeter, in new and sometimes surprising directions.

We should note, first, that the very status of national poet is, in fact, integrated into transnational or even transcontinental institutions. Consider, for instance, the Icelander Jónas Hallgrímsson (1807–1845), the Uruguayan Juan Zorrilla de San Martín (1855–1931), and the Angolan António Agostinho Neto (1922–1979): three continents, two centuries of history, yet basically the same mechanisms of canonization, through which each author becomes emblematic for his own culture. Second, acquiring national poet stature takes an international affiliation, which, as Alex Goldiş shows in his contribution to this collection, is most often articulated by a direct connection or comparison with a prestigious model or prototype in Western literature. For instance, it is not by accident that Karel Hynek Mácha has been called "the Czech Byron,"[4] and that Hristo Botev has been dubbed "the Bulgarian Victor Hugo,"[5] whereas Adam Mickiewicz was exported to the United States during the First World War sometimes as "the Polish Goethe"[6] and sometimes as "the Polish Shakespeare."[7] All these authors gained legitimacy *as* national poets also through "at-distance" associations of various kinds with authors belonging to other cultures—if you think about it, the very granting of the title of national poet implies or, to my mind, should imply that the author in question does double duty as a transnational poet, that his or her work and his or her overall figure are a kind of business card one literature offers to the others. Third, being a national poet also requires some delimitation from other authors, whether they are national poets belonging to other cultures or transnational poets, as only such a compare-and-contrast routine can guarantee that the poets under scrutiny are "truly" national poets and not mere Czech, Bulgarian, or Polish clones of various transnational poets. The very status of national poet inevitably implies, then, a multiple if often elusive inscription into a global or, at least, transnational literary circuit.

But how can this be? How can a national poet become a transnational poet given the constraints, ties, obligations, advantages, calculations, allegiances, cultural-aesthetic decisions, political reasoning, and ideological unreasoning that keep him or her nation-bound, locally committed and meaningful? And, should the poet manage to break through his or her national aura, can then he or she represent or "typify" solely his or her own nation any longer? More importantly still perhaps, what are the literary traits preventing him or her from crossing the boundaries of his or her culture into larger regions? And what are the literary-cultural mechanisms poets need to activate to take this leap, to catch bigger worlds in their literary nets? Below, I attempt to answer these questions by turning to the work of Mihai Eminescu (1850–1889), Romania's "national poet."

1. An Unlikely Candidate

If exceptionalism is the opium of small literatures, then Romanian literature is a good case in point. Stronger than any other Romanian writer's is the case provided by Eminescu, whom Romania's critics regard as one of a kind, nonpareil, alpha, and omega of all things literary. "Eminescology" is still the name of a growth industry, and it is reputable "Eminescologists" who have proclaimed the author an absolute ending of a sublime era ("the last major European Romantic"), an absolute beginning (precursor of Symbolism, modernism, and even Existentialism),[8] and also an irreducible exception (he is "the unparalleled poet" too).[9] Interestingly enough, in trying to play up Eminescu's originality in relation to major writers of Western literatures, the critics have overlooked precisely the rather atypical status of the writer not only relative to other "national poets" of his part of Europe but also within his own culture. I might note, along these lines, that, unlike most East-Central European poets—the Polish Adam Mickiewicz (1798–1855), the Greek Dionysios Solomos (1798–1857), the Slovenian France Prešeren (1800–1849), the Czech Karel Hynek Mácha (1810–1836), the Serbo-Montenegrin Petar II Petrović-Njegoš (1813–1851), the Hungarian Sándor Petőfi (1823–1849), and the Bulgarian Hristo Botev (1848–1876)—Eminescu lived and wrote not in the first but in the second half of the nineteenth century. But this detail is less relevant than the poet's position within his country's cultural–historical moment. That is, in the 1860s, when he stepped on the Romanian political and literary scene, the "national rebirth" of his country had already taken place. Unlike Solomos, Mickiewicz, Petőfi, or Botev, he did not participate in any of the armed insurgencies of his own people, nor did he carry out any revolutionary activities for that matter. No wonder he could not do that, for, by the time he reached adulthood, all the heroic moments of the rising modern Romanian State seemed to have already been occurred. Thus, Eminescu, born in 1850, could have participated neither in the national uprising of 1821, which ended the Greek-Ottoman regime and put Moldavia and Wallachia on their path to modernization, nor in the Revolution of 1848–1849, which advanced the idea of uniting the Danube Principalities and all other regions inhabited by Romanians. He was too young to have anything to do with the union of Moldavia and Wallachia when it finally happened (1859) or with the preservation of this great accomplishment under a newly arrived foreign prince (1866). The only historical turning point on which Eminescu could have left his mark was the 1877–1878 Romanian War of Independence, but at that time his attitude as a publicist for the main newspaper of the conservative opposition was predominantly critical of the liberal government, which had been accused of having neglected the Romanian army. As a result of this historical and political context, Eminescu virtually played no role, except, at most, for a critical one, in Romania's mid-nineteenth-century "national revival."

More interesting still is where Eminescu fits within the Romanian ideological landscape of the era. After his debut as a teenager in a Transylvanian magazine in 1866 with a poem dedicated to the memory of his former gymnasium teacher, Eminescu would be soon noticed by Titu Maiorescu (1840–1917), the most influential Romanian critic of the time, and invited to join the Junimea (Young Generation) cultural society. Significantly, unlike many such nineteenth-century East-Central European societies, which had a liberal-progressive agenda modeled on the famous anti-Absolutist *Junges Deutschland* of the German Romantics, Junimea had a conservative orientation. It did not lack certain nationalist accents, but, unlike most East European nationalist movements, which regarded France as the world's emancipation engine, Junimea was manifestly pro-German. Both ideological positions were actually worked into Maiorescu's cultural-political theory of "forms without substance," which doctrine rejected the "revolutionary" achievements of the previous generation—the Romantic revolutionaries of 1848, also known as the "Forty-Eighters"—in whose accomplishments he saw an expression of a hollow and phony nationalism, advocating instead a "natural evolution" and an "organic," internally driven development of Romanian culture and society.[10] I might add that not only would Eminescu adopt such view, but he would also ramp them up and develop them into a vehement wholesale critique of the young Romanian State's modernization.

No less intriguing is, or at least was for a while, Eminescu's place among the country's literary greats. His quick recognition as a top literary figure and even "national poet" must have appeared odd because the position seemed to have been filled already by an elder and distinguished writer, Vasile Alecsandri (1819–1890). Alecsandri surely fit the job description. Truth be told, he was overqualified. Not only did he take part in the 1848 Revolution in Moldavia, but he also played a decisive role in the unification of the two Romanian Principalities, not to mention that, in 1859, when he had been offered the throne of Moldavia, he turned it down in order to force the appointment of the Wallachian candidate to this position, which led to the effective unification of the two Principalities. Besides, Alecsandri's writing covered more than honorably all the literary forms of the era, checking off all the available generic boxes: comedies, historical dramas, folk-inspired poems, intimate poems, epic poems on historical themes, satirical poems, novellas, epistles, and more. In effect, in 1869, that is, the year before Eminescu published his first notable poems, Alecsandri had published his most important volume, *Pasteluri* (Poetic Pastels), which would make Maiorescu proclaim him the "leading poet of the past generation."[11] Last but not least, let us not forget that Alecsandri's artistic talent, which went hand in glove with his diplomatic activity, seemed to render him the kind of cultural "personality" suitable for major international recognition. And, indeed, the conditions for enjoying some substantial European prime time existed. In 1878, during the second edition of the Floral Games held in Montpellier, he had been awarded a prize by a jury chaired by Provençal poet Frédéric Mistral, the 1904 Nobel Prize laureate.

Over the next two decades, however, Eminescu would make quick work of the Alecsandri in the fairly public competition for "national poet" status. Before long, "Mircești bard" would be no more than a sort of "official" poet of the Romanian nineteenth century.[12] However, the victory would prove costly, and the price paid had to do, one more time, with where Eminescu stood inside the cultural-aesthetic latticework of his time and place. This time around, the issue is the looming modern age complete with its inherited and evolving formal codes and preferred genres. As John Neubauer points out, "[a]t the center of a national poet's work we usually find an epic verse narrative (never a prose one) that became exemplary for the poet and his nation, though the degree to which such a work participated in the construction of a national identity greatly varied."[13] Yet, among the East-Central European poets mentioned above, Eminescu is the only one who failed to put out this kind of narrative. Prešeren won his designation as "national poet" with his 1836 *Krst pri Savici* (Baptism at the Savica), Petrović Njegoš with his 1847 *Gorski vijenac* (The Mountain Wreath), Mickiewicz with his 1834 *Pan Tadeusz*, Petőfi with the 1845 *János Vitéz* (John the Valliant), and Botev, even if he did not leave any epic text of comparable size, evoked the heroes of Bulgaria in poems such as the 1873 *Hadzi Dimitar* and the 1876 *Obesvaneto na Vasil Levski* (The Hanging of Vasil Levski). The only text Eminescu published during his lifetime in which he revisited the heroic past of the Romanians is his 1881 "Scrisoarea III" (The Third Epistle), where the poet symbolically reenacted the 1395 Battle of Rovine where the Wallachian army led by Voivode Mircea the Elder made an honorable stand against the Ottoman troops of Sultan Bayezid I. But the overall purpose of the poem is far from heroic. Taking up less than half of the work, the hostilities are flanked by a description of the rise of the Ottoman Empire and a blistering diatribe against the author's contemporaries. The text's inclusion in the series of five satires indicates that the poem's overall goal is not to eulogize the past but to lampoon the present.

2. Homer, Shakespeare, Goethe . . .

This does not mean that Eminescu overlooked the main themes of Romanian history. To the contrary, the over 14,000 manuscript pages donated by Maiorescu to the Romanian Academy in 1902 show clearly that the poet had given a lot of thought to the idea of treating national history systematically, in large-scale literary undertakings covering three major areas. First, this material attests to his ambition of writing an epic poem, an epic dramatic series, or at least a drama inspired by the clashes between the armies of Decebal, the last Dacian King, and Trajan, the Roman Emperor. It seems that Eminescu had in mind a Homeric approach, given that his subject was this foundational historical myth of the Romanian people. The poet had also outlined a "dramatic Dodecameron" that, when completed, would have chronicled in Shakespearean fashion the history of the Mușat dynasty, which had ruled Moldavia between the fourteenth and the sixteenth centuries. Finally, heavily inspired by Goethe, a third work of this sort was to bring back events and personalities of Romania's more recent history, as for instance in his unfinished novel *Geniu pustiu* (Wasted Genius) or in his dramatic poem "Mureșan." To sum up, all these projects, already underway and partly written, tell us that he had been indeed serious about tackling Romanian history in a heroic or tragic manner. And yet they had not been published, and most of them had not been even finished, which forces us to conclude that these endeavors ended up, spectacularly but irrevocably, in failure.

The question is why. We get a preliminary answer in the 1870 poem "Epigonii" (The Epigones), one of the texts included in the cluster of works that propelled Eminescu to the forefront of national literature.[14] "Epigonii" evokes the most important of his Romanian predecessors while also copying their styles in elaborate pastiches. There are eighteen writers mentioned in it, beginning with Antioch Cantemir (1709–1744) and ending with Alecsandri, who is crowned "king of poetry." On the other hand, the generation that Eminescu himself belongs to is dismissed as decayed and skeptical. The reasons for this treatment are unambiguously laid out:

> And we, epigones, their offspring? Chilly feelings, broken harps,
> Too big-headed, too small-minded, impotent and worn-out hearts,
> Each a grinning mask adjusted aptly on a scurvy mind,
> All Our Holy is a phantom and our homeland merely bluster,
> With us everything is varnish, everything but surface lustre.
> You believed in your own writings, *we to all belief are blind.*

Living in a postromantic era, Eminescu stands, as one can see, under the spell of a belatedness complex not unrelated to the cultural "delay" discussed by other critics in *Romanian Literature as World Literature*. A symptom of this complex or anxiety of cultural "tardiness" is the nostalgia of a Golden Age of poetry, which came to an end with Romanticism and yet was, according to Eminescu, the only period in whose aesthetic temporality the homologous Golden Age of national history could have been represented. In a letter addressed by the poet to his editor, the author explains, in no uncertain terms, what lies behind the poem's great show of pessimism. "Our predecessors," Eminescu writes, "believed in their writings, just as Shakespeare believed in his fantasy; however, consciousness also brings along the thought that such images are just a game; in my opinion, this is when skeptical mistrust in one's own creations rears its head."[15] At the same time, the reference to Shakespeare underscores an additional cause: it is not only a particular *Zeitgeist* but also another complex, a certain sense or suspicion of inferiority in relation to the great writers of world literature that triggers Eminescu's "skeptical mistrust" in his own work, a work whose ability to match theirs he doubts and which, in his eyes and for this reason, remains condemned to keep imitating authors from "greater" cultures by means of an epigonic literary mechanics that yields, as Maiorescu had just warned, "forms" but no "substance."

This awareness or angst may not have been a writer's block proper, but its effects were largely the same and wound up affecting other sectors of Eminescu's writing such as the dramatic projects dealing with Romanian history. In this department, he only managed, as George Călinescu observed, to sketch out a number of types and motives also Shakespearean in nature. Irina from "Gruie-Sânger" and Bogdana from "Bogdan-Dragoş" seem to copy Lady Macbeth; in the latter play, the coronation scene, with Dragul as protagonist, reminds one of *Henry IV, Part 2*; in "Mira," the main character recalls Ophelia, and a *Hamlet*-inspired, theater-in-theater kind of "comedy" is performed at the court of Moldavia's prince; the draft of "Mihai cel Mare" is placed by the poet himself under the tutelage of *Julius Caesar*, and so on.[16] In fact, not only did Eminescu consider Shakespeare "the greatest poet who has ever walked the Earth," but the Romanian author was fully aware that an imitation of the English writer would result in an epigonic product.[17] Read in this light, the harsh words Eminescu had for the historical plays of fellow Romanian poet Dimitrie Bolintineanu (1819–1872) as early as in 1870 may also help us understand why Eminescu left incomplete, and subsequently gave up on, his own artistic projects. "The root cause of Mr. Bolintineanu's deep failure in these writings," he ventures, "might be the fact that he happened to take a glance at the works of Shakespeare, the genius eagle of the North .... Indeed, when you turn to Shakespeare's works, loose and disconnected from one another as they may strike you at first blush, it might seem an easy task to write like him and maybe even better than him. And yet, perhaps no other author of tragedies has ever been more in control over his subject matter, better at spinning all the threads of his writings .... Shakespeare should not just be read quickly; he should be studied, so as to get to know exactly that which, in him, you may be able to imitate according to your own talent and ability... ."[18]

What Eminescu tells us about Shakespeare holds by and large true for Johann Wolfgang von Goethe as well. Ever since his adolescence, the Romanian poet had been working on a novel inspired by the German author, and also on a *Faust*-based dramatic poem, which he dedicated to Transylvanian poet Andrei Mureșanu (1816–1863). Titled *Geniu pustiu*, subtitled *Tasso-n Scoția* (Tasso in Scotland), and following the *Bildungsroman* structure used in *Wilhelm Meister*, the novel had been given up by Eminescu early on, during his student years. The poem, however, would go through several drafts in 1869, 1871, and 1876 before Eminescu would give up on it too. As he explained to his publisher when he decided to drop the project, "My drama will amount to nothing, since I cannot figure out what its form should be, which is because it is no drama in the first place." "It might be," thought Eminescu, "much better suited for an epic poem, but in this case the vivacity of the scenes and characters that come to my mind would be missing ...; I can feel how the whole is divided into its constituent parts, each of them claiming is autonomy. Had it come to an end, it might have been similar to *Faust*, though not really."[19] How can one write a major work, which is "similar to *Faust*, though not really"—this is the paradox tormenting the young Eminescu.

What about Homer? Although the Romanian poet had limited knowledge of Greek, his manuscripts show some attempts to translate the beginnings of *The Iliad* and *Odyssey*, and Eminescu's poems themselves make ample references to Homeric characters and motifs. But the poet just did not manage to get his bearings on heroic, Homeric ground. On the contrary, his isolated incursions in this territory would one more time drift into the parodic. For instance, in 1877, when the former Conservative Government, including many members of the Junimea group, was sued, Eminescu started working on a poem painting the episode with a mock-Homeric brush, composing a scenario where the Society's members would have real and imaginary figures as stand-ins on the model of the allegorical novel (Maiorescu = Odysseus, V[asile] Pogor = Ve Pogoros, etc.), and one of the judges was nicknamed "the

Cyclops," with an allusion to his physical deformity.[20] The 1873 poem "Mitologicale" (Mythological Stanzas) followed a similar recipe, where the "Hurricane," personified as a deity of Romanian mythology, would return to his mountain-palace he inhabited and dry out his boots by "the Fire of Hell." Not unlike the aborted efforts of Shakespearean or Goethean inspiration, the texts evolved from a Homeric structure betray, then, a certain basic incongruity with the epic ideology, be it tragic, Faustian, or heroic, a discrepancy that subtends all these tutor authors, works, and genres. This incompatibility accounts, I think, for his inability to compose a *Romanian* Homeric epic poem, a *Romanian* Shakespearean dramatic cycle, or a *Romanian* Faustian poem. But, I would offer, said incapacity runs deeper than "skill." It is a matter of conviction, of an aesthetic philosophy, if you will, in which notions of nation, national tradition, culture, and the world of *cultures* take center stage. That is to say, as long as such heroic and lofty literary elaborations bodied forth a *Weltanschauung* into which Eminescu had stopped buying and which were only making him "skeptical," they were bound to remain mere imitations ("localizations") of foreign literary patterns, "forms without substance" resembling, in fact, those previously criticized by Eminescu himself with reference to Bolintineanu. Furthermore, *as* imitations, as half-hearted undertakings forcing their author to second-guess himself, they could only move in one, self-subverting direction, hence their rapid spiraling downwards into pastiche, parody, and ultimately the author's bin of abandoned projects.

3. "Memento Mori" or, The National Epos that Failed

The question that bears asking, then, is: What did Eminescu *believe* in? And, above all, what happens when the poet tries to fill in the heroic, tragic or Faustian "forms" with the "substance" of that belief, with his own ideology? The answer to both questions could be found in "Memento mori. Panorama deșertăciunilor" (Memento Mori: Panorama of Vanities), the longest poem ever written by Eminescu (1,302 lines in sestinas), which was completed in 1872 and published integrally only in 1932 by Călinescu.[21] At first glance, "Memento mori" reads like a typically Romantic text recapping and lamenting the rise-and-fall cycles of various civilizations throughout history, which is why Romanian critics compared the poem to Constantin-François de Volney's 1791 philosophical treatise *The Ruins*, to Victor Hugo's 1876 poem series *The Legend of the Ages*, and to Imre Madách's 1861 drama *The Tragedy of Man*. All such comparisons are more or less pertinent, but perhaps the most relevant is the parallel to the Hungarian writer. What counts, in this case, is not so much the common theme but the skeptical Madách's position in his own national cultural system and literary history. This place was isomorphic to the one Eminescu occupied in the history of Romanian literature, which, strangely enough, allowed him to try and carry through, in his *own* system, Petőfi's nationalist program.

The poem is organized so as to make this objective clear. Although the outer narrative frame seems to announce an overview of the world's civilizational pageant complete with the *corsi e ricorsi* of Babylon, Egypt, Palestine, Greece, Rome, the invasion of Germanic tribes, and France during the reign of Napoleon I, almost half of the text (104 sestinas out of 217) is dedicated to Romanian ethnogenesis and therefore showcases an Edenic depiction of Dacia and a mythical reenactment of the wars between Dacians and Romans. Even more surprising is that, by contrast to the typically Romantic, overall pessimistic philosophy of the work, the Dacian interlude draws from pre-Romantic prototypes, particularly from the literary giants discussed in the previous section. Thus, the Homeric component of the episode is set off primarily in the hyperbolic construction of a mythical world inhabited by demigods. Here is, for instance, how Eminescu portrays Dacian nobles:

> The dukes are men like mountain firs, strong as rock.
> Their great eyes are cruel, but the look in them is sad,
> Red lion and tiger skins decorate their shoulders.
> There are strong, long-backed, broad-chested, bright
> beneath their great helmets, black as granite,
> and their long black hair is like the hair of demi-gods.

Moreover, in Homeric fashion, gods themselves would engage in battle. In fact, they are the ones waging the war between the two peoples, and the action basically consists in a *mano a mano* between Jupiter and Zalmoxis, whereas mortals are mere spectators just like the Norse gods, who also watch the bout ("Far away, serene and far away under a soft sun/in a blue sky, the gods of the North lie armed with lance and shield"). Such details foreshadow the Goethean dimension of the poem, for, in a manner similar to *Faust*, Eminescu's intention here is to build a pantheon where Dacian mythology crosses paths with the Greco-Roman and Norse gods and goddesses *and is thus recognized and legitimized by them*, sanctioned not only as national gallery of deities but also as segment of a transnational literary mythology system or archive and comparable to this world repertoire's other national sections. As for the Shakespearean model, this becomes noticeable when, immediately after Zalmoxis is defeated by Jupiter and the Dacian army routed, King Decebal curses Rome much like King Lear does Goneril (*King Lear*, 1.4), except that, in Eminescu, the specter of genetic "degeneration" haunts not only a single individual's descendants but the whole nation:

> Curse you, power of Rome. Dust and ashes
> shall be all that survives of your greatness. Your lips
> shall be silent. A time shall come when children understand
> nothing of their ancestors. As great as your rise to power
> has been, as great shall be your fall. Wise men
> shall despair as they drink, drop by drop,
> the wine of degradation, on which the mad shall rage.

The poem seems, then, to have met the main requirements—cultural, thematic, formal, and otherwise—for becoming a or perhaps *the* Romanian national epic poem, and yet it comes up short. Why? To answer, let me point out first that the heroic-tragic-Faustian poetic apparatus of the Dacian scene works against the very ideology underpinning the poem's main narrative frame, in that the heroic implies exception and singularity whereas the parade of empires and cultures foregrounds the history's cyclical tug-of-wars.[22] But how can we define this ideology? It is not Jewish-Christian because, despite the poem's title and subtitle—which were actually assigned posthumously by Călinescu—the explanation behind the sad fate dooming all civilizations is biological rather than moral. Nor is this ideology Hegelian, for the poem effectively rules out progress, even though—and this will turn out to matter a great deal—the poet appears to be pointing to an evolutionary, ascending course of history from East to West. At any rate, on this issue Eminescu was influenced by the dark pessimism of Arthur Schopenhauer, in whose view history is mere phenomenological expression of the individual Will and hence a spectacle of the universal Evil unleashed by the instinctual selfishness secretly governing humankind. The ontological preeminence of Evil is actually the reason in chapter 38 ("On History") of his comments on the second edition of *The World as Will and Representation* (1844), Schopenhauer considers, in the spirit of well-known Aristotelian dissociations, that history is, as a representation of the particular, inferior to poetry, which is appreciated for its intuition of the universal. On the other hand, Schopenhauer takes to task Hegel and the study of civilizations based on the Hegelian philosophy of history. To him, this study is misguided given that, contends Schopenhauer, the plurality of cultures is just the panorama of the One's different incarnations:

> In every microcosm lies the macrocosm, and the latter contains nothing more than is contained in the former. Plurality is phenomenon, and external events are mere configurations of the phenomenal world; they therefore have neither reality nor significance directly, but only indirectly, through their relation to the will of the individuals. Accordingly, the attempt to explain and expound them is like the attempt to see groups of persons and animals in the forms of clouds. What history relates is in fact only the long, heavy, and confused dream of mankind.[23]

Eminescu's poem reflects both Schopenhauerian positions. Thus, first, in "Memento mori" world civilizations are de facto reduced to culturally emblematic individuals, whether they are historical or mythical figures: Semiramis (in Babylon), the unnamed Magus (in Egypt), Solomon (in Palestine), Orpheus (in Greece), Caesar (in Rome), Decebal (in Dacia), and so forth. Second, Eminescu symbolically concludes his poem by drinking from the cup of "fiery" poetry while declining to sip from the lake of "immortality"—after all, the most that time-bound human life can afford, as history has "shown" the poet throughout its evolution, is a front-row seat at the same, monotonously ever-reiterated, misanthropy-inducing spectacle of vain passions, pseudo-virtues, and wickedness. Nonetheless, the poet's essential pessimism does not take the wind out of the heroic deployment of the Dacian episode, which begs the question of this part's driving force, of its "ideology," so to speak. In the fifty-three sestinas preceding the showdown between Dacians and Romans, Eminescu paints the canvas of a mythical-archetypal Dacia whose fantastic geography is replete with silvery streams, woods abloom, palaces carved into mountain walls, diamond bugs, sparkling rivers, cohorts of butterflies, boats pulled by swans, and fleets of clouds. This "heavenly, fairy-like landscape" surrounds a dome whose paintings preserve the "Dacian myths."[24] Which are these myths? More to the point, what do they *mean*? What are the ideas, the "pictorial" ideology of the images?

If Eminescu does not even hint at an answer, that is because he does not have one. At the time he was working on what it was supposed to be his epic poem, Romanian historians were still arguing whether Dacians had been wiped out by the Romans or not. It was only in 1860 that, in his study "Perit-au dacii?" ("Did the Dacians Disappear?"), Bogdan Petriceicu Hasdeu brought forth evidence suggesting that the local population had not been completely exterminated by the conquering Romans. As to scholarship on Dacian mythology, the situation was pretty much the same. Romanian historians and folklorists began exploring this ground only at the beginning of the twentieth century, through works such as Vasile Pârvan's 1926 *Getica*, and even then most of the available work was sheer speculation. Therefore, what we are here dealing with, as far as the poet's situation goes, is *a country without an ideology* and perhaps with one without a mythology also, if one takes into account the ambiguous auras with which the poet surrounds Zalmoxis and Dokia, the only figures of the Dacian pantheon that are evoked in his text. This is, then, Eminescu's Dacia in "Memento mori": a country without an ideological, culturally-mythologically distinct profile—in a nutshell, a country without an *ethos* of its own. But a nation cannot recognize itself in an *epos* without ethos. If the poem fails, as I think it largely does, then, this is the main reason for the failure.

Undoubtedly, the poet himself was aware of this difficulty. He attempted, therefore, in "Memento mori" already, to work out a compromise. Thus, while putting a curse on the Romans, Decebal beseeches the "barbarians" of the North to help him out, and, whether solely to oblige the Dacian or not, the German tribes, led by Odin, would destroy Rome. Furthermore, the episode was developed in another poem, written the same year (1872) but also left unpublished, "Odin și poetul" (Odin and the Poet), where, answering Odin's invitation to Valhalla, the unnamed "Poet" would meet Zalmoxis and tell him about the decay of Rome's unworthy Romanian heirs. The narrative pretext may be clever, but it misses the target, for, if a nation cannot identify itself with a country whose core mythical-historical imaginary is lacking in ethos, it cannot see itself in a foreign ethos either.

4. A Passage to India: Eminescu across Deep Space

Eminescu would find the solution to his problem more or less unexpectedly. That is, he would not be looking for it locally or, rather, vertically, by digging deep into national time in search of the elusive traces and meanings of Dacian mythology, but horizontally, across continents, as he gradually approached, in the 1870s, a place that will become his definitional "deep space."[25] This place is India. Most likely, the Romanian poet was drawn to the culture of the Indian subcontinent, beyond his personal "problem," by a combination of factors. The first was philosophical, specifically, Schopenhauer's oeuvre, with which Eminescu became acquainted between 1869 and 1872, during his student days in Vienna. This was not at all surprising. As a result of the success of his two-volume 1851 work *Parerga and Paralipomena*, as well as a consequence of the interest artists such as Richard Wagner had taken in his ideas during the 1850s and 1860s, Schopenhauer was at the height of his popularity in the German-speaking world, where he was considered the most prominent authority in metaphysics.[26] It did not hurt, of course, that Schopenhauer was appreciated, both as a philosopher and as an aesthetician, at Junimea as well, especially by Maiorescu. Equally noteworthy is that Schopenhauer inspired Eminescu to seek a broader knowledge of India as the philosopher belabors numerous themes and concepts belonging to Hindu thought. In *The World as Will and Representation*, which made a lasting impression on Eminescu, the German thinker writes that, throughout the nineteenth century, "the influence of Sanskrit literature will penetrate no less deeply than did the revival of Greek literature in the fifteenth century,"[27] and that, from the point of view of epistemological intuition, Buddhism's "preeminence" over all other religions should be acknowledged.[28]

Eminescu continued his studies of Hindu culture in Berlin, between 1872 and 1874, when, as his manuscripts prove, he seemed to be increasingly interested in linguistics, mythology, and comparative ethnopsychology. At that time, Berlin was a leader in "Oriental" scholarship. It was in the capital of the new German Empire that linguist Franz Bopp had ended his highly acclaimed academic career only five years prior to Eminescu's arrival. Author of the famous six-volume *Comparative Grammar of Sanskrit, Zend (Avestan), Greek, Latin, Lithuanian, Old Slavonic, Gothic, and German* (1833–1852), Bopp demonstrated the common origin of Indo-European languages. The German scholar's argument must have given Eminescu the idea of more profound parallels between Dacia and India. The fact is, in any case, that the poet was not only well acquainted with Bopp's research, but that, toward the end of his life, around 1884–1886, he even began to translate some of the German linguist's works, such as the 1845 *Critical Grammar of Sanskrit Language*.[29]

The Romanian writer took the natural step from Bopp's comparative linguistics to comparative mythology at home, and this step was the big jump I allude to in the opening of my presentation, for it gave him the decisive impetus to pursue his cultural-ideological homologies and flesh out an imaginary equivalence between India and Dacia. It is, again, a leap made at home but into the world. Returned from Berlin, Eminescu made friends, between 1875 and 1876, with the Jewish folklorist Moses Gaster (1856–1939), whom he introduced to the Junimea crowd, before which the scholar read the manuscript of his work *Literatura populară română* (Romanian Literary Folklore). Although the book would only be published as a volume in 1883, it is much earlier that Eminescu may have become familiar with the gist of Gaster's "theory of East European folklore as Indian mythology by-product."[30] The filiation became central to Eminescu's thinking, or so one would gather from one of his polemical interventions, in which he argued for the Romanian origin of the Raven, a symbol featured on both the Corvinus (in Transylvania) and Basarab (in Wallachia) coat of arms. To back up his thesis, Eminescu invoked a legend told by the Moldavian

historian Miron Costin (1633–1691), in which a raven swallows the ring of the
Corvinus house and is then killed by a Basarab. "The ... legend," claims Eminescu,
"proves not only the connection between the Corvinus and Basarabs, but much more,
namely, the persistence of myths of Aryan origin in the memory of our people. Costin's
legend is the legend of Sakuntala, dramatized in Sanskrit by Kalidasa. It is the same
story, only that in Sakuntala the raven is replaced by a Ganges fish."[31]

Farfetched as it may be, Eminescu's argument bespeaks the strength of the spell
such a comparative fiction cast on the poet. A possible common origin of Hindus
and Dacians would supply not only a potentially noble ancestry for Romanians but
also a solution for the creative dead-end the poet experienced in "Memento mori."
More specifically, such a fiction furnishes him with a *substance* and even with an
ethos that will help bring his "national" projects to fruition. Whether it was the Vedas,
Buddhist wisdom, or the work of Kālidāsa, at the end of the 1870s Eminescu began to
regard ancient Hindu texts as belonging to Romanian folk tradition or, at least, to a
cultural heritage common to Hindus and Romanians. In his poetry, this radical shift
in perspective starts with his 1879 poem "Rugăciunea unui dac" (A Dacian's Prayer),[32]
where the description of the birth of the universe reenacts the homologous episode of
Rigveda. Here is the beginning of Eminescu's poem:

When death did not exist, nor yet eternity,
Before the seed of life had first set living free,
When yesterday was nothing, and *time had not begun*,
And one included all things, and all was less than one,
When sun and moon and sky, the stars, the spinning earth
Were still part of the things that had not come to birth,
And You quite lonely stood ... I ask myself with awe,
Who is this mighty God we bow ourselves before.

It would be instructive to compare the lines above and the following opening of the
Vedic hymn (*Rigveda*, 10:129.1–3):

Then was not non-existent nor existent:
there was no realm of air, no sky beyond it.
What covered in, and where? and what gave shelter?
Was water there, unfathomed depth of water?
Death was not then, nor was there aught immortal:
no sign was there, the day's and night's divider.
That One Thing, breathless, breathed by its own nature:
apart from it was nothing whatsoever.
Darkness there was: at first concealed in darkness
this All was indiscriminate chaos.
All that existed then was void and formless:
by the great power of Warmth was born that Unit.[33]

The reader who goes to the trouble to set the two fragments side by side cannot miss how denotative, matter-of-fact-like, and literally expository Eminescu's poem is by contrast to the Vedic prototype. This does not mean that the Romanian poet did not take the time to polish his work. His manuscripts indicate that he first did a translation of the hymn into Romanian by comparing several German and English translations with the original Sanskrit text.[34] But this is not the only explanation. Eminescu simply viewed the Vedic hymn, along with all the other Hindu literary texts, as *part of "Romanian" folklore*, and so he felt free to handle the Vedas as *he would domestic material*, that is, immune to any anxiety-inducing pressure to prove himself by equaling and possibly outshining the model in the originality department. This explains, in a way, why his mode of adapting *Rigveda* differs radically from his borrowings from Homer, Goethe, and Shakespeare. For, even when Eminescu imitates the European greats in the most obvious fashion, he appropriates from their works either small expressions and allusions no longer than a line or macrostructural technique but hardly ever whole chunks of actual text. This is not only because his Western models are authors of marked individuality, but also because they were, must have thought Eminescu, "foreigners" without a substantial connection with Romanian culture. If, on the other hand, the Vedas *are* part of "national" patrimony, as Eminescu would have it, then originality becomes almost a moot point, hence the high degree of similarity between the Romanian poem and the Vedic hymn. And, indeed, Eminescu views the latter just as such, as a subset of a cultural archive both national and shared across national boundaries and vast swaths of space, which in turn would not be possible if he did not see entire Hindu tradition as a *"folkloric" unit*. That this is indeed his view is confirmed by the ingenious shift his text's rhetoric and mythology undergo. If the poem "Rugăciunea unui dac" begins, as we have seen, as a hymn of praise and gratitude to God who gave life to mankind, the final part ends with a chiasmus, on a defiant and self-imprecatory note as the Dacian hero asks the Creator to put an end to his life of endless misery: "To gain eternal blessings my head I do not bow,/But rather ask that you in hating compassion show./Till comes at last the evening, your breath will mine efface,/And into endless nothing I go, and leave no trace." Late as it comes in the economy of the text, this is a true rhetorical watershed. The poem's mythological tributaries, which initially flow in the direction of the *Upanishads*, are now, at the end, reversing course and running toward Buddhist philosophy, helping the poet illustrate "the doctrine … of coming out of the *saṃsāra*, the circle of birth," and the access to *nirvāṇa*, which is quite befitting given that the first version of Eminescu's poem was entitled "Nirvana."[35]

The revelation of Hindu tradition sent, during the second half of the 1870s, shock waves throughout the poet's aesthetic vision and practice, bringing about pivotal clarifications and helping him, apparently, sort things out. At this point, Eminescu seems to have overcome both the complex of Western "forms" and the lack of "substance" or "meaning"—the ethical "scarcity"—of Dacian "tradition." On the one hand, he spends a lot of time now studying popular literature and composing poetic adaptations of Romanian folk tradition, which he rereads through a perspective informed by Hindu philosophy in poems such as the 1879 "Revedere" (Return) or the 1883 "Mai am un singur dor" (One Wish Alone Have I), where he contrasts the ephemeral nature of mankind and the eternity of nature. On the other hand, Eminescu gradually abandons his heroic poems, tragedy, and drama, and turns instead primarily to folk poetry genres. After he comes back from Berlin, he writes mainly legends and fairy tales in verse, as well as ballads and folklore-inspired lyrical poems locally known as *doine*, and he gets them in print too. The masterpiece of this stage of his work and of his entire career is the long, 1883 poem "Luceafărul" (Legend of the Evening Star), which tells the story of the impossible love between an emperor's daughter and the immortal celestial body to which the text's title refers.[36] Somehow similar to "Rugăciunea unui dac," "Luceafărul" opens with the princess's portrayal, which is done in a fairy-tale style ("... Now, once upon enchanted time,/As time has never been,/There lived a princess most divine/Of royal blood and kin."), and ends with a description of the lofty isolation of the Evening Star, in a way that reminds one of the Hindu concept of *nirvṛti*[37] ("bliss," "pleasure," but also "peace" and "extinction"): "In human sphere of narrow lore/May that your luck will hold,/As I remain forever more/In my eternal cold."

The fantastic tale provides just one of the mythical, philosophical, and literary threads and motifs woven into the smooth fabric of the poem. They are borrowed not only from Romanian and Hindu cultures but also from Western narrative traditions, and it is time to make it clear that Eminescu may have found an inspirational passage to India, but, as he turns East, he is not turning his back to the West either. The deep space into which he is diving affords him, in fact, multiple, culturally less "Euclidian" positionings, so much so that he can look to Hindu literature while pivoting to meaningful models and archival resources located on other meridians, including European. Thus, some of his best poems, with "Glossă" (Gloss, 1883), "Odă. În metru antic" (Ode in Classical Meter, 1883), and the five "Scrisori" (Epistles, 1881) coming out around this time, illustrate with superb elegance the multimillennial history of Western forms and poetic motifs. Only that—and this is truly remarkable—after his imaginary journey through India, Eminescu rereads and rewrites this tradition differently. More notably still, he revisits his own work, to the extent that it was molded by this tradition. This "Hindu" self-emendation—this Hinduization—of the "national poet" is perhaps most obvious in his tinkering with older poems. For instance, he rewrites the 1879 "Pajul Cupidon ..." (Cupid ...)[38] nine years after its original composition and retitles it, quite tellingly, "Kamadeva."[39] A comparative analysis of the two versions shows right away how central is Eminescu's knowledge of Hindu mythology to his late work. While both texts are clustered around their original mythical figures by retaining the specific symbolic accoutrements of both deities, in this case their representative weapon, namely, the bow and arrow of love, as well as their childlike appearance and playful behavior, the similarities end there. "Pajul Cupidon ..." is longer (nine stanzas), has a more markedly narrative composition, and its introduction of the main character is more descriptive and done on a casually genial but overall "objective" tone: "Cupid, dreadfully spoiled rascal,/Many a hoax stored in his head,/With the children romps and scampers,/With the ladies sleeps in bed." However, when Eminescu attempts to put a more "subjective" twist on the text, he does so by pulling the reader in as an impersonal "you," while the "I" remains outside the poem's world. The text ends on a ribald note:

"While if you should beg him nicely,/Quite enough a scamp is he/Just to part the veil a little/And a moment let you see," the final stanza, follows a fragment where "the scamp" grabs a "double armful" of a "maiden breast," which now he "hide[s] with his hands." "The veil," we gather, conceals the woman's naked body, and the reader's chance to catch a glimpse of the hidden secret only lasts "a little." "Kamadeva," on the other hand, has only five stanzas and sounds like a confession from the very beginning. It starts with the poet's appeal to the god: "With the balm of lover's torment/Dreaming thus my soul to heal,/I, to Kama, God of India,/Kamadeva, did appeal." As one can notice, the impersonal "you" in the earlier poem is replaced here by a poignantly personal voice, while the playful overtones, although still present, are accompanied by a description of the torture of love and lovesickness. Most significantly, the poem's ending acquires a completely different meaning: "Thus it was a poisoned flower/Deep within my breast did send/India's child of purple heavens/And illusions without end." No less important is that "the veil" is never lifted ("illusions without end"), and that, unlike in "Pajul Cupidon …," where the veil conceals carnal reality, in "Kamadeva" the shroud's nature is the same as that of "purple heavens." This is, then, a *divine* veil whose job is to conceal not an erotic object but the world itself. This may look like a trivial detail, but it is not. For it helps us to pinpoint both the major difference between the two poems and the reason Eminescu decided to retell the story of Cupid/Kamadeva from another and, I would stress, absolutely revealing perspective (no pun intended), namely, that of a Roman deity who seems to be merely a desacralized, secular counterpart of the Indian god. Indeed, Cupid has all but lost his hallowed identity, while Kamadeva has managed to preserve it—to survive mythologically, in a sacred world and as an index of this world, which now Eminescu is tapping into to fulfill needs that are as mythopoetical as they are "ethical."

5. The Secret Master

In his 1876 poem "Cărțile" (The Books), Eminescu confesses that he had "three sources" or "masters."[40] The first was Shakespeare, "the gentle brother of my soul," who taught him "more than hosts of centuries." The second, whose name is never disclosed, was a "wise man" who helped him solve the mystery of the "end of the world." This person was most likely Schopenhauer. The identity of the third master was also kept "untold": Eminescu only lets on that this person falls asleep in his arms, and that he or she taught him even more than Shakespeare did. According to Romanian critic Caius Dobrescu, Eminescu's "secret master" may have been the woman he loved. This may be true within the framework of the poem but questionable or, at any rate, limiting if we look at Eminescu's work as a whole.[41] We can see now that the true "hidden master" of the poet was not a specific person but many, and not even persons or cultural personas but a *space*; it was not an author, set of authors, or even a "national" culture, but a cluster of related cultures. This cluster, this *spatialized* cultural web was India. The contact with its cultures was, for Eminescu, a poetic therapy of sorts. Once "plugged" into Hindu philosophical-mythological energies, Eminescu got over his "complex" and stopped seeing himself as a poet from a "minor" country with no longstanding tradition, who was doomed to remain a "peripheral" imitator of Western literature. In brief, India enabled him to find his own voice. On the other hand, it is true that, in order to pull off this self-reinvention of sorts, he had to give up his dream of writing a Romanian "national" epic. Give up he did, but this was exactly what presented him with the opportunity to thoroughly explore folk tradition, to top Alecsandri, and thus become the "national poet" of his own culture. Moreover, the "discovery" of India put Eminescu in a position to be the one to jumpstart, only two decades before Romanian modernism took off, a real Far Eastern tradition among his compatriots, as Bogdan Crețu shows in the essay included in this volume.

Eminescu was not the only one to benefit from his imaginary journey to India, but Indian cultures themselves as well; he did not actually travel to India, but, via his work, India did cut its own passage to Romania. By helping Indian ancient cultures communicate with one another, by mixing them with Romanian folk traditions and revisiting them through lenses provided by Western texts, discourses, and epistemologies, Eminescu brings out not only new shades of India but also a new way of connecting Europe to it. Needless to say, the Romanian poet was not the first European to reveal India's literary wealth to the world. As is well known, before him, translations from *Bhagavad-gītā*, Kālidāsa, and the Vedas, and especially "Indian" verse tales adapted by Romantics such as Lord Byron, Percy Bysshe Shelley, Walter Savage Landor, Robert Southey, and Thomas Moore had made major inroads into, and have thrown solid bridges to, the Asian subcontinent. Sometimes, though, the literary value of all these European responses to India notwithstanding, the images of India— Eminescu's "ideology"—painted by these poets only managed to consolidate resilient stereotypes of its "exoticism" and "Orientalism." Michael J. Franklin is only one of the critics who, in the Saidian line of anti-Orientalist and postcolonial critique, have rightly insisted that "[t]he growth of Romanticism and [O]rientalism was synchronous [in] the West, and European Romantic imagination was saturated with [O]rientalism."[42] In this view, the case can be made that Eminescu, who got to a point where he saw Hindu tradition as his own, was well positioned to try and be one of the first European writers to *de-Orientalize India*. My sense is that, deliberately or not, he did that, at least in part. Furthermore, by uncovering the Eastern roots of European culture, as he did in the pair of poems "Pajul Cupidon ..."-"Kamadeva," and by taking an intercultural-intertextual approach closer to William Butler Yeats, T. S. Eliot, and Hermann Hesse rather than to the early-nineteenth-century Romantics, Eminescu also attempted to *Easternize* or, better yet, re-*Easternize the West*.

Would it then be, I wonder, a big stretch to see, along these lines, Eminescu as one of the "secret masters" of European or even world literature? True, he may not have started his extraordinary journey on the right path, but he found another one, a whole cultural portal, and, in the final analysis, he redeems himself insofar as the end results of his Indian turn outweigh his errors and failures. Setting out to find the national, the very "substance" of "Romanianness," Eminescu plunges into the *prenational* of *Hindu* cultural-philosophical treasures and by the same token discovers—and participates in—the *trans*national, recharging his work and in turn reactivating Indo-European connections.[43] In plainer English, Eminescu looks for the nation but finds the world, a Euroasian, shared, more complex, and richer world than the West alone. And he does not just find it; he embraces it as his "national" tradition. This is how, starting with the mid-1870s, Eminescu reads *world literature as Romanian literature* and, conversely, *writes Romanian literature as world literature*.[44]

Notes

1   For the distinction between "globe" and "planet," see Christian Moraru, *Reading for the Planet: Toward a Geomethodology* (Ann Arbor, MI: University of Michigan Press, 2015), 19–76.

2   According to Marijan Dović and Jón Karl Helgason, "the gap between national and transnational cultural saints is becoming increasingly visible in the globalized world." See Dović and Helgason, *National Poets, Cultural Saints: Canonization and Commemorative Cults of Writers in Europe* (Leiden: Brill, 2017), 202.

3   See Mads Rosendahl Thomsen, *Mapping World Literature: International Canonization and Transnational Literature* (London: Continuum, 2010), 33–60. An excellent example of the autonomous functioning of the two literary circuits is the case of Hans Christian Andersen, an author who, although he gained significant international prestige, was long regarded as a minor author in Denmark. For a more recent analysis of Andersen's case, see Karin Sanders, "A Man of the World: Hans Christian Andersen," in *Danish Literature as World Literature*, ed. Dan Ringgaard and Mads Rosendahl Thomsen (New York: Bloomsbury Academic, 2017), 91–114.

4   Richard Burton, *Prague: A Cultural and Literary History* (Oxford: Signal Books, 2003), 40.

5   Milan V. Dimić, "Romantic Irony and the Southern Slavs," in *Romantic Irony*, ed. Frederick Garber (Amsterdam: John Benjamins, 1988), 252.

6   Anthony J. Zielinski, *Poland in the World of Democracy* (St. Louis: Laclede, 1918), 96.

7   Edmund Obecny, "Translator's Note [to Juliusz Słowacki's *In the Tomb of Agamemnon*]," *Free Poland* 4, no.17 (June 1, 1918): 208.

8   Edgar Papu, *Poezia lui Eminescu* (Iași: Junimea, 1979), 204.

9   George Călinescu, "Eminescu, poet național," [1964] in *Opere*, vol.3, ed. Nicolae Mecu, Ileana Mihăilă, and Daciana Vlădoiu (Bucharest: Fundația Națională pentru Știință și Artă, 2016), 528. Călinescu coined the phrase "unparalleled poet" to suggest that, in Romanian literature, one could not find Eminescu's match. The expression was subsequently taken to designate the poet's exceptional stature nationally *and* internationally.

10   Titu Maiorescu, "În contra direcției de astăzi în cultura română," [1868] in *Opere*, vol.1, ed. Dumitru Vatamaniuc (Bucharest: Fundația Națională pentru Știință și Artă, 2005), 157–166.

11   Maiorescu, "Direcția nouă în poezia și proza română," [1872] in *Opere, vol. 1, 170.*

12   George Călinescu, *Istoria literaturii române de la origini până în prezent* (Bucharest: Fundația Regală pentru Literatură și Artă, 1941), 253.

13   John Neubauer, "Figures of National Poets–Introduction," in *History of the Literary Cultures in East-Central Europe: Junctures and Disjunctures in the 19th and 20th Centuries*, vol.4, ed. Marcel Cornis-Pope and John Neubauer (Amsterdam: John Benjamins, 2010), 12.

14 Mihai Eminescu, *Poezii-Poems*, trans. Leon Levițchi and Andrei Bantaș (Bucharest: Teora, 2000), 45–53.

15 Mihai Eminescu, "Scrisoare către Iacob Negruzzi," [June 18, 1870] în *Opere*, vol.16, ed. Perpessicius, Dumitru Vatamaniuc, and Petru Creția (Bucharest: Editura Academiei, 1989), 34.

16 Călinescu, "Opera lui Mihai Eminescu," [1947] in *Opere, vol. 1, 1061.*

17 Călinescu, "Opera lui Mihai Eminescu," [1947] in *Opere*, vol. 1, *1057.*

18 Eminescu, "Repertoriul nostru teatral," [1870] in *Opere, vol. 9, 8.*

19 Eminescu, "Scrisoare către Iacob Negruzzi," [February 6, 1870] in *Opere*, vol. 16, 38.

20 For Eminescu's Homeric parodies, see Călinescu in *Opere*, vol. 1, 891–896.

21 Mihai Eminescu, *Poezii-Poems*, trans. Roy MacGregor-Hastie (Cluj-Napoca: Dacia, 1980), 190–247.

22 "A panorama of vanities, a *memento mori* could not (and could never) be … extracted from a national history in which the selfish feeling of preserving the nation and its worth reigns supreme," argues Călinescu in *Opere, vol. 1, 561–562.*

23 Arthur Schopenhauer, *The World as Will and Representation*, vol.2, [1849] trans. E. F. J. Payne (New York: Dover Publications, 1969), 443.

24 Mircea Cărtărescu, *Visul chimeric* (Bucharest: Litera, 1992), 48. For a more detailed interpretation of the Eden *topos* in Eminescu, see Radu Vancu, *Eminescu. Trei Eseuri* (Sibiu and Cluj-Napoca: InfoArtMedia-Argonaut, 2011), 89–91.

25 Wai Chee Dimock is one of the critics who has theorized "deep space." "Literature," she posits, "is the home of nonstandard space and time. Against the official borders of the nation and against the fixed intervals of the clock, what flourishes here is irregular duration and extension, some extending for thousands of years or thousands of miles, each occasioned by a different tie and varying with that tie, and each loosening up the chronology and geography of the nation." See *Through Other Continents: American Literature across Deep Time* (Princeton, NJ: Princeton University Press, 2007), 4.

26 On Schopenhauer's popularity in the mid-nineteenth century, see David E. Cartwright, *Schopenhauer: A Biography* (New York: Cambridge University Press, 2010), 524–548.

27 Schopenhauer, *The World as Will and Representation*, vol. 2, XV.

28 Schopenhauer, *The World as Will and Representation*, vol. 1, 169.

29 Amita Bhose, *Eminescu și India* (Iași: Junimea, 1978), 19.

30 Radu Cernătescu, *Literatura luciferică. O istorie ocultă a literaturii române* (Bucharest: Cartea Românească, 2010), 53.

31 Eminescu, "Mai lesne se torc …," [1883] in *Opere*, vol. 13, 164.

32 Mihai Eminescu, *Poezii-Poems*, trans. Corneliu M. Popescu (Bucharest: Editura Fundației Culturale Române, 1999), 51–53.

33 *The Hymns of the Rigveda*, trans. R. T. H. Griffith (New Delhi: Motilal Banarsidass, 1995), 633.

34 Amita Bhose, *Eminescu și India*, 115–120.

35 Amita Bhose, *Eminescu și India*, 91.

36 Mihai Eminescu, *Poezii alese-Selected Poems*, trans. Adrian George Sahlean (Bucharest: Univers, 2000), 55–95.

37 Bhose, *Eminescu și India*, 127.

38 Eminescu, *Poezii-Poems* (1999), 41–43.

39 Eminescu, *Poezii-Poems* (1999), 370.

40 Mihai Eminescu, *Poezii-Poems* (2000), 379.

41   Caius Dobrescu, *Mihai Eminescu: Imaginarul spațiului privat. Imaginarul spațiului public* (Brașov: Aula, 2004), 39.

42   Michael J. Franklin, "Orientalism: Literature and Scholarship," in *Encyclopedia of the Romantic Era, 1760–1850*, vol.2, ed. Christopher John Murray (New York: Fitzroy Dearborn, 2004), 834.

43   Wai Chee Dimock, "Scales of Aggregation: Prenational, Subnational, Transnational," *American Literary History* 18, no.2 (2006): 219–228.

44   According to Thomas O. Beebee, the notion of a "world literature as German literature" was not alien to Goethe's concept of *Weltliteratur*. "Why not posit," asks the American critic, "the origins of German literature as multiple, and as including Greek tragedy, Tacitus, Horace, and the Bible, Italian *novelle*, and so forth—so Goethe seemed to argue implicitly?" See Beebee's "Introduction: Departures, Emanations, Intersections," in Thomas O. Beebee, ed., *German Literature as World Literature* (New York: Bloomsbury Academic, 2014), 17.

2

Aux portes de l'Orient, and Through: Nicolae Milescu, Dimitrie Cantemir, and the "Oriental" Legacy of Early Romanian Literature

Bogdan Crețu

In line with other contributions to this volume's opening section, my essay sets out to lay bare the ideological construction of Romania's literary historiography, a scholarly genre that, after Romanticism, has not shied away from articulating and pursuing political ideas and ideals throughout Europe. To that effect, I will trace, first, the ways in which representative Romanian literary histories have placed the medieval and, in particular, late medieval period—the country's "old" or "early literature"—into the service of state, national, and nationalist agendas. For, as I argue below, not only have such political platforms been conspicuously present in this scholarship, but they also account for the dominance of both benignly nationalistic and overtly nationalist takes on cultural phenomena that were *trans*national and occurred *well before* the birth of the nation-state and its attendant discourses of nationhood and nationalism.

To foreground this transnationalism and highlight, accordingly, the various layers of the palimpsest-like conglomerate of cultural ingredients that went into the making of Romanian literature during its pre-national era, I will focus on two writers of the time: Nicolae Milescu Spătarul (1636–1708) and Dimitrie Cantemir (1673–1723). Major international figures of the seventeenth and early-eighteenth centuries, these authors grew up, were educated, lived, and wrote in a quintessentially transitional space where goods, ideas, values, cultural forms, and mentalities shuttled back and forth between Europe and Asia. Reflecting this intersectional positioning in the wider world, their works were fashioned by and circulated in both Western and Eastern lands. This intercultural movement shaped not only Milescu's and Cantemir's oeuvres but an entire literature's saliently complex notions, themes, and styles, translating into a fertile presence of the Middle and Far East in a culture that, beginning with the second half of the nineteenth century, would more and more pride itself on its Europeanism, sometimes by downplaying the significance of stimuli from outside Europe. In fact, as I will show in the last section of my intervention, while, especially after nineteenth-century Romantics such as Mihai Eminescu, Romanian writers will periodically rediscover, from a Western, increasingly "Orientalizing" perspective, the Eastern world into which scholars and travelers like Milescu and Cantemir had made their forays, the twentieth century will witness a widening of the gap between "Romanian literature," understood as an expression of national identity, and Eastern traditions, which will be increasingly perceived as external and alien.

1. Literary Historiography, Nationalism, and Pre-National Literature

As Theo D'haen has pointed out, the development of national literary histories in the post-1800 era, a time that also witnessed the rise of Goethean *Weltliteratur*, was influenced by political shifts in the formation of modern nation-states. "Goethe," the Belgian critic observes, "pushed the idea of a world literature in an age of intense nationalism. In Germany as in the rest of Europe, and later also in the Americas, during the nineteenth and twentieth centuries most effort would go into the writing of national literary histories." "This was," D'haen concludes, "the logical cultural counterpart to the relentless process of political nation-building or consolidation going on across Europe. According to the tenets of Romanticism, each nation strove to ground its legitimacy in its own literary antecedents. Consequently, we see the first systematic histories of Europe's various national literatures appearing in the first part of the nineteenth century."[1] Occurring about a century after their European models and in rough-hewn forms, the first attempts at a history of Romanian literature date back to the end of the nineteenth century.[2] Basically, they were textbooks and anthologies consisting of portraits of writers and sketchy analyses of literary fragments and purporting to explain what was "specifically Romanian" in the authors at hand. Lacking proper design and following no clear criteria, these undertakings barely met the requirements of critical scholarship, let alone of modern literary historiography.[3] It was not before the beginning of the twentieth century that the first true histories of Romanian literature were published. Coming out during moments of national crisis and political tension, many of these works were eager to assume ideological functions accordingly. This explains why literary histories of the first part of the twentieth century such as those by Nicolae Iorga (1901), Sextil Pușcariu (1901), Nicolae Cartojan (1940–1945), and George Călinescu (1941) do much more than merely describe the evolution of literature or propose aesthetic-criteria-based hierarchies of values. Instead, they are *national projects*, and problematically so. For, in taking implicitly or explicitly on the ideological task of imagining and arguing for the coherence, longstanding tradition, continuity, self-sufficiency, and, in particular, for the nationally defining and unifying characteristics of the literary texts produced by Romanians in Romanian territories, said projects' presentation of these works is strategically selective and streamlining. Not only does this body of primary sources seem to be often at war with itself, self-conflicted about its direction, and imitating, sometimes indiscriminately and incongruously, foreign styles, formulas, and authors belonging to different, even discrepant movements and periods, but this complexity of structure and content is paralleled by one of scale. As Wai Chee Dimock notes,

My own conclusion is that literary studies require the largest possible scale, that its appropriate context or unit of analysis is nothing less than the full length and width of our human history and habitat. I make this claim from the standpoint of literature as a linguistic form with agency in the world, a linguistic form compelling action. This action gives rise to a jurisdictional order whose boundaries, while not always supranational, are nonetheless not dictated in advance by the chronology and territory of the nation-state. As a set of temporal and spatial coordinates, the nation is not only too brief, too narrow, but also too predictable in its behavior, its sovereignty uppermost, its borders defended with force if necessary. It is a prefabricated box. Any literature crammed into it is bound to appear more standardized than it is: smaller, tamer, duller, conforming rather than surprising. The randomness of literary action—its unexpected readership, unexpected web of allegiance—can be traced only when that box is momentarily suspended, only when the nation-state is recognized as a necessary but insufficient analytic domain, ceding its primacy upon scale enlargement.[4]

"Start[ing] to serve as institutionalized forms of national memory, ... [the] national literary histories" coming out in Romania during the country's post-1918 consolidation as a nation-state are precisely the "prefabricated boxes" Dimock talks about. They are simply inadequate for a content whose formal-thematic and scalar constitution calls not only for different critical containers but also for a methodology more accommodating than the restrictively nationalist approach that left out a sizeable part of the very cultural material it was supposed to retrieve.[5] Notably enough, the segment in question covers some major Southeast European and Asian aesthetic and religious paradigms, patterns, and orientations. Instrumental to the genesis of premodern Romanian letters, all these took, beginning with the second half of the nineteenth century, a back seat to Western and, before long, Westernizing cultural models. National literature's priority became—as many a Romanian critic would put it—to "catch up" or "synchronize" its "progress" with literary developments in the West, and it was national literary historiography's job to document this process and, by the same token, make a two-pronged case for Romanian literature as testimony to an identity at once nationally unique and European.

Given this brief's inbuilt epistemological constraints, one should not be surprised by how critics have handled early literature, including some key issues such as timeline, the "origins" of Romanian literature, and the relationships between language and literature or between literature "per se," done for primarily "aesthetic" purposes, and literature in a more general, utilitarian, administrative, historical, or religious sense. Thus, when addressing the birth of Romanian literature, most scholars have been tempted to push it farther and farther back into the past so as to "prove" the existence of a long-established, "organic" literary tradition on national soil. The question they invariably raise is: Which are the first *literary* texts written in this space? If Iorga, for example, thought that the Greek language and culture represented "the generally shared knowledge [across] the Orient [Near and Middle East]" and in the Romanian kingdoms at the time,[6] and if Cartojan considered the old, Slavonic religious texts fragments of "Romanian soul translated into Slavonic,"[7] Călinescu cherry-picked works composed in a reasonably polished, artistically functional Romanian language—"[l]iterature," he insists in the preface to his *Istoria literaturii române de la origini până în prezent* (History of Romanian Literature from Its Origins to the Present), "includes solely writings expressing the intellectual and emotional processes aimed at or at least resulting in an aesthetic response."[8] Similarly, in his 2008 *Istoria critică a literaturii române* (Critical History of Romanian Literature), Nicolae Manolescu recognizes that "during the Romanian Middle Ages, it was common to write in several languages" but declines to "consider those texts [composed in idioms other than Romanian] as belonging to Romanian literature."[9] If Manolescu's history is, like Călinescu's, keen on the nexus language-literature, that is because both are premised on the notion that through language—it goes without saying, Romanian—literature becomes an exclusively national product, connecting with the nation-state's identity genetically and thus "naturally" instantiating and indexing it. As Pascale Casanova reminds us,

> [t]hrough its essential link with language—itself always national, since invariably appropriated by national authorities as a symbol of identity—literary heritage is a matter of foremost national interest .... [t]he link between the state and literature depends on the fact that, through language, the one serves to establish and reinforce the other. Historians have demonstrated a direct connection between the emergence of the first European states and the formation of "common languages" (which then later became "national languages").[10]

But neither language—more exactly, a *single* language, the one that would eventually rise to the rank of national idiom—nor the territory inhabited by its native speakers in medieval or modern times can, alone, define a literature, account for its growth, and supply a rationale for its "specificity." In all actuality, Romanian literature would not have come about, and the richness of its beginnings would not still intrigue us today had the mobility and interweaving of the works, ideas, stylistic patterns, and motifs incorporated into early Romanian literary texts obtained solely within the linguistic, territorial, and ethnic borders of the nation-state or of its historical, pre-national-era regions. No doubt, the idiom matters, including the rhetorically specialized medium of written, nonutilitarian, "artistic" texts. Likewise, the ethnic origin of an author cannot be ignored either. But they are not sufficient conditions for the emergence of a literature, and early Romanian literature was no exception. In point of fact, if we really need a concept broad enough to accommodate the genetic dynamic leading to this literature's appearance, that concept—or cultural formation, rather—is *tradition*, more precisely, the tradition*s* to which belonged the various texts coming out during this period. Furthermore, on the one hand, these traditions were religious and largely spiritual, philosophical, political, as well as—and certainly not only—"artistic" or "literary." On the other hand, they were all under no circumstances "national" linguistically, ethnically, politically, territorially, or otherwise. In effect, what scholars commonly refer to as "old Romanian literature" was part and parcel of a cultural swath stretching across Southeastern Europe and synthesizing phenomena originated in a range of traditions covering an even wider area. This cultural perimeter forms in the shadow of the Eastern Orthodox Church and as an outlying subset of Byzantine and post-Byzantine civilization. In 1935, Iorga put forth an argument on the survival of Byzantine culture, especially in the Orthodox Christian countries, after the 1453 fall of the Byzantine Empire. As his "Byzantium after Byzantium" theory has it, it is hard to talk about a sufficiently individualized, "national" Romanian culture from the sixteenth to the eighteenth century, when, with the gradual weakening of the Phanariote rulers' grip on Moldavia and Wallachia, the Byzantines' legacy also wanes in the Romanian Principalities of Wallachia and Moldavia.[11]

The impact of Iorga's vision was short-lived, however. Making a splashy appearance a mere six years after *Byzance après Byzance*, Călinescu's *History* authoritatively recharted the course of Romanian literary historiography in an entirely different direction, one that played up the national and the aesthetic, with the latter assigned the task of couching the former's "unmistakably" Romanian nature. Granted, the book was immediately attacked by the far-right-wing press, which resented the critic's references to the contribution of "foreign," especially Jewish writers to the fostering of "national specificity" and accused him of *lèse-nation* ("anti-national") crimes. Otherwise, the *History*'s political, indeed nationalist agenda is fairly clear, as are the bearings of this program on Călinescu's treatment of old Romanian literature. In brief, his approach involves a reading scenario meant to "heal" the so-called complexes of the Romanian literature—collective self-representations organized around a set of insecurities about the rise, age, and originality of national literary culture. In response to these anxieties—more bluntly put, to make up for the lack of a reassuringly distinctive culture of this sort in the early period—the *History* hatches a series of "founding myths" of Romanian literature while overstating the aesthetic value of the medieval texts in Romanian.[12] In them, the critic appreciates not only literary artistry but also the potential for identity construction, which will remain a top priority for the historiographers following in Călinescu's footsteps and ultimately explains why their archival forays are devoted to the recovery of old texts. Yet again, their endeavors are not unprecedented. It was, in fact, by no means uncommon in nineteenth-century European literary historiography to focus on "imaginative literature" at the expense of multilingual religious, historical, and philosophical works, and to do so for *ideological* reasons, to wit, because, understood as *belles letters* written in the vernacular, literature presented itself as the discourse best equipped to portray the "national soul."[13]

These notions of literature and literary history held sway well into the post–Second World War epoch in scholarly and political contexts such as Romania, where, while not always doing the bidding of official nationalisms, critics were nonetheless at pains to "uncover" early literature's aesthetic virtues and its later, "organic," cultural coherence-inducing circulation in the modern nation-state. It is true that, as Casanova also comments, literature gains its "autonomy" as object—and as an object of study as well—once its history is no longer derived from national history. "Little by little," she remarks,

literature succeeded in freeing itself from the hold of political and national authorities that originally it helped to establish and legitimize. The accumulation of specifically literary resources, which involved the invention and development of a set of aesthetic possibilities, of forms, narrative techniques, and formal solutions (what the Russian formalists were to call "procedures")—in short, the creation of a specific history (more or less distinct from national history, from which it could no longer be deduced) allowed literary space gradually to achieve independence and determine its own laws of operation. Freed from its former condition of political dependency, literature found itself at last in a position to assert its own autonomy.[14]

In Romania, literature's "political dependency" took effect later and lasted longer than elsewhere, what with the interwar decades' disputes between traditionalists and modernists spilling over into the Cold War years and beyond and inflecting the conversation around the early literary patrimony, its artifact status, dating, role in the obsessively renewed case for the culture's Latin origin, "unique" profile in the region and in Europe, and the like.

2. Comparatism and the Geography of Originality

All these problems remain, to this day, pivotal to the national and nationalist platform. As such, they pressure periodically the participants in this debate to reinstate aforementioned "dependency" by dint of a series of critical maneuvers that deemphasize, render insufficiently visible, and otherwise give less play to early Romanian literary culture's transnational formation and its partaking in geocultural systems hardly coextensive with the terrain that would only centuries later fall under the jurisdiction of the nation-state. By mapping this culture onto the national territory so as to limit, analytically speaking, the former to the latter, critics have severed the truly "organic" bond of their object with its "natural," worldly matrix, that is, with the Byzantine, post-Byzantine, and Southeast European cultural space, whose *transnationality*—a transnationality of the *pre*-instead of *post*national world—was a true hotbed for a whole array of interrelated aesthetic practices and manifestations. In the age of nations, these phenomena would evolve and advertise themselves accordingly, as more spatially, culturally, and linguistically discrete, more "national." But for the premodern, Orthodox Christian European Southeast, including places like today's Romania, it would be a mistake, for example, to try to come to grips with print culture and with books' production, circulation, and meaning by relying exclusively on scalar models such as the one provided by post-1918 Romanian territorial sovereignty. Critics who have chosen to do so have retroactively assigned the borders of the *later*, modern nation-state to Romania's *earlier* culture and have thereby confined the movements, inspirations, and interchanges engendering and defining this culture to a spatial and political domain that, because it did not exist as such back then, cannot serve as an analysis unit either. All the same, under the sway of nationalist politics, Romanian scholars have overlooked the glaring scalar incongruity in play here. As a result, they have celebrated as "Romanian" literary works that in fact were common assets of the European-Levantine regional system centered on

Orthodox Christianity and Byzantine heritage. Moreover, not only were these works "Romanian," but they were also "original," for, to reiterate, the objective here has been to recover old texts that were both ethnically and aesthetically "peerless," not evocative of, or derived from, "outside" texts and contexts. That is why these early Romanian works have been often read in isolation from their actual genetic environments and sources, as self-explanatory, autochthonous, and "new," when in reality they are, for the most part, translations, adaptations, or versions of books that, once again, make up the premodern cultural commons of this part of the world. Thus, what has reinforced the "originality" argument has been, besides nationalist epistemology, the scarcity of thorough comparative studies, for the competent and diligent comparatist was bound to discover sooner or later that the written heritage of his or her national culture came about, in earlier times more than ever, by compilation, translation, adaptation, remake, imitation, collage, and the like. This should not surprise us either because, more than in the West, the basic creative protocol of the region in the early age was *erudition*.[15] Dealing with a subject and more generally "expressing" "new" knowledge about it meant gathering together *all* available knowledge on the topic in one place. This was both reproductive work, in that it did rehash extant stuff, but also productive insofar as it produced the writer's authority, or rather set it up as a reflection of the authority of the problem at hand and of those who had formerly tackled it. Questioned only infrequently, such an authority over time becomes tradition, and the job of an author in this culture was principally to allow tradition to manifest itself and pass itself along. The personal, subjective, or "creative" take on things came second or, better still, to create *was* to recreate, to rehearse, transmit, and preserve. This helps us understand why the vast majority of old texts written in Romanian compiled, catalogued, recapitulated, and recycled much more than they "invented" or started from scratch, and why they did so without "plagiarizing"—a term quite out of place in this context. Thus, historical chronicles consistently drew on one another as they unabashedly borrowed and reworked lengthy excerpts from previous works of this kind; books of religion, philosophy, ethics, and pedagogy largely translated their Byzantine prototypes; and the era's "popular" books or novels such as *Barlaam and Josaphat* and *Aesopica* underwent a dazzling array of adaptations while remaining easily recognizable as they traveled and morphed across the lands and vernaculars of this sector of the Eurasian continuum.

The style- and narrative structure-oriented analyses to which critics of early Romanian literature have been so partial have been demonstrably unprepared to do justice to a material whose makeup required a comparative tack. While the situation has improved after 1990 with the first academic inroads of interdisciplinary studies, the New Historicism, and cultural materialism, close reading still keeps its "distant" cousin and, by the same movement, comparative interpretation at bay.[16] As Franco Moretti has insisted, "the trouble with close reading (in all of its incarnations, from the new criticism to deconstruction) is that it necessarily depends on an extremely small canon."[17] Put another way, this sort of perusal both preserves its effectiveness when applied to a limited amount of texts *and* reinforces this limit, for, scalewise and otherwise, the latter is apposite to close reading's narrow scope and methodological inability to reach beyond the textual and the national into the contextual, more exactly, into transnational and world contexts. In other words, close reading attends to, and endorses, a national canon set up solipsistically, at "close quarters," and organized into an ossified hierarchy that is as grand as it is isolated from the competition as well as from the potential sponsorship of world literature. Approaching "distance *[a]s a condition of knowledge* ... allow[ing] you to focus on units that are much smaller or much larger than the text[, such as] devices, themes, tropes[,]or genres and systems," distant reading has, instead, access to cultural spaces, structures, and meanings to which textual analyses of the close kind do not.[18] Positioned as they were across and beyond the languages, ethnicities, and national territories marked on the modern maps of Southeastern Europe, and thereby in no way centered exclusively on Western hubs of prestige and innovation, these stylistic, thematic, and geocultural domains were crucial to the development of early Romanian literature. This is the reason the latter calls for a germane reading algorithm, viz., for one capable to handle the intrinsically supra- and transnational, "at-distance" formation of a body of work that splices together the near and the far, the West and the East.

3. Before the Great Wall

Milescu and Cantemir epitomize this synthetic and still insufficiently elucidated process by which worlds apart merge and spawn new worlds in the writings of early Romanian authors. To this day, the former cuts a somewhat enigmatic figure in Romania's literary-cultural history. For one thing, many of the works translated into or compiled in Romanian during the seventeenth century and whose authorship is either disputed or unknown have been attributed to him, from the translation of Herodotus' *Histories* to the *Pearls* of Saint John Chrysostom and from Agapios Landos's *Salvation of the Sinners* to *Apology against Muhammad* by fourteenth-century Byzantine emperor John VI Kantakouzenos. Following the steps and curricular concentrations typical of the Southeast European scholarly instruction of the epoch, Milescu's training pursued both religious and secular interests and built expertise in Western, Byzantine, as well as Middle Eastern and other Asian traditions. After studying in his native country, Moldavia, under the supervision of Greek scholars, he went to the Academy of the Patriarchy of Constantinople (Istanbul) where he was in a select company—one of his peers was Dositheus Nottaras, the future Patriarch of Jerusalem. Later, Milescu served in various political and diplomatic positions for the rulers of Moldavia and Wallachia, which allowed him to travel not only to Constantinople but also all over Western Europe. Thus, in 1666 he went to Stockholm and in 1667 to France, where he spent time at the court of King Louis XIV. He visited Berlin and Italy too. Between 1699 and 1671, he was back in Constantinople, where Dositheus Nottaras had recommended him for a position in diplomacy with the Czar of Russia. It is in this capacity that, in the spring of 1675, he left for China, where he would be "the first Romanian to stand before The Great Wall."[19]

Documented as some of these journeys and encounters are, Milescu's life is still something of an unknown for his biographers, hence the myths and enigmas swirling around him, from the espionage suspicions to the rumors sparked by the cutting off of his nose, a punishment, at the time, for pretenders to the throne. It is, however, not his adventures but his no less spectacular and multivalent work that makes him one of the most extraordinary figures of Romanian culture, a kind of *uomo universale*. Fluent in a number of languages including Slavonic, Latin, and Ancient Greek, he translated the Old Testament into Romanian, which version was incorporated into the first edition of the Romanian Bible (1688). In response to a challenge by the French ambassador, he wrote, in 1677, a short text in Latin on Orthodox Christianity's doctrine of transubstantiation, a hot topic of the moment and bone of contention in the disputes between the Jansenists and the Reformed. The piece's title was *Enchiridion sive Stella Orientalis Occidentali Splendens, id est Sensus Ecclesiae Orientalis, scilicet Grecae, de Transsubstantione Corporis Domini, aliisque Controversiis, a Nicolai Spadario Moldavolaccone, barone ac olim Generali Wallachiae, conscriptum Holmae anno 1667, mense Februarii*. In 1669, it was included by Antoine Arnauld and Pierre Nicole in *La Perpétuité de la foy de l'Église Catholique touchant l'Eucharistie, défendue contre le livre du sieur Claude, ministre de Charenton*, which assured Milescu's essay a wide readership in the West.

What brought him fame across and beyond the Western world was, however, chiefly his journey to the Far East. The trip led to two of his best-known works, which came out in Russian, were translated into New Church Slavonic and Greek, and circulated throughout Southeastern Europe. These are travelogues: the 1675 *Book Describing the Journey through Siberia, from the Town of Tobolsk to the Border of the Kingdom of Kitaia, Year 7183, Month of May, Day 3*, and the 1676 *Description of China*, his "report" as a diplomat assigned to check out unknown Asian lands and establish contacts. The *Description* consists of fifty-eight chapters presenting, in an encyclopedic fashion, China's geography, history, culture, religion, language, customs, education, institutions, administration, military, roads, and main towns. The text is not so much a collection of an explorer's "impressions" but the official account of an emissary and explorer whose job was to gather accurate and useful information. Occasionally, the writer compares what he discovers with things and places he was already familiar with—a river reminds him of the Danube, for example—and his general reaction is not that of a traveler dumbfounded by the exotic forms of other geographies and civilizations. Notably, if the Far East does not come through, in Milescu, as a *terra mirabilis*, as the "land of miracles" it did in the West, that also had to do with the functional, expository style, which in turn echoed the informative nature and official purpose of the *Description*, a "report" that did not set out, nor did it claim, to be the work of an "author" in the modern, individualizing, and proprietorial sense of the term.

Further compounding the "expressive" issue as well as the problem of the authenticity of the *Description* is its "intertextual" makeup: in their fascination with Milescu's aura, most Romanian critics skirt around the authorship question altogether, ignoring conveniently in the discussion of his "originality" that the work represents, to a large extent, a translation of the Jesuit Martino Martini's *Novus Atlas Sinesis*, which was published in Amsterdam as part of Joan Blaeu's 1655 *Atlas Maior*. This detail is highly relevant. Much in line with the knowledge-production conventions and literary-cultural customs of seventeenth-century Eastern Europe, a scholar like Milescu, charged though he had been with laying out what he encountered and experienced firsthand, chose to acquit himself of the task by translating a Western scholar's work. To grasp the meaning of his decision, it bears repeating that "originality" as we know it did not exist yet, and that erudition—a presentation protocol the era held in high regard—often meant unearthing relevant sources, as well as appropriating and adapting them to the specific parameters of the project. Granted, it may seem odd to us today that the procedure entailed, at the "gates of the Eastern world," data gathering and other kinds of "on-site" documentation about the East that were, to no negligible degree, a Western writer's prior treatment of the subject.[20] And yet the procedure is only apparently paradoxical, for Milescu's method fits in with the modus operandi of his age's scholarship. The latter required research and composition practices such as quasi-encyclopedic familiarity with the widely disseminated European literature covering a vast geocultural zone beyond Europe and ability to translate, marshal, and tweak these sources so as to work out, in a peripheral culture such as the one evolving in the Romanian territories of Milescu's time, syntheses that served ends and carried the material and philological echoes of a much broader, European and Asian cultural realm.

Taking advantage of the limited circulation of its sources, Milescu's *Description* played an important part in the formation of the Western image of the East. Beside its translations into Slavonic and Greek, it was also summarized in Floy de la Neuville's *Relations curieuse et nouvelle de la Moscovie*. Thus, circling back to the Western intellectual archives where its genesis had started out, the book's geo-philological route charts a trajectory quite common to the manuscripts, publications, and ideas of Milescu's world and goes to show that, simply put, in this space, cultural material belonged to everyone during the seventeenth century. Equally remarkable is, once more, that the geography of this belonging, this cultural zone of sharing, inspiration, and intellectual-artistic production, was much wider than the creative and spatial-administrative rubrics and domains under which modernity classifies and ascertains scholarly and aesthetic creativity. Learned works were not necessarily assumed to come from an individual author, just as they were not attributed to a "national culture." In fact, literature was not yet divided into national literatures. Certainly, as a philologist and translator, Milescu is considered today, as he should be, a Romanian scholar. But the diplomat, the author of the books on China and of the compilation of treatises on the education of Russian noblemen, such as the 1672 *Aritmologhia, adică știința despre numerele tuturor lucrurilor* (Arithmologion), *Cartea despre sibile* (The Book of Sibyls), also published in 1672, and the 1673 *Cartea pe scurt despre cele nouă muze și despre cele șapte arte liberale* (Brief Book on the Nine Muses and the Seven Liberal Arts) draw a more complex portrait nationally, scholarly, and otherwise. Their author does not shy away from using his knowledge and talents to serve political authority, in this case the Czar's, whose imperial autocracy *The Book of Sibyls* seeks to legitimize. A few decades later, Cantemir's learning will go down the same path in the service of Peter the Great.

4. A World Citizen's Posthumous Career: From Transnational Scholar to National Symbol

Cantemir stands front and center particularly in the scholarship devoted to reinforcing the notion of a substantial and sophisticated early Romanian literature. Was the Cantemir we know formed in a Romanian area, though? Did he operate in it? Then, even if he indeed did, was there such a neatly delimited, national—let alone "Romanian"-designated—cultural domain in the seventeenth century? Aside from the private lessons taken with Jeremiah Cacavelas, one of the most renowned theologians of the East, Prince Cantemir too was educated at the school run by the Patriarchy of Constantinople. His acknowledged role models were both Westerners such as philosopher, alchemist, and physician Jan Baptist van Helmont, whose works Cantemir diligently summarized as a young man, and Asians like Persian poet Saadī Shīrāzī, author of the *Gulistan*. Son of the ruler ("Voivode") of Moldavia, Cantemir reigned twice, lived for almost twenty years in Constantinople, and sought and was granted asylum in Russia, where he became a counselor of Czar Peter I. Besides Romanian, his mother tongue, he spoke New Church Slavonic, Latin, Ancient and Modern Greek, Persian, Turkish, and Russian. Like Milescu, he is a perfect example of the premodern cosmopolitan intellectual at home in many worlds, citizen of a cultural, religious, and geographical world spanning not only Orthodox Christian Europe but also the Eastern traditions beyond it. His training, his interdisciplinary and cross-cultural activity, the sheer amount and complexity of his work, as well as the scholars he looked up to are as many reasons to think twice before describing him as a product chiefly, let alone exclusively, of Romanian culture in the national-territorialist sense that marks literary and cultural history after Romanticism.

And yet this understanding of Cantemir's personality and work still prevails, making him into an early symbol of the excellence, sophistication, and "universalism" of national culture. In fact, drawing on his historical writings—which seek to prove the Latin origin of the Romanian language and the Roman roots of the Romanian people, a subject very popular with Eastern Europe's late humanists—some critics have gone to great lengths to present him as a precursor of nationalist ideology. To build this argument, they have pointed to the lasting influence of those contributions in the country's cultural history, from the Romanian Enlightenment, particularly the nineteenth-century Transylvanian School (Școala ardelcană"), all the way to the "protochronists" who, echoing Romanian Communism's late 1960s' nationalist turn, would pull all-nighters to demonstrate that the world's modern breakthroughs in the arts and sciences had been made or anticipated in Romania or by Romanians. However, from his very first book, the 1698 *Divanul sau Gâlceava Înțeleptului cu Lumea sau Giudețul Trupului cu Sufletul* (translated into English as *The Salvation of the Wise Man and the Ruin of the Sinful World*), which 25-year-old Cantemir published in Romanian, in Moldavia (Iași), it became clear that the author's overall affiliations and allegiances were ecumenical rather than "national" in that they extended far beyond his homeland and were "disciplinary," philosophical and theologian, rather than Moldavian. The *Salvation* is an Orthodox Christian pedagogical and political handbook of sorts that places a lot of stock in an encyclopedic training whose curricular content and objectives are both attuned to European humanism and geared to broader political goals. A beneficiary of this kind of instruction, Cantemir represents the new type of well-educated Southeast European leader who, at the turn of the seventeenth century, proves himself not so much on battlefields but in the library while wielding learning as a political weapon.[21] Considered by some the first Romanian philosophical work, the *Salvation* does not depart from the Orthodox Christian doctrine common to the post-Byzantine world of which, once again, Moldavia was just a small part. Along these lines, it is noteworthy that, featuring Jeremiah Cacavelas's translation, the book appeared in a bilingual, Romanian and Modern Greek edition, which speaks to the author's ambition to reach audiences and otherwise intervene in a geocultural system spreading past the territorial and linguistic borders of his birth country. Unifying this non- and supra-national system were primarily religion—Orthodox Christianity—and language, namely Greek, the new lingua franca supplanting New Church Slavonic. Also informing the system were, as mentioned earlier, composition protocols in which authoring and borrowing, textuality and intertextuality, originality and translation or adaptation characteristically bled into each other. These writing procedures were transregional, that is, in use throughout the cultural geography marked by the legacy of the Byzantium, but also trans-European and even intercontinental. Accordingly, the allegorical dialogue of the *Salvation*'s first part and the expository segment of the book's second part cite a large spectrum of authorities, from those approved by the Eastern Orthodox Church to Catholic thinkers to secular and ancient writers, while the third big section is an adapted translation of a treatise by Unitarian theologian Andreas Wissowatius, *Stimuli virtutum, fraena peccatorum*, which had come out in Amsterdam in 1682. Furthermore, the Moldavian Prince's interest in the "Orient" is also obvious. On one occasion, for example, he mentions Saadī—who, writes Cantemir, "although pagan, beautifully spoke"—a reference that is rather unexpected in a book of Orthodox Christian persuasion.[22] In relation to the Saadī passage, it also bears noting that the *Salvation* circulated in print and in a whole array of manuscripts in Romanian—critic Virgil Cândea uncovered more than fifteen in Moldavia, Wallachia, and Transylvania[23]—and in Greek, but also in Arabic, under the title *Salāh al-hakīm wa-fasād al-'ālam al-damīn*, in a translation by Athanasios Dabbās, Patriarch of Antioch and Metropolitan of Aleppo.[24]

If Cantemir is familiar with "Oriental" traditions such as Persian, on Turkish culture he is a true expert. While fulfilling his peculiar envoy-cum-hostage duties in Constantinople on behalf of his father, he wrote, in Turkish, a music manual entitled *Kitab-i 'ilm al-musiqi* (Book of the Science of Music), where he proposed a notation system he then used to preserve hundreds of musical pieces and compose a few dozen himself.[25] This is an important contribution to Turkish musicology; in fact, Turkish cultural history recognizes him primarily as a musicologist. But the *Book* is also a landmark in world music history, making its author a resource for contemporary artists active in the recovery of Eastern musical traditions, such as Jordi Savall and his orchestra Hespèrion XXI, who, since 2009, have toured the world with their popular show "*Le*

Livre de la Science de la Musique" et la Tradition Musicale Séfarade et Arménienne.
Furthermore, Cantemir was not only entirely at home in Ottoman music. In his 1717
Incrementorum et decrementorum Aulae Othmanicae sive Aliothmanicae historiae …
(History of the Rise and Decline of the Ottoman Empire …), he also compares it to
European music. "I may certainly venture to say," he offers in the *History*, "that the
Turkish Music for metre and proportion of words is more perfect than any European,
but withal so hard to be understood, that in [the] spacious city of Constantinople, you
will scarcely find above three or four, who understand the grounds of this Art."[26] Here
and elsewhere, Cantemir's scholarship shows off not only impressive command of an
exceptionally diverse, Eastern and Western material but also his ability to unearth
cross-cultural parallelisms and contrasts and work out syntheses in which whole
cultural traditions converge, overlap, and mesh.

In fiction, his most significant synthetic effort of this sort is by far the 1705 *Istoria
ieroglifică* (Hieroglyphic Story), which was written in Romanian. Some have identified it
as the country's first work of literature in the narrower, modern sense of the term, while
others have described it as the most elaborate "bestiary" of seventeenth- and eighteenth-
century European literature.[27] At any rate, literariness is in this novel both intentional and
ostentatiously flaunted, which has also prompted comparisons with Baroque "sensibility"
and its intricately ornate, highly wrought stylistics. Notably, because *Hieroglyphic Story*
did not benefit, and so could not draw, from a local tradition in the art of fiction, let
alone in the art of novelistic form, it marks a beginning rather than a continuity in that
tradition, or, better yet, could have marked one had it indeed had a chance to furnish the
steppingstone for future novels or fictional prose generally. Unfortunately, Cantemir's
masterpiece, completed in 1705, was published much later, in 1883, and so it missed an
opportunity to give birth or contribute in some way to an indigenous novelistic tradition.

In all actuality, it is tenable that *Hieroglyphic Story* could have made a difference in
the admittedly slow rise of the Romanian novel. In his work, Cantemir is no longer
chiefly a learned compiler but an individualized author whose well-configured,
personal take on things is on full display. No pre-nineteenth-century text of Romanian
culture showcases such a subjective engagement with the world. As a matter of fact,
the novel introduces, historically speaking, a whole new shift in authorial perspective,
more specifically, in what it means to create by moving into a quasi-modern writer's
position. That is to say, with Cantemir, the Romanian literary text finally becomes a
work of art, i.e., something the writer imagines, makes, and colors subjectively, so
much so that he or she, up to that moment a secondary element, now becomes a
primary, individualized factor, who has not just the initiative but also the authority
to fashion raw material and rationales as well as to rework previous aesthetic and
intellectual formulas according to the intended message. Assuming this authorial
position, Cantemir's prose takes liberties with some of the norms of religious thinking
of his time and place and, when necessary, steps outside the geocultural boundaries
of Orthodox Christianity altogether. Massively indebted to the literatures of the East,
Hieroglyphic Story acknowledges as its model Heliodoros's romance, *Aethiopica*, whose
narrative chronology Cantemir borrows. He does the same with Persian fables, which
he recycles into his animal allegories. Major sources also include *Halima*, Saadī, and

Kalīla wa Dimna, a Persian rewriting of *Panchatantra*, an Indian collection of fables Cantemir could have read in its Turkish version, *Hümayanname*, or in Simeon Seth's Greek rendition, *Stefanites kai Ihnilates*. In fact, many of the novel's exotic characters, such as the Jackal, originate in these works, and it would be only fair to say that *Hieroglyphic Story*'s fictional fauna is neither Western nor Eastern but both, as the author, much like Milescu, saw the European and Asian literary patrimonies as a single cultural reference system.[28]

A similar argument can be made on the book's language. The latter is, of course, a Romance and therefore European idiom, but it must have sounded to its contemporary reader, much as it does to us, artificial, "synthetic" in a sense evocative of trial-and-error laboratory experiments. Engineered in Cantemir's literary-encyclopedic vitro, *Hieroglyphic Story*'s Romanian is chock-full of neologisms and imitates convoluted, Latin- and Turkish-inspired syntax and grammar structures. Beyond language, Turkish literature and culture, as well as Islamic written tradition, along with their stylistic patterns, have also influenced *Hieroglyphic Story*, particularly in the fragments of rhymed and rhythmic prose, which echo the *Koran*.[29] These are some of the linguistic, cultural, and religious resources the author puts to use in his endeavor to do something about the conceptual and expressive limitations of his era's Romanian. For, at the time, Cantemir's mother tongue was far from ready to become a medium for sophisticated literary and scholarly projects, and so the novelist sets out to enrich and refine it through crosspollinations with Eastern and Western, ancient and modern idioms and with grammatical, stylistic, and rhetorical formulas of emblematic works written in those languages.

What Cantemir's linguistic syncretism is after was in no way detrimental to Romanian. Not only that, but it may well have sped up what Michiel Leezenberg calls the language's "emancipation." This process, through which the idiom becomes ripe for specialized, literary usage, was, according to the critic, part and parcel of broader, Europe-wide, "pre-nationalist," and "vernacularizing" developments. "Cantemir's literary writings," claims Leezenberg, "mark an important phase in the emancipation of Romanian as a language of literature and learning; as such, they may be seen as an example of the vernacularization that generally preceded the rise of nationalisms in the strict sense of the word."[30] True, having been employed in writing for almost two centuries before Cantemir, albeit not necessarily for literary purposes proper, Romanian was likely ready to graduate to aesthetic medium status in *Hieroglyphic Story*. But the author picks his native language not so much for its pre-national or outright nationalist affordances as for the political decoding it enables. For, on the one hand, this *roman à clef* allegorizes real events in Moldavian and Wallachian politics, which, on the other hand, the book relitigates passionately by addressing an audience knowledgeable about and even involved in those disputes. Thus, a whole host of elements, including the location of these conflicts, the identity of their main actors, as well as the language of Cantemir's intended public, made Romanian an obvious choice.

Absent these circumstances, other languages would strike him as a better fit. Latin was one of them. In Moldavia and Wallachia, where Orthodox Christianity required Slavonic and, later, Greek, Latin was not popular. However, after *Hieroglyphic Story*,

Cantemir resorted to it in works whose topics were more "international," whose stakes—he thought—were higher, and through which he was hoping to enter broader, European circuits of intellectual exchange and, ultimately, that World Republic of Letters in which Latin was still a lingua franca.[31] The work that grants him this kind of scholarly and cosmopolitan citizenship is *History of the Rise and Decline of the Ottoman Empire*. A mix of historiography, anecdotes, and memoir, this significant achievement speaks to Cantemir's academic and literary training, as well as to his knack for mining for relevant information both historical archives and his personal experience. Researched and, as it appears, partially written in Constantinople, where its author lived for twenty years, completed in Russia, translated into, and published, in English in 1734 and then in French and German in 1743, the book played a foremost role in the shaping of the Western view of the Ottoman Empire for about a century. The *History*'s considerable impact on Enlightenment and Romantic literature can be traced through the works of Voltaire, Byron, Chateaubriand, Victor Hugo, and other major figures of the eighteenth and nineteenth centuries.[32]

Indeed, although it was elaborated in Russia and its subject is the Ottomans, the book was read mainly in the West, and so it bears asking: Which culture does the *History* belong to? Romanian? Russian? Ottoman or Turkish? Is the work a part of the humanist Europe in which Latin was still reigning supreme? Is its strongest association perhaps with European culture as a whole? Moreover, and setting one more time aside the anachronistic use of the term here placed within scare quotes as to designate a geopolitical reality still centuries away, is Cantemir an author affiliated with a single "national" culture? Modern Romanian critics have rushed to bill him as an icon of national creativity and advancement and even as a forerunner of nationalism tout court, but this portrait misses the bigger picture and the world behind it. His multilingual and pluricultural education, his life experience, his many travels and residences, his firsthand access to Western and Eastern sources, his recognized authority on a range of subjects and in a vast geography of knowledge production and prestige from Moldavia to Constantinople and from the Russian intellectual circles to the Royal Academy of Berlin, whose member he was, testify to this world—to the several words, in fact, whose intermingling accounts for the transnational character of eighteenth-century culture in the territory of the future Romanian nation-state.

5. East by West

One of the main worlds participating in these cultural synergies, the East continued to captivate Romanian artists and thinkers after Milescu and Cantemir and into the nineteenth century. This period witnessed spectacular progress on the country's modernity project. A two-track process, this undertaking entailed a feverish import of Western institutional models, social structures, and literary-intellectual forms in parallel with the blooming of a nationalist mythology and attendant discourses, which was also echoing similar developments in the West. In this context, where modern Romania was reinventing itself by emulating its European "sisters," primarily the other siblings of the Romance family and most emphatically France, the "Orient"'s pull ebbed gradually without ever fading away completely. Its remarkable endurance in the Romanian literary imaginary testifies to the writers' inspirations from and aspirations to cultural spaces wider than the nation-state to whose building up they were otherwise channeling their energies in the second half of the nineteenth century.

Their efforts paid off before long. By the time Moldavia and Wallachia sealed their "little unification" as United Principalities in 1859 and shook off, after the Independence War of 1877, their vassalage to the Ottoman Empire by achieving full sovereignty, the culture had evolved a clearly national and even nationalist program across all Romanian regions, including Transylvania. Again, this platform's model was Western. In 1848, well-traveled poet and revolutionary Vasile Alecsandri, whom many regarded as the "national bard" until the arrival of Eminescu on the literary scene, pointed out that visiting Eastern lands was fashionable for Romanian boyars. But that was no longer the case with many authors of travel memoirs, such as Teodor Codrescu, Dimitrie Ralet, Dimitrie Bolintineanu, Teodor Burada, and Mihail Kogălniceanu, for whom going East and especially to Constantinople made for a sort of culturally, politically, and historically "regressive" if not "reactionary" journey. Definitely, the East had become the past.[33] The West was the modern present Romanian literature wanted to be part of, and cultural mimesis was neither too high a price for the admission ticket nor at odds with the nationalist agenda. That was also because, whereas the West and its assimilating thrust were not felt as threats to national identity, the East and its "Orientalizing" adjacency were. Consequently, Romanian writers started seeing and imagining the Eastern world as remote, radically different, and "other" from and to the identitarian space in and from which they were defining themselves and their burgeoning nation.

It is essentially with the Romantics that, in Romanian and other European traditions, the Middle East and other parts of Asia became the enticing, "feminine," exotic, and sometimes fantastic geography and object of the hackneyed representations and "othering" mentalities Edward Said and his followers would expose so diligently. But the Romantic turning point in the history of the European cultural imaginary was as "Orientalist" as it was nationalist.[34] This twin shift also shaped modern Romania, its literature, and the study thereof after the mid-nineteenth century. It is at this juncture that the basic ideas about nation and national identity are defined and literature begins to hew to these ideas and carry, openly and proudly, their combined payload: the ideology of patriotism. This ideology—how the Romantics identified themselves, their compatriots, their country, and its history—needed the "Orient" as a contrasting backdrop against which to set itself off, and this background, this "world-not-us," was "discovered" through the lens of Western media and literature.[35] Thus, the images, landscapes, literary characters, mythical and historical figures, and popular heroes of the East were summoned as references in arguments about "typically" Romanian features of national culture. Given the odds in a geopolitical and cultural environment in which the Ottomans and other "Orientals" had posed major "contamination" risks for centuries, this culture's survival was nothing short of a "miracle." Moreover, it was not only radically distinct from its Eastern and Islamic vicinities but also "superior" to them. This is the gist of the national mythology concocted by poets such as Alecsandri, Bolintineanu, Alexandru Pelimon, Constantin D. Aricescu, and Alexandru Depărățeanu, members of a "transitional" generation of writers for whom the East was neither entirely passé nor the source of authentic and culturally formative dialogue that it had been for previous authors.

From a literary-historical standpoint, these early Romantic—but largely eclectic—authors are transitional insofar as they also lay the groundwork for Eminescu (1850–1889). Where this discussion is concerned, however, his case is not so easy to sort out. A full-blown if belated Romantic as well as *the* "national poet" of Romanian literature, Eminescu is probably its most influential Romanian writer to this very day. Still considered by many the greatest Romanian poet ever and therefore incontrovertibly central to the culture's aesthetic canon, Eminescu draws on the "Orient" abundantly and originally. He even tried to gain direct access to the sacred Hindu texts in the original, for which purpose he translated Franz Bopp's Sanskrit grammar into Romanian. What might be defined as the "Indian intertext" in Eminescu's work is also quite extensive. From the early poem "Venere şi madonă" (Venus and Madonna*),* where Amita Bhose detected echoes of Kalidasa's *Shakuntala,* to "Memeto Mori," which paints enormous Oriental panoramas with Romantic brushstrokes, "Rugăciunea unui dac" (Prayer of a Dacian), "Glossă" (Gloss), and "Scrisoarea I" (The First Epistle), many of his masterpieces are influenced by Buddhist spirituality.[36] Their cosmogony is visibly indebted to the *Vedas'* "Hymns of Creations," and so is, at times, the wording itself of some of Eminescu's lines. Intriguingly enough, "Rugăciunea unui dac" meshes the nationalist theme of Dacian "autochthonism" with the suggestion of a common spirituality that both spans a geography much vaster than the nation's and, in line with Romantic genealogic fantasies, assigns Romanian people a culturally prestigious and venerable ancestry. Likewise, Eminescu's prose works such as *Sărmanul Dionis* (Poor Dionysus), *Geniu pustiu* (Wasted Genius), *Archaeus,* and especially *Avatarii faraonului Tla* (Pharaoh Tla's Avatars) are as many riffs on the Buddhist notion of reincarnation. Here as elsewhere, the author's in-depth knowledge of Eastern cultures and religions is indisputable even though he discovered and mined them via European Romanticism and more generally as a result of his German education and interest in Arthur Schopenhauer's philosophy[37] rather than in response to a genuine Hindu influence on him or to the inherent cultural and spiritual "affinities" between the Romanians and the Hindus.[38]

The lack of such "organic" kinship did not prevent Eminescu from canvassing, like Milescu and Cantemir before him, greater cultural spaces inside and outside Europe. His friend Ion Luca Caragiale (1852–1912), the most important Romanian playwright, would follow suit, most prominently in short stories such as "Kir Ianulea," "Abu Hassan," and "Pastramă trufanda" (Freshly Cured Pastrami). After him, the East does remain a common reference for twentieth-century writers, but in them the "Orient" gets more and more "Orientalist," treated as a strange realm defined by obscure beliefs and outlandish customs. In Liviu Rebreanu's 1925 "metempsychotic" novel *Adam şi Eva* (Adam and Eve), for instance, a couple is reunited for seven times in various periods and in places like India, Egypt, and Babylon. The Far East "spiritualizes" sexuality in Mircea Eliade's 1933 novel *Maitreyi* (Bengal Nights) as well. This widely read book tells the story of a young Romanian scholar who falls in love with his Indian mentor's daughter and has, through her, the revelation of a totally different world and love philosophy—a cultural perspective to which, I might add, the female character's presumed prototype responded in 1974 with her own fictional account, *It Does Not Die*. Eliade, who lived in India between 1929 and 1931 and later became a well-known historian of religions, also described his Indian experience in his 1934 book *India*, as well as in other essays. In 1940, he published two short stories on the same subject: "Secretul doctorului Honigberger" (Doctor Honigberger's Secret) and "Nopți la Serampore" (Nights in Serampore).

But the author who has tried the hardest to recover the umbilical nexus connecting Romanian and Eastern traditions in the modern era is Mihail Sadoveanu. In the 1933 novel *Creanga de aur* (The Golden Bough), he attempts a cultural-religious synthesis between the pre-Roman world of Dacia and Christianity through his protagonist, Kesarion Breb, the last priest of the Dacian god Zalmoxis, who had been, according to Herodotus, a disciple of Pythagoras, and it is interesting to note that Breb first travels to Egypt, to be initiated, and then to Byzantium, whose "decadence" dismays him. Also, in his 1940 set of interlinked "Oriental" short stories *Divanul Persian* (The Persian Divan), Sadoveanu rewrites an old popular book of Indian origin, *Povestea lui Sindipa filosoful* (The Story of Philosopher Sindipa). Here he offers, according to Marcel Cornis-Pope, "a genuine cross section of Oriental narrative lore (Turkish, Syrian, Arab, Mongolian), demonstrating the value of intercultural dialogue at a time of sharp political polarizations."[39] Six years after *Divanul Persian*, in 1946, in *Fantazii răsăritene* (Eastern Fantasies), Sadoveanu also recycles Turkish stories, legends, and factual historical information. This is something Romanian writers find harder and harder to do under Communism, which considered Eastern spirituality "obscurantist" and therefore "subversive." Nonetheless, fiction writers and poets of various generations, from Cezar Ivănescu—who worked Buddhist philosophy into his 1979 volume of poetry *La Baaad*—to Mircea Cărtărescu—who published his postmodern epic poem *Levantul* (The Levant) in 1990—keep returning to Eastern cultural geographies for themes, formal patterns, and worldviews whose full measure in the formation of national literature Romanian literary historiography still needs to take.[40]

Notes

1   Theo D'haen, *The Routledge Concise History of World Literature* (London: Routledge, 2011), 9.

2   The first literary histories appeared in Italy (1723) and in France (1733), followed by a slew of similar works at the beginning of the nineteenth century, as D'haen reminds us in *The Routledge Concise History of World Literature* (10).

3   Examples include Aron Pumnul, *Lepturariu rumânesc cules de'n scriptori rumâni pre'n Comisiunea denumită de către naltul Ministeriu al învățământului ... spre folosința învățăceilor den clasa I și a VIII-a a gimnaziului de jos*, vol. I–IV (1862–1865);

Gheorghe Gh. Arbore, *Noțiuni de Istorie a Literaturii Românești pentru uzul școlilor comerciale și licee* (1886); Miron Pompiliu, *Antologie română pentru uzul școalelor secundare* (1885); Ioan Lăzăriciu, *Istoria literaturei române. În uzul tinerimei studioase* (1884); I. Nădejde, *Istoria limbei și literaturei române cu probe de limbă, de ortografie și de toate neamurile … Pentru cursul superior liceal* (1886). Wilhelm Rudow published in Leipzig a German history of Romanian literature, *Geschichte des rumänischen Schrifttums bis zur Gegenwart* (1892), on which, see Horst Fassel, "Două vechi istorii literare românești în limba germană: Wilhelm Rudow (1892) și Gheorghe Alexici (1906) și literatura și cultura română," *Philologica Jassyensia* 22 (2015): 147–164.

4   Wai Chee Dimock, "Planetary Time and Global Translation: 'Context' in Literary Studies," *Common Knowledge* 9, no.3 (Fall 2003), 489.

5   D'haen, *The Routledge Concise History of World Literature*, 12.

6   Nicole Iorga, *Istoria literaturii române în secolul al XVIII-lea (1688–1821)*, vol.I, revised ed., pref. and ed. Barbu Theodorescu (Bucharest: Editura Didactică și Pedagogică, 1969), 5.

7   Nicolae Cartojan, *Istoria literaturii române vechi*, revised. ed., pref. Dan Horia Mazilu, ed. Rodica Rotaru and Andrei Rusu (Bucharest: Editura Fundației Culturale Române, 1996), 56.

8   G. Călinescu, *Istoria literaturii române de la origini până în prezent*, pref. and ed. Al. Piru (Bucharest: Minerva, 1982), 3.

9   Nicolae Manolescu, *Istoria critică a literaturii române: 5 secole de literatură* (Pitești: Paralela 45, 2008), 27.

10   Pascale Casanova, *The World Republic of Letters*, trans. M. B. DeBevoise (Cambridge, MA and London: Harvard University Press, 2004), 34–35.

11   Nicolae Iorga, *Byzantium after Byzantium*, trans. Laura Treptow (Iași, Oxford and Portland: Center for Romanian Studies, 2000).

12   The main interventions in this discussion are works by Mircea Martin and Andrei Terian: *G. Călinescu și "complexele" literaturii române* (Bucharest: Albatros, 1981) and *G. Călinescu. A cincea esență* (Bucharest: Cartea Românească, 2009), respectively.

13   John Neubauer, "Introduction" to "Part IV. Literary Histories: Itineraries of National Self-Images," in *History of the Literary Cultures of East-Central Europe: Junctures and Disjunctures in the 19th and 20th Centuries*, vol.3, ed. Marcel Cornis-Pope and John Neubauer (Amsterdam: John Benjamins, 2007), 346.

14   Casanova, *The World Republic of Letters*, 37.

15   Michel Foucault, *The Order of Things: An Archaeology of the Human Sciences* (London: Routledge, 2002), 37–38.

16   On distant reading and comparative analysis, see Franco Moretti, "Conjectures on World Literature," *New Left Review* 1 (2000): 54–68, and also Franco Moretti, *Distant Reading* (London: Verso, 2013), 43–62.

17   Moretti, "Conjectures on World Literature," 57.

18   Moretti, "Conjectures on World Literature," 57.

19   This is one of the most common clichés surrounding Milescu's personality.

20   In 1900, Raymond Poincaré famously declared: "Que voulez-vous, nous sommes ici aux portes de l'Orient, où tout est pris à la légère"—"What would you expect? Around here, we are at the gates of the Eastern world, where things are taken lightly." Reproduced by Romanian newspapers, Poincaré's pronouncement became famous—and, in

some quarters, infamous—after novelist Mateiu I. Caragiale used it as an epigraph of his 1929 novel *Craii de Curtea Veche* (The Old Court Libertines). On this issue, see Monica Spiridon's essay "On the Borders of Mighty Empires: Bucharest, City of Merging Paradigms," in *History of the Literary Cultures of East-Central Europe: Junctures and Disjunctures in the 19th and 20th Centuries*, vol.2, ed. Marcel Cornis-Pope and John Neubauer (Amsterdam: John Benjamins, 2006), 100.

21 Virgil Cândea, "Les intelectuels du Sud-est européen au XVIIe siècle," *Revue des études sud-est européennes* 2 (1970): 181–230.

22 D. Cantemir, *Opere complete, I. Divanul*, pref. and ed. Virgil Cândea (Bucharest: Editura Academiei Republicii Socialiste România, 1974), 251.

23 Cantemir, *Divanul*, 77–81.

24 D. Cantemir, *The Salvation of the Wise Man and the Ruin of the Sinful World [Salāh al-hakīm wa-fasād al-ʿālam al-damīm]*, ed. and trans. Ioana Feodorov, Introduction and Comments by Virgil Cândea (Bucharest: Editura Academiei Române, 2006); Ioana Feodorov, "The Arabic Version of Dimitrie Cantemir's *Divan*. A Supplement to the Editor's Note," *Revue des études sud-est européennes* 1–4 (2008): 195–212.

25 On Cantemir as a musicologist, see Eugenia Popescu-Judetz, *Prince Dimitrie Cantemir: Theorist and Composer of Turkish Music* (Istanbul: Pan Yayıncılık, 1999); Stefan Lemny, *Les Cantemir. L'aventure européenne d'une famille princière au XVIIIᵉ siècle* (Paris: Complexe, 2009), 84–86; Michiel Leezenberg, "The Oriental Origins of Orientalism: The Case of Dimitrie Cantemir," in *The Making of the Humanities, vol. 2: From Early Modern to Modern Disciplines*, ed. Raens Bod, Jaap Mat, and Thijs Westeijn (Amsterdam: Amsterdam University Press, 2012), 252–253.

26 See Leezenberg, "The Oriental Origins of Orientalism," 253.

27 Marcel Cornis-Pope considers Cantemir's novel as marking the "prehistory" of Romanian historical fiction. He notes that *Hieroglyphic Story* is "written against the background of a traditional literature composed of historical annals and religious homilaries." For these and other related comments, see Marcel Cornis-Pope, "The Search for a Modern, Problematizing Historical Consciousness: Romanian Historical Fiction and Family Cycles," in *History of the Literary Cultures of East-Central Europe*, vol.1, ed. Marcel Cornis-Pope, John Neubauer (Amsterdam: John Benjamins, 2004), 499.

28 On these aspects, see Mircea Anghelescu, *Literatura română și Orientul* (Bucharest: Minerva, 1975), 28–30; Alina-Georgiana Focșineanu, *Kalīla wa Dimna și Istoria ieroglifică. O posibilă filiație* (Iași: Ars Longa, 2015).

29 Anghelescu, *Literatura română*, 24–25.

30 Leezenberg, "The Oriental Origins of Orientalism," 259.

31 "Latin—together with Greek, reintroduced by humanist scholars—had accumulated all of the literary and, more generally, cultural capital then in existence," argues Casanova in *The World Republic of Letters* (48).

32 See Lemny, *Les Cantemir ...*, 136–144; Leezenberg, "The Oriental Origins of Orientalism," 253–258. Cantemir is evoked in Byron's *Don Juan*, Canto V as follows: "His Highness was a man of solemn port,/Shawl's to the nose, and bearded to the eyes,/Snatch'd from a prison to preside at court,/His lately bowstrung brother caused his rise;/He was as good a sovereign of the sort/As any mentioned in the histories/Of Cantemir, or Knolles, where few shine/Save Solyman, the glory of their line" (Lord Byron, *Don Juan* [London: Hodgson & Co., 1823], 219).

33 Florin Faifer, *Semnele lui Hermes. Memorialistica de călătorie (până la 1900) între real și imaginar* (Bucharest: Minerva, 1993), 75.

34 Joep Leerssen calls early nationalism "political Romanticism" and defines it as "not just as a politics inspired by Romantic concepts and attitudes, but also [as] a Romantic literature inspired by national politics" in *National Thought in Europe: A Cultural History* (Amsterdam: Amsterdam University Press, 2006), 21, 177.

35 Mircea Anghelescu, *Lâna de aur. Călătorii și călătoriile în literatura română* (Bucharest: Cartea Românească, 2015), 106.

36 Amita Bhose, *Eminescu și India* (Iași: Junimea, 1978), 47–52.

37 See Ilina Gregori, *Știm noi cine a fost Eminescu? Fapte, enigme, ipoteze* (Bucharest: Art, 2008).

38 This is what Bhose argues in *Eminescu*, X–XI.

39 Marcel Cornis-Pope, "The Search for a Modern, Problematizing Historical Consciousness: Romanian Historical Fiction and Family Cycles," 501.

40 Harold B. Segel, *The Columbia Literary History of Eastern Europe since 1945* (New York: Columbia University Press, 2008), 202.

3

"Soft" Commerce and the Thinning of Empires: Four Steps toward Modernity

Caius Dobrescu

If critics have dwelled at length on empires' politically oppressive, economically exploitative, and culturally reductive thrust, they have done so for obvious reasons that need not be rehearsed here. The havoc imperialism has wreaked throughout the world is a matter of evidence, and this observation too is a commonplace. But such truisms are exactly the point, more precisely, the jumping-off point of my essay: to this day, imperialism has been a major driving force of world history, part and parcel of the very fabric of history. Not only that, but, in all sorts of ways—some of them more egregious than others—empires have set in motion sociocultural and political processes without which, for better or worse, neither most of the national entities as we know them today nor supranational aggregates such as the EU would exist.

One could suggest, in fact, that one of the less intended but enduring consequences of imperial advancements in areas such as the European Southeast was exposure to other worlds and, through characteristically imperial and imperialist ideologies, policies, and sociocultural practices of "holism," "universalism," "totality," all-encompassing "order," "commonality," and the like, even to a certain vision of a "worlded" world beyond the local, the regional, the "provincial," the "insular," the ethnic, and the national. This is, in effect, the gist of my argument in the following critical sketch of modern Romanian cultural and literary history. As I further suggest by extrapolating from a sequence of case studies and succinct overviews of pivotal cultural movements and figures from Dimitrie Cantemir to Ion Budai-Deleanu, Nicolae Bălcescu, Titu Maiorescu, and Ion Luca Caragiale, Romanian modernity and principally its literature came into being at the crossroads of and amidst centuries-long conflicts among Euroasian empires and through dialogue with their "metropolitan" worldviews and discourses. This was, I also contend, a complex, multidirectional, and evolving engagement that went through several stages and cultural strategies and, around the turn of the twentieth century, ended up with a quasi-self-empowering, culturally differentiating, "transmetropolitan" moment—one that both asserts, powerfully and originally, Romanian culture's European and planetary belonging and reminds us that this affiliation is, to a notable degree, the result of creative responses to imperial pressures in this part of the continent. In other words, such influences did not always have assimilationist or colonizing effects. Imaginative pushback against various empires' hegemonies *and* tactical absorption of imperial cultural and political leverage set the stage, instead, for a gradual awakening to a sense of a worlding world, of vaster horizons beyond imperial actors and subaltern status and thus spawned new, nonderivative, and even anti-imperial cultural forms.

I write "actors" advisedly. For key to the genesis of such forms was the plurality of imperial agents jockeying for supremacy in the area. Notably, modern Romanian culture did not arise in the sphere of influence of a single empire, but at the intersection of multiple such zones and sometimes astride the frontiers—ever porous, shifty, and contested—separating a number of empires and hubs of power geographically adjacent to Romanian lands, encroaching on them (Byzantine, Ottoman, Russian and Soviet, Austrian–Hungarian), or distant, exerting their mimetic pull from afar (French, German, British, and, of late, arguably American). The range of interactions and overall modalities of experiencing a wider world and echoes of other places, people, and cultures in this polyimperial space, coupled with the ability to play, when convenient, one empire or co-opting force, fashion, and cultural model against another transformed over the course of a few centuries this corner of Europe into a hotbed of creativity. This process involved an intuitive, nonsystematic, two-thrust approach to imperialism that pushed against empire as cultural–political, annexing and controlling *imperium* while reaping the direct and indirect benefits of the worldly realities, traffics, and opportunities imperial geocultural and demographic dynamics sometimes afforded. Thus, a disjuncture between empires' dominating, selfsameness-oriented drive and what their world-integrating impetus allowed, as it were, against their "better" imperial judgment—a "syncope" of imperialist self-reproductive rationality— could and did occur and left its imprint on modern Romanian literature.

This disconnect and its positive upshots in human life and cultural expression have not been a prerogative of recent times, however. According to J. G. A. Pocock, the first modern scholar to have considered this aspect is Edward Gibbon, who, says Pocock, pointed to Roman sociocultural formations that came about alongside and sometimes via imperial expansion and domination but grew completely distinct from them. In Pocock's assessment, Gibbon's sharp eye for the unstable and ambiguous couplings and decouplings of *imperium* and *libertas* throughout Roman history enabled him to notice that "peace and prosperity had endowed the citizens of the empire with a shared fabric of manners—the fruit of *commercium* rather than *imperium*—which had endured for some time after the political and martial spirit to defend it had been lost."[1] The distinction between *commercium* and *imperium*, which Pocock borrowed from Gibbon's celebrated *History of the Decline and Fall of the Roman Empire* but had been already in play in Voltaire's philosophical letters, specifically in their references to *le commerce des pensées, le commerce des idées*—the interchanges of thoughts or ideas—is central to my presentation.[2] As we will discover, the rise of modern Romanian literature is to no negligible degree an outgrowth of active trade in ideas, themes, fashions, cultural forms, and paradigms—of the *soft commerce*, if you will, that the imperial presence in this part of the world allowed or stimulated, in parallel and sometimes at odds with the more brutally exploitative and domineering, "hard" forms it took up in the lives of peoples and in the countries under its heel. As my outline also implies, the history of modern Romanian literature and modern Romanian culture in general can thus be viewed as a complex, by no means teleological narrative whose basic plot may nonetheless be summarized as an incremental "thinning out" of this presence and of imperial authority overall in Romanian space and as a correspondent "thickening" of a national literature and culture increasingly capable to authorize themselves as legitimate and independent actors on the world stage.

1. Interimperialism

In her explorations of the relationships between the empires clashing in Southern and Southeastern Europe during the late Renaissance, E. Natalie Rothman dwells revealingly on the "cultural brokers" who served as mediators between Venice and Istanbul and whose activities, she maintains, help us trace "some of the genealogies of our own analytical vocabulary of *in-betweenness, transculturation, diversity,* and *mixedness*" all the way to "colonization, state formation, and interimperial rivalry in the early modern Mediterranean."[3] The cultural or, better yet, intercultural brokerage Rothman deems as characteristically developing in conjunction with sixteenth-century Venice's hegemonic claims extended, however, past the zenith and territorial reach of Venetian influence. In the seventeenth and eighteenth centuries, the Romanian Principalities of the Danube corridor, Wallachia and Moldavia, made for one of Europe's saliently "interimperial" areas whose intellectual elites assumed, more or less deliberately, various intermediary roles with respect to surrounding empires. "Caught in the web of complex imperial mechanisms" as they stood, these elites were "essential to producing the means to calibrate, classify, and demarcate imperial alterities" so as to articulate "the actual location of sociocultural boundaries, the prototypical centers of different categories, and the meaning of their own 'in-betweenness.'"[4] These go-betweens were active in a number of fields and genres inside and outside literature. Grigore Ureche (1590?–1647), Nicolae Costin (1660–1712), and Ion Neculce (1672–1745), for instance, were historians and translators who had humanist training, served in diplomacy and other official capacities, moved back and forth between their Moldavian homeland and neighboring countries, and set up Romanian-language historiography as a geoliterary "triangulation" of the tensions among Poland, Russia, and the Ottoman Empire. Similarly interimperial positions took up religious figures such as Dosoftei (1624–1693), Metropolitan of Moldavia, and Anthim the Iberian (Antim of Georgia or Antim Ivireanul [1650?–1716]), Metropolitan of Wallachia, as well as more secular umanists like Udriște Năsturel (1596?–1659) and Constantin Cantacuzino (1650?–1716). They laid the foundations of print culture and promoted translations into Romanian and other languages of the region while doing their best—and, like Antim and Cantacuzino, sometimes failing tragically—to walk along or across the fine lines separating the East and West, the Hapsburgs and the Ottomans, the Russians and everybody else, and so forth.

The consummate "interimperial subject" of this time and part of Europe was, however, Moldavian prince, philosopher, and author Dimitrie Cantemir (1673–1723). He spent some of his youth in the capital of the Ottoman Empire, where, as Bogdan Crețu reminds us in the essay preceding mine in this book, Cantemir was both a student at the Greek Academy of the Orthodox Patriarchate and a diplomatic "collateral" of sorts guaranteeing, as required by the Turkish custom, the allegiance of his father Constantin, Moldavia's "voivode," to the Sultan. If Crețu attends to Cantemir's *avant-la-lettre* "transnationalism," here I propose we shift gears somewhat to pursue Cantemir's trans- or, better still, interimperialism in Rothman's sense, which, incidentally, foregrounds allegiance—more exactly, multiple, changing, or conflicted loyalties—to a specific imperial authority or authorities as a defining element of the work done by cultural brokers. To this end, I will touch briefly on two of Cantemir's books that articulate back-and-forth movements between several imperial systems and, by the same token, some of the initial chapters of his country's cultural narrative. Before I turn to those works, though, it is worth remembering that Cantemir participated from an early age in a uniquely textured knowledge hub where Western traditions, the Byzantine legacy, and Persian and Arab science and wisdom intersected.[5] He occupied the Moldavian throne for a short time, between 1710 and 1711, when he attempted a radical cultural and political realignment by following Peter the Great's Western-inspired program of modernization. The experiment was cut short by the defeat, on Moldavian soil, of the Czar's army in the 1711 Russian–Turkish war, after which Cantemir fled the country and joined the multiethnic aristocracy swarming around the Sankt Petersburg court.[6] The first Russian ambassador to Paris and London, his son Antiochus (1709–1744) is a poet and, like his father, an intellectual associated with the European Enlightenment.

More importantly in light of this discussion, Cantemir is the first Romanian scholar to elaborate a full-dress theory of empire. Aside from the many and variegated contributions he made in his impressively encyclopedic oeuvre, the work that brought him international fame was *Historia incrementorum atque decrementorum aulae othomanicae* (History of the Rise and Decline of the Ottoman Empire).[7] Written in Latin between 1714 and 1716, the *History* was among the first studies of this sort to analyze the dwindling of Turkish power and predict its demise. The book was translated into English and published by Nicholas Tindal in 1734 and, as Hugh Trevor-Roper observes, constituted a major source of inspiration for the last part of Gibbon's *History*.[8] Even more relevant here is one of Cantemir's previous works, the 1705 novel *Istoria ieroglifică* (Hieroglyphic Story).[9] The first lengthy narrative fiction ever completed directly in Romanian, *Hieroglyphic Story* is a *roman à clef* in which Moldavians are four-legged creatures, while Wallachians are birds and Turks aquatic beings. In it, the Unicorn, the novel's protagonist and authorial alter ego, manages to overcome a world dominated by conniving sycophants and powerful adversaries and reach the end of his ordeal without compromising his moral standards. Coached in allegorical language, a compelling exercise in Euroasian politics takes center stage in the novel's third part. This section purports to recount the presumed voyage of another imaginary creature, the Camilopardalus—i.e., Alexander Mavrocordatos, a great scholar but also a rival contender for the Moldavian throne and therefore sworn enemy of the Cantemirs— to the fabled Mountains of the Moon, from which the Nile was supposed to spring, whereas the Camel-Leopard is actually set to visit Water-Creatures' capital city, that is, Istanbul.[10] In the novel, the latter is called Epithymia ("lust," in Ancient Greek), and in this segment of the story Cantemir draws from his background in alchemy and the symbolism of precious metals and stones in occultism to describe the city and shrine of goddess Pleonexia (Ancient Greek for "greed").

The way Cantemir handles his characters as a fiction author, specifically the fashion in which he negotiates his authorship inside the novel by processing philosophically and encoding literarily his own political experience as a young prince, is telling for his later career *outside* his fiction, as an interimperial courtier, European personality, member of the Royal Academy of Berlin, at whose behest he wrote his 1714 *Descriptio Moldaviae* (Description of Moldavia), and cultural middleman in the real and hotly contested spaces where empires border on each other, intersect, and collide. No doubt, the future Moldavian ruler has plenty of inside knowledge about the public and backchannel machinery of the intra- and international power struggle of his age. The novelist transfers the politician's information and expertise to a world of talking beasts, some of which are actual animals, and some of which are either mythical or Cantemir's own concoctions. One way or another, all of them join in the allegorization of his imperially interstitial positioning, translating into the language of fiction a mode of being in the world and of negotiating politically, intellectually, and otherwise one's place in it that proves remarkably keen on the many worlds—bigger, often violent, threatening, yet not infrequently alluring—crisscrossing little worlds such as Moldavia and repurposing them as stages for a drama much larger than their territory. In this context, it would be not too much of a stretch to read *Hieroglyphic Story* and other works by Cantemir informed by such efforts to discern the wider and the multifarious in the deceptively small and simple as endeavors similar to more recent attempts at formulating, across the arts and academic disciplines, insights into a geopolitically and culturally worlding[11] order beyond Moldavia, beyond the nation-state that would later on incorporate it, beyond a Europe that did not fail to acknowledge Cantemir's stature, as well as beyond the empires whose bidding he did, or so it seemed, at one point or another.

2. Paraimperialism

In 1698, after the Hapsburgs had driven the Ottomans out of Transylvania, an important part of the Romanian Eastern Orthodox higher clergy of the province signed the so-called "Union" agreement with Rome.[12] In exchange for the recognition of Papal authority, Romanian clerics were allowed to preserve their Eastern Christian traditions and were promised social emancipation for the new converts to Christian Orthodoxy.[13] As a result of the deal, Jesuit colleges started admitting and educating generation after generation of Transylvanian intellectuals of Romanian origin, with the brightest of them receiving scholarships to continue their studies in Vienna and Rome. This is how, over time, "Uniatism" created the conditions under which Transylvania's Romanian Greek Catholics, or the "Uniates," became a thriving and culturally active middle class, so much so that, toward the end of the eighteenth century, its scholarly and artistic energies cohered into an entire movement—The Transylvanian School.[14]

While polymaths like Petru Maior (1756–1821), Gheorghe Șincai (1754–1816), and Samuil Micu-Klein (1745–1806) are among its intellectual leaders, the most fascinating writer associated with it is Ion Budai-Deleanu (1760–1820). On the one hand, Budai-Deleanu was a cog in the great wheel of Hapsburg bureaucracy. On the other hand, he managed to carve out for himself a private world within the imperial system. I would call this world *paraimperial* in that it participated in that system at the same time that it afforded Budai-Deleanu a "tactical" self-positioning with regard to the homogenizing pressure of the Empire so that, inside this world, one that was shaped by both the empire and peripheral, if not completely immune, to the empire's fiat, he preserved and nurtured his freedom of thought and of the imagination. In short, Budai-Deleanu was good at "compartmentalizing," as we might say nowadays, a sociopolitical ploy he may have borrowed from the "cameralists"—the philosopher–administrators who embodied the very spirit of the Austrian Enlightenment.[15] This compartmental approach to empire's workings across public and private spheres, official discourse and personal, sometimes counter-discursive creativity accounts for his marginal place in the School's loose hierarchy of thinkers, pedagogues, and ideologues, as it does for his analogously less-than-prominent location on the Empire's map—the reader will recall that Budai-Deleanu spent the last part of his life in Lemberg, or Lviv, in present-day Ukraine, first as an attorney and then as "royal counselor" in the Hapsburg administration of Galicia.[16] This relative, paraimperial isolation did make a difference, for it sheltered and even gave a boost to the free play of the imagination fueling his masterpiece, the mock-epic poem *Țiganiada* (The Gypsiad).

Still unknown to the public for more than half a century after his death, *Țiganiada* was published as late as in 1877.[17] While, for a number of political and theological reasons, other School luminaries concentrated on proving the direct descent of Romanians from the ancient Romans, Budai-Deleanu's imagination wandered in other directions and toward other ages. He was particularly drawn to an epoch when Italy, Rome's "official" successor, even though it found itself politically fragmented and, comparatively speaking, insignificant as a military power, was becoming the breeding ground for various types of empires themselves paraimperial in relation to traditional imperial structures. These empires or institutional-symbolic systems were financial (with Florence at its core), commercial (centered on Venice), but also literary—empires of the imagination. Joining one of the latter, *Țiganiada* helped its author withstand the draw of the real empire, Budai-Deleanu's employer. The poem's Italian associations are indeed fairly obvious. Its main formal and thematic model is the Renaissance epic tradition of Luigi Pulci's 1483 *Morgante*, Lodovico Ariosto's 1532 *Orlando furioso*, and Torquato Tasso's 1581 *Gerusalemme liberata*.[18] Not only does the recognizable mix of historical realism and fantasy, heroism and comedic antiheroism, pathos and parody mark *Țiganiada*, but it also "relaxes" Budai-Deleanu's work culturally and politically, imparting a healthy measure of relativism and humanist tolerance to some of the poem's core concepts and situations.

Prominent among these are race and ethnicity alongside identity more broadly. For all these, *Țiganiada* supplies literary constructions that testify to the author's active involvement in all sorts of "soft" transactions and discourse formation barterings

Transylvania's imperial location allowed somebody in his position at the turn of the eighteenth century. The bulk of this ideological commerce concerns the Gypsies/Roma, Budai-Deleanu's unlikely heroes and heroines. Not only is the author sympathetic to this enslaved, historically disenfranchised, stateless, voiceless minority of the Hapsburg Empire and Central-Eastern Europe largely—in Moldavia and Wallachia, the Roma's serfdom will be abolished decades after Budai-Deleanu's death. But the writer identifies with their vulnerable and acutely subordinate condition, as well as with their fluid, supranational identity and instinctive rejection of the social order and its disciplinary apparatus. In his foreword, the narrator of what is presented as a historical "chronicle," an enlightened and cosmopolitan "Bohemian" (in all senses) whose name is Leon(aki) Dianeu (anagram of Ion Deleanu), explicitly warns that "the whole story is an allegory, where by Gypsies one should also understand those who did or do the same as the Gypsies had in times of old. The wise one will understand …."[19] Granted, Dianeu/Deleanu here vents, albeit obliquely, the frustrations of the emerging Romanian elite with its low ranking within the outdated *cursus honorum* of the Hapsburg social system, which de facto took into account not only class but also ethnicity. At the same time, the lowly, Roma-like status and the abovementioned "identification" therewith are not a source of anxiety. There is, instead, a lot of potential in this Roma—or Roma-modeled—identity paradigm, which clearly intrigues and draws the writer. What is more, this model is further modulated or negotiated within a stratified "commercial" framework. In the latter, the classical, Renaissance, and early Baroque literary crosscurrents carrying conventions of epic comedy ran over, dovetailed, and merged with undertows of life and administrative procedure indicative of the trans-ethnic makeup and geopolitical convulsions of the Hapsburg system, to whose budding, "proto-multicultural" environment and appetite for wider geographies the Empire's Enlightenment bureaucrats were fine-tuning their *Weltanschauungen*. Thus, Dianeu tells us a bit about his own, heroic adventures on the world stage as someone who took part in the imperial wars of his age—notably enough, on *both* the Austrian and the French side. First, he discloses, he fought the French as a conscript in the Austrian army, but then he was taken prisoner and ended up a soldier under the command of Napoleon himself, whose expeditionary force he followed to Egypt, where, after losing a leg in battle and retiring from military service, he set shop and delivered himself to the pleasures of literature—hence his alleged authorship of *Țiganiada*.

As one can see, Dianeu is a Roma twice: by birth and by virtue of his Bohemian exploits. Not unlike the poem itself, their narration in the preface evokes playfully and imaginatively an order that is imperial—or multi-imperial, rather—in a worldly, complex, and, easygoing kind of way and does not try to exorcize disorder, nomadism, and nonconformism but to integrate them with amused tolerance. In fact, mayhem and anarchy are euphuistically celebrated as expressions of exuberant vitality painted with Rococo brushstrokes in *tableaux vivants* featuring characters wearing deceivingly "primitive" Roma garments. Whether they confront actual threats or deliberate on the best form of government for their future state, Budai-Deleanu's fictional Roma are constantly stepping back and forth across the divide between coherence and chaos and in that are symbolic of broader conflicts and human predicaments. Granted, as with other authors of ages past, the pervasive and rather blunt references to skin color and implicitly race remain likely to bother contemporary readers, and for good reason. One would be hard pressed to argue that *Țiganiada* is, as far as the Roma's portrayal goes, racial prejudice-free. It is also fairly apparent, however, that these and related formulas allude to realities beyond the racial, the racist, and the ethnic, and even beyond a certain ethno-racial group. Furthermore, these allusions have a paraimperial logic to them in that they harness the rich complexities of Roma life, language, and politics not only to Budai-Deleanu's own poetic endeavor but also to an equally imaginative, uninhibited, sophisticated, and "proto-multicultural" project of national community that is as Roma as it would be, within decades, Romanian and whose blueprint the poet draws by dipping his quill in the various inks, colors, and shades of imperial discourse available to him. And so, highly sensitive as he proves to be to the imbrications of the local into the international and the remote, of the past into the present, and of the marginal and the oppressed into the Enlightenment's emancipatory philosophy, Budai-Deleanu too remains relevant in the context of ongoing conversations around the expanding imaginaries of "planetarity" and their knack for catching intimations of a "macro" world in the rustle of the "micro," the humble, and the idiomatic.[20]

3. Metaimperialism

One way or the other, soft commerce involves cultural mimesis. As Raoul Eshelman points out in his discussion of "performatist" relationality in film, "[humans] share one common trait: they have a primarily mimetic and intuitive, rather than a discursive and intellectual, motivation." "'Mimesis'" the critic specifies, "is used here in the way that is understood by René Girard and Eric Gans: it assumes that foundational or primary forms of human interaction occur through imitation of others. Such imitation has both a violent and a reconciliatory potential .... "[21]

Piggybacking mainly on the final segment of Eshelman's observations, I would note that, so far, we have come across Romanian imitative formations that were primarily literary and obtained by dint of quasi-symbiotic, co-participatory, less contentious engagements with empires and the transregional circulation of ideas, values, and representations imperial systems set in train or filtered. This would change with the modern era. In effect, Romanian modernity in literature and other areas of individual and public expression, including politics, can be seen as a shift away from largely nonantagonistic to more "pugnacious," agonal mimesis. The latter was a complex, sociocultural, and existential mechanism whose activation was triggered by Wallachia and Moldavia's intensifying interactions with imperial powers in the first half of the nineteenth century, a mechanism that was at least partly responsible for the rise of a new social class: the scions of Wallachian and Moldavian nobility of the olden days. Members of the new, largely bourgeois and international elite, the "boyars'" progeny were the leaders of the 1848 Revolution that, in emulating the democratic ideals and rhetoric of the 1848 French revolutionary movements, steered Romanian society in the direction of a Western-inspired modernity.

This change followed a logic that I would call metaimperial. I find this coinage descriptively apt because said logic played out as a scenario of cultural dissemination and transformation that, after importing the self-aggrandizing rhetoric of the imperial sublime and its references to "glory," "honor," and other dignified derivatives and symptoms of the Ancient Greek *thymos*, reworked it and tailored it to Romanian traditions, actual or imaginary, and redistributed it to the "people" in an effort keyed to demonstrating not only how much all these values applied to the nation but also that such legitimately ascribed attributes made it eligible to join broader humanity. The public recirculation of this ideologically and emotionally charged grandstanding phraseology was meant as a pep talk for the Romanian multitudes that, so energized, would try harder to "keep up" with their neighbors, be they arrogant imperial powers or peoples experiencing proud "national awakenings." In adopting and then ramping up and spreading what would eventually become the template of the country's nationalist discourse, the Romanian revolutionaries of the mid-nineteenth century responded to an international—regional as well as European—context of ever-increasing socioeconomic, cultural, diplomatic, and military interactions among older empires and rising nation-states. This was a contested and raucous landscape in which one was expected to save face if not to come ahead in a tough competition that measured one's ability to show off one's ethnic or national sense of pride, self-esteem, and collective worth. Various empires may have fostered the scripts and vocabularies of such agonal spectacle, but, through their very performance, the contestants—whether they were individual or groups, and whether they "proved" themselves on behalf of themselves or of their communities—sought to *transcend* their initial mimetic dependency as well as the ethnic and national purview of their "act" and thus move *beyond* ("meta") empire's cultural-rhetorical and political authority.

Concurrently a matter of national and cultural poetics, this transcendental performance addressed, then, a double audience. One was international and included primarily imperial "spectators." Illustrative of their reaction—and of the effectiveness of the spectacle overall—is a note sent from Bucharest by Consul-General Robert Colquhoun to Stratford Canning, the British ambassador to Istanbul, on the "moral" atmosphere inside Wallachia's 1848 revolutionary provisional government. "A sense of real chivalrous honor," comments Colquhoun, "pervades one or two of the Chiefs and as long as they maintain their Influence I have no fear of the movement being stained by any Act of violence."[22] The other public is domestic. It is this readership Nicolae Bălcescu (1819–1852), the main ideologist of the 1848 generation and central Wallachian figure of rising Romanian Romanticism, hoped to reach by recasting the traditional cosmopolitanism and universalism of the Christian elites of the Ottoman Empire into a pathos for liberal-democratic crusading.[23] This is, in effect, a main goal of his historical monograph *Românii supt Mihai-Voievod Viteazul* (Romanians under Michael Voievode the Brave). Published in 1863, after Bălcescu's untimely death in exile, the book dramatizes Michael the Brave's short-lived 1600 unification of Wallachia, Moldavia, and Transylvania as a divinely sponsored prefiguration of the nation's manifest destiny. In his book's preface, Bălcescu writes:

> After showing us in the Gospel[s] the moral law, absolute [and] unconfined, *the law of righteousness*, and after prompting humanity on the never-ending road of harmonious, progressive development by subduing nature, brutal might, [and] the external world to the absolute power of mind and thought, the Savior reveals to us, through the blood He shed in His death, the practical law, the law of the act, the law of sacrifice, of love and brotherhood, the manner in which we can save our souls, overcome evil, and fulfill the moral mission of humanity, primarily through the word, the idea, and consequently through our deeds, [and] sacrificing, in the process, our individuality to our family, the latter to our fatherland, and the fatherland to humanity [and] to the future.[24]

Bălcescu's political–theological, exalted messianism was echoed in Moldavia by Alecu Russo (1819–1859), chiefly in the 1855 prose poem *Cântarea României* (Song to Romania). Like Bălcescu's diorama of past heroism, Russo's biblical incantations purported and succeeded to consolidate, around a range of variations on the national sublime theme, a Romanian secular religion of sorts by working the same universalist aspirations of post-Byzantine multiethnic elites into a Romantic, French-inspired cosmopolitan exhortation that both called out to the nation and urged it to "look" beyond itself: "Look south, [and] look north[—]people[s] are raising their head[s]; the mind emerges luminously above […] darkness. [… the] mind, the godly spirit that constructs, the faith that gives life; the old world is falling, and over its ruins your freedom rises! Awaken!"[25] The "South" is most likely Greece, which had already won its independence war against the Ottomans, and the "North" is apparently revolutionary Poland—a safe conjecture since the influence of Paris-based, Polish Romantic messianism was strong on Romanian expatriates like Russo. This is the geopolitical and intercultural frame of reference for a poetic prophecy that updates "aspirationally" the map of the Romanian territory so as to deemphasize the latter's client status as imperial junction by making less visible the former imperial suzerains while underscoring the young nation's presence on bigger maps, as a hub of "universal," progressive-liberal agency where various revolutionary axes intersect.

This metaimperial remapping and its agonal scenario are even better marked in the Romantic literature produced around Romania's own War of Independence, most prominently by Vasile Alecsandri (1818–1890), the leading poetic voice of the 1848. A politician and diplomat highly sensitive to the emerging international image of sovereign Romania, Alecsandri was involved in Paris and London, after the crushing of the 1848 Moldavian revolution, with a quasi-underground network of political radicals from all corners of Europe.[26] He was a major player in Wallachia and Moldavia's 1859 unification, which he supported as a foreign minister and ambassador to several European countries.[27] Little surprise, then, that his poetry is the mise-en-scène of an entire "diplomacy" geared toward symbolic capital acquisitions meant to benefit Romania on the world stage, where the nascent nation advertises its proud self-determination in terms both derived from and transcending imperial discourses of exceptionalism. A telling example of his metaimperial poetics and politics of pride is the cycle of propaganda poems *Ostaşii noştri* (Our Troops),[28] which he penned in support of the 1877 war Romania waged alongside the Russian Imperial Army against the Ottomans in today's Bulgaria.[29] These texts exalt models of bravery over and against a lofty backdrop enlivened by Turkish feats of valor and the presumed gallantry standards of the Russian allies.[30] Allegorical self-boasting is pressed into the service of settling the score with the former Ottoman overlords in the emblematic poem "Balcanul şi Carpatul" (The Balkans and the Carpathians), in which the two mountain chains face off as two "formidable giants" and do battle through their champions, two "agile" and equally "formidable" eagles. A transparently imperial synecdoche, the topography identifies the political antagonists, viz., the Ottomans, who stand accused of being "sorrow-bringing through fanaticism [and] powerful through cruelty," and the United Danube Principalities, which, as a consequence of the war's outcome, will become the Kingdom of Romania—an aspiration expressed through grandiosely provocative declarations thrown at the "declining" opponent ("Your motto is *enslavement*, but mine is *no submission!*"). No less significant is the attitude toward the Russians, though, for maintaining composure and cutting a "noble" figure in their company and in relation to their own imperial credentials seem equally important to the poet-ambassador. Illustrative of these metaimperial theatrics is the poem "Sergentul" (The Sergeant), where Alecsandri imagines an encounter between a wounded and ragged-looking Romanian soldier on his way back home and a Russian cavalry unit. The haughty demeanor of the Russian officers, who are not battle-tested yet but predictably arrogant, suddenly flips over into its opposite as they ceremonially salute the warrior when they catch a glimpse of the Russian and Romanian military medals pinned on his tattered jacket.

4. Transmetropolitanism

A sovereign monarchy after 1881, with a King, Carol of Hohenzollern-Sigmaringen, and a Constitution borrowed from the Germans and the Belgians, respectively, Romania nuanced and accelerated its metaimperial dynamics into an increasingly emancipatory modality of cultural poesis that roughly completed the building of the fundamental structures and institutions of Romanian modernity in literature and other areas. I would term this modality transmetropolitan. It goes without saying, much like with the other prepositional varieties of my essay's imperial vocabulary, "transmetropolitanism's" appeal is primarily heuristic. At the same time, the label does help pinpointing, as I will below, authors, works, and whole directions that provide thumbnail descriptions of episodes, initiatives, and accomplishments symptomatic of a broad, sociopolitical, ideological, and aesthetic movement by which the nation-state largely settled into geoculturally identifiable modern forms of art, philosophy, scholarship, and so forth. This crystallization continued to be predicated on frictions with imperial spaces of artistic influence, mimetic pressure, prestige, and legitimation. This "stabilization" took reiterated and creative crossings into and *past* these metropolitan zones of authority. This was a transgressive effort that, this time around, appropriated the imperial sources and their purviews and rhetorics and retooled them as steppingstones to a cosmopolitan-universalist discourse that billed itself and began to be recognized internationally as Romanian. Entering their transmetropolitan phase around the dawn of the twentieth century, Romanian literature and literary ideology showed that, under certain circumstances, less central domains of regional and world cultural systems can design cultural programs and evolve aesthetic repertoires for articulating world pictures embracing far more than just their geographical turfs and developing an acute awareness of others. Transmetropolitanism, then, moves across, as much as it challenges, this spatiality schematically represented as a topological distribution of metropolitan centers and colonial outposts, but this horizontal axis has a vertical counterpart along which transmetropolitan artists and critics advance to the position "major" cultures set aside for themselves, viz., to the top of a hierarchy presumably warranting their pro-cosmopolitan, anti-parochial pronouncements.

Now, earlier modes of imperial mimesis had run the gamut from outright imitation to "commensal" acculturation to the "self-colonization" Bulgarian critic Alexander Kiossev has theorized in his attempt to prove that the imperial associations sought out by societies of this part of the continent spoke to a distaste for one's Southeast European "condition" and neighbors. Instead, Romania's transmetropolitan interactions with the West started forefronting internalizations of a trans-ethnic, universalist ethos that were locally empowering in that they allowed for bottom-up self-definitions less and less dependent on the empire's benevolent, top-down descriptive gaze.[31] New kinds of soft commerce and with them the bourgeoning "tradition of the new" stepped up the thinning of imperial structures and spawned, correspondingly, flexible, inventive, plural, and alterity-minded formations of cultural sovereignty in which metropolis and colony, colonial status "by domination" and imperial membership "by invitation," subordination and equal footing, and influence and originality began to balance out.[32] Understood as a "balancing act" in this particularly transmetropolitan sense, Romanian culture also became open to other West European stimuli beyond French, and it would be probably fair to say that the spreading sensitivity to pluralism within it reflects the pluralization of its interest in the world outside of it.

This multiplication of potential cultural models—as well as of notions *of* model, of what such a paradigm might call for—brought German philosophy and literature into the orbit of Romanian culture. This happened primarily through the Junimea (Young Generation) Society, the quintessentially transmetropolitan literary circle and intellectual orientation at this juncture in Romanian history. The Society's leader was the founder of modern Romanian criticism and the era's foremost cultural ideologue, Titu Maiorescu (1840–1917), who was also a politician and served as the country's Prime Minister. With Maiorescu at its helm, Junimea and its magazine, *Convorbiri literare*, promoted at the end of the nineteenth-century writers who would become and remain the unchallenged canonical benchmarks of national literature—its "great classics" such as poet Mihai Eminescu (1850–1889), memorialist and folktale author Ion Creangă (1837–1889), fiction writer Ioan Slavici (1848–1925), and Ion Luca Caragiale (1852–1912), a playwright who also composed short stories. A conservative whose philosophical sources were German idealism and British meliorism, Maiorescu took to task the 1848 Romantics, whose sometimes operatic nationalism had been, as we have seen, the conduit for the country's "Westernization." If unchecked, the rush to "imitate" others—the French, that is—was bound, contended Maiorescu, to keep Romania stuck in a marginal, culturally subservient mode, and he spoke against this sort of hurried imitation wherever he ran into it, whether in a poem or in the way the government did business. His critique is by no means without nuances, however. As he maintains in his 1872 landmark essay "Direcția nouă în poezia și proza română" (The New Direction in Romanian Poetry and Prose"),

> When a nation lives next to another that is more advanced culturally, the latter necessarily influences the former. This is because one of the hallmarks of cultural advancement inheres in one's ability to leave behind the narrow quarters of more individual interests and, without losing sight of the national aspect of this, to discover and formulate ideas for all humanity. Identifying and carrying through these ideas have often been painful. And yet, once the sacrifice required by trying them out has been made, they have become gifts bestowed on entire humanity, on which they now call to share in them and reap their bountiful benefits. You just cannot turn a deaf ear to this call—coming together in and through the basic culture-making forms is the inevitable fate of all European nations. The question is if they can fulfill their destiny as equals to other nations or as slaves ....[33]

It is clear that, in Maiorescu, the nation and the world are not opposed. In point of fact, they seem to be structurally isomorphic, comparable, and alike due to the analogies, overlaps, and "cultural plasticity" that render one pliable and, as such, compatible with and homologous to the other's forms. Quite deliberately, the critic employs his ideological keywords loosely so as to keep the boundaries between the national and the universal porous and thus permeable to crossings in either direction. Far from rejecting inspiration from the outside, his intervention stresses the unavoidable interplay of the country and the world, with the proviso that one cannot ignore culture's call as much as, in responding to this call—in playing by culture's rule (*principiile de cultură*)—one may either come into one's own and thus "unite" as a national culture or become like somebody else if not that somebody else altogether.

Sometimes cogently reasoned and other times pushed to a conservative extreme, this ambivalence about cultural mimesis permeates the literary work and cultural philosophy of other Society members, including Eminescu, who also studied in imperial metropolises of the German-speaking world such as Berlin and Vienna and took up in his work, with various results, the ethno-cultural, economic, and military forays into Romanian territories of empires (old and new), industrial progress (railroads, trade), minorities, and "foreigners." Born in Transylvania, Slavici is an even more typical product of Hapsburg education. His 1894 novel *Mara*, which tells the story of a poor woman whose obstinate desire to improve her family's station in life leads to tragedy, sheds revealing light on the multiethnic mesh of Transylvanian life. Wholly socialized into his region's multicultural and multilinguistic kaleidoscope, Slavici experienced the empire's cross-identitarian environment firsthand, as an everyday reality that does not threaten but is there, a given that makes who you are. This is, again, a cultural poesis of the transmetropolitan kind, whose mechanics Slavici witnessed inside the "universal-order" rhetoric and socio-administrative apparatus of the Hapsburg Empire and carried with him south across the Carpathians, into a Romanian Kingdom that looked, despite the coeval onset of an assortment of vociferously chauvinistic nationalisms, ready to heed Slavici's "naturally" cosmopolitan message.

Some of these nationalisms became favorite targets of the sarcastic realism and acid irony of Caragiale's theater and "sketches" of urban life. Plays such as the 1879 *O noapte furtunoasă* (A Stormy Night), the 1884 *O scrisoare pierdută* (A Lost Letter), and the 1885 *D'ale carnavalului* (Carnival Stuff), as well as the short stories gathered in *Schițe* (Sketches [1897]) and *Momente* (Moments [1901]) are part of a broader, literary and political critique of accelerated mimetic modernization and modernity overall. They convey both conservatism à la Maiorescu and a progressive radicalism that, intriguingly enough, rendered Caragiale, both thematically and formally, an acknowledged precursor of modernist experiments such as Eugène Ionesco's theater of the absurd. Traditionally, Caragiale's work has been viewed as an all-out ethical indictment of the Romanian elites of the Romantic era, specifically of their rushed, sometimes demagoguery-ridden and perfunctory attempt at "enslaving" the culture, as Maiorescu would have put it, to Western fashions, phraseologies, and cultural-institutional modes damaging to the young nation. This reading is not off beam, but it is also simplifying insofar as it misses the literary case Caragiale enters for a transmetropolitan sovereignty by focusing insistently on the linguistic, aesthetic, and sociopolitical dialogics of a world acculturation show in which Romanians may every now and then look like buffoons but out of which they cannot opt. As a participant in and spectator of this spectacle, he critiques but does not condemn. Nor is he repelled by the cultural hybridity that, he feels, is the very script and the lifeblood of the comedy of modernity, in which people are forced, sometimes with mixed results, to work out existential compromises between the "Westernizing" present and the country's not too remote Balkan and regional multicultural past. Thus, his oeuvre documents critically the at once challenging and fertile intersection in the Romanian system of several imperial circuits of cultural evolution, with his comedies and narrative sketches homing in on West- and future-oriented, modernizing trajectories and novellas such as the 1909 "Kir Ianulea" (Mr. Ianulea) featuring situations and mores characteristic of Romania's movement on older, Greco-Ottoman tracks.[34]

As if to dramatize intertextually the West and East's clashes and mutual interpellations in the pre-modern Mediterranean world, "Kir Ianulea" rewrites Niccolò Machiavelli's novella "Belfegor arcidiavolo."[35] Rehearsing some of his tutor text's plot, Caragiale has Ianulea, a low-ranking "devil" in Hell's hierarchy, travel to Bucharest to test the shrewdness of local women back in the eighteenth century, when the Romanian Principalities were run by Greek rulers recruited from Istanbul's Fanar neighborhood. Ultimately losing the war of nerves against his wife, Ianulea cannot wait to bail out and regain his peace of mind back in the underworld. Perhaps more than the gender troubles the story obviously, and occasionally tongue-in-cheek, stirs up, what catches the eye here is the panorama of a "hesitantly contemporaneous"

Kingdom of Romania, which still has to work out fully its peripheral position in the cultural network of "Europe"—shorthand in Caragiale for progress, ahead-looking, and modernization but also source of anxieties, inhibitions, and "complexes," as other essays in *Romanian Literature as World Literature* show. Caragiale's point here is that Levantine cosmopolitanism, which had left its mark on Romanian tradition already, is not only worth salvaging but also inscribing into the country's fast-expanding worldly horizons, which is actually what the author does ideologically and literally, through his writings. Along these lines, he suggests that the other shorthands pervading domestic ideological debates during his time as much as they are today—"Balkans" and "Balkan," "Byzantium" and "Byzantine," "Levant" and "Levantine," "Fanar" and the "Fanariotes"—and, beyond them, the rich human realities designated by an "Oriental" nomenclature that has little to do with Edward Said's "Orientalism" should all count as part of a cosmopolitan symptomatology through which Romanian culture signals the deepening of its feel for and connection with a changing, bigger world. Insistent, witty, parodic, and intertextually allusive, this suggestion and Caragiale's energetic transmetropolitanism more generally have drawn generation after generation of innovative Romanian writers from Ionesco to the postmoderns of the 1980s and the young prose authors of the twenty-first century.

Notes

1   J. G. A. Pocock, *Barbarism and Religion,* vol. 4., *Barbarians, Savages, and Empires* (Cambridge: Cambridge University Press, 2005), 332.

2   An extensive discussion of the soft commerce notion takes place in *Le commerce des idées philosophiques*, ed. Louis Pinto (Paris: Croquant, 2009).

3   See E. Natalie Rothman, *Brokering Empire: Trans-Imperial Subjects between Venice and Istanbul* (Ithaca, NY: Cornell University Press, 2015), 4.

4   Rothman, *Brokering Empire,* 13.

5   A sympathetic if West European approach to the cultural melting pot of post-Byzantine, Ottoman Istanbul characterizes *The Works of M. de Voltaire*, vol. 3, chapter 78: "On the Taking of Constantinople by the Turks," trans. from the French by T. Smolett et al. (London: J. Newbery et al., 1761), 97–108. Cristina Bîrsan provides a detailed overview of Cantemir's exposure to Ottoman-style cosmopolitanism in *Dimitrie Cantemir și lumea islamică* (Bucharest: Editura Academiei Române, 2005).

6   Ștefan Ciobanu dwells at length on this period in Cantemir's life in *Dimitrie Cantemir in Rusia* (Bucharest: Elion, 2000).

7   See Paul I. Cernovodeanu and Alexandru Duțu, eds., *Dimitrie Cantemir. Historian of South East European and Oriental Civilizations: Extracts from the History of the Ottoman Empire* (Bucharest: Association internationale d'études du sud-est européen, 1973).

8   See Hugh Trevor-Roper, *History and the Enlightenment* (New Haven, CT: Yale University Press, 2010), 54–70.

9   A reliable edition of the novel is Dimitrie Cantemir, *Istoria ieroglifică*, P. P. Panaitescu and I. Verdeș, eds. (Bucharest: Minerva, 1997). There is no English translation of the text, except for two short fragments. They are "The Hieroglyphic History:

Glossary," trans. Florin Bican in *Plural* 3 (2000), http://icr.ro/uploads/files/125581the
-hieroglyphic-historydimitrie-cantemir.pdf, and "The Hieroglyphic History," trans.
Alastair Ian Blyth and available at http://dialognaporoge.blogspot.ro/2009/04/
-hieroglyphic-history.html

10   The rivalry as well as the affinities between Cantemir and the son of Alexandru
Mavrocordat, Nicolae, himself a scholar and writer who is credited to have authored the
first Greek novel of modern times and who also ruled both in Moldavia and Wallachia,
is discussed in Tudor Dinu's monograph *Dimitrie Cantemir și Nicolae Mavrocordat.
Rivalități politice și literare la începutul secolului XVIII* (Bucharest: Humanitas, 2011).

11   Amy J. Elias addresses this process apropos of Elinor Ostrom's economic concept of
the *commons* in "The Commons… and Digital Planetarity," in *The Planetary Turn:
Relationality and Geoaesthetics in the Twenty-First Century*, ed. Amy J. Elias and
Christian Moraru (Evanston, IL: Northwestern University Press, 2015), 37–70.

12   Mary B. Cunningham and Elizabeth Theokritoff present the historical context of
the "Union with Rome" of some Romanian and Ukrainian Orthodox churches in
"Who Are the Orthodox Christians? A Historical Introduction," in *The Cambridge
Companion to Orthodox Christian Theology*, ed. Mary B. Cunningham and Elizabeth
Theokritoff (Cambridge: Cambridge University Press, 2008), 9–10.

13   See among others, Keith Hitchins, "Religion and Rumanian National Consciousness
in Eighteenth-Century Transylvania," *The Slavonic and East European Review* 57,
no. 2 (1979): 214–239.

14   On this issue, see: Stefan Lemny, "Die rumänische Aufklärung. Mit einer
Grundlagenbibliographie," in *Aufklärung(en) im Osten*, ed. Carsten Zelle (Gröningen:
Wallstein, 1995), 36–57; John Neubauer, Marcel Cornis-Pope, Sándor Kibédi-Varga,
Nicolae Harsanyi, "Transylvania's Literary Cultures: Rivalry and Interaction," in
*History of the Literary Cultures of East-Central Europe: Junctures and Disjunctures
in the 19th and 20th Centuries*, vol. 2, ed. Marcel Cornis-Pope and John Neubauer
(Amsterdam: John Benjamins, 2006), 245–282, 255–256.

15   See Franz A. J. Szabo, *Kaunitz and Enlightened Absolutism 1753–1780* (Cambridge:
Cambridge University Press, 1994), 210–211.

16   See Marius Turda's brief introductory note "Ion Budai-Deleanu: The Gypsy Epic,"
in *Discourses of Collective Identity in Central and Southeast Europe (1770–1945).
Texts and Commentaries*, vol. 1, *Late Enlightenment—Emergence of the Modern
"National Idea,"* ed. Balázs Trencsényi and Michal Kopeček (Budapest: Central
European University Press, 2006), 177. On the Hapsburg Empire's multiethnic and
cosmopolitan bureaucracy, see Iryna Vushko, *The Politics of Cultural Retreat: Imperial
Bureaucracy in Austrian Galicia* (New Haven, CT: Yale University Press, 2013), 18–45
and 46–82.

17   The best edition is *Țiganiada sau Tabăra țiganilor*, ed. Florea Fugaru (Timișoara:
Amarcord, 1999). The book is available in French as *Tsiganiada ou Le Campement des
Tsiganes*, trans. by Romanița, Aurélia, and Valeriu Rusu, put into verse by Françoise
Mingot-Tauran (Port-de-Bouc: Wallâda 5, Bucharest: Biblioteca Bucureștilor, 2003).
There is also an Italian version: *Zingareide o l'accampamento degli zingari*, trans. A.
Senatore (Bari: Carucci, 2015). Mária Kovács has translated a fragment into English
in *Discourses of Collective Identity in Central and Southeast Europe (1770–1945). Texts
and Commentaries*, vol. 1, *Late Enlightenment—Emergence of the Modern "National
Idea,"* ed. Balázs Trencsényi and Michal Kopeček, 179–181.

18 This influence is thoroughly investigated by Dimitrie Popovici in *La littérature roumaine à l'époque des Lumières* (Sibiu: Centrul de Studii și Cercetări cu Privire la Transilvania, 1945).

19 See *Ţiganiada sau Tabăra ţiganilor*, ed. Florea Fugaru, 61–64.

20 On the "macro" and "micro" interplay, see Christian Moraru, "Decompressing Culture: Three Steps toward a Geomethodology," in ed. Elias and Moraru, *The Planetary Turn*, 211–244: 222, 223.

21 Raoul Eshelman, "Archetypologies of the Human: Planetary Performatism, Cinematic Relationality, and Iñárritu's *Babel*," in ed. Elias and Moraru, *The Planetary Turn*, 90.

22 Quoted in Angela Jianu, *A Circle of Friends: Romanian Revolutionaries and Political Exile, 1840–1859* (Leiden: Brill, 2011), 83.

23 Dan Berindei, "Nicolae Balcescu" in *Encyclopedia of 1848 Revolutions*, ed. James G. Chastain, http://www.ohiou.edu/~Chastain/ac/balcescu.htm

24 Nicolae Bălcescu, *Românii supt Mihai-Voievod Viteazul* (Bucharest, Romania-Chișinău, Republic of Moldova: Litera Internaţional, 1998), 9.

25 Trans. Mária Kovács, in Trencsényi and Kopeček, *Discourses of Collective Identity in Central and Southeast Europe (1770–1945). Texts and Commentaries*, vol. 1, *Late Enlightenment—Emergence of the Modern "National Idea*," Balázs Trencsényi and Michal Kopeček, eds., 282. Excerpts from Russo's poem are available in English as "Hymn to Romania," trans. Mihaela Anghelescu Irimia in *European Romanticism: A Reader*, ed. Stephen Prickett and Simon Haines (London: Bloomsbury, 2014), 729–30. On Russo's impact as ideologue, see Paul E. Michelson, "Alecu Russo and Historical Consciousness in 19th-Century Revolutionary Romania," in *Temps et changements dans l'espace roumain*, ed. Al. Zub (Iași: Editions de l'Académie Roumaine, 1991), 139–149.

26 The subversive activities of the Romanian Romantic emigration are described in Jianu's *A Circle of Friends*, 189–290.

27 On Alecsandri's political and diplomatic career, see: Alexandru Ciorănescu, *Vasile Alecsandri: A Monograph* (New York: Twayne, 1973). Also see Alexander Drace Francis, "Alecsandri, Vasile," in *Encyclopedia of the Romantic Era, 1760–1850*, ed. Christopher John Murray (New York: Taylor & Francis, 2013), 9; Jean T. Michelson, "Vasile Alecsandri," in *Encyclopedia of 1848 Revolutions*, ed. Chastain, http://www. ohiou.edu-/~Chastain/ac/alecsandri.htm; E. D. Tappe, "Alecsandri and the English," *Revue des études roumaines* 2 (1954): 154–168.

28 The poems were first collected in a volume in Vasile Alecsandri, *Soldaţii noștri: ediţie pentru soldaţi* (Bucharest: Socec & Co., 1878).

29 On the international context of the 1877 war, see Frederick Kellogg, *The Road to Romanian Independence* (West Lafayette, IN: Purdue University Press, 1995).

30 On this subject, see Harsha Ram, *The Imperial Sublime: A Russian Poetics of Empire* (Madison, WI: The University of Wisconsin Press, 2003).

31 Vasile Alecsandri's work also features disturbingly anti-Semitic remarks. As a politician and diplomat, he stood with those who opposed the naturalization of citizens of "Israelite persuasion." On this issue, see Leon Volovici, *Nationalist Ideology and Antisemitism: The Case of Romanian Intellectuals in the 1930s* (Oxford: Pergamon Press, 1991), 10.

32 David Edward Tabachnick, "Empire by Invitation or Domination? The Difference between *Hegemonia* and *Arkhē*," in *Enduring Empire: Ancient Lessons for Global Politics*, ed. David Tabachnick and Toivo Koivukovski (Toronto: University of Toronto Press, 2009), 41–53.

33   Titu Maiorescu, "Direcția nouă în poezia și proza română," in *Critice*, ed. Domnica
     Filimon, preface by Gabriel Dimisianu (Bucharest: Editura Albatros, 1998), 185.
34   "Kyr Ianulea," trans. into English by Alina Cârâc, *Plural*, 6 (2000). http://icr.ro/
     uploads/files/125701ky-ianuleail-caragiale.pdf
35   Șerban Cioculescu, *Caragialiana* (Bucharest: Editura Eminescu, 1974), 203–204.

4

Beyond Nation Building: Literary History as Transnational Geolocation

Alex Goldiş

"There is no people that have not borrowed from other peoples. European culture has been created by a number of nations, which goes to show that each of them owes something to the others—Germanic nations have adopted Roman culture; all modern nations have expanded ancient culture; eighteenth-century France borrowed from the English, eighteenth-century Germany from the French, contemporary French literature from the Scandinavians and the Russians, and this or that literary school from one country is the offspring of this or that literary school from another, not to mention borrowings in sciences, and so on and so forth": remarkably, these observations have not been made by a contemporary World Literature theorist but by a Romanian critic at the beginning of the twentieth century, Garabet Ibrăileanu (1871–1936).[1] In addressing the connections of Romanian literature with other literatures, Ibrăileanu does not espouse a transnational position explicitly but basically casts light on the relations among national literatures. Moreover, one could hardly claim that this perspective entirely guides his writing. In fact, a more nationalist attitude pervades his work, much as it has most European literary histories. As Stephen Greenblatt notes in the introduction to his 2009 "cultural mobility" manifesto, "the established analytical tools have taken for granted the stability of cultures, or at least have assumed that in their original or natural state, before they are disrupted or contaminated, cultures are properly rooted in the rich soil of blood and land and that they are virtually motionless."[2]

In spite of its limitations, Ibrăileanu's statement points, instead, to an interactive model of national cultures in turn based on the dynamic character of global space. Taking center stage much later, with cultural historians and comparatists of Greenblatt's generation, this notion is pivotal to the following critical reassessment of Romanian literary historiography. If this world dynamism reflects indeed the "natural" situation of cultures, and, further, if this modality of being can be viewed as a continuous flow of cultural material and as a flourishing of relationships unconfined to certain political jurisdictions, then the emphasis on the nation-state as a "basic unit" of analysis and on nationalism broadly can be defined, it seems to me, as a tendency of a system, be it literary, critical, or otherwise, to restrict cultural mobility. As one such system, literary history becomes subsumed under a nationalist project when it adopts strategies for keeping this circulation within territorial bounds even though, as Greenblatt also insists, "the reality [of literature and culture] … is more about nomads than natives."[3] In all actuality, most traditional literary studies, wedded as they have been to the ideology of a presumed "national soul," of a fixed geography of cultural development, and of a rigid sense of time, have relied on a static understanding of literature and, by the same token, have adopted the epistemological framework of nationalism.

This framework, I contend, needs to be overhauled so that fresh readings of Romanian literature, attuned to our geopolitical, cultural, and theoretical moment, become possible. To that effect, I will rely on Itamar Even-Zohar's polysystems theory—in my opinion, one of the most convincing accounts of interaction, or, as he puts it, "interference" among cultures—to bring to light the generative pattern subtending most historical descriptions of national literary systems in Southeastern Europe and particularly in Romania, a pattern characteristically informed by *structural correspondence*. Embodying the latter analytically, literary histories illustrating the nationalist paradigm are more or less deliberately built on a closed system of relations involving rigid and discrete notions of time and space. Such notions and the historiographic approach they enable paint a fragmented, often isolationist, stationary, monolithic, and hierarchically organized panorama of world literatures and of the collective selves these literatures articulate. Instead, what I propose in rounding off my argument is an *interactional* model liable to reconstruct Romanian literary history on the premise that such a scholarly enterprise cannot overlook the worldly exchanges that, while they may be more visible today than in the past, have nonetheless given birth to Romanian literature, old and new. When such transnational traffic is factored in, it affords, I finally submit, an entirely new "geolocation" of national literature and identity, no matter how "marginal," stable, all-of-a-piece, and well configured most literary histories picture them.

1. Literary History as National Project

If "nationalism … is a relation," as Pascale Casanova asserts, it is not at all clear that the Herderian aftermath she is referring to was marked, in Europe and elsewhere, by relations geared toward fostering dialogue among cultures.[4] In *The World Republic of Letters*, she sees the nineteenth century as witnessing the emergence of a shared, "worldly space" wherein the cultures of the world suddenly intensified their contacts and reached out to each other across political boundaries. However, this international arena was a hierarchically organized domain in which each sovereign actor strove to shore up its borders so as to better position itself. Under those circumstances, and contrary to Casanova's stance on the matter, the defining relationship among nations was not interaction understood as a give-and-take between two or more cultures, but *homology*, to wit, the pursuit of a structural isomorphism between cultures viewed separately, as monads. Laying claim to a particular spot in this world space reinforced one nation's identity, which explains the paradox of cultural commerce within the post-Herderian nationalist framework: on the one hand, as these national cultures came into being, they had to reckon with the influence of global power structures while seeking to relocate themselves on the planet's map of values—this is what Casanova aptly calls "competition among nations;"[5] on the other hand, cultural interchanges were oftentimes discouraged and even blocked because they were seen as threatening originality and "national specificity." For this twofold reason, the members of the dominant oppositions underpinning the European discourse of literary historiography such as tradition–modernity and Europeanism–autochthonism should no longer be viewed antagonistically. Instead, they should be collapsed into a single, coherent cultural symptomatology of nationalist entrenchment, project in which most histories of literature continue to participate as they remain, like all national histories, highly receptive to collective identity-driven discourse and "national values" more generally.

The issue, of course, is what we mean here by discourse and values. This question bears raising especially when we talk about "marginal" or presumably "marginal" cultures such as those of the European Southeast, for these cultures all share a great potential for building as well as for dismantling and complicating national identities. Interestingly enough, this notion chimes in with Casanova's observation that peripheral and semi-peripheral countries are keen on the discourse on nationalism. It is true that her critics have taken her to task, and rightly so, for her Eurocentric and, more to the point, Gallocentric bias, which follows from the assumption that, at least in the first half of the last century, Paris functioned as the "center" of world literature. It is also obvious that Casanova's "world-system" reformulates in economic and egalitarian terms the nationalist notions variously put forward by French critics at the end of the nineteenth century. If Gustave Lanson's 1894 *Histoire de la littérature française* sought to illuminate the unity of French literature and Hippolyte Taine's 1864 *Histoire de la littérature anglaise* chronicled the clash between, on one side, the indigenous substance provided by Romantic English writers and, on the other, the imported forms of classic literature, Ferdinand Brunetière maintained that "[a]s for us, the French, our role ... has been to tie together, meld, and somehow unify under the idea of a general society of the human race that which otherwise could have remained a bunch of mutually contradictory and ill-disposed elements."[6] Rehearsing Brunetière's pronouncement a century thereafter, Casanova's iterations on the "French" aptitude for "exporting" a unifying "law of universality [to] the world of letters" do not prevent her, though, from granting more "marginal" spaces the propensity for insistent preoccupation with the struggle for international recognition. For, admittedly, while centrally positioned literatures can afford to be less self-reflective about the workings and identitarian upshots of the mechanisms of cultural capital accumulation, literatures from the system's outer reaches dwell relentlessly on the nuts and bolts of world competition for symbolic goods and status.[7] On this account, even though the closed-circuit model of the nation is not an exclusive hallmark of Central and East European collective imaginaries, these do offer, I believe, a particularly instructive terrain for exploring the part identity issues have played in the genesis of national literatures and literary historiographies.

Geographically and scholarly, this holds true especially for Central-Eastern Europe and for literary history, respectively. Ever since Romanticism, literary historiography has been one of the intellectual genres most actively involved in defining national identity and the communal "values" associated with it, as well as in disseminating the definitions thus formulated, always doing more than simply recovering, compiling, organizing, and assessing literary works. This should come as no surprise given that the majority of such projects were undertaken in times of political and social crisis and therefore have played, to some extent, the role of compensatory fictions. The first "national" literary history of Hungary, Ferenc Toldy's 1851 *A magyar nemzeti irodalom története* (History of Hungarian National Literature), for instance, was written after the defeat of the 1848 revolution, and the 1881 history of Piotr Chmielowski, *Zarys literatury polskiej z ostatnich lat szesnastu* (An Outline of Polish Literature of the Last Sixteen Years), also tried to provide a symbolic counterbalance to the crushing of the 1863 Polish national independence movements by Czarist Russia and the German Empire. One can point, consequently, to a political agenda or bias that sometimes makes historical narrative and, more broadly, the scholarly, on one side, and the mythical and fictional, on the other, difficult to tell apart.

Students of East European literary historiography have not missed this entanglement. As Robert B. Pynsent reminds us, "Each literary historian based his writing on three things": "his predecessor's manuscripts and books discovered since his immediate predecessor, and his own understanding of national mythology. He had thus to enrich national mythology by demonstrating its continuum on the basis of an ever larger number of texts."[8] Romanian critics are no exception, invested as they too are simultaneously in the exploration and glorification of the nation's archive as a way of consolidating collective mythologies in hard times. Eugen Lovinescu's *Istoria literaturii române contemporane* (History of Contemporary Romanian Literature [1926–1929]), for example, was written right after Romania's 1918 political unification into "Greater Romania," while G. Călinescu's 1941 *Istoria literaturii române de la origini pînă în present* (History of Romanian Literature from Its Origins to the Present) was published following a sizeable loss of Romanian territory as a result of the 1940 Vienna Agreement. In fact, the case can be made that, in response to the constant threat to national identity in the region, twentieth-century Romanian and East-European literary historiography more largely have remained markedly indebted to the nineteenth-century Herderian imperative that rendered the genre a "reflection" of, and thus an argument for, the "national soul."

2. Time, Space, Cultural Complex

Multipronged, the argument unfolded along temporal, spatial, and critical-aesthetic trajectories, all of which intersected in a fairly coherent set of cultural anxieties or "complexes." For Romanians, their "marginality" in the European historical and geocultural system—the "belated" birth of their literature, coupled with the latter's "peripheral" location on the continent's political and axiological map—is one such resilient fixation, shaping as it has an entire metacritical discourse throughout modern Romanian literary scholarship. A symptom of this obsession is a nationally engaged criticism's constant preoccupation with a symbolic reterritorialization of Romanian culture from the outskirts of Europe to its core. Of course, Central and East European historiography has been steadily built around spatial metaphors, so much so that, on one side, the discipline as a whole can be understood as a subset of geoaesthetics, and, on the other, this understanding entails a "Euro-systemic" view of space and time. Thus, in the seventeenth and eighteenth centuries, Romanians would refer to Western Europe as a place lying "inside" a larger yet familiar world. To "leave for the West" did not mean back then to go *abroad*, as one might say nowadays, that is, to "leave" or to step outside their world, but to go *inside*, to enter or return to an established space of civilization.[9] It is from this both externally and internally situated zone that the literature concept arrives in places like Romania, "delayed" by history and geography alike. In his research on the relationship between literacy and national identity, Alex Drace-Francis observes that, in Romanian, the term "literature" is a neologism that dates back to the beginning of the nineteenth century, when the first literary institutions were created: "The idea of literature made its appearance in Romanian culture in the 1810s and early 1820s, and was not initially distinguished from the idea of learning in general." Soon after that, he further comments, the connection between literature and the nation became inextricable, which is why most Romanian scholars consider literary accomplishments an "index of national levels of civilization."[10]

Typical of Eastern Europe, the correlation between the dawn of nationhood and the "late" rise of literature props up national identity while fueling certain insecurities about its place in the world's history, geography, and cultural system. Over and over again, Romanian scholars tell us that by the time the country's literature was born, Italian, German, English, and French literatures had already gone through their "golden ages," an insistence that, some have ventured, bespeaks a "cultural complex" of sorts. Drawing from psychoanalyst Alfred Adler, Romanian critic Mircea Martin has suggested, for example, that such complexes occur in various literatures and function similarly to individual complexes.[11] Essentially, a complex stems from a self's sense of worth and recognition, takes shape through skewed, often unfavorable comparisons to others, and, accordingly, shows discursive symptoms ranging from overstatements— or, to the contrary, underestimations—to abusively restrictive assessments—or, as the case may be, generalizations—and other misrepresentations of this kind. All of these concern, in our situation, national culture's rank among other cultures and perform a compensatory function in terms of how and where in the world the nation is seen as positioning itself. Giving away the complex are the characteristically distorted self-perception of those affected by it, as well as its highly recurrent manifestation, which in turn accounts for the never-ending debates around Romanian literature's location in European history and on the continent's aesthetic maps. This is one reason the claim that "the time-space vectors constituting the nation became deeply embedded in most historiography of the twentieth century" is borne out most emphatically by Romanian and other peripheral and semi-peripheral cultures, where critics wrangle over identity issues with reference to such maps.[12]

The limitations of the cartographic imaginary undergirding such disputes are readily apparent, however. A case in point are the simplistically one-directional understandings of temporal and spatial relationships mentioned earlier and on which histories of Romanian literature fall back by invariably taking Western cultures in general and French culture in particular as references. Over and over again, these works basically set out to *reposition* Romanian culture on the world map by converting the inferiority complex into a superiority complex through an elaborate critical legerdemain that, to many, has the makings of providential intervention. The most influential among these histories and also the model of all such "counter-cartographies" is by G. Călinescu. Published the year after Romania lost the regions of Bucovina and Bessarabia and a large chunk of Transylvania, his *History of Romanian Literature from Its Origins to the Present* is a critical fiction that takes upon itself to evince the integrity of Romanian literature so as to reestablish symbolically the country's territorial sovereignty. To that effect, the preface to this *History* posits the "organic" character of national culture. As the critic writes on the first page of his book, "the organic is present in Romanian culture."[13] Routinely employed by nineteenth-century literary historiographers, the biological metaphor is here designed to rescind rhetorically the "complex" of an absent or discontinuous national tradition, hinting, instead, that Romanian literature has been functioning and growing "naturally," like a living body whose parts have been historically integrated and "organically" tied to one another.

Serviceable politically, the organicist fantasy has little bearings on Romanian literature and its development even if one insists on the literature's systemic makeup and evolution and perhaps especially if one does so. In that case, however, more apposite to literary-historical reality would be, it seems to me, a different and effectively "relational" kind of system, such as the one Even-Zohar defines as "the assumed set of observables supposed to be governed by a network of relations."[14] In fact, the Israeli critic's system model comes in handy particularly when one weighs the outcomes of the analysis of the relationship between autochthonous and foreign writers and phenomena in literary histories indebted to the epistemological framework of nationalism. Thus, Even-Zohar's polysystemic approach to culture makes it easier to notice that, to account for the "organicism" of Romanian literature, Călinescu resorts to a whole series of relational strategies. Strongly argued in his book's "Preface," the most ingenious one consists, however, in setting up an entire web of internal references meant to link up tightly *domestic* movements, tendencies, and affinities among writers. "With few exceptions," he contends,

> our critics have little knowledge of national literature and are skeptical about "closed-circle," *intra*-national comparisons. The mere mention of [Costache] Conachi, [Dimitrie] Bolintineanu, or Anton Pann in an article on Ion Barbu appears to them ridiculous and even outrageous. A Romanian poet is usually compared to foreign poets such as Edgar Poe, Mallarmé, and Paul Valéry. Nevertheless, the legitimate method is the one comparing the nation's authors among themselves.[15]

Acting on his author's methodological manifesto, Călinescu's history epitomizes, in Romanian culture, a nationalist literary historiography whose comparative thrust appears bent, oddly enough, on playing down the amount and significance of external stimuli. Even when he is forced to admit that local writers have been heavily influenced by outside authors, Călinescu does his best to deemphasize the impact of those authors by putting in place what Andrei Terian calls a "policy of minimizing and, sometimes, even negating the external influences on modern Romanian literature."[16] This is most obvious in the way Călinescu's *History* deals with Romanian classics, whom he strives to "protect" from foreign associations, which is why the Ion Barbu chapter focuses on the hermetic poet's emancipation from the "pure poetry" of Paul Valéry, while the fragment on Lucian Blaga does not even mention his affiliation with Expressionism. In the section on Tudor Arghezi, despite the poet's explicit association with Charles Baudelaire in the volume bearing the telltale title *Flori de mucigai* (Flowers of Mildew) and elsewhere, the name of the French writer is nowhere to be found. Instead, the critic goes out of his way to "nativize" Arghezi. To do so, he "uncovers" the writer's predecessors within national literature's "internal circuit" by a critical sleight-of-hand equivalent to what Paul Ricouer terms "retrodiction"—that is, by reading backwards, from the present cultural effect or echo (Arghezi) back to its (his) putative "cause" or "forerunner."[17] Likewise, Călinescu leaves no room for any potential dialogue with world literature when he discusses Hortensia Papadat-Bengescu, a pioneer of the modern Romanian novel, who was familiar with Freudian psychology and Proustian narrative techniques. "Parallels between Hortensia Papadat-Bengescu's writing and the 'Proustian method,'" the critic acknowledges, "have been drawn." Yet, he goes on, "they are all flawed. [In her work, t]he narrative is plain, continuous, oriented toward the outer world, and even if characters travel from one novel to another, this is an old technique that Duiliu Zamfirescu borrowed, through Zola, from Balzac."[18]

What Călinescu is after differs from the goal pursued by Nicolae Iorga, high-profile nationalist politician and most influential figure of Romanian literary historiography in the pre-Călinescu era. Iorga openly argued for a "cultural protectionism" that, incidentally, went so far as to propose raising the taxes on imported books. As a representative of *sămănătorism*, a conservative movement that extolled ethnicity, he believed that his initiative would stimulate national creativity. Nonetheless, turning a blind eye to international references while plying a strictly "domestic comparatism" does make for a *symbolic protectionism*, and for a widely popular one to boot since it will be pursued by all Romanian literary histories framed by the nationalist paradigm. Ramiro Ortiz, Italian literary historian and professor at University of Bucharest's Faculty of Letters in the years before the Second World War, finds this protectionism and the overall reluctance to attend to literary interactions among national traditions rather peculiar. "While Shakespeare, Goethe, Carducci, [and] D'Annunzio are studied in conjunction with their sources," he notes, "the Romanian writer feels belittled if his sources are mentioned."[19]

Might the Romanian critic—Călinescu himself but also the country's critics in general—feel the same? Truth be told, foreign "sources" are not completely dismissed in Călinescu. However, the way they are handled is worth another look. Thus, when they are referenced at all, they are dealt with as abstract entities lying outside concrete space and time, and so they do not present themselves as that which they actually are, to wit, as junction points between cultures. Instead, they are pressed into the service of a strategy of symbolic legitimation. In the *History*, the procedure is most visible in the segment on Alexandru Macedonski, the rival of Mihai Eminescu, "the national poet." While Călinescu ignores foreign influences in the beginning of the chapter, in closing, when the writer's portrait has been completed and no longer runs the risk of coming across as a reflection of better-known figures, the critic finds that "something of Dante's brilliant solemnity, of Byron's ferocity, [and] of Blake's mystic genius is transferred, albeit without identical effects, into the poetry of this bizarre poseur."[20] The same, "tactic" comparatism is in play in the Eminescu chapter. If, in the 1934 monograph on Eminescu foreign influences are accurately documented, in the *History* chapter, where the pressure of the nationalist paradigm is higher, they are deemed irrelevant. "Eminescu," writes Călinescu, "is, first and foremost, a traditional poet who absorbs all the elements of the literature before him. All his themes are rooted in Romanian tradition, no matter how patchy this tradition might be, while the foreign influences ... only bring nuances and details."[21] It is, again, just at the end of the chapter, when Eminescu's work is presented as transcending all contingent dealings, that the critic turns to a more relational approach by placing the poet in the aesthetic and spatial proximity of Johann Wolfgang von Goethe, George Gordon Byron, Alphonse de Lamartine, and Friedrich Hölderlin. The message is clear: Eminescu is neither a descendant nor a follower of the great European writers, but their rival—the Romanian contender in the world tournament of letters. Călinescu's point as a "comparatist" is not that Eminescu and Macedonski are indebted to Goethe and Byron, but that Romanian writers take up, in their literature, *the same space* claimed by Goethe and Byron in German and British literatures, respectively.

3. Discrete Spatiality and Cultural Homology

Therefore, although domestic and international authors are set side by side and even related to one another in Călinescu and his followers' account, this does not mean that these writers and, more broadly, their cultures actually interconnect. The "relationship" the critics describe is static and acknowledged post factum. This description does not shed light on the transnational flows, exchanges, and influences inevitably giving rise to this relationship, but, largely speaking, on the structural symmetries popping up in national literature *deus ex machina*-like and unveiling a pattern of similitudes between this and other literatures. According to the logic of cultural production or, rather, *re*production at work here, to be competitive on a world scale, a culture must replicate internally the structure of another, more "established" one. Yet again, the replication in question somehow takes place without effective commerce between the two. As the same logic would have it, they are both closed systems even though the capacity of a marginal or quasi-marginal cultural system or subsystem of this kind to compete with the more central areas of a regional or world system hinges, paradoxically, on the ability of a presumably closed system such as a "core" nation to engender forms and themes recognizable in another closed system. Generated "spontaneously" rather than relationally, by means of de facto relations, the argument for these forms and themes and for the homologies they are supposed to lay bare among nations represents the nationalist framework of analysis' awkward attempt to work through conundrums such as "universalization without internationalization" and "comparison without interaction."

Underlying this argument is the "territorial trap"[22] notion, which implies that any national culture is equipped with and ideologically invested in "a firm sense of territorial grounding or enclosure."[23] Drawing on Immanuel Wallerstein and other world-systems theorists, World Literature critics have become of late increasingly aware that "the state as the unit of analysis" is no longer able—if it has ever been— to explain "actually existing" literary relations, and yet the literary historiography of emergent cultures, whose sovereignty has been in balance until recently, remains particularly anchored in a territorialist "geographical unconscious," as John Agnew has dubbed it. This unconscious lies behind spatial homogenizations, that is, behind critical mappings of entire national territories as one culturally uniform continuum. Such maneuvers are not uncommon in modern literary scholarship. Branko Vodnik, for example, in his 1913 history of Croatian literature (*Povijest hrvatske književnosti*), gives a boost to the idea of national Croatian literature by downplaying the regional differences among Dalmatia, Slavonia, and the rest of Croatia.[24] Or, the same deep apprehensions drive Călinescu's cognate notion of Romanian literature as a territory under siege. His *History* purports precisely, and symbolically, to recover, on behalf of his country, the location the political map of Central-Eastern Europe no longer affords Romania after 1940. To draw this map—and to make his geopolitical statement—he fills in the blanks of Romanian culture by assigning highly praised writers to all three Romanian provinces, with Eminescu and Ion Creangă as stand-ins for Moldavia, Ioan Slavici and Liviu Rebreanu for Transylvania, and Ion Luca Caragiale for Wallachia.[25]

Parting company with Călinescu in other respects, Lovinescu is also invested in repositioning national culture in the world through a critical foregrounding of international isomorphisms. As noted above, the presumed lack of "organicism" of Romanian culture called for a territorial solution, which, in Călinescu, translated into a thoroughgoing critical coverage of the entire area administered or claimed by the Romanian state. Instead, Lovinescu responds to the same problem with a temporal solution: where Călinescu's approach is chiefly spatial and results in topological operations such as symbolic geopositionings and quasi-exhaustive mappings of national cultural space, Lovinescu's tactic involves temporal charts and temporally relocating moves. A critical rationale for assigning Romanian culture a better place in the chronology of Western culture, his *History of Contemporary Romanian Literature* handles the thorny issue of its object's comparative "belatedness" in European context by deploying concepts such as "mutation" and "synchronism." His contention is basically that, if during the nineteenth century Romanian society was still trying to catch up with the more advanced West by deliberately "imitating" Western institutions, the gap already closed in the early-twentieth century. "While in cultures shaped by smooth evolutionary processes the changes in affect and taste happen gradually," Lovinescu maintains, in societies such as ours, which are brought into being by revolutionary convulsions, transformations are swift in all the fields, and so, through a precipitous synchronization with the forms of art of Western Europe that was meant to put us all of a sudden on an equal footing with the West, the slow, organic, and intermediate phases of Romania's evolution have been suppressed.

Illustrating such synchronizing changes, the group of writers Lovinescu himself promoted in the Sburătorul literary circle and designates as "the modernist movement" in his book is the overdue but well-deserved release of Romanian literature and culture from their "peripheral" status. This is how he retools the "belatedness complex" into a quasi-positive category by laying compensatory emphasis on the role of "modernism" in the country's recent cultural history. Furthermore, as a social critic, Lovinescu openly advocates the infusion of foreign capital, and, many decades prior to Franco Moretti's insights into the planetary spread of the novel, theorizes "[writers'] merging of foreign literary techniques with national topics so as to foster [new,] valuable pieces of art."[26] In this regard, his stance may seem different from Călinescu's. On closer inspection, it becomes clear, however, that outside influences are referenced perfunctorily, in comments on literary movements and periods. When it comes to individual writers, one cannot miss Lovinescu's reluctance to compare, juxtapose, and connect. Not unlike Călinescu in his discussion of external factors that have contributed to the formation of Romanian literature, Lovinescu too tends to discount them in order to "protect" the originality of domestic writers. He does name such European sources of inspiration, but, in these instances, his method could be described as "reference without comparison," a technique specific to the construction of collective identity-oriented narratives and frequently used, among others, by the author of the most important early-twentieth-century histories of Estonian literature, Mihkel Kampmann. In *Eesti vanem ilukirjandus* (1908) and *Eesti kirjanduseloo peajooned* (1912–1936), Kampmann sketches out the evolution of Estonian literature by subsuming it under Romanticism and Realism but abandons these movements' comparative contexts when he dwells on specific Estonian writers.[27] Most likely, Lovinescu did not read Kampmann, but his reaction to Papadat-Bengescu, whom he saw as a pioneer of the modern Romanian novel, is akin to Kampmann's response to Estonian writers, as much as it is, the reader will recall, to Călinescu's own take on Papadat-Bengescu. "While [Papadat-Bengescu's] name has been repeatedly linked to that of Proust, this association," Lovinescu too argues, "should not be mistaken for an identification between the two, nor should it concern more than her knack for psychological analysis."[28] In discussing her work, the critic seems rather irritated by the parallels to the French author, but when he adopts a bird's-eye view of the place of Romanian literature among world literatures, he does not hesitate to underline the structural homology between the two novelists. "Kindred spirits if not equal in talent," Lovinescu insists, "both Baudelaire and Proust can be found in Romanian literature through the writings of Mr. T. Arghezi and Ms. Hortensia Papadat-Bengescu."[29] Retained as far as the cultural system goes but ignored analytically, at the level of the writer's own textual system, isomorphism works hand in glove with the pseudo-comparative tack mentioned earlier to resolve two crucial issues entailed by the "national unit of analysis" that reflect the tension between superiority and inferiority complexes: on the one hand, "homologist" reading sets these writers side by side, suggesting that they *all* make up a common pool of international values of shared rank; on the other hand, this reading modality carries the implication that marginal authors, whose originality claims would be jeopardized by a truly comparative inquiry, are self-reliant in their efforts and that, by the same token, their work is *not* derivative.

Marginal as they may appear in the European scheme of things, such authors constitute by no means an exotic fringe in Romanian letters, and so intercultural correspondences of this type abound in Lovinescu's *History*. In effect, the critic strives to identify local counterparts to every major movement of modern French culture, on the premise that the national literary system managed, over a mere few decades, to make up for the lost time in a cultural contest in which older traditions had given themselves a civilizational head start. Thus, "[Vasile] Alecsandri nationalized elements borrowed from Hugo," while Gheorghe Brăescu and Liviu Rebreanu are native satellites of Honoré de Balzac and Émile Zola—"What French naturalism ... accomplished more than a half century ago through Balzac, Zola and, especially, Maupassant," Lovinescu lets us know confidently, "is about to be achieved ... by Mr. Brăescu's work"; as for Rebreanu's writings, they avail themselves of "the formula of the naturalist novel, of the *Comédie humaine* ... [and of] the world of Balzac's peasants in *Les paysans*, and, especially, of Zola's in *La terre*," with similar effects.[30] In poetry, if Arghezi can be considered Baudelaire's emissary to Romanian culture, George Bacovia is Paul Verlaine's spokesman, while Ion Pillat writes in the name of Francis Jammes, as it were. One could argue, in fact, that the critic sets out to build a Romanian replica of the functional dynamics of the French literary system, for he seeks not only to locate autochthonous equivalents to the French masters but also to match each function of the "master system" with an identical or comparable protocol or structural principle at work in the literature of his country. If the totality of the laws governing production within a literary system forms, as Even-Zohar has proposed, a "repertoire," then Lovinescu lays out the Romanian repertoire as a formal thematic inventory completely analogous to the French one. More specifically, if "secondary" (or conservative) repertoires feature traditional formulas characteristic of nineteenth-century literature, and, under this heading, the critic pairs up Victor Hugo and Alecsandri and Zola and Rebreanu, respectively, with a revival in the twentieth century in the direction of the Jammes-Pillat duo, "primary" (more innovative) sets of techniques and motifs comprise literary manifestations tilted, in Romanian literature at least, to the twentieth century, with couplets like Marcel Proust-Papadat-Bengescu, Baudelaire-Arghezi, and Verlaine-Bacovia.

Such pairings and symmetries, as well as the systemic homology model of literary-historical analysis turning them out point to a cultural symptom Gregory Jusdanis has defined as "belated modernity." Extrapolating from the situation of modern Greek literature at the dawn of the last century, the critic reflects on the sometimes simplistic and "geo-positivistic" understandings of "modernization" in the cultures of the European periphery, where the term often designates "an inexorable process of change ending in the complete reproduction of western paradigms."[31] Jusdanis's *Belated Modernity and Aesthetic Culture* details the workings of a cultural dynamics that pivots on the conflict between intellectuals with a Westernizing agenda and those keen on "national specificity," a dispute as common to modern Greece as it has been to its neighbors. Pleading for a more nuanced view of East European cultural developments, Jusdanis advocates a critique of Eurocentrism that is at once spatial and temporal. Thus, this critique "demands European motifs, strategies, and concerns from non-European societies" while urging a "search for modern concepts in earlier cultures."[32] Rarely subject to this kind of scrutiny in this cultural zone, ideological antinomies such as "tradition" and "modernity" and "East" and "West" are, Jusdanis stresses, mere upshots of the "developmental" model[33] according to which modernity and modernization are synonymous with the West and Westernization, respectively.[34]

4. Toward an Interactional Historiography

It seems to me, though, that both those who picture national culture as an "autochthonous" phenomenon occurring within self-sufficient and self-confining structures and those who place this process within Westernizing narratives of progress and equate it with a sort of cultural emancipation rely on a "separatist" notion of national space or, better yet, spaces, which they see as determining each other rather mechanically. Indebted to a one-to-one, one-directional model of cultural exchange or, more precisely, influence, the "Westernizers" think within the framework of the aforementioned structural correspondences between so-called "core" and "marginal" cultures, although the assumption that the former boast a steadfast and coherent identity that serves as a preordained reference for the latter due to their presumably less "organic" makeup has been debunked during decades of multicultural and postcolonial analysis. Instead, what the same scholarship has shown, and what I reiterate in the Romanian context, is that even if cultural trade among nations has often been conducted on unequal terms, literary modernity has brought about a world space of knotty intersections wherein the East has also helped construct the West. Gerard Delanty is just one of the critics who have pointed out that "The rise of the West and European modernity, for instance, cannot be explained without taking into account how the West interacted with the East and with other parts of the world."[35] Nevertheless, whether they throw their lot with the "autochthonists" or with the "Westernizers," Călinescu and Lovinescu both tend to reduce such interactions to "a one-way account of colonial appropriation."[36] Even Lovinescu's insistence on French culture as *the* model for Romania's modernization upholds nationalism—the nationalism, if not the cultural imperialism, of the model—supranationally, on a European scale. For, in his work, internationalization and French literature's reproduction on Romanian soil are all too often interchangeable, and, in that, the *History*'s relocating "reparations" remain perfunctory.

When critics like Bulgarian essayist Alexander Kiossev determine this sort of reproduction as "self-colonization," they set little store by the pressures said imperialism applies on emerging literary cultures to reincarnate entire structures and even emblematic figures of the world-system's core.[37] These pressures create problematic expectations at the system's center too. Here, they lie behind something that could be diagnosed as the "Saul Bellow complex," for, to be sure, metropolitan hubs are not immune to complexes either. "Who is," infamously asked Saul Bellow, "the Tolstoy of the Zulus? The Proust of the Papuans?" as though, to become globally relevant, each national patrimony had to restage better-known literatures complete with their particular writers.[38] Otherwise, in the system's outlying stretches this reinstantiation of French or German classics, styles, and trends has had at times a cheerfully intentional dimension to it, and quite a few literary historians have assumed that genres and schools naturally—and purposefully—reproduce Western prototypes. Since the effectiveness of this reenactment has been held in high esteem across the region throughout modernity, identifying native representatives of Classicism, the Baroque, Romanticism, modernism, and even postmodernism has been tantamount to issuing a certificate of value. It comes as little surprise, then, that Central and East European scholars have scrambled to substantiate the presence of these movements in their countries, as Antal Szerb did in *Magyar irodalomtörténet*, the 1934 history in which Hungarian literature is presented as "a miniature copy of European literature."[39] Not to be outdone, those unable to back up their "structural correspondence" claims with literary documents went ahead and fabricated them, à la the nineteenth-century Czech writers who adduced forged manuscripts as proof positive that an "organic" national culture had existed in their country prior to more extensive interactions with the rest of Europe.[40]

Whether they involve honest scholarship or fraudulent philology, these episodes of post-Romantic literary historiography speak to the same, crude conception of skill and accomplishment that made Eugen Ionesco aver, back in his Romanian days, that "There is a limited number of positions and roles in culture, and each of them can be held or fulfilled by only one individual."[41] Deeply embedded in historiographic homologism, this view of culture is mechanically "distributive" as it is territorialist–separatist. On the other hand, its dismantling does not entail doing away with the national framework of understanding literature altogether either. Instead, the critique seeks to redefine the territorial unit of literary studies as "copresence of the national and the wordly."[42] According to Casanova's "relational" paradigm, for example, cultures consist in a closed-shop kind of interminglings, and so when these cultures deal with one another, such dealings are quintessentially inter*national*, whereas truly *trans*national interchanges occur throughout national traditions across, over, and the expense of political borders, not only allowing for the free play of transcultural interactions but also assigning the latter a major role in the formation of national culture. What Wai Chee Dimock has observed of the United States applies to any other national patrimony in the world system: a country's literature is a "tangle of relations"[43] that exceeds by far national space, more exactly, the territory under that country's administration. To echo here a point this volume hammers home forcefully and repeatedly, it bears underscoring that there is nothing natural or self-evident about the concept of literary history as a territorially organic construct, according to which literary and national borders are the same. The argument from their coincidence is in fact inseparable from a specific juncture in the history of European ideas, when, as prominent Hungarian literary historian János Horváth showed, under the pressure of various national platforms, the onset of a "narrowing" of "the literary mind" changed the theory and practice of literary historiography forever. In Hungary, this tightening of scope was already heralded by Ferenc Toldy's 1851 *A magyar nemzeti irodalom története*. The "Hungarian nation" phrase in Toldy's title signals the genre's increased focus on the literary life of a single people or nation inhabiting a well-defined territory under precise historical circumstances. However, in Pál Wallaszky's 1785 *Conspectus reipublicae litterariae in Hungaria*, the first Hungarian literary history, literature had included "all forms of writing" and "all kinds of texts written in Hungar[y] in any kind of language," and similarly ecumenic, narratively schematic yet multilingual and fairly multicultural "protohistories" of literature had been written throughout Central and Eastern Europe before the nationalist turn.[44]

5. Translation and Transcultural Intertextuality

If, as Even-Zohar stresses, "[interaction] cannot be divorced from literary history, since it is part of the historical existence of any cultural system,"[45] then few histories of literature can be said to attend in the aftermath of this shift to what I would define as systems' real "life forms." Here, I will briefly zero in just on two of these forms—or formations, rather—through which such systems arise *inter*culturally and acquire a recognizable, even "original" contour: translation and intertextuality. In closing, I will assess the play these practices have been given in Central-East European and especially Romanian literature and literary history.

Ironically enough, it is translation, the most tangible form of cultural interactivity, to begin with, that post-Herderian literary historians have failed to take into account more than anything else, all the more so that, as Even-Zohar also posits, translations are the most active subsystem of a literature.[46] Corroborating his insight, Franco Moretti shows in *Atlas of the European Novel 1800–1900* that, in the nineteenth century, while England and France imported a rather limited number of novels, in Poland, Italy, and Russia these imports exceeded 50 percent.[47] But these foreign-made literary commodities have been all but ignored in the theoretical articulation and analysis of "national literature," a concept that was created in a critical vitro where the actual functioning of the cultural field simply could not and cannot be studied, given that this sort of ideologically controlled environment had been designed to stifle or disparage the junctions and commerce with other milieus. The paradoxical stance of Mihail Kogălniceanu (1817–1891), prominent figure of national Romanticism and director of the Iași National Theater, who famously proclaimed that "translations do not make a literature" while he was adapting French plays to supplement his institution's repertoire, speaks precisely to this gulf between literary reality and critical discourse.[48] A similar position was adopted around the same time by Maurycy Mochnacki, the leading ideologue of Polish Romanticism. One of his main assumptions was that translations stunt a culture's development, which is why his 1830 *O Literaturze Polskiej w Wieku Dziewiętnastym* (On Polish Literature in the Nineteenth Century) celebrates "Romantic originality" at the expense of cultural exchange. "After all," Mochnacki contended, "Montaigne, Montesquieu, Kant, Fichte and other authors wrote original things: they neither translated nor imitated anything."[49] The other presupposition at work here is, of course, that translation, imitation, and the like occur primarily in "noncore" literatures, a lopsided view of transcultural relationality into which not all Romanian critics have bought. Ibrăileanu, as we have noted, is one of those who saw things somewhat differently. In *Spiritul critic în cultura românească* (The Spirit of Criticism in Romanian Culture), he actually pictures interactivity across cultural spaces as a financial tug of war whose actors are foreign capital and indigenous material, and he attempts to sort out productive (creative) and nonproductive (reproductive, superficially imitative) influences. His 1909 book marks one of the first East European efforts to assess intercultural traffic from the "target culture's" perspective. Many decades ahead of Dionýz Durišin's theory of the interliterary process, Ibrăileanu's take on cultural reception foregrounds what he determines as "mutual selection," viz., an operation during which certain items are imported, provided they fulfill a culture's structural "needs."[50] But because translation is mostly absent from Ibrăileanu's examination of these imports, so is the translational component of his transnational literary history.

More visible in less central and emergent traditions, where "import rates" are higher, overlooking or underappreciating a national culture's translational subsystem otherwise characterizes all literary histories indebted to what Ulrich Beck seizes as "methodological nationalism."[51] Trying to restore "the sense of belonging" to the literary works translated into English, Stuart Gillespie acknowledges, in this vein, that,

> in every phase of English literature, and for that matter [in] many phases of other western literatures too, much of the innovative impulse comes directly or indirectly through translation from ancient Greek and Roman texts, and in some eras their impact is fundamental … [T]he eighteenth-century literary world is a translating culture, with the greatest prestige attaching to classical translation. Once this fact comes into focus, the absence of this dimension from the received literary-historical account becomes equally obvious.[52]

Gillespie's is a timely reminder that translations, which had initially furnished *primary* forms of interaction among cultures, became a *secondary* system only with the nationalist circling of the wagons that took place in historiography at the middle of the nineteenth century. Before that, translations had been deemed more significant, and so cultural zones particularly drawn to rendering ancient and foreign authors into national idioms had not been automatically assigned "newcomer" or "derivative" status. As Gillespie also remarks, during the seventeenth and the eighteenth centuries, when, across Europe, translations had exceeded domestically composed works by far, English culture had been as "emergent" and "imitative" as East European cultures would be only a century thereafter.

Pivotal to comparative and historical studies for hundreds of years, the classical source-influence, original-translation (imitation) model of analysis has, then, all this time fallen short of its very goal, for it has missed a vital dimension in which literatures talk to each other and, more basically, "emerge." Challenging this model, the interactional scenario accentuates, instead, that foreign writers and currents oftentimes acquire multiple cultural memberships, belonging originally to the "source" culture but becoming eventually, through various processes of translation, adaptation, and dissemination, part and parcel of other cultural environments as well. The interactional approach may have come to the fore with new comparatism, World Literature, world-systems, and polysystems theory, but, I would suggest, it is well suited to tackle virtually any period, given that the literary and cultural formation notion this approach rests on predates modern times. For that reason, no study of interwar Romanian literature, for instance, can afford to pay no heed to how much European classics such as Charles Baudelaire and Stephane Mallarmé have made themselves "at home," as it were, in and through Romanian authors. And yet nationalist literary histories have preferred to relate pre–Second World War writers like Barbu and Arghezi chiefly to traditional figures like Dosoftei or Bolintineanu. At the same time, a history of Cold War-era Romanian poetry remains incomplete without a chapter on the American Beat poets. For, led by Mircea Cărtărescu, the Romanian "generation of the 1980s" sought, in fact, to break with local tradition, that is, with the previous, "neomodernist" literary generation, by taking up a poetry formula that, incorporating as it did massive amounts of autobiographical elements, had little appeal to previous Romanian writers. Nevertheless, rather than acknowledging Allen Ginsberg's imposing presence in contemporary Romanian literature and, more broadly, the co-spatiality or intersection of autochthonous and American letters in the early 1980s, most critics fell back, by means of a pseudo-relational protocol once again redolent of Ricoeur's retrodiction, on an "internal" tradition. One more time, their organicist objective was to "fill the gaps" and "connect the dots" on—and predeterminately within—the national map, whereas the interactional method requires something quite opposite: unearthing the geocultural nodes that enable the meeting of two or more cultures and ultimately engender them. To read Romanian literature in such transculturally intertextual terms means, and requires, to effectively relocate it and thus, at long last, stop reining in its in-built back-and-forth among and across the networks of other literatures and cultures.

Notes

1   G. Ibrăileanu, *Spiritul critic în cultura românească*, ed. Pavel Balmuş (Chişinău: Cartier, 2000), 11.

2   Stephen Greenblatt, "Cultural Mobility: An Introduction," in *Cultural Mobility: A Manifesto*, ed. Stephen Greenblatt, with Ines G.Županov, Reinhard Meyer-Kalkus, Heike Paul, Pál Nyíri, and Friederike Pannewick (Cambridge: Cambridge University Press, 2009), 3.

3 Greenblatt, "Cultural Mobility," 6.

4 Pascale Casanova, "La guerre de l'ancienneté," in *Des litteratures combatives*. *L' internationale des nationalismes littéraires*, ed. Pascale Casanova (Paris: Éditions Raison D' Agir), 19.

5 Casanova, "La guerre de l'ancienneté," 18.

6 Ferdinand Brunetière, "Sur le caractère essentiel de la littérature française," in *Études critiques sur l histoire de la littérature française* (Paris: Hachette, 1903), 275.

7 Pascale Casanova, *The World Republic of Letters*, trans. M. B. DeBevoise (Cambridge, MA: Harvard University Press, 2004), 87.

8 Robert B. Pynsent, "Nineteenth-Century Czech Literary History, National Revival and the Forged Manuscripts," in *History of the Literary Cultures of East-Central Europe. Junctures and Disjunctures in the 19th and 20th Centuries*, vol. 3, ed. Marcel Cornis-Pope and John Neubauer (Amsterdam: John Benjamins, 2007), 367.

9 See Mircea Martin, *G. Călinescu și "complexele" literaturii române* (Bucharest: Albatros, 1981).

10 Alex Drace-Francis, *The Making of Modern Romanian Culture: Literacy and the Development of National Identity* (London: Tauris Academic Studies, 2006), 129.

11 Martin, *G. Călinescu și "complexele" literaturii române*, 34–35.

12 Prasenjit Duara, "Civilizations and Nations in a Globalizing World," in *Reflections on Multiple Modernities: European, Chinese and Other Interpretations*, ed. Dominic Sachsenmaier, Jens Riedel, and Shmuel N. Eisenstadt (Leiden: Brill, 2002), 92.

13 G. Călinescu, *Istoria literaturii române de la origini pînă în prezent*, 2nd revised ed., preface and edition by Alexandru Piru (Bucharest: Minerva, 1982), 3.

14 Itamar Even-Zohar, "Polysystem Studies," *Poetics Today* 11, no. 1 (1990): 27.

15 Călinescu, *Istoria literaturii române*, 4.

16 Andrei Terian, *G. Călinescu. A cincea esență* (Bucharest: Cartea Românească, 2009), 290.

17 Paul Ricoeur, *Time and Narrative*, vol. 3, trans. Kathleen Blamey and David Pellauer (Chicago: University of Chicago Press, 1988), 173.

18 E. Lovinescu, *Istoria literaturii române contemporane*, vol. 3 (Bucharest: Minerva, 1981), 230.

19 G. Călinescu, "Eminescu în italienește. De vorbă cu dl. Ramiro Ortiz," in *Opere. Publicistică*, vol. 1, ed. Nicolae Mecu, Ileana Mihăilă, and Daciana Vlădoiu, foreword by Eugen Simion (Bucharest: Editura Fundației Naționale pentru Știință și Artă, 2006), 252.

20 Călinescu, *Istoria literaturii române*, 528.

21 Călinescu, *Istoria literaturii române*, 388.

22 John Agnew, "The Territorial Trap: The Geographical Assumptions of International Relations Theory," *Review of International Political Economy*, 1, no. 1 (1994): 53–80.

23 Paul Giles, "The Deterritorialization of American Literature," in *World Literature in Theory*, ed. David Damrosch (Malden, MA: Wiley Blackwell, 2014), 419.

24 See John Neubauer, "Literary Histories: Itineraries of National Self-Images. Introduction," in *History of the Literary Cultures of East-Central Europe*, ed. Marcel Cornis-Pope and John Neubauer, vol. 3, 349.

25 Călinescu, *Istoria literaturii române*, 6.

26 Lovinescu, *Istoria literaturii române*, vol. 1 (Bucharest: Minerva), 118.

27 Epp Annus, Luule Epner, and Jüri Talvet, "Shifting Ideologies in Estonias Literary Histories, Textbooks, and Anthologies," in *History of the Literary Cultures of East-Central Europe,* ed. Marcel Cornis-Pope and John Neubauer, vol. 3, 356.

28 Lovinescu, *Istoria literaturii române*, vol. 3, 230.

29 Lovinescu, *Istoria literaturii române*, vol. 1, 142.

30 Lovinescu, *Istoria literaturii române*, vol. 3, 243.

31 Gregory Jusdanis, *Belated Modernity and Aesthetic Culture: Inventing National Literature* (Minneapolis: University of Minnesota Press, 1991), XIV.

32 Jusdanis, *Belated Modernity and Aesthetic Culture*, 10.

33 Brian James Baer, "Introduction: Cultures of Translation," in *Contexts, Subtexts, Pretexts: Literary Translation in Eastern Europe and Russia*, ed. Brian James Baer (Amsterdam: John Benjamins, 2011), 5.

34 Gregory Jusdanis, *Belated Modernity and Aesthetic Culture*, XV.

35 Gerard Delanty, *The Cosmopolitan Imagination* (Cambridge: Cambridge University Press, 2009), 192.

36 Delanty, *The Cosmopolitan Imagination*, 192.

37 Alexander Kiossev, "The Self-Colonising Cultures," in *Cultural Aspects of the Modernisation Process*, ed. Dimitri Ginev, Francis Sejersted, and Kostadinka Simeonova (Oslo: TMV-Centeret, 1995), 76.

38 Saul Bellow had reportedly asked the infamous questions in an interview that elicited reactions so vocal that the writer felt compelled to follow up, a few years thereafter, with an explanation in "Op-Ed: Papuans and Zulus," *The New York Times* of March 10, 1994. See http://www.nytimes.com/books/00/04/23/specials/belloe-papuans.html

39 John Neubauer, "The Narrowing Scope of Hungarian Literary Histories," in *History of the Literary Cultures of East-Central Europe*, vol. 3, 388.

40 A detailed account of the "forged manuscripts" scandal can be found in Robert B. Pynsent, "Nineteenth-Century Czech Literary History, National Revival, and the Forged Manuscripts," in *History of the Literary Cultures of East-Central Europe*, vol. 3, 366–377.

41 Eugen Ionescu, *Nu* (Bucharest: Vremea, 1934), 168.

42 For a detailed argument on this issue, see Christian Moraru and Andrei Terian, introduction to *Romanian Literature as World Literature*.

43 Wai Chee Dimock, *Through Other Continents: American Literature across Deep Time* (Princeton, NJ: Princeton University Press, 2006), 3.

44 John Neubauer, "The Narrowing Scope of Hungarian Literary History," in *History of the Literary Cultures of East-Central Europe*, vol. 3, 384–385. Similar to Wallaszky's *Conspectus* are Petru Maior's 1812 *Istoria pentru începutul românilor in Dachia*; Ulrich Ernst Zimmermann's 1812 *Versuch einer Geschichte der Lettischen Literatur*; Feliks Bentkowski's 1814 *Historya literatury polskiey*; and Josef Jakub Jungmann's 1825 *Historie literatury české*.

45 Itamar Even-Zohar, "Polysystems Studies," 54.

46 Efim Etkind observes that

The importance of the translation system has been noted since the nineteenth century. Russian literary writer and critic Nikolai Chernyshevsky declared in the mid-nineteenth century that "literature in translation should be seen as an organic part of a national literature. The latter cannot be studied in its entirety, and its social significance cannot be entirely understood, if the facts of literature in translation are ignored."

See Efim Etkind, "Introduction," in *Mastera poeticheskogo perevoda Mastera russkogo stikhotvornogo Perevoda* (Leningrad: Sovetskii pisatel, 1968), apud. Brian James Baar,

"Introduction: Cultures of Translation," in *Contexts, Subtexts and Pretexts: Literary Translation in Eastern Europe and Russia*, ed. Brian James Baar (Amsterdam: John Benjamins, 2011), 5.

47 Franco Moretti, *Atlas of the European Novel 1800–1900* (London: Verso, 1998), 151–157.

48 Paul Cornea, "Conceptul de istorie literară în cultura românească," in *Conceptul de istorie literară în cultura românească*, ed. Paul Cornea (Bucharest: Eminescu, 1978), 13–14.

49 Jerzy Jedlicki, *A Suburb of Europe: Nineteenth-Century Approaches to Western Civilization* (Budapest: Central University Press, 1999), 29.

50 See Dionýz Durišin, *Communautes interlittéraires spécifiques* (Bratislava: Institut de Littérature Mondiale, 1993).

51 Ulrich Beck, "Toward a New Critical Theory with a Cosmopolitan Intent," *Constellations* 10, no. 4 (2003): 453–468.

52 Stuart Gillespie, *English Translation and Classical Reception: Towards a New Literary History* (Malden, MA: Wiley-Blackwell, 2011), 13.

5

After "Imitation": Aesthetic Intersections, Geocultural Networks, and the Rise of Modern Romanian Literature

Carmen Muşat

"To be human is to be intended toward the other," writes Gayatri Chakravorty Spivak in the last chapter of her 2003 book *Death of a Discipline*.[1] Bearing the imprint of a different time, place, and vocabulary and variously formulated, this claim has been made by one twentieth-century Romanian critic after another. By and large, they all point to the same complex and ultimately originality-inducing mechanism of national culture production. The functioning of this apparatus, they note, is also oriented toward others and their literatures, and this orientation has been deeply formative of the country's literature. But, as I argue below by drawing from the same commentators, the pull of other worlds has not prompted mere "imitation," nor has it yielded a "derivative" body of work. Furthermore, my critical sketch of Romanian intellectual history shows that, on the one hand, within this tradition, imitation is rarely understood univocally, and mimetically so, and, on the other hand, no matter how one views imitation in a culture whose main authors have often positioned themselves interculturally, past a certain point originality and singularity here come about not so much as these writers "imitate" trends and aesthetic formulas forged inside "major" cultures but by a different kind of engagement with those cultures and with the literary world-system broadly.

Accordingly, my two-pronged argument will dwell, first, on a redefinition of imitation in modern Romanian criticism where the concept is no longer at loggerheads with creativity and much-touted "national specificity," and, second, on how said concept and related practices take a back seat to concordance, kinship, and other nonimitative, more markedly exchange-like types of cultural, indeed, intercultural and interlinguistic aesthetic production that force us ultimately to rethink national literature itself and its ties to idiom, ethnicity, territory, and even the world beyond. For, situated in a geopolitical zone shaped throughout its history by remarkable ethnolinguistic and demographic fluidity and shifting borders, Romanian literature arose in a multinational and multicultural region, borrowed early on from the Central and Southeast European neighbors, and responded enthusiastically but originally to remoter cultures such as French centuries later. Stemming from this openness to the vaster world without and within are, I maintain, multiple literatures, which have formed not only inside the same nation-state but in the same national language as well. Engendered through aesthetic protocols in which cultural mimesis and creativity are two sides of the same coin, this multiplicity goes to show that, even though the criterion of language remains probably the most relevant in defining Romanian literature, the geography and cultural milieus surrounding and overlapping with present-day Romania have been equally important in fostering the identity of its literature. Therefore, this identity is not only plural but also "intersectional" and "nodal," attributes that apply to countless Romanian writers from Paul Celan and Emil Cioran to Benjamin Fondane and Tristan Tzara, as they do to so many other authors on the planet, who belong to more than one tradition and geo-linguistic and cultural system and whose works call on us to take another look at the relationships between the writer and his or her community, between national literature and literatures by ethnic minorities, as well as between national and world literature.

1. Influence and Originality

As Eugen Lovinescu (1881–1943) puts it in the second volume of his *Istoria literaturii române contemporane* (History of Contemporary Romanian Literature, 1926), "Man is not an abstract or isolated being; his spiritual action is affected by the pressure of the moral atmosphere of the age, just as the surface of a body is impacted by the pressure of the physical atmosphere."[2] Attempting to capture the specifics of Romanian literature's evolution during the first decades of the twentieth century, Lovinescu is fully aware that because cultural forms, techniques, and "ideas" originating elsewhere get "nationalized" as they "undergo considerable refraction while passing through new cultural territories," national literature's tendency to "synchronize" with the broader "spirit of the age" need by no means result internally just in imitation of outside sources and externally in an increased uniformity of supranational literary space. In his argument, Lovinescu turns to Roman historian Tacitus and his all-embracing, "worldly" concept of *saeculum*, distinguishing between the latter and *spiritus loci*, which, by contrast, brings to the fore the differences between coeval cultures. As is well known, the distinction crossed into the modern era with the *philosophes* of the Enlightenment such as Voltaire, who referred to the "spirit of the age" (*l'esprit du siècle*) in a sense closer to ours, then with Johann Gottfried von Herder, who coined the German equivalent, *Zeitgeist*, in 1769, and with William Hazlitt, who redefined the term in *The Spirit of the Age: Or Contemporary Portraits* (1825) as encapsulating "the progress of intellectual refinement, warring with our natural infirmities."[3] Opposed to the Herderian *Volksgeist* and the ethno-cultural theory behind it, the Voltairean "spirit of the age" concept underscores the role played by an interactive cultural system unifying, within the same historical period, different local developments and highlights the spread of the Enlightenment along with the emergence of European public consciousness. Keen on this system, Lovinescu insists that literary movements and artistic phenomena in general are not "spontaneous creations" of a people but endeavors specific to a given geographical and historical context and, on that ground, they crystallize the spirit of the age in a certain fashion. In so doing, they do incorporate material from "source" cultures, but this material is selected, interpreted, and otherwise filtered through a particular sensibility, which in turn is a sociohistorical rather than ethnic formation.

Setting out to uncover the "local" features of Romanian literature, Tudor Vianu (1897–1964), one of Lovinescu's disciples, reaches somewhat similar conclusions. In his view, the continuation of medieval life structures into seventeenth- and even eighteenth-century Romania had major consequences for the culture's evolution. The most notable among such repercussions was, according to Vianu, the lack of a true Renaissance, and, indeed, while a Renaissance corpus does exist in Romanian cultural history, this body of work is primarily scholarly.[4] Vianu thinks this absence accounts for Romanian literature's strong "popular" character, which, granted, is quite obvious in the constant interest the country's writers have shown in folklore.[5] But Alecu Russo, Vasile Alecsandri, Mihai Eminescu, and other examples adduced by the critic attest, perhaps more forcefully, to the influence exerted by European Romantics on Romania's nineteenth-century authors and to the Romantics' overall return to *völkisch* traditions. It is true that the choice of folkloric themes as well as the predilection for the militant and political side of Romanticism—obvious in most nineteenth-century Romania's minor poets—also responded to a sociopolitical reality marked by the emergence of civic and national consciousness. Otherwise, as Vianu cogently observes, although European Romanticism laid the aesthetic groundwork for modern Romanian literature, the dominant characteristic of this literature is "realist classicism" rather than a taste for Romantic excess.[6] Besides, did the discovery of Greek and Roman Antiquity happen simultaneously in Florence and France in the fourteenth century? Or, more likely, did the "law of imitation" not play a part in the configuration of the Italian and French Renaissance? And, one might wonder as well, does the fact that Romanticism arose almost concomitantly, albeit with differentiating artistic emphases, in Germany, France, and England not bespeak the cross-national interpenetration of cultural phenomena and the significant role of "national particularities" in the constitution of any literary doctrine? In his *History*, Lovinescu treats *poporanism* and *sămănătorism* as "mere imitative waves of Romantic ideology" and by no means isolated phenomena, thereby demolishing the case made by the proponents of a "native" traditionalism, who saw in the two movements a coming to fruition of local processes.[7]

Lovinescu's analysis brilliantly demonstrates the extent to which even the most "particular" cultural manifestations are ultimately *phenomena of synchronism* achieved through absorption, assimilation, and adaptation of a foreign cultural ideology to the national geo-historical context. Valid, in all actuality, for most literary movements regardless of historical moment and geographical location, the critic's conclusion has been borne out worldwide even more saliently in recent decades, when national borders are no longer the obstacle they used to be in the path of free circulation of people and ideas and when information reaches most corners of the world almost instantaneously. As for the "imitative spirit," Lovinescu simply turns the phrase on its head, likening imitation to "the bee's process of assimilation and elaboration" and defining it as "the most common way of being original."[8] Repeatedly arguing for the dissociation of the ethnic from the aesthetic, Lovinescu claims that "the aesthetic is an autonomous value achieved through language and the spiritual basis within an ethnic material,"[9] a remark that underlines the importance language "as a principle of artistic creation"[10] accrues when originality is at stake. To him, it is evident that "originality in art is to a large extent reabsorbed in talent and in the capacity to produce aesthetic emotion," a point he illustrates by adducing two powerful examples. One is several epic poems by Alecsandri, in which Charles Drouhet identified numerous influences by Victor Hugo. After reading Alecsandri's ballads, Lovinescu concludes that the poet's "epic work, which derives in such various respects and in such a powerful way from a foreign work, is overall a Romanian work."[11]

The other piece of evidence is a poem by Eminescu (1850–1889), "Sleepy Birds," an adaptation of the German lullaby "Gute Nacht." To be sure, the thorny question of the relationship between originality and influence presents itself most emphatically in Eminescu's work. One of Europe's belated Romantics, the author is acknowledged as both *the* "national poet" and, in Lovinescu's words, as "the point of intersection of multiple influences, more powerful and more fecund than the influences of French Romanticism on [other, less responsive creative] temperaments."[12] Complex and multiform, Eminescu's work is indeed an intersection point weaving together various threads into an original configuration of generic and local features that foregrounds relatedness and interaction as the driving forces behind *original* cultural production. Thus, each and every literary work is, in effect, a subjective synthesis of multiple influences, which stem not only from different yet synchronous spaces and cultures but also from the recycling and reinterpretation of older themes and techniques belonging to other epochs and literary movements. For, "worlding the world, making it a world of relations," to quote from Amy J. Elias and Christian Moraru's introduction to their essay collection *The Planetary Turn,* involves not only spatial interrelatedness in the present.[13] In calling for a contemporary "world of relations" in which all cultures participate, we need to take into account not just the present but the past as well, the incessant dynamic process of literary exchanges, stimuli, influences, reception, and translations that includes, besides voices and phenomena of our time, earlier writers and works. And while "cross-reading" may well be the most effective way of dealing with this material's original harnessing of cultural mimesis, we would do well to keep in mind that this sort of perusal, theorized as such only recently, has been part and parcel of writing practices since Classical Antiquity.

Speaking of originality makes more sense, however, at the individual rather than at the collective level. I would offer, in fact, that *a national literature is not an "original" literature* but an institutional framework within which different tendencies play out by materializing in sometimes unique and unrepeatable literary works. Originality has nothing to do with literature as an institution, given that the qualifier "original" applies only to individual creations; at the same time, the concept of "national specificity" bears no relevance to reading and understanding original literary works other than those whose authors are anonymous and collective, as in folk literature, for instance. The distinctness of each separate "national literature," on the other hand, is a wholly different issue. Addressing the "particular character of Romanian literature," Vianu sets out from the idea that this character is consolidated over time and is therefore more obvious in older literatures.[14] But, although within a given movement (Romanticism or *sămănătorism*) or within a certain moment or period (the 1848 Revolution or the first decades of the twentieth century) the model worked out by Vianu appears reasonably effective, none of the "specific" features he identifies can be extended to the entirety of Romanian literature.[15]

2. "One and unequal": Center, Periphery, Kinship

Because literature and, more generally, culture are practices that contribute decisively to the constitution of a people's identity, they also provide a solid foundation for the identitarian policies promoted by the relevant institutions of any state. Yet a people, and even less so a culture, is not a monolithic structure, but rather an orchestra in which, ideally, various players harmonize with each other while each performs from his or her own musical score. Resulting from this performance—and, again, this describes the ideal case—is a diversity in unity, all the more distinct the more it succeeds in bringing together different instruments and personalities. Or, to borrow a phrase used by Spivak in *Death of a Discipline*, a thorough knowledge of a national literature highlights "the internal line of *cultural* difference within 'the same culture.'"[16] It is this cultural difference that has generated, fashioned, and complicated the dichotomies of traditionalism/modernism, rural/urban, nationalism/cosmopolitanism at every stage of Romanian culture's evolution. In the contemporary era, where the country's borders no longer obstruct the movement of individuals, beliefs, and books, this process has been accelerating, and so internal cultural differences are multiplying exponentially. Boosting up this phenomenon are: the thriving, within the same moment and space, of literatures by Hungarian and German ethnic minorities, as well as of literature written in Romanian by authors of Armenian, Jewish, Russian, and other backgrounds; the intensifying assimilation by national culture of the literary production of Romanian exiles and diaspora; somewhat symmetrically, the steadily growing dialogue between today's Romanian and foreign writers, exchanges strengthened by the fast-increasing number of translations and by growing interaction, whether face-to-face at international book fairs, through creative writing residencies abroad, during meetings with audiences and readings organized by various cultural institutions, in cultural magazines and in the mass media, or online. These contacts are just some of the signs that post–Cold War Romania too has become part of Zygmunt Bauman's "liquid" world, one in which we are witnessing interesting changes in patterns of cultural influences.[17] Essentially, the latter no longer seem to be a one-way street where the geocultural system's marginal areas are simply "influenced" by the core. And yet there still is, among critics, an obvious tendency to overlook the impact cultural and geographical periphery also makes on those cultures considered central or "major."

We should be mindful of this shortcoming while welcoming, as I am, the entering of the study of world literature into the planetary era. The insights of planetary critics such as Franco Moretti and Spivak, I hasten to acknowledge, are particularly relevant to Romanian literature. While Bauman maintains that there is no such thing as "an unequivocal and uncontested hierarchy of cultures"[18] nowadays, to Moretti, the literary world-system, made up of interconnected national literatures as it is, presents itself as profoundly unequal since it reflects the power relations between states. According to him, "the destiny of a culture (usually a culture of the periphery, as Montserrat Iglesias Santos has specified) is intersected and altered by another culture (from the core) that 'completely ignores it.'"[19] Moretti views inequality as a consequence of what he takes to be the one-sided nature of influence, a presupposition that fails to account, however, for situations in which the bilateral aspect of influence cannot be ignored. Invoking the opinions of various literary historians and theorists, he concludes that "in cultures that belong to the periphery of the literary system (which means: almost all cultures, inside and outside Europe), the modern novel first arises not as an autonomous development but as a compromise between a western formal influence (usually French or English) and local materials."[20] Partly correct, such contentions remind one of the cultural advancement algorithms proposed at different junctures in modern Romanian history and from various ideological angles, starting with Titu Maiorescu's nineteenth-century theory of "contentless forms" and continuing, in the first decades of the twentieth century,[21] with Lovinescu himself, who posits that "high literature is the result of the refraction of foreign ideology through the ethnic individuality of the Romanian people."[22] Interestingly enough, he interprets the rise of some of his country's literary movements by deploying a metaphor also used by Moretti, namely, the "wave." *Sămănătorism* and *poporanism*, offers Lovinescu, are "imitative waves of Romantic ideology"[23] that, once they reach Romanian soil, acquire specific features through a "compromise" between what Moretti would call "foreign form and local material."[24] But the "local material" existing at a given time is in turn the product of previous compromises, since the dynamic behind the cultural phenomenon entails a continuous interpenetration of tendencies and influences that, in Romania and elsewhere in the world, have always been highly variegated. That is to say, despite appearances, "borrowings" do not function unilaterally; if we examine more closely whole national literary histories or histories of genres and other literary forms, we come across multiple instances where this "unilateralism" does not pan out but something else—the genres and discourse modalities dominant today in the West, which, past a certain point, have evolved autonomously and differently in response to their geopolitical contexts, arguably have as their starting points Indian and Egyptian epic poems, the prose of Greek and Latin Antiquity, and the narrative models supplied by Arabic prose in *A Thousand and One Nights*, to give only a few of the better-known examples. Available for the first time in French in a 1704 rendition that expurgated everything contravening the norms of French society at that moment, *A Thousand and One Nights* was subsequently translated and republished countless times throughout Europe, and its impact on the evolution of Western literature has been overwhelming. Under the systemic pressures exerted over centuries by works like it, not only has the relationship between center and periphery changed over the course of history, but influences have shifted their functions and coordinates as well. Contemporary literary movements and, among them, postmodernism perhaps more than any other, illustrate the complexities of the center/periphery and Eastern/Western interplays inside literary European and world-systems most powerfully. But earlier epochs, too, supply plenty of similar examples, from the rediscovery of Greco-Roman Antiquity during the Renaissance to the Romantics' fascination with far-away places such as India and the Middle East. In fact, the very beginnings of European literature bear the imprint of its contacts with other civilizations and cultures.

In discounting the role such interactions played in the rise of the novel in England, France, Germany, and Spain, Moretti disregards the interest writers from these countries showed in Eastern literatures.[25] For instance, the gothic novel, "invented" by Sir Horace Walpole (*The Castle of Otranto*), has its origins in the Persian and Arab tales he knew and valued. Likewise, Murasaki Shikibu, the author of what is regarded as the world's first novel, *The Tale of Genji* (1010), was Japanese, while the text itself presents most if not all the features of a seventeenth-century French novel such as Madame de la Fayette's 1678 *Princess of Clèves*. Thus, as far as this issue, too, goes, remembering that the history of literature does not begin with the modern period is key, much like recognizing that later on, as a result of the extension of power relations from the political into the cultural sphere in modernity, the reciprocity of influence seems to subside. Actually, Moretti himself notes that "World literature was indeed a system—but a system of *variations*," adding that "The pressure from the Anglo-French core *tried* to make it uniform, but could never fully erase the reality of difference."[26] Moretti's commonsense observation is backed by the systemic dynamic of literary phenomena, which, receptive as it is to multiple influences and tendencies, works against uniformity. Even more adequate is the phrase Spivak uses to describe continuous exchange between different cultures: "the incessant shuttle" that enables the evolution of literary ideas, techniques, and forms, allowing them to be carried not only across space but also from one epoch to another.[27] For, revisiting the past periodically from constantly changing perspectives fashioned by the present results in the constant renewal of the literary system. And what makes the difference between one literature and another when it comes to "inventing" literary forms is not necessarily priority understood as chronological antecedence but rather writers' ability to assimilate and filter through their own individuality structures, themes, and devices that otherwise, more often than not, do not belong to any particular individual. Refocusing attention on this ability might lead us to rethink, in Romanian and other contexts, the politics of influence and more broadly the power relationships between the world's literatures. This is one of the ramifications of G. Călinescu's intervention in "Tehnica criticii şi a istoriei literare" (The Technique of Literary Criticism and Literary History), where he proposes that concepts such as "the Renaissance" advanced by Jakob Burckhardt and "Romanticism," for whose understanding we are still indebted in large part to Madame de Staël, could be reconfigured so as to realign their constitutive elements into structures of signification indicative of more complex commerce and feedback loops between real and presumed centers and margins separated by space and time.[28] Of course, what ultimately matters is the critical viewpoint from which geographical and historical intervals between cultures are surveyed, a notion whose appreciation Călinescu shares with later critics such as Wai Chee Dimock.

Leaning in her genre approach on Claude Lévi-Strauss's anthropology and especially on Benoit Mandelbrot's fractal geometry, Dimock works toward a spectacular albeit sensible rethinking of the history of the novel.[29] Suggesting that "the never-ending saga of the epic and the novel can truly become the saga of the world," she underscores the common growth and interpenetration of literary forms from ancient times to the present day.[30] In fact, the critic's analysis rejects the hypothesis of the autonomous evolution of the novel in eighteenth-century Europe and makes a strong case for kinship between all the categories of the epic, a relation that transcends time and space. Granted, we can question the appropriateness of the term "kinship," as opposed, for instance, to *creolity*, which Spivak prefers because her concept is, as she puts it, "about the delexicalization of the foreign," where "[t]o lexicalize is to separate a linguistic item from its appropriate grammatical system into the conventions of another grammar," thus "yield[ing] us a history and a world."[31] But kinship does unfold histories and worlds too. In support of this "lexical" option, we might turn to a pertinent argument developed by Paul Cornea more than three decades ago. Involving the problem of "influence" in comparative literature, Cornea's premise is the "implicit similarity" between recipients and producers of cultural discourse, a phenomenon he calls *concordance*. The latter "subsists between members of various European families—these have formed," the Romanian literary historian and theorist specifies, "through conquests, wars, migrations, reciprocal relations, in the melting pot of the same history, undergoing the same socioeconomic transformations, feeding on the same legacy of Greek and Roman Antiquity and Judeo-Christian monotheism."[32] In other words, besides language, the shared historical, political, socioeconomic, and geographical circumstances lead to the appearance of similar traits within kindred literary systems. Thus, the fact that the Balkans and Southeastern Europe more broadly were under the influence of the Ottoman Empire from the fall of Constantinople till the beginning of the twentieth century has not been without consequences in the literature and culture of those places. Exploring the principal affinities among the peoples of this part of the continent in a study whose goal is precisely the description of the main traits of Southeast European Romanticism, Cornea reminds us that

these [peoples] were all subject to Ottoman rule, which isolated them for centuries from the major movements of European civilization and delayed their economic development; they were all hindered from asserting their national identity and forced to accept as an expression vehicle, for a longer or shorter period, a superior culture's foreign language (Greek for the Bulgarians, Serbs, and Romanians, Hungarian for the Croats); at the end of the eighteenth century and the beginning of the nineteenth century, with the decline of Ottoman power and the major upheavals brought about by the French Revolution and the Napoleonic Wars, they equally found themselves faced with the same fundamental tasks: the rediscovery of a particular identity, the construction of unitary and independent nation states, and the rapid closure of the political, socioeconomic, and cultural gap that separated them from Europe's advanced nations.[33]

The disparity persisted in the countries behind the Iron Curtain for almost half a century after the Second World War, a situation at which Cornea's study, published during Communism, could only hint. Despite the aforementioned similitudes, one registers, however, neither uniformity nor identical evolutions across the region's cultures; as Cornea also points out, "the common features of the 'zone' never blur the particularities of each people."[34] Thus, what arises in Romania and elsewhere in this part of Europe, and what the critic appreciates, is a creative fusion of heterogeneous elements, and, as he stresses, it is this synthesis—if not necessarily each of its ingredients—that is original, one of a kind. To uncover this uniqueness, the critic works out, as early as 1980, an approach to Southeast European Romanticism that calls for "taking into account the works belonging to various national Romanticisms,"[35] a method that, in its applications at least, recalls Moretti's "distant reading." This sort of method has the advantage of highlighting the parallel and synchronous developments of cultural systems among which there are exchanges, interactions, and contaminations that cannot be explained away as narrowly understood influences and imitations. And even when sheer imitations are at play—whether they are good or mediocre, or whether, more generally, they do or do not "make a literature," or the object of comparative literature for that matter[36]— what counts is the novelty effect the assimilation of exterior models produces. For, as Cornea quotes Paul Valéry, "[there is] nothing more original, nothing that suits oneself more than to feed on others. The lion is made of assimilated sheep."[37] As Cornea insists, imitation and originality do go hand in hand, just as every writing act entails rewriting.

On the other hand, it becomes obvious that imitating, borrowing, rewriting, and the like work only insofar as there is *consubstantiality* between the cultural systems these operations bring into contact; conversely, the birth of specific literary forms hinges on the ways in which each culture processes external elements. Following French comparatist René Étiemble but anticipating issues on which Dimock and Moretti will touch frequently and characteristically, Cornea speaks of the "typological concordances" occurring within cultures separated by large geographical distances and between which direct commerce and interminglings are unlikely—that is, unlikely but not impossible, if we remember that people have always traveled to unfamiliar lands on other continents and brought back not only silk and spices but also information that has subsequently circulated throughout Europe. A case in point is the world history—or histories, rather—of the novel. For example, comparing Chinese novels written between the fifth and the eighteenth century AD and the eighteenth-century European novel, Étiemble points to the "scandalous" similarities between them. The "scandal" or "shock" of unexpected resemblances and "kinship" of sorts presumably has to do with the limited interface of Chinese and European literatures during this period even though, especially since the late thirteenth century, after Marco Polo had reached China (a land that fascinated him and which he describes at length in his travelogues), Chinese culture was not unknown to Europe, and so contaminations between the two cultural paradigms cannot be ruled out.

3. Intersection, Creolity, Nodality

What part have such contaminations, imports, and echoes played in the history of Romania and its literature? As twentieth-century Romanian literary historiographers and comparatists have shown extensively, the beginnings of modern national literature were marked by intense contacts with European, particularly French and Italian cultures. Until the end of the nineteenth century, most of these relationships obtained via Polish, Greek, Russian, and Ottoman intermediaries. Especially during the Middle Age, these neighbors acted, successively or all at once, as cultural "filters" between the wider world and the country and, as such, held a significant role in the configuration of the Romanian cultural system. Accordingly, besides Latin and Ancient Greek, the first Romanian writers also learned Old Slavonic (as well as Russian and Polish), Modern Greek, Turkish, and even Arabic. Grigore Ureche, Miron Costin, Dimitrie Cantemir, Nicolae Milescu Spătarul, Constantin Cantacuzino (known as the "Stolnic"), and other sixteenth- and seventeenth-century Moldavian and Wallachian historians, humanists, and literati knew foreign languages, traveled abroad frequently, and otherwise moved freely and curiously in the world, which inspired them to create works that were as original as they were adapted, thematically and otherwise, to the authors' homeland. One of Romania's first globetrotters—the "Romanian Marco Polo"—Milescu set off on his first long journey to China in 1675, returning there twice thereafter. His writings about Chinese history, geography, customs, and politics circulated widely throughout Eurasian countries from the eighteenth to the twentieth century. An English translation of his works, along with texts by other authors, was published in London in 1919 in a monumental two-volume edition compiled by John F. Baddeley under the title *Russia, Mongolia, China*. Similarly fascinated by remote places and cultural alterity and leaving behind a relevant body of work were, among others, Cantacuzino (1640?–1716), who owned an impressive library and was the first Romanian to gain in-depth knowledge of the Italian Baroque; Cantemir (1673–1723), a leading political figure of his region and Enlightenment-influenced ruler of Moldavia who was also a historian, a fiction writer of great skill, and a composer; and Dinicu Golescu (1777–1830), whose family numbered several writers and who was a journalist and an author known primarily for his 1826 *Însemnare a călătoriei mele* (My Travelogue). The collective commitment to integration into the grand concert of Europe originated with these writers, but the idea that Romanian literature was lagging behind other European literatures did not become a constant of public discourse until the nineteenth century. As is well known, also on the rise during that time across the continent was an awareness of national differences and particularities, which, in Central and Southeastern Europe, were harnessed by artists, critics, and politicians to various projects of national identity. Testimonies to the birth of modern thought, which is bound up with the desire to step outside known space and to open up to other cultural horizons, such undertakings too were indebted to foreign travel, prompted as they were by discoveries of new places and customs, by the inevitable comparisons the traveler draws between himself or herself and those he or she encounters, and by the tendency to relate to them not just as different but as a potential *cultural model* as well.

Such models were increasingly available to Romanians in the nineteenth century, when going abroad for educational purposes became the norm. Whereas in the first half of the century the main cultural centers frequented by Romanian intellectuals were in Poland, Ukraine, the Ottoman Empire, and Russia, after the 1820s it was Paris, Vienna, Rome, Padua, and Berlin that started attracting an increasing number of young Romanian students. Direct contact with Western Europe also provided exposure to non-European cultures, as it did in the case of Eminescu, who, as Andrei Terian shows in his contribution to this volume, had the revelation of Egypt and India during the 1872–1874 interval spent in Berlin. As more and more young Romanians studied in the West and traveled abroad ever more frequently, the places and traditions they came across served as filters and casts orienting and shaping Romanian identity and lending the country's "cultural pioneers" not only literary themes, forms, and techniques worthy of adoption and adaptation but also a particular vision of the European cultural system and, at the same time, of the Romanian writer's place in it and in the world at large.[38]

As we approach the twenty-first century, more and more Romanian critics come to the realization that this place is a geocultural crossroads. Practicing Orthodox Christianity, speaking a Romance language in a region dominated by Slavic nations, lodged at the intersection of Western and Eastern influences, forced to contend for centuries with the brutal expansionism of the Ottoman Empire, on one side, and of Russia, on the other side, Romanians have evolved a culture by steadily assimilating, adjusting, and combining various outside tendencies and inputs. A series of internal and external factors, both intra- and extra-literary, have worked together over the course of time to give birth to an eclectic yet original culture characteristically marked by a *créolité* of sorts, by an *amalgam* of literary styles, typologies, forms, and procedures. Numerous studies dedicated to modern-era literary schools and movements from humanism to the Enlightenment and from the Baroque to classicism, Romanticism, realism, modernism and its derivatives such as Parnassianism, symbolism, the avant-garde, expressionism, and, more recently, postmodernism dwell consistently on what appears to be a characteristic of Romanian culture: given the time gap between the moment when various literary trends arise in Europe and when they are received in Romanian culture, the latter habitually treats all these directions and their corpuses as if they were coeval, hence its tendency to absorb multiple aesthetic doctrines concurrently even when, in their birth countries, they were articulated at different historical moments and, what is more, from positions hardly compatible with one another, as in the case of classicism and Romanticism, for example. In point of fact, this is why, in Romanian literature, classicism sometimes presents features specific to Romanticism and there are no literary works that can be classified solely as products of the Enlightenment. For the same reason, the Romanian Enlightenment is difficult to distinguish from humanism and the Baroque, and so are classicism and Romanticism and Romanticism and modernism. In effect, one would be hard pressed to find any Romanian canonical writers who belong exclusively to a certain movement such as Romanticism or Symbolism. This may also explain why these authors' response to influences and internationally circulating, doctrinal, thematic, and formal repertoires has been largely interpretive and creative, frequently yielding original works. The situation differs especially where less important literary figures are concerned, who have been inclined to reproduce mechanically, closely and recognizably, ideological tenets, themes, genres, and devices emblematic to a given literary movement. This mimeticism is one of Fondane's main arguments in his assessment of Romanian culture as a "French colony."[39]

Among the first Romanian critics to take issue with Fondane, Lovinescu adduces a series of counterarguments, including a more nuanced view of the "laws" governing the interaction between distinct and synchronous cultural systems, general principles that do allow, he insists, for original processing of a "universal" material whose creation at the "center" is contemporary to its "peripheral" recreation. But if one takes into account the broader historical picture, the diachronic evolution of the relationships between the Romanian "periphery" and a French culture presumably "central" to the European and world-system, it appears that what we have here is an *exchange*, rather, even if the give-and-take looks at first blush unequal and asymmetrical, along the lines drawn by Moretti and Itamar Even-Zohar.[40] In this and other cases, what complicates the putatively one-directional flows between core and periphery in spite of the pressure applied by the former's political leverage and symbolic capital on the latter is the historical logic of *cultural debt*. That is, such a debt can be paid off in spectacular ways over the course of time, which is what happened with a Romanian writer like Fundoianu himself, who, once relocated in France, would become Fondane and publish such essays as *Rimbaud le Voyou* (1933) and *La Conscience Malheureuse* (1936). But Fundoianu/Fondane is not the only Romanian author participating in this two-way traffic of cross-systemic indebtedness. Eugène Ionesco and Cioran, who have written extensively in Romanian, also left deep and distinct marks on French and, indeed, European literature following their move to France during the Second World War. Nor can the European avant-garde be properly understood if one ignores the essential contribution of the small but exceptionally innovative group of Romanian writers and artists who arrived in Zürich in 1916, with Tzara, Victor Brauner, and Constantin Brâncuși among them.

These are "nodal" writers and artists who belong simultaneously to multiple literatures and can be found in almost every culture. As noted at the outset of my essay, theirs is not an isolated case. Many world-acclaimed modernists fit into this category: Joseph Conrad, who "transferred" from Polish to British culture; Vladimir Nabokov, who grew up in Czarist Russia, studied Slavic and Romance languages in the United Kingdom at Trinity College, Cambridge, between 1919 and 1922, lived in Berlin between 1923 and 1937, spent three years in Paris, moved to the United States and wrote in English there, and relocated in 1961 to Switzerland, where he died in 1977; or Samuel Beckett, an Irishman living in Paris and a bilingual author who expressed himself with the same ease in French as in English. The nodal type is even more popular among postmodern and contemporary writers, who routinely build their fictional worlds and not infrequently their real lives too at the intersection of at least two cultural traditions, namely, that of their countries of origin and that of the countries whose languages they have adopted and, no less, have *adapted* to their own vision, mother tongue, and culture. Milan Kundera, the Czech novelist who left for France after the Prague Spring and is claimed by both Czech and French literature, Indian–British (and, of late, American) author Salman Rushdie, who is currently residing in the New York City area, and Haruki Murakami, who writes in Japanese but contributes to the translation of his novels into English and shuttles back and forth between the United States and his native Japan, are also among the best-known examples. Pivotal to various literary histories, the nodality the lives and works of such authors embody belies arguments, still made by some, for the autonomous evolution of national literary-artistic and cultural systems or, at the other end of the old-fashioned comparative spectrum, for absolute priorities, servile imitations, and the like. No doubt, such propositions are easier to debunk in a contemporary world in which officially recognized geopolitical units and the boundaries separating them overlap less and less, even when they remain unchanged, with cultural realities, the space they cover, and their political map.

Ignoring this asymmetry risks distorting the very dynamic of cultural phenomena. The risk is probably higher when one turns to modern Romanian culture than in other situations. Nurtured by sustained international intellectual exchanges and constituted at the intersection of the Romantic doctrine with the irreverent spirit of Ion Luca Caragiale and the taste for the absurd of Urmuz, Romanian modernism represents a triumph of cosmopolitanism in Romania's *and* other countries' cultural histories. Cultural hybrids in their own right, these writers boast immigrant and multicultural backgrounds and life experiences. Caragiale (1852–1912), a Romanian writer who had Greek roots and spent his last years in Berlin, is Romania's "national" playwright, and his comedies, which are still widely performed although the writer died more than a century ago, greatly influenced Ionesco. Younger than Caragiale, Urmuz (1883–1923) was a forerunner of the Romanian and European avant-garde, with Tzara one of his followers. Gathered in 1930 in a volume titled *Pagini Bizare* (Weird Pages), his absurdist short prose and poetry also left their mark on Ionesco.[41] Both writers continue to fascinate generation after generation of Romanian writers all the way to the 1980s and into the 1990s.

True, after the Communist-era hiatus, the culture's openness to the world grows by leaps and bounds, but even during the Cold War, especially since the 1960s and in spite of political circumstances, Romanians were hungry for the ideas and books produced elsewhere. A few years of intellectual liberalization in the late 1960s and early 1970s were sufficient to allow French structuralism and Noam Chomsky's generative grammar to make their forays into universities and publishing houses to bring out, in print runs of tens of thousands of copies, translations from the latest works by the proponents of the French Nouveau Roman, substantial anthologies of modern and contemporary American poetry, and impressive collections of theoretical studies exposing Romanian readers to the latest critical theories and methods developed in the West. When this period ended, there followed, in the opposite direction, an exodus of important writers, critics, and university professors such as Matei Călinescu, Virgil Nemoianu, Mihai Spăriosu, Marcel Corniș-Pop, Thomas Pavel, Norman Manea, Andrei Codrescu, George Banu, and Dumitru Țepeneag. They all succeeded in making a name for themselves in their countries of adoption by publishing influential books and becoming part of intellectual life on both sides of the Atlantic.

While Romanian academics were rebuilding their careers on American campuses, a new series of writers—the "1980s Generation"—integrated for the first time North American literary experiments into the country's culture during the last decade of the Communist regime. Although it was not until 1985 that Moraru introduced the term "postmodernism" into the discourse of the Generation and of Romanian criticism more broadly,[42] the young writers who would come into prominence in the 1980s had been talking about major changes in the writing and understanding of literature as early as 1979, roughly at the same time and in the same postmodern spirit as their American counterparts.[43] Romanian postmodernism managed in the post–Second World War era to quash Romanian literature's "European complex" by producing highly sophisticated and innovative works whose significant political implications were also clear both to the writers themselves and to their critics. After the interbellum generation, the Generation constituted, in the country's literary history, the second moment of perfect synchronization with a dominant cultural movement in full swing abroad. Sensitive to new developments in American and other literatures, Romanian postmoderns such as Mircea Cărtărescu, Matei Vişniec, and Mariana Marin also extended local traditions of aesthetic insurgence such as the avant-garde. This stylistic and chronological alignment with world developments was, on this account, hardly an "imitative" operation, stemming instead from a lengthy process of recovering and reclaiming lesser known or underappreciated authors of Romanian tradition (such as Ilarie Voronca), whom the young Romanian postmoderns reread through the post-1960s French, English, and American theory while they were also discovering the Beat Generation, J. D. Salinger, Sylvia Plath, Ken Kesey, Truman Capote, John Updike, Thomas Pynchon, John Barth, Philip Roth, Kurt Vonnegut, Frank O'Hara, Diane Wakowski, and other contemporary American writers, whether in the original or in the translations already in circulation since the 1970s. Highly bookish, the poetics of this group entailed writing protocols in turn dependent on extensive and cross-pollinating readings from a range of twentieth-century literary school and intellectual traditions: Continental and American critical theory from Mikhail M. Bakhtin and Herbert Read to T. S. Eliot, William Empson, and *Rezeptionsästhetik*, United States poetry and prose, European literature and philosophy (mainly phenomenology but also Ludwig Wittgenstein), and structural and generative linguistics. They all shaped post-1980s Romanian literature both as an institution and as a writing practice as the latter brought them all into the same postmodern present of textual and intertextual processing. As Ernst Robert Curtius wrote in *European Literature and the Latin Middle Ages*, "[f]or literature, all the past is present, or can become so."[44] This transformative fusion of past and present and familiar and remote voices, this creative "presentification" of the material regardless of its origin in time and space, is not only postmodern Romanian writers' revisionary approach to literary history but, as we are noticing more and more these days, also a defining modus operandi of major contemporary cultural projects, be they national, planetary, or anything in between.

Notes

1   Gayatri Chakravorty Spivak, *Death of a Discipline* (New York: Columbia University Press, 2003), 73.

2   E. Lovinescu, *Istoria literaturii române contemporane*, vol. 2 (Bucharest: Editura Minerva, 1973), 362.

3   William Hazzlit, *The Spirit of the Age: Or, Contemporary Portraits*, in *The Complete Works of William Hazzlit*, vol. 12, Centenary ed., ed. P. P. Howe (London: Dent, 1931), 128–129.

4   Drawing from Goethe, Tudor Vianu was the first Romanian theoretician to define "world literature." Vianu foregrounded what he viewed as the specific traits of Romanian literature in his 1959 essay "Asupra caracterelor specifice ale literaturii române" (On the Specific Traits of Romanian Literature), in *Studii de literatură română* (Bucharest: Editura Didactică și Pedagogică, 1965), 545–559.

5   Vianu, *Studii de literatură română*, 550.

6   Vianu, *Studii de literatură română*, 557.

7   Lovinescu, *Istoria literaturii române contemporane*, vol. 1, 128.

8   Lovinescu, *Istoria literaturii române contemporane*, vol. 1, 122.

9   Lovinescu, *Istoria literaturii române contemporane*, vol. 1, 154.

10 Lovinescu, *Istoria literaturii române contemporane*, vol. 1, 150.

11 Lovinescu, *Istoria literaturii române contemporane*, vol. 1, 133.

12 Lovinescu, *Istoria literaturii române contemporane*, vol. 1, 135.

13 Amy J. Elias and Christian Moraru, "Introduction: The Planetary Condition," in *The Planetary Turn: Relationality and Geoaesthetics in the Twenty-First Century*, ed. Amy J. Elias and Christian Moraru (Evanston, IL: Northwestern University Press, 2015), xxiv.

14 Vianu, *Studii de literatură română*, 545–559.

15 One of Romania's ideological-artistic movements at the beginning of the twentieth century, *sămănătorism* posits the superiority of rural over urban life. *Sămănătorism* takes its name from a cultural magazine, *Sămănătorul* (The Sower), a conservative-agrarian publication that offered up peasant culture and cognate archaic traditions as a "developmental" model for Romanian society.

16 Spivak, *Death of a Discipline*, 96.

17 See Zygmunt Bauman, *Culture in a Liquid Modern World*, trans. Lydia Bauman (Cambridge: Polity Press, 2011). In Bauman's liquid world, "none of the consecutive forms of social life is able to maintain its shape for long" (11), and incessant migration produces "a neighbourhood of meandering, spongy and porous boundaries, in which it is difficult to ascertain who legally belongs and who is a stranger, who is at home, and who is an intruder" (36). In this globalized world, the ties between identity and nationality are put to the test, and "no culture can demand or be entitled to subservience, humility or submission on the part of any other simply on account of its own assumed superiority or 'progressiveness'" (37).

18 Bauman, *Culture in a Liquid Modern World*, 38.

19 Franco Moretti, "Conjectures on World Literature," *New Left Review* 1 (January–February 2000), 56. As Moretti implies, there is "*one* literature (*Weltliteratur*, singular, as in Goethe and Marx), or perhaps, better, one world literary system (of interrelated literatures); but a system which is different from what Goethe and Marx had hoped for, because it's profoundly unequal" (55). See also the essays in Elias and Moraru's collection *The Planetary Turn*.

20 Moretti, "Conjectures on World Literature," 58.
21 Titu Maiorescu's 1868 essay "În contra direcției de astăzi în cultura română" (Against Romanian Culture's Current Direction) sparked a long-lasting debate around the "import" of cultural "forms" and institutions into a culture presumably lacking the substance they require. In Maiorescu's view, the content comes first and calls for specific forms. It cannot be the other way around. At the beginning of the twentieth century, Lovinescu rejected Maiorescu's position. Bringing in outside forms and institutions, Lovinescu maintained, is a necessary step for Romania on its way to modernization.
22 Lovinescu, *Istoria literaturii române contemporane*, vol. 1, 149.
23 Lovinescu, *Istoria literaturii române contemporane*, vol. 1, 128.
24 Moretti, "Conjectures on World Literature," 60.
25 Moretti, "Conjectures on World Literature," 61.
26 Moretti, "Conjectures on World Literature," 64.
27 Spivak, *Death of a Discipline*, 13. Following Melanie Klein, Spivak underscores the major role comparative literature plays in coming to terms with alterity and difference. Spivak points out the necessity of translating "not from language to language, but from body to ethical semiosis, that incessant shuttle that is a 'life'" (13). "The incessant shuttle" metaphor also captures the mechanics of cultural exchanges.
28 This essay is included in Călinescu's book *Principii de estetică* (Bucharest: Editura Fundației pentru Literatură și Artă, 1939), 101–125.
29 See Wai Chee Dimock's essay, "Genre as World System: Epic and Novel on Four Continents," *Narrative* 14, no. 1 (January 2006), 85–101. Mandelbrot's theory appeals to Dimock mostly because it highlights "a tangle of relations, one that counts as a 'system' precisely because its aberrations are systemwide, because pits and bumps come with many loops and layers of filiation. Even literary forms that look quite different at first sight turn out to have these quirks in common" (89).
30 Dimock, "Genre as World System," 91.
31 Gayatri Chakravorty Spivak, "World Systems and the Creole," *Narrative* 14, no. 1 (January 2006), 106.
32 Paul Cornea, "Conceptul de 'influență' și paradigmele sale" (The Concept of "Influence" and Its Paradigms), in *Regula jocului. Versantul colectiv al literaturii: concepte, convenții, modele* (Bucharest: Editura Eminescu, 1980), 106.
33 Paul Cornea, "Romantismul sud-est european: Schiță de caracterizare zonală" (Southeast European Romanticism: Sketch for a Regional Description), in *Regula jocului*, 201–202.
34 Cornea, "Romantismul sud-est european," 203.
35 Cornea, "Romantismul sud-est European," 205.
36 Mihail Kogălniceanu (1817–1891), politician, historian, and writer, was a prime minister of Romania (1863), minister of Home Affairs (1868–1870), as well as of Foreign Affairs (1876–1878). His introduction to the first issue of the magazine *Dacia literară*, published in January, 1840, is the manifesto of Romanian Romanticism. He famously insisted that translations, among which he included imitations and adaptations of works from other cultures, "do not make a literature." A typical Romanticist, he encouraged his country's writers to turn to folklore and national history as their sources.
37 Paul Valéry quoted in Cornea, "Conceptul de 'influență' și paradigmele sale," 109.

38 See Paul Cornea's 1974 book *Oamenii începutului de drum* (Bucharest: Editura Cartea Românească, 1974).

39 Born Benjamin Wexler into a Jewish family of intellectuals in Bukovina in 1898, Benjamin Fondane lived in France after 1923 and died in the Auschwitz-Birkenau Nazi camp in 1944. Fondane or Fundoianu, as he was known in Romania, was a Romanian and French writer, poet, critic, and existentialist philosopher. In 1922, he published *Imagini și cărți din Franța* (Landscapes and Books from France) (Bucharest: Socec Publishing House), in whose introduction he called Romanian culture a "French colony." Lovinescu was among the first to reject Fundoianu's harsh pronouncement.

40 Moretti, "Conjectures on World Literature," 65. The critic builds on Itamar Even-Zohar's concept of "interference" to describe the "difficult" relationship between source and target literatures. Moretti quotes Even-Zohar, who asserts in a 1990 article that "There is no symmetry in literary interference. A target literature is, more often than not, interfered with by a source literature which completely ignores it" ("Conjectures on World Literature," 56).

41 Urmuz's writings were gathered in a book posthumously, in 1930. After that, they have been reissued in various editions. A few of his works had appeared in literary magazines shortly before the author's death, while others were published in Romanian periodicals after his tragic suicide.

42 Christian Moraru's essay, "Către o nouă poetică" (Toward a New Poetics) appeared in *Ateneu*, 9, September 1985 and was republished in Gheorghe Crăciun's anthology, *Competiția continuă. Generația 80 în texte teoretice* (Pitești: Paralela 45 Publishing House, 1999), 25–29.

43 For an overview of the Romanian debate on postmodernism and the latter's connections to modernism, see my book, *Strategiile subversiunii. Descriere și narațiune în proza postmodernistă românească* (Bucharest: Editura Cartea Românească, 2008), 81–99, and my essay "Is There a Romanian Postmodernism?" *Euresis. Cahiers Roumains d'Études Littéraires et Culturelles* 1–4 (2009): 305–320. In his article on postmodernism and postmodernity published in the same *Euresis* issue, "D'un postmodernisme sans rivages et d'un postmodernisme sans postmodernité" (11–22), Mircea Martin argues for a postmodern literature that came about in Romania in the obvious absence of the economic and political context of American postmodernism.

44 Ernst Robert Curtius, *European Literature and the Latin Middle Ages*, trans. Willard R. Trask, with a new introduction by Colin Burrow (Princeton, NJ: Princeton University Press, 1983), 14.

Part II

Literature in the Plural

I think the very concept of *heritage* needs to be redefined because the notion does not designate only what comes down to us from our own ancestors or what we inherit from them as their *heirs*. The concept also refers to what makes its way to us from others' forebears. It is up to each of us how much of this "external" inheritance we are willing to accept and integrate into who we are.

—Mircea Martin, "Cosmopolitism: scurt istoric şi implicaţii actuale"
(Cosmopolitanism: Brief History and Contemporary Implications)

6

Reading Microliterature:
Language, Ethnicity, Polyterritoriality

Mircea A. Diaconu

Since nation-states and areas inhabited by distinct ethnolinguistic groups seldom overlap fully, literatures in different languages have developed side by side within and astride national borders. Defying the latter, the boundaries of such idioms and literary cultures are even more disputed than political frontiers. Applicable to most regions of the world, these basic observations hold true particularly of Eastern Europe. And yet, driven by an autarchic territorialism that flew in the face of official "internationalism," Communist-era scholarship largely assumed that the Hungarian- or German-language writers from Romania, as well as their Romanian-language counterparts from Serbia belonged to a literary system that ended at the borders of these authors' countries. Nor did this nationalist–sovereignist model of national literature differ from what was epistemologically and institutionally *de rigueur* in the former Soviet Union itself, as the impetus behind "USSR literature," which also comprised the Romanian writers from today's Republic of Moldova and Ukraine, was an ideologically colonizing, politically hegemonic, and artificially unifying Russian hub that sponsored a literature multiply subordinated to it while the writers themselves were longing either for autonomy from the Kremlin or for joining "greater" Romanian literature.

In the post–Cold War era, however, such presumptions and the whole national literature paradigm encouraging them start taking a back seat to uncertainties and even questions, some of which bear reiterating here. For example, do Romanian authors writing in Romanian and living outside Romania belong to Romanian literature? The problem is compounded by the difficulties Romanian-language writers from the Republic of Moldova, Bukovina, or the Serbian sector of the Banat region have faced historically in their struggle to integrate into Romanian literature. Conversely, one might ask if Romania's Hungarian- and German-language poets or novelists could be included in the Romanian literary system, or if Romanian writers from Serbia's Timoc Valley are part of Serbian literature. Moreover, once we begin to wonder along these lines, the inherited definitions of this European area's national literatures and national literary histories no longer seem dependable either, and so we are compelled to further ask: How helpful are such notions and representations in the twenty-first century? Can we keep leaning on them today without factoring in the literatures of the ethnic populations whose homelands straddle the political borders between East

European states? And, if we at long last agree that we cannot, then how can we do justice to these literary cultures given that they are stuck in an affiliational double bind that reinforces their subaltern or peripheral condition in relation to *both* their country of residence's administrative center—by which they are rarely appreciated, and with which they are reluctant to be associated—and to their own, ethno-political and literary-canonical center, which lies in the country where they are the majority, a real as well as symbolic cultural kernel that they are drawn to and idealize and whose recognition they seek?

These last questions in particular are pivotal to this essay, which dwells on a set of representative authors to revisit the status of East European national and ethnic literatures, especially of those flourishing in and around the Romanian geoliterary zone in the contemporary era. Prompted by transnational world developments such as the upswing in multicultural and globalization phenomena, my intervention remains mindful that the "national" itself as well as the literature practiced or conceptualized around it project "force fields" of sorts, domains constantly changing shape and *moving* under the impact of various tensions, influences, and geopolitical vectors. These show, in spite of recent nationalist and anti-immigration flare-ups, how fragile, deceptively stable, and conventional borders can be, how "soft"—shifty, ever contested, historically fluid, and ultimately "open"—the geographical body of the nation-state has been and is likely to stay. Nonetheless, most critics are still following in the long line of thought that has presumed to be dealing with self-enclosed national literary spaces and, by the same token, with "hard" identitarian territories, that is, with ethno-political units considered well contoured and "naturally" structured around a single center of authority. I would call, for lack of a better word, the understanding of literature and literary tradition beholden to this "centralism" *statal*. I would also argue that, insofar as it refers, simply speaking, literature generally and, particularly, minority literature back to a unique geo-jurisdictional core, the statal approach's shortcomings have become conspicuous.

In response to this methodological crisis, I propose a reading algorithm featuring a more flexible dynamic of discourse and territoriality. This interpretive model, I submit, would actually allow for a discussion of literature in terms *closer to the "reality in territory"*—or, better yet, to literature's "real" territoriality—by taking into account the concrete parameters of literary practices' geohistorical formation and expression, processes that involve specific textual and contextual elements as well as ties and negotiations with *multiple* centers. In this sense, literature becomes—better still, it has always been—concurrently *extra-* and *intraterritorial*, arising as it does in relation to both its ethnic "capital," which is situated elsewhere, in another, usually adjacent country, and to the majority group with which the minority producing this literature coexists. In other words, a Serbian-language writer from Romania is "extraterritorial" when read alongside Serbian-language authors from Serbia or former Yugoslavia, and he or she is "intraterritorial" when looked at against the backdrop of Romanian literature from Romania. Yet again, the playwright or novelist in question is usually both at the same time—and, as we shall see, possibly more.

Extraterritorialism, intraterritorialism, and frequently also bi- if not plurilingualism: these are the three main attributes simultaneously characteristic of every modern-era East European ethnic or minority literature. Their consistent copresence renders this literature what I would determine as a *microliterature*, to wit, a literary culture that builds up its identity cross-statally and in conjunction with another or several other literatures within and without the host country. Obtaining at the intersection of other, oftentimes better consolidated, national or "macro" kind of literatures, microliterature aches, on one side, for *territorialization* or extraterritorial incorporation into the system of its macro- or "parent" literature, fantasizing—in the Romanian case—about a "greater" or "global Romanian literature," as if the temporarily disjointed fragments of the Osirian body of national letters could once again acquire, as Gilles Deleuze and Félix Guattari theorize, a "totalizing" logic allowing the scattered parts to gel into the majestic whole;[1] on the other side, microliterature struggles to safeguard its individuality with respect to *all* literary traditions around it. Thus, it is conceivable that the Republic of Moldova's Romanian literature might join the larger Romanian literature system one day, but for the extraterritorial Romanian literatures of Serbia and Bukovina, not to mention the Aromanian (Macedo-Romanian) microliteratures of the Balkans, this is unlikely, and the same goes for Hungarian and German literatures from Romania, which also dream the impossible dream of rejoining a long-lost cultural totality. But, again, history has also shown that microliteratures are keen on what sets them apart, no matter what the element of contrast may be.

In my view, these aspirational or effective multidirectional and asymmetric engagements with their surroundings define not only the high-stakes identity project of microliteratures but also their links with the various hubs of power, culture, and prestige of the East European regional system. For here, I would also stress, microliterary subsystems arise by way of successive and vastly intricate de- and reterritorializations that, especially in our global age, challenge the dependent and marginal status traditional literary history has mechanically assigned ethnic minority authors writing in their mother tongues.[2] In effect, their actual position is seldom merely secondary or peripheral—they do manage to encroach on "hard" cultural spaces and their "macro" patrimonies, and they do leave their marks on them although they rarely receive full appreciation, but they cannot isolate themselves completely either, in hopes that they might preserve their ethnic identity. In their turn, "national" literatures have repeatedly failed to adequately co-opt extraterritorial writers into their historical narratives. This failure or, in some case, sheer disinterest, has added more than moral insult to critical injury as "micro" poets and playwrights have felt rejected by national or "macro" literatures and so have frequently distanced themselves from them. Symptomatic of microliterature, the aesthetic of affect engendered by the expression of this feeling of being nowhere at home, of being displaced and disregarded or underappreciated runs the gamut from endemic dependency, provinciality, and periphery "complexes" to assimilation anxieties, nostalgias for extraterritorial ethno-cultural origins and kinship, and, in some extreme situations, to opposite, anti-nostalgic if not utterly anti-ethnicist and overall anti-microcultural apprehensions.

1. Politics, Ethnicity, Mother Tongue: The Moving Parts of the Literary System

"In spite of the rather aspirational view of 'Bessarabian' [Moldovan] literature as part of Romanian literature," posits Andrei Terian in the "Romanian Literary History in the Era of Globalization" chapter of his 2013 book *Critica de export*, "it is highly possible for the literary relationships between Romania and [the Republic of] Moldova to become, in the not-too-distant future, similar to those between Germany and Austria, two countries that share the language but constitute different literary systems." "Conversely," the critic goes on, "we are facing the same ethnogeographical problem" if we examine the situation internally, from within the Romanian literary system, and so we should also ask ourselves "if there is any reason to include in Romanian literary history the literatures written in the languages of Romania's ethnic minorities."[3] But, Terian also wonders, "can we really understand Romanian literature from Transylvania if we fail to take into account its interactions and rivalry with the Hungarian and German literatures in the area?"[4] The last interrogation is as radical as it is rhetorical. But if the answer is indeed negative, then, I would suggest, the microliterature concept helps framing it so as to bring into sharp relief most salient, geocultural and theoretical ramifications. For it is time to own up to the historical picture limned by the influences, contacts, exchanges, and transfers among literatures and among idioms in this European neighborhood, an image that is markedly different from how national literatures have been seen traditionally. It is well known, for example, that Romania's Hungarian-language theaters are much more integrated into Romanian entertainment culture than they are into Hungarian theatrical life. For classification and analysis purposes, what still takes precedence, however, as if by intellectual inertia, is ethnic identification or, if you will, an *a priori* ethnicist activism of sorts according to which literature and cultural performance broadly are expected to index and even assist in the recovery and propping up of collective ethnic identity. Therefore, when they decide to break free from such expectations and write "for the bigger world," extraterritorial writers risk being left out of local, largely ethnicity-oriented microliterary canons, which is what has happened to authors such as Herta Müller (1953–), Ioan Miloş (1930–2015), and Ion Druţă (1928–), as we shall see later on. When microliteratures themselves attempt this kind of emancipation—that is, from parent literatures and implicitly from the countries where extraterritorial writers would be the ethnic majority—they should have first reached a certain maturity, which does not necessarily mean a long history behind them but the capacity to make a well-thought-out break that would bode well for their future rather than sound their death knell. Paradoxically enough, it is when microliteratures maintain their ethnicity focus that their authors can attempt more successfully to forsake the limitations and redundancies of the ethnic agenda, and individual departures from such group platforms become both possible and a sign of value.

A basic equation of interdependency is, in fact, in play here: the "micro" writer feeds on the national and the ethnic just as the ethnic and the national are legitimized and boosted by literature, with the exceptions bearing out the rule. In practice, though, the literary-historical account of the mechanics of this reciprocity has been lopsided. More to the point, gaining access to the regular, homologating circuit—publication, dissemination, interpretation, canonicity—of national literature has been difficult and sometimes even traumatic for extraterritorial literary production. In this vein, illustrative is how Romanian critic G. Călinescu (1899–1965) tackles this thorny issue in his 1941 *Istoria literaturii române de la origini până în present* (History of Romanian Literature from Its Origins to the Present). As a "national manifesto" advocating explicitly and implicitly, as method and vision, a self-sufficient and "organically" integrated identity of Romanian literature, the *History* should have covered the body of work originated across the territory of 1918 Romania. But, despite its nationalist program, Călinescu's *magnum opus* fails to paint the image of a "one and only, and indivisible" literature, for not only does he foreground geographically differentiating features in writers from Moldavia, Wallachia, and Transylvania, Romania's three major historical provinces, but his modus operandi also proves inconsistent throughout.[5] Thus, we are told, well-seasoned Transylvanian writers such as Lucian Blaga and Liviu Rebreanu, "founders" of modern poetry and prose, respectively, in Romanian literature, make for an integral part of Romanian literature, indeed, even encapsulate and secure its "national essence," although Rebreanu, just like his forerunner, Ioan Slavici, a Romanian classic, was raised as a good citizen of the Austro-Hungarian Empire, and his first works to come out were in Hungarian. On the other hand, Călinescu does not attend to Bessarabian authors at all, except for the few names mentioned only in his book's bibliography, while the Romanian writers from Bukovina, on whom he had not written prior to the *History*, are all lumped together in an overview. In this as in most other cases, then, extraterritorial Romanian writers' endeavors to be acknowledged by and reclaim their "natural" place in "greater" Romanian literature—"integration by assimilation"—have not worked out, largely on allegedly "aesthetic" grounds. Notably, such assimilating efforts have been frustrated in literary history—and *by* histories of literature such as Călinescu's—as they have been in literary life. Instructive are, on this score, the comments Nicolae Costenco made on the tensions between the Romanian-language authors from Bessarabia and from the rest of Romania (Old Kingdom) in a 1934 programmatic article published in the traditionalist cultural magazine *Viața Basarabiei*. "Those who know Russian," maintains Costenco,

> are overwhelmingly superior, in their dignified, cultured composure, to the their big-mouthed and cheeky brethren from the Old Kingdom …. We, as Bessarabians, are happy that the Bessarabian people are not falling for the poisonous warmth of today's Romanian culture. We are nourishing the hope, at least, that those attuned to our ideals will come along in the near future.[6]

When they did come along, those in agreement with Costenco—the Soviets, that is—would promptly dispatch him to Siberia, from where he was not to return for over a decade. Could, then, his have been the reaction of someone dedicated to an anti-ethnic position? Not at all. More likely, Costenco overreacted to the cold-shoulder treatment his peers got after 1918 from Bucharest and its modernizing experimentalism, which Greater Romania's new, ethnically oriented, "provincial," and neglected periphery did not quite go for. It bears therefore asking: to which literary system do the Romanian-language writers of Bessarabia—and later, the Republic of Moldova—belong? To Romanian literature, which, granted, has rediscovered them after 1990? To the literature of the Soviet Union before that? Or do they form, perhaps, their own, separate literary world?

One faces similar dilemmas regarding the Hungarian writers from Romania, who identify themselves in relation to two different literary systems at once, Romanian and Hungarian. A survey conducted by the Transylvanian cultural magazine *Vatra* and posing the question "What does it mean to be a Hungarian writer in Romania these days?" has made it clear that the very identity of the polled authors is at risk. "What kind of writers are we, Hungarian writers from Romania," asks Péter Demény (1972–).[7] This is *the* question of the extraterritorial writer, an interrogation largely behind the inherently national problematic of any microliterature. And the other question resoundingly implicit in it—"Where do we belong?"—is indeed indicative of a need to belong, to be part of a community. Cut off politically and otherwise from its "macro-" or "mother"-literature while routinely avoiding extensive contacts with surrounding "majority" literature, microliterature is forced into self-subsistence, and yet it yearns nostalgically for its native place. It is definitely no happenstance that extraterritorial writers often use the world "exile," for they do feel, in their own country of birth— provided they have not been deported or forced out—as if they were living in exile. Even when it is actively pursued, whatever recognition they might receive alongside and from the majority culture in the country of residence does not always satisfy since the only accomplishment seems to be "macroliterary"—an acknowledgment by parent literature that equals a symbolic return to origins, to the ancestral homeland. "The Hungarian magazines from Romania," observes Péter, "are more than eager to publish us, but those from Budapest not so much." And he adds: "There are times when I contemplate moving to Hungary."[8] Relocating to the center—back home, that is—has been also the dream of Romanian writers from Bessarabia and, after the Second World War, the Republic of Moldova, as well as from Serbia and Bukovina, who were all hungry for integration into, and attention from, the literary macrosystem. This remains the measure of success although, at least in places such as Bessarabia, the literature was, and is, at home in the very territory where it manifests itself, where its authors reside in their homeland, come from the ethnic majority, and express themselves in their mother tongue. But even so, or perhaps all the more so, the wretchedness of their estrangement from the country's spatio-cultural heart—Bucharest—is more than they can bear. What they gain by writing in the national idiom is lost geographically and politically, for they are lodged at Romania's unsettled periphery, on an orbit whose distance and connection with the system's center remain unnerving and historically uncertain. Hence the twofold, frustration-cum-alienation trauma unfolding on the stage of Bessarabian/Moldovan microliterature: on the one hand, the actors on this stage seek shelter in their own yet denied home and comfort in a being-at-home feeling in which they are not allowed to bask; on the other hand, they cannot but assume and live out their "minor," "peripheral," and "anonymous" condition, with all its implications. For the extraterritorial writer can be and frequently is an unknown entity not only to his or her country of residence's majority literature but also to the "greater" or "macro" literature in whose concert, alas, his or her voice remains unheard.

2. Writing in No Man's Land?

This situation has barely changed after 1989. Although they circulate more freely and are no longer censored, Eastern Europe's extraterritorial writers continue to feel alienated and exiled. They still do not "belong" either. Or, if they do, this belonging of sorts only corroborates their suspicions about their quintessential solitude. As Demény admits, authors like him may "[belong] to themselves," after all, but, he offers, this is hardly enough.[9] For at stake here is not so much the individual novelist or poet but a broader and dramatic reality, in which his or her ethnic community *and* reception are intimately intertwined. "The writer's dilemma," Demény reveals,

> is that he is writing for a few people living in no man's land. If you are a Hungarian writer in contemporary Romania, you have to ask yourself over and over again: for whom do I write actually? ... For a bunch of people in the boonies who are constantly fretting over trifles and cannot see that life goes by and we do not get to leave anything behind?[10]

The corollary to the question, "For whom does the extraterritorial author write?" is more painful interrogations such as "Do others share my experiences so that they could understand me?" and "Can others benefit from what I have been through, or will my testimony fall on deaf ears?"

Those others—others *like* him or her, from within his or her ethno-cultural group—do matter a great deal. Danilo Kiš's exhortation "Don't write for a minority!" which Slavco Almăjan (1940–), a Romanian writer from Serbia, took to heart, has been heeded by few for the simple reason that the "experiences" conveyed by the extraterritorial writer are bound to pertain to his or her multiply peripheral and minority condition. Historically speaking, only a handful of microliterary figures have overcome this status, whether we are talking about Romania's Hungarian authors, who find themselves in a marginal position with respect to both the Hungarian literature from Hungary and the Romanian literature from Romania, about Serbia's Romanian poets, who live in a double, at once internal and external exile from Romanian and Serbian literatures, respectively, about the Republic of Moldova's Romanian novelists, who see themselves in the context of the Romanian literary system, or about Romanian-language authors living in Ukraine's Northern Bukovina, who define themselves in relation to their Bucharest and Chişinău peers.[11] Budapest, Bucharest, Belgrade, and Chişinău, all these cultural capitals, are places where the extraterritorials would readily go, or "go back to," rather, so as to recover their "true" homes. Their exilic condition, however, cuts their homecoming short, and so they remain stuck, as German–Romanian (and, since 1969, Romanian–German) writer Dieter Schlesak has put it, "between our native country [Romania] and our mother tongue [German]."[12] Nostalgia for the fiction of a primeval totality does not subside, though, and so, time and time again, microliterature dramatizes reterritorializations whose goal invariably consists in symbolic returns "home," recoveries of publics and prestige, and other forms of "true" acknowledgment. Thwarting these repositioning maneuvers and complicating the predicament described by Schlesak is another, also twofold and also contradiction-ridden offshoot of the extraterritoriality scrutinized here: where microliteratures aim at joining macroliteratures while pushing ethno-regional specificity, central, politically "territorialized" (or "majority") literatures may encourage the pursuit of such objectives but lack the tools required by them.

Bessarabian literature is a case in point and a rather disheartening one to boot. Although he argues for a specifically Bessarabian literary identity, critic Mihai Cimpoi, author of a history of Bessarabia's literature, also contends that "The Bessarabian [literary] phenomenon awaits its natural integration into the global Romanian context,"[13] its "homecoming."[14] Roughly the same statement is made by a younger critic, Mircea V. Ciobanu, who asserts that "the pan-national histories of Romanian literature are yet to make room for us[, Bessarabians]."[15] No doubt, here Ciobanu puts his finger on a perennial shortcoming of national literary historiography. Pointing to the failure of Călinescu's history to attend to Bessarabia's literature alongside the rest of Romania's, Grigore Chiper, a writer from the Republic of Moldova, bitterly notes in 2004 that "the perception in Romania's Old Kingdom regarding Bessarabia's literature as something separate, regional, and backward reflected at that time [when Călinescu's history came out] an objective situation, for this literature was only arising after a century of alienation [from the main body of national letters], of a quasi-total lack of Romanian culture in Bessarabia."[16] "Decimated after World War II, cut off from its Romanian matrix, and forced into a survival mode comparable to the Stalinist Gulag, this fragile literature," Chiper goes on,

> had no choice but to follow its own path, which, like it or not, was not the widest. The best the Bessarabian writers could do under the circumstances … was to draw on pan-Romanian literary models found one step behind the times, and so they failed, to a significant degree, to connect with the [Romanian] developments of the day.[17]

At the other end of this connective dynamic, though, Romanian literature and criticism themselves proved, during the Communist years, incapable of reaching out to, and assimilating, the body of work from across the Prut river. This was due not only to said Gulag conditions and to the isolation of various part of the Soviet Empire from one another but also to Bucharest's dismissive attitude toward Bessarabian writers' "outmoded" ways, to Romanian intellectuals' ever-troubling obsession with "cultural tardiness" or "belatedness." Obfuscating any historical and stylistic alignments and overall narrative of "pan-Romanian" catch-up are the asymmetric plays of the national and the aesthetic. That is, in Communist-era Romania, the former seemed to have been monopolized by official ideology and, in literature, by Socialist Realism, while the "aesthetic" option consisted, in its extreme expression, in their rejection and has remained so; in post-USSR Bessarabia, however, breaking free from the Soviet political and cultural straitjacket and upholding the national ideals have taken on the meaning of an *aesthetic* gesture, indeed, of a counterintuitive "recovery" of the aesthetic.

The linguistic particularities of extraterritorial writing are also something to keep in mind when considering such disjunctions and discrepancies, as well as any "macro" apprehensions riding on them. In Bessarabia, the influence of Russian, coupled with the region's forcible removal from the broader, enlivening circuit and evolution of Romanian, has had consequences whose seriousness have not escaped commentators. Almăjan, for instance, quotes Silviu Berejan, a linguist from the Republic of Moldova, who has worried that the languages of minorities such as those represented by Almăjan have become "unusable at a superior level of culture."[18] Almăjan himself admits, in fact, that "the idiom we speak is a dialect, slightly archaic, sometimes neurotic, and even 'mixed.' Romanians from Vojvodina combine Romanian and Serbian words, expressions, and phrases …."[19] Moss-grown, rural, and overall "flawed," their language is seen—from the outside, at least—as old-fangled and "belated," and so is the "topical" ("ethnicist") literature written in it. Therefore, no matter how innovative poets and playwrights may be in their extraterritorial, Bessarabian or Serbian contexts, they are viewed by most of their Romanian counterparts and critics as meekly following the lead of Romanian macroliterature, echoing its latest trends while always trailing a step behind.[20] What Almăjan fears, actually, is not that the gap will never be closed, but that soon there will be nobody left to close it. "I must confess," he says, "that [we,] Romanians from Vojvodina[,] are nowadays obsessing over our looming disappearance, just as the Native Americans were not long ago,"[21] and similar statements could be made by the extraterritorial German or Hungarian writers from Romania, whom their intended audiences and forums of cultural authority and aesthetic canonization from outside their birth country ignore, treat with superiority, and otherwise patronize. Peter Motzan, a German critic born and raised in Romania and who emigrated to Germany in 1990, touches on this sore subject when he talks about the regional variety of German spoken by Transylvanian Saxons and Swabians. This dialect, it is widely assumed, could only sustain a culturally conservative and ethnicity-centered literature of limited macrosystemic appeal. But even when Romania's Germans stopped continuing down the path of their precursors' ideals, ethnicity-informed literature, and dialect, they remained little known. Likewise, residing across the border from their Hungarian brethren, extraterritorial Hungarian writers from Transylvania are only apparently better positioned. They may "belon[g] to Hungarian culture because [they] write in [Hungarian] and preserve [Hungarian] traditions," and yet "[their] presence is resented," says Jánosházy György, "here [in Transylvania], at home, but also in their Hungarian fatherland, where they are considered mere tourists [and where,] in the eyes of local writers, critics, and readers, they rank—provided they are noticed at all—a priorily below their Hungarian peers."[22] Misunderstandings crop up in the other direction too, as Bölöni Domokos allows. "'Over there,' in the 'fatherland,'" he remarks, "battles are fought for purposes too deep for a [Hungarian] 'yokel' from [Transylvania's] Mureș [backwater]."[23]

These are typical and sobering comments. For extraterritorial writers, lost home is a desert mirage, and the aesthetic quest for it is usually appreciated neither "over there" nor "over here." All the same, they keep going, whether they do so as fiction authors or critics, laboring to reshape the literary present into a place more hospitable to extraterritorial writing or reworking the past into histories that would retroactively—if questionably—reterritorialize microliterature into a cultural system compatible and coeval with macroliterature. So does a critic like Cimpoi, for instance, when he ties Bessarabia's literary "Generation of the 1970s," whose national militantism presumably "rediscovered" the aesthetic, to Romania's "1960s Generation," which did make a similar move but by connecting with domestic and Western modernist tradition. Oddly enough, Cimpoi also thinks that the Bessarabian 1980s Generation descends from Nichita Stănescu, a major Romanian poet of the 1960s Generation, and displays "a propensity for symbols and parables," whereas, quite to the contrary, the poets of the parent literature of the 1980s—the "macro" Generation of the 1980s, to which Cimpoi's description of the writers of the Bessarabian 1980s obviously alludes—characteristically struggle to cast aside symbolic and allegorical language.[24]

As one can notice, microliterary history is here a narrative of cultural mimesis chronicling the formation of individual and collective literary identity as adjustment to "macro" trends and schools. Microliterature writers go so far as to publish in or even relocate to Romania, where they take part in macroliterary life, while the close attention microliterature critics pay to their Romanian colleagues shows through in book titles and whole works. Thus, Ciobanu writes *Deziluziile necesare* (Necessary Disillusions), which points to the "demythologizing" project of Romanian critic Eugen Negrici, *Iluziile literaturii române* (The Illusions of Romanian Literature); a collection of essays, *O istorie critică a literaturii române din Basarabia* (A Critical History of Romanian Literature from Bessarabia), echoes Nicolae Manolescu's *Istoria critică a literaturii române* (Critical History of Romanian Literature); and a 1995 anthology of 1990s Bessarabian young poets, *Portret de grup* (Group Portrait), replies to the 1990 *Antologia poeziei generației 80* (Anthology of Poetry by the 1980s Generation) put together by Alexandru Mușina in Romania. The list of such examples could go on, bringing into view a phenomenon one might term Bessarabian microliterature's aesthetic and critical-epistemological "self-colonization." The questions are if this extraterritorial gambit could lead to macroliterary "integration" and, more importantly still, what this integration might mean. The answers are not encouraging: whether it is rescinded mimetically, in imitative aesthetic and critical practice, or cancelled out literally, as the German writers from Banat have left for Germany and almost all those from Bukovina have moved to the Republic of Moldova and Romania, extraterritoriality seems to be on the wane. And with it, so is microliterature itself, which is treated—and all too often presents itself also—as a fringe, second-order phenomenon whose *raison d'être* lies outside itself and is a function of the umbilical cord tying it to a space and cultural paradigm in which kinship and tutelage are two sides of the same coin.

3. Microliterature and Intraterritoriality

Caught between a rock and a hard place, microliterary cultures fare no better inside the borders where they have been forced to evolve in an uneasy if not utterly adversarial relationship with the literature of the ethnic majority or, as was the case of Romanian-language letters in USSR-ruled Bessarabia, with officially endorsed Romanian ("Moldovan") and Russian literature. For, intraterritorially, a microliterature's authors get a similarly chilly reception in principle apprehensive of writers coming out of poor, rural, isolated, and minority communities and whose ethnic focus is deemed as "excessive" as "lacking" and "unpolished" is their literary idiom thought to be. Therefore, on this front too, "integration" proves a tough proposition, when the intraterritorials want it at all. In Communist Romania, the regime did push for it, and the reasons were no different from those behind the "united" nation-state propaganda apparatus, hence the early setting up of ethnic minority artists' unions, magazines, scholarly journals, and publishing houses. All of these were geared toward providing a smattering of multiethnic yet "common" literary life "transcending" nationalism and offering a glimpse into the happily internationalist future whose blueprint was being drawn in the USSR. The officially sanctioned "integration" rhetoric yielded, in Bessarabia, the "Soviet-Moldovan literature" notion and, in Romania, the idea that Hungarian writers from Romania were "Romanian authors writing in Hungarian," as well as the ideological concoction that went by the name of *rumäniendeutsche Literatur,* "Romanian–German literature," which lumped together the Transylvanian Saxons and Swabians. But rhetorical fiction was no substitute for reality, and it is noteworthy that the somber reality further deteriorates after 1989, when, although postcommunist regimes stop enforcing aggressive policies of cultural assimilation, microliteratures' marginalization within national or "majority" literary systems worsens.

So do, as a result, the intraterritorials' "complexes," which turn out to be as resilient as the insecurities beleaguering them, as we saw earlier, in extraterritorial ambiances. Unequivocal in this respect, Almăjan rehearses the belatedness fixation. "Arriving late on the cultural scene," he predicts, "minority writers will remain unappreciated for a long time, marginalized in advance."[25] But then the "marginalized" respond with a superiority complex that turns geocultural excentricity on its head, proudly recycling remoteness and, implicitly, backwardness with respect to the nation-state's center into access to multiple, broader, and non-parochial cultural centers and horizons. "Romanian literature from Vojvodina," Almăjan specifies, "has developed in a country where bilingualism and [even] plurilingualism had been common. This literature has not arisen in [the Romanian] diaspora, nor are its authors people who have disowned their own community. One should add right away that [these authors'] language is Romanian, but their life-giving space is Vojvodina. One should then conclude that this literature comes into being under the aegis of two cultures and two temperamental categories, one of which is Balkan, the other European."[26] Yet, Almăjan also observes, a 1982 world literature history published in Zagreb barely sets aside "room for the Romanian literature of Yugoslavia." As for the rest of the region, "we will be hard pressed to find many places where the existence of this literature is acknowledged in the context of national literatures."[27] Prevailing in these and other situations is a derogatory "majority" view—Serbian in this case—according to which Vojvodina's Romanians are a backwoods bunch living "on the outskirts of culture" and out of their depth "in the circles of intellectual elites,"[28] for their cultural comportment is as provincial and uncouth as it is childish—they are said to walk around the world of culture wearing kids' clothes.[29] Similarly unflattering opinions have ventured cultural apparatchiks of the former USSR and members of the Russian intelligentsia of the Republic of Moldova.

By comparison, at least, the German and Hungarian literatures of Romania have enjoyed a modicum of "intraterritorial" appreciation. There have been several extensive studies on Romania's Hungarian writers by Romanian critics and historians fluent in Hungarian, from Ion Chinezu's 1930 *Aspecte din literatura maghiară ardeleană* (Aspects of Transylvanian Hungarian Literature) to Nicolae Balotă's 1981 *Scriitori maghiari din România* (Hungarian Writers from Romania) and Mircea Popa's 1998 *Apropieri literare și culturale româno-maghiare* (Romanian-Hungarian Literary and Cultural Exchanges). Also, Cluj-Napoca's Dacia press brought out, in Romanian, the 1979 anthology *Tineri poeți maghiari din România (Generația Förras)* (Young Hungarian Poets from Romania: The Förras Generation), and two years later Albatros publishing house, from Bucharest, put out another anthology of this kind, *Dincolo de formă. Pagini de poezie și proză maghiară din România* (Beyond Form: A Sheaf of Hungarian Poetry and Prose from Romania). It is surprising, though, that Kantor Lajos's milestone *Literatura maghiară din România: 1944–1970* (The Hungarian Literature from Romania: 1944–1970), published in Hungarian by Bucharest's Kriterion press and awarded an important prize by the Romanian Academy in 1975, has not been translated into Romanian yet. Again, after 1989, one wonders what the reasons might be.

Some have suspected lack of interest on both sides. What is beyond doubt, though, is that, overall, Romanian critics and audiences are vastly unfamiliar with the country's Hungarian literature. In "Fața românească. Cultura ignoranței" (On the Romanian Side: The Culture of Ignorance), an article accompanying a 1999 survey conducted by the Târgu-Mureș *Vatra* magazine, critic Al. Cistelecan bluntly concludes that "For Romanian writers *as* readers, the Hungarian literature from Romania is something that just does not exist at all."[30] Also quite telling is what polled contemporary Romanian writers themselves have to say. "Romanians," argues critic Ioan Buduca, "know just as little about the Hungarian literature from Romania as they do about the Turkish literature from Turkey."[31] In the same vein, noted novelist Petru Cimpoeșu lets us know that this literature feels like a "foreign literature" to him and that, if he were a Hungarian writer who lived in Romania, he would rather be published in Hungary.[32] Likewise, Mircea Cărtărescu, perhaps the most renowned Romanian writer of our time, declares curtly: "I know nothing about the Hungarian literature from Romania."[33] In turn, Liviu Ioan Stoiciu, a poet from Cărtărescu's generation, wonders for whom Romania's Hungarian-language authors write, given that they are ignored by "today's Hungarian critics" as well as by "Hungary's literary history." Do these writers, Stoiciu asks, not have a country already? And if they do, and if this country is Romania, then, he continues—in a direction opposite to Cimpoeșu's comments—"I find it impossible to understand why they would not publish in Romanian and tap into the [market provided by the] Romanian majority ..." Stoiciu seems convinced that such writers, unlike poets and novelists of "Jewish, German, Armenian, Macedonian, Gypsy [Roma], Turkish, Serbian, or Ukrainian ethnic background from Romania, who write and publish in Romanian as well," have repeatedly turned down the overtures made by Romanian writers, who "have learned their lesson" and have stopped taking notice of the accomplishments of Hungarian microliterature. He recognizes, however, that this aesthetic production testifies to a specific "inner content," to an "affective profile" different both "from that of the Romanian writer who writes and lives in Romania and from that of the Hungarian writer from Hungary," and suggests that the literary expression of this particular sensitivity should be acknowledged and revalued by the history of the literature written in Romania.[34] Unfortunately, this revaluation is an uphill battle due to the very setup of public education, curricula, and the like. Adrian Suciu, a young poet who graduated from a Transylvanian university proud of its "multicultural" mission, thinks that

> we, Romanians, have been actually taught to ignore the Hungarian literature from Transylvania. In five years of college in the Faculty of Letters of Babeş-Bolyai University in Cluj-Napoca, we did not spend a single class session on Hungarian literature [from Romania] ... in their lectures, our professors did not cover—even just for the sake of appearances—any Transylvanian authors belonging to the Hungarian minority.

Opening up in school, the "gulf separating us," says Suciu, widens later on as "we do not cross paths in the same publications, do not follow the same models, do not communicate, [and] no one cares to try and bring us closer together."[35] There is both cynicism and realism in such comments. Where Serbia's Romanian writers own up to their exile, the rift in the Romanian literary system along ethnic lines seems to be a given on all sides. Historically, participation in this system has not been a top priority for the Hungarian intraterritorials. There have been, however, some important exceptions such as poet Sziklágyi Domokos, whose work thrives on contacts with Romanian literature and culture, and critic Ştefan Borbely, who is bilingual, writes exclusively in Romanian, often on Romanian topics, and arguably belongs to Romanian literature. In the postcommunist years, the number of such exceptions has increased, more and more Hungarian writers envisaging an "internal" emigration of sorts, viz., an affiliation with Romania's linguistic, literary, and cultural macrosystem.

4. The Many Faces of Exile: The Predicament of the Extraterritorial Writer

Since, on the one hand, extraterritorial writers feel nowhere at home, and, on the other hand, home and public are, to them, one and the same, their biggest worry has been that they will end up writing for nobody. On this account, "system switching" has had an understandable appeal, driving them to consider shaking off their minority writer status and modus operandi. What would be, they have thus asked themselves, the way out of their traditional quandary? Should they leave behind their mother tongue and ethnic platform and enlist in the exclusive—putatively ethnicity-"blind"—service of Literature? Might, then, they ever be able to proclaim wholeheartedly, with Danilo Kiš, that "everything is literature and nothing else"?[36] Kiš, the reader will remember, issued this provocative statement in Paris, away from his compatriots and certainly not—or not solely—on their behalf. Nor was the Jewish-Hungarian-Serbian writer's brazen self-deterritorialization the only remedy available to extraterritorial writers. As we have seen, they have tried out both "external" emigration—physical relocation— to parent literature and "internal" or intraterritorial repositioning through a range of acculturating protocols including bilingualism, the switch to a literature in a language different from the mother tongue, and critical self-distancing from ethnicity, its tradition, and strictures.

The former, internal "solution" has been the most dramatic if not tragic, for it has led to the virtual disappearance of the microliterary cultures of Transylvanian Saxons and Swabians, most of whom had left before 1989 for their "mother-tongue country," Germany, although, as they would quickly discover, they were quasi unknown in their linguistic *Vaterland*. In this light, the title of a debate hosted by a 1989 Marburg literary forum, "Obituary for the German Literature from Romania," says it all.[37] On this occasion, the discussions homed in mainly on the split between *rumäniendeutsche Literatur*, a notion many German-language writers from Romania had bought into, and the literature promoted by the 1972–1975 movement *Aktionsgruppe Banat*. Where the highly artificial construct dubbed *rumäniendeutsche Literatur* had been designed to cover aesthetically, contain politically, and otherwise play up Romania's German literature as a whole, which the Communist-era German-language textbooks had already been billing triumphantly as "the fifth German literature" besides those of the Federal Republic of Germany (FRG), the Democratic Republic of Germany (DRG), Austria, and Switzerland, the *Aktionsruppe Banat* young poets did not only discard their ancestors' rural dialect, ethno-political objectives, and literary tradition, but they also "repatriated" themselves to "macro" (German) literature when they did not give up writing altogether. This may explain why this microliterature has been categorized, apropos of 2009 Romanian Banat-born Nobel Prize winner Herta Müller, as *Anti-Heimatliteratur*. But taking this label, as some have, to denote a simply "antipatriotic" or anti-communitarian literary orientation directed against these writers' "homeland" misses *Aktionsgruppe Banat*'s polemically complex message of resistance and protest. This is precisely what Richard Wagner, a group member, Müller's ex-husband, and currently Berlin resident, accentuates in his characterization of *Aktionsgruppe*. "Our dissent," he reveals,

> played out within the minority to which we belonged. We were not, as intellectuals, representative of the German minority from Romania. To the contrary, we worked, thought, and wrote against this minority.... We were a minority within the minority, for we stood against its self-sufficient, provincial consciousness,

conservative to the point of being reactionary, which had developed, throughout history, a particularly ethnocentric, colonizing attitude toward other peoples and had presented itself as a "civilizing" force in Southeastern Europe …. As far as the German literature from Romania is concerned, we, as an "action group," started writing against this literature. We did not think of ourselves as part of the German literature from Romania, but as a kind of anti-German literature from Romania.[38]

It is therefore no accident that Müller's 1982 debut book, *Niederungen* (Nadirs), rubbed people the wrong way, wherever her "people" and their "home" were at the time—whether in Romania, where Banat's Swabian readers felt slandered, or in Germany, where the Swabian–Romanian community mounted a whole campaign against the novelist, considering her a collaborator of the Romanian equivalent to Stasi, the no less infamous Securitate. Even a literary historian such as Horst Fassel, who was born in Timişoara, not far from Müller's birthplace, thinks that her early work kowtowed to the regime's ideology. However, "Swabian Bath," a short story from the same book, "demolishes and destroys 'Germanness' from the inside." This is, according to Wagner, precisely what the community's survival required, for Romania's Germans were in dire need of unsparing self-scrutiny and, overall, of a language different from the one they got used to as a community.[39]

Critical of its ethnicity, Wagner's "minority within the minority" produced, then, a microliterature that, in an important sense, was also a *minor literature* à la Deleuze and Guattari. As the French philosophers famously posited, "minor literature" is not what an author might write in a "minor language" but the kind of literature a "minority" manages to compose in a "major language."[40] Since Romania's "major language" is Romanian, the *Aktionsgruppe*'s linguistic medium was not "major" either. Nor did they take up the minority vernacular as such. They expressed themselves in their mother tongue, namely, in German, but they plied the Banat Swabians' dialect—an idiom burdened by complicity with the country's authoritarian politics and dogmatic aesthetics—in ways that had deeply deterritorializing effects for "tradition," "home," "ethnic group," and the like. In Müller, who wrote and writes neither for the Swabian nor for the Romanian communities but largely "against" them, such deterritorializations have given rise to symbolic—that is, Deleuze and Guattari would also specify, eminently political—distancing whether from the image of the father, former Nazi or Nazi sympathizer, like other members of Banat's Swabian community during the Second World War, or from the Romanian regime. And so, while many of Romania's German-language writers were, like Almăjan, "minority" authors, the *Aktionsgruppe Banat* poets were not. Or they were perhaps *more* than that, a "hyperminority" consciously twice self-marginalized with respect both to the country and their ethnicity. But, as Wagner disclosed in a piece included in the *Aktionsgruppe*'s 1982 landmark poetry anthology *Vînt potrivit până la tare. Tineri poeţi germani din România* (Moderate to Strong Wind: Young German Poets from Romania), this linguistic and cultural detachment was a form of ontological "engagement," a tactical, "anthropological" disconnection designed, with an apparent paradox, to reconnect him and his friends with "reality." For, as he insisted, "We must think through the best ways of latching onto surrounding reality. The specificity of minority life comes second. The preoccupation for reality should be our main concern."[41]

This "realism," which had a huge influence on 1980s Romanian literature, involved another departure, namely, one from literary tradition, especially modernist, whether German or Romanian, insofar as this tradition had basically conflated poetry and metaphorical lyricism. Thus, the *Aktionsgruppe* program made provisions for "a fight against poetization."[42] As critic Dan Petrescu has commented on *Vînt potrivit până la tare*, this battle entailed an "indifference to talent," that is, a rejection not only of a certain aesthetic talent notion but also of a whole poetics resting on this concept during Communism. "Thus modified, transformed, that is, into the very arena in which the expression of revolt occurs," observes Petrescu,

> poetry is indifferent to talent. I am not implying that the young poets, German or Romanian, have no talent, but that "talent" does not amount to much given what freedom of expression means these days. "Talented" poets who versify adequately only go through well-rehearsed motions, merely taming the rebel specter of language and by the same token doing the bidding of dictatorial discourse. Consequently, such poets find themselves on the other side of the barricade ...[43]

This side of the barricade, the German writers of 1970s–1980s Banat went instead for an aesthetic practice in which stylistic, intentional "self-marginalization," rejecting as it did the mimetic and ultimately self-colonizing position some Romanian-language authors from the Republic of Moldova eagerly accepted, attested to "an acute political consciousness and a firm ideological option" that wound up radicalizing their work.[44] This radicalization is the kind of politicization of the linguistic and of the aesthetic that gives birth to minor literature and by the same, critical and formally innovative movement—rather than thematically—opens up room for collective survival. Müller, for example, does not seem especially invested in "preserving" her communal identity. She has not assumed the typically *Aktionsgruppe* excentricity only to fall back on ethnocentrism, and this may well be the secret of her triumph on the world stage. Kiš too took this route with his *Anatomy Lesson*, which was published in Belgrade in 1978 and performed, as Pascale Casanova argues, a veritable in vivo dissection of the Yugoslavian literary body. Refusing to rehash in his book the assortment of anachronisms and nationalisms that were de rigueur in the Josip Broz Tito era, the author was forced into exile, much like Müller.

Where the exile leaves one national literary system for another, ordinarily external to it politically or administratively, but keeps his or her language of expression, as Müller and Kiš did, the extraterritorial writer may choose to deterritorialize himself or herself linguistically without doing so territorially—or without deterritorializing himself or herself literally, by moving to another country. In this case, the author composes, and oftentimes also publishes, in a language other than his or her native tongue, which language is usually the idiom of the ethnic majority. But, as the career of Romanian–Serbian writer Vasko (Vasile) Popa shows, the shift can be more than linguistic. Born in Serbian Banat in 1922, Popa spearheaded the Romanian literary revival of post–Second World War Vojvodina as a first editor-in-chief of the Romanian-language magazine *Lumina*, which initially promoted an ideologically engaged literature, and as a poet writing in Romanian and Serbian. If his manifesto "The Journey of Our Becoming" advocated the necessity to follow in the footsteps of Romanian literary classics and traditionalism overall with an eye to passing them off as Socialist Realism's forerunners, in 1948 he left the magazine and quit writing in Romanian. The change from Romanian to Serbian also paralleled a sharp turn in his trajectory as an artist, with the modernist Vasko leaving behind Vasile's dogmatic and regionalist clichés. After all, he had started out as a writer in Romania during his years as a medical student in Bucharest, where he had come into contact with the Romanian avant-garde, the Surrealists, poet Gellu Naum, and other major figures of Romanian modernism such as Tudor Arghezi and Ion Barbu. Itself highly inventive in ways reminiscent of Romanian modernists, his 1953 debut volume, *Kora*, marked a true revolution in Yugoslavian poetry, and the question is whether the quantum leap from an unsophisticatedly politicized treatment of ethical and ethnic issues to aesthetic-driven poetic expression was, and perhaps generally is, predicated on another, linguistic shift away from the mother tongue—viewed, in this case, as a culturally "aging," artistically "rusty," possibly "defective" medium—to the more "advanced" language of the ethnic majority. It appears, in any event, that he had tried his hand at poetry in Romanian in the late 1940s, but the only formula he could have taken up as a Romanian author affiliated either with Romania's official, macroliterary system or with his own microliterature would have been quasi folkloric or agitproplike. Almăjan, who has published both in Romanian and Serbian and has wrestled with the same ethnic, linguistic, and political conundrums, is probably right to suggest that

we would not want to guess what would have happened to Vasko had he stayed at *Lumina* and kept on writing in Romanian; we can only imagine the kind of different adventures this poetic talent would have embarked on and whether or not his name would have participated in the questioning and diversification of literary modernity in this part of the world.[45]

What matters is that Popa did switch to Serbian, and once he did it, his move allowed him to take advantage of Tito's falling-out with Stalin and to return to literature—to a literature of a certain kind, which folded one national literary system within another. For, although he wrote in Serbian, his poetic models were Romanian and subsequently French, which, in hindsight, renders his "insurgence" a bridge across space, time, and cultures, an element of continuity with respect to the history of modernist poetry in Romania and elsewhere. A Janus-like figure fording the divisions between tradition and innovation, micro- and macroliterature, and Serbian and Romanian languages and literary systems, Popa became a Serbian writer whose contacts with Romanian culture were not negligible. In 1956, with Romania at the height of ideological dogmatism, he was a member of Yugoslavia's official delegation to the first Convention of Writers of the Popular Republic of Romania, where he gave a nonconformist speech that, under the guise of Socialist Realist rhetoric, argued for a morally uncompromising, truthful literature. Then, in 1966, he met Nichita Stănescu, who would translate his work into Romanian and do the preface to one of his volumes, which, given Stănescu's quasi-mythic aura, was the ultimate endorsement a writer could get in the country. All the same, he did not write literature in Romanian, nor did he live on the presumed territory of "national literature," and this "hard" territorialism excludes him from all histories of Romanian literature.

Popa is featured, however, in the *Dicționarul general al literaturii române* (General Dictionary of Romanian Literature) edited by the Romanian Academy, and so is Ion Druță. Born in 1928 in Bessarabia, Druță too jettisoned the Socialist Realism clichés after Stalin's death and has composed most of his works in Russian, especially after 1969, when he moved to Moscow. Much of his oeuvre has been translated into the languages of the former Soviet republics, where he met with notable success, whereas in the Republic of Moldova his writings were blacklisted after his self-exile to Moscow. Back home, we are told, he had "defied" the "official" feedback received from the self-appointed standard-bearers of an ethnic ideal that was rapidly taking center stage. Initially, the criticism was coming from those Bessarabian writers who, as mentioned earlier, had rediscovered the aesthetic in and *as* ethno-national thematics and were militating for a recovery, through literature, of Romanian identity. Later on, Druță's own equivocal stance on such hot-button issues, compounded by the absence of well-defined and consistently applied principles of microliterary evaluation and classification, would further muddle the writer's position and significance. Thus, some commentators feel that he has introduced "into the Soviet literary space a distinct universe, to wit, the Romanian ethos."[46] Others, like Cimpoi, have opined that "since 1994, the writer has paradoxically given in to his earlier critics and started manifesting conservative tendencies of cultivating [in his work] the 'seeds of Socialism' alongside Moldovenism and Russian-inspired Christianity," which "tendencies" would only corroborate Druță's earlier "literary regionalism-cum-anti-Romanian aesthetic" argument.[47] No less damaging is the charge that, during Bessarabia's Romanian awakening, Druță chose to champion a noncommittal "writing profession" rather than deliver speeches on behalf of the national cause. "Our profession, dear friends," he is reported to have said, "comes from the verb 'to write,' not from the verb 'to speak,'" but many believe that his plea for a literature whose job is to throw aside the constraints of ethnicity was a diversion covering up his belief in a Moldovan literature affiliated to the Russian macrosystem.[48] In Cimpoi's words, "Ion Druță is a bilingual author who stands out, however, by virtue of the lasting aspects of his work as a *Romanian* writer despite the Russian cultural environment he embraces and the programmatic endorsement of 'Moldovenism' ... [H]e has," adds Cimpoi, "a very good command" of Russian, whereas his Romanian is "poor," requiring massive editing before publication.[49] The question that bears raising, then, is how could one reconcile such verdict or, for that matter, Druță's own view of himself as a writer belonging to a Moldovan literature that, to his mind, is different from Romanian literature, with the claim that his works, "having sustained the [Bessarabian] continuity of Romanian literature,"[50] are "a monument of Romanian literature from Bessarabia."[51] Such contentions were admittedly borne out by his recognition by the Romanian Academy, whose member he became in 1990. At the same time, though, back home, in the Republic of Moldova, he was being attacked by those who in the 1970s had been pushing the nationalist aesthetic and who were the same who were also rejecting the new poetry and pioneering Bessarabian writers such as Emilian Galaicu-Păun, who set no store by Moldovan cultural myths, pseudo-patriotic parochialism, and localist aesthetics, turning instead to bookish allusiveness, literary artifice, and intertextuality. In the process of acquitting themselves of their traditional task, ethnicity's self-styled guardians once more moved to cast out and exclude.

Two other writers of former Yugoslavia, Ioan Miloș and Adam Puslojić (1943–), have received similar treatments. In 1957–1958, Miloș published in *Lumina* a two-part article titled, with a Leninist allusion, "Ce-i de făcut?" (What Is to Be Done?). The text was read as "a break with the traditionalist line of the magazine" and as "a settling of accounts with Banat's literary situation" and with the dogmatic conformism plaguing it. Bold and forward-looking, the piece disparaged the "political meeting-type" of "declarative poetry" and the "literature of compilation, of data-gathering, and speeches" Popa had freed himself from. As critic Catinca Agache observes,

> The pushback [against Miloș] from Proletkult and traditionalist authors was so strong that it nipped in the bud the rise of what could have been the 1960s generation [of Romanian-language writers from Serbia], who were thus forced to flee to Serbian language zone, go into exile [outside Yugoslavia], or seek a kind of "inner" exile[, without leaving the country].[52]

Accused of being a "dangerous avant-gardist" by fellow Serbian-born Romanian literati at a time of mounting tensions between Romania and Yugoslavia and quickly become a pariah inside his microliterary milieu, Miloș chose exile, and, as a result, his work was banned in Serbia for more than two decades.[53] He had gone to school there, graduating from University of Belgrade's Faculty of Philosophy with a thesis on Surrealism, and he also made his debut as a poet in Serbia, in 1953. But his second volume of poetry would be published only in 1977, in Bucharest, with the third, in Swedish, coming out in 1978, in Sweden, where he had settled in 1959, after a year spent in Paris on a research grant, during which time he met legendary figures of post–Second World War Romanian exile such as E. M. Cioran, Eugène Ionesco, Mircea Eliade, and Constantin Brancusi. Before 1989, he would visit Romania only in 1968, at the International Congress of Romanian Studies, which prompted members of the Paris Romanian diaspora to pillory him for allegedly taking Nicolae Ceaușescu's side and for being a "spy." In Vojvodina, he would give an interview as late as in 1989. Meanwhile, he had stopped writing in Romanian for a while but had instead taken up writing in Swedish and translating Romanian or Serbian literary works into Swedish or Swedish authors into Romanian. However, in Romania, where some of his books would come out in the 1980s, he is still less known than in Sweden—if better known than in Serbia—and so one wonders if his literary citizenship "declaration" from his poem "În trei limbi" (In Three Languages) has fallen on deaf ears: "My country/Is the language in which I was born/Romanian. /I will never leave it."[54]

Also born in Romanian, in the Timoc Valley, to a Romanian mother and a Serbian father, Adam Puslojić has followed a different trajectory. Based in Belgrade since 1962, he served as Secretary of Writers' Union of Serbia, wrote exclusively in Serbian for decades, and, also because the Timoc Romanians were considered "Wallachians" and their language was not recognized officially, started using Romanian for literary purposes only after 1995. Under these circumstances, assigning him a reasonably well-defined identity profile—or just one, or one at a time—is a fairly daunting task, for it cannot be easily determined if indeed his Serbian-language work conveys a Romanian "affect structure" and therefore makes him a Romanian poet of Serbian expression, or if he is a Serbian poet who happens to have an important work in Romanian also. He does describe himself as a Serbian author of Wallachian origin and passionate about Romanian poets Mihai Eminescu and Stănescu. But such allegiance statements are primarily cultural or, more precisely, cross-cultural, while the moves they often presuppose inside or outside national territories and their respective microliteratures and national literatures may not matter as much. Another Romanian writer from Serbia, Ioan Flora, for example, migrated in the 1970s to Romania and became, most likely by virtue of his familiarity with Serbian literature, one of the most important contemporary Romanian poets, whereas Petru Cârdu, who shares Flora's background, did not change his Vojvodina residence and edited a large number of books by poets of a plethora of ethnicities and languages. "In [such] books," he said, "a Serbian and a Croatian may live together even in time of war."[55] His agenda was neither ethnic-separatist nor nationalist but a poetic solidarity derived from cosmopolitan commitment to literature. As he also confessed, "I was not born as a Romanian, but as an individual who must leave behind a message to mankind."[56] This message may well be microliterature's quintessential albeit less obvious brief. Devoted as they seem principally to their various ethnic-identitarian projects and national "republics of letters," microliteratures also thrive in a transnational age that facilitate their postethnic, multiply de- and reterritorializing literary-cultural protocols.

Notes

1   Gilles Deleuze and Félix Guattari, *Mii de platouri*, trans. from the French by Bogdan Ghiu (Bucharest: Editura Art, 2013), 296.

2   In his 1999 book *Globalization and Culture*, John Tomlinson dedicates a whole chapter to deterritorialization, which he defines as "the cultural condition of globalization." See the Romanian translation of his book, *Globalizare și cultură* (Timișoara: Amarcord, 2002), 152.

3   Andrei Terian, *Critica de export. Teorii, contexte, ideologii* (Bucharest: Editura Muzeul Literaturii Române, 2013), 297.

4   Terian, *Critica de export*, 298.

5   G. Călinescu, *Istoria literaturii de la origini pînă în prezent*, 2nd revised ed., preface and edited by Alexandru Piru (Bucharest: Editura Minerva, 1982), 976.

6   Nicolai Costenco, in Eugen Lungu, "Spații și oglinzi," in *O istorie critică a literaturii din Basarabia* (Chișinău: Științа—Arc, 2014), 134–35.

7 Péter Demény, "Înseamnă a te teme," *Vatra* 8 (1999): 4.

8 Demény, "Înseamnă a te teme," 4.

9 Demény, "Înseamnă a te teme," 4.

10 Demény, "Înseamnă a te teme," 4.

11 See Slavco Almăjan, *Rigoarea și fascinația extremelor* (Panciova: Editura Libertatea, 2007), 68.

12 Dieter Schlesak, in Réka Santá-Jakabházi, "Cenzura literară și consecințele ei pentru lirica lui Franz Hodjak," *Vatra* 1 (2012): 21.

13 Mihai Cimpoi, *O istorie deschisă a literaturii române din Basarabia*, 3rd revised and augmented ed. (Bucharest: Editura Fundației Culturale Române, 2002), 21.

14 Cimpoi, *O istorie deschisă a literaturii române din Basarabia*, 155.

15 Mircea V. Ciobanu, *Deziluziile necesare* (Chișinău: Editura Arc, 2014), 45.

16 Grigore Chiper, *Proza scurtă între diletantism și profesionalism*, in *O istorie critică a literaturii din Basarabia*, 78.

17 Chiper, *Proza scurtă între diletantism și profesionalism*, 78.

18 Almăjan, *Rigoarea și fascinația extremelor*, 37.

19 Almăjan, *Rigoarea și fascinația extremelor*, 36.

20 Almăjan, *Rigoarea și fascinația extremelor*, 39.

21 Almăjan, *Rigoarea și fascinația extremelor*, 67.

22 György Jánosházy, "Dezavantajele de a fi scriitor și de a fi maghiar," *Vatra* 8 (1999): 10.

23 Domokos Bölöni, "Fără prispă," *Vatra* 8 (1999): 8.

24 Cimpoi, *O istorie deschisă a literaturii române din Basarabia*, 228.

25 Almăjan, *Rigoarea și fascinația extremelor*, 73.

26 Almăjan, *Rigoarea și fascinația extremelor*, 63.

27 Almăjan, *Rigoarea și fascinația extremelor*, 31.

28 Almăjan, *Rigoarea și fascinația extremelor*, 44.

29 Almăjan, *Rigoarea și fascinația extremelor*, 23.

30 Al. Cistelecan, "O anchetă cu două fețe (despre literatura maghiară din România)," *Vatra* 8 (1999): 3.

31 Ioan Buduca, "Putem fi naționaliști și prin ceea ce *nu* facem," *Vatra* 8 (1999): 53.

32 Petru Cimpoeșu, "Dacă aș fi scriitor maghiar din România ...," *Vatra* 8 (1999): 55–56.

33 Mircea Cărtărescu, "Situația mi se pare anormală," *Vatra* 8 (1999): 58.

34 Liviu Ioan Stoiciu, "Există un ferment al autodistrugerii la scriitorii maghiari din România," *Vatra* 8 (1999): 59–60.

35 Adrian Suciu, "Prăpastia care ne desparte," *Vatra* 8 (1999): 66.

36 Quoted in Pascale Casanova, *Republica Mondială a Literelor*, trans. from the French by Cristina Bîzu (Bucharest: Editura Curtea Veche, 2007), 210.

37 Cf. Bianca Bican, "O controversă nu doar literară. Ce este 'rumäniendeutsche Literatur,'" *Vatra* 1 (2012): 25–26.

38 Richard Wagner, quoted in Mihaela Bereschi, "Sub ochiul 'broaștei germane' prin *Niederungen* ale Hertei Müller," *Vatra* 1 (2012): 41.

39 H. Schneider, quoted in Bereschi, "Sub ochiul 'broaștei germane' prin *Niederungen* ale Hertei Müller," 41.

40 Gilles Deleuze and Félix Guattari, *Kafka. Pentru o literatură minoră*, trans. from the French and afterword by Bogdan Ghiu (Bucharest: Editura Art, 2007), 43.

41 Richard Wagner, "Texte programatice," in *Vânt potrivit pînă la tare. Tineri poeți germani din România*, anthology by Peter Motzan, 2nd ed., and preface by Ion Bogdan Lefter (Bucharest: Editura Tracus Arte, 2012), 219.

42   Peter Motzan, *Cuvânt înainte la ediția I*, in *Vânt potrivit până la tare*, 174.

43   Dan Petrescu, "Poezia mizeriei—mizeria poeziei?" in *Vînt potrivit pînă la tare*, anthology by Peter Motzan, 254.

44   Ion Bogdan Lefter, "Prefață. Vîntul potrivit bate tot mai tare ... Despre "poezia germană din România,"" in *Vânt potrivit până la tare*, anthology by Peter Motzan, 7.

45   Almăjan, *Rigoarea și fascinația extremelor*, 135.

46   Catinca Agache, *Literatura română în țările vecine* (Iași: Princeps Edit, 2005), 85.

47   Cimpoi, *O istorie deschisă a literaturii române din Basarabia*, 174.

48   Ion Druță, quoted in Gheorghe Erizanu, "Incomodul Druță," http://erizanu.cartier .md/incomodul-druta-6402.html http://erizanu.cartier.md/incomodul-druta-6402 .html (accessed December 15, 2016).

49   Cimpoi, *O istorie deschisă a literaturii române din Basarabia*, 264.

50   Agache, *Literatura română în țările vecine*, 80.

51   Agache, *Literatura română în țările vecine*, 81.

52   Agache, *Literatura română în țările vecine*, 105.

53   Quoted in Agache, *Literatura română în țările vecine*, 166.

54   Quoted in Agache, *Literatura română în țările vecine*, 208.

55   Petru Cârdu, "Fac ce vreau în cultura sârbă," *Secolul 21*, 7–12 (2013): 83.

56   Petru Cârdu, "Despre literatură, poezie și condiția poetului," *Secolul 21*, 7–12 (2013): 90.

7

Trees, Waves, Whirlpools: Nation, Region, and the Reterritorialization of Romania's Hungarian Literature

Imre József Balázs

In the context of the last decades' geopolitical shifts and especially in relation to the expansion and transformation of the EU and to the new tides of immigrants sweeping across Europe, Arjun Appadurai's earlier comments on the nation-state remain particularly relevant. In his widely read 1999 book, the critic perceptively points out that "nation-states, for all their important differences (and only a fool would conflate Sri Lanka with Great Britain) make sense only as parts of a system."[1] The recent nationalist and anti-globalist backlash notwithstanding, the critic's observation captures a reality defining not only our century but also "modernity at large." Taking my cue, on the one hand, from Appadurai's definition of the national as a component of greater aggregates and, on the other, from the *histoire croisée*'s revisiting of traditionally one-dimensional, homogenizingly nation-centered comparative studies, I seek to revisit, in what follows, our understanding of Romania's Hungarian literature.[2] This operation hinges in turn, as we shall notice, on a new, "intersectional" way of looking at this body of work, an interpretation model sensitive to the literature's own, self-defining, thematic and formal, symbolic and overt efforts to articulate its inscriptions into and associations with spaces and traditions bigger or simply different than those of the nation-state, its territory, and surroundings.

Does this mean that the nation—Romanian or Hungarian—the region as a culturally and historically distinct zone inside a national territory, and other such sub- or peri-statal categories and scales of analysis no longer matter? Hardly. They do to Appadurai and his fellow explorers of cultural globalscapes as they do me. It is just that, in a fashion analogous to the way the Indian critic and his followers map out the world in their fields, I read Hungarian literature produced in Romania as an evolving, geoculturally roving, multiply affiliated discourse system that reworks such classifications and foci so as to open up and position itself in and astride domains, conversations, and meanings neither "methodological nationalism"—a legitimate target throughout this volume—nor "methodological regionalism" has been capable to get a handle on. Thus, with a nod at Franco Moretti, I propose a critical dive into this literature's "whirlpool" to uncover the inner workings of literary mechanisms writers activate to take apart and complicate selfhood, belonging, community, territory, and other similar notions. As we will learn from our encounters with several contemporary

Transylvanian-born Hungarian authors, these elements and the practices articulating them are paramount and hint that individuals, groups, locations, idioms, and polities are no longer as settled, well marked, and rationalized as they were or seemed to be. "De-essentialized" and disseminated, identity sprouts ramifications and is otherwise reterritorialized in these writers across wider, fluid, and unorthodoxly canvased, "rhizomatic" geographies that come to define the personal and the collective, the fictional and the historical—what happens in this literature, as well as where this literature is, how it sees itself, and how it relates to sites and systems of culture such as nation-state, region, world diaspora, planet, and so forth. The first two segments of my intervention perform a critical–theoretical house cleaning of sorts by shedding light on the limited ability of older, nationally and regionally minded analyses to do justice to "minority" literature, in particular to the trans-territorial and cross-cultural aspect of its identitarian spectacle. The last section examines how this intersectionality plays out in Ádám Bodor's 1992 *Sinistra körzet* (The Sinistra Zone), Zsolt Láng's 1997–2012 trilogy *Bestiárium Transylvaniae* (Transylvanian Bestiary), and István Szilágyi's 2001 *Hollóidő* (Time of Ravens), specifically in these works' strategic handling of narrative voice.

1. Regionality, Historicity, Reading

In his 1930 monograph on Transylvanian Hungarian literature, Romanian critic Ion Chinezu tells his readers that his book's ultimate objective is "Transylvanianism." "Restricting the discussion to the realm of literature," Chinezu specifies,

> we shall try to see if there really is an art-generating Transylvanianism, a specific soul of this region, a Transylvanian way of thinking capable of crystalli[z]ing [...] into its own form of literature. Such an approach [to] the issue is within the field of literary geography. Well, it is beyond doubt that a Transylvanianism of this kind does exist, and that it also existed when it was being ignored, the same way one could discern a Moldavian, Muntenian, Transylvanian[,] and Oltenian soul in Romanian literature.[3]

In a slightly modified Herderian line of thought, the critic points to a region-specific "soul," a scaled-back variety of the Romantic national soul. Long overdue, any attempt at reassessing the interconnection between Hungarian literature from Romania and Romanian literature by situating their dynamic within the framework of new developments in world literature viewed as both literary and methodological domain would have to acknowledge, first, the remarkable resilience of this Herderianism in the criticism on Hungarian literature created in Romania. In fact, this scholarship, whose beginnings date back to the early 1920s, has placed this type of literature squarely under the regional rubric. More precisely, Hungarian literature written in Romania was for its first commentators and has largely remained a regional variant of Hungarian literature from around the world, of world or "universal Hungarian literature," an appellation some have used to designate the totality of literary works in Hungarian no matter where they have been composed or published—in Hungary or across its frontiers, past or present, within the Hungarian diasporic communities cropping up on various continents during the last two centuries, and so forth.

In effect, throughout the twentieth century, the historians of Hungarian literary modernity have been keen on the issue of extraterritoriality. Arguably, their focus has been a direct consequence of certain milestones in Hungarian and world history and politics. The first is the 1920 Trianon Treaty, through which a significant part of the Hungarian population was stripped of its citizenship and found itself inhabiting neighboring states, whose boundaries had been redrawn so as to mark these countries' incorporation of lands previously under Hungarian sovereignty. Therefore, post-1920 Hungarian literature has also originated outside Hungary's current boundaries, in territories of present-day Romania, Slovakia, Serbia, and Ukraine. Responding to this historical reality, the concept of Hungarian regional literatures has been pivotal to a series of regional literary histories. These cover the Hungarian body of work coming out from these countries by taking them either as regions, viz., as areas of study separate among themselves and from the literature done in Hungary, or together, in more synthetic, interregional surveys. The latter paint a broader picture of Hungarian-language literatures, featuring as they do representatives of "regional" literatures from outside Hungary such as Jenő Dsida, Áron Tamási, András Sütő, Ottó Tolnai, and Lajos Grendel among many others and considering them part and parcel of the Hungarian literary system in its entirety.

The second major event accounting for the extraterritoriality of the Hungarian literature is the 1956 anti-Communist revolution's brutal crushing, which, forcing Hungarians to flee their homeland in droves, gave a spectacular boost to Hungarian-language "exile literature."[4] Ever since, the study of this literary production has expanded steadily, further complicating the ways in which critics handle literature and its definitional associations with the author's language, ethnicity, location, citizenship, the nation-state, and national literature. In fact, as Mircea A. Diaconu also suggests in his contribution to *Romanian Literature as World Literature*, the historical, historically consequential, and geoculturally complex presence of regional ("ethnic-minority") literatures inside and alongside national literary ensembles leaves little room for a treatment of the latter as homogeneous, organic, all of-a-piece monolith. It is true that, over time, critics can manage to work out, across cultural-linguistic and political divides, trans-ethnic canons in which minority groups are also present. By and large, though, these have been a token presence. The ethno-linguistically "inclusive" canonical structures put forth by specialists for various national literatures of Central and Eastern Europe and beyond have been only perfunctorily incorporated into curricula and collective patrimonies and memories outside the academy, which, in the wake of multiculturalism, postcolonialism, and feminism, has led to the breakout of veritable "canon wars" in the area.

It is noteworthy, however, that Chinezu's undertaking was premised on an overall pluralism of literary culture in this European zone, whether said pluralism characterized Hungarian-language regional literatures developing in countries around Hungary or, inside national literatures such as Romania's, the local varieties emerging in Moldavia, Muntenia, Oltenia, or Transylvania in modern times. At any rate, Chinezu's sensitivity to regional diversity within and without Hungarian literatures has an entire critical tradition behind it. I might note along these lines that the second half of the nineteenth century had already seen the establishment of Transylvanian literary-cultural societies and related institutions such as Erdélyi Múzeum-Egyesület (Society for the Transylvanian Museum), which was founded in 1859, Kemény Zsigmond Társaság (The Zsigmond Kemény Society), established in 1876, Erdélyi Magyar Közművelődési Egyesület (The Hungarian Culture Society of Transylvania), created in 1885, and Erdélyi Irodalmi Társaság (The Literary Society of Ardeal [Transylvania]), which was formed in 1888. In Romanian literary and academic history, the situation is different, especially in the post-1900 period, when the pursuit of regional specificities declined due to the widely felt urgency of a quintessentially trans-regional project aimed at fostering a "unitary" nation-state. There are exceptions, though, and they have occurred mainly during the postcommunist years. One of them is Cornel Ungureanu's post-2000 work, where he seeks to develop a "geography of Romanian literature today," which objective is loosely related to the scholarly agenda of the Third-Europe Group of Timişoara and the collective's pursuit of a Central Europeanism of Romanian literature; the other is Mircea Muthu's research on Romanian literary "Balkanism."[5] It also bears mentioning here, as it did earlier apropos of post–Second World War Hungarian literature, the steadily growing body of exile literature by Romanians, which boasts highly interesting literary works. Their true integration into Romanian literature requires, however, as it does for other literary and critical traditions, reading and assessment frameworks genuinely appreciative of the inherent multiplicity and, once more, of the inbuilt "pluralism" of literary and aesthetic systems.

In my view, the critical–theoretical work that has come to the fore on the heels of new comparative analysis, planetary studies, and *histoire croisée*'s interest in "intersecting" cultural histories has the potential to bring to light the plural makeup and positioning of Romanian literatures, as well as their cross- and supranational affinities and links to the worlds these literatures are and open windows into. In drawing on this work, my goal is to formulate an approach to, and a broader concept of, "ethnic" literature—Hungarian, in this case—for an era demonstrably marked worldwide by speedy advances no less than by crises in this late-global epoch's trans- and post-national economic, financial, demographic, and cultural mobility. The first step in articulating this approach entails a critique of authors like Chinezu who, not unlike the Hungarian theoreticians of "Transylvanianism" of the early-twentieth century, spoke of the "soul of the region" and its literary expression, namely, regional literature. As is well known, underlying is both a metaphysical, idealist—or, with a more recent term, "essentializing"—and typically Romantic notion of nation. Rooted in Johann Gottfried von Herder's thought, this idea, schematic and essentialist as it proved to be, was not applied to an ethnic-majority-ruled nation-state but was instead retrofitted for the smaller territory of the multi-ethnic region of Transylvania.

It was precisely this pluricultural aspect that gave hope to the young Hungarian men and women of letters of the 1920s, who envisioned a cultural project that would be shared by all Transylvanian writers, be they Romanian, Hungarian, or German Saxons, on the basis of the regional platform of "Transylvanianism." Started out through reciprocal translations, joint public lectures, and writers' meetings, the initiative lost momentum toward the end of the previous century's third decade, when the political and cultural interests of the three major Transylvanian ethnic groups grew more and more divergent. Before that, there had been a short period during which such goals had overlapped and sometimes had even coincided as they carried forward, one way or the other, the commonly Transylvanian heritage of earlier, cross-ethnically unifying organizational structures and mentalities, which the 1918 rise of Greater Romania suddenly put to the test of a new political reality. Indeed, utopian or not, the Hungarian "Transylvanianists'" initial idea was that regional "specificity" was as much a socioculturally coalescing factor for Transylvanians as ethnic identities and, beyond them, national self-identifications and aspirations were. As Chinezu also reminds us, "[m]uch attention has been given to the centur[ies]-old contacts between Romanians and Transylvanian Saxons [and to] the various mutual influences resulting from [these] contact[s], which gradually [led scholars to conclude that] Romanians, Transylvanian Saxons, and Hungarians share, to various degrees, [a common mind-set]."[6]

Have these interchanges yielded the *same* brand of "Transylvanianism" in all of Transylvania's three main regional literatures, though? Granted, one does come across entire thematics, let alone motifs, threading through Transylvanian literary production across linguistic divides in the years between the First and the Second World Wars, and yet it is hard to make a strong case for a sufficiently marked commonality of this kind. In fact, what recent comparative scholarship such as the multivolume *History of the Literary Cultures of East-Central Europe* edited by Marcel Cornis-Pope and John Neubauer brings into sharp relief is not principally the distinctiveness of the common denominator but, to the contrary, the central role played by the distinctions themselves among such "cultures." Accordingly, the *History* supplies separate coverages for the works published in each of the three major Transylvanian languages, and its contributors show how each community keeps focusing on its own ethnic group according to a specific, individualizing agenda. "What divided the three national literatures, namely their focus on their own ethnic traditions, was," contend the editors, "precisely what made them also similar: they all tended to uphold rural values against 'decadent' urban ones."[7] But, in critical practice, the "similarity" could not, and did not, sustain over time a regionally "holistic" approach to Transylvanian literatures. Besides, the interpretation model in question was conceptually flawed, and the flaws, one more time, come down basically to an overly streamlined, "essentialist" view of ethno-cultural community.

In a 1996 article on contemporary regional literatures, R. M. Dainotto argues that "essentialized" takes on regionalism in all actuality rehearse the epistemological homogenizations previously applied to national cultures. This is, the critic observes, a nationalist revival with an organicist vengeance in that the region is billed as a more "organic" community, one that, given its presumably more tightly knit fabric, is less fragmented and more "authentic" than the nation-state. In his opinion, "It is in this re-evaluation of notions of authenticity, of a natural and organic community, that I see regionalism as an attempt to revive some peculiarly nationalist ideals by passing them off as 'new' regionalist ones."[8] The critic's point is germane to my essay's own endeavors to move the interpretation of Hungarian literature from Romania past nostalgically "organic," uniformity-inducing definitions and readings. Elsewhere, I have offered a regional literature concept based, in effect, on the reception of literary works and not so much on their thematic content and their origin.[9] Expanded below, my argument has been, very simply speaking, that we *read* these texts *into* certain ethnic, national, spatial, and cultural classifications and memberships; it is our reading, I have insisted—and I reiterate here—that places this literature both under such headings and in the world. And so, more redundantly put, but arguably with a meaningful redundancy, "Hungarian literature from Romania" is that body of writings that is *read* as "Hungarian literature from Romania" or as "Romania's Hungarian literature," with all that such formulations and annexations might entail. One of the benefits provided by such a reading-centered approach and especially by the particular reading protocol I have in mind is that, in opening up their "regional" object to the world along both the synchronic and diachronic axes, they help us see how the criteria of this object's belonging to a literature itself regional shift historically to reflect new situations and realities. In so doing, this reading methodology alerts us to a sense of mutating, temporality-bound cultural identity reminiscent of Wai Chee Dimock's glosses on nonstandard and fluctuating time.[10] What is more, when looked at through the lens of the abovementioned interpretive procedure, the literature of a certain region and cultural regionality overall call for meaning-making operations that can be both regionalizing and de- or trans-regionalizing in that they can link up the poem, play, or novel at hand with the regional perimeter as well as with zones, worlds, and traditions beyond it, as the case may be. These frameworks too are not ahistorical or given a priorily; it is in the practice of this kind of reading that such spaces and worlds, such defining affiliations and contexts emerge. For Hungarian literature from Romania, they run, as we shall notice, the whole gamut from the patrimony of all Hungarian-language works or "national" Hungarian literature to Hungarian literature from across the world, Central-European literature, world literature, and Romanian literature.

2. Minority Literature, Minor Literature, and the Politics of Cultural Networks

When judged over and against the latter's backdrop, the efforts of Romania's Hungarian authors are quasi-invariably addressed *qua* minority literature. Directly or indirectly, the elucidating connection or reference here seems to be dominant, Romanian culture. Having lost the definitional force and overall relevance they preserve in other circumstances, territorial and native claims to a real or virtual, imaginary or familiar, everyday geography now play second fiddle to the power relationships with—and de facto to the political subordination to—the country and its majority culture. In this situation, where Romania is the putatively pertinent, epistemologically guiding context, the ties of these writers to Romanian literature appear stronger and wield, accordingly, superior explanatory force by comparison to the play such bonds were given in classical theories of regionalism. Specifically, what marks the connections between these minority authors and the majority environment, as well as what ultimately reinforces these poets, novelists, and playwrights' minority condition and treatment in a very palpable kind of way is the nation-state's institutions, mainly—but not solely—those directly involved in cultural production. Before the Second World War, the "institutionality" of "minority" cultures was still a living reality, suggesting as it did a sense of continuity with the regional cultural institutions of the nineteenth century. Moreover, a couple of new magazines, publishing houses, and literary-historical societies were founded after the First World War as literature became even more serious about expressing the identity of Romania's Hungarian and German populations in light of their recently acquired "minority" status. During this interval, the country's coexisting ethnicities wrote, published, engaged in debate, and otherwise manifested themselves through parallel networks of authorship, dissemination, and communication venues and channels. Multilingual magazines such as *Aurora* (1922–1923) and *Cultura* (1924), which, in principle, made for cross-cultural, less ethnocentric, and more "commonalty" geared exchanges and culture were very few, and their presence was marginal. Insofar as this period's literary societies are concerned, the PEN Club episode stands out as the only institutional platform of this type. We might recall, apropos of the Romanian history of the Club that, although the negotiations for its local chapter's setup had begun as early as 1928, it was only in 1932 that a section for the Hungarian writers from Transylvania was established inside the Romanian PEN Club. Yet again, the latter was an exception to the rule, that is, to the predominance of arenas and webs of literary expression that rarely intersected. Intercultural communication did occur, but it was neither systematic nor encouraged in an institutional sense and reflected rather individual initiatives of writers representing various Transylvanian literatures. Translation programs did exist, and public readings featuring authors of different backgrounds were held as well, but they were all projects underpinned primarily by Transylvanianism conceived in the traditional sense of this regionalist ideology.

This all changed dramatically after the Second World War, mainly due to the nationalization of private property, including presses, magazines, and the like, as well as to the aggressive Sovietization of Romanian culture. Up until the early 1960s, all publications and events even remotely related to "intercultural communication" had to conform strictly to the ideology of proletarian internationalism and, during the Gheorghe Gheorghiu-Dej and Nicolae Ceaușescu regimes, to official "minority" policies. Thus, Romania's Hungarian writers were forcibly rendered cultural actors beholden to the same, nationally centralized and Soviet-inspired structure of ideological vetting and politically motivated promotion and censorship as their Romanian, German, or Serbian peers, with the still existing Writers' Union of Romania a prime example for the homogenizing and monitoring workings of this institutional system of cultural management and control. Also, these authors' writings came out, sometimes in several languages, from the same state-owned publishing houses, for the publishers—newspapers, weeklies, academic journals, the broadcasting media, and the media at large—participated in the weaving of this "common" institutional fabric.

The scare quotes are warranted because this mandated commonality was artificially induced and therefore constituted no more than a façade: forcing Romania's literatures into the same, highly ideologized and centralized institutional apparatus did little to foster creative synergies among them. What it actually accomplished, was, on the one hand, to ward off such exchanges and, on the other hand, to consolidate the subaltern position of the country's Hungarian literature—to literalize its "minority" condition. Interestingly enough, this status was further sanctioned by another institution, namely, literary criticism, which between 1944 and 1989 seemed quite keen on the "minority" voices of literature by Romanian Hungarians. Interestingly enough, both Romanian and Hungarian critics joined this pseudo-integration campaign as they all appeared to endorse the participation of Romanian territory-originated Hungarian literature in two national traditions, Hungarian and Romanian. Underpinning this perspective was a crudely historicist or "realist" aesthetics stipulating what a short story or a drama does, is, and attests to. That is to say, if literature constitutes a reflection of its author's milieu, which in our case is Romanian, then the point of convergence and reference of all works composed in Romania was bound to be some kind of Romanian reality as well, irrespective of these texts' language, of their authors' background, and so on. This twofold cultural inscription remains a major tenet of Romanian critic Gavril Scridon's 1996 *Istoria literaturii maghiare din România* (History of Hungarian Literature from Romania). "[Romania's Hungarian-language] literature, which is intimately tied, through the language in which it is written, through its entire panoply of expressive forms, and through its cultural heritage, to Hungarian literature," maintains Scridon, "is a distinct literature with its own particular features, some of them organically close to Romanian literature, alongside which it has formed and has grown by way of permanent exchanges of ideas, suggestions, and experiences."[11] Notably enough, keynote here is "organically." Following from it is the implication that minority literature undergoes continuous transformation leading logically and harmoniously to a sort of hybrid in which Hungarian heritage goes hand in hand with the increasingly seamless "incorporation" into Romanian literature.

In 1990, Gusztáv Láng raised serious objections to the "hybridization" theory and the conceptualizations, labels, and definitions derived from it. As he aptly remarked,

Sooner or later, we should realize that these two factors [the socio-political environment, on one side, and, on the other, the cultural-linguistic and historical connection between Hungarian literature from Romania and entire Hungarian literature] are not complementary, but that, in fact, they can be diametrically opposed to each other. This is because the pressure social influences bring to bear on literature generally varies according to the degree to which the minority individual identifies—at the level of everyday life rather in [this or that consciously undertaken aesthetic project]—with the objectives pursued by the country whose citizen he or she is. The more democratic the political structure of that country, the easier and more spontaneous this identification, which can also make that person distance himself or herself from the country [where his or her brethren are the majority, i.e., Hungary] and can therefore weaken the ties with the very cultural heritage that defines the Hungarian character of Romania's [Hungarian] minority.[12]

Demonstrably, the cultural and political logic Láng unpacks here was borne out by the history of Communist Romania. It is this logic too, one of "dis-identification," of opting out of the country's integrative circuits of culture, that accounts for the era's missing or ineffective intersections and crosspollinations between Romania's Romanian and Hungarian literary networks. No doubt, high-quality translations, anthologies, and literary histories came out during this time in both languages, presenting one tradition to another's audience. Likewise, Romanian writers and their Hungarian colleagues worked together within the Writers' Union and occasionally in the pages of various magazines. Especially significant in this respect was Kriterion Press's multilingual program. In addition to books in the languages of national minorities of Romania, Kriterion published Romanian versions of works by "minority" authors, as well as scholarship such as critic Nicolae Balotă's highly appreciated monograph on Hungarian writers from Romania.[13] But these joint projects and publications did little to ensure a substantial reception and presence of "majority" literature in its "minority" counterpart, and vice versa, for the long haul. Quite instructive is, in this view, the 1999 *Vatra* magazine survey, which addresses, in the new context of postcommunist Romania, some of the causes of this situation. Answering one of *Vatra's* questions, Mircea Cărtărescu, a prominent figure of contemporary Romanian literature, recalls vividly the impact *Vânt potrivit până la tare* (Moderate to Strong Wind), a 1982 anthology of poetry by young German authors from Romania, had on him and on the "1980s Generation" broadly.[14] No influence of this caliber on Romanian literature has been identified, by Cărtărescu or anybody else, in Hungarian literature from Romania, and most contemporary critics agree that there have been scant interactions between the two literatures overall.

Despite the abovementioned institutionally enforced integration of Romanian literatures under Communism and the comparable periodization of these literatures' histories which also reflect, and in the first place perhaps, international timelines and dynamics of supranational movements such as Romanticism, modernism, and so forth—the two traditions seem to evolve decidedly on separate tracks. If indeed, as I will show below, their trajectories start intersecting somewhat one another and with other, world circuitries of values and symbolic expression freely, that occurs in the postcommunist years. This happens because the democratic setup of society is "naturally" conducive to such crisscrossings but also because intertextuality, collage, literary remix, bookish allusion, and other techniques that, with postmodernism, become de rigueur in such interweavings are now dominant. These procedures represent, in effect, a formally-thematic apposite protocol in that the textual and intertextual mutations and permutations they set in train inside individual works reenact the genetic scenarios lying behind the production of minor literature in its entirety. When read with an eye to this aesthetic protocol, those works become so many incentives to rethink Hungarian literature and its place as minority literature in Romania and as literature *tout court*, in Romania and in the world.

In a 2008 essay, I took the first steps toward this reading model and the reconceptualizations it enables.[15] That article leans, perhaps inevitably, on Gilles Deleuze and Félix Guattari's *Kafka: Toward a Minor Literature*, but it does so in order to make a particular argument about how this literature bespeaks the "minor" as well as the "minority" condition in two ways or with respect to two "major" and or "majority" traditions, Romanian and Hungarian.[16] *Both*, I underscore in my piece, apply on the Hungarian literature of Transylvania certain pressures whose ultimate effect is reductive and, in a sense, colonizing insofar as they cram the region's Hungarian-language authors and their complex works into historical and critical–theoretical constructions designed to facilitate annexations by either national culture. However, as we will notice momentarily, some of these writers resist such appropriations by rejecting them altogether or by supplementing them with links and contacts in other directions and with other traditions and geographies. When effective, resistance assigns these artists a less marginal place in the literary world-system, a location and a significance less mediated by the central position claimed by, and mechanically granted to, national literatures in this setup.

The way I see it, the problem is not the effectiveness of these oppositional tactics but our ability to *read for* and assess the scope of their world-systemic realignments. If this is true, then Moretti's comparative morphology of cultural traffics and ensuing relationships across the system might well provide a solution—or at least a starting point for one. For, it seems to me, "Conjectures on World Literature's" frequently invoked analytic tropes, the "tree" and the "wave," *both* ultimately describe flows out of or away from an "originating" to a "receiving" point and thereby a process of derivation and subordination. On this score, appealing as these figures might be as allegorizing how minority literature comes into being, what it does formally and thematically, and how it situates itself in the world, the "whirlpool" might furnish, I believe, a more aptly descriptive metaphor.[17] This is because, in complicating, nuancing, and merging the cultural dynamics dramatized by the trees and waves of Moretti, vortexes, swirls, and such paint a more accurate picture of minority literature, increasing our awareness of the fluid and tumultuous, predictable and unexpected, sequential and concomitant, one- and multi-directional ripples and swells, currents and countercurrents, and ebbs and flows that pull it, sometimes concurrently, in a number at directions and enrich its meanings. Thus, as a whirlpool or set of loosely communicating, decentered and decentering crosscurrents and eddies of discourse, minority Hungarian literature becomes isomorphic with Deleuze and Guattari's *minor* literature, emulating its ability to capture a disjointed and fragmented world of culture, identity, language, and narrative voice.

As we will see in my chapter's final part, it is particularly this last element, voice, and its centrifugal dynamics that allow for gestures to and insertions into other worlds. Complete with its plurality, instability, and ventriloquizing echoes in other voices and places, narration, its human root, and the outlooks embedded in storytelling acts are particularly instrumental to these mutations, diversifications, and ramifications across all kinds of category designations and geocultural frontiers. In calling attention to how voice functions in the Western novel's forays into Eastern cultural traditions such as Japan's, Moretti discloses that, unlike Fredric Jameson's emphasis on the form-content binary, "[f]or me, it's more of a triangle: foreign form, local material—*and local form*. Simplifying somewhat: foreign *plot*; local *characters*; and then, local *narrative voice*: and it's precisely in this third dimension that these novels seem to be most unstable."[18] The voices making themselves heard especially after 1970 and particularly under the influence of postmodernism in fiction by multiply affiliated, Romanian-born Hungarian figures such as Bodor, György Dragomán, and Attila Bartis, who wrote most of their oeuvres after they had emigrated to Hungary, may seem "local" as Romanian readers may hear in them echoes of situations, names, people, and places from their country's contemporary history, art, and literature. But, in the whirlpools of novels like those discussed below, this locality frays and decomposes but only to disseminate across a wide expanse of other locales. In these works, Hungarian literature asserts its "minority" through "vocal" and cognate narrative techniques that tear apart ossified classifications and collectivist–totalist grand narratives of culture, idiom, and creativity to project new and "worlding" categories, identifications, and sodalities at the shifting crossroads of other voices, spaces, and cultures.

3. In the Whirlpool: Reading Intersectional Fiction

Bodor's *Sinistra körzet*, Láng's *Bestiárium Transylvaniae*, and Szilágyi's *Hollóidő* have all made quite a splash in Hungary. Bodor has also reached a fairly wide international audience in translation, including the Romanian public. There are no Romanian versions of Láng's and Szilágyi's remarkable books, however. Their authors are both living in Romania, but their residence does not seem to have made a difference so far. Instead, *Sinistra körzet*'s, that is, where the novel is set does—or, better still, where the book is *not specifically set* and, relatedly, how it handles actual and invented geographical and cultural references across an extremely elaborate structure in which each chapter can be read as an independent short story. The novel's subtitle, *Egy regény fejezetei* (Chapters of a Novel), points, in fact, to this loose narrative assemblage. Nonetheless, the fragments are linked to the text's general architecture through characters and occurrences that keep resurfacing throughout the narrative.[19] Cross-graining real with imaginary locations and historical with fictional events, the author builds a geoculturally plausible, seemingly self-contained possible world around the small town of Dobrin, which is situated, we are told, somewhere in the Carpathian Mountains, close to the Ukrainian border. This is Sinistra, a "zone" under army control, in reality a vast penitentiary for convicts placed under home confinement. The political system of the zone appears to be an absurd military dictatorship, with the latter running everything, from distribution of supplies to a mysterious flu with no cure. Those "diagnosed" with this epidemic are quarantined in isolation, a "therapy" well in line with the carceral microsociety characteristic of the area. The civilians forced to reside here have primitive and mostly pointless occupations whose meaninglessness brooks large over the meandering exploits of Andrej Bodor, the novel's protagonist. Andrej comes to this remote region to find his adopted son, Béla Bundasian, who has been missing for several years. After repeated attempts, Andrej manages to find Béla, who has been living on a nearby natural reservation, but does not succeed to convince him to break out of the zone. Andrej's failure speaks to the ambiguities of interpersonal relationships, which the novel's storytelling technique destabilizes by dint of a "selective" narrative voice that holds back information strategically. Although first-person, Andrej-focused, and third-person narrations alternate across the novel, the reader rarely gets a clear sense of what the characters think or feel, for, whether they are truly bereft of emotional life or not, the heroes and heroines often react to various events corporeally, through crying, nausea, and the like. This narrative chiaroscuro is further complicated by the moral ambivalences paving Andrej's trajectory. At some point, he falls in with the commander of the military units in the region, Coca Mavrodin, and so becomes, as Béla accuses him, a cog in the repressive system, even though Andrej decides to flee the zone, which he does eventually.

Vagueness-inducing narrative style works hand in glove with a similarly open-ended fictional onomastics to "delocalize" what, at first blush, looks like an isolated and self-enclosed environment and to tie it into other spaces, cultures, and identities. What we are dealing with is, indeed, a veritable novelistic whirlpool in which formal, thematic, and cultural currents carry, break up, and recombine voices, viewpoints, historical milestones, and toponyms into amalgamations evocative of broader or remote places and stories. Thus, characters' names such as Cornelia Illafeld, Mustafa Mukkerman, Elvira Spiridon, Béla Bundasian, Aranka Westin, Nikifor Tescovina, Géza Kökény, and Coca Mavrodin draw a picture one would be hard pressed to recognize on Europe's actual political map. Granted, the reader may identify certain Central-European and even Asian resonances—Hungarian, German, Jewish, Russian, Romanian, Armenian, and so on—in all these names. None of the latter, however, can be attributed unequivocally to any particular ethnicity or homeland, and so the novel's narrative turbine of disassociations-cum-reassociations preempts any allegorical reading that, in turn, would pinpoint the book's world by grounding itself in a set of elucidatory historical, geographical, political, ethnic, or linguistic inferences.

In the narrative swirl of *Sinistra körzet*'s polyvocal and multilayered world, the category of minority literature itself liquefies but only to gel subsequently into new and provocative meanings as the reader draws his or her own cognitive map in response to the "clues" the novel drops to prompt such conjectures. More than anything else, place and territoriality more broadly bear the brunt of the writer's tactics of indeterminateness. Going out of his way to make strange and outlandish a geography with which his Central and East European audience should be familiar, Bodor works into the zone's description toponyms that are either imaginary or belong on different charts and guides. But plays of deliberate displacement and misplacement rework not just space. They affect—deconstruct and reconstruct—identity as well, and, once again, it is in the book's onomastic vortex that its de- and re-territorialization takes place. "Ethnic-sounding" first names appear in heterogeneous combinations with family names that also hint at certain ethnic backgrounds, and they are all bestowed on characters who are renamed by the zone's authorities, while the original names remain unknown. But, beyond names, the named itself, Bodor's dramatis personae, are enigmatic as the narrators' somewhat impersonal, feeling-neutral stories withhold information that would help trace people's origins back to actual locales and events or even to previous episodes that would supply readers with expectations or rationales of some kind. Thus, character development obtains in Bodor a little counterintuitively, through a *dehistoricization* of sorts that does not annul history proper but, to the contrary, yields an *excess* of historical possibilities as it presents visual, auditory, or olfactory reactions to the world on the heroes and heroines' part but no narrative commentary that would circumscribe that fictional universe to attested histories and sociocultural ambiances. In the world or worlds, rather, whose panoramas the author spreads out before us, family bonds and the family overall as a traditional site of identity origination and determination are deconstructed, as they also are in the 1999 *Az érsek látogatása* (The Archbishop's Visit) and in the 2011 *Verhovina madarai* (The Birds of Verhovina), novels whose fictional worlds Bodor populates with orphans, adopted children, and stepparents.[20] Generally speaking, the profiles he ascribes his characters are fluid, untraceable to identifying birthplaces or milieus, fragmented, ever incomplete, and, in the spirit of Deleuzian and Guattarian minor literature, making and remaking themselves outside and even against traditionally "organic" or linear narratives.

This holds true of Láng's *Bestiarium Transylvaniae* as well.[21] Informing the author's destabilizing manipulation of spatial, temporal, and cultural context this time around is chiefly the classical bestiary genre, which features a mix of real and fantastic beasts. Voice and narrative form broadly also play into these maneuverings, and so the book's "reality" coalesces *qua* story, fluctuating as it follows fiction's pendulum swing between the recognizable and the made up. Thus, the ontological status of various references oscillates accordingly between imaginary and the effectively existing. The first volume is an echo chamber of sorts for an anonymous narrative voice mimicking those of authors of historical chronicles and memoirs of sixteenth- and seventeenth-century Transylvania, when the region was an independent Principality. Otherwise, the book is only archaic as vision, as worldview, in the same way as the vision of medieval bestiaries. The text is the hub of a thick intertextual web of relations mainly with accounts of events also occurring in late Middle Ages Transylvania. Yet in *Bestiarium*, too, places, names, and chronologies lose their localizing and meaning-stabilizing impetus as they dissolve into seemingly random combinations intimating that book-spawned realities are merely textual upshots à la Linda Hutcheon's "historiographic metafiction" even when they convey themselves under the guise of historical prose.[22] Again, the narration's ultimate effect, despite the formal conventions at work, is anachronistic and ahistorical or dehistoricizing in the sense specified apropos of *Sinistra körzet*, and, also much like in Bodor, a similarly disembodied narrative voice orchestrates these games of actual and not-so-actual chrono-topological reference.

In the second volume, the source of narrative information is better individualized, but this does nothing to change the games' basic rules. The narrator has actually a name now, Eremie. A name does not necessarily translate, however, into the name bearer's well-settled, solidly constellated identity or historically identifiable position, and so Eremie does not seem to be one but many in one, as it were. He is introduced as a monk living in the Moldavian monastery of Noroieni, but, as the story unfolds, who he actually is and even whether he has ever existed become subject to debate. A possible figment himself, Eremie's voice fictionalizes the chain of events spanning the plot and swirling around Eremie's time, the present in which he tells his story and through which his persona takes shape, as well as around the narrated past, namely, around the lifetime of Despot, ruler of sixteenth-century Moldavia. But Láng does not stop here. He ups the ante of this imaginary reworking of histories and geographies further in the trilogy's third segment, which is set in the months preceding the Romanian antitotalitarian uprising of December 1989 and whose protagonist is Bori, a high-school girl. It is basically through her that the final volume of *Bestiarium* offers a microhistorical perspective on Romanian Communism, but she is not the only narrator. Nor are all storytellers human beings—one is an officer of the secret police, the infamous Securitate, and the other a gigantic blue rat—and yet they are all capable of self-reflexive comments, alternate and sometimes ironic accounts, as well as of different, "meta" perspectives on fictionality and narrativity and, more importantly, on history, on what "really" happened during the 1989 upheaval. Along with the rest of Láng's novel, the closing section highlights the often underappreciated role of the imagination in the articulation of historical consciousness and, more generally, in the cultural formation of representations and denominations that all-too-eagerly chalk up the book's humanity—"Transylvanians," "Moldavians," and so forth—to restrictive rubrics, locales, and world pictures.

Narrative modulations and ambiguities of voice are also behind the narrative critique of such narrowly stereotypical headings and cubicular views of subjectivity, habitat, and culture in Szilágyi's *Hollóidő*. Another metahistorical and metafictional novel, Szilágyi's work pursues more pointedly the workings of power across a wide swath of time that stretches as back as the anti-Ottoman struggle and Protestant debates of centuries past. Interestingly enough, though, religion—theology, more exactly—accrues, not unlike history, an aesthetic and cultural–philosophical dimension in the book. In the first chapter, Illés Fortuna, a schoolmaster, ventures before his students a personal hypothesis of a biblical Genesis still underway, in which the creation of humankind is still ongoing. As in Bodor and Láng, this notion of an "in-progress," unsettled civilization applies to people and to their homes and histories, as well as to space and time more broadly. *Hollóidő* is, one might say, a novelistic meditation on temporality, specifically on the nonlinearity and discontinuity of time, on their disrupting bearings on geography, and on how communities and individuals see themselves and their worlds when traditional, stable chronologies and spatial structures acquire unexpected fluidity, future events are wedged into the present, and labyrinthine memory sends people on the wild-goose chase of things past. Likewise, in a fashion reminiscent of *Sinistra körzet*'s fictional toponymy, Szilágyi messes with real place names, which makes it hard for the reader to determine the location of this or that plot development. Further, similar indeterminacy stratagems obscure the narrator's identity. In the book's second part, the story is related from a first-person-plural point of view, but it is difficult to tell whom or what exactly this narrative "we" refers, given their (its?) constant, ironic shifts back and forth between an entire group of young men who leave their home village, destroyed by the Turks, and join the anti-Ottoman resistance, to only two or three individuals. Either way, we are getting few reports of noble gallantry, for the author seems preoccupied mainly by how power works. Yet political authority, imperial or otherwise, and the opposition thereto come in many shapes and forms in Szilágyi's novel. These can be brutal, mindlessly aggressive, but also intellectual, of a kind one might define as narrative or discursive, with the latter sort wielded by Fortuna or Tentás, the "intellectual," another character who exerts a strong influence on those around him and under whose sway various narrators blend together fictitious and real, detail-rich and nebulous, individual and collective histories into antiheroic and relativist, "fuzzy" and polymorphic stories, destinies, and worlds.

These worlds are and are not recognizable. Sometimes they belong on official maps. But sometimes they do not, and so they draw their own. The books' fictional cartography, however, runs afoul of what we know or think we know about Transylvania, Hungarian literature written on its territory, and this territory itself as a stage of self-other encounters, history, identity, communal definitions and moorings in time, space, idiom, culture, and interactions with Romanian literature and with Romania overall as a nation-state. As the novels briefly examined above suggest, while all these elements matter, they should not be absolutized either, and this applies to a range of territorial jurisdictions, claims, and communities, recognized or contested, real or imagined.[23] I wanted us to descend in this minority literature's narrative maelstrom precisely because what the workings of this textual apparatus ultimately reveal is how all these factors intermingle so as to suggest a genuinely intersectional and thereby less hegemonic commerce between Romanian literature and Hungarian literature from Romania. From the standpoint of this cultural dynamic, it would be counterproductive to base a celebratory reading of the former's "plurality" on the latter's retrospective, ahistorical, and hasty integration into Romanian culture's presumably hospitable multicultural and multilinguistic ensemble. Such an approach would once more lead to a schematic and undifferentiated concept of Romania's Hungarian-language literature, as it did in the past, when Socialist Realism and its colonizing, Soviet cultural model were deployed to make a case for how neatly integrated East European literary cultures were with each other and how similar they were to one another.[24] Instead, watching out for the intense traffic at the geographical and historical crossroads of this literature and listening for its concert of cultural voices afford, as we have discovered, more flexible, more mutually beneficial, and, in all likelihood, more historically accurate relationships between Romania's national literature and the body of works by the country's Hungarian authors. At the same time, these interconnections, to do what they are supposed to do, must bring together open structures on both sides. This is as much as saying that, at its end, Romanian culture must respond to the whirlpool-like, crisscrossings-prone configuration of Hungarian literary discourse with an analogously inclusive and receptive critical and cultural apparatus, that is, with real interest in and adequate reactions to this discourse on the part of both lay and literary-academic publics.

Notes

1 Arjun Appadurai, *Modernity at Large: Cultural Dimensions of Globalization* (Minneapolis, MN: University of Minnesota Press, 1999), 19.

2 See Fuyuki Kurasawa, "Critical Cosmopolitanism," in *The Ashgate Research Companion to Cosmopolitanism*, ed. Maria Rovisco and Magdalena Nowicka, (Farnham: Ashgate, 2011), 287; Michael Werner and Bénédicte Zimmermann, "'Beyond Comparison': Histoire Croisée and the Challenge of Reflexivity," *History and Theory* 45 (February 2006): 38.

3 Ion Chinezu, *Aspects of Transylvanian Hungarian Literature (1919–1929)*, trans. Liviu Bleoca (Cluj-Napoca: Centrul de Studii Transilvane—Fundația Culturală Română, 1997), 45. In the original, the passage can be found in the Romanian edition of Chinezu's book, *Aspecte din literatura maghiară ardeleană (1919–1929)* (Cluj: Editura Revistei Societatea de Mâine, 1930), on page 15.

4 A comprehensive survey of exile Hungarian literature supplies *The Exile and Return of Writers from East-Central Europe. A Compendium*, ed. John Neubauer and Borbála Zsuzsanna Török (Berlin: Walter de Gruyter, 2009).

5 See Cornel Ungureanu, *Geografia literaturii române, azi*, vol. 1 and 4 (Pitești: Paralela 45, 2003, 2005); Mircea Muthu, *Balcanismul literar românesc* (Pitești: Paralela 45, 2008).

6 Chinezu, *Aspects of Transylvanian Hungarian Literature*, 46.

7 John Neubauer, Marcel Cornis-Pope, Sándor Kibédi-Varga, and Nicolae Harsanyi, "Transylvania's Literary Cultures: Rivalry and Interaction," in *History of the Literary Cultures of East-Central Europe: Junctures and Disjunctures in the 19th and 20th Centuries*, ed. Marcel Cornis-Pope and John Neubauer, vol.2 (Amsterdam: John Benjamins, 2004), 271.

8 R. M. Dainotto, "'All the Regions Do Smilingly Revolt': The Literature of Place and Region," *Critical Inquiry* 22.3 (Spring 1996): 488.

9 Imre József Balázs, "Histories of Transylvanian Hungarian Literature," *Transylvanian Review* 4 (2004): 52–59.

10 Wai Chee Dimock, *Through Other Continents: American Literature across Deep Time* (Princeton, NJ: Princeton University Press, 2006), 132–133.

11 Gavril Scridon, *Istoria literaturii maghiare din România* (Cluj-Napoca: Promedia Plus, 1996), 8.

12 Gusztáv Láng, "Plimbare în jurul unei definiții," in *Travers. O antologie a literaturii maghiare din Transilvania*, ed. Imre József Balázs and Ciprian Vălcan (Iași: Polirom, 2002), 21.

13 Nicolae Balotă, *Scriitori maghiari din România* (Bucharest: Editura Kriterion, 1981).

14 *Vînt potrivit până la tare. Zece tineri poeți germani din România*, ed. Peter Motzan (Bucharest: Kriterion, 1982). See Mircea Cărtărescu, "Situația mi se pare anormală," *Vatra* 8 (1999): 58.

15 Imre József Balázs, "Hungarian Literature from Romania between the Minor and Majority Language Usage," in *Identité nationale: réalité, histoire, littérature*, ed. Ioana Bot and Adrian Tudurachi (Bucharest: Institutul Cultural Român, 2008), 245–257.

16 Gilles Deleuze and Félix Guattari, *Kafka: Toward a Minor Literature*, trans. Dana Polan (Minnesota: University of Minnesota Press, 1986).

17 Franco Moretti, "Conjectures on World Literature," *New Left Review* 1 (January–February 2000): 66–67.

18 Moretti, "Conjectures on World Literature," 65.

19 Ádám Bodor, *Sinistra körzet* (Budapest: Magvető, 1992).

20 Ádám Bodor, *Az érsek látogatása* (Budapest: Magvető, 1999), and *Verhovina madarai* (Budapest: Magvető, 2011).

21 Zsolt Láng, *Bestiárium Transylvaniae. Az ég madarai* (Pécs: Jelenkor, 1997); *Bestiárium Transylvaniae. A tűz és a víz állatai* (Pécs: Jelenkor, 2003); *Bestiárium Transylvaniae. A föld állatai* (Pozsony: Kalligram, 2011).

22 On this issue, see Linda Hutcheon, *A Poetics of Postmodernism* (New York: Routledge, 1988).

23 On this aspect of territoriality, see Roxana M. Verona, "The Intercultural Corridor of the 'Other' Danube," in *History of the Literary Cultures of East-Central Europe: Junctures and Disjunctures in the 19th and 20th Centuries*, vol. 2, 233. On imagined communities, see Benedict Anderson's classical work *Imagined Communities: Reflections on the Origin and Spread of Nationalism* (London: Verso, 2006).

24 For an extended discussion on this topic, see Imre József Balázs, "Creating the 'New Man': Propaganda and Its Alternatives in Hungarian Literature from Romania, 1948–65," in *War of Words: Culture and the Mass Media in the Making of the Cold War in Europe*, ed. Judith Devlin and Christoph Hendrik Müller (Dublin: University College Dublin Press, 2013), 180–191.

8

Cosmopolites, Deracinated, *étranjuifs*: Romanian Jews in the International Avant-Garde

Ovidiu Morar

The avant-garde literature published in Romania between the First and the Second World Wars bears witness, as I will show in what follows, to a remarkably cosmopolitan orientation in a context otherwise deeply marked by the aggressive spread of nationalism across the whole spectrum of cultural, social, and political life. In this vein, it is noteworthy that avant-garde Romanian poetry, which was represented mainly by Jewish authors like Tristan Tzara, B. Fundoianu (aka Benjamin Fondane), Ilarie Voronca, Mihail Cosma (who will rename himself Claude Sernet), Sașa Pană, Gherasim Luca, and Paul Păun, was modeled, beginning with the second decade of the previous century, not so much on local poetic tradition, but on some of the most radical strains of European experimentalism in literature and the arts. Whereas, aside from major modernist figures such as Tudor Arghezi and Lucian Blaga, a sizeable segment of the Romanian poetry of the time was still held back by old-fashioned rhetorical formulas of Romantic and neo-romantic, pastoral-nostalgic origin like *sămănătorism, poporanism*, and Symbolism, the paths Futurism, Dadaism, and Surrealism were cutting in the world arena seemed more appealing to Romanian avant-gardists. Sometimes following these trails and other times blazing their own, these authors—to whom one might add Paul Celan and Isidore Isou (born Isidor Goldstein), who were less prolific in Romanian—made, as we will learn, landmark contributions to international modernism's aesthetics and cosmopolitan climate. If indeed, as Guy Scarpetta insists, cosmopolitanism's lifestyle and philosophy of culture push for alternatives to any "ideological mechanism[s] of enrooting," to any *dispositif* or sociocultural setup threatening to tie down people, thought, and expression to insular, shortsighted, and parochial views and cultural practices, then, as I also argue, these avant-garde artists' overall agenda was quintessentially cosmopolitan.[1] For, to be sure, they "uprooted" themselves, aesthetically and otherwise, so as not only to "deracinate" themselves and thus set in motion and open up Romanian culture, its tradition, and styles but also to reroute and reroot them across larger geographies and thus inscribe them into the wider, trans- and supranational world. Pursuing these processes of literary radicalization, the first section of my presentation sketches out a brief history of Jewish-Romanian and Jewish-Romanian-French avant-garde, complete with its major figures, milestones, influences, and textual–contextual features; the remaining segments focus chiefly on two prominent figures of the movement, Tzara and Luca, to take a closer look at the formal and thematic mechanisms activated in their works by the dual, uprooting–rerooting, literary and cultural dynamic typical of avant-garde poetry.

1. Poetics and Politics of Uprootedness

In its various guises, Romanian avant-gardism was a highly effervescent and creative phenomenon through which Romanian culture not just finally "caught up" with European developments—a true fixation of the country's cultural ideologues—but, to a significant extent, also became, literally and otherwise, the advancing forefront of world literature and art. Here, I can only rehash some of the moments and actors of this spectacular progress. Thus, in 1916, to being with, Tzara and painter Marcel Iancu, who had been born into a Jewish family in Bucharest in 1895, cofounded, in Zürich, Dadaism, which would in turn inspire the Surrealism André Breton launched in France after 1920 and whose headway owed much of its global impact to Jewish Romanian poets and artists, including Luca, Victor Brauner, Jacques Hérold, and Jules Perahim. Around the same time, painters Iancu and M. H. Maxy, a Romanian Jew born in Brăila the same year as Iancu, were involved in the international Constructivist movement. They participated in individual and collective exhibits and, in Bucharest, ran cultural magazines such as *Integral* (1925–1927) and *Contimporanul* (1922–1932). The latter was the brainchild of Iancu and Ion Vinea. Some of the most distinguished artists of the moment took part under its auspices in a series of international Constructivist art shows organized after 1924 in the Romanian capital. Also before the Second World War broke out, the works of poets Voronca, Fondane, and Claude Sernet rippled across the Parisian avant-garde circles. During the war, back in Bucharest, Luca and Gellu Naum founded in 1940 the Romanian Surrealist group, whose membership also comprised painters like Dolfi Trost and poets such as Păun and Virgil Teodorescu. The group gained recognition on the international stage between 1945 and 1947 while, in Paris, Isou was establishing Lettrism, which cultivated a form of poetry drawn to the melodic beauty of alphabetic combinations.

This already long list of names could be further extended to include M. Blecher, H. Bonciu, and Ion Călugăru, Jewish-Romanian writers who went out of their way to promote the avant-garde in pre–Second World War Romanian fictional prose. Their primary cultural-literary sources too, with the Viennese *Sezession*, German Expressionism, and French Surrealism among them, belonged to a modernist lineage that was neither autochthonous nor limited to a single national cultural system. I hasten to point out, however, that the Romanian avant-garde had a strikingly original native precursor in Demetru Dem. Demetrescu-Buzău (1883–1923), whose pen name was Urmuz and who is known for a minimalist-absurdist prose that is similar, but in no way indebted, to French writer Alfred Jarry's. Urmuz's narratives had been circulating orally during the 1910s around Bucharest's cafés, until Arghezi published two of them, "Pâlnia și Stamate" (The Funnel and Stamate) and "Ismail și Turnavitu"

(Ismail and Turnavitu), in the magazine *Cugetul românesc* in 1922. For his followers, Urmuz embodied the very spirit of the avant-garde, and in that is comparable to Jacques Vaché, the French poet who had so much contempt for literature that he had never written any line, and who, after committing suicide—probably "absurdly," without an apparent or "trivial" motive—became an idol for the Surrealist group led by Breton. Consistently rejecting literary fame, Urmuz chose anonymity throughout his life, which he ended, without any explanation, with a self-inflicted gunshot in 1923. It was primarily the radicalism of the ethical stance implied in his abrupt departure that made him an acknowledged precursor and supreme model for all Romanian avant-garde writers. But it is beyond question that his writing as such drew them as well, and, indeed, a whole set of distinguishing features of the Urmuzian style—*anti-literary* par excellence—is noticeable in Romanian avant-garde poetry, especially in Surrealism. These include playful demythologization of cultural and political values; polemical engagement with literary tradition through parodies of consecrated forms, techniques, and communication structures from literary character and portrait to literary discourse's "literariness" and everyday linguistic constructs organized around a certain logic, myths, and literary topoi such as heroism, religiosity, metaphysical reasoning, awe before the natural sublime, and other ethical and aesthetic reactions and postures presumably befitting "elevated spirits;" wordplay and *calembour*-engendering verbal automatisms, both in use or made-up; absurd juxtapositions of logically incompatible objects and qualities; dark humor; and out-of-the-blue metamorphoses of people and things. All these were instrumental to Urmuz's subversively decompositional project, which became typical of the avant-garde as well, one that, in his wake, sought to tear apart the truisms and knee-jerk patterns of thought and expression by frustrating systematically, with method, readers' expectations regarding conventional literature's mechanical rehearsal of overused and lackluster schemes, stock phrases, and languages.

Romanian avant-garde poetry, whose beginnings can be said to coincide roughly with Urmuz's first prose experiments, was driven by a similarly intense dissatisfaction with ossified tradition, literary and otherwise. It was fairly obvious, in fact, that, during an early, transitional stage, Romanian avant-garde poets, just like their European counterparts, felt the need to set poetry free from the constraints of shopworn literary formulas that no longer reflected the *zeitgeist* at the dawn of the twentieth century. Like Jarry and Guillaume Apollinaire in France, F. T. Marinetti in Italy, or Hans Arp in Germany, Romanian poets Tzara, Vinea, and Adrian Maniu, who in 1912 formed a group around the Bucharest magazine *Simbolul* (The Symbol), began their careers by defying the hackneyed anachronisms of the belated Romanticism and Symbolism that were still dominating the poetic landscape at the time. It would take, however, ten years for an avant-garde movement proper to take shape and develop a coherent platform and distinct forms of manifestation, which happened when *Contimporanul* was launched in Bucharest. By then, Romanian modernism had already taken off with the literary magazine and circle *Sburătorul*, which had been founded by critic Eugen Lovinescu in 1919, and modernist poets such as George Bacovia, Ion Barbu, Arghezi, and Blaga had become household names on the domestic literary scene. Their post-Symbolism, hermeticism, and Expressionism, sometimes filtered through archaic-mythical and traditionalist styles and worldviews, presented the public with a modernism that seemed, and arguably was, more moderate than the radical version fostered by the literary and artistic avant-garde of the early-twentieth century, which, by comparison, determined a complete paradigm shift across a range of aesthetic media and forms.

This turn was one big gesture of contestation, a negation that, in practice, boiled down to a weeding out or an "uprooting" of traditional, overused, and "bourgeois" prescriptions, constraints, and platitudes from the hotbed of writing. Setting out to break with stylistic and even linguistic and cultural conventions, the avant-garde sought to afford absolute freedom to a poetic discourse that, instead of encoding a preexisting idea in literary form or of pointing to a certain exterior referent, generated meaning in and through the very temporality of writing, as the text unfolded under the reader's eyes. Consequently, the poem became an "openwork," as Umberto Eco would say, or a "work in progress" where the emphasis shifted away from a certain signified already implied by available commonplaces and dictionary meanings to the endless play of signifiers. In this sense, neither Romanian postmodern poetry of the last century nor that produced by subsequent generations can be imagined independently from the revolutionary avant-garde "tradition," as Mircea Cărtărescu, the leading figure of the 1980s Generation, makes it clear in his book *Postmodernismul românesc* (Romanian Postmodernism). This holds true of other literary genres and even of art as a whole. In literary prose, the avant-garde abolished the conventions of realism, those regarding place and time, as well as those concerning plot and characterization, so much so that a character could now act and be portrayed as a complex, multifaceted being, behaving in contradictory ways. Likewise, in the visual arts avant-gardism advocated, in fashions conspicuously analogous to the insurgent realignments it triggered in literature, total freedom of expression by rejecting the classical principle of mimesis and creating a self-contained world that was not beholden to the shapes and hues of the objects and phenomena recognizable in empirical reality.

Furthermore, the avant-garde revolution was not confined to aesthetic matters either. Its transforming impetus resonated loudly across society. Openly weary of the nation-state-sponsored policies and "blood-and-soil" stratagems of "enrooting," avant-gardism's innately cosmopolitan spirit broke across all sort of professional, ethnic, religious, and linguistic divides, mobilizing people belonging to a remarkable variety of sociocultural groups. It is true that, in Romania, the great majority of avant-garde figures were Jewish, but the explanation is the specific political situation of Romanian Jews. As elsewhere in Europe, in Romania the history of Jews has always been truly traumatic. Treated ordinarily as undesirable foreigners and denigrated by the state and the Church alike, they enjoyed few rights until after the end of the Second World War. In general, they were not allowed to own land, practice certain trades, occupy administrative and military positions, participate in political life, and so forth. In 1923, they were officially granted Romanian citizenship but only to lose it with the coming to power of the 1937 Octavian Goga-A. C. Cuza government. Moreover, the latter introduced new discriminatory measures and absurd anti-Semitic regulations, which would be further ramped up during the military dictatorship of Ion Antonescu

(1940–1944), one of Adolf Hitler's allies. Dead set on "purging the Romanian nation of all Jewish parasites," Marshall Antonescu issued a number of orders intended to expel the Jews from the army and remove them from public office. His government also banned "interracial" marriages, denied Jews the right to work in factories, practice law, medicine, and journalism, and enroll in state-run schools and universities. Moreover, Antonescu moved them forcibly from villages and towns to bigger cities for surveillance purposes, stripped them of property, and sentenced them to forced labor. All these measures culminated with the Jewish massacres committed by the Romanian army, starting in 1941, in Moldova, Bessarabia, and Northern Bukovina, as well as with the mass deportations of Jews from the occupied territories to the Transnistria concentration camps. As a result, from the roughly 800,000 people of Jews who had been living in the territories of "Greater Romania" and represented Europe's second largest Jewish minority, only half survived the war.

Under such circumstances, Jewish writers and artists felt, as one might expect, that their chances to "assimilate" into national tradition were scant, and so it should come as little surprise that they moved in other directions, saliently at cross-purposes with said tradition and promoting shockingly unconventional forms. Thus, before long, these authors were labeled "anarchists"—an early, 1932 book on Romanian modernism by critic Constantin I. Emilian was titled *Anarhismul poetic* (Poetic Anarchism).[2] Alongside and sometimes conflated with their "cosmopolitanism"—or, as critic G. Călinescu preferred to say, "internationalism"—their "anarchism" was widely frowned upon.[3] As a general rule, these descriptors were used pejoratively, and they were accompanied by accusations of "Bolshevism" especially in the nationalist press, which routinely denounced the Jews en masse as Bolshevik agents bent on destroying the social order. Circulated by the country's official propaganda around the late 1930s, a phrase such as "Judeo-Bolshevism" (*iudeo-bolşevism*) implied, as later theorists would also argue extensively, the charge of cosmopolitanism—indeed, as Scarpetta explains, the fight against the cosmopolitan "threat" in culture was a corollary of anti-Semitism, based as it was on the assumption that Jewish artists were inherently radical and antisocially so, championing an extreme modernism predicated on the dismantling of established conventions inside and outside art.[4] Otherwise, while a comparatively small segment of Romanian Jewry had Communist affiliations, the Bolshevism of the avant-garde was not a complete fabrication. Taking their cue from their French comrades, the majority of Romanian avant-gardists upheld the ideals of the proletarian revolution openly. Many of them actually joined the Communist Party early on, when this was operating illegally, and when the Romanian government was making no secret of its backing of the chauvinist and anti-Semitic nationalist Far Right. Variously discriminated against and socially marginalized, the avant-gardists found the idea of an egalitarian society naturally attractive, and so their political choices must have struck them as both obvious and warranted. They made no bones about their commitments either. In 1930s left-wing publications like *Viaţa imediată* (Life Unfiltered), *Cuvântul liber* (The Free Word), *Reporter, Umanitatea* (Humanity), *Meridian, Tânara generaţie* (Young Generation), *Era nouă* (New Era), the major figures of the Romanian avant-garde denounced the exploitation of the workers, the officially condoned anti-Semitism, the

Fascist threat, and the increasingly ominous specter of war, while also calling for an "engaged" or "revolutionary" literature.

Stemming from the political project lying behind the rhetoric of this journalism were specific literary genres such as "the proletarian poem," "the proletarian novel," and the "reportage poem," but the idea of the revolution largely drove the avant-gardists' work, which is why they were viewed from the get-go, according to Eugène Ionesco, as dangerous enemies who, from within the walls of their society's "fortress," conspired with secret outside forces to tear it down.[5] Therefore, there was nothing nugatory about the insistent anti-avant-garde attacks either. In a recent study, novelist and critic Stelian Tănase has made public the classified files Romania's pre–Second World War secret police (*Siguranța Statului*) was keeping on Geo Bogza, Brauner, Scarlat Callimachi, Călugăru, Gheorghe Dinu (aka Stephan Roll), Eugen Ionescu, Luca, Maxy, Naum, Pană, Perahim, and other writers for alleged subversive activities instigated by the Romanian Communist Party.[6] It bears remarking, however, that, contrary to the conclusion reached by Tănase, who maintains in his preface that Romanian avant-gardists were hoping to see the Russian tanks roll into Bucharest, the Surrealists—the last wave of Romanian avant-gardists—picked up promptly on the "ideological mechanism of enrooting" on the rise at the time, rejected it categorically, and distanced themselves, accordingly, both from Stalinism and from the Socialist Realism that, after 1947, would become the only officially approved aesthetic formula. For this very reason, the group was charged with bourgeois "decadence" and forced to break up shortly after the installation of the Communist regime. Ironically enough, the texts published by the group's members during this period, most of them written in French, are entirely apolitical, which, with another irony, only made matters worse. For, *not* engaging in politics—more exactly, declining to follow approved political scripts—was becoming fast the ultimate political heresy and, insofar as the heretics were rejecting the emerging "tradition" of conformist slogans, platitudes, and regimenting conventions, made for a subversive "uprooting" tactic.

This tactic was, of course, keyed to the *art of uprootedness* the avant-garde had always been and would remain regardless of the specific cultural-political consensus, expression codes, and collective fantasies—"kin," "people," "nation," or "party"— it has taken an exception to and disentangled itself from at one historical juncture or another. In the sense of this dissent, of this ever-vigilant critique that assumes its marginal and fluid position inside national cultural systems and astride the boundaries between them, the literary avant-garde overlaps substantially with "minor literature" as theorized so influentially by Gilles Deleuze and Félix Guattari in their Franz Kafka book.[7] As is well known, for the French philosophers, the Jewish-Czech author is *the* "minor" writer, a reading challenged lately by Pascale Casanova in an article eventually worked into *The World Republic of Letters*.[8] Personally, I find Deleuze and Guattari's analysis apt not only as far as Kafka goes but also as a platform for working out a literary model as well as for employing the latter to frame a discussion of the avant-garde that would not lose sight of the twin, formal-aesthetic and cosmopolitan-internationalist gambit of avant-gardist deracination strategy. Thus, over and against official, nationally enrooting injunctions in culture, politics, and so forth, the

Romanian avant-garde has pursued "internationalizing" goals from the outset. Since interchanges with germane European trends and phenomena were so vital to it, its very modus operandi was transgressive in a trans- and extraterritorial way, which is why the avant-garde devotees ignored the expectations and calls to ply one's trade solely within national borders. Not only did they write for foreign magazines and took part in conferences, shows, and similar events abroad, but a host of artists based in other countries had their work featured in Romanian publications such as *Punct* [Period], for instance, the 1924-established "magazine of international constructivist art," and in modern art exhibits in Romania. Furthermore, de- and reterritorialization did not involve just physical territory. It affected language too, and not only through what Jewish Romanian avant-gardists did in and to the national idiom but also through what they did outside it, in other languages. Uprooting themselves linguistically, they either exiled themselves in a *sui generis* Romanian, a truly international poetic idiom of their own making, or stepped outside their homeland's main language altogether by switching to French, the lingua franca of the early-twentieth-century arts. This exile became literal during and after the Second World War, when many members of Romania's avant-garde expatriated themselves. Their enthusiasm for Zionism was low, and this seems to be a main reason few of them settled in Israel, choosing instead other adoptive countries, primarily France, the quintessentially cosmopolitan home of avant-gardism, and quickly receiving wide recognition as major figures of modern poetry and art.[9]

2. Tzara, the National Blues, and *dictée automatique*

The true measure of these authors' distaste for enrooting languages, entrenched habits, and ingrown culture overall is the thematic-formal mechanics of avant-garde poetry. Immediately noticeable is the anti-national or, better yet, *a*national thrust of this literature, in which references that otherwise usually serve more descriptive, inevitably "localizing" purposes do not point specifically to an autochthonous, *Romanian* "national specificity," to a "national soul," or to other putative markers and "roots" of "Romanianness." If the Romantic-populist myths swirling around a "uniquely" Romanian, natural or ethnic sublime were identitarian indexes in the literature of the past—if, in other words, their reiterations in a certain text made that text "Romanian,"—then it would be only fair to say that Romanian avant-garde literature is hardly Romanian. Whenever such traditionalist *idées fixes* turn up, it is only to be subjected to parody and critique. For instance, from his early, pre-avant-garde poems, published around the First World War, Tzara announces his decision to break definitively with poetry as it had been written until then, rejecting it as contrived and parodying its clichés. What annoys him most is those emotions, postures, and notions deemed "poetic," such as the saccharine adulation of nature, the presumed "purity" of rural life, spiritualized love, and religiosity. Anticipating later, more outrageous Dadaist assaults on the hypocrisy and falseness of a world stuck in vacuous attitudes, the poet invites his lover to the town's public park to "scandalize the city" in "Înserează" (Dusk Is Falling) and his friend (Vinea) to strip off his clothes "to scandalize the priest, to cheer up the girls" in "Vacanță în provincie" (Countryside Vacation). In "Glas" (Voice), he wonders why "Lia, blonde Lia" has not hanged herself, for he would have enjoyed watching her dangle like a "ripe pear." This desire to shock, to violate bourgeois "common sense" would soon become the defining features of the avant-garde. "Vacanță în provincie," which appeared in the inaugural, October 4, 1915 issue of the magazine *Chemarea* (The Call), already captures this rebelliousness accurately in terms of theme and genre, insofar as the text disembowels the classical conventions of "poetic" scenes of nature, as well as at the level of discursive logic:

> The still birds in the sky/Like smudges left by flies/Servants chatting in front of the stable/And on the path the cattle's manure has bloomed // The gentleman in black and his little girl go down the street/The beggars' joy at dusk/But at home I have a Polichinelle with little bells/To entertain my sadness when you cheat on me // My soul is a mason returning from work/Memory that smells like a clean drugstore/ Tell me, old maid, what was once upon a time/And you, cousin, let me know when the cuckoo will sing ...[10]

Characteristic of this poem and, in effect, of Tzara's entire pre-Dada stage is the complex, uprooting–rerooting mechanism the author cranks up to rub the reader the wrong way, as it were, by upending, one by one, the banalities that have infiltrated his or her aesthetic-literary education and cultural formation. If the first line seems to wave us into the enchanting atmosphere of traditional poetry through the quasi-transcendent suggestion of birds frozen in atemporal flight, the second plunges us into the "anti-aesthetic" realms of the trite and the paltry. Now likened to the dirty traces of bugs, the trajectories of the same travelers of the skies nip in the bud any nascent lofty "poetic emotion." The same strategy of syntagmatic combinations based on opposition rather than contiguity informs the following lines, which crystallize around antithetic categories such as the elevated and the sublime, on one side, and the sordid and the scatological, on the other. By virtue of this deracination-with-re-embedding formal and cultural poetics, relationships of contrast are logically rerouted as relationships of similitude, while paratactic structures glue together disparate realities whose juxtaposition is devoid of any apparent logic. Not only are causal explanations conspicuously absent, but the poet also constantly pokes, jostles, and provokes an increasingly bewildered reader, who must be wondering why the gentleman in black and the child bring such joy to the beggars, and why this detail, registered so matter-of-fact, is somehow set off against the sadness the poet feels when his lover betrays him. The free verse, ostentatiously prosaic poetry, and, conversely, poetic prose, alongside the collage-like, arbitrary agglutinations of heterogeneous information, and the jarringly illogical analogies are among the stylistic hallmarks of the Romanian avant-garde's uprooting–reenrooting poetics.

Published in the next issue of *Chemarea*, Tzara's poem "Furtuna și cântecul dezertorului" (The Storm and the Deserter's Song) is a masterpiece of anti-war literature, flying in the face of the warmongering hysteria and bellicose nationalism that marred the era and rendered Romania the suffocating environment where all artists could do was dream up their at once hope-shattering and hope-giving deracination scenarios. It is in this world about to plunge into the inferno of the Great War that the author, born Samuel Rosenstock, must have thought up his famous *nom de plume*, in which texts such as "Furtuna și cântecul dezertorului" help us discern the reason Tzara exiled himself to France in 1919. To be sure, Romania gave Tzara the nationalist blues around 1915, made him feel depressingly out of place and "sad in [his own] country," "trist în țară," *triste en son pays* (or *tzara*, as the Romanian word for "country" would read in French transliteration), and pushed him down the international pathway of Tristan Tzara's celebrated career. Surveying the war-torn homeland, the poem canvases an apocalyptically incoherent landscape whose chaotic violence seems to shake up, disjoin, and then recouple the text's contiguous syntactic units, and so, much like this martial geography cannot possibly provide a stage for the high-drama of heroic sacrifice—the speaker is a deserter—"cântecul dezertorului" (the deserter's song) founders into incoherence:

Light blew out of the exploding shells/and sparked off the lightning bolts of our anger/Broke up into five fingers like God's hand/We catch up with those stragglers and cut them down/Crush the corpses left in the snow/Open a window into the flooded dark/Through the valleys that sucked in the enemies/We killed them all the way to their bluest horizon // Frost: breaks up bones, feasts on flesh/We let our heart cry // ... On scabby hills down into the gulley/Is like the skull's eye socket/ We found shelter for our storm terrors/And one of us just started babbling/In there // I harvested his ramblings—as many/Clear-sky moonscapes are getting through to me like ghouls/As needed to make you a shark-tooth necklace/Swirling into whorls of bad dreams. // The rusted-out crosshairs aim fire/We get into the mouth of the faraway/And, under the fort's row of teeth, the others/Are waiting // It is so dark only the words are glowing.[11]

Later Dadaist poems by Tzara and others would take such rejection of ideological, literary, and linguistic conventions to an extreme. Formally, these "babblings" constitute one big deconstructive enterprise, pursuing their decompositional goals at all levels, from punctuation to semantics. The outcome is a "phonetic" kind of poetry partial to particular sound associations and dissociations, to collages whose only genetic principle seems to be randomness, to strings of unrelated words sometimes in multiple idioms, or to the *dictée automatique* that becomes increasingly prevalent across a range of avant-garde strains. It is as if the authors of these experiments turn to "automatic dictation" and to language's own illogisms and automatisms out of fear of being co-opted by more "disciplined" and "rational" forms of expression back into "entrenching" national idioms and ideologically fraught groupthink. For, what one may arguably distinguish in Romanian avant-gardists' wrestling with language is the same problem of the "world" Ludwig Wittgenstein's notion of "linguistic play" touches on, viz., a concept of language reinvented or appropriated for a usage tainted as little as possible by "cloistering," "political" interests—in our case, particularly those of a national community and its institutional and culturally intellectually "disciplinary" apparatus. As the reader will remember, Wittgenstein famously wrote in his *Tractatus Logico-Philosophicus* that "The limits of my language are the limits of my world," a dictum that may well serve as a motto for most avant-garde poetry after the momentous breakthrough Tzara accomplished by playing with language so as to "replay" it into sound and meaning poetic constellations liable to push the frontiers of what can be uttered and experienced in order to unleash other expressive possibilities and other worlds with them.[12]

It is these intertwined, cosmopolitan emendations and expansions of one's language, cultural repertoire, and material ambiance that gave birth to *pictopoezia*. A version of Dadaist collage, "picture poetry" or "picto-poetry" was introduced by Brauner and Voronca in the October 1924 issue of the *75 HP* magazine and was designed to fuse poetry and painting into a new interarts alloy. This cosmopolitanism of genre became one of form broadly in the "linguistic" poetry promoted by the same publication. Consisting of random word combinations that defy logic à la Tzara's wartime ramblings and borrowing their material from multiple idioms, these poems are as many critical statements on canned language and its debilitating effects on thought. Literature of this sort started appearing in other publications as well, and, in fact, one of the best examples of this kind, Cosma's absurdly titled "automatist" text "Binomul cu exponentul de argint" (The Binome with the Silver Exponent), came out in the second issue of the magazine *Punct* in November 1924:

> (c'est un conte à dormir debout que il y a trois jours me télégraphia de Venise et de Philibert Le Voyer seigneur de Lignerolles et de Bellefille ma nourrice nommée la Sultane aux seins de fine ouate). inventează prohibițiunea în nocturn cu ambalaj megaloman, scena reprezintă un om—linda dama en la cama. le binôme est un bonhomme à quatorze abonnés 3, 7, 8, 11, c, M, x, f, ut, fa, mi bémol, Londres et 100 cartes de visites. o dar pieptănul matrimonială e complect tifos. îngerul mecanic plictisit în omnibus maniac de aceea domnul meu, mylord, sênor, mein herr, monsieur, signore, bunăziua Doamnă! dispariția mâine—mâna dreaptă în suspensie. cette négation armée d'un perroquet: hic, ubi vir non est, ut sit adulterium, circ circular circular circulară în circatrice circumcisă etc. atunci ți-ai fost mamă cu un dinam. semnul de întrebare a fost mult mai mare la început. stinge steaua no. 8 din stalul al III-lea. eu mă elefant tu te elefanți el se elefante (nu el e fante), aplauze în contumacie sau costum național și tren mixt incognito, un tânăr belgian negru fuge răgușit. trapez la trap se accident. steamer în pantofi de lac ent haupft vers l'amérique con paraguanto. în gând tramwaye simultane. dansatori pe sârmă ghimpată imită gloanțe dum-dum. 1740 etaje la pătrat. Trotuarul automat întrerupe: le crocodile mystique est téléphone PUNCT[13]

A poetic prelude to the linguistic bacchanalia of *Finnegans Wake*, Cosma's work is as translatable—or untranslatable—as Joyce's 1939 book. Bits and pieces in French and Romanian, the odd quote from Roman poet Martial, words, phrases, and even entire "logical" sentences are recognizable, and so they can be translated individually.

But, from the outset, this self-acknowledged "conte à dormir debout" proves to be the ultimate cock-and-bull story of poetic meaning itself, suggesting that disparate references could be isolated and made sense of ("this scene represents a human being," "one hundred business cards," etc.) if only they stayed so, that is, isolated from one another. The problem is that they do not. Instead, they slide homophonically into one another ("elefante [... el e fante") or, vice versa, decline to fulfill each other's semantic expectations, and wind up throwing everything out of whack.

3. Luca, or the Art of Stammering

Born Zolman Locker in Bucharest in 1913 and resettling in France in 1952, Luca takes the absurdist din of this polyglot cosmopolis to a whole other level. In Cosma's incoherent-absurdist Babel, people may be rambling, and so the overall meaning may elude us too, but we do understand words and expressions, and we may even get a pun or two. In Luca, there is no language to speak of and in any more but only babbling. A fundamentally cosmopolitan artist and central figure of the Romanian avant-garde, he distinguished himself in the context of international Surrealism through an ingenious method that intrigued, among others, Deleuze. In his 1996 dialogue with Claire Parnet, Deleuze called Luca "a great poet among the greatest" and credited him with the invention of a babbling kind of writing—a "prodigious stammering [*bégaiement*], his own"—or a *style*. For, according to Deleuze, developing a style, which is to say (if redundantly), a personal one, means nothing else but "to stammer in one's own language," speaking one's own language like a stranger and so putting one's own language to a "minor" use.[14] Deleuze's description of Luca's "deracinating"—and self-deracinating—handling of language is on target, but worth adding right away is that the poet behaved "like a stranger" not only in his adoptive language and culture but also in Romania and in Romanian, as his early work shows. One of the best examples in this sense is "Niciodată destul" (Never Enough), a poem written around the same time as the better-known "Passionnément" and in the same, "prodigiously stuttering" style.

But Luca "stammered" not only in his writing. He did so in his life as well. Long before "mumbling with method" as an artist, he had made a point to acknowledge his disruptive presence in his own country and language, the incoherence and strangeness he was bound to spawn as a "stranger" self-exiled in his own tongue and native land, and it can be argued that, no matter where he lived, he always remained an *étranjuif*, as he called himself. An "alienjew"—or, better still, a "foreignew"—like Kafka and Celan, he was the consummate *eccentric* writer always busy disrupting and decentering deeply seated forms, values, and himself ultimately, resisting the pull of various centers of discourse, culture, and power. Nor would he try to rein in this instinctive, genuinely avant-gardist, centrifugal impulse. In fact, he flaunted this eccentricity from his very first poems. As critic Iulian Toma has observed, the majority of these epic-lyrical texts, which came out in the avant-garde magazine *Alge* in the early 1930s, are organized around the same narrative scheme, namely, the repression of any kind of dissent by the establishment.[15] Their narrator-protagonist is usually an alienated figure, an outsider at war with the bourgeois status quo, much though the idea of class struggle is not explicitly spelled out yet. Variations on the rebel and pariah themes include burglars, murderers, and rapists, while the poet's avatar seems to be a dog, as he lets on in the 1933 poem "Câinii ar putea juca un rol important în relațiile mele intime cu oamenii" (Dogs Could Play an Important Role in My Intimate Relationships with People"):

> and as I have told you what pains me is that my dog is a poet/and never will you be able to realize that at the moment I'm indeed walking down the middle of the street/and that in reality the poet and dog gherasim luca is howling in the middle of the road/and that in reality the poet and dog gherasim luca is howling in the middle of the road/this dog is a valuable dog/we will send him our congratulations and rank him the 3642nd in Romanian literature.[16]

Other poems are built around eroticism, another major theme that fits in with the Surrealist project to "transform the world, to change life."[17] Some of them unfold purely phantasmagoric, libido-driven scenarios.[18] As for the texts published between 1933 and 1937 in the second series of *Alge* and in other left-wing magazines such as *Viața imediată*, *Cuvântul liber*, or *Meridian*, most of them are in the mold of the "proletarian poetry" theorized by the author in a 1935 set of articles from *Cuvântul liber*, where Luca advocates a "revolutionary" poetry that needs, in both form and content, to integrate into "the process of doing away with existing frameworks."[19] Part and parcel of this program is an all-out attack on the aesthetic, which Luca targets as a core category of "purist," "transcendent" bourgeois poetry. To overcome the latter's aery conformism, "proletarian poetry," contends Luca, must first gut conventional lyricism's generic infrastructure by incorporating ostentatiously prose-like, bare-bones reportage sprinkled with outrageous gestures and crude language such as that tested by Bogza in poetry collections such as the 1929 *Jurnal de sex* (Sex Diary) and *Poemul invectivă* (Profanity Poem).[20] In the texts enacting this antiaesthetic, Luca's radical views are on full display, positioning the author as an anarchist and *agent provocateur* instigating violent opposition against the alienated and alienating world. Thus, in "Tragedii cari trebuie să se întâmple" (Tragedies That Should Happen), he calls on the poets with "fingers shaking like poplars and as short as bullets" to break the shop windows on the big boulevards;[21] in "Poem de dragoste" (Love Poem), he tells us how he smeared his beloved with "all the trash in the street," spat on her, and dropped her into a sewer;[22] in "Poem cu un domn în frac" (Poem Featuring a Gentleman in a Tuxedo), we learn how he shot a certain "gentleman in a tuxedo" because of "the social class to which [that individual] belonged";[23] and, in "Sfânta împărtășanie" (Holy Communion), we find out that, after working late at the "gas factory," he let himself seduced by a bourgeois lady with "curly hair and a car" only to end up, after a night of lovemaking in her "luxurious apartment," with his mouth symbolically "filled with spit," as his class distaste got eventually the better of him.[24] The central theme of these poems, if there is indeed one, could be "class struggle" itself, as they are built around the antithesis between exploiters and the exploited. "Poemul oamenilor blânzi" (The Poem of Gentle Folk), for example, exposes the hypocrisy of the "stuffed" bourgeois. The fake smile, the poet warns, should not fool the starving workers: "beware, comrades, of the godly smile of gentle folk/.../they are gentle because they are not hungry/and those who are full have plenty of time on their hands to feel pity for those who have nothing to eat/but they continue to be full/and you continue to have nothing to eat// comrades,/the burglars who break into people's homes at night to rob them/are just as dangerous, whether they are masked or not/their mask, their smile, their pious words of Church and God/have to be unmasked, once for all."[25] The plain, prosaic diction, purged of superfluous stylistic embellishments, and the vehement, equally non- and even antipoetic tone are defining features of this poetry. They all work according to the same "negative" logic of deracination not to "enrich" poetic language in an ornamental sense but to take it in the opposite direction of the "deliberately impoverishment" Deleuze and Guattari deem paramount to minor literature practices. This stylistic and political reduction of the poetic to the antipoetic is also in play in the two novels—or antinovels, rather—Luca published in 1933 (*Roman de dragoste* [Love Novel]) and, respectively, in 1937 (*Fata Morgana*). They both pursue the same programmatic goal of undermining consecrated literary conventions and "beautiful," "logical" artistic representation more generally. In *Roman de dragoste*, this objective is clear from the outset:

> this railway station is the dirtiest railway station in the world no wonder that every night so many desperate women commit suicide in this railway station no lantern, no porter, no lemonade seller, no tree, no bon voyage. Tomorrow I'm going to see my friend, the minister of communications and tell him to tear down this dirty railway station in which so many desperate women end up dead. I think that you've guessed from the very beginning that the novel I want to write is a love novel, perhaps the most terrible love novel. Needless to say, the only one to blame is the minister of communications.[26]

After 1937, however, given the increasingly hostile political climate, Luca was forced to abandon proletarian literature, and, after failing to move to Paris, which had been under Nazi occupation since 1940, went back home and switched to an oneiric literature with a Surrealist bent. But his writing did not lose its subversively "uprooting" edge. Thus, in 1947, the Bucharest Surrealist press Negarea Negației (Negation of Negation) brought out his volume *Niciodată destul* (Never Enough), which anticipated the French experiments that would later make him famous. One long poem, the book is one of the few texts published by Luca in Romanian after 1945 and a deliberate attempt to sabotage language's meaning-making mechanisms:

> propopopopoporpor proporporporți
> proporțiporți porțiproporporți proporpopor poporpopor
> proporțisorți proposorți proposorți prea mulți morți
> prea multe torțe propoforțe prea multe propoforțe
> propropropormor promoprotozor mori în zori proton

proporproton care ton protonproprotoni care toni
protoni propropropriul meu plop ploproprod
aprodafrod proprafrodiziacprozaicpro propor
porpor por în cor rog por pentru popor
propor rog popor să mori
contrapropopor fără bor la popor
la cotor un singur por proporporpor
proporproporți proporțiporți
proporționproporționapro
proporționpion prospion propor
proporspion spion la pion la pian
prosperi popor protosferă prompt la popor
proporporpor
proporporporporporc un porc de popor
proporționpopor proporționapropro apropo
asta propun propropropopun un porc
de popor proporțional[27]

Once again, while basic grammatical units and phrases are in play and, as such, are identifiable, what dominates and "unwrites" the poem as much as it carries it along is something comparable to the Derridean "endless deferral of meaning." The text zeroes in on a word, "proportional," takes it apart relentlessly, and breaks it into syllables that then, through mechanical repetition and aleatory recombination with other homophonically related syllables, morphemes, and chunks of words, generate a fluid poetic assemblage that can be seen as a *mise-en-scène* of the thought process close to the pre-discursive stage where the obscure and meandering itineraries of the unconscious are still visible. With them, some of the author's obsessions—and possible clues for an interpretation of the text—rise to the surface. A closer look at the poem may thus stabilize its quicksilver flow and volatile linguistic combinations and puns into, say, a critique of "the people" and of nationalist ideology. Arguably, it is in this direction that most of the references point, including the rabidly anti-Semitic behavior of his Romanian conationals during the war. Phrases such as "too many dead people," "too many torches," "dead at dawn," "pray for the people," "pray the people will die," and "a pig-like people" paint an unflattering portrayal of the citizenry and country for and in which Luca felt like a stateless *străinevreu*, at once a foreigner and a Jew—a "foreignew," as he would describe himself.

This self-identification as *străin*—"alien" and "strange" at once—also entails a "strangeness" or estrangement in and of poetic language and language overall. Quite telling is in this respect Luca's French poem "Passionnément," in which critics such as Moshe Idel have seen a "phonetic kabbala."[28] Here, writing accrues a mystically initiatory dimension via an ontological "transmutation" of reality that obtains in and *qua* language through a formal "outrooting" or liberation of contents but bears on the poetic subject as well. In a revealing 1978 interview, Luca disclosed that

In the language that helps me designate objects ordinarily, a word has only one or two meanings, and so, in it, the potential of meaningful sonority is hemmed in. Now, if you break open the form in which this potential is trapped, new relations and, with them, new possibilities arise. This expressive play of sound is enhanced, and the secrets lying dormant inside words come out. Whoever listens to these transformed words is waved into a vibrant world that engages that person physically and mentally. If you set free the breath held captive inside language, every word becomes a signal …. [For] the word is nothing but the material foundation of a search whose end is to transmute the real …. The poem is an operational space wherein the word undergoes a series of sound mutations, each of its facets issuing forth a multiplicity of meanings with which it is already charged. Nowadays, I dwell in a dimension in which the hubbub and silence clash, where the poem takes the very form of the soundwave it has set off. Better put yet, the poem effaces itself in the face of its own upshots. In other words, I become oral, speech-like—I am "vocalized" by my own writing.[29]

Writing-as-vocalization, as "sonorous" disappearance of the poet himself, whose obsessive goal is to "destroy language, to deconstruct its Freudian legacy," as French writer Sarane Alexandrian remarked, is one reason Luca appeared to the same fellow Surrealists as "a very tragic man."[30] But, of course, this is not just a matter of appearance. For it speaks to the same uprooting and self-uprooting poetics and, by the same token, to Luca's profoundly cosmopolitan understanding and exercise of minor literature.

In an identically Deleuzian and Guattarian vein, in which the struggle with language and personal existential torments alike dramatize the same, aesthetic as well as ethnocultural problematic of Kafkaesque deracination and self-deracination, marginalization and self-marginalization, the poet is also in the company of Celan, Issou, and many other Jewish-Romanian luminaries of the European avant-garde and modernism. The most highly acclaimed among them all, Celan, for example, shared Luca's background, lived through the same traumatizing history, and built a career along similar lines. Born Paul Antschel into a German-speaking Jewish family from Cernăuți in 1920, when the town, along with its surrounding region, Northern Bukovina, still belonged to Romania, he did write in Romanian too but preferred German. In 1948, he moved to Paris where, in 1970, anticipating Luca's 1994 final liberating act of uprooting, committed suicide by jumping in the Seine. After an apprenticeship to Romantic-Symbolist poetry between 1938 and 1944, during which time he wrote in German, Celan left for Bucharest and started writing in Romanian and in a different style, which was influenced by Surrealists such as Luca, Naum, Păun, and Teodorescu. The inspiration they provided would reverberate throughout Celan's work, marking its obscurity, strangeness, and hallucinating mix of realistic detail and dream-like scenes. Initially published in Petre Solomon's Romanian translation under the title "Tangoul morții" (The Tango of Death) in *Contemporanul* in May 1947, Celan's masterpiece, "Todesfuge," clearly echoes this influence. Pulling himself out of his native landscape a few years after the war during which his parents had died in Transnistria's extermination camps, Celan did not simply return to German as to a more accommodating, presumably more "international" instrument of expression. Instead, he sought to destroy and recreate it poetically, reinventing it in response to what the language and writing in it became culturally, politically, emotionally, and otherwise in the wake of the Holocaust. This reinvention, this de- and concomitantly reconstruction of the linguistic medium and of the literary-cultural intertextuality built into it or informed by it had made Celan, too, a favorite example and source for philosophers and critics. As is well known, Jacques Derrida dwells at length on the poet's amphibological *shibboleths*.[31] More notably yet, several German critics, with George Steiner among them, have commented that even Celan's late poems leave the impression of having been "translated" from German.[32] Made by George Steiner among others, this point does not so much imply that Celan's command of the language is somehow lacking as it hints at the idiom's deracinating and deterritorializing handling in a poetry that gets its subversive, compositional and decompositional energies from its experimental beginnings. Along with the Romanian Surrealists and avant-gardists of the wartime years, Celan strove to accomplish a "total revolution" in the arts as much as in social life. They all dedicated themselves to a radical and radically liberating transformation of expression and of the human. Thus, they set their ambitiously cosmopolitan agenda around an absolute, unnegotiable freedom idea, which they brought to bear on a wide panoply of enrooting and uprooting instruments, sites, forms, and concepts, from native language, genre, literary tradition, community, and nation to international style, revolutionary pathos, and hunger for the bigger world.

Notes

1   The main cosmopolitan themes are, writes Scarpetta, "the impossible community, a lack of a sense of belonging, [and] an individuality irreducible to 'roots' or 'social relationships.'" See Guy Scarpetta, *Elogiu cosmopolitismului*, trans. Petruța Spânu (Iași: Polirom, 1997), 82. Ideologically, and very simply speaking, cosmopolitanism values, according to Scarpetta, the first member of binary oppositions such as internationalism/nationalism, diaspora/native country, discourse/nature, individual/species, universal/local, and progress/regression. As the critic specifies, the avant-garde seeks to jam "the mechanism of enrooting" of culture through irreverence toward origins, national traditions, "racial patrimony," and "purity of language," as well as through transgressions of all kinds of territorial, linguistic, and cultural borders (85).

2   Constantin I. Emilian, *Anarhismul românesc* (Bucharest: Institutul de arte grafice "Bucovina"—I. E. Torouțiu, 1932).

3   In 1941, at the height of the fascist dictatorship, G. Călinescu published his *Istoria literaturii române de la origini până în present* (History of Romanian Literature from Its Origins to the Present). The book quickly became Romanian criticism's national benchmark and established a national literary canon that has remained virtually unchallenged to this day. The political climate of the mid-1940s exerted a strong influence on the *History*, which concludes, quite revealingly, with an essay about "national specificity." This coda teems with old, racist and anti-Semitic biases and preconceptions, which during the war became widely accepted. "Jews, naturally few within the majority population," claims Călinescu,

are present in our literature as they are in all others, but they remain a factor lying outside [our] racial circle, serving as a bridge between the national and the universal .... [Jewish writers] are well-informed disseminators of the newest trends, anti-classicists, modernists, losing sleep over tormenting issues. They compensate for the inertia of tradition by forcing it to reinvent itself. Their genuine humanitarianism transforms, in terms suggestive of a higher Christian perspective, a conservative spirit that could otherwise degenerate into closed-mindedness. These traits are tied into typically irritating flaws such as a total lack of interest in creation as one's ultimate goal, exaggerated "existentialism," the disavowal of criticism—which criticism, we, as a constructive race, are in need of—[and] a humanitarianism pushed as far as to deny our national rights and specific characteristics. Due to such tactless behavior, here as everywhere else, Jews bring up on themselves periodically all kinds of troubles. (*Istoria literaturii române de la origini pînă în prezent,* 2nd ed., preface and ed. by Alexandru Piru [Bucharest: Minerva, 1982], 976)

Regarding the Jewish Romanian writers discussed in the *History,* worth noting is that, while Călinescu takes them to task for their alleged "Judaic tendentiousness" and unwillingness to limit themselves to aesthetic matters, he reads their work ideologically, assessing it from a saliently nationalist standpoint. Adding insult to injury, he routinely fails to differentiate between writers and their fictional characters, censuring the former for the latter's ideas.

4   Thus, for instance, poet Horia Stamatu maintained in an article published in the far-right-wing newspaper *Buna Vestire* in 1937 that "left-wing literature and art (the avant-garde) go hand in hand with left-wing politics, ... sullying the things this nation cherishes most and putting on a show of a 'spirituality' that is a mere cover for the idea of class struggle." The fragment is cited by Gellu Naum, Paul Păun, and Virgil Teodorescu in their collective manifesto *Critica mizeriei* (Bucharest: Colecția Suprarealistă, 1945), 15.

5   Ionesco defined the avant-garde as "opposition and rupture," considering the avant-garde writer the qintessential opponent of the "system." On this issue, see Eugène Ionesco's essay "Discours sur l'avant-garde," in his book *Notes et contre-notes* (Paris: Gallimard, 1998), 77–78.

6   See Stelian Tănase, *Avangarda românească în arhivele Siguranței* (Iași: Polirom, 2008).

7   According to Deleuze and Guattari, "minor" (or "marginal") literature should be understood not as qualitatively inferior to "major" literature but as any kind of literature that relates subversively ("revolutionarily") to the latter. Therefore, "'minor' no longer refers to a particular literature but to the revolutionary tendencies of any literature nested inside a so-called major (i.e., instituted, officially recognized) literature." Thus, "minor" designates the subversive function of this literature in relation to mainstream literature and culture and to their institutions and centers of power. In "deterritorializing" a certain national or vernacular language, "minor" literature becomes politically charged, setting itself up in irreversible opposition not only to official literary culture and this culture's values but also to the "languages of power." "To deterritorialize" the national idiom, then, means "to oppose the oppressed character of this language to its oppressive quality, to find points of non-culture and underdevelopment, linguistic Third World zone through which language escapes and 'breathes,' an animal grafts itself into structures, and

an assemblage forms." See Gilles Deleuze and Félix Guattari, *Kafka. Pentru o literatură minoră*, trans. and prefaced by Bogdan Ghiu (Bucharest: Ed. ART, 2007), 31.

8 Pascale Casanova first critiques—not very convincingly, to my mind—Deleuze and Guattari's reading of Kafka in her essay "Literature as a World," which came out in *New Left Review* 31 (January–February 2005): 85.

9 Before settling in Paris, B. Fundoianu had adamantly insisted in the preface to his 1922 book *Imagini și cărți din Franța* that, far from having a distinct character, Romanian literature had until then been "a mere parasite" of French literature and therefore should be regarded as its appendage. See B. Fundoianu, *Imagini și cărți din Franța*, ed. Vasile Teodorescu, trans. Sorin Mărculescu (Bucharest: Minerva, 1980), 24.

10

Pe cer păsările nemișcate/Ca urmele ce lasă muștele/Stau de vorbă servitori în pragul grajdului/Și-au înflorit pe cărare rămășițele dobitoacelor // Trece pe stradă domnul în negru cu fetița/ Bucuria cerșetorilor la înserare/Dar am acasă un Polichinelle cu clopoței/Să-mi distreze întristarea când mă-nșeli // Sufletul meu e un zidar care se întoarce de la lucru/Amintire cu miros de farmacie curată/ Spune-mi, servitoare bătrână, ce era odată ca niciodată,/Și tu verișoară cheamă-mi atenția când o să cânte cucul ...

The poem was published in *Chemarea* 1 (1915): 12.

11

A plesnit lumi\na din obuze/Și a crăpat fulger în mânia noastră/Ca mâna Dumnezeului în cinci degete s-a despicat/Ajungem din urmă cetele și le culcăm/ Stâlcim stârvurile lepădate în zăpadă/Deschidem întunericului înecat fereastră/ Prin văile ce-au supt dușmanii ca ventuze/I-am ucis până în depărtarea lor cea mai albastră, // Gerul: oasele fărâmă, carnea mănâncă/Noi lăsăm inima să plângă .... // Pe dealuri leproase în văgăună/E ca ochiul craniului/Ne-am adăpostit noi spaima de furtună/Și pornise unul să vorbească fără șir/Acolo. // Am cules vorbele lui—câte/Îmi pătrund ca vârcolaci seninătățile lunare/Să-ți fac mărgele cu dinți de rechin/Ce joacă vârtejuri de vise urâte. // Ochiul de rugină mâncat, foc îndreaptă/Noi intrăm în gura depărtării/Și sub șirul dinților de fort, ceilalți/ Așteaptă /E atât de întuneric, că numai vorbele-s lumină.

This is the original text for Tzara's "Furtuna și cântecul dezertorului," in *Chemarea* 2 (1915): 26–27.

12 Ludwig Wittgenstein, *Tractatus logico-philosophicus*, trans. Mircea Dumitriu and Mircea Flonta (Bucharest: Humanitas, 2012), 167.

13 Mihail Cosma, "Binomul cu exponentul de argint," *Punct* 2 (1924): 3.

14 Gilles Deleuze and Claire Parnet, *Dialogues II*, trans. Hugh Tomlinson and Barbara Habberjam (New York: Columbia University Press, 2002), 4.

15 Iulian Toma, *Gherasim Luca ou l' intransigeante passion d' être* (Paris: Honoré Champion, 2012), 87.

16 The poem came out in *Alge* 2, no. 1 (March 1933): 4.

17 André Breton, *Les vases communicantes* (Paris: Gallimard, 1970), 170.

18 On the eroticism of these poems, see Toma, *Gherasim Luca ou l' intransigeante passion d' être*, 90. Representative texts of this sort include "Femeia Domenica d'Aguistti" (The Woman Domenica d'Aguistti), published in *Alge* 1, no. 6 (July 5, 1931): 1, and

"Se caută potcoave de inimă moartă" (Horseshoes of Dead Heart Wanted), which appeared in the magazine *Muci* (Snot) (February 7, 1932): 2.

19 Gherasim Luca, "Denaturarea poeziei" (The Denaturation of Poetry) in *Cuvântul liber* 27 (May 11, 1935): 5.

20 Gherasim Luca, "Prezenţa poeziei" (The Presence of Poetry) in *Cuvântul liber* 17 (March 2, 1935): 5.

21 "Tragedii cari trebuie să se întâmple" came out in *Viaţa imediată* 1 (December 1933): 3.

22 "Poem de dragoste" was published in *Alge* 2 (April 1933): 2.

23 "Poem cu un domn in frac" appeared in *Alge* 2 (April 1933): 3.

24 "Sfânta împărtăşanie" came out in *Meridian* 11 (1937): 9.

25 "Poemul oamenilor blânzi" was published in *Cuvântul liber*, 43, September 1, 1933, p. 3.

26 In the original, the text reads:

> gara asta e cea mai murdară gară din lume nu e de mirare că în fiecare noapte se sinucid atâtea femei disperate în gara asta nici un felinar, nici un hamal, nici un vânzător de limonadă, nici un pom, nici un voiaj bun. mâine am să mă duc la prietenul meu ministrul comunicaţiilor şi am să-i spun să desfiinţeze gara asta murdară în care atâtea femei disperate îşi găsesc sfârşitul. Cred că de la început aţi bănuit că romanul pe care vreau să-l scriu e un roman de dragoste, poate cel mai teribil roman de dragoste. Singurul vinovat e desigur ministrul comunicaţiilor.

See Gherasim Luca, *Roman de dragoste* (Love Novel), in *Inventatorul iubirii* (The Inventor of Love), ed. Ion Pop (Cluj-Napoca: Editura Dacia, 2003), 101.

27 Gherasim Luca, *Niciodată destul* (Bucharest: Negaţia negaţiei, 1947).

28 See Moshe Idel's *Kabbalah and Eros* (New Haven, CT: Yale University Press, 2005).

29 Luca's interview with Serge Bricianier, "Gherasim Luca and Serge Bricianier, "Le poeme s'éclipse devant ses conséquences," *Oiseau-tempête* 2, no. 4 (Hiver 1998): 32–33.

30 Nina Zivancevic, *With Sarane Alexandrian in Paris*, http://nyartsmagazine-.com/67/ nina.htm. Accessed December 31, 2002.

31 On Derrida and Celan, see in particular the philosopher's *Sovereignties in Question: The Poetics of Paul Celan*, ed. Thomas Dutoit and Outi Pasanen (New York: Fordham University Press, 2005).

32 George Steiner makes a number of such references to translation, poetry in general, and Celan's work in *The Poetry of Thought: From Hellenism to Celan* (New York: New Directions), 2011.

9

Communicating Vessels: The Avant-Garde, Antimodernity, and Radical Culture in Romania between the First and the Second World Wars

Paul Cernat

As several contributors to this collection insist, the Romanian avant-garde and the existentialist–spiritualist "Young Generation" of the 1930s came about within, and consolidated, European and world networks of literary-artistic discourse and cultural–political reflection. If this is true, then, as I argue, these two movements and the considerable body of work they engendered inside and outside Romanian culture should be read accordingly, as subsets of an assemblage or system of communicating vessels that is at once domestic and transnational, aesthetic and ideological. More specifically, the multiply comparative reading I am proposing sets out to show that the modernity models undergirding these two movements are different facets of one and the same radical cultural paradigm whose purview spans discrete and sometimes inconsonant spaces, politics, and formal repertoires. To map out the vivid discrepancies and surprising juxtapositions underpinning this conflict-ridden yet coherent geoaesthetic and ideological ensemble, I will extend and complicate a line of argument that, in recent decades, has gained considerable traction in modernist studies, particularly with concepts like "reactionary modernism" (Jeffrey Herf), "epiphanic modernism" (Roger Griffin), and "antimodernist modernism" (Antoine Compagnon). Notably, the new critical perspective embedded in this vocabulary no longer views innovative, "progressive" aesthetics, on one side, and conservative-nationalist or reactionary politics, on the other side, as opposite but as intertwined phenomena. Much like in a formula such as "conservative revolution," the notions of revolution and conservatism are not at odds here, and, as we will also note, this correlation had its geocultural correspondent. For, aside from various aspects endemic to the circumstances of Romanian modernism, the situation described below neither differed substantially nor occurred independently from what happened in the rest of Europe; there were, indeed, Romanian artists and writers who joined radical modernity or the avant-garde while taking up ultraconservative and, at times, even Fascist or pro-Nazi positions, as did Gabriele D'Annunzio, Julius Evola, Ezra Pound, and Louis-Ferdinand Céline.

It is, then, worth asking: Do 1930s Romania's avant-gardists such as Tristan Tzara (1896–1963) and Ion Vinea (1895–1964) and Young Generation members like Mircea Eliade (1907–1986), Emil Cioran (1911–1995), and other followers of ideologue and *maître à penser* Nae Ionescu (1890–1940) really belong to completely opposite camps? The answer today is, I maintain, a qualified "no." In fact, about two decades ago, critics stopped looking at the "progressive" modernity of the pre–Second World War avant-garde and at the largely "reactionary" modernity of the same period as ideological polar opposites, that is, as epitomizing the Fascism–Communism antinomy.[1] The growing tendency has been, instead, to view the two modernities as different thrusts of the same radical critique of the rationalist and bourgeois establishment, which this critique targeted as a symptom of a broader, systemic crisis of European modernity. Not only that, but the era's avant-garde and *arrière-garde* are now seen as complementary, as two sides of the same coin. Romanian literary critics such as Sorin Alexandrescu[2] and Matei Călinescu[3] have also pointed out that the notion of an antithetical relationship between modernism and traditionalism—an idea that has shaped most debates on cultural identity in post-1918 Romania—is now outdated.[4] In his foreword to a 2008 volume of interdisciplinary essays, Romanian critic Sorin Antohi too highlights the obsolescence of this opposition. The "traditionalism-modernism binary," Antohi says, "has survived as a 'received idea' of Romanian history and culture." "[T]he assumption has been," he goes on, "that the elements in the conceptual chain modern(ist)-Western-progressive-Communist (or leftist)-democratic-antifascist were equivalent, and that so were the elements of the diametrically opposed series, traditional(ist)-antimodern(ist)-autochthonist-reactionary-authoritarian/dictatorial/totalitarian."[5] Bringing together scholars such as Griffin, Alexandrescu, Hayden White, Jörn Rüsen, Liviu Antonesei, Victor Rizescu, and Valentin Săndulescu, Antohi's collection seeks to collapse the "false dichotomy" of modernism and antimodernism by tackling the two phenomena's Romanian interplay as reflecting the "simultaneous, ambivalent, and sometimes mixed answers to the challenges of modernization" in a country that, in the 1930s, "was stuck on the margins of this process."[6]

1. Mazeway Modernism

On July 31, 1926, Nae Ionescu published in the magazine *Cuvântul* an article that echoed, directly and indirectly, some of these challenges. The piece was titled, revealingly enough, "Sufletul mistic" ("The Mystical Soul"). In it, Nae Ionescu, who had not become the Far Right's leading ideologue yet, engages in a friendly polemic with philosopher and psychologist Constantin Rădulescu-Motru, who, in a piece that had come out in the magazine *Gândirea*, had deplored, from a rationalist and moderately conservative position, the European resurgence of "mysticism." Noting that Motru had rejected "commercialism" as the root cause of the "offensive launched by the mystical soul," Nae Ionescu asks: "Would the merchants of ideas, attitudes, and beliefs have been equally successful in 1925 had they hawked, instead of mysticism, eighteenth-century encyclopedism and the philosophy of the Enlightenment? I have, it would seem, every right to doubt that." Both the question and the answer are fair, but Nae Ionescu goes on to present himself as a spokesperson for the bourgeoning development. "So far," he informs his readers, we have been only trying to stamp out rationalism. However, we have no problem with genuine rationalism, with which mysticism has always been getting along most fruitfully, but with Cartesian rationalism, which is a reversal and, indeed, a misleading, one-sided misrepresentation of true rationalism. We have been wiping out [this Cartesian variety] in philosophy through the latter's new anti-intellectualist trends … [,] whose critical impact is often deeply undermining and does damages beyond repair; in politics, by scrutinizing the parliamentary and democratic regime, [and] by shifting our interest toward working, concrete forms of administration … [,] in brief, by allowing an organic life philosophy to prevail over a contractual one; in art, where Cocteau, von Unruh or Hasenklaver, Satie, Poulenc, or Schoenberg, Picasso, Brâncuşi, or Kokoschka have isolated the conceptual components of art, attempting original syntheses … [, and] in religious life, through repeated and sustained attacks against Protestantism, against this trite, nearsighted desecration of heaven and "humanization" of God.[7]

Antimodern and mystical as revolution struck Nae Ionescu, he nonetheless championed it, and he saw irrationalist philosophies and artistic modernism as "childhood illnesses" of the approaching New Middle Ages but also as a means of doing away with Cartesian rationalism and all its implications. The names listed above included mostly, but not only, avant-garde, Abstractionist, and Expressionist artists. Nae Ionescu's agenda was, however, crystal clear: Jean Cocteau, who was admired by his followers, had converted to Catholicism under the influence of neo-Thomist thinker Jacques Maritain, while composers Francis Poulenc and Arnold Schoenberg were Cocteau's friends. All these references reinforce the impression that, setting aside the political "conservative revolution" they would endorse, Nae Ionescu and the young essayists contributing regularly to *Cuvântul* such as Eliade and Mihail Sebastian (1907–1945) were, intellectually speaking, plugged into a modernity network that was artistically and epistemologically more advanced than the international liberal-rationalist system of culture Eugen Lovinescu (1881–1943), Romania's main ideologue of modernism between the two World Wars, was urging his country to join; overall predicated on what he called the "autonomy" of the aesthetic, Lovinescu's modernism was, by comparison, moderate not only politically but also aesthetically. The more pointedly avant-garde tastes of Nae Ionescu's disciples were only apparently at odds with their "neomedievalist," Christian-Orthodoxist, and ethno-culturally "organicist" views. Running through and, to a notable degree, accounting for all these distinct and sometimes divergent preferences and options were the common denominator of unmitigated change and its intellectual instrument, the critique of the liberal bourgeoisie and of the secular, universalist, and progressive rationalism rooted in the French Revolution, Martin Luther's Reform, the philosophy of René Descartes and Francis Bacon, Enlightenment secularism, and Jean-Jacques Rousseau's contractualism. Originated with the Romantics, the conflict between two of modernity's central sociocultural "types," the artist and the bourgeois, characteristically shaped both the progressive avant-garde and the conservative-right-wing *arrière-garde*.

Summarizing his authoritative 2007 book *Modernism and Fascism: The Sense of a Beginning under Mussolini and Hitler*, British historian Roger Griffin articulates persuasively these similitudes and intersections in a comprehensive definition of modernism as a "palingenetic response to Western modernity"[8] in his 2008 article "Modernity, Modernism, and Fascism: A 'mazeway resynthesis.'"[9] Drawing from Frank Kermode's 1967 *The Sense of an Ending* and Peter Childs's 2000 *Modernism*, Griffin distinguishes between two major categories of modernism: "epiphanic modernism" and "programmatic modernism." He describes the former as "an exclusively artistic expression, often involving extreme experimentation with new aesthetic forms conceived to express glimpses of a 'higher reality' that throw into relief the anomie and spiritual bankruptcy of contemporary history." As for "programmatic modernism," Griffin specifies, it "focus[es] on the creation of a 'new world,' either through the capacity of art and thought to formulate a vision capable of revolutionizing society as a whole, or through the creation of new ways of living or an entire sociopolitical culture that will ultimately transform not just art, but humankind itself, or at least a chosen segment of it, under the leadership of a new elite."[10] In other words, while "programmatic modernism" is driven, as its name implies, by a social "program," and by a progressive one to boot, "epiphanic modernism" is basically an aesthetic affair and speaks to the need for "transcendence" in a disenchanted modern society. Foreshadowed by Friedrich Nietzsche's "Dionysian modernism," the epiphanic responds to the time's spiritual "crisis" and, as such, is discernible across a range of endeavors to bring about a cultural "regeneration" in the face of *fin-de-siècle* "decadence."[11]

When judged over and against the backdrop of Griffin's mazeway Euromodernism, the Romanian culture of the years preceding the Second World War seems more similar to the Italian and, to a lesser extent, the French situation. However, the avant-garde had a more massive presence in France, where Leftist intellectuals also were, comparatively speaking, more numerous, as existentialism had a markedly Marxist component, and the Catholic intelligentsia, from Jacques Maritain to the Personalist contributors clustered around the journal *Esprit*, espoused significantly anti-Fascist views. By contrast, Romanian existentialism between the two World Wars—or *Trăirism* (an "ism" derived from the Romanian verb for "to live" or "to exist"), as it has been pejoratively dubbed—was strongly marked by Vitalism, whether German (Nietzsche, Ludwig Klages), Orthodox Russian (Nikolai Berdyaev, Lev Shestov), or Spanish (Miguel de Unamuno), and was largely—but not entirely—reactionary ideologically. What we should also keep in mind is that the relationships between the avant-garde and the Young Generation, and more broadly between the Far Right and the Far Left were characterized by baffling overlaps, similitudes, associations, as well as an intense circulation of authors and ideas in *both* directions. In a book chapter on Surrealist poet Gherasim Luca and his politics prior to his resettling in France after the Second World War, Romanian critic Marta Petreu highlights precisely the commonalities, overlays, and intersections determining and redirecting the cultural–political flows in the communicating vessels inside which avant-gardists and the likes of Eliade and Cioran were moving alongside other representatives of the group she dubs, following literary critic Dan C. Mihăilescu and by analogy with the Spanish Generation of 1927, the "Generation of '27." "From a history of ideas standpoint," Petreu observes, the Romanian avant-garde and the Generation of '27 crossed paths[. B]efore the dramatic political watershed would emerge in Western Europe and in Romania alike, that is, before the 1932–1933 interval, the Romanian Generation of '27 partly consisted of avant-garde artists, and[, vice versa,] some of the avant-garde artists of the late 1920s and the early 1930s belonged to the Generation of '27 .... These were mostly visual artists, as the Generation of '27 included young people from all areas of intellectual and artistic life, such as Mac Constantinescu, Marcel Janco, Milița Petrașcu, Max Hermann Maxy, and Margareta Sterian. They were moving from one group to another quite naturally, were publishing in newspapers and magazines edited by the members of the Generation of '27, and were showing their works in exhibitions like the one organized by the Criterion Association in February 1933.[12]

The reader may recall that the Criterion Association was set up by essayist, art critic, historian, and Americanist Petru Comarnescu to promote interdisciplinary and cross-ideological debates, and that its name, as well as the title of the *Criterion* magazine—which was founded in 1934, after the Association had been dismantled by the authorities—were inspired by T. S. Eliot's famous publication. Further, in Petreu's assessment, "the difference between the avant-gardists and the Criterionists" was largely one between "materialism" and "spiritualism." Politically speaking, the two groups were divided "solely by the *nature* of the revolution they were dreaming of: the avant-gardists were envisaging a proletarian revolution modeled after the Soviets, while the right-wing elite of the Generation of '27 (the rightist Criterionists) was planning a nationalist revolution. At the same time, they all shared an anti-bourgeois stance, a rejection of individualism, and an endorsement of revolution and collectivism," which, according to Petreu, does not mean that ideological "extremism" was a dominant characteristic of the generation.[13]

The picture is, indeed, more nuanced within and without Romania, reflecting complexities, ambiguities, and coincidences circulating and complicating a great deal cultural realities across national borders. A closer look at Eliade, Cioran, Eugen Ionescu, Constantin Noica, Mircea Vulcănescu, Comarnescu, Sebastian, and others like them suggests that, despite the confusing array of sodalities and trends it comprised, this new orientation in Romanian culture bodied forth, as far as the aesthetic choices of this direction go, both of Griffin's categories. It would be a mistake, then, I think, to generalize and extrapolate the ideology of the Fascist commitments of some of these authors to the whole modernist movement to which they belonged. True, names running through the supranational communicating vessels of European modernism included, aside from Eliade, Cioran, and Noica, figures like Gottfried Benn, Pound, Wyndham Lewis, Giovanni Papini, Evola, and Céline, but those who did not heed the siren calls of right-wing ideologies were equally numerous. Besides, the epiphanic positions many of these authors staked up in the arts shed, at most, some clarifying light on these modernists' political allegiances; the latter were hardly "determined" by aesthetic epiphanism. A propos of this disjunction, two important points bear making here. First, many of those who championed Futurism, Dadaism, Surrealism, or Imagism, from Hugo Ball and Pound to Evola and Papini, would not renew their avant-garde memberships after the First World War, embracing instead various religious and mystical beliefs and philosophies, and such conversions, I should stress, whether they were spiritual, political, or aesthetic, were typical of the radical European culture of the era. Second, where the Romanian avant-garde of the 1920s borrowed the radicalism of its aesthetic insurgence from anarchism and Filippo Tommaso Marinetti's Futurism while showing little interest in the latter's pro-Fascist rhetoric, the Young Generation was drawn to Italian Fascism. Lured as it was by the tragic-agonal tones of the metaphysical existentialism of Nietzsche, Søren Kierkegaard, Shestov, Berdyaev, Martin Heidegger, Klages, and Miguel de Unamuno, the group's "new spiritualism" was nonetheless fraught with ambivalences.[14] Nae Ionescu, for instance, regarded "particularist" and "autocephalous" Eastern Orthodoxy as occasioning direct spiritual contacts and opposed it to Catholic rationalism and Protestant pragmatism, which he viewed as "universalist" vehicles of imperial domination. By contrast, his disciples thought that, just like sexuality or politics, religion could foster extreme and multiply transgressive experiences of the sacred. Steeped in a blend of Orthodox, Catholic, and Islamic mysticism, some of them—including esoteric figures such as Vasile Lovinescu and Mihai Vâlsan, who would actually serve as a Mufti of the Paris mosque—were familiar with Sufism. Others spiked this altogether antimodernist religious-theosophical cocktail with the occultism of René Guénon's "primordial Tradition," with pre-Christian practices such as Orphism and Hermeticism, and even with atheism and agnosticism.

2. Ethics, Aesthetics, and Politics in "Greater Romania"

To be sure, the eclectic and sometimes incongruous medley featured ingredients beyond the religious and the spiritual. Addressing this and related issues in a 1999 book, Alexandrescu offers that, defined as it is by formalism and by the aesthetic autonomy doctrine ("aestheticism"), Romania's 1930s mainstream literary modernism constitutes an epiphenomenon of the liberal culture developing in the wake of the 1918 final unification of Romanian regions into the nation-state of "Greater Romania." As the critic remarks, despite the unquestionable ideological differences between them, the avant-garde, on one side, and Eliade and his friends, on the other, composed a loosely integrated, anti-"aestheticist" and antibourgeois *ethical* front opposed to *aesthetic* modernism. "The rise of *aestheticism*," Alexandrescu elaborates,

> coincide[d] with the triumph of liberalism in "Greater Romania." The setting up of the forms and foundations of the [nation-state] continued into the 1920s in politics (with the rise of new parties), in legislation (with reformist laws), as well as in literature (with the publication of the first modern novels and with the new poetic movements) and in the visual arts. In contrast to this aestheticism stood an entire cluster of *ethical* concerns, a whole ethical attitude and domain of public life. While this ethics was also born in the 1920s, it expanded over the next decade as a

result of a desire to dismantle the aforementioned forms and foundations. Giving vent to this desire were political parties, essayists, and regimes on the Right, which targeted what they saw as a failure of democratic institutions, but also the avant-gardes [seeking] new, non-figurative art forms, [and in general all] those who, in their search for completely new ideas and experiences in the novel, experimental theater, and the essay, were looking to reach beyond Romanian and even European traditions. No matter how different, all of these activities had in common fierce opposition to bourgeois society and mentality, to the principles of democracy, and, *at the same time*, to modernism.[15]

The clash between generations and their different mindsets took center stage in the conflict between establishment "aesthetic modernism" and antiestablishment "ethical modernism," an antagonism that sharpened around the First World War. For the war brought about a traumatic rift separating those who had been educated before 1916, in a patriarchal culture dominated by secular rationalism, positivism, and strict "moral principles," and those whose spent their childhood and teenage years witnessing the horrors of the hostilities and the massive social upheavals unfolding in their aftermath. Even though the age difference between the two series of authors is no more than a decade or so, the latter group saw the former as "old" and themselves as "young." In reality, the gap between the two is tantamount to a hiatus between two *saecula*, in the sense of the term used by Tacitus and adopted, from the Latin historian, by Lovinescu in his 1925 book *Istoria civilizației române moderne* (History of Modern Romanian Civilization). This concept, which has to do with a certain cultural atmosphere or "dominant" more than with historical periodization—let alone with a timeline broken into centuries—would suggest, in our context, that the nineteenth century ended *de facto* in 1914, while the twentieth century truly began with the collapse of the Russian and Austrian–Hungarian Empires. Overlaying the formative rites every child goes through, the ordeal of the war period left an indelible mark on the rising writers and intellectuals of 1920s Romania, placing them from a very early age in the proximity of collective death and exposing them to the brutal irrationality of history. Arguably, there had been little to prefigure, before the 1914 Sarajevo assassination of Austria's Archduke Franz Ferdinand, the proportions of the ensuing global disaster, whose unpredictability and consequences in turn severely undermined the reigning philosophical systems and the explanatory "Grand Narratives" grounded in them, along with the primacy of reason, Enlightenment universalism, and confidence in progress. Social instability, institutional chaos, widespread corruption, and a series of cascading cultural–political emancipations combined to create an environment in which the teenagers of the 1920s were witnessing the dramatic breakdown of traditional values, were experimenting with sexuality, were facing death and failure anxiety, and were, as a result, becoming vulnerable to nihilism, irrationalism, mysticism, and religiousness. Concomitantly, in the face of society's fragmentation, they were thirsty for new forms of community, which is why their Oedipal rejection of their parents' values went hand in hand with a certain joy of living and with a strong desire to create that showed little respect for old formulas and moral-aesthetic constraints.

This radicalism upped the ante of the progressivism of the decade immediately following the First World War. Those years were marked by new land ownership regulations, by the 1923 Constitution, by the passing of the universal suffrage bill—although the right was extended to men only—and by other similar legislation initiatives of the National Liberal Party. It was a time of hopes and headway in the modernization of institutional structures despite acute social problems, spreading discontent, and serious administrative challenges in a country whose territory and population doubled after the 1920 Trianon Treaty and where projects of cultural unification and emancipation were still driven by a sense of constructive enthusiasm. With the next decade, however, things took a turn for the worse, in Romania and throughout Europe, as different, oftentimes alarming events, political developments, ideas, themes, and rhetorics started passing back and forth across borders and through the geocultural system of Euromodernism. Most worrisome were transnational disintegrations occurring in parliamentary democracy and, what with the Great Depression just around the corner, in economy and society generally. Similar erosions and breakdowns threatened literature and culture. If the consolidation of the Romanian liberal national-state led to a boom in the novel, literary criticism, and poetry, which reached unprecedented levels of sophistication, the onset of systemic crisis brought on or sped up an anarchic unraveling of forms and genres. Inherited from the pre–First World War era, the Victorian culture of prudishness and privacy, of formalism and conventions increasingly made room in the 1930s for the values of authenticity, intellectual and affective intensity, and transgressive experiences. It is under their banner that both the avant-garde and the Young Generation graduated from an initially moderate and eclectic phase to an all-out antiestablishment stance. But while the avant-gardists rejected nationalism as an outgrowth of bourgeois militarism, the new spiritualists adopted it in the name of Leninist and Trotskyist internationalism, as a form of antiimperialist and anticolonial resistance to the hegemony of the liberal West. In this vein, Marxist essayist Petre Pandrea pointed up explicitly Romania's status as a "Western semi-colony." Neither was his critical and self-critical attitude isolated. To be sure, it marks his whole generation, which was literally obsessed, as we will notice below again, with overcoming the condition of a "minor" and ignored culture at the European periphery.

Various strains of radicalism and revolutionarism cross, link up, and refine, then, Romanian modernisms and experimentalisms within the new system of national and European culture on the rise after the First World War. If we were to apply Alexandrescu's classification to this situation, we could subsume aesthetic modernism to a culture of moderation intent on preserving the status quo, whereas ethical modernism would correspond to a culture of contestation keen on doing away with the constituted order. In that case, setting side by side the avant-garde—which has been ordinarily associated with Left- and Far-Left-wing politics—and Eliade's group—which was close to the extreme Right—within the same modernist cultural "bloc" or assemblage becomes a plausible and perhaps inevitable critical move. Granted, the two movements do make for strange bedfellows, but they do share a loosely unifying, transformative-revolutionary élan of the either "progressive-Communist" or "conservative-reactionary" variety. After all, inside the bigger, European maze of cultural-aesthetic modernism, too, Italian Futurists tended to embrace Fascism—which, I might add, was itself a revolutionary, national-socialist movement seeking to "deprovincialize" Italy by revivifying Roman imperialism—while Russian Futurists were, on the contrary, drawn to Bolshevism.

But revolutionary heterodoxy as a quintessentially antibourgeois rejection of one-dimensional, standardized life was not the only bridge and communication channel inside this highly complex system. Other affinities and contact points included the myth of energetic and creative youth, Vitalism, and a discourse of "authenticity," which all suggest—to me, at least—that it would be a stretch to claim, as Compagnon has, that the historical avant-gardes and antimodernity are equivalent. As is well known, following in the footsteps of Charles du Bos and Jacques Maritain, Compagnon has contended that the antimoderns were in fact the "true moderns, as they would no longer allow themselves to be deceived or to entertain any grand illusions about modernity."[16] Putting his rose-tinted glasses on to measure the otherwise reactionary politics of the "veritable" moderns with the yardstick of their "aesthetic" achievements, the French critic tells us that "the antimoderns, those *charming reactionaries*, [were] disenchanted or exasperated moderns; indeed, they [were] the very spice of modernity."[17] It is true that Compagnon leans on Roland Barthes's dictum about the avant-garde and death to raise the stakes of literary history so as to nuance things himself. "Being in the avant-garde," Barthes famously said, "means knowing what is dead; being in the arrière-garde means still loving that which has died,"[18] and Compagnon invokes the Barthesian pronouncement so as to explain why he locates his antimoderns not only in the "rearguard of the avant-garde" but also in the very avant-garde of the avant-garde, as it were—"we tend to regard them," he acknowledges, "as more modern than the moderns themselves and the historical avant-gardes,"[19] and, along the same lines, elsewhere the critic describes antimodernity "not as neoclassicism, academicism, conservatism, or traditionalism, but as resistance and ambivalence on the part of those who are genuinely modern."[20] More broadly, in Compagnon's view, the antimodern is "a modern who got caught up in the maelstrom of history but was unable to let go of the past."[21] This definition affords him a presentation of "antimodern tradition" with references to a saliently heteroclite panoply of figures from the historical and political (including the ideologues of the counterrevolution) to the philosophical (anti-Enlightenment authorities), moral, existential (pessimist thinkers), religious and theological (writers on the "original sin"), aesthetic (philosophers and artists of the sublime), and stylistic (literati plying the rhetoric of vituperation or imprecation)—a deeply heterogeneous cluster of writers among whom very few fit into the classical taxonomies of the historical avant-garde.

A similarly heterogeneity characterized traditionalist currents, tendencies, and authors in post-1918 Romania. Thus, historian and critic Nicolae Iorga, who staunchly opposed modernism in literature and the arts, was still advocating an antiquated sort of nostalgically agrarian, backward-looking, yet secular traditionalism around the dawn of the twentieth century. Distinct from his antimodernism was the spiritualist neotraditionalism of the group formed around the magazine *Gândirea*, whose ideologues, Nichifor Crainic and Radu Dragnea, were upholding the values of Orthodox mysticism and were hoping to bring back the late medieval grandeur of the Byzantium. In its radicalized political version, this traditionalism quickly drifted to the Right and wound up sponsoring, in the 1930s, a fundamentalist notion of a nation-state ruled by religious ethnocracy. Further compounding *Gândirea*'s cultural and political situation, the publication's commitment to Orthodox Christianity—which was, in some respects, not incompatible with Russian Slavophilia either—also opened the door to influences by cultural phenomena of Austrian and German origin such as Expressionism, the literature of the psychological depths and the unconsciousness, and abstract art. *Gândirea* also nurtured the growth of the young radicals of the 1930s, including the authors of one of Romania's earliest generational programs, "The 'White Lily' Manifesto." But the spiritualism of these rebels lacked a clearly defined cause; rather eclectic, it pursued different, somewhat less "political" goals. To give an example, when Hermann von Keyserling visited Bucharest, he was greeted with enthusiasm both in the neospiritualist circles and by the editors of the avant-garde magazine *Contimporanul*. The Baltic philosopher thought, actually, that the Balkan Orthodox countries of Eastern Europe could provide an "opportunity" to reinvigorate a fast-aging, burned-out Europe, with Romania a potential regional leader in a "new Europe."[22]

If the neospiritualists of *Gândirea* pictured Romania at the vanguard of a twenty-first-century Byzantine Commonwealth, at *Contimporanul*, Vinea, its editor-in-chief, believed in the emancipatory mission of "new" Romanian art in the European Southeast. He was confident that, as, apparently, many of his friends from abroad were telling him,

> it will not be long before the intellectual elite of our metropolis [i.e., Bucharest] will stop playing catchup with the defining driving agent of the century we live in, namely, with [the] motion-speed-power [constellation of creative elements]; [our artists and thinkers] will join[, sooner than one might expect,] the ranks of creators proper and will lead the backward societies of the Balkans.[23]

Picking up on similar—and similarly mixed—cultural signals coming from a variety of directions, Romanian critics have drawn attention to important aesthetic resemblances among the divergent cultural trends surfacing in the 1920s. Ovid S. Crohmălniceanu, for instance, stressed that the constructivist avant-garde thinkers from *Contimporanul* and the champions of "neo-Byzantinism" from *Gândirea* such as Lucian Blaga and Francisc Șirato shared a common interest in Expressionism and abstract art, which they had adapted to suit their own agendas, which were progressive and secular in the avant-gardists' case and, at *Gândirea*, ethno-spiritualistic.[24] Constantin Brâncuși's sculpture itself was subjected to this kind of double decoding, valued as it was both as an abstract avant-garde exemplar and as a vehicle for boiling down to an abstract essence and for universalizing Romanian folklore and archetypal mythology. Also, within a post-Romantic, post-Nietzschean frame of thought, the avant-gardes' interest in "primitivism," on the one hand, and, on the other, Eliade and his group's stress on the "universality" of the archaic and on the prevalence of newly revealed Asian spirituality over the "exhausted" West were not far apart either. What differed, in Romania and elsewhere in the modernist geosystem, was these programs' stakes, as Hayden White has shown. The avant-garde artist, White expounds in his "Modernism and Primitivism" essay, came on the "primitive" in worlds opened up by imperialist conquest and exploitation, where this new reality was treated as a mysterious and mesmerizing "Other," as something or somebody radically different from, and in that deeply appealing to, the 1920s avant-garde painters, sculptors, and writers.[25] In the West, fascination and threat alternate in ways enabling White to differentiate between the avant-garde and the high modernism of Eliot, Pound, James Joyce, Virginia Woolf, Marcel Proust, Franz Kafka, Thomas Mann, Ungaretti, Eugenion Montale, and Italo Svevo. In the European East, especially in Romania, this distinction applies much less, for, unlike Western modernists, who were oftentimes apprehensive about this kind of primitiveness, Eliade and his fellow spiritualists sought to employ its mythical thinking—which they deemed typical of a "young" and "non-modern" culture such as Romania's—as a weapon against ossified "Old Europe."

If the cultural–philosophical grids powering the 1930s radicals' critique spread far beyond Romanian lands and modern times, so did this critique's scope. Extending along the same intellectual routes past domestic liberalism, this radicalism challenged the French-led project of European liberal universalism, which had laid the ideological foundations of the Romanian state after the 1859 Union of the Danube Principalities and was reaffirmed at the Versailles Peace Conference and by U.S. President Woodrow Wilson's 1918 "Fourteen Points" speech. Thus, the young rebels were fulfilling an old dream of the culture: becoming "synchronous" with Europe. And, indeed, in Euromodernism's system of communicating vessels, their dissent followed trajectories across vast intervals of coevality in which they were joining a larger chorus speaking out against liberal democracy, contractualist politics, and Eurocentrism. Both the Left and the Right had their vocal representatives in this steadily growing oppositional mass, for, in Romania and everywhere in Europe, angry young men and women had been ready for *any* political model capable of furnishing an alternative to what they saw as the bankrupt universalist and humanist ideal of Old Europe and of governmental bodies such as the League of Nations. Hungry for change, the radicals of the pre–Second World War years were eager to support a wide spectrum of political regimes and experiments, from the recently established authoritarian governments of Central Europe to the Soviet Union and the United States; they could sympathize with Japanese militarism, but also with the anticolonial upheaval of Mahatma Gandhi's India; they showed interest in the Chinese Boxer Rebellion, and it does bear mentioning that radical Islam starts attracting its followers roughly around the same time; and, as for new types of social organization, they seemed drawn to communitarian (*gemeinschaftliche*) concepts, be those corporate or collectivist.

3. The Two Arms of the Modernist Scissors: The Avant-Guard and the *arrière-garde*

Discrepant political visions circulated in the era's system of national and international modernism as much as asymmetric literary and aesthetic formulas did. Mircea Vulcănescu, a Young Generation leader and conservative defender of "autochthonous" values, was a traditionalist whose anti-urban, "ruralist" views did not prevent him from endorsing aesthetic tenets of avant-garde art and "epiphanic" modernism. In a February 1933 speech honoring the Criterion Association, Vulcănescu praises "Orphic" poet Dan Botta and Sebastian, as well as avant-gardists such as Ion Călugăru, Maxy, Marcel Janco, and Vinea.[26] In fact, he was close to the latter. Vinea was a pioneer of the avant-garde movement and a leftist opponent of the rising Romanian Fascist organization, the violent Iron Guard. In 1927, when *Contimporanul* stopped coming out due to financial troubles, Vinea contributed regularly to the newspaper *Cuvântul*. Subsequently, when *Contimporanul* resumed appearance, he did not think twice before soliciting articles from Sebastian and Eliade. Likewise, sociologist and economist Paul Sterian, who wrote several volumes of religious poetry, published Christian Orthodox-inspired pieces in *Gândirea*, and was an editor of *Cuvântul*, also authored modernist and experimentalist texts. More notably yet, one of his contributions was titled "Poezia agresivă sau poemul reportaj" (Aggressive Poetry or, the Reportage Poem) and was featured by the avant-garde magazine *unu* alongside interventions by numerous Jewish and anti-Fascist artists and journalists, many of whom were either Communists or Communist sympathizers. Sterian's was a full-dress, high-pitched Futurist manifesto demanding "the reporter show up" and replace lyricism in poetry writing with a more direct engagement with reality. It is equally interesting that critics have assumed that some of his works were Dada parodies of Orthodoxism, and, moreover, that their author was Jewish, which, incidentally, he was not—he only had been married, before drifting to the Far Right, to Margareta Sterian, a painter and writer of Jewish origin.

Odd as they may look to those less familiar with the nuances and imbrications of Romania's radical cultures between the First and the Second World Wars, such collocations, alliances, and permutations within and across disciplines, expression forms, and politics were uncommon neither domestically nor internationally. Once again, the Romanian context was somewhat similar to what went on in Italy up until the late 1930s, when Benito Mussolini's anti-Semitism showed Il Duce's true colors to Jewish intellectuals like Curzio Malaparte and others. Instead of a system of clearly and stably demarcated positions, meanings, functions, and aesthetic-political correlations, what we are dealing with in Romania, Italy, France, and elsewhere is a complicated and evolving vanguard–rearguard interplay similar to the one theorized, also after Barthes, by French critic William Marx and his contributors in their 2004 essay collection *Les arrières-gardes du XX-e siècle. L'autre face de la modernité esthétique.*[27] In "L'arrière-garde vue de l'avant," the volume's opening chapter, Vincent Kaufmann sets the avant-garde apart from the *arrière-garde* by pinpointing the latter's distinctive features. In his opinion, these include religiosity; anti-democratic and socially nostalgic elitism; nationalism and respect for classical culture (the *arrière-gardes*, says Kaufmann, are "nationalist and classicist, whereas the avant-gardes are internationalist"); anti-intellectualism (as opposed to the "intellectualism" of the avant-gardes); and a view of social community as a project one might describe as "essentialist" or stamped by an "essence" or nature hard and unwise to redefine because it has already been defined by the past—for avant-gardists the "social" is a "construction" yet to undertake, whose building plans are still to be drawn, while the *arrière-gardistes* finds the whole enterprise pointless because it has been done.[28] It is clear, though, that for Marx, much like for Kaufmann in the dissociations made above, the two concepts go hand in hand and complement each other. This is exactly what Marjorie Perloff emphasizes in her commentary on *Les arrières-gardes du XX-e siècle.* "When an avant-garde movement," stresses Perloff, "is no longer a novelty, it is the role of the arrière-garde to complete its mission, to ensure its success."[29] Of course, Charles Baudelaire himself understood the modern as a tension between the lure of fleeting novelty and the nostalgia for classical order, and the question is whether these two forces historically operated in tandem, coevally, in sequence, as Perloff seems to be suggesting, and so forth.

The answer is all of the above. An outcome of such cycles and juxtapositions, actions and reactions, exploratory ventures and skeptical pushbacks, Romanian modernism is a dazzlingly diverse and contradictory phenomenon—or a constellation of phenomena, rather, for, as elsewhere, Romanian modernism is not one but several, not a current or stream of culture but a tangle of polychromous, ambivalent, and paradoxical crosscurrents.[30] This system of communicating vessels complete with the cultural lifeblood running through it is a *fluid ensemble* where worthy of the critic's attention are *both* elements that appear to move swiftly forward politically and otherwise and the slower or backward-drifting flotsam and jetsam. What counts here is the circuitries and the flows but also the incoherent coherence, the *concordia discors* kind of unity in disunity or cultural–political logic that renders that progressive and revolutionary impetus of the avant-garde and the largely reactionary radicalism of the Young Generation elements of the same unit. We are talking about philosophers, historians, writers of various sorts of fictional literature, journalists, artists, and other humanists, academics, and intellectuals who shared the same generational mindset; who had similar intellectual sources and formative experiences; who were hostile to the same bourgeois establishment that had emerged within the positivist, historicist, and secularist–rationalist late-nineteenth century; who were driven by the same radical ethos; and who witnessed the collapse of Europe's *ancien régimes* and Austro-Hungarian, Czarist, and Ottoman empires, as well as the deepening crisis of archaic electoral systems and of an education apparatus too narrowly focused on classical Greco-Roman and Judeo-Christian inheritance. The "Young Turks" of the moment, be they avant-gardists or nationalist–existentialists, found all these traditions passé or lacking one way or the other. Clinging to this patrimony, they suspected, was a sure sign of a culture that had run out of steam. By contrast, the Romanian equivalent of the *jazz age* or the French *années folles* was permeated, much like in some of F. Scott Fitzgerald's novels, by a sense of liberation, hedonistic euphoria, and rejuvenation. The overall atmosphere mirrored the era's governing ethos of change, whose young and brash social heralds were building a whole new life philosophy around the values of youth, novelty, energetic transformation, adventure, the body, and extreme existential experiences whether private or public, individual or social. Political experimentation—or experimentations, rather—was part of them, in Romania and Europe at large, and they prompted or intersected with trials and experiments in other domains, again, nationally and internationally, after the war and in response to it, when whole groups, classes, and countries attempted to fill the vacuum left by empires by recycling former imperial power into neoimperial, Soviet proletarian internationalism or by investing rising nationalisms with expansionist ambitions, as was particularly the case of Italy and Nazi Germany.

Making death a collective, immediate, and material reality—the ultimate "extreme experience"—the war had also hastened the breakdown of scientific, positivist reason, which in turn led to a resurrection of the "religious sentiment" as a mystical and, once more, "authentic" life of the mind and spirit, which was one of the constitutive elements of the abovementioned ethos. Following from the latter was a whole set of aesthetic-ideological choices and priorities, with "genuinely" lived-out life, brutally direct communication, the unembellished and directly accessed "truth" of nonfiction, personalized informal relations, the fragmentary, the aspiration to sexual freedom, the instinctual, and community preferred over the weak euphemisms of classical rhetoric, the "deceitfulness" of fiction, the disembodied rationality of systemic wholes, the bureaucratic formalism of impersonal institutions, prudishness, sexual repression, social disintegration, and alienation, respectively. By and large, these options cut across the divides between the political visions of the avant-garde and the Young Generation. Granted, where the former was dreaming of a classless society, the latter was insistently visited by the phantasm of a neo-feudal regime with an elitist–corporatist twist, and yet both were exercised by the pathos of a messianic *renovatio mundi*, with Romania as *the* project of the exalted present.

4. Trading Modernisms: Centers, Peripheries, and Cross-Systemic Exchanges

For both groups, the national project entailed not only a radical transformation of the country but also a change of Romania's position within the European geocultural system. In the essay with which part III of *Romanian Literature as World Literature* opens, Mihai Iovănel shows at length what it took for prominent 1930s figures such as Ionescu, Eliade, and Cioran to relocate within this system and even take up world positions of influence and prestige beyond it. Here, I would like to underscore, in line with Ovidiu Morar's contribution to this book, that, after expatriating themselves and working their way into their adoptive cultures, representatives of both camps acquired international recognition, whether they were avant-gardists such as Brâncuși, Tzara, and Victor Brauner or members of Eliade and Cioran's movement. For all of them, being "peripheral," relegated to the continent's margins, expected to echo more "central" voices but otherwise practically voiceless or unheard in vaster arenas turned into a cultural complex of sorts. While its roots push deep into Romanian history, this complex reached a cultural boiling point before and around the Second World War, and the tensions, decisions, and transformations following from it were unprecedented across the forms, itineraries, and locations of modernism. After the war, Cioran, who had emigrated to Paris and morphed into a latter-day French skeptic, and Noica, who had remained in Romania to be imprisoned by the Communists and reemerge in the 1960s as a Heideggerian proponent of an ethnolinguistic ontology of "Romanianness," had an extensive exchange on this subject, where they adduced the divergent trajectories of their lives as arguments in a debate in which leaving or not leaving the homeland behind is part of the broader controversy around said complex and its solutions. Similarly instructive was the earlier disagreement between Vinea and his friend Tzara after Dada's Zurich world premiere.[31] Previously, both writers had contributed to several short-lived post-Symbolist magazines including *Simbolul* and *Chemarea* and had spent holidays together writing nonconformist poems, some of which would be read by Tzara on the stage of Cabaret Voltaire. Unlike Tzara, who went on to build a widely acclaimed career, Vinea, who was at least as good a poet as his friend, did not leave Romania, and, in Bucharest, unlike Noica, would become increasingly bitter in the face of a world to which he remained unknown and "marginal."

A few years after the First World War, Vinea was still hopeful, though. In a 1924 article published in *Cuvântul liber* and titled "Modernism şi tradiţie" (Modernism and Tradition), he points to Brâncuşi, Tzara, and Janco, who had met with success abroad and who were, according to Vinea, living proof that Romanian artists were in a good position to try and reduce the historical trade deficit of the culture by reversing the inflows through its communicating channels. Romanian modernism, Vinea claimed, was no longer an import, peripheral mimesis at best, but a product flowing out into the bigger world, an "export modernism" (*modernism de export*). "As for the modernism beginning to proliferate especially after 1917," he wrote,

> it goes, in the bargain, against the grain of our entire literature and art: it is an *export modernism*. It is for the first time we have given the world outside something this world has recognized as such. Today it is universally acknowledged that sculptor Brâncuşi has influenced the entire field of the modern arts through his students, Liepschitz and Arhipenko, who have become much more famous than the master himself. All art circles abroad are aware of the role Marcel Janco had played in the spread of Cubism since as early as 1915. It is also well known that this great artist is the first to create Cubist plaster reliefs in Western Europe. Finally, our friend Tristan Tzara, who had published his lyrics in *Chemarea* in 1915, sparked off an entire literary movement that pulled the youth in France, Germany, Switzerland, and America away from the conventions of outdated Symbolism. Every newly founded magazine in these countries is a testimony to the insignificant feat planned around here before the war and that clears Romanian modernists of any "import" charges.[32]

The reference to the "insignificant feat" or "accomplishment"—in the original, the Romanian *ispravă* is both ironic and self-deprecating—conveys a frustration that would only deepen in years to come. Even more exasperated already was, around the same time, Vinea's friend Benjamin Fundoianu (1898–1944) in his 1921 book *Imagini și cărți din Franța* (Images and Books from France). Like Vinea, Fundoianu, a modernist poet and essayist, had been the product of *fin-de-siècle* culture and decadent Symbolism. Before his 1923 expatriation to France, he published articles in *Contimporanul* and frequented avant-garde circles but was weary of the latter's revolutionary dogmas. He was, if for a little while, a bridge between the avant-garde and the Existentialist-mystical *arrière-garde* but also between Romanian and French culture, for he introduced new French poetry to the Romanian public and, after 1923, translated various Romanian writers into French. In *Imagini și cărți din Franța*, however, Fundoianu describes in harsh terms the "importing frenzy" of Romanian writers and their unbridled desire to copy French authors. In his volume's cynical preface, he claims not only that Romanian literature is utterly dependent on French literature—and that the latter's imitation has willy-nilly become the former's *raison d'être*—but also that his country's writers have produced, *as* Romanian writers, nothing that would enrich the pantheon of world culture. "We are no longer doing," Fundoianu thinks,

> poor and deliberate imitations—we are no longer copies of this kind but are in the process of most diligently working our way toward a different kind of situation, where we belong to a different category. Our culture has evolved, and now cuts a particular figure, has acquired a certain status—it has turned into a colony—a colony of French culture.

Going on to expand on his severe verdict, Fundoianu adds insult to injury:

> We are dependent on French literature because of our bilingualism—at least insofar as the upper-class is concerned. We cannot write in French, even though this would be the only logical thing to do. And, when we write in Romanian, all we do is imitate [and so] we hardly contribute anything to world culture, to which we are useless. As a separate literature, we cannot be of interest to anyone. We will have to convince France that we are, intellectually speaking, a province of its larger geography, and that, in its greatest achievements, our literature is a contribution to French literature.[33]

Intent on making his contribution direct and without delay, Fundoianu left Romania for good, settling in Paris in 1923, where he changed his name to Benjamin Fondane. A follower of Nietzsche and Jules de Gaultier, he combined Judaic traditionalism of Hasidic inspiration and French modernism with avant-garde twists that did not exclude, however, classicist nostalgias and some "untimely" Nietzschean posturing. In France, he became known mainly as an existential thinker and as a disciple of Shestov. He is, in brief, an *antimodern* in Compagnon's sense. Fundoianu's insurgent antirationalism fascinated Cioran, who befriended him in Paris at the time of the Nazi occupation and who tried unsuccessfully to save him from Auschwitz. Cioran would later paint a touching portrait of Fundoianu in his 1986 book *Excercices d'admiration*.

Fundoianu's Jewish background, intertwined interests in the avant-garde and existentialist "authenticism," and tragically cut short career define another prominent member of the generation, Max Blecher (1909–1938). If Fundoianu is an antimodern, Blecher presents us with a case of "epiphanic" modernism. Having come down with Pott's disease, he was confined to his bed during the last ten years of his life, and so this "Romanian Kafka," as some critics have called him, had little chance of "exporting" his extraordinary gifts to the wider world. He admired Kierkegaard and Heidegger and was deeply fond of both Kafka and Kafka's "official" East European counterpart, Bruno Schulz. Blecher's 1936 masterpiece *Întâmplări în irealitatea imediată* (Adventures in Immediate Unreality), recently retranslated into English by Michael Henry Heim, is steeped in an original and haunting version of Surrealism. A generic and literary-philosophical hybrid, the book is at once a poetic novel of sorts, an essayistic meditation, and the personal diary chronicling the identity crises of a hallucinating teenager in a nameless and godforsaken small town.[34] Like Fundoianu, Blecher did not have the time to serve as the intermediary he could have become between the radical avant-garde and the *arrière-garde* of the Romanian 1930s. But, if Blecher's striking blend of Surrealist–realist–absurdist perception and intimations of a higher reality nested in the drabness of the "immediate" everyday drew the admiration of Eugen Ionescu, that was also because Ionescu himself was ready to play this part, which he did at various historical junctures and sites of the Euromodernist continuum.

Ionesco's French theater, for instance, was explicitly influenced not only by Romanian playwright Ion Luca Caragiale, as a number of critics remind us in *Romanian Literature as World Literature*, but also by Urmuz (Demetru Dem. Demetrescu-Buzău), the great role model of all Romanian avant-gardists, while the peculiar strain of slapstick nihilism of *No* (1934), an essay book launching a devastating metaphysical-existentialist attack on the literary critics of Ionescu's time, is akin to the carnivalesque relativism of Tzara's manifestos. If, inside the communicating vessels of modernism, Ionescu makes for a tributary flowing smoothly into the broader stream of Ionesco's oeuvre, the author's *entire* Romanian–French body of work seems split between a nihilistic, rebellious, and iconoclastic impulse, on one side, and a religious search for divinity, on the other. Noticing, to his dismay, that the vast majority of his friends in Romania had joined the Far Right, which he detested, Ionesco looked for a personal, political, and philosophical solution equally distant from Christian Orthodox fundamentalism and Communist atheism, and he found it in the leftist Catholic Personalism of Emmanuel Mounier, who edited the French magazine *Esprit*. His friends included—in Bucharest as well as later on in Paris—Eliade and Cioran, who relied, however, on different maps to navigate the same rough waters of culture and history. And yet instructive intersections, parallels, and confluences obtain within this quasi-mythic triangle as well. Eliade, for example, *was* indebted to Italian Futurism but not aesthetically, although he was as an admirer of Papini, a Futurist dissenter; the University of Chicago historian of religions was drawn to Futurism ethically and politically, and by the same token to the "aestheticization of violence" Frankfurt School critics would tie to Fascism. Remarkably enough, however, in a 1950s journal entry Eliade would pinpoint, in hindsight, several important similitudes between his ideas about "transgression" and André Breton's.[35]

Eliade's "Surrealism" is just one element of a vast and multifaceted work in which the correlation avant-garde–*arrière-garde* becomes visible in the Romanian 1930s and beyond Romanian cultural history and geography. Cioran's case is equally telling—and equally special. His anti-rationalist *forma mentis* was Nietzschean but also shaped by Oswald Spengler's morphological approach to history and by *Lebensphilosophie*, hence Cioran's back-and-forth between a decadent stylistics and Expressionist *Formlosigkeit*. Against the grain of Spenglerian *Kulturpessimismus*, though, Cioran published in 1936 a fiery and politically extremist manifesto, *Schimbarea la față a României* (Romania's Transfiguration), where he proclaims that "Romania is the fruit of a modernist passion" and praises the "historical leap" and "fertile break with the past" whereby "smaller cultures" can at long last overcome their subaltern and marginal condition.[36] Addressing his country as a self-styled prophet of the Apocalypse, revolutionary provocateur, and instigator of a national "regeneration," Cioran develops a Vitalist philosophy of history and cultural–anthropological morphology that is more akin to Italian Fascism and German National Socialism than to the Romanian Iron Guard. Vehemently opposed to traditionalism, ruralism, Orthodoxism, and the like, he urges immediate "synchronization" with the Messianic "progressivism" he thinks characterizes Europe's rising dictatorships. At this stage in his career, he is an advocate of totalitarian modernism and of a drastic change of history's direction. As I have shown, he is, at this point, hardly the only one hungry for this change, in Romania and abroad. Violent or less so, couched in aesthetic languages, in political discourse, or in both, this transformation's theme and the rhetoric swirling around it constitute the unifying cultural undertow of a radical modernity running across the divides between Left and Right, Fascism and Communism, the progressives and the reactionaries, and the artistic avant-garde and the moderate and conservative aesthetes whose lives and works make up the system of the Romanian and European modernism of the 1930s.

Notes

1   See, for example, Jeffrey Herf, *Reactionary Modernism: Technology, Culture, and Politics in Weimar and the Third Reich* (Cambridge: Cambridge University Press, 1984), 1–18.

2   See Sorin Alexandrescu, *Privind înapoi, modernitatea*, trans. Mirela Adăscăliței, Șerban Anghelescu, Mara Chirițescu, and Ramona Jugureanu (Bucharest: Univers, 1999). The critic revisits his views on this issue in his essay "Modernism și antimodernism. Din nou, cazul românesc," in *Modernism și antimodernism. Noi perspective interdisciplinare*, ed. Sorin Antohi (Bucharest: Cuvântul and Muzeul Literaturii Române, 2008), 103–161.

3   See the theory of the two modernisms—progressive-bourgeois *vs.* anti-bourgeois, left-wing *vs.* right-wing—in Matei Călinescu's book *Cinci fețe ale modernității. Modernism, avangardă, decadență, kitsch, postmodernism*, 2nd rev. ed., trans. Tatiana Pătrulescu and Radu Țurcanu (Iași: Polirom, 2005).

4   See, in particular, Eugen Lovinescu, *Istoria literaturii române contemporane*, vol. 1–6 (Bucharest: Ancora, 1926–1929); G. Călinescu, *Istoria literaturii române de la*

origini până în prezent (Bucharest: Editura Fundaţiilor Regale, 1941); Z. Ornea, *Tradiţionalism şi modernitate în România deceniului al treilea* (Bucharest: Minerva, 1980).

5 Sorin Antohi, "Cuvânt-înainte: Modernism şi antimodernism," in *Modernism şi antimodernism*, ed. Sorin Antohi, 7–8.

6 For an international bibliography of the relationship between modernism and anti-modernism, see also T. J. Jackson Lears, *No Place of Grace: Antimodernism and the Transformation of American Culture, 1880–1920* (Chicago: University of Chicago Press, 1981); Lynda Jessup, ed., *Antimodernism and Artistic Experience: Policing the Boundaries of Modernity* (Toronto: University of Toronto Press, 2001); Hal Foster, Rosalind Kraus, Yve-Alain Bois, and Benjamin Buchlon, *Art since 1900: Modernism, Antimodernism, Postmodernism* (London: Thames & Hudson, 2011); Diana Mishkova, Marius Turda, and Balazs Trencsenyi, eds., *Anti-modernism: Radical Revisions of Collective Identity; Discourses of Collective Identity in Central and Eastern Europe, 1770–1945*, vol. 4 (Budapest: CEU Press, 2014); Susan Stanford Friedman, "Planetarity: Musing Modernist Studies," *Modernism/Modernity* 17, no. 3 (September 2010): 471–499; Mark Wollaeger and Matt Eatough, *The Oxford Handbook of Global Modernisms* (New York: Oxford University Press, 2012), which was reviewed by Christian Moraru in "Modernist Studies after Modernism," *symploke* 22, no. 1–2 (2015): 303–306.

7 Nae Ionescu, *Roza vânturilor. 1926–1933*, ed. Mircea Eliade (Bucharest: Cultura naţională, 1937), 23–25.

8 Roger Griffin, "Modernitate, modernism şi fascism: O 're-sintetizare a viziunii,'" in *Modernism şi antimodernism*, ed. Sorin Antohi, 62. Griffin's widely acclaimed book on the subject is *Modernism and Fascism: The Sense of a Beginning under Mussolini and Hitler* (London: Palgrave Macmillan, 2007).

9 Roger Griffin, "Modernity, Modernism, and Fascism: A 'mazeway resynthesis,'" *Modernism/Modernity* 15, no. 1 (2008): 9–24. On this problem, see also Fredric Jameson, *Fables of Aggression: Wyndham Lewis, the Modernist as Fascist* (Berkeley, CA: University of California Press, 1979).

10 Griffin, "Modernity, Modernism, and Fascism, 15.

11 Griffin, "Modernity, Modernism, and Fascism, 15–16.

12 Marta Petreu, *De la Junimea la Noica. Studii de cultură românească* (Iaşi: Polirom, 2011), 420.

13 Petreu, *De la Junimea la Noica*, 298.

14 *Anarhismul poetic* (Poetic Anarchism) was the first doctoral thesis on Romanian avant-garde poetry. Written by Romanian scholar Constantin I. Emilian (Bucharest: Tipografia Bucovina, 1932), it views almost entire modernist and avant-garde poetry and, in fact, nearly all modern culture of the period as "anarchism."

15 Sorin Alexandrescu, *Privind înapoi, modernitatea*, 134–135. For a definition of the Romanian modernism between the First and the Second World Wars, see *Modernismul literar românesc în date (1880–2000) şi texte (1880–1949)*, vol. 1–2, ed. Gabriela Omăt (Bucharest: Institutul Cultural Român, 2010).

16 Antoine Compagnon's *Les cinq paradoxes de la modernité* (Paris: Seuil, 1990) has been translated into Romanian as *Antimodernii. De la Joseph de Maistre la Roland Barthes*, trans. into Romanian by Irina Mavrodin and Adina Diniţoiu (Bucharest: Art, 2008). The passage can be found on p. 12.

17   Compagnon, *Antimodernii*, 537.

18   Compagnon, *Antimodernii*,18.

19   Compagnon, *Antimodernii*, 13.

20   Compagnon, *Antimodernii*, 20.

21   Compagnon, *Antimodernii*, 18.

22   Graf Hermann Keyserling, *Das Spektrum Europas* (Heidelberg: Niels Kampmann Verlag, 1927).

23   Ion Vinea, "Pentru contimporani," *Contimporanul* 34 (1923): 1.

24   Ovid S. Crohmălniceanu, *Literatura română și expresionismul* (Bucharest: Eminescu, 1971).

25   Hayden White, "Modernism and Primitivism," in *Modernism și antimodernism*, ed. Sorin Antohi, 18.

26   Mircea Vulcănescu, *Tânăra generație*, ed. Marin Diaconu (Bucharest: Editura Compania, 2004), 220.

27   William Marx, ed., *Les arrières-gardes du XX-e siècle. L'autre face de la modernité esthétique* (Paris: PUF, 2004).

28   Vincent Kaufmann, "L'arrière-garde vue de l'avant," in *Les arrières-gardes du XX-e siècle*, 27–34.

29   Marjorie Perloff, *Unoriginal Genius: Poetry by Other Means in the New Century* (Chicago: University of Chicago Press, 2010), 53.

30   This is Compagnon's overall argument in *Les cinq paradoxes de la modernité*.

31   I have discussed this problem in my book *Avangarda românească și complexul periferiei. Primul „val"* (Bucharest: Cartea Românească, 2007).

32   Ion Vinea, "Modernism și tradiție," *Cuvântul liber* 1 (1924): 101–102.

33   B. Fundoianu, *Imagini și cărți din Franța* (Bucharest: Socec, 1921), 11.

34   Max Blecher, *Adventures in Immediate Unreality*, trans. Michael Henry Heim, with essays by Andrei Codrescu ("Max Blecher's Adventures") and Herta Müller ("Every Object Must Occupy the Place It Occupies, and I Must Be the Person I Am") (New York: Directions, 2015).

35   Mircea Eliade, *Fragments d'un journal* (Paris: Gallimard, 1973), 62.

36   Emil Cioran, *Opere*, vol. I, ed. Marin Diaconu (Bucharest: Academia Română, Fundația Națională pentru Știință și Artă, 2012), 510–511.

Part III

Over Deep Time, Across Long Space

When we talk about research, the role played by national space is limited. This space does supply research topics, but it is too small to host the network of specialists with whom the researcher must necessarily engage in dialogue. The space required by this network is, as the Renaissance taught us, supranational. And, if we still insist on going back to the good all times, then we might as well remember that this space was the Republic of Letters, not the Socialist Republic of Romania, and not even the Romanian Kingdom. We might notice too that the new Republic of Letters has capitals also in Asia, in America, and in Europe.

Alexandru Matei, "Introducere în noua ecologie a criticii literare"
(Introduction to the New Ecology of Literary Criticism)

10

Temporal Webs of World Literature: Rebranding Games and Global Relevance after the Second World War—Mircea Eliade, E. M. Cioran, Eugène Ionesco

Mihai Iovănel

Drawing on world-systems theory, on the historical analysis model developed by Pascale Casanova, and on similar contributions by critics such as Franco Moretti, Wai Chee Dimock, Eric Hayot, and Christian Moraru, my essay explores the transcultural protocols by which three Romanian writers—Mircea Eliade, Emil Cioran, and Eugen Ionescu—acquired major author status in the French culture of post–Second World War Paris. As I suggest below, after they had become popular in interwar Romania—a "peripheral" country in Immanuel Wallerstein's terminology—these authors managed to reinvent themselves across deeper space and time by rebranding themselves in a central cultural arena and by "exporting" themselves to the wider world, thus receiving global recognition. As is well known, Eliade (1907–1986) is renowned internationally first and foremost as a student of religions, as well as an author and editor of books that participated prominently in the epistemological shifts taking place between 1940 and 1980.[1] These works also carved him a popular culture niche as a guru of sorts of the 1960s' hippy generation, which was drawn to the Eastern philosophies that were Eliade's chief specialty. But he also enjoys a certain reputation as a fiction author translated into several languages and was even mentioned as a potential Nobel Prize laureate during the 1980s.[2] Cioran (1911–1995), or E. M. Cioran, as his name reads on his French books' covers, is an essayist who around the age of 35 switched from Romanian, in which he had shocked the literary establishment of his native country, to an old-fashioned French of the kind used in the seventeenth century, which did not prevent him from emerging as one of the great post–Second World War French masters of literary style.[3] Eugen Ionescu (1909–1994), or Eugène Ionesco, as he signed his name in French, became known worldwide as a representative of the "theater of the absurd."[4] He is one of the few authors featured during their lifetime in the prestigious collection La Pléiade, which released his Théâtre complet volume in 1991. Cioran's 2011 Œuvres, too, is included in the Pléiade. One could argue, consequently, that these authors do deserve a place in the twentieth-century Western canon, possibly even in one of its shorter versions. More notably yet, together they speak to a phenomenon that is quite typical of their native country. For, although whether any writer from Romania has achieved genuine world fame during the last two centuries remains something of an open question, several Romanian-born authors, starting with avant-garde poet Tristan Tzara (1896–1963),[5] managed to remake themselves into successful presences in cultures such as those from Western Europe and the United States.[6]

Underlying such a success, this very tension between peripheral roots and subsequent prestige in a central culture constitutes the focus of my discussion. As already mentioned, my approach follows in the line of recent theoretical tendencies in comparative studies, World Literature, and world-systems interpretation. More to the point, I turn, with some reservations, to Casanova's *The World Republic of Letters*. In spite of its Gallocentrism and other problematic aspects, which I take up later on,[7] her 1999 book is instrumental to my efforts insofar as it provides a dynamic model of literary system, "one of incessant struggle and competition over the very nature of literature itself—an endless succession of literary manifestos, movements, assaults, and revolutions."[8] Then, leaning on Moretti, I ground my analysis in a series of assumptions regarding the "evolutionary" type of developments within world-systems and, in particular, within literary world-systems. Finally, from Dimock I borrow the concepts of "nonstandard time" and "supranational time,"[9] which help me refine the usual, spatial-geographical model for tackling "globalization," *mondialisation*, and "planetarity" by adding a temporal component to it.[10]

This element is key to my undertaking, which starts from the premise that literary geography also performs a temporal function.[11] To clarify, I should point out that, in view of my argument, temporality makes for a milieu twice. First, writers need to work out their relationship to it the same way players have to figure out their offensive and defensive tactics on a chessboard—a move forward that is too quick ("avant-gardist"), for instance, or one that is too cautiously slow ("defensive" or "conservative") may compromise the global front strategy, which in our case is geared toward the writers' advancing into, and gaining recognition in, a major cultural domain and network. Also, temporality constitutes an environment insofar as it comprises an inextinguishable supply of nonlinear, heterogeneous scenarios and trajectories where a sequence of seemingly energetic and well-effected moves such as those making up a writer's career may stop suddenly, if not arbitrarily, or where, on the contrary, a move that was apparently blocked in the past may undergo a resuscitation that is as spectacular as it is unpredictable. In other words, as I show in what follows, the predictability of the center–periphery type of spatial relations is offset temporally, at the level of long-term duration, insofar as later developments in an author's career may trigger retroactively countervailing games of repositioning and reassessment involving that author and his or her original (native) cultural system. On the one hand, this game may surprise us because those specific junctures in the future that will eventually erase, reset, and otherwise alter what has already occurred cannot be foreseen in the present of the occurrence, which will in turn become, from their perspective, a scene from the past. On the other hand, the game's course may be somewhat anticipated as mechanism, in terms of how the game is played. The more complex and cross-culturally interconnected the literary networks accessed by a certain work or writer, the greater the chance future networks will recoup and reclaim the work or writer in question. In fact, as we shall see below, networks are an important conceptual operator for mapping out the primary sources and for unifying the terminology of my essay. Of interest here are, specifically, those webs and web-like structures of national, transnational, and planetary organization that work through intertextuality, all sorts of ideologies, and other connectors of varying degrees of power and that integrate the spatial and the temporal vectors. Elucidating this multilayered convergence is one of my main goals. Inspired by Moraru's 2015 geomethodological manifesto *Reading for the Planet: Toward a Geomethodology*, the pursuit of this objective involves the tracing, however sketchy and limited in scope, of a "chronogeomethodology."[12]

1. The Players' Initial Positions: Divergences and Convergences

When one mentions Cioran, Eliade, and Ionesco together, this triggers, in Romania and elsewhere, certain associations almost automatically.[13] To many, the very narrative of success implied by the "Cioran, Eliade, and Ionesco triad" synthesizes and highlights the "periphery complexes" of Romanian culture.[14] Young, truly born under Romantic auspices in the nineteenth century despite some scattered medieval precedents that had not cohered into a system, Romanian literature shares said complexes with other peripheral and recent literatures. One such fixation or anxiety has to do with Romanian authors' stature, which fluctuates dramatically depending on whether they are read and judged inside or outside their country. Thus, the triumvirate's success story indirectly references, at the same time, the failures of Romanian writers who have *not* achieved world recognition even when they have been deemed "great" in Romania, as with Mihai Eminescu (1850–1889) himself, who is, according to a *locus classicus* of Romanian criticism, not only "the national poet" but also "the last great European Romantic."

Now, the clichés accumulated around their own careers aside, what substantive connections and commonalities are there among Cioran, Eliade, and Ionescu? First, it is worth mentioning that they all belong to the so-called Young Generation that arose around 1927 and consists of Romanian intellectuals born circa 1907, Eliade's birth year.[15] Second, each bears the characteristics of this group: the "match" the young writers played against their "elders," that is, against all other authors over 30; the obsession with "de-provincializing" Romania and, relatedly, with the grandiose "quantum leap" of the individual as well as of the culture as a whole into "universality;" the cognate ambition to finally put Romania on the world's cultural map, which betrays the anxiety of the country's perceived status as a "province of France," as B. Fundoianu had defiantly proclaimed in 1922;[16] left-wing or right-wing extremism, and sometimes both at once; the apparently contradictory propensity, on one side, for the "primacy of the spiritual" over the "material conditions of existence," which, at the time, our writers dismissed offhand as vulgar Marxism, and, on the other side, for all kinds of ethnic essentialisms. Third, all three authors produced a significant body of work in Romanian, with Eliade's the most substantial. In addition to his popularity as an essayist, which earned him the title of "leader" of the Generation, the "Romanian" Eliade already distinguished himself as a religious studies scholar through a trailblazing 1936 doctoral dissertation on Yoga, which stirred the interest of several European specialists, and as a fiction writer. His wildly variegated literary output ranges from experimental novels à la André Gide (*Isabel și apele diavolului* [Isabel and the Devil's Waters], 1930) or James Joyce (*Lumina ce se stinge* [The Light That Is Failing], 1931) to the exotic–erotic romance *Maitreyi* (*Bengal Nights*, 1933) to "Balzacian" novels about his generation such as *Întoarcerea din rai* (Return from Paradise, 1934) and *Huliganii* (The Hooligans, 1935) to the "pornographic" vampire narrative *Domnișoara Christina* (Miss Christina, 1936). In his turn, Cioran made waves with his five "scandalous" books published before 1940, especially *Schimbarea la față a României* (Romania's Transfiguration, 1936), an inflammatory, anti-Semitic manifesto fantasizing wildly about Romania's entry into the world's "greater history," and *Lacrimi și sfinți* (Tears and Saints, 1937), an assault on Christianity. As for Ionescu, his collection of aggressively iconoclastic essays *Nu* (No, 1934) tears down, cavalierly in some cases, more thoughtfully in others, canonical Romanian authors while questioning the very disciplinary foundations of literary criticism with a radicalism that puzzled the era's cultural establishment.

Fourth, one should keep in mind that not only did all three authors participate in politics, but that their involvement was also official. Eliade, for example, was sent on a diplomatic mission to London, where he was apparently involved in intelligence-gathering activities, and after that to Lisbon, where he was in charge with propaganda on behalf of the Fascist-authoritarian regime led back home by Marshall Ion Antonescu, a military ally of Nazi Germany.[17] Cioran and Ionesco were both affiliated with the Vichy bureaucratic apparatus. Cioran had gotten an assignment there based on his relations with the Iron Guard during the short yet disastrous interval between September 1940 and January 1941 when this Fascist organization took part in the Romanian Government, but he was deemed inefficient and was quickly demoted by Antonescu himself. Between 1942 and 1944, Ionesco served as a representative of the Propaganda Ministry in the Romanian mission at Vichy. It was due to their shady political past that all three writers ended up staying in France, where they entered the cultural game that would propel them as cultural players to be reckoned with globally. Past missteps, whether big or small—Cioran's and Eliade's overt Fascist allegiances or Ionescu's short stint as member of a far-right regime—would prevent them from returning to Romania after August 23, 1944, when their country, which had already been partly occupied by advancing Soviet troops, turned against its German ally. Up until then, each of them had maintained ties to their native land. Eliade's were the strongest, even though the history of religions was in the Romania of those days a target of ironies in the popular media and not much of an academic discipline despite Eliade's substantial work and exchanges with distinguished scholars from France, Italy, and Germany. Had it not been for the country's fall into the Soviet sphere of influence, which made it virtually impossible for him to go back home after the war, Eliade would have most likely returned in order to keep playing his twofold, home-and-away kind of game involving building a career in Romania and Europe concomitantly. For Cioran too, cutting himself off from Romania and, in particular, from the Romanian language was a traumatic event. Nonetheless, he all but stopped using his native tongue for the rest of his life. Ionesco also gave up on his Romanian ambitions in 1948, after his homeland had become Communist officially and by the same token a USSR satellite.

Until then, he had been making plans to publish a number of books in Romania and had continued to write in Romanian pieces such as *Englezeşte fără profesor* (*English without a Tutor*), an early version of a future play, *La Cantatrice Chauve* (*The Bald Soprano*), which would earn him worldwide acclaim.[18]

2. Repositionings

This is what the situation looks like when the "match" really gets under way—that is, when our players become exiles. On the one hand, there is Paris, "the capital of the nineteenth century," as Walter Benjamin aptly called it, but which continues to remain in the years immediately following the Great War one of the few planetary metropolises spawning the "universality" our writers were so much yearning for; on the other hand, here are three writers forced to undertake a radical career reset, viz., to start a process of cultural rebranding so as to reinvent themselves under circumstances totally different from those under which they became known. If one weighs, at this point, the chances they stood to win their game, one might conclude that the most odds seemed to have been stacked in Eliade's favor, as he was the most culturally versatile and polyglot among all three and had already enjoyed a good reputation in scholarly circles outside Romania. Thus, Georges Dumézil would invite him as early as 1945, right after Eliade's arrival in Paris that September, to teach at the prestigious École Pratique des Hautes Études, where his lectures started in February 1946. He would not be paid for them, and his French made him nervous as he suspected that it was barely acceptable "even in an elementary school."[19] At any rate, his teaching contract would be terminated before the end of the year as a result of the pressures exerted by the Romanian Government, which denounced Eliade's Fascist past.[20] Coming right after him, Ionescu occupied the second-best position at this juncture. Unlike Cioran, who picked up his French late, and unlike Eliade, who used it minimally until the end of his life, Ionesco was precociously bilingual due to his mother's Romanian–French roots and to the childhood years spent in France. Cioran too knew French, but he was not as fluent as Ionesco. In fact, he knew German much better, but this would not help him much at the time. During the war, he also began—quite literally—to learn English without a tutor, but since his newly acquired language skills did not come in handy either, he made a decision that, in hindsight, turned out to be right, namely, to learn to write in French and to fashion a distinct literary style for himself as a French writer. In any case, even though each author did it in his own way, all three authors ended up winning the global fame lottery.

How did they manage to pull it off, though? To answer the question, I should note, to begin with, the obvious: given their background, the writers found themselves arguably in one of the best places they could be in after the Second World War, and, in this place, they also made the smartest decisions possible, for which a good example is Cioran's giving up on Romanian and switching to French. But there are more substantial explanations for their success. The balance of my essay will offer three of them.

The first is that the cultural networks to which they would eventually gain access were more complex than Paris, which was rather "one-dimensional" despite its claims to work, according to Casanova, as a "universality" factory of sorts.[21] Eliade is a case in point for, in 1957, when he arrived in Chicago as a university professor, he joined a spectacularly expanding network.[22] He settled in Chicago permanently even though he continued to spend a lot of time in Paris. He also maintained good relationships in Germany, where he published one of his major books, *The Sacred and the Profane*, in 1957, which will be translated into French only in 1965. It was also in the 1960s that Cioran entered the American cultural market as Susan Sontag, one of the decade's rising intellectual celebrities, devoted an essay to his work in 1967.[23] In the United States, he also had the chance to be rendered into English by a poet and exceptional translator like Richard Howard.[24] Also, Paul Celan, who knew Cioran personally, translated Cioran's 1949 *Précis de décomposition* (A Short History of Decay) into German in 1953, only four years after the original French edition. Let us not forget, however, that during these years Cioran was a "niche" author. True, his books were published by a major press like Gallimard and were awarded several distinguished prizes, which, incidentally, were turned down by Cioran, except for the first one, the Rivarol (1950). But they would start appealing to wider audiences only in the 1980s, when *Syllogismes de l'amertume* (a 1952 book that would be later reissued in a *poche* edition), *Exercises d'admiration* (1986), and *Aveux et anathèmes* (1986) would enjoy high sales. As for Ionesco, he took advantage of the opportunity to become part of a genre global network, the "theater of the absurd," which linked him up with authors such as Samuel Beckett and Arthur Adamov in a cultural and historical context favorable to dramatic experiments of this kind.

The second explanation has to do with the *innovative* nature of each of these writers' work. Furthermore, not only did they all bring something new on the time's literary and intellectual scene but their innovations also placed them in a powerful position relative to the cultural center to which they had moved, for none of them tried to merely fit in by simply imitating trends then dominant in the West. Timely as it was in the aftermath of the Second World War carnage and following the 1942 publication of Albert Camus's *L'Étranger* și *Le Mythe de Sisyphe*, Ionescu's theater of the absurd fleshes out originally elements only vaguely present in the atmosphere of the age and well before the genre's formula would lose its avant-gardist edge. Recalling the 1950 staging of *La Cantatrice chauve*, one of the directors would ascribe the difficulty of figuring out how to approach the play's production to Ionesco's text itself, which was just too unusual and unprecedented.[25] In his turn, Cioran may have imitated the French moralists of the seventeenth and eighteenth centuries, but he did so at a time when injecting their classic and pure style with a desperate and blasé nihilism was strikingly singular.[26] And, finally, although the roots of Eliade's original thoughts on the history of religions are scattered throughout the interwar period and thus traceable to authors ranging from Raffaele Pettazzoni and Rudolf Otto to Ananda Coomaraswamy and René Guénon, he too brings a fresh interdisciplinarity and encyclopedic spirit to the table. Behind these innovations lie his acute provincial anxieties, which he often acknowledges in his essays, diaries, memoirs, and interviews, and also a certain

Romanian intellectual tradition centered on a well-rounded, Renaissance scholarly type, which had been illustrated by Dimitrie Cantemir, Bogdan Petriceicu Hasdeu, and Nicolae Iorga, all of whom Eliade admired a lot. Just like Ionesco, he had played one round of his cross-cultural match of self-reinvention before the rules of the game became a matter of public knowledge and drew other players, thereby seizing on the opportunities offered in the 1950s–1970s interval by a cultural and academic climate dominated by all kinds of speculative-ahistorical discourses such as phenomenology and structuralism—his "epistemic" decline would coincide, tellingly enough, with the rise of historicist approaches and "micronarrative" interpretation models, which arguably challenge the integrative thrust of Eliade's universalism.[27]

Each of the three writers manages, therefore, to become competitive by forging a nonmimetic relationship with adoptive culture. But, notably, this originality strategy is inconsistent. Like Beckett's, Ionesco's culturally nonimitative drive is *revolutionary*, for the works he starts producing have, at the time, no equivalent in the literary archives. Cioran's anti-mimetic approach lies in its *regressive* component in that he rediscovers something so old that it becomes new. His placement by Casanova alongside V. S. Naipaul in the "Assimilated" section of *The World Republic of Letters* makes sense only insofar as they both are quintessentially conservative, come from a "peripheral" culture, and invent a creative identity by "converting" to a central linguistic-cultural paradigm such as classical France for Cioran and imperial Great Britain for Naipaul.[28] Otherwise, Naipaul's fiction is perfectly synchronous with the times in which it was produced, even in its innovative character—his 1971 novel *In a Free State*, which consists of three apparently independent narratives, was awarded the Booker Prize amidst controversies regarding the work's adherence to the genre's conventions. By contrast, Cioran leaves the impression of a "body snatcher" sort of author whose contemporary look provides the cover for the reactivation of the stylistic manner of an eighteenth-century writer.

Equally worth exploring in Ionesco's and Cioran's cases alike is the relation between the innovative elements on which they based their rebranding in French culture and the Romanian body of work they had left behind. *La Cantatrice chauve*, for example, incorporates a good portion of a previous Romanian text, *English without a Tutor*. As a matter of fact, Ionesco would mine throughout his entire career Ionescu's writings. These were influenced—but also amplified and reconfigured according to Ionesco's unique personality—by Ion Luca Caragiale (1852–1912), the most important Romanian playwright, and by Urmuz (1883–1923), one of the world pioneers of absurd literature,[29] both of whom were marked by the typically Romanian feel for the absurd, for those "'Kafkaesque' moments of absurdity that are [everyday] realism in Romania"[30] and that stand out to many who visit the country or even to those Romanians who return home after a long absence. Of course, as Jorge Luis Borges hints in "Pierre Menard, Author of *Don Quijote*," what a text *literally* is, in its textuality, and what it can designate *literarily*, in terms of its meaning and literary-cultural significance, are not the same thing. This is, essentially, what Matei Călinescu suggests in an observation that has nothing paradoxical to it. *The Bald Soprano*, comments Călinescu, is, from a literary point of view, superior to *English without a Tutor*, although at least a third of it is a translation or verifiable adaptation .... Seen in the context of Romanian literature, *English without a Tutor* remains a marginal text, and a strange one to boot. By contrast, in the context of French literature, *La Cantatrice* ... is a powerfully original work consistent with and consolidated by the works Ionesco wrote after it, *the beginning of a series* and, at the same time, *the renewal of a comic tradition* that starts with Alfred Jarry, and, in a sense, can be traced back all the way to Rabelais .... What lends this French avant-gardist "anti-play" classic status, one that would have been inconceivable in Romanian literature, is not so much the fact that it was written in a widely circulated language but that it has *survived* a tough competition in this language and culture and that it has outlasted easily and gracefully the literary fads of the 1950s .... For, in Europe, the Romanian cultural milieu was and still is a peripheral and "poor" space, which cannot confer universality even on those writings that would fully deserve it.[31]

Cioran's game of cultural rebranding can be viewed along similar lines. The difference between *Pe culmile disperării* (On the Heights of Despair [1934], the first book he published in Romania), and *Précis de décomposition*, his French debut, is quite negligible as far as their anguished-nihilistic themes go, even though one may note the dissimilarity between the lyrical pathos and volcanic rhetoric of the 1934 volume and the blasé skepticism and austere style of the one that came out in 1949. The true distance here, however, is marked by the passage from a peripheral cultural system of reference (Romanian) to a central cultural system (French). The key to success lies in the deployment of an innovative strategy within the latter. True, Cioran had been an original Romanian writer as well, but his originality within his native culture had been both irrefutable and, from a broader, transnational perspective, irrelevant.

Eliade's career too shows, in a negative sort of way, just how important the radical change of the reference system is. For not only did he abandon the Romanian language, which would force him to rely on translators and would make him known solely "indirectly," in renditions of an original never in international circulation, but, if in his scholarship he broke, at the time, new ground, in his post–Second World War literary work he went for a literary strategy that proved inadequately anti-mimetic; in fact, in a 1950s Paris where writers were experimenting with the *Nouveau Roman*, Eliade attempted to break into the French cultural market by opting for one misguided strategy after another. First, in 1950, he translated, under the title *La Nuit bengali*, the exotic novel *Maitreyi*, which had been very popular with audiences from a wholly different place and time, namely, Romania in the 1930s. Then, he published *Forêt interdite* (Noaptea de Sânziene [1955]), translated into English as *The Forbidden Forest* (1978), a *roman-fresque* written in the typically Balzacian manner that was by then anything but new in France. Especially helpful in understanding Eliade's miscalculations as a fiction writer in Paris could be a comparison with Witold Gombrowicz. Having immigrated to Argentina before the Second World War, Gombrowicz did not renounce his native language, Polish, either and tried to gain access to the more marginal Argentine system through the 1947 translation of his 1937 novel *Ferdydurke*; he would eventually achieve global recognition but only through the translations published in France later on. Unlike Eliade, however, he is an innovator of the novelistic formula, so much so that his novels would be in the 1980s associated with postmodernism, as their freshness did not wear off with the transition from the French *Nouveau Roman* to the postmodern novel. It was only the fantastic prose, toward which Eliade channeled his creative energies after the failure of his novels, that emerged as a more suitable strategy in the 1960s and 1970s, when magical realism flourished in Latin America and was exported to Europe and the United States. Nevertheless, although the genre remains the best-known sector of his literary oeuvre, not even the fantastic would bring Eliade the world renown he sought. The film adaptation of his novella "Tinerețe fără tinerețe" by Francis Ford Coppola in *Youth without Youth* (2007) did not improve the situation much; the movie was deemed almost unanimously a "flop," with a score of 43 on Metacritic.com.[32]

As one can notice, what differentiates the moves made by the three writers engaged in their rebranding games is the temporal positions the players take up with respect to the major cultural processes unfolding at the French center—their new home—right after the Second World War. These positions can be defined as avant-gardist (with Ionesco a case in point as his emerging work was ahead of the cultural curve); coeval or synchronous (Eliade's religious studies scholarship); anachronistic-innovative (Cioran); and anachronistic-asynchronous (the novels Eliade republished in the 1950s). As the reader will recall, the unequal relationships of exchange that characterize the center–periphery dynamic have in Casanova's argument a temporal dimension;[33] the center *qua* center has an advantage over the periphery, and this advantage can never be entirely cancelled out, as in the ancient paradox about Achilles and the turtle, in which Achilles can no longer catch up with his opponent. However, this scenario does not seem to apply to the writers analyzed here. Although it is true that, as a national system, Romanian literature does not occupy the prominent position the French literary system holds in the world, and, in that, Romanian writers seeking to appeal to an international readership can be said to be a priori at disadvantage, individual inventiveness can overcome this handicap in fields such as literature, whereas in economics, commerce, and the like the collective and financial-material aspect of the "competition" makes the underdog's situation far more difficult. Well known in Romanian culture, the "synchronism" theory critic Eugen Lovinescu borrowed from Gabriel Tarde acknowledges this problem. According to Lovinescu, it is necessary for "small" (i.e., "young") cultures, in their search for a more or less utopian "synchronization" with the wider world, to follow the lead of "big" cultures, in which they find a sort of guiding "lighthouse." But, oddly enough, even though it was formulated around 1924–1925, Lovinescu's theory overlooks the Romanian avant-garde, the most spectacular "leap" made by the country's literature and by this literature *as* literary system, whose creativity rendered it a partner on equal footing with other systems engaged in experiments across Europe at the time. As an example, Tzara once again comes to mind first, a Jewish-Romanian writer who found it extremely easy to transition, during the first two decades of the twentieth century, from the Romanian system, replete as this was with ideologically and culturally rudimentary forms, to the full-blown Dadaism he helped invent.[34] It is also true, however, that any individual "leaps" in relation to a peripheral reference system require a new reference point—

in this case, the central system—in order to be not only validated but also "noticed," registered, culturally speaking. This "unequal exchange" between competitive peripheries and monopoly-like centers is perfectly illustrated by the difference-cum-similitude or discontinuity-in-continuity sort of dynamic obtaining, as we saw earlier, between *English without a Tutor* and *The Bald Soprano*.[35] A related aspect of this kind of cultural commerce lies in the particularity of the raw material to be exported (as such or processed) to the center. This bolsters the originality of experimental games relying on anti-mimesis. Moretti's hypothesis regarding the process through which marginal cultures adapt the Anglo-French novel by mixing it with elements of local tradition can be applied in the opposite, centripetal direction: the writer who, having moved into a central literature, innovates in it, brings over, from his or her native margins, material specific to the latter, and this stuff may pertain to form (e.g., the orality of the African novel) or to cultural tradition and milieu broadly, such as the fantastic-realistic atmosphere of Latin-American magical realism.[36]

But these repositionings and repurposing maneuvers involving formal or thematic elements have a political dimension as well. As far as Cioran, Eliade, and Ionescu are concerned, one cannot help noticing, in this view, a compromise in how they approached the conversion of their national capital into French and international cultural currency during the rebranding game. For instance, their early tendency toward political radicalism gave way quickly to a rather calm acceptance of bourgeois and mainstream values, with Ionesco going so far as to join the French Academy, a membership that carried conservative, indeed reactionary implications, bespeaking as it did an anti-Left attitude reaching beyond the anti-Communism[37] that, I might mention in passing, proved quite serviceable during the Cold War.[38] The three writers also laid aside their native language and the "peripheral" themes associated with it. In this respect, Eliade presents us with the most instructive situation: after the Second World War, he continued to write literature in Romanian, but he would not make it as a fiction author although his intricately encoded, cryptic-esoteric narratives were formally well positioned to be met with interest in a context in which fantastic literature by writers like Borges or Julio Cortázar was quickly infiltrating, also via French channels, the global reputation network. But our writers' "outgrowing" of their "Romanian" subject matter did not bring about a wholesale repudiation of their early writings. Instead, these were rather integrated into the authors' post–Second World War works: Cioran turned his Romanian hysterics into a literary subject, which he contemplates from the distance of the fairly well-controlled cynicism that informs his French writings; Ionesco made the most of Caragiale's and Urmuz's legacy; and Eliade introduced a Romanian problematic into a broader, world conversation through his scholarship, in *De Zalmoxis à Gengis-Khan* (1970), through his fiction, as well as through nonfictional prose such as his memoirs and diary. One could conclude, then, that they made the right moves as far as their Romanian beginnings go. After all, there are times when a "peripheral" culture pins its most realistic hopes for world recognition on the capacity to export to a "central" culture, in quantities as sizeable as possible, raw material ranging from anecdotes and subjects to entire cultural narratives such as those disseminated by our Romanian "informants" during their post-Romanian careers.

3. Temporal Networks

A third explanation for the success of the rebranding operation propelling these careers onto the world stage, I argue, would have to take into account the *critical mass* these writers made up over time, that is, the distinctively marked and self-supporting "mini-network" their books and personalities wove over a few decades. The well-known 1977 photograph taken in the Parisian Place de Furstenberg consecrated iconically the sociocultural effectiveness of the authors *as a group* both in their country of origin, where the success they all enjoyed abroad in similar circumstances made their association routine, but also in France. Attesting most saliently to this critical reflex is Alexandra Laignel-Lavastine's 2002 book *Cioran, Eliade, Ionesco. L'oubli du fascisme: trois intellectuels roumains dans la tourmente du siècle*, which focuses on the conspiratorial interpretation of the photo—all the writers under scrutiny, Laignel-Lavastine suggests, have built their French and international careers on "moves" meant to cover up their blemished past.

Be that as it may, the concept of network—mini-networks, national networks, or global networks—informs all of these explanatory elements. Cioran, Eliade, and Ionesco started off by distinguishing themselves in a local or national network of interwar Romania. Later, they managed, through a cultural rebranding operation, to carve out a space for themselves in the larger, French network, which in turn makes it possible for them to take their place in world networks, be they literary ("the theater of the absurd" for Ionesco, fantastic literature and the history of religions for Eliade, and nihilistic literature for Cioran), national (France, Germany, Great Britain, the United States), or global. Far from being merely spatial or territorial, as the relation between a center and a periphery might suggest, these networks also have a temporal dimension. This comes into play in the chronology that undergirds the lopsided exchange between an influencing, "central" culture and influenced culture's usually belated response, in the temporal aspect of the recognition strategies deployed by the very trio discussed here, in the network "shelf life" or authors and works, or in these writers' capacity to start over once they have become part of such a network. As Dimock has shown,

> *Deviation* from the national timetable surely matters as much as the synchronization under the sign of the nation. Such deviation challenges not only the sequence of events dictated by a territorial regime, it also challenges the sequence of events dictated by a literary canon. Neither of these official narratives can line everyone up, for the effect of offbeat reading is to generate a temporal bond at odds with the chronological progression of the nation, and at odds with the chronological succession of sanctified texts. What results is a kind of serial unpredictability, the unexpected contact between points of time numerically far apart.[39]

Now, once Casanova's symbolic capital has reached an amount sufficient to form a critical mass equivalent to the writers' "validation" or "recognition" on a local or global scale, the "cash value" of the cultural assets thus established moves, over time, neither in a straight line nor over a homogenous space. Some authors lose their symbolic capital fast without ever recuperating it, while others—Ionesco, for instance—consolidate it. And writers like Eliade deplete their funds completely yet manage to replenish them in a new asset configuration. In short, a writer's symbolic capital or brand takes up various forms, which register inevitable ups and downs. So has, accordingly, the world's interest in the three Romanian authors even though the fluctuations have been less dramatic than those affecting, say, some postcolonial writers, whose life cycle on the global market depends more closely on the planet's political "stock market."[40] Again, in this regard, Ionesco's trajectory is the smoothest although his oeuvre is the most radically innovative. After achieving and consolidating his fame in the 1950s and 1960s, when he wrote his most characteristic works—*La Cantatrice chauve* (1950), *Les Chaises* (1952), *Rhinocéros* (1959), and *Le roi se meurt* (1962)—Ionesco focused mainly on maintaining it: he became a member of the French Academy, received honors and had his plays produced all over the world, published in *Le Figaro* essays later on collected in volumes, composed more dramatic pieces, gave interviews, and so on. Being published in the *Pléiade* during his lifetime was also an honor and helped secure his place both in French culture and in the global arena, where scholarship on his output would also grow steadily, in the English-speaking world and beyond.

Cioran's and Eliade's situations are different. The authors benefitted from a belated shockwave that reanimated their posterity, keeping it alive as a globalized or globally present text but also deeply altering it. Triggering both processes was the resurfacing, in the last years of the previous century, of their Fascist past. Ionesco's little Vichy episode did not have any significant consequences. Bits and pieces about it had come out in previous decades, but in a scattershot kind of way and under circumstances that failed to lend them long-term critical force. These revelations had more enduring effects for the other two. These repercussions were paradoxical especially in Eliade's case: on one side, they gave his public persona a new lease on life, and, on the other, affected, even destroyed his credibility as a history of religions scholar.[41] Incremental disclosures such as those from *Jurnalul portughez* (The Portugal Journal), which had been left unpublished for a long time, sparked political controversies to which the interest in Eliade's scholarship had to take a back seat.[42] At the same time, Eliade was cast as a character in recent novels such as Saul Bellow's *Ravelstein* (2000), Norman Manea's *Vizuina* (2009)—translated into English as *The Lair* in 2012—and Caius Dobrescu's *Minoic* (2011), which puts an ironic spin on a host of conspiracy theories. In parallel with his afterlife as a protagonist of intellectual thrillers, Eliade became target of a detective sort of reading. Only this line of interpretation did not pursue his work's ahistorical symbolism, which would have been an approach he would have probably appreciated, but, with critics such as Daniel Dubuisson, Matei Călinescu, and Marta Petreu, a political subtext or "code" that, once broken, would expose his disguised Fascism.[43] Interestingly enough, as Eliade's links with Fascism became a matter of public record, he would all but lose his position, if not as an inquiry topic then as a scholar firmly established in academic culture, at the same time as he would consolidate his presence in mass culture, where Fascism remains, largely for entertaining purposes, a theme popular with thriller authors and big-budget movie producers alike.

Cioran, on the other hand, had less to lose than Eliade, for, although his posthumousness is similar to his friend, he had no academic reputation to defend. He had also been more honest about his past, to which he had owned up occasionally. Nevertheless, for him too Fascism played an oddly revitalizing role, which was similar to the one that turned Eliade into a fictional character. Brought to light in the 1990s, Cioran's Fascism conferred the author a "menacing," "radical" edge, a sort of ominous "seriousness" that, after his earlier despairs had lost their original punch, worked to discourage the sentimentalist responses that would have relegated his books to young adult literature status. A measure of Cioran's posterity is given by his presence in *True Detective*'s season 1 (2014), "an instant classic" as far as TV series go. Not only does the show's most charismatic character, detective Rust Cohle (played by Matthew McConaughey), talk like Cioran, but Cohle also plagiarizes the philosopher via Thomas Ligotti, author *The Conspiracy against the Human Race: A Contrivance of Horror* (2010), where Cioran is one of the main references.[44]

4. Recursive Globalization

If the world-system in general and the Western world-system in particular can be said to involve an actual canonical hierarchy, no matter how restrictive and even "reactionary," and, further, if this hierarchy's makeup changes according to the trends of the international stock market built into the system, then such variations, I propose, warrant an analysis of globalization as a *recursive* process, to wit, as a spatial-temporal world phenomenon that, because it is not a perpetuum mobile, requires periodic jumpstarts to keep going. This can be done in different ways, but all of them bring into question Casanova's glosses on the autonomy of the literary field in relation to the historical-material and political domains.[45] Specifically, it is the heteronomous, multidirectional nature of what I determine as recursive globalization that raises serious doubts about her claims on this issue. In other words, the stepping of a (semi) peripheral culture writer into the global system is a complex act involving more than exchanges between a center and a periphery, as Casanova's limitedly Gallocentric reading model implies. Nor is this move complete and done with once for all but rather reiterative, for it needs occasional restimulation to maintain its functionality and vitality. Moreover, this operation depends, to a large extent, on the political as well as on the ideological map. It is in this vein that Carlo Ginzburg suggests that "One day [Eliade's] *The Myth of the Eternal Return* might be taken up as an antiglobalization, postcolonial, ecological manifesto."[46] At the same time, one must recognize that there is also an element of arbitrariness to an author's access to global significance, and that this component is at least as important as whatever, in the success narrative, may point to a world celebrity achieved rationally, programmatically, and otherwise by design. Accounting for this is not only—and most basically—the inscrutable nature of time but also the literary system's lack of autonomy with respect to history, as borne out, in fact, by the very careers of Cioran and Eliade.[47] The ever-increasing curiosity about the Fascist past of Cioran, Eliade, or Paul de Man, for that matter, coupled with the post-1980s transformation of the Holocaust into a critical and public inquiry "macro-theme," as well as the unpredictable developments in popular culture are all external factors rather than "immanent" to the cultural field. By the same token, this field's "autonomy" is a fallacy. To be sure, the literary world-system plays the game of real history; the latter throws the dice, and culture rolls with them. This is why it is only in hindsight that one can draw some broader conclusions from the case of writers who, like Eliade, Cioran, and Ionesco, come from an economic and cultural periphery, cannot but reinvent themselves in a central milieu, succeed in this operation of cultural rebranding, and ultimately achieve global fame in the post–Second World War years. One can argue, in effect, that, whatever rules drive the evolution of the literary system, they will always become discernable retrospectively; looking forward, the system can hardly help us predict anything due to the close yet oftentimes arbitrary relation between culture and history. This does not mean, however, that one cannot pinpoint certain circumstances favorable to peripheral cultures and their writers' advancement into the global arena. As we have seen, paramount among these is the ability to play, in and with one's own work, games in which the final score depends on the author-player's capacity to innovate, on the ambiguity of potential interpretations of his or her oeuvre, on his or her spatial mobility, and, last but not least, on his or her integration into more and more complex and far-reaching networks.

Notes

1   Florin Țurcanu is the author of the most important Eliade biography, *Mircea Eliade, le prisonnier de l'histoire* (Paris: Découverte, 2003). See also Matei Călinescu, *Despre Ioan P. Culianu și Mircea Eliade. Amintiri, lecturi, reflecții*, trans. Mona Antohi (Iași: Polirom, 2002); *Hermeneutics, Politics, and the History of Religions: The Contested Legacies of Joachim Wach and Mircea Eliade*, ed. Christian K. Wedemeyer and Wendy Doniger (Oxford: Oxford University Press, 2010); Moshe Idel, *Mircea Eliade: From Magic to Myth* (New York: Peter Lang, 2014).

2   Țurcanu, *Mircea Eliade*, 501–502.

3   Ilinca Zarifopol-Johnston, *Searching for Cioran* (Bloomington, IN: Indiana University Press, 2009); Nicolas Cavaillès, *Cioran malgré lui* (Paris: CNRS Édition, 2011); Nicolas Cavaillès, "Chronologie," in *Œuvres*, ed. Emil Cioran (Paris: Bibliothèque de la Pléiade, 2011), XXXI–LVI; Marta Petreu, *An Infamous Past: E. M. Cioran and the Rise of Fascism in Romania*, trans. Bogdan Aldea (Chicago: Ivan R. Dee, 2005); Marin Diaconu, "Cronologie," in Emil Cioran, *Opere*, vol. I (Bucharest: Fundația Națională pentru Știință și Artă, 2012), CLIX–CCLXXII; Eugen Simion, *Cioran, une mythologie de l'inachevé*, trans. Virgil Tănase (Le Mesnil-Mauger: Soupirail, 2016).

4   Matei Călinescu, *Eugène Ionesco: teme identitare și existențiale* (Iași: Junimea, 2006); Marta Petreu, *Ionescu în țara tatălui* (Iași: Polirom, 2012); Eugen Simion, *Le jeune Eugen Ionescu*, trans. Virgil Tănase (Paris: L'Harmattan, 2013); Alex Drace-Francis, "Eugen Ionescu's Selves, 1934–60," in *The Traditions of Invention: Romanian Ethnic and Social Stereotypes in Historical Context* (Leiden: Brill, 2013), 201–212.

5   For a discussion of Romanian cultural exports, see Andrei Terian, "Romanian Literature for the World: A Matter of Property," *World Literature Studies* 2 (2015): 3–14.

6 On the *Gallimard* website, there are no references to Ionesco and Cioran's Romanian origins. Both are listed as French nationals, whereas Georges Simenon, who spent most of his life in France, is presented as Belgian. A short note does indicate that Cioran was "born in 1911 in Romania," but there is no mention of Ionesco's Romanian roots and identity. See http://www.la-pleiade.fr

7 For critical reactions to Casanova, see especially Christopher Prendergast, "The World Republic of Letters," in *Debating World Literature*, ed. Christopher Prendergast (London: Verso, 2004), 1–25; Ebjani Ganguly, "Global Literary Refractions: Reading Casanova's *The World Republic of Letters* in the Post-Cold War Era," in *Literature for our Times*, ed. Bill Ashcroft et al. (Amsterdam: Rodopi, 2012), 21–33.

8 Pascale Casanova, *The World Republic of Letters*, trans. M. M. DeBevoise (Cambridge, MA: Harvard University Press, 2007), 12.

9 "Supranational time," writes Dimock, "seems to me especially important, if currently undertheorized, in the context of globalization. What I have in mind is a duration antedating the birth of any nation and outlasting the demise of all. The unit of analysis here is large-scale but not standardized, due in part to the context-dependent time frames and in part to the vectorial arrow running in both directions. Supranational time goes backward (a recursive loop into the past), and it goes forward (a projective arc into the future). This bidirectional arrow maps the entire length of history as a field of globalization. World governance takes on new meaning as a result." See Wai Chee Dimock, "Planetary Time and Global Translation: 'Context' in Literary Studies," *Common Knowledge* 9, no. 3 (2003): 490–491.

10 For an astute analysis and groundbreaking manifesto for a "planetary" reading, see Christian Moraru, *Reading for the Planet: Toward a Geomethodology* (University of Michigan Press: Ann Arbor, 2015), 39–76. Also relevant here is Eric Hayot's recent work *On Literary Worlds* (Oxford: Oxford University Press, 2012).

11 Casanova, *The World Republic of Letters*, 351.

12 Moraru explicitly foregrounds the temporal component of his planetary project. As he writes in *Reading for the Planet*, "there is no fully constituted 'planetarized' order or spatial planetarity. What we have instead is an ongoing, polydirectional, and uncoordinated planetarization process whose twin *axis* is spatial and temporal *depth*: 'deep space' and scope, scale, and spatiality overall, and Dimock's 'deep time,' both unfolding over and against globalization's compression of cultural spaces and temporalities, respectively" (56–57).

13 Alexandra Laignel-Lavastine, *Cioran, Eliade, Ionesco. L'oubli du fascisme: trois intellectuels roumains dans la tourmente du siècle* (Paris: PUF, 2002); Marta Petreu, "Eliade, Sebastian, Ionescu, Cioran, 'copii din flori' ai României interbelice," in *De la Junimea la Noica. Studii de cultură română* (Iaşi: Polirom, 2011), 441–454; Matei Călinescu, "Eliade and Ionesco in the Post-World War II Years: Questions of Identity in Exile," in *Hermeneutics, Politics, and the History of Religions*, ed. Christian K. Wedemeyer and Wendy Doniger, 103–131.

14 See Mircea Martin, *G. Călinescu şi "complexele" literaturii române* (Bucharest: Albatros, 1981).

15 For a short introduction to the problematics of "The Young Generation," which is known in Romanian historiography as "The Generation '27," see Mihai Iovănel, *Mihail Sebastian. Evreul improbabil: o monografie ideologică* (Bucharest: Cartea Românească, 2012), 47–72.

16 B. Fundoianu, *Imagini și cărți din Franța* (București: Institutul Cultural Român, 2001), 6–7.

17 Țurcanu, *Mircea Eliade*, 384.

18 *Scrisori către Tudor Vianu*, vol. 2 (Bucharest: Minerva, 1994), 303–304, 309–310.

19 Țurcanu, *Mircea Eliade*, 436.

20 Țurcanu, *Mircea Eliade*, 437–438.

21 Casanova, *The World Republic of Letters*, 87.

22 In his 1966 devastating anthropological critique of Eliade's work, Edmund R. Leach reviewed as many as thirteen works Eliade had published in English, most of which having come out after his settling in the United States. See Leach's review-essay, "Sermons by a Man on a Ladder," *The New York Review of Books*, October 1966, 28–31.

23 This would be reprinted by Susan Sontag in her 1969 book *Styles of Radical Will*, for which see the 2002 edition (New York: Picador, 74–95).

24 See, among other titles: E. M. Cioran, *Fall into Time* (Chicago: Quadrangle, 1970), *The New Gods* (New York: Quadrangle, 1974), *A Short History of Decay* (New York: Viking, 1975), and *The Trouble with Being Born* (New York: Viking, 1976).

25 See Monica Lovinescu, *La apa Vavilonului* (Bucharest: Humanitas, 2008), 101, for more on how *The Bald Soprano* posed challenges to the two directors who "kept rehearsing (one act took [them] six months) because [they] didn't know how to approach this new theater with characters devoid of psychology."

26 I do not mean to imply that, in another context, he would have necessarily written a different kind of literature. I am just suggesting that he had the chance to be "selected" by a favorable context.

27 For a critical look at Eliade's scholarly legacy, see the concluding chapters to Moshe Idel, *Mircea Eliade*.

28 Casanova, *The World Republic of Letters*, 209–212, 215–217.

29 Monica Lovinescu and Ionesco would actually translate Caragiale and Urmuz into French.

30 See Ilinca Zarifopol-Johnston, *Searching for Cioran*, 190.

31 Matei Călinescu, *Eugène Ionesco*, 134.

32 See http://www.metacritic.com/movie/youth-without-youth

33 "There is," writes Casanova, "a time specific to literature, measured with reference to what I called the literary Greenwich meridian, in terms of which it becomes possible to draw an aesthetic map of the world, the position of each national space being determined by its temporal distance from the center"; "time, the sole source of literary value (converted into antiquity, into credit, into literariness), is also the source of inequality of the literary world" (*The World Republic of Letters*, 351, 352).

34 For a discussion of Tzara, see Andrei Terian, "Romanian Literature for the World."

35 On "unequal exchange," see Immanuel Wallerstein, *World-System Analysis. An Introduction* (Durham: Duke University Press, 2004), 28.

36 In "Conjectures on World Literature," Moretti writes: "In cultures that belong to the periphery of the literary system (which means: almost all cultures, inside and outside Europe), the modern novel first arises not as an autonomous development but as a compromise between a western formal influence (usually French or English) and local materials." See *Distant Reading* (London: Verso, 2013), 50.

37 Ionescu's situation was slightly different because he was initially a left-wing anarchist.

38 Cristiano Grottanelli, "Wartime Connections: Dumézil and Eliade, Eliade and Schmitt, Schmitt and Evola, Drieu La Rochelle and Dumézil," in *The Study of Religion*

under the Impact of Fascism, ed. Horst Junginger (Leiden: Brill, 2008), 303–314; Anne T. Mocko, "Tracing the Red Thread: Anti-Communist Themes in the Work of Mircea Eliade," in *Hermeneutics, Politics, and the History of Religions*, ed. Christian K. Wedemeyer and Wendy Doniger, 285–306.

39 Wai Chee Dimock, *Through Other Continents: American Literature across Deep Time* (Princeton, NJ: Princeton University Press, 2008), 133.

40 Robert J. C. Young, "World Literature and Postcolonialism," in *The Routledge Companion to World Literature*, ed. Theo D'haen et al. (London: Routledge, 2012), 217–218. See also David Damrosch, "The Hidden Code of World Literature in a Postcanonical, Hypercanonical Age," in *Comparative Literature in the Age of Globalization*, ed. Haun Saussy (Baltimore: The Johns Hopkins University Press), 48–50.

41 See Carlo Ginzburg, "Mircea Eliade's Ambivalent Legacy," in *Hermeneutics, Politics, and the History of Religions*, ed. Christian K. Wedemeyer and Wendy Doniger, 307–308.

42 Mircea Eliade, *The Portugal Journal*, trans. Mac Linscott Ricketts (Albany: Suny Press, 2010).

43 See Daniel Dubuisson, *Twentieth-century Mythologies: Dumézil, Lévi-Strauss, Eliade* (London: Equinox, 2006); Matei Călinescu, *Despre Ioan P. Culianu și Mircea Eliade*; Marta Petreu, "Codul ascuns al *Nopții de Sânziene*," in her book *De la Junimea la Noica*, 361–387.

44 In 2010, Charles Simic was nonetheless wondering: "Who reads E. M. Cioran nowadays? … At universities where graduate students and professors are familiar with every recent French philosopher and literary theorist, he's practically unknown, though he was a much finer thinker and wrote far better prose than a whole lot of them." See Charles Simic, "Insomnia's Philosopher," *The New York Review of Books* (November 11, 2010): 30–43.

45 Casanova, *The World Republic of Letters*, 350.

46 Ginzburg, "Mircea Eliade's Ambivalent Legacy," 322.

47 Paul Ricoeur, *Time and Narrative*, vol. 3, trans. Kathleen Blarney and David Pellauer (Chicago: The University of Chicago Press, 1988), 261–274.

11

A Geoliterary *Ecumene* of the East: Socialist Realism—the Romanian Case

Mircea Martin

Understood and practiced as a mechanical reflection of ruling ideology in literature, art, and culture broadly, Socialist Realism was a "creative method," as Soviet theorists had already described it in the early 1930s, but also an officially promoted "ism" for at least two decades after the Second World War in Romania and other countries that experienced Communism as a historical *reality*. I emphasize the previous sentence's last word because, in Europe, Asia, and elsewhere in the world, Communism was indeed "real," effectively existing as such. This does not mean, I hasten to add, that it was also "true," corresponding or even coming close to the reality or world one imagines or hopes Karl Marx and Friedrich Engels had called for. The distinction between real and true is not academic either. An actual historical, socioeconomic, and cultural-political phenomenon, Communist or, better still, Socialist reality—more precisely, the material reality of life inside existing Communist nations—was oversaturated with, and papered over by, the *un*reality of ideology. What is more, this ideology was both utopian and totalitarian, which made it, as Pope John Paul II observed, a tragic utopia. The program of this utopian vision was carried out by a panoply of "hard" means ranging from sheer force, persecution, surveillance, unprecedentedly brutal social engineering, and completely centralized control over the decision-making and administrative apparatuses by Communist Party oligarchies to "softer" forms of proselytizing and indoctrination that played out obliquely, through various aesthetic and cultural media. Falling under the latter category, Socialist Realism served as a vehicle for the ideological and, by the same token, was—ironically enough—as *un*realistic as ideology itself. Implausible and "untruthful," lacking a correspondent in the very social reality it referenced so insistently, and, as we will learn, rife with paradoxes and contradictions, Socialist Realism was nonetheless endorsed and disseminated by the same political machinery that lay behind ideological activism and political "vigilance." In fact, never before had a literary and cultural current been so dependent on a politically totalitarian power both economically and ideologically, what with Socialist Realism's overall agenda, stakes, and instruments, which were all set, made available, and enforced by a Party that had become equivalent to the state itself. This economic, logistic, and doctrinal dependence on and subordination to the authoritarian Party-state and its specialized propaganda, censorship, and repression agencies mark the radical novelty and oddity of Socialist Realism as an aesthetic trend or orientation that concomitantly did the bidding of its totalitarian backer and benefitted from the patron's enormous resources.

Thus, while it did not expand "naturally," as less generously sponsored currents and movements such as historical realism or Symbolism had, Socialist Realism quickly flooded a vast area of Europe and Asia. Aggressively pushed by the Soviets and widely perceived, in and after its heyday, as a mode of Sovietization put into effect by various Communist satellites in ways and through channels that were everywhere largely identical, resting on the same few dogmas no matter where it was transplanted, and reducible to an equally limited set of formal and thematic stereotypes, Social Realism was an artificial cultural–ideological construct whose uniform and simultaneous implementation across this transcontinental expanse gave birth, as I argue in this essay, to a *geoliterary ecumene*. Forced on countries, their artists, and their audiences, this was, I further propose, a *negative* ecumene or a *pseudo*-ecumene that, much like the community implied by a phrase such as "proletarian internationalism," did not truly exist and that, in this sense, was as unreal—or, as "social" and "realistic"—as the reality represented by literature and art under the auspices of Socialist Realism. As a body of literary-artistic and theoretical–ideological work complete with its institutional infrastructure of funding, training, vetting, publication, and reward, this ecumene did exist, however, in very concrete terms inside the Eastern Bloc. Having been tested for more than a decade in the former USSR, Socialist Realism spread like wildfire on the heels of Soviet imperialism after the Second World War to the Eastern part of the Northern hemisphere from East Berlin to Beijing and Pyongyang, as well as to Vietnam, under Ho-Chi-Minh, and later to the Cambodia decimated by Pol Pot, demarcating across the world-subsystem of Communism a loosely structured, transnational collective or mass of artists, venues, and institutions where, painstakingly policed aesthetically, ideological homogeneity balanced out linguistic, ethno-racial, cultural–historical, and geographical diversity.

1. Anti-Traditionalism, "Engagement," and the New "Canon"

After 1989, when critics from the former Communist countries could finally, and openly, take a hard look at Social Realism, many of them underscored its anti-traditionalism. An intensely advertised priority of Socialist Realism, a clean break with tradition is not this geocultural formation's distinguishing feature, though. As other essays in *Romanian Literature as World Literature* show, the avant-gardes attempted and sometimes brought about such fractures in the cultural–historical continuum. Otherwise, the parallel goes only so far. While there are similarities between the radical novelty promoted by avant-gardists and Communists' revolutionary repudiation of the past, the differences dwarf the resemblances especially if one compares avant-garde independence of thought, imagination, and action to Socialist Realists' playing along and docilely buying into the notion of a "necessity" to operate with narrowly defined, oftentimes restricting concepts and theoretical premises so as to ensure art's "authentic engagement." Moreover, in its very rejection of the past, Communist activism pursued recuperative goals in history as well as literature and the arts, for it demonstrably tried to rewrite tradition, including literary tradition, to create one of its own, so much so that, when set side by side with historical avant-gardism's extreme anti-traditionalism and anti-classicist position, Socialist Realism looks, paradoxically enough, like a version of neoclassicism.

But then the idea of "engaged art," of artists and intellectuals' being in the service of "the people," was not new either. The democratic Russian revolutionaries of the first years of the twentieth century had already proclaimed it with great success, just like the Narodniks before them and, later on, the Romanian Socialists and the self-styled advocates of the "people" (*popor* in Romanian), the *Poporanists*. Yet neither an intellectual's "duty" as described by Narodniks and *Poporanists* nor the "commitment" displayed by writers inspired by the Social-Democrat platform was anything like the task dictatorially foisted on writers by the Communist Party to depict "reality" from a politically partisan, self-consciously assumed standpoint. In fact, "tendency," literature of a certain bent such as the *roman à thèse*, and even art with a more explicit bias were also old news. However, Socialist Realism took them all to a whole other level by turning moralizing "thesis" and political "penchant" into absolutely uncompromised, quasi-mystical, officially sanctioned, expected, and ruthlessly enforced partisanship. Simply speaking, with Social Realism, hewing to the Communist Party line became writers, artists, and critics' job, and doing this job effectively was billed as a superior stage in a painter or poet's arduous progress toward "sincere" social engagement.

This engagement emerged as the defining characteristic and *raison d'être* of Socialist Realism gradually. As late as 1934, the idea of "fellow travelers" was still entertained and even encouraged at the First Convention of Soviet Writers, which was attended by Boris Pasternak, Vsevolod Ivanov, Isaac Babel, Konstantin Fedin, and Leonid Leonov, among others, and where Communist ideologue, former Politburo member, and *Izvestia* editor-in-chief Nikolai Bukharin was still talking about the necessary *quality* of literature. Between 1930 and 1938, however, during a period of major mock trials, many writers and artists were sent to the Gulags, with Ossip Mandelstam, Babel, Boris Pilniak, and Vsevolod Meyernold among the better known. After the victorious war, terror seemed to abate for a while. Authors such as Andrei Platonov and Anna Akhmatova, who had been banned since the 1920s, could publish again, which made intellectuals and artists hopeful. 1946 was actually "the year of great expectations," as the title of a chapter from E. Dobrenko and G. Tihanov's 2011 *History of Russian Literary Theory and Criticism* reads.[1] But that same year, 1946, I. V. Stalin ordered Andrei Zhdanov, one of his top ideological henchmen, to reverse course, switch back to the dogmatic hardline, and take repressive measures against writers, artists, and intellectuals in general. Complying with the boss's directions, Jdanov's "Report" on the *Zvezda* and *Leningrad* magazines mounts a violent attack on "art for art's sake," cosmopolitanism, and the "servile" admiration of Western, "petit bourgeois" literature. The "Report" brings back the buzzword of "Party commitment" or *partisanship* (*partiinosti* in Russian), which had been introduced by V. I. Lenin and was headed for a spectacular career, and this is also where Zhdanov demands from literature a content high in "ideas" (*ideinosti*) and equates ideological defects or writers' "failure" to "educate" readers' "souls" with the Soviet's industry defective products. Harshly criticized here are Mihail Zoscenko and Akhmatova while *acmeism* overall is frowned upon as "aristocratic–bourgeois."[2] Later, Zhdanov would take to task composers Sergei Prokofiev and Dmitri Shostakovich, who would be ostracized for the "anti-popular" character of their music. Known at the time as *jdanovcina*, the "Report" and the program stemming from it entailed a top-down, unmitigated politicization of culture and society, as well as a total break with Western traditions.

Notably, it was this radical and radically prescriptive and repressive Zhdanovian version of Socialist Realism that was exported to Romania and other regions of the Soviet Bloc. Imposed by Moscow, the new metropolitan center of the imperial system in which the Communist countries were absorbed, Socialist Realism was, then, initially not so much a movement, "ism," or current—let alone a freely flowing one—as a canon formation of sorts. Strongly normative and coercive, the Zhdanovian "canon" was a set of principles predating and external to literature and regulating literary form and content. It goes without saying, this is very different from what we mean these days when we talk about the literary canon. For Socialist Realism was not so much produced and illustrated by a literature out of which its "poetics" would be eventually fleshed out by scholars, as, quite the other way around, literary works were expected to illustrate it by abiding by its preexisting rules. An ideological *a priori* rather than an aesthetic *a posteriori*, Socialist Realism was, as far as contemporary works went, projective–restrictive, hence the multifaceted incompatibility between the Socialist Realist and the Western canon, whether we understand the latter how Harold Bloom does or how his critics do. It may even be argued that Socialist Realism is not a canon proper, and that "canon" may be a misnomer here insofar as no other canons, "creative methods," or measuring instruments were really conceivable alongside it, for, despite occasional and rather specious debates around it, no diversity, competition, or alternative were tolerated in the trans-Communist ecumene during this "ism's" late 1940s–mid-1960s iron-fist reign. In this era, Socialist Realism did appear and basically was rock solid, incontrovertible, and unchallengeable because its profound identity was ideological and political, not aesthetic, which made it part and parcel or, better yet, a cultural-aesthetic facet and function of a much broader canon or prescriptive code undergirded by an assortment of Marxist, Leninist, and Stalinist precepts, injunctions, guidelines, and imperatives. It is true that, whether we think of it as a body of work, as an aesthetic modus operandi, or both, any canon takes shape in a particular climate that is social, political, as well as literary artistic. In this case, however, the hegemony of the extra-aesthetic is overwhelming and absolutely unnegotiable in that the political and its all-pervasive ideology supply the only protocols and criteria both for literary production and for its assessment. Where any canon is *influenced* by sociopolitical factors, Socialist Realism was governed, guided, and ultimately *structured* by them. Its principles applied to literature and the arts, but these rules' normative power stemmed from the supposedly infallible and immutable Communist ideology, which imparted to Social Realism a quasi-sacred quality that made for another paradox of this resolutely antireligious and secular geoliterary ecumene.

2. The Birth of a Literary World-Subsystem

Although the countries of the aptly called "Socialist camp" had their own, individual traditions and were, at the end of the Second World War, at different stages of sociocultural development, the doctrine and then "style" of Socialist Realism were put into practice, much like Communist ideology at large, in the same authoritarian and indiscriminate fashion across the board. As Social Realism was going world-systemic to become the aesthetic lingua franca in the workers' paradise, local particularities were ignored, which is why they would come back later on retrofitted as "dialectical" arguments in the "revisionist" cases various Communist countries entered for the right to choose their own "paths" to Socialist society and culture. Such a path was proclaimed by the leaders of Popular Republic of Romania in 1964 and by the German Democratic Republic's government when it began to encourage a Socialism built by an "educated nation" (*gebildete Nation*). The revisionist argument was not the only one, nor were these "itineraries" the only ways of circumventing Moscow's imperial fiat inside and outside cultural policies.

Whether this kind of revision, deflection, and detours was effective or not, it should be obvious to critics both in the East and the West by now what was fairly clear across the Communist world from the get-go, and what I have underscored upfront: Socialist Realism was no more than a conduit of a Soviet colonization that, as Bogdan Ştefănescu shows at length in the essay following mine in our collection, unfolded primarily on two continents, Europe and Asia, where it took on various guises, chiefly ideological and politico-economic, but also territorial, with countries such as Moldova and the Baltic States swallowed up by the imperial conglomerate of the USSR.[3] Otherwise, despite the Empire's disregard for local minutia, Socialist Realism was bound to give rise to different sub-formations in each literature that was forced to adopted its program, and even this program itself was occasionally tweaked—without being substantially modified, however—across the history and the geocultural system on which it left its imprint. Equally significant is the inherent and, in a sense, unquenchable diversity of literary works, which were bound by the very nature of their medium to incorporate the Soviet orthodoxy of Socialist Realism in different ways and to varying degrees. Yet again, the "variety," to the extent that there is one, obtains within a paradigm not unlike the ecumenic camp housing the artists and the writers themselves, and so a synthetic overview is not only possible but also once more necessary in the new context of World Literature, before turning to the specifics of the Romanian situation.

Among the variables mentioned earlier, language and ethnicity are among the more important elements accounting for the fluctuations inside the Socialist Realist continuum. A case in point is Czech literature, whose important circumstances need to be factored in. These include the country's belonging to the Slavic family, the Czechs' gratitude, in the years after the war, for the liberating Russian troops, the dispute over Sudetenland, and the German occupation. Coupled with a robust industrial tradition and a well-established working-class culture, all these paved the way for Socialist Realism. Thus, Hana Voisine-Jechova, author of a recent *History of Czech Literature*, is right to point out that "'Socialistic' if not outright socialist tendencies had played an important role in Czechoslovakia between World War I and World War II, and so, after 1948, the authorities could present Communist hegemony as the coming to fruition of those tendencies already embedded in Czech culture."[4] Even more "Socialist Realism-ready" was East Germany (GDR), where the proto-Socialist, labor, as well as outright Socialist and proletarian movements boasted longer and richer traditions. The German Revolution of 1918–1919, the activity of the "Spartakus" group, the 1928 founding of the Association of Proletarian-Revolutionary Authors (*Bund proletarisch-revolutionärer Schriftsteller*), the decidedly anti-Nazi and sometimes Marxist cultural life in the Weimar Republic, as well as the anti-Hitler opposition of German exiles during the Second World War were all fresh in the mind of a population that, after losing a war of conquest, may have found itself under foreign occupation but was pressured to adopt an ideology that was anything but foreign. The founders of the Association included fiction writer Anna Seghers and poet Johannes Becher, both of whom fled Germany in 1933, the first to Paris and then Mexico, the second to Moscow, then Taşkent, where he met György Lukács, who had also sought asylum in the USSR. The 1938 exchange between Seghers and Lukács over realism and the writer's function in society prefigured postwar debates about Socialist Realism, as did the polemic between Lukács and Bertolt Brecht with respect to the Marxist position on modernism and the avant-garde. Unlike Brecht, Lukács took a more conservative and antimodernist approach beholden to the Marxist–Leninist orthodoxy, and yet he would be attacked for his "revisionism" in the 1960s by Soviet, East German, and Romanian defenders of Socialist Realism. Of course, Brecht's own experimental and highly influential dramatic oeuvre deserves a special mention here, and not only for its "agitprop" and other techniques ostensibly political in nature and objective. With others, Brecht had also written little didactic plays (*Lehrstücke*) for community theater with the purpose of raising awareness of social injustice among workers. Later on, GDR writers would incorporate such initiatives into a full-dress Socialist Realism that, we can see in hindsight, Brecht had laid the ground for without completely fitting its formula.

Lukács himself presents us with a somewhat similar situation in his own country where, breathing new life primarily in the intellectual circles, a powerful revolutionary impetus led to the 1918–1919 Hungarian Soviet Republic. Lukács was, I should note, a political commissary in the Fifth Red Army, and this detail had significant implications not just for the biography of this Marxist philosopher and critic. His 1930 self-imposed exile to the USSR, like that of other Hungarian thinkers and writers, spoke to his Communist convictions, which several years later would be tested by the Stalinist "purges." Upon his 1947 return to Hungary, he immediately became an ideologically central figure and thus an element of continuity in the Communist history of modern Hungary. His authority as a Marxist critic and aesthetician, let alone the political positions he held in both Communist and reformist governments in Hungary from the end of the First World War to the 1956 anti-Soviet Revolution, made him into the influential figure and theoretical resource on which crudely doctrinal projects such as Socialist Realism could draw to accrue a modicum of flexibility and build up their credibility.

For various reasons, nothing like this was possible in countries like Poland and, beyond Europe, in China. In the former, a proletarian literature did exist before the Second World War but no interest in Socialist Realism. Neither the tragic aftershocks of the Nazi invasion nor the propaganda efforts of the group formed around the Lodz literary magazine *Kuznicza*[5] created an ambiance sufficiently favorable to the new aesthetic program; truth be told, even the *Kuznicza* contributors themselves proposed a "broad realism" that eschewed the Zhdanovist strictures, which explains the magazine's disappearance in the 1950s following Socialist Realism's official arrival in Poland.[6] In China too, the "ism" failed to allow for significant departures from the formulaic. The "local" twists noticeable in the Chinese sector of this geoliterary ecumene derive, as one might expect, from the Maoist emendations of Communism and Stalinism. At a great cultural and geographical distance from Europe, the leverage of Soviet Communism had grown after 1919 exponentially and wound up pushing out the humanist and individualist spirit of the Enlightenment, which gradually gave way to the ideology of class struggle and of workers and peasants' revolution. Left-wing activists' calls for a "literature for the masses" would later be taken up by Mao Zedong and echoed by his 1940s speeches. These would set the stage for the 1949 establishment of Chinese Socialist Realism and for its Cultural Revolution excesses, which remain unmatched throughout Communist history.[7]

3. Joining the Geoliterary Ecumene: Romanian Socialist Realism and the Leninist "Two-Cultures" Model

As in countries like Poland, in Romania there were neither favorable conditions nor earlier manifestations or anticipations of Social Realism. A Socialist movement had coalesced between 1870 and 1880 around the Iași magazine *Contemporanul*, but one of the publication's founders, Marxist critic Constantin Dobrogeanu-Gherea, had drawn sharp distinctions between "tendency"- and "thesis"-driven art. Gherea found the former inevitable and innate to all art, while a thesis, he thought, was imposed from outside and constituted an agenda or politics to which artists were expected to cater. He was wary of the 1918 Revolution, and so were not only other left-wing Romanian intellectuals but also the general population. Established in 1921 and outlawed three years thereafter, the Communist Party had been a negligible presence in the Romanian political landscape and imaginary due to fears of a Bolshevism that had looked even more ominous against the backdrop of the territorial conflict with Russia and its imperial heir, the USSR, over Bessarabia and Northern Bukovina. In Romania, the Bolsheviks had been synonymous with "collectivization" at gunpoint, kolkhozes, and the like—which is understandable given that the overwhelming majority of the population had been living in rural areas—but also with the threat of brutal meddling in domestic affairs, which apprehension had been equally unsurprising. In 1944, when the Romanian Communist Party resumed its lawful operations, only 10 percent of its less than a thousand members were of Romanian ethnicity. Nonetheless, along with a Soviet Army that was doing double duty as a liberating and occupying force, the postwar years brought to Romania a new revolutionary élan, which, emboldened by Soviet tanks, would before long manage to overturn both social and cultural values. The 1945–1948 interval was marked by a simulacrum of freedom and democracy, even though the 1946 parliamentary elections were rigged. Around this time, censorship began to rear its ugly head also, but, compared to what was to come after 1948, the press was still relatively free and so able to host national debates such as the one raging in 1946 around the "crisis of culture."

No doubt, the subject was controversial. But the barbs traded on this occasion in no way anticipated the draconic interdictions to follow, all the more so that those who dismissed the notion of a "crisis" as a fib included reputable authors and critics such as George Călinescu, Şerban Cioculescu, and, from a younger generation, Adrian Marino, who would be sentenced before long, I might add, to nine years in prison and seven years of house arrest. In effect, as long as writers and scholars participated in the discussion, everything seemed business as usual. But when Communist Party activists and even ministers in the new puppet government such as Gheorghe-Gheorghiu Dej, the future leader of the Party and of the country until 1964, joined in, the tone abruptly changed. "We need," declared apparatchik Nicolae Moraru, "to hit reactionary currents in the arts and culture with all we have got, to expose the tendencies to isolate the artist and his creation from reality."[8] Romanian critic Sanda Cordoş is therefore right to observe that "this is the moment advancing Communist literary ideology laid down its rudimentary, Soviet-inspired tenets."[9] Indeed, given the culture's crisis, to which figures as different as Călinescu and Moraru turned a blind eye for equally different reasons, the issue of what had caused it in the first place was unavoidable, as was also the elephant in the room, viz., the very problem of freedom of creation and opinion. "The crisis of culture," insisted Ion Caraion, a poet and essayist who would also spend his youth in the prisons of Romanian Communism, "is the crisis of individual liberty."[10] Another participant in the discussion, modernist poet Tudor Arghezi, summed up a concept of literature that was at the time widely shared by Romanian writers. "Art," said Arghezi

> is never "for" someone or "for" something; it inherently lacks a "for." The mistake here is to consider the audience more stupid than it is, even though, as far as intelligence and deep feeling go, the public has got them both. The challenge is not to open a literature sweatshop that cranks out stuff by working with existing stencils and formulas, but to write beautifully, which is harder than exploiting clichés and commonplaces.[11]

Neither in Arghezi's article nor elsewhere in the "crisis of culture" polemics is Socialist Realism explicitly mentioned. But the subject does cast a dark, premonitory shadow over the entire affair, and, within a mere few years, the still vaguely portentous if crudely utilitarian and partisan "for-art" (*artă pentru*) dismissed by Arghezi became reality. So did, with it, the subordination of literature and the arts to the Party-State and their transformation into means of "education" and propaganda. Under these circumstances, the prohibition of any aesthetic alternative—and, it seemed, of the aesthetic altogether—was the next logical step. Anything Romanian or foreign that could not be used for ideological purposes was rejected as "elitist," "cosmopolitan," or "bourgeois decadence." These were serious charges and were aimed particularly and systematically at the domestic modernist canon, which was both present in the nation's cultural memory and the least compatible with Socialist Realist "stencils and formulas." In 1948, when its ideological and administrative eradication got under way, literary and artistic modernism had not yet finished its course in Romania as it had not elsewhere in the world. Important poets such as Arghezi, George Bacovia, Lucian Blaga, Ion Barbu, and Alexandru Philippide and fiction writers like Camil Petrescu, Hortensia Papadat-Bengescu, and Călinescu, who had brilliantly embodied it, were still in full creative swing, while critics such as Călinescu, Vladimir Streinu, Tudor Vianu, and Cioculescu, who had supported these world-class authors, were about to complete major scholarly syntheses. All of a sudden, they would all be out, simply speaking. So would be younger avant-garde artists too, unless they renounced their previous radicalism. But that was easier said than done because, their left-wing ideals notwithstanding, Socialist revolution proved incompatible with the revolution they had envisioned in poetry and the arts, and so they had to be forced to ramp up and proclaim explicitly their enthusiasm for the "revolution" underway, revisit their political as well as creative principles accordingly, and otherwise get on with the Communist program. This is how poets such as Virgil Teodorescu and Gellu Naum, through whose work Bucharest sent out a last wave of European Surrealism, ended up publishing agitprop poems dedicated to various political events even though they must have noticed that the Communist dream turned out a far cry from the oneiric landscapes of the unconscious. Obviously, Louis Aragon, rather than André Breton, could have served as a model to Teodorescu, Naum, Gherasim Luca, and others like them, and only with some of his poems and by virtue of his membership in the French Communist Party, for, otherwise, his reputation as a Surrealist whose work was too obscure for the "masses" was hardly a credential in the book of Socialist Realist ideologues. Even more typical are, in this vein, the career U-turn of Geo Bogza, a rebel poet before the Second World War who wrote the 1929 *Jurnal de sex* (Sex Diary) and *Poemul invectivă* (Profanity Poem) but also the 1953 pro-Soviet panegyric *Meridiane sovietice* (Soviet Meridians), and the similarly ironic about-face of avant-garde painter M. H. Maxy, who would become director of the Art Museum of the Popular Republic of Romania.

Sincere or less so, such "changes of heart" abounded after the Second World War, so much so that, as Romanian critic Ion Pop has concluded, "The former avant-garde would actually turn into an *arrière-garde,* an aesthetic caboose of sorts following the lead of the governing Party and its forcibly imposed ideology."[12] Since in the last essay included in this book's part II Paul Cernat dwells at length on the *arrière-garde* and its place in the geosystem of Romanian and European modernism, here I only point to the human dramas—and sometimes tragedies—behind such conversions and splits that occurred in the works and lives of Romanian avant-gardists, as they did, in fact, in the lives and works of most artists and intellectuals who had made a name for themselves before or immediately after the war and did not flee the country.

Officially and pompously designated as forms of "revolutionary transformation," such metamorphoses, reconstructions, and reinventions involved incarceration, hard labor, and death for some, silence for others—or, more often than not, their silencing, their banning from the social arena—and for the rest sliding down the slippery slope of moral, political, and ultimately artistic compromises. The combination or sequence in which these occurred were a function of people's moral fiber and so varied from case to case, but this is not just a matter of what happened to this or that poet or playwright. A similar and equally violent rupture between a "before" and an "after" was inflicted on the entirety of Romanian literary history and, in effect, on the history of Romania generally, whose less "revolutionary" record was about to be scoured off while the brave new present was looking increasingly bizarre in its radical and artificial difference from a past still vivid in people's mind.

This schism was a temporal feature of the Leninist "two-cultures" model Socialist Realism brought to bear on the Romanian literary-aesthetic system old or recent so as to weed out any elements that might obstruct the nascent cultural order. This duality was reinforced synchronically and diachronically by a parallel disjunction between the "noble" culture of the exploited, invariably nurtured by lofty and progressive ideas, and the exploiters' retrograde, reactionary, and "hostile" culture. A polar opposite to the unconditioned devotion to the Party—"Partysanship," or *partinitate* in the Romanian Communist lingo of the time—"hostility" (*dușmănie*) was the term of choice to describe the "class enemy" and its inherently "inimical" culture. A writer would automatically belong to this category and would therefore forfeit public presence of any kind unless he or she had a "healthy" working-class background, a highly acute "social consciousness" and critical attitude toward the old bourgeois regime, and a never-flagging "revolutionary spirit" documentable by his or her work itself in ways easily accessible to "the people." In this sense, Socialist Realism also made for the "best practices" of a very real and busy human resources office whose employees were deciding who and what would get published and otherwise participate in the culture. Remarkably, such decisions affected living and dead writers alike. Everybody and everything ever written or done were screened for "social origin" and for the "hostility" or, as the case may be, "proletarian progressivism" presumably following from such biographical accident. Along with entire Romanian history, the country's cultural tradition was combed for moments, authors, and works that were liable to illustrate and support the idea of social revolt and anti-bourgeois resistance.

In the process, a thorough overhaul of the Romanian literary value system was afoot. The "national poet" himself, Mihai Eminescu, was allowed in the new and politically hyperfocused Romanian curricula only with the proletarian's speech from his poem "Împărat și proletar" (Emperor and Proletarian) and with various fragments of social and moral criticism from "Scrisori" (Letters) and other poetic works, all of them not only truncated but also accompanied by Marxist–Leninist glosses providing, in no uncertain terms, guidelines for how the texts were supposed to be read. Thus, both as a set of primary sources and as a modality of dealing with them, the emerging canon did not set out to furnish an "alternative"; instead, it purported to be the only one, hence its aggressiveness, its invasive-species behavior in the expanding cultural ecology.

This conduct comes through the Manichean extremism of a two-cultures dualism whose clear-cut ideological dyad was deployed to constantly sift through, scrutinize, vet, and reshuffle the past and the present, domestic and international patrimonies. The latter were particularly regarded with suspicion, especially if they did not belong to the "socialist camp," for the cultural and artistic products of the capitalist system, which, as per Lenin, had reached its terminal stage, had to be rejected, ignored, or adduced solely as negative examples. Long after Stalin's death and even after repeated denunciations of the *Proletkult*—which would remain, however, a pivotal component of Social Realism—this multilayered rigid Manicheanism would still reign supreme.

While classical and especially modern authors' texts were republished in blue-penciled editions or completely banned, obscure but politically acceptable writers such as "cobbler poet" Theodor Neculuță were retrieved and pushed for the purpose of inventing a proletarian pantheon—again, not *another* tradition but *the* tradition and, by the same movement, a genealogy of rising culture. The literary canon thus forged did not include any authors from the First World War–Second World War interval unless they were Communists or Communist sympathizers like the mediocre novelist Alexandru Sahia or unless they were willing to shift gears, as prose writer Mihail Sadoveanu did in his 1949 didacticist novel *Mitrea Cocor*. But Sadoveanu was not the only one who caved in. Another major novelist and playwright, Camil Petrescu, managed to stay afloat only by playing along through his 1948 drama *Bălcescu* and the sprawling but unfinished 1957 novel, *Un om între oameni* (A Man among Men), which he also dedicated to Nicolae Bălcescu, a hero of the 1848 Revolution. Major poets who had also established themselves before the Second World War, such as Blaga, Ion Pillat, Adrian Maniu, and Vasile Voiculescu, were banned for reasons that had to do with their biographies as well as with certain aspects of their works. Arghezi too shared the same fate until he decided to play ball in the poems from *Cântare omului* (Song to Man) and *1907*. As far as a belated Symbolist such as Bacovia went, he was easily retrofitted by critics as a poet of proletarian suffering and revolt.

All of these cuts, purges, pressures to recant and "self-reconstruct," and critical "reconsiderations" were cynically palmed off, in Romania and across the Socialist Realist ecumene, as recovery of national literary "values," while the very notions of "value" and "national" were sorely missing from the entire equation. The sole criteria of this reassessment operation were ideological, and its effects on the traditions undergoing it were equally devaluing and denationalizing. On this account, the critical impact of Socialist Realism has been felt, in Romania an elsewhere in the Soviet zone, as a traumatic assault on the identity of the nation and literature alike. For, extremely limited in all sorts of ways, the corpus that passed the Socialist Realist test was, in reality, quite "exclusive" also, in that, at least initially, it met with the approval only of a small clique of apparatchiks whose abecedarian concept of literature it was bound to mirror. Therefore, not only was the number of works that survived ideological screening and made it into the new canon fairly small and shockingly alien to various national patrimonies, but this material was expected to be effortlessly legible. Consequently, reprimanded were not only the deviations from the Party line but also those from straightforward literary exposition and, more broadly, any case of ambiguity, subtlety, obscurity, "excessive" intellectual depth and use of neologisms, as well as erudite references, linguistic playfulness, and abundantly metaphorical language, which were seen as an insult to "the simple man." They all were ground for censorship and for denying publication to a sizeable literature that, for these reasons, did not come out in its time or at all and that began to give rise in the 1950s to a *negative canon*, as it were, which was part and parcel of the culture Socialist Realism was struggling to suppress. In the early years of Romania's own *Proletkult* period, this canon comprised a list of banned titles, whether they were available or not. Where they were, they were made unavailable. This is why, during this era, people's books were confiscated or destroyed while "anti-revolutionary" volumes and works by "subversive" writers were purged from all public libraries, and landmark establishments such as the Romanian Academy's Library and University of Bucharest's Library had restricted-access holdings.

Since, as Mihaela Ursa shows in this book's final essay, translation plays such a key role in the formation of any canonical structure, the negative canon had inevitably an international component. The *excess* of Soviet and Russian authors among the epoch's translations was an aspect of the Sovietization campaign going on all over the Socialist Realist ecumene, whereas the flipside of this abundance, the *scarcity* of Romanian renditions of non-Soviet, non-Russian, and non-Soviet Bloc non-"ideological" writers, spoke to the rapid growth of a canonical body that became, as I have suggested, more and more remarkable *negatively*, through its glaring absence from bookstores, libraries, schools, and public conversation. For, from other literatures, only classical authors were translated and from among twentieth-century authors only those who were Communists, who expressed support for Communist causes, or who dealt with social and political issues in ways deemed sufficiently compatible with said causes. Thus, Theodore Dreiser, Walt Whitman, Martin Andersen Nexø, Henri Barbusse, Howard Fast, Nazim Hikmet, and Yiannis Ritsos were among the approved foreign writers. One should also acknowledge, however, the opportunity given Romanian audiences of these dark decades to read great Russian authors such as Alexander Pushkin, Nikolai Gogol, Leo Tolstoy, Anton Chekhov, Fyodor Dostoevsky, and Ivan Goncharov.

4. What Society Ordered: The Rise of a New "Poetics"

Not the only form of "engaged" art, Socialist Realism literalized the engagement notion by striving to fulfill what the moment's ideologues called, quite appositely, "society's order" or "command"—*comanda socială* in Romanian. The phrase was not intended to "sound" militaristic; it was so. That is, it conveyed a clear order, which was to be followed thematically and stylistically according to the Communist Party's political objectives. This is how a recognizable—because exceedingly hackneyed—Socialist Realist poetics crystalized in the 1950s and 1960s across a huge Eurasian swath. This poetics' main feature was an immediately identifiable *thematics*, that is, a set of intrinsically political themes in which the message or lesson to be learned was conspicuously rolled into the subject matter. Inside and outside Romania, such thematics comprised praise for those enthusiastically working on the big projects of rising Socialist economies, for "disinterested" labor generally, and for the wiping out of private land ownership and the forced "collectivization" of family farms into kolkhozes; the awakening of class consciousness among the poor; the ever-"sharpening" social conflicts; the struggle against the enemies of the new order and against "obsolete mentalities." At least two related themes were especially recommended: the liberation from the yokes of Fascism and bourgeois oppression, and working-class heroism in Romanian modern history. The first was illustrated in novels like *Străinul* (The Stranger) by Titus Popovici, *Bariera* (The Barrier) by Teodor Mazilu, *Şoseaua Nordului* (The North Highway), by Eugen Barbu, *Ieşirea din Apocalips* (Escaping the Apocalypse) by Alecu Ivan Ghilia, and *Pe muchie de cuţit* (On a Knife Edge) by Mihai Beniuc. The second was a bit trickier because it had to be dealt with so as to foreground the "self-sacrificing spirit" of Communists back in the day when the Party was outlawed and when, unfortunately, its members were few and far between. The titles of works nonetheless taking on this multiply fictional task speak for themselves, from the novels of Valeriu Emil Galan (*Zorii robilor* [The Dawn of Slaves]) and Ion Pas (*Lanţuri* [Chains]) to dramas such as *Cetatea de foc* (The Fortress of Fire) by Mihail Davidoglu and *Citadela sfărâmată* (The Torn-Down Citadel) by Horia Lovinescu to poems by Mihai Beniuc ("În frunte" [First in Line], "Comuniştii" [The Communists], "Balada anului 1933" [The Ballad of 1933]), Maria Banuş ("Slavă eroilor Doftanei" [Ode to Doftana's Heroes]), Marcel Breslaşu ("Cântecul de leagăn al Doncăi" [Donca's Lullaby]), Veronica Porumbacu ("Mierla lui Ilie Pintilie" [Pintilie's Thrush]), and Victor Tulbure ("Balada tovarăşului care a căzut împărţind "Scânteia" în ilegalitate" [The Ballad of the Comrade Who Fell Distributing 'The Spark' in the Days When the Party Was Outlawed]).

The working-class focus was not new, but the crushing social determinism accounting for everything in this literature was. As a result, the fictional humanity of prose and drama consisted in flat, mechanical instantiation of characters' respective social categories, and the conflicts into which these heroes and heroines were automatically drawn lacked credibility precisely because, in line with the new poetics, authors were discouraged from "individualizing" their dramatis personae. Instead, a novel character kept reoccurring in Socialist Realist novels, plays, and even poems. He or she had a vast life experience and so was if not all knowing then always capable to solve the most difficult problems; initiated into the Party's theoretical and practical wisdom, he or she had seen the light and was obviously eager to pass his revelation on and help others see it too; thus, this exceptional and yet so common human being was prepared to persuade the proletarian comrades to fight together the bourgeois regime, past or still agonizing as "mentality," the peasant brothers and sisters to join the collective farms, and his or her intellectual associates, who happened to be more "hesitant" by nature, to pledge allegiance to the Revolution. This individual was the Party activist, and his mission was the "building" of "Socialist consciousness."

Poetry's brief was no different. Because of that, the genre had to become declarative, didactic, and frequently narrative in nature, and so poets had to abide essentially by the same "realistic" principles as prose and drama. The only difference lay in prosody. As an effective carrier of ideology, poetry had to meet presumably mimetic standards, which is why the latter would be the main target of the young Romanian critics of the 1960s.

Until then, lyricism was pegged, however, as a symptom of bourgeois individualism. If, in prose, the officially encouraged approach was the theme at hand's comprehensive treatment—the *fresque sociale* or social panorama—in poetry most cultivated was the so-called *poem de largă respirație*—"the ample-breadth poem." Fairly lengthy, oftentimes paying homage to a certain political occasion or event, this poetic species had a moralizing and mobilizing tone, toggling between praise and condemnation and reaching rhetorical intensities whose pathos came dangerously close to bathos and whose self-righteous vehemence teetered on the brink of involuntary comedy. No wonder very few of these poems outlived the 1950s, despite the reputation of their authors, some of whom had distinguished themselves before the onset of Socialist Realism, such as Eugen Jebeleanu, Beniuc, Banuș, and Nina Cassian. Among partial exceptions to the dismaying lack of quality of this poetry were, again, Jebeleanu, with fragments of his extensive poem "Surâsul Hiroșimei" (Hiroshima's Smile) and the short poem "Lidice," as well as the group of poets clustered around the Cluj literary magazine *Steaua*, who favored a confessional and personal style that at the time looked like outright artistic dissent. Even more than fiction, the declarative agitprop poetry of the 1950–1960 interval marked a striking involution of the genre, which seemed bent on circling back to a naïve neoromanticism of sorts for which the post-Symbolist modernist revolution had never taken place. Thus, "contemporary" Romanian poetry of the decade was a travel back in time to an aesthetic form and period that had never existed in the first place, but if they did, they could have been placed somewhere in the early-nineteenth century. The issue here is not so much the return to rhyme and to neoclassical style—again, to one that no literary history records—but this ironically "retrograde" poetics' preset formulas and, above anything else, the thesis-driven message.

Comanda socială required the latter be basically the only "content" of the work, but also that this content be readable without difficulty. Therefore, it would be an understatement to say that form, a key element distinguishing literature from other kinds of discourse, played second fiddle to "ideas" in Socialist Realism. At best, form was treated as insignificant, as a coat in which thoughts were dressed; at worst, it was a distraction or obstacle blocking out the shining message. This is why expression was looked at with suspicion and writers' preoccupation with form, a concern presumed to index a neglect of the "content," triggered routinely charges of "formalism." Any interest in the formal aspects of writing risked, in fact, being considered a first step toward recognizing a certain particularity or aesthetic distinctiveness characteristic of literature and, worse, toward acknowledging art's "autonomy" with respect to utilitarian or even social purposes that would thus be seen as not necessarily constitutive of a poem or short story. This implication would have gone against the grain of a poetics of transparency or of self-effacing form where the latter's role was to be the vehicle of an "educational" tenor, to intermediate the instruction of the masses as directed by the Party. One consequence of such a content-oriented literature was that almost all of its encoding mechanisms were political–ideological, while the protocols pertaining to literary form, from narrative viewpoint to irony and metaphor, were viewed as derivative and were barely tolerated or taken into account. Moreover, much like the poets and novelists reverted to outmoded styles, Socialist Realist critics fell back, for obviously propagandistic reasons, on discredited concepts and approaches such as authorial intention, which mattered as much as the actual play or novella. A writer's own, direct "message" was appreciated, and so public statements and confessions were encouraged but had to match the work's message, whose interpretation was not left solely to the reader either, being guided instead by the *professional* reader, namely, by the ideologically vetted critic. Thus, across the Eastern geoliterary ecumene, the literary phenomenon was closely monitored at both its inception and reception ends, and the plurality of interpretations was limited, if it existed at all. On the off-chance that they might occur, any amphibologies were promptly explained away as "ideological confusion" by commentators whose revolutionary vigilance was regularly stoked and called for by Communist activists. Clarity of style was at a premium because, again, it let the message shine through but also because it was thought to echo the unambiguous ways in which the author embraced the Party's teachings. Valued in similar terms was verisimilitude, and, as noted earlier, not because Socialist Realist literature was "truthful" to whatever it was allegedly "reflecting," but because how the reflected object was handled in turn conveyed and reaffirmed, whether in prose, drama, or poetry, ruling ideology. The effectiveness of this reaffirmation was the measure of the writer's success, and this efficacy, and with it the success itself, was a function of the abovementioned poetics of transparency, for the author's ideological position, the strength of his or her political convictions, had to come across unfiltered and undistorted by expression. Conversely, artistic failure was a sign of an author's vacillation and indecision, and these were suggestive of a lack of conviction—political conviction, that is—all the more so when it came or seemed to come into play in the handling of preferred themes. Indeed, even the approved thematics of Socialist Realism was ranked according to sociopolitical content, and picking out a "major" topic scored points instantly with the era's "committed" critics. The choice for such a subject matter remained a risky proposition, though—the more political the subject matter was, the more politically unambiguous and emphatically formulated the writer's own position was expected to be.

This vicious circle engendered a body of work that was not only informed by a certain ideology but actually identified programmatically and practically with it. This literature was, simply put, ideology by other means. The conflation of literature and political ideology raises, of course, the question of how *literary* or *artistic* content-driven Socialist Realism was in a critical environment where, from Berlin to Beijing, literariness was equated to formalism and formalism, a "residue" of international modernism, was a sign of bourgeois cosmopolitanism and, with it, target of periodical witch hunts across the ecumene and of vituperations at the meetings of various Communist Parties' Central Committees. With another paradox, then, while critics can talk—as I have—about a Socialist Realist *poetics* or *aesthetics*, while these disciplines were studied in the universities of the Soviet Union and its satellites, and while books in these fields were written during that time, the poetics and aesthetics *of* Socialist Realism had almost nothing to do with the appreciation and cultivation of literary means, with a writer's specific trade and instruments, and the like. In the same vein, it is indeed a bit of a puzzle that Socialist Realism provided the conceptual framework for the world's *first network of literary theory departments* or, if you will, for one big school of literary theory with branches at different higher education locations throughout the Communist geocultural subsystem, where "school" should be understood both institutionally, as a university unit, and culturally, as a coherent, conceptually, historically, and, in this case, also geopolitically circumscribed body of ideas. There was, of course, as far as "schools" fitting some aspects of this definition go, the Russian Formalist precedent, but its orientation—including the work done in the Mikhail M. Bakhtin circle—had been and remained radically different. Viktor Shklovsky, for instance, had famously defined art as "device" or "technique" and thought that "defamiliarization" (*ostranenie*), which increases a literary text's obscurity or "strangeness," represented a general law. Likewise, Yury Tynyanov had dissociated literary and artistic "facts" from "the fact of life." Retrospectively, it is quite amazing that, only two decades after the Russian Formalists had truly revolutionized the analysis of literature, one of their fundamental concepts, *literaturnosti* (literariness) was officially replaced by the Socialist Realist theory "school" with the likes of *ideinosti* and *partiinosti*.

Absolutely pivotal to the new poetics, this substitution subtended and oriented all the other moves of Social Realist critics and theorists with an inflexibility that, as suggested upfront, rendered Socialist Realism rather unrealistic *qua* literature. Now, *partiinosti*, the ecumene's ideologues would have replied in today's language, is no photoshopping of reality because the facts themselves are always subject to interpretation; it is only misguided objectivists who fail to get it. Explicitly countering "bourgeois objectivism" and "empiro-criticism," Leninist philosophy, which informed literary and critical theory throughout the Eastern ecumene, featured an activist ontology that made tactical provisions for a strict ideological compliance that did not entail, or was advertised as not entailing, rather, a narrow perspective on reality, much less a sectarian distortion thereof. For the sacrosanct origin of ideology was the Communist Party, which represented the interests of the working class, which, in turn, was the only class that, as a driving force of historical progress, was "objectively" interested in a genuine understanding of social reality in order to transform it. By way of this "dialectical" legerdemain, Leninism set up *partiinosti* as a hard core of a mimetic theory and literary practice that supposedly gave the short shrift neither to historical accuracy nor to literary verisimilitude because such a politically and epistemologically guided understanding tackled reality in its "revolutionary" development. From Lenin's 1905 article "The Party Organization and Party Literature" all the way to the 1980s, when Socialist Realism drew its last breath in its Soviet world subsystem, representing reality along these developmental lines—which stipulation required impeccable *partiinosti*—remained the impossible yet *sine qua non* task of cultural producers and their ideological handlers across a vast expanse of the world. Regardless of country or language, Socialist Realism demanded, while, with a huge irony, de facto nipping in the bud, a literature "close" to "the daily life" of workers and peasants—read close to the directives of the Communist Party at that particular moment. Society's actual experience of the totalitarian and destitute present surely did not match the propagandistic representation of the everyday in Party documents, government-controlled media, or school, a quotidian that was always dressed up as an idealized reality to come, always in the making. Thus, the contradiction between realism and historical Socialism derives not only from the "Partysan" perspective but also from the fact that Socialism saw itself as a sort of just-around-the-corner future, thereby projecting itself into a steadily deferred futural present rather than effectively striving, its declarations notwithstanding, to transform the surrounding world and make itself comfortable in it. Picking up on this paradox, Albert Camus astutely observed in a 1957 Nobel Prize acceptance speech that "the true object of Socialist Realism is, in fact, what has no reality yet," and that "ultimately, this art will be Socialist precisely to the extent that it will not be realistic."[13]

With yet another incongruity, what prevented new "realism" from being one was exactly what its supporters deemed pivotal to its poetics: the *typical*. A work's acceptance hinged on whether or not the text was capturing the "typical" in the subject at hand. This was a clever strategy designed to reinforce the ideological determinism of literature without giving the impression that the "direct contact" with the religiously invoked reality of a novel or short story was being discouraged or obstructed—quite the contrary, actually, for the typical served as an interface between representation and the represented, a means of controlling the creative process by charting its course in advance so as to prevent any "deviations" from the Party line by writers who might be tempted to adopt too critical of a perspective, to place the wrong kinds of emphasis, and so forth. Ideologically precooked, the typical came before reality and oriented its literary processing. In that, the realism relying on it *was* one, but in a medieval, vaguely classical, or, once again, neoclassical sense, with a smattering of Romanticism thrown into the ideologically selective mix. The cherry-picking of facts, people, and ideas required by the typical was somewhat similar to the classical paring down of worldly variety to a "universal" essence, except that the typical was here not that of the human universal but one intimately bound up with and even produced by a particular historical epoch. This historicity, actual or claimed, coupled with the antithetical vision of one class always pitted against another, brought Socialist Realism close to Romanticism, specifically, to a hypermeliorist, "revolutionary" Romanticism. Only, "typical" meant "exponential"—or what was considered to be so—rather than "characteristic" and "historicity" an idealized, ideologically streamlined picture of history. This automatically ruled out a naturalist approach, which Socialist Realist critics faulted, along Marxist–Leninist lines, with "trite" and "false" objectivity as much as they denied any "idealization" of history while demanding it in the same breath—writers were expected to paint historical pictures complete with their social conflicts, but to do so with a brush dipped in *partiinosti*.

The central figure or type of such typical canvasses was the positive hero or heroine, who had to serve as a social role model, and so the realist-critical formula of the typical put forth by Engels himself—"typical characters under typical circumstances"—had to be amended by a Romantic desideratum—"exceptional characters under exceptional circumstances"—and further fine-tuned to the revolutionary objective that demanded the present be seen and interpreted, according to its futural logic, as an arduous, ongoing but somehow already "victorious" march toward Communism. The positive hero in literature, painting, and film was conceived as a harbinger, amid the trials of the "now," of what was bound to emerge after the lengthy and laborious process of fostering Socialist society: "the new man" (*omul nou* in Romanian), who managed to shake off the petty-bourgeois mentality and, generally, the prejudices of the past. The most important mission of Socialist literature and culture was the very building of this new man or mankind, a task that was simultaneously pedagogical, literary, political, and dialectical. Thus, the whole theory of the typical reflected the optimist epistemology of the era's historical materialism, which posited that reality can be known but only if it was considered in its totality and typicality, with the latter providing a corrective to the former, a discriminating selection of the meaningful and the relevant from the world's bazaar of data and occurrences. Whereas the totalizing perspective was needed to step beyond the limitations of individual experience and leave "bourgeois individualism" behind, the typical presupposes focus on those aspects and qualities seen as truly defining for a society headed to a necessarily bright future.

5. A Wrinkle in World Cultural Time: The Assault on the Western Canon and the Deceleration of Modernity

Socialist Realism was short lived in Romania. Established in1948, at the same time as the new regime, it gained momentum in the 1950s, lost steam in the early 1960s, and came to a grinding halt after 1965. Its demise suggests a historical parallel, for, if the rise of this Eastern geoliterary ecumene had been a vector of Sovietization, Socialist Realism's departure was a form of de-Sovietization and cultural–political decolonization more broadly. Little if anything of the Socialist Realist canon has passed the test of time, and the attempts to salvage chunks of it in the 1970s and 1980s under touched-up forms and designations such as "Socialist humanism," "revolutionary humanism," and finally just "humanism" have all failed. True, the control and censorship by the totalitarian State did not go the way of Socialist Realist orthodoxies, and some of the restrictions, after being officially "removed" in 1977, actually increased in the 1980s. However, a key distinction began to operate, in Romania more than elsewhere in the East in the late 1960s between the role of the Party in the administration of literature and *partiinosti* inside literary texts. That is to say, the Party's national leadership was recognized—or rather tacitly deemed as something hard to do away with—and the Party-State authority over various institutions including literature and its publication was not challenged either. The regime's direct, ideological involvement in the *making* of literary works, in the author's private "workshop," became a thing of the past, though. With the exception of an "official" literary production consisting mainly in widely despised yet still lucrative encomia catering to the Party leadership, post-late 1960s Romanian literature settled for this kind of relative autonomy. While incomplete, the casting aside of the Socialist Realist straightjacket became a reality in Romania more than elsewhere and before it occurred in other areas of the geoliterary subsystem.

Though short-lived, Socialist Realism brutally interrupted local cultural narratives across vast geographies. Its ecumene can be thus viewed as a topological wrinkle in world literary time, as it were. This is, at any rate, what the Socialist Realist intermezzo meant in Romanian literary history, which it managed to throw off its course. I might note that, in the 1930s, the country's literature had roughly got on the same page or pages with Western literatures, no pun intended. For, what we are talking about is not just discursive similitude and compatibilities but also creative participation, especially through the avant-garde, in the expanding of a cross-European canon, in both meanings of the term employed in my essay, that is, as a repertoire of textual protocols and as a set of valued works. In this light, Socialist Realism, complete with its theory and criticism, represented a first, *avant la lettre*—if unsuccessful— contestation of the Euroatlantic canon, an assault whose only upshots were an aesthetic "restoration" and a deceleration of modernizing and modernist processes. Temporary as it was, this slowing down gave rise, together with the entire Cold War, to serious and complex handicaps and asymmetries between the cultural domains formerly separated by the Iron Curtain, so much so that the themes, issues, and crises foregrounded in contemporary West European literature differed significantly from those in Eastern Europe. This is why, when Romania began recovering from Socialist Realism in the mid-1960s, the priorities did not coincide with those of French or U.S. literature. Understandably, retrieving national tradition and resuming modernist experimentation struck Romanian writers and critics as more urgent than critiquing modernism and possibly moving into the postmodern, a move that, along with the first domestic inroads of poststructuralism, would have to wait almost two decades. In the same vein, if the humanities on both sides of the Atlantic saw a paradigmatic shift that prompted a revaluation of the aesthetic, a renewed interest in "context," "culture," and identity issues, as well as a 1968-type of politicization of theory and criticism increasingly premised on resistance to state apparatuses and on a deconstruction of their discursive effects, many Romanian intellectuals and artists felt solidary with a nation-state whose sovereignty continued to be threatened by the USSR. While recent scholarship from outside the former geoliterary ecumene of Socialist Realism seems to be drawn to the latter's "exotic" aspects and similitudes with admittedly comparable literary production from the United States, the postcolonial world, and elsewhere, to the overwhelming majority of Romanian and East European critics and cultural historians the phenomenon looks—to paraphrase Stephen Dedalus—like a nightmare from which they are happy to have awakened.

Notes

1   Evgheny Dobrenko and Galin Tihanov, *A History of Russian Literary Theory and Criticism: The Soviet Age and Beyond* (Pittsburgh, PA: University of Pittsburgh Press, 2011).
2   Andrei Zhdanov, quoted in Dobrenko and Tihanov, *A History of Russian Literary Theory and Criticism*, 169–171 and 179–180.

3   On Soviet colonization, I refer the reader to my essay "Le communisme comme colonialism," which came out in *Euresis* 1 (2005): 3–26.

4   Hana Voisine-Jechova, *Histoire de la littérature tchèque* (Paris: Fayard, 2001), 598.

5   Another group bearing the name of *Kuznitsa* was founded in Soviet Russia in 1919 and was against Proletcultism.

6   Czeslaw Milosz, *Histoire de la littérature polonaise* (Paris: Fayard, 1996), 615.

7   Su Wei, *The School and the Hospital: On the Logic of Socialist Realism in Chinese Literature in the Second Half of a Modern Century. A Critical Survey*, ed. Pang-yuan Chi and David Der-wei Wang (Bloomington, IN: Indiana University Press, 2000): 65–75.

8   Nicolae Moraru, "Criza culturii române?" *Contemporanul*, October 11, 1946, 8.

9   Sandra Cordoş, *Literatura între revoluţie şi reacţiune* (Cluj-Napoca: Apostrof, 1999).

10 Ion Caraion, "Criza culturii româneşti," *Jurnalul de Dimineaţă*, October 17, 1946, 2.

11 Tudor Arghezi, "Artă pentru," *Adevărul*, October 27, 1946, 2.

12 Ion Pop, *Din avangardă spre ariergardă* (Bucharest: Editura Vinea, 2010), 212.

13 See Albert Camus's essay "L'artist et son temps," *Essais* (Paris: Gallimard, 1965), 1087.

Romanian Modernity and the Rhetoric of Vacuity: Toward a Comparative Postcolonialism

Bogdan Ştefănescu

Around the mid-1990s, I stumbled across an unexpected topos of Romanian culture: the void. As I learned during the research I was doing at the time, this recurrent figure comes in different guises as members of modern Romania's cultural elite keep referring to the country's "absence" from history and to its various "wants" and "deficiencies." These critics and philosophers ply the trope of "foundational void" to talk about a cultural trauma supposedly lodged at the core of the Romanian "soul" and "destiny." At some point, I even gave a paper on this subject, but then I dropped the issue, for I thought there was not much to it. However, I came across it again more than a decade later as I turned to the comparative study of postcommunism and postcolonialism. Suddenly, the persistence of the void motif in the identitarian imaginary of formerly colonized cultures from distinct world-systems became an eye-opener. For, as I was wrestling with this theme and with the world dynamic of trauma and postcoloniality more broadly, it dawned on me that an entire comparative remapping of Romanian culture might be possible, and, what is more, that such an undertaking need not follow nationalist or universalist orthodoxies' overemphasis on the supposed untranslatable singularity or on the aspiring, decontextualized, and generic nature of the country's aesthetic patrimony, respectively.

Thus, in what follows, I will be focusing on the imagery of vacuity and bareness in Romanian and other postcolonial trauma cultures around the globe. The literary and critical inflections of this imagery occur, I argue, in a counterintuitive yet conspicuous pattern shared by the otherwise loosely interconnected subsystems of what development theory used to identify as the "Second" and "Third" World. The consistent deployment of the void thematics both in the ex-colonies of Western empires and in the former Soviet republics and satellites seems to indicate, I further submit, that all these countries instantiate the same postcolonial situation, namely, a widespread sense of lack and emptiness that comes from viewing one's culture as irreparably traumatized by an alien and malignant modernity. One of my aims here, then, is to draw attention to this similitude—to what I call the nodal convergence of postcolonial discourses. To clarify, what I mean by "nodal convergence" is the echoing and interplay of certain tropes and *topoi* in collective self-representations from cultures that have all been colonized one way or the other but that have had no direct contacts among themselves and have been shaped by different geo-historical and political contexts as well. By the same token, my intervention warrants a reexamination of the emerging theories and methodologies of World Literature comparative studies. As is well known, comparatists have traditionally imported divisions from geography and history and have mostly relied on regional or temporal contiguity to explain how literatures interact within such units. Instead, alongside critics like Wai Chee Dimock, I propose a "reterritorialization" of our scope and discipline altogether and push, accordingly, the boundaries of comparative accounts past such limited spatial and temporal categories to expand the scale of analysis so as to include and bring together cultures that are, literally and otherwise, worlds apart.

1. Postcolonial Symptoms of Cultural Trauma: Malignant Modernity

Historically speaking, modernity has been Janus-faced, smiling generously on its promoters while turning a malicious face to those who, pushed by modernity's discourse of dominance, see themselves as lagging behind, on the margins of the modern world, outside it, in dissonance with it, or its powerless object. Likewise, cultures embracing the ideology of progress perceive modernity as a blessing or at least as a given of historical evolution. But there also are plenty of cultures that present "subaltern" discourse patterns suggesting that such cultures tend to view themselves as victims of modernity. For such cultural voices, the latter struck like a calamity or felt like a foreign intrusion in the natural course of their history. The ruthless drive of modernity robbed them of territories, material resources, and individual lives, as well as of their own sense of identity and historical destiny. In short, subordinate cultures experienced modernity as colonization of not only space and time but also of body and mind. Elsewhere, I have offered the phrase "malignant modernity" to indicate precisely this kind of historical representation in colonized cultures.[1] While the expression may strike some as odd, the phenomenon it names is certainly not. The imposition of Western modernity on colonized lands has been a commonplace theme in radical anticolonialism ever since the 1950s discourse of *négritude* and has persisted as a critical concern in Africa, Asia, and, indeed, most colonized cultures. In fact, the collective psychological response to the historical intrusion of modernity has remained inscribed in the mentalities and national metanarratives of these communities as a "cultural trauma." This concept has been amply discussed and employed.[2] My own use of the term is consistent with Piotr Sztompka's claim that cultural trauma is a mental construct whereby historical change is negatively encoded as abrupt, radical, brought on by an external agent, and repulsive.[3] I would only add to Sztompka's account the necessity of what I would designate as "canonical encoding," that is, a process by which individual anxieties become collective self-representations, are gradually instituted and accepted as tradition, and thus turned into *cultural* traumas.

I find this traumatic identity construction to be an experience generally shared by "postcolonies" of both Western and USSR empires. If Cathy Caruth is right when she says that "trauma itself may provide the very link between cultures," then postcolonial trauma may well be one such link between the former Western and Soviet colonies. The connection was set up in the twentieth century, when colonial trauma was inflicted worldwide in ways that, different from those of earlier modernity, expanded and modulated the very significance of modernity itself.[4] For, to be sure, new forms of colonialism appeared in the late nineteenth and especially in the twentieth century. One such case is Czarist Russia, whose imperialist tactics of land-grabbing colonialism in Transcaucasia, Central Asia, the Baltic region, and Eastern Europe were carried on by the USSR under the propagandistic slogan of "liberating" all nations in its imperial grip, as they are applied these days by Russia under new pretexts. True, the practice and ideological legitimation of Soviet colonialism differed from those of other empires. However, the postcolonial aftermath presents notable similitudes no matter where you look. In the former British, French, or Belgian possessions, the new independent states were coopted into a world-system arguably geared toward informal, discreet, and indirect recolonization or neocolonization. In this global context, these colonies continue to be culturally dominated and driven to view themselves as falling behind by Western standards of progress. The same goes for the former Soviet colonies or "semicolonies," as some critics consider them. After being forced to follow the Kremlin's supposedly more progressive and enlightened lead for almost half a century, some of them have resumed, in the postcommunist age, the pursuit of various national destinies as part and parcel of European and planetary modernity but still with the sense of delay with respect to the more "advanced" West, while others chose to preserve their subaltern position toward Russia as a regional superpower. Whatever their new geopolitical affiliations and subordinations, virtually all previous colonized countries have been faced with the same double challenge, though: on the one hand, they have realized that their recently acquired political independence does not shield them from a novel, subtler, and more perverse form of colonization; on the other hand, these countries have found that underdevelopment, endemic corruption, a weak state, frail social structures, marginal placement in the networks of international power, and other marks and remnants of the crippling colonial past do not go away that easily, pressing them to endlessly remember and relive the traumas of the past and, more generally, to picture modernity and modernization as traumatizing and damaging.

In Western and Soviet colonies and postcolonies alike, during and after colonial times, the veritable "identitarian malaise" caused by what I term malignant modernity shows a symptomatology that includes memory lapses, blockages, and other disorders of this kind, ostentatious silence, irreversible loss, the feeling of abandonment, of being ostracized and stigmatized, humiliation, deprecation, self-loathing, and passive-aggressive behavior. One symptom category I would like to dwell on in my essay is what I define as the *tropology of the void*, that is, a central imagery of absence and lacking around which the cultural identity of the colonized is fashioned. To reiterate, this set of images obtains in geographically and culturally unconnected environments, which both bears out and complicates those comparative theories of "nodal" reading that rely on contextual determinism. As we have noticed during the past twenty years or so, recent World Literature approaches have introduced such new concepts as "nodes,"[5] "nodal points,"[6] "nodal cities,"[7] or "marginocentric cities"[8] to focus more effectively on the "loci where Europe has historically encountered otherness and defined itself against and through it."[9] These conceptual innovations speak to an effort to move critical understanding away from static, nationalist or nation-centered teleologies and toward a dynamic and transnational mapping of cultural convergence and influence. However, these attempts invariably operate within geographical and historical contiguity, failing to take into account not only that literature and culture are dual phenomena drawing from and attesting to both our material and mental worlds but also that parallelisms and even crosspollinations arise among literatures and cultures *separated* by large swaths of time and space. Thus, my work on the postcolonial imagination of former Soviet and Western colonies helped me uncover a *transregional* and *trans-period* interplay of discursive topoi working at a distance. This leads me to propose the notion of *spectral nodality* in order to conceptualize a type of comparison that may seem counterintuitive, but that, I maintain, comes in handy when one deals with the complex phenomenon by which discourses from geographically and historically unrelated cultures echo or interpellate each other. For, indeed, *haunting* images of distant places both repel and attract the traumatized postcolonial subject, and, across traditions, they constitute, to paraphrase Lucia Boldrini, mental loci for a self-defining encounter with otherness.[10] The obsessive figures of the identitarian void, which I will briefly review in the next section, operate as such a spectral nodality, for it brings together and sets up exchanges between discourses from former colonies whose dealings with one another historically have been indirect at best.

2. Avatars of Vacuity in Western and Soviet Postcolonies

In the postcolonial discourse of Asia and Africa, the *topos* of the void is anything but marginal.[11] In fact, Homi Bhabha posits the void as a founding trope for the concurrent rise of modern colonialism and of modern nations with their "homogenous empty time," as well as for the linguistic and existential experience of native intellectuals in the postcolonies of the West.[12] Likewise, Achille Mbembe repeatedly employs the metaphor of the void to represent a number of issues marking the historical development of formerly colonized countries, maintaining that the blank gaze of the colonist actually constructs the colonized as ontological and historical emptiness.[13] Other postcolonial critics, such as Anne McClintock, Aparajita Nanda, Janet Wilson, Emman Frank Idoko, Ania Loomba, Bill Ashcroft, Gareth Griffiths, and Helen Tiffin have also touched upon figurative networks of identitarian vacuity.[14] But the recursive figure of the void does not feature only in criticism; it is also copiously present in the fiction of Western postcolonies. Guyanese writer Wilson Harris sees the experience of the colonized as a descent into the subjective vacuum left by the displacement of one's language and culture.[15] In turn, Nigerian novelist Chinua Achebe protested against the Orientalist notion that Africa had been a cultural void before the arrival of Western colonists.[16]

For him, this void is rather the effect of cultural intrusions, and in *Things Fall Apart* he presents Christian converts as "empty men" (*efulefu*), a dismissive tag for men who sold their machetes and wore empty sheaths to battle. The same *topos* of Africa as one great "metaphysical vacuum" is invoked by Ghanaian–American philosopher Kwame Anthony Appiah when he comments on the work of Nigerian author Wole Soyinka. In *Death and the King's Horseman,* Soyinka depicts acculturation as a form of vacuity: "... there is only one shell to the soul of man: there is only one world to the spirit of our race. If that world leaves its course and smashes on boulders of the great void, whose world will give us shelter?"[17] Finally, on a different continent, Indian artist Gajanan Madhav Muktibodh also captures this traumatic experience of emptiness in his poem "The Void," in which critic Vinay Dharwadker has identified "the late colonial self as a thing that is still alive but emptied out of all its human qualities, and reduced to a violent, retaliatory animal presence-that-is-an-absence.[18]

In all these situations, although the *topos* of the identitarian void engendered by imperial modernity rolls across the national or even the continental boundaries of Western powers' former colonies, it nevertheless plays out within a world-system or subsystem whose components are adjacent or close to one another when they do not make up a homogenous, geocultural and, in places, linguistic continuum. But how does one explain the circulation of that same trope across the nation-states that were under colonizing Soviet rule until the dismantling of the Berlin Wall? Unlike the former colonies of the West, Eastern Europe was a colonial territory where Russian, the language of the imperial center, did not function very effectively as a *lingua franca* throughout the entire expanse and history of the Soviet Empire—no wonder Russian all but withered away in the former Soviet republics and satellites, which further disintegrated their regional linguistic environment. In spite of the quasi disappearance of the colonist's language, however, a great deal of post-Soviet Central and Eastern Europe's identitarian discourse revolves around the spectral imagery of the void. In the early 1990s, the fall of the Soviet colonial system came to be associated with the trope under scrutiny here. Thus, in 1992, Jean Baudrillard referred to an "ascent of the vacuum toward the periphery" and famously proclaimed that "the 'victory' of the West is not unlike a depressurizing of the West in the void of communism, in the void of history."[19] A year later, Slavoj Žižek's meditation on the virtues of spiritual dismemberment and revival turned to the image of the 1989 Romanian revolution's hole in the flag with its Communist symbol cut out. Addressing the voided cultural identity of postcommunist countries like Romania, Žižek observed that "instead of the symbol standing for the organizing principle of the [*sic*] national life, there was nothing but a hole in its center."[20]

Notably, the country's symbolic self-image reverberated throughout the crumbling Communist Bloc. Some East European writers were quick to add, however, that the void in question was the result of their nations' Soviet colonization, thus placing themselves and their postcommunist societies in a "spectral" sort of juxtaposition not just with one another but also with other, faraway postcolonies, bound together as they felt by the nagging sense that the confrontation with a traumatizing modernity left their cultural selves "empty inside." Following Indian–American anthropologist Akhil Gupta, Maria

Todorova has suggested, for instance, that such a "historical consciousness of lack" is the "curious though not fundamental trait" shared by countries that, whether in Africa or in Eastern Europe, were feeling that they were lagging behind modernity.[21] Another Bulgarian cultural historian, Alexander Kiossev, had already drawn attention to the obsessive, cultural discourse-spawning image of an absence in his culture, which he found to be symptomatic for many marginalized East Europeans. In his view, Bulgaria and other nations in the region have grounded a "self-colonizing" identity of sorts in their angst of "lacking" a homegrown civilization model.[22] In his discussion, Kiossev pointed to a recurrent theme in many East European cultures that were subjected to multiple colonizations in the course of their history. For these traumatized cultures, Sovietization only reinforced an older sense of historical vacuity. Adding insult to injury after the collapse of the Soviet Empire, the patronizing Western "guidance" on the road to democracy only rekindled earlier apprehensions of a modernity whose shockwaves made them feel culturally empty, inadequate, or belated. In the same vein, historians like Israeli-born Omer Bartov and Argentine Ezequiel Adamovsky resort to the void metaphor to account for a postcoloniality that connects the experiences of Eastern Europe and the developing world,[23] while Croatian philosopher Boris Buden deems postcommunism an entire sequence of "vacuums," given that Soviet colonialism itself lacked an ethnocultural center.[24] Likewise, for cultural theorist Boris Groys, "communism yet again appears as a specter: a Nothing materializing and, after its disappearance, dissolving into Nothing,"[25] whereas Polish sociologist Zygmunt Bauman contends that the overall experience of modernity fosters a defining obsession with the void (*horror vacui*) and passes this fixation on to postmodernity as well.[26]

But, just as in Western postcolonialism, the image of identitarian emptiness in postcommunism is by no means restricted to critical writing. This image also turns up in fictional literature all over post-Soviet Eastern Europe. At the former center of the Soviet colonial empire, to begin with, the figure occurs in recent Russian literature. Thus, in his 1999 novel *The Underground, or a Hero of Our Time*, Vladimir Makanin invokes Chekhov to describe the alienating void not only as a result of postcommunist confusion but also as a paradoxical "foundation" of Russian identity throughout its own history of trauma as "all sorts of different things … push into your (post-slave) vacuums of emptiness from the outside. And it's not immediately that you observe the alien element in yourself."[27] Published in the same year as *The Underground*, Viktor Pelevin's novel *Generation "P"* alludes, along the same lines, to Russia's rediscovery of its identity of nothingness in the postcommunist, consumerist age. Here, the void is featured as a commercial for the chain of Gap stores in the country. "Russia," writes Pelevin, "was always notorious for the gap between culture and civilization: now there is no more culture: no more civilization: the only thing that remains is the gap: the way they see you."[28]

In post–Cold War Polish literature, this gap becomes a crack. In *On the Road to Babadag*, for example, Andrzej Stasiuk records his attraction to uncharted, unknown, historically blank spots in Eastern Europe as he looks for "cracks in the scenery that imagination might slip into," and this preoccupation has been noted by commentators such as James Hopkin and Marek Kohn. In effect, Kohn joins Todorova, Kiossev, Bartov, and Adamovsky to propose, in an analogy with Orientalist representations of the West's colonial lands, that "the emptiness, the disconnectedness and the stasis deep inside Europe can be as emotionally transfixing and revelatory as the tumult of a city crowd on the Indian subcontinent."[29] Dawid Bieńkowski, another Polish writer, also spins a narrative of traumatized postcommunist identities around the constitutive image of hollowness and inner void in his 2005 novel *Nic* (Nothing).[30] There is even something called "the Nothing Generation" (*pokolenie nic*, also known as Poland's "Generation X"), which includes writers Dorota Masłowska and Sławomir Shuty and which recasts the traumatic void brought about by Communist oppression as postcommunist "resignation from intellectual aspirations."[31] In Hungary, *pokolenie nic*'s equivalent is the so-called "generation of absence." Its members are Géza Bereményi, György Spiró, and Mihály Kornis, among other Hungarian playwrights of the 1970s and 1980s who "have grown up with a vacuum in their own past" and whose "absence of self-identity" compelled them to "dramatize the unspoken."[32] But there is, as Rajendra A. Chitnis suggests, also a Czech way and a Russian-Slovak way of "living with emptiness" of this kind. For Czech authors like Daniela Hodrová and Jáchym Topol, writing is "a metaphor for the unceasing dynamic struggle of being against emptiness," whereas Slovaks such as Ivan Kolenič, Dušan Mitana, and Ján Litvák, and the Russian Vladimir Sorokin display "a paradoxical yearning to give way to silence and emptiness once and for all."[33] These are only some of the authors who cast light on spectral avenues of nodality weaving together East European literatures not just among themselves but also with the remote literary world-system of former French or British colonies. Larry Wolff is one of the critics who have shown that these far-flung regions have been present in East European consciousness since the eighteenth century as a result of Western authors and publics' representing Europe's Eastern outskirts as a colony of sorts[34] while, I might note, conversely, the post-Ottoman- and post-Habsburg-era Balkans are sometimes pictured in African anticolonial writing as a culturally and politically subaltern zone.[35]

3. *Ex nihilo*: A Genealogy of the Romanian Void

As early as 1981, before Bhabha and Mbembe, or Todorova and Kiossev, Romanian critic Mircea Martin highlighted the symptoms of a persistent cultural trauma of modernity in Romanian literature by outlining the "complexes" marking some of his country's authors. In an analysis on which I build in this section of my essay, Martin points to the "obsessive search for identity," or to the "handicap" stemming from a belated adoption of Western models of modernity and driving writers like Benjamin Fondane—or Fundoianu, as he signed his Romanian works—to dismiss Romania's literary patrimony as no more than a "colony" of French literature.[36] Martin's choice of critical vocabulary is revealing. He describes the trauma in question through the familiar motif of vacuity as "an inventory of constitutive lacunae in Romanian literature" and as "an acute sense of a void"[37] that, we are told, preceded the belated, mid-nineteenth-century beginnings of modern Romanian letters.[38]

Resonating powerfully to this void throughout his oeuvre, philosopher Constantin Noica (1909–1987) is an important agent of the nodality at hand—viz., of the thematization of a vacuity-obsessed imagery that echoes a far-flung yet similar, anxiety-ridden tropology. A casualty of modernity himself—and quite literally so—Noica began his career between the two World Wars with critical meditations on Romanian culture's marginal status by comparison to the West's self-proclaimed central position. During the Soviet colonization of the post–Second World War years, the Communist authorities first sentenced him to forced domicile and then imprisoned him for six years.[39] Responding to his ordeals, his work reiterates insistently the interwar topos of a Romania absenting itself from history as a paradoxical strategy for cultural survival and regeneration; specifically, he contended that an individual's "spiritual" survival comes from willfully severing one's social ties in a "subtle exile, an exile among your own people, sometimes even at home, in your own world and yet in one from which the concrete world has been emptied out."[40] In fact, Noica tried to work out an entire genealogy of vacuity for his country by connecting tradition and the cultural elites of which he was part in the 1930s and early 1940s. Thus, he traced the "traumatic" lineage of Romanian thought and the culture's cognate, "periphery" and "inferiority" complex all the way back to Moldavian scholar and ruler Dimitrie Cantemir (1673–1723).[41] Indeed, in *Descriptio Moldaviae* (1714–1716), a work actually commissioned by his peers at the Berlin Academy, Cantemir does fall back on the symbolic arsenal of the void when invoking a historical hiatus and emptiness as "origin" of his people,[42] which claim Noica interpreted as a "lack of harmony" in Cantemir's estranged soul as well as an effect of having "internalized" the standards of Western civilization.[43] Notably, Noica set up a major nodal convergence of the rhetoric of the vacuous self in Romanian literature and history overall by linking this inaugural moment to his own generation, naming his friend Emil Cioran (1911–1995) as Cantemir's latest descendent, and for good reason, too. In his 1936 book *Schimbarea la față a României* (Romania's Transfiguration), Cioran made heavy-handed references to Romanians' presumptive "lack" of historical substance, which for him pinpointed "a substantial flaw in the psychic structure of the Romanian, an original void generating a series of failures throughout our past."[44]

The historical void image broached in the writing of young Noica and Cioran had been introduced by historian A. D. Xenopol and his disciple G. I. Brătianu[45] and was already a commonplace in Romanian identitarian discourse of the late 1930s and early 1940s. By then, philosopher and modernist poet Lucian Blaga (1895–1961) had been working toward a "national metaphysics" liable to counter the infamous "historiographic void" in the country's remote past and the notion that Romania might be a mere "blank spot" on the map of the region.[46] Blaga's view of national history was building, however, on an older founding myth featuring a peasant people that, for a long period of time following the breakdown of the military and administrative structures in the Eastern regions of the Roman Empire, withdrew from history and even started to "boycott" it, for they somehow spontaneously decided to choose a peaceful and anonymous spiritual communion with nature over an epic world destiny and a place in the nations' hall of fame.[47] Mircea Eliade (1907–1986), a friend of Noica and member of the same generation of Romanian intellectuals, echoes Blaga's apologetic narrative in his 1943 *Los Rumanos. Breviaro historico* (The Romanians: A Concise History) and actually paraphrases him in "The Fate of Romanian Culture" (1953) and *L'épreuve du labyrinthe* (1978) by famously referring to the "terror of history" his people had to confront.[48] "The Fate of Romanian Culture" is particularly relevant due to its *postcolonial* perspective on national history. Here, Eliade sketches out an ethnogenesis of Romanians by explicitly bringing together Roman colonization, the settling of early medieval migratory populations among the natives, the Ottoman Empire's domination of territories inhabited by Romanians, the Soviet hegemony of the Cold War era, and the colonial as well as postcolonial marginalization of "minor" and indigenous cultures by the West—in sum, Romania's virtually uninterrupted colonial status in premodern, modern, and even postmodern times.[49]

Having tied together the recent contributions of Brătianu, Blaga, Cioran, and Eliade to Cantemir and Romanian tradition more largely, Noica carried over the inherited motif of the vacuous self into yet another colonization episode of Romanian culture— the dark age of Communist dictatorship. De facto colonized by the Soviets in the decade that followed the Second World War, Romania went through an initial, partial, and drawn-out decolonization until 1989. During this time, the country's Communist leaders acted at first as a veritable comprador oligarchy on behalf of the Kremlin but eventually opted for a gradual desovietization by first replacing Moscow loyalists, then negotiating the 1958 retreat of the Red Army, and finally veering toward nationalist Communism and even objecting openly to Moscow's policy of colonial domination, as they did, for instance, during the 1968 invasion of Czechoslovakia. The final stage of decolonization from Soviet-style Communism started in 1989 with the precipitated demise of the system officially put in place in 1947. Thus, Noica spent the last forty years of his life under Communist rule, and so, in order to be allowed to publish once again after his release from prison, he negotiated an uneasy cohabitation with the propaganda of Nicolae Ceaușescu's authoritarian regime. In such works as the 1978 *Spiritul românesc în cumpătul vremii: Șase maladii ale spiritului contemporan* (The Romanian Spirit in History: Six Maladies of the Contemporary Spirit), *De dignitate Europae*—the German translation had come out two years before the Romanian original, which was published in 1990 as *Modelul cultural European*—or in the 1990 *Rugați-vă pentru fratele Alexandru* (Pray for Brother Alexander), he revisited and expanded the theme of a presumptively hollowed-out Romanian identity troubled by colonial modernity.[50]

The theme will haunt the early postcommunist years too. In his 1991 book *The Hole in the Flag*, Romanian-American poet Andrei Codrescu ponders this very subject on his way back to his native land after years of exile when he sees the Romanian revolutionary flag before crossing the border: "[i]t's through that hole ... that I am returning to my birthplace."[51] In recent memory, this is an important "nodal" moment or multilayered echo of the traditional discourses of emptiness and absence that, as Codrescu also suspects, lies at the core of Romania's colonial identity. These discourses trace a lineage that, even though it comprises canonical figures such as his beloved literary masters Blaga, Cioran, and Eliade,[52] makes some feel uncomfortable.

Commentators such as Horia-Roman Patapievici, for instance, reject this line of thought as a sign of his people's historical inertia. Recalling Noica's "nodal" positioning in this tradition, he blames Communism for perpetrating a cultural trauma that all but annihilated the national character and reinforced the "identity of nothingness" (*identitate de neant*) collective mentality.[53] Apt or not, Patapievici's stance goes to show that Romanian artists, critics, and public intellectuals have had diverging attitudes toward modernity, modern Western values, and the urgency of modernizing Romanian culture.[54] But, whether or not one accepts outside modern influences on Romanian culture, and whether or not one views the identitarian void figure as beneficial to it, comparing national culture with the (Western) modern "civilized world" has been a constant cause for anxiety, uneasiness, and embarrassment. Even those who embraced the rational and progressive ideals of modernity felt compelled to theorize and endorse "catching up" with the West and had to face, historically speaking, ideological resistance from more conservative groups, as well as the reluctance of a largely traditionalist and poorly educated general population. Such mix of pro-modern enthusiasms and antimodern apprehensions and identity-related anxieties explains, according to Martin, why Romanian literature presents itself as a "simultaneity of contradictory options" and large spectrum of "[t]heoretical constructions whose broad social and political implications exceed the strictly literary and originate in the impulse either to disguise and reject such 'complexes' or to assume and dwell on them more deeply so as to overcome them eventually."[55]

4. Nodality: Cultural Reality and Comparative Approach

If Romanian and overall Central and East European responses to the collective identity trauma induced by colonial and postcolonial modernity are oftentimes ambivalent, critics from the former colonies of what used to be known as the Third World appear more inclined to ascribe an unambiguously negative value to the cultural void modernity and modernization have hegemonically associated with identity formation in those sectors of the world-system. A major factor accounting for this somewhat disorienting diversity of reactions in Europe's Eastern half after the Second World War is the long and convoluted history of colonization in this region, where country after country had already undergone multiple waves and forms of colonization before Sovietization. Above this and other distinctions, however, the shared imagery of an emptied-out, insubstantial, and belated identity provides, across centuries and continents, a "nodal" kind of convergence and coherence to the world's different idioms of colonial trauma and makes it possible for Eastern Europe and the Third World to become "spectral" relatives, as it were. This kinship, I propose, calls on us to rethink our approach to Romanian, East European, as well as world postcoloniality. For, as we have noticed, whether in Western colonies or in Central and Eastern Europe, similar symbolic mechanisms of national identity constitution operate. Belonging to geographically discrete cultures as they do, the images engendered by such mechanisms may nonetheless be recontextualized and thus integrated critically into spectral literary and cultural networks spanning continents so as to supplement or even substitute for missing or negligible interactions derived from direct contact and vicinity. I find this type of comparative approach effective because it accounts for the striking discursive similarities between disparate postcolonial contexts. It is, as I submit, the phenomenon of spectral nodality that calls for a revisiting of Romanian literary and intellectual tradition from this new comparative perspective whereby historical formation of cultural discourse, including the discourse of identity and self-representation, and historicity most generally, is understood in a broader, sociologically and spatially less deterministic fashion that is, by the same token, less dependent in its analysis on the existence of physical contacts among neighboring individuals or cultures. As we have seen, this perspective facilitates the comparison of discourses from world-systems that have been kept apart by ideological and geo-historical differences. In highlighting the vacuity rhetoric common to the broad spectral circuits of identitarian discourse typical of Eastern Europe, Asia, Africa, and other formerly colonized zones of the world, one uncovers, as I have above, major nodes of a *transhistorical* and *transregional* postcoloniality. "Transhistorical," I might add, here fruitfully complicates the historical from the perspective suggested by Fernand Braudel's *long durée*, Maria Todorova's "relative synchronicity,"[56] and Dimock's concept of "deep time."[57] Transhistoricity, I would also specify, does not depend on the chronological contiguity of events, just as transregionality, analogously seen as "deep space," does not involve the geographical juxtapositions of regions. Instead, these "trans-" concepts rather point to those geocultural remappings that are made possible by discursive similarities or proximities in a "complex tangle of relations … a crisscrossing set of pathways, open-ended and ever multiplying, weaving in and out of other geographies, other languages and cultures."[58] The transhistorical and transregional nature of postcolonial trauma connects world cultures on the basis of generic, structural, and relational similarities constructed discursively. This is because traumatic postcoloniality does not possess an inherent, geohistorically circumscribed ideology, and so its "situatedness" exceeds the bounds of certain spatial and temporal localizations.[59] Indeed, there may be no direct contact or influence between Noica and other intellectuals or cultures in Eastern Europe, or between writers from Romania and their counterparts from Africa, Asia, or the Americas, and yet for all such traumatized subjects the inner void is, individually and collectively, as painful and as actual as underdevelopment and the empire's military presence. The world we inhabit, they rightly feel, is no less imagined than it is real, and so the counterintuitive comparisons and associations effectuated by the imagination, anachronistic and "anatopic" or "out of place" as they may appear, can nevertheless set in motion "multidirectional" memories[60] and connections allowing traumatized subjectivities that are worlds apart to come together by virtue of their shared formal and generic features, as Robert Eaglestone has shown in his comparative analysis of post-Holocaust and postcolonial literature.[61] No doubt, the material, physical contact among languages, literatures, and cultures through economic, political, and social interactions is highly relevant to the study of world literature. But if identities are produced discursively, then "untying" the nodes of identitarian discourses, no matter where and when these discourses come about in the world's postcolonial history, is also an important part of our work as twenty-first-century comparatists.

Notes

1   See Bogdan Ştefănescu, "Marginal Romanian Meets European Model: Noica and Modernity as Colonial Trauma," in *European Integration/ National Identity; Plurilingualism/Multiculturality—Romanian Language and Culture: Evaluation, Perspectives*, ed. Ofelia Ichim (Roma: Aracne Editrice, 2014), 289–290.

2   See Jeffrey C. Alexander and Piotr Sztompka, eds., *Rethinking Progress: Movements, Forces, and Ideas at the End of the 20th Century* (Boston: Unwin Hyman, 1990); Dominick LaCapra, *Representing the Holocaust: History, Theory, Trauma* (Ithaca, NY: Cornell University Press, 1994); *History and Memory after Auschwitz* (Ithaca, NY: Cornell University Press, 1998); *Writing History, Writing Trauma* (Baltimore, MD: Johns Hopkins University Press, 2001); Cathy Caruth, *Trauma: Explorations in Memory* (Baltimore, MD: Johns Hopkins University Press, 1995); Kirby Farrell, *Posttraumatic Culture: Injury and Interpretation in the Nineties* (Baltimore, MD: Johns Hopkins University Press, 1998); Piotr Sztompka, "Cultural Trauma: The Other Face of Social Change," *European Journal of Social Theory* 3, no. 4 (2000): 452.

3   Sztompka, "Cultural Trauma: The Other Face of Social Change," 452.

4   Caruth, *Trauma: Explorations in Memory*, 11.

5   Marcel Cornis-Pope and John Neubauer, eds., *History of the Literary Cultures of East-Central Europe: Junctures and Disjunctures in the 19th and 20th Centuries*, vol. 4, *Types and Stereotypes* (Amsterdam: John Benjamins, 2010), 5.

6   Linda Hutcheon and Mario J. Valdés, eds., *Rethinking Literary History: A Dialogue on Theory* (Oxford: Oxford University Press, 2002), 8. See also Mario J. Valdés and Linda Hutcheon, "Rethinking Literary History—Comparatively," *American Council of Learned Societies*, occasional paper no. 27, 1995.

7   Ania Spyra, "Between Theory and Reality: Cosmopolitanism of Nodal Cities in Paweł Huelle's *Castorp*," *Comparative Literature* 63, no. 4 (2012): 287.

8   Marcel Cornis-Pope and John Neubauer, eds., *History of the Literary Cultures of East-Central Europe: Junctures and Disjunctures in the 19th and 20th Centuries*, vol. 2 (Amsterdam: John Benjamins, 2010), 9.

9   Lucia Boldrini, "Comparative Literature in the Twenty-First Century: A View from Europe and the U. K.," *Comparative Critical Studies* 3 (2006): 17.

10 Boldrini, "Comparative Literature in the Twenty-First Century," 17.

11 For a more detailed discussion of the void trope in the former colonies of Asia and Africa, see Bogdan Ştefănescu, "Filling in the Historical Blanks: A Tropology of the Void in Postcommunist and Postcolonial Reconstructions of Identity," in *Postcolonial Europe? Essays on Post-Communist Literatures and Cultures*, ed. Dobrota Pucherova and Robert Gafrik (Amsterdam: Brill/Rodopi, 2015), 107–112.

12 Homi K. Bhabha, "DissemiNation: Time, Narrative, and the Margins of the Modern Nation," in *Nation and Narration*, ed. Homi K. Bhabha (London: Routledge, 1990), 291, "Making Emptiness," http://anishkapoor.com/185/Making-Emptiness-by-Homi-K.-Bhabha.html. Accessed August 27, 2016; *The Location of Culture* (London: Routledge, 1994), 37.

13 Achille Mbembe, *On the Postcolony* (Berkeley, CA: University of California Press, 2001), 187.

14 See Ştefănescu, "Filling in the Historical Blanks," 107–120.

15 Wilson Harris, *Tradition, the Writer and Society* (London: New Beacon, 1973), 60, 62.

16   Bernth Lindfors, ed., *Conversations with Chinua Achebe* (Jackson, MS: University Press of Mississippi, 1997), 29.

17   Quoted in Kwame Anthony Appiah, "Myth, Literature, and the African World," in *Perspectives on Wole Soyinka: Freedom and Complexity*, ed. Biodun Jeyifo (Jackson, MS: University Press of Mississippi, 2001), 167.

18   Vinay Dharwadker, "Late Colonial and Postcolonial Selves in Hindu and Marathi Poetry," in *Self as Image in Asian Theory and Practice*, ed. Roger T. Ames, Thomas S. Kasulis, and Wiman Dissanayake (Albany, NY: State University of New York Press, 1998), 243, *passim*.

19   Jean Baudrillard, *The Illusion of an End*, trans. Chris Turner (Cambridge: Polity Press, 1994), 49.

20   Slavoj Žižek, *Tarrying with the Negative: Kant, Hegel, and the Critique of Ideology* (Durham, NC: Duke University Press, 1993), 1.

21   Maria Todorova, "The Trap of Backwardness: Modernity, Temporality, and the Study of Eastern European Nationalism," *Slavic Review* 64, no. 1 (Spring 2005): 145, 160.

22   Alexander Kiossev, "Notes on Self-Colonising Cultures," in *Art and Culture in Post-Communist Europe*, ed. B. Pejic and D. Elliott (Stockholm: Moderna Museet, 1999), 114–115.

23   Omer Bartov, *Erased: Vanishing Traces of Jewish Galicia in Present-Day Ukraine* (Princeton, NJ: Princeton University Press, 2007), ix, and Ezequiel Adamovsky, *Euro-Orientalism: Liberal Ideology and the Image of Russia in France* (Bern: Peter Lang, 2006), 282.

24   Boris Buden, "Ce este postcolonial în postcomunism?," trans. Cristian Cercel, *Suplimentul de cultură* 144, no. 8–14 (September 2007): 2.

25   Boris Groys, "Situația postcomunistă," trans. Maria Magdalena Anghelescu, *Ideea* 21 (2005), http://idea.ro/revista/?q=ro/node/40&articol=318

26   Zygmunt Bauman, *Intimations of Postmodernity* (London: Routledge, 1992), xvii–xviii.

27   Quoted in Hans Günther, "Post-Soviet Emptiness (Vladimir Makanin and Viktor Pelevin)," *Journal of Eurasian Studies* 4, no. 1 (2013): 100.

28   Quoted in Günther, "Post-Soviet Emptiness," 104.

29   James Hopkin, "*On the Road to Babadag* by Andrzej Stasiuk—Review: A Eulogy for the Peripheral Corners of Eastern Europe," *The Guardian*, July 8, 2011, http://www.theguardian.com/books/2011/jul/08/road-babadag-andrzej-stasiuk-review; Marek Kohn, "*On the Road to Babadag*: Travels in the Other Europe" by Andrzej Stasiuk, trans. Michael Kandel, *The Independent*, October 23, 2011, http://www.independent.co.uk/arts-entertainment/books/reviews/on-the-road-to-babadag-travels-in-the-other-europe-by-andrzej-stasiuk-trans-michael-kandel-2327564.html. Tomasz Zarycki thinks that "self-Orientalizing" is a commonplace not only in Polish culture (Lublin is "a hole somewhere in the east"), but also in that of neighboring Belarus, a land of "emptiness," "absence," and "non-existence"—Tomasz Zarycki, *Ideologies of Eastness in Central and Eastern Europe* (New York: Routledge, 2014), 219.

30   "Dawid Bieńkowski," The Book Institute. http://www.bookinstitute.pl/autorzy-detal,literatura-polska,3700,bienkowski-dawid.html. Accessed November 15, 2016.

31   Kuba Wandachowicz quoted in Christine Henseler, *Generation X Goes Global: Mapping a Youth Culture in Motion* (New York: Routledge, 2013), 92.

32   Péter P. Müller, "Hungarian Drama Available in English Translation," in *Babel Guide to Hungarian Literature in English Translation*, ed. Ray Keenoy, Vivienne Menkes Ivry, and Zsuzsanna Varga (Oxford: Boulevard Books, 2001), 102.

33　Rajendra A. Chitnis, *Literature in Post-Communist Russia and Eastern Europe* (London: Routledge, 2005), 136, *passim*.

34　Larry Wolff, *Inventing Eastern Europe: The Map of Civilization on the Mind of the Enlightenment* (Stanford, CA: Stanford University Press, 1994), *passim*.

35　Cf. Benyamin Neuberger, "The African Concept of Balkanisation," *The Journal of Modern African Studies* 14, no. 3 (September 1976): 523–529; Rob Nixon, "Of Balkans and Bantustans: 'Ethnic cleansing' and the crisis in national legitimation," *Transition* 60 (1993): 4–26.

36　Mircea Martin, *G. Călinescu și "complexele" literaturii române* (Bucharest: Editura Albatros, 1981), 13–15, 29.

37　Martin, *G. Călinescu*, 14, 16.

38　Also see, on this issue, my previous work on the identitarian trope of the void: "Voices of the Void: Andrei Codrescu's Tropical Rediscovery of Romanian Culture in *The Hole in the Flag*," *University of Bucharest Review* 10, no. 2 (2008): 11–21; "The Regenerative Void: Avatars of a Foundational Metaphor in Romanian Identity Construction," *Philologica Jassyensia* 7, no. 1 (13) (2011): 127–139; "Filling in the Historical Blanks."

39　More on Constantin Noica's life and writings in Bogdan Ștefănescu, "Constantin Noica," in *The Literary Encyclopedia*, http://www.litencyc.com/php/speople. php?rec=true&UID=13291

40　Emil Cioran, *Istorie și utopie* (Bucharest: Humanitas, 1992), 157.

41　Constantin Noica, *Istoricitate și modernitate* (Bucharest: Capricorn, 1990), 29, *passim*.

42　In Dimitrie Cantemir's unoriginal account, after the retreat of the Roman colonizing army in the third century AD, the Romanized local inhabitants had to find shelter from the invading hordes during the great migrations of the late Antiquity–early Middle Ages period and live in the mountains for hundreds of years, leaving the fertile plains of today's Romania only to return to this forsaken territory (*habitatoribus destitutas*) and resettle it in the fourteenth century.

43　Noica, *Istoricitate și modernitate*, 33.

44　Emil Cioran, *Schimbarea la față a României* (Bucharest: Humanitas, 1990), 42, 44, 48 (the quotes come from the third chapter, "Romania's Historical and Psychological Voids").

45　See Ștefănescu, "Voices of the Void" and "Filling in the Historical Blanks."

46　Lucian Blaga, "Getica," in *Dreptul la memorie*, vol. 4, ed. Iordan Chimet (Cluj-Napoca: Dacia, 1993), 32–33.

47　Lucian Blaga, *Spațiul mioritic* (Bucharest: Humanitas, 1994 [1936]), 177.

48　Mircea Eliade, *The Romanians: A Concise History*, trans. Rodica Mihaela Scafeș (Bucharest: Roza vînturilor, 1992), 19.

49　Mircea Eliade, *The Fate of Romanian Culture*, trans. Bogdan Ștefănescu (Bucharest: Athena, 1995), 30–31.

50　See Ștefănescu, "Marginal Romanian Meets European Model," "Voices of the Void," and "The Regenerative Void."

51　Andrei Codrescu, *The Hole in the Flag: A Romanian Exile's Story of Return and Revolution* (New York: W. Morrow & Co., 1991), 67.

52　See Ștefănescu, "Voices of the Void," 11–21.

53　Horia-Roman Patapievici, *Cerul văzut prin lentilă* (Bucharest: Nemira, 1995), 86, 89, 118.

54　Cf. Katherine Verdery, *National Ideology under Socialism: Identity and Cultural Politics in Ceaușescu's Romania* (Berkeley, CA: University of California Press, 1991); Zigu Ornea, *Traditionalism și modernitate în deceniul al treilea* (Bucharest: Editura

Eminescu, 1980); Keith Hitchins, *Rumania: 1866-1947* (Oxford: Oxford University Press/Clarendon Press, 1994).

55 Martin, *G. Călinescu*, 25-27.

56 Maria Todorova, "The Trap of Backwardness," 149. On my views on colonialism and historicity, see Bogdan Ştefănescu, *Postcommunism/Postcolonialism: Siblings of Subalternity* (Bucharest: Bucharest University Press, 2013), 106-107.

57 See Wai Chee Dimock, *Through Other Continents: American Literature across Deep Time* (Princeton, NJ: Princeton University Press, 2006).

58 Dimock, *Through Other Continents*, 3.

59 Cf. Nancy Van Styvendale, "The Trans/Historicity of Trauma in Jeannette Armstrong's *Slash* and Sherman Alexie's "Indian Killer," *Studies in the Novel* 40, no. 1-2 (2008): 203-223.

60 On "anatopic" associations and "multidirectional memory," see Michael Rothberg, "Decolonizing Trauma Studies: A Response," *Studies in the Novel* 40, no. 1-2 (2008): 225.

61 Robert Eaglestone, "'You Would Not Add to My Suffering If You Knew What I Have Seen': Holocaust Testimony and Contemporary African Trauma Literature," *Studies in the Novel* 40, no. 1-2 (2008): 72-85.

13

Gaming the World-System: Creativity, Politics, and Beat Influence in the Poetry of the 1980s Generation

Teodora Dumitru

Focusing on the young Romanian poets of the 1980s, this essay joins in the ongoing attempts to revisit literary phenomena through the lens of the world-systems theory put forth by Immanuel Wallerstein and, in various combinations with Goethean *Weltliteratur*, fine-tuned to world literature inquiries by critics such as Pascale Casanova, Franco Moretti, Wai Chee Dimock, Christian Moraru, Emily Apter, and Ursula K. Heise. Before I get started, though, a few caveats are in order about the applicability of world-systems analysis to literary scholarship. I should point out, in this vein, that Casanova and Moretti's "world literature" notion, in which the first term designates a geographical whole—whether this aggregate is "global," "planetary," and so on—does not quite chime in with the Wallersteinian "world-system," which is less spatial than functional and structural. Underscoring the hyphen in the spelling of the world-systems term, Wallerstein has actually maintained that such systems do not necessarily cover the entire world.[1] Furthermore, he has been skeptical about the broader concept of "world culture" itself,[2] which has made some wonder about culture's ability to function as a "constitutive" part of the world-system alongside economic and political elements or to "resist," especially in the humanities and in its scholarly humanist form, the idea of system and to world-systems theory more broadly.[3] Such questions and, underlying them, objections to the cross-disciplinary epistemological extrapolations entailed by a world-systemic take on literature and culture—or by a literary-cultural analysis of the world-system, for that matter—have proliferated of late. They have led many to conclude that the geographies of literary-artistic and political-economic hegemonies do not overlap as a matter of course,[4] and that, by the same token, the taxonomies and laws of the capitalist world, as well as what defines that world qua system—the so-called "division of labor"—neither reflect nor coincide with the intricate makeup and problematics of fiction, poetry, or drama.[5]

Nevertheless, as a working hypothesis or heuristic metaphor—that is, without taking economic determinism too seriously—this epistemological framework, grounded in Wallerstein's "world-system" but also in Fernand Braudel's "longue durée," is still useful to literary studies, including the one that follows.[6] My intervention, however, will not try out Wallerstein's theory of the capitalist world-system on cultural forms that have emerged inside the same market environment. As mentioned earlier, I am here primarily interested in road testing the theory in the 1980s East European zone of Socialist economies, and this does raise certain issues. For instance, as some have pointed out, this political-economic area could be seen as anti-systemic insofar as, in relation to the capitalist world-system economy, the Soviet satellites of the Eastern Bloc, as well as nationalist and Social Democratic regimes, spawned "anti-systemic movements;"[7] still others have envisioned this region as part and parcel of the global system or as a "subsystem."[8] Given these reservations on and qualifications of the classical theoretical model, it bears asking, first: How should we treat the literatures of Eastern Europe's former Communist countries? Second, how can these literatures' examination help us reinforce or, as the case may be, rethink the world literature idea, as well as the interpretive and conceptual compatibility of world-system analysis and literary criticism? Third, how effective is world-systems methodology when applied to a "local" material such as 1980s Romanian poetry? Specifically, can we still talk about centers and peripheries in a typically world-systemic sense? If we can—but especially if we cannot—what would that tell us about the aesthetic and political claims implicitly or explicitly made by the new poets of late Cold War-era Romania?

1. Literature, Economics, Ideology: The Generation of the 1980s in Context

All these misgivings and questions aside, these authors' works can be approached as "world literature" in Casanova and Moretti's sense—that is, in relation to an international canon and cultural prestige center such as post–Second World War North American poetry—but also in a way opened up by postcolonial studies. The nexus involved by the latter would link up national culture and the metropolitan center of sorts from which late 1960s and 1970s Romanian letters had by and large strained to distance themselves, that is, the USSR, which was locally, if nominally at times, represented by the Communist Party and its leader, Nicolae Ceaușescu. Since this connection has been attended to in this volume and elsewhere, I will turn below to the relationship between Romanian writers and cultural centers to which they were drawn during the last years of Communism, when colonizing Sovietization was subsiding.[9] As I argue, what drives the emerging poetry of the 1980s is a complex manipulation of or "game" with the late-twentieth-century cultural and political world-system and its subsystems. More to the point, I suggest that the rising writers of Romania's last Communist decade "import" poetic models from the United States, one of the time's world centers, to articulate a "double discourse" that, on the one hand, reworks, relocates peripherally, and ultimately decenters symbolically this center itself and, on the other, critiques the Soviet world subsystem of which Communist Romania had been part. What defines the 1980s Romanian poets' endeavors is, then, a geocultural project in which whatever lesson they learn from a faraway cultural–political hub is brought to bear on Romanian space and becomes, not without certain ambiguities, a source of resistance and aesthetic performance inside their country, its political system, and evolving literary tradition.

Acutely mindful of Romania's premodern economic structures, social-governmental institutions that wore the appearance of modernity, and subaltern status as one of Europe's "internal" colonies, Romanian cultural ideologues had by the dawn of the twentieth century done little more than provide rationales for adopting Western "forms" compatible with indigenous "contents." After the Second World War, Romania's economy, along with the other economies of the Soviet Bloc, finally worked its way through the initial stages of European modernity and, like most of the Communist world, did so without being part of the capitalist global market proper. Its developmental narrative rehearsed, albeit imperfectly, the first step of modernity, which was geared toward heavy industry and the extraction and processing of raw materials, at the same time that it neglected services and the manufacturing of everyday commodities. Incomplete and multiply flawed, the Soviet-imposed model could not compete with the technologically-driven, services-based, and more ecologically minded economies of postindustrial modernity.[10] If Communist Romania modernized its structures and institutions and, at least compared to the country's pre–Second World War situation, gained access to a superior form of modernity, compared to Western countries it was as economically "poor" as it was administratively inefficient, ideologically nationalist, and politically totalitarian.[11]

Especially during the heydays of Socialist Realism (1950–1964), Romania was also twice isolated culturally as its incorporation into the Soviet sphere of influence curtailed the interactions with the West and other parts of the world while the officially sponsored Socialist Realist "aesthetic" itself found meager appeal beyond the Iron Curtain. After 1970, when the regime decided that Romanian society's "revolutionary" modernization had been accomplished and, as a result, stopped pushing the agitprop formula aggressively, writers found it easier to try their hands at other kinds of literature, primarily modernist, with major 1960s and 1970s poets such as Nichita Stănescu (1933–1983), Ana Blandiana (1942–), Marin Sorescu (1936–1996), and Mircea Ivănescu (1931–2011) combining high-modernist elements and prosaic forms. The end of the 1970s witnessed, however, the arrival of a different group of writers, who will be known as "the 1980s Generation." They will systematically reject the legacy of conceptual–metaphorical modernism, dwelling instead on the dreary day to-day existential routine, urban realism, and the "common man." Many of these authors were members of the "Monday Literary Circle" (*Cenaclul de luni*) founded in 1977 and led by critic Nicolae Manolescu (1939–), who had also championed the aesthetics of his own generation since the 1960s. The most prominent figures among the new poets included Mircea Cărtărescu (1956–), Florin Iaru (1954–), Traian T. Coșovei (1954–2014), Mariana Marin (1956–2003), and Alexandru Mușina (1954–2013). Due to political censorship as well as to the economic austerity policies of the 1980s, most of them had, at least at first, a tough time getting their work published.[12] Therefore, they turned initially to student literary groups, festivals, and publications, and other alternate and underground venues. In these forums, they struck their audiences through a new poetics, which flaunted a brutally prosaic makeover of the lyrical genre, and through denotative diction and an American-, generally postmodern-inspired straightforwardness of expression at the expense of the more hermetic, obscurely self-reflexive, and abstract ("pure") tone of the 1960s poets, who were associated with French modernism and dismissed as passé.[13]

2. "Postmodernism without Postmodernity": American Echoes and Subversive Potential in the Poetry of the 1980s

Under the guise of a more "realistic" approach to contemporary Romania, the poems of Cărtărescu's volume *Faruri, vitrine, fotografii* (Headlights, Shop Windows, Photographs [1980]), *Poeme de amor* (Love Poems [1983]), and *Totul* (All [1985]), Coşovei's *Ninsoarea electrică* (Electric Snowfall [1979]), Iaru's *Cântece de trecut strada* (Songs for Crossing the Street [1981]), Muşina's megapoem *Budila-Expres* (1982), and Mariana Marin's *Un război de o sută de ani* (A Hundred Years War [1982]) all developed a somewhat ambiguous relationship with Communist modernity. Especially after Ceauşescu's rise to power, this modernity abandoned the internationalist ideals in favor of a vehemently nationalist and isolationist agenda, which brought about a rapid worsening of living conditions. In this context, the sordid, the fragile, and the trivial aspects of human life and social reality overall transfigured by this poetry did seem to convey an anti-regime stance. Thus, in his first poetry collection, principally in the "Georgicele" (The Georgics) section, Cărtărescu derides the agrarian revolution and the peasants' "modernization." In his turn, Iaru manages to sneak in, amidst linguistic puns and surreal images, the truth about food shortages—"we have," he writes, "a circle but we don't have π./We have a Pope [*papă*] too but no glop [*Papy*]."[14] Likewise, Coşovei hints at the ravages of misguided industrialization—"An iron car/ an iron plain/an iron grass/an iron air wafting noisily beneath the stuck gate/of the iron factory,"[15] which reprises the "artificial worse-than-dirt-industrial-modern" from Allen Ginsberg's "Sunflower Sutra"—while Marin invokes utopias, disasters, death, and a reality as bountiful as "steel production per capita."[16] On the other hand, this poetry appeared to eschew a more direct expression of dissent, taking refuge in a writing that remained too playful, too literarily allusive, and too evasive to truly mount a political challenge to anybody. Nonetheless, most commentators have considered the generation a movement of programmatic alignment with the Western literature of the time, open to the world, cosmopolitan—if primarily "American-oriented," even "Americanist"—critical of the official, autarchically nationalist discourse, and they have promoted it as a local embodiment of postmodernism.

Granted, there is plenty of thematic evidence in this regard. For one thing, the group's representative poets liked to dwell on the material emporia of capitalist modernity, particularly on consumption items as signifiers of "luxury." The emblematic references to Western-made appliances, cars, clothing, makeup, cigarettes, movies, music albums, hard currency, and the like encapsulate as many disparaging glosses on "homemade" modernity. This is dismissed as a Communist failure and widely equated, during the regime's last years, with food shortages, lack of heat in people's apartments, and the alienating desolation of cities devastated by ill-conceived urban and economic planning. Hence the obsession with metal, the "welding flame," and "electric" power in Coşovei's poems, the exaltation of foreign and unaffordable brands of audio-video equipment in Iaru's, and the frequent allusions to the precarity and semirural traits of Communist city life, which was marked, as in the work of Mircea Dinescu (1950–), an older poet but stylistically close to the "realists" of the 1980s generation, by the invasion of canned food, the omnipresent potato, cheap fabric, and other poor-quality goods.[17] As if to make up for all these deprivations, the lyrical hero of the 1980s poetry dreamed of another world—the consumerist mirage of an idealized America whose iconic exports became privileged objects of desire.[18] This is why some love poems of the era read like advertisements for U.S. and Western commodities. Shot through with ambivalent irony, these texts, in which erotic and brand-name objects traded places constantly, depended for effect on the reader's socioeconomic frustrations while simultaneously disavowing and aestheticizing them. Cărtărescu is particularly skilled at this game: "You've got so much helena rubinstein in your look, so much donna summer in your voice;" the beloved's "eyes are as blue as two freshly washed Mercedes."[19] True, other poems seem to incriminate American "imperialism" or at least the bellicose impulses ascribed to it by the New Left. Coșovei, for instance, appears to mock the alliance between technological progress, epitomized by Western Europe and the United States, and the predicament of a sophisticated civilization pursuing advanced weaponry: "On the freshly paved park alleys,/the paralytic is pushing his quiet and polished wheelchair/with the same care as others would show the amazed world/the latest offspring of the arms race."[20] But even in these cases, the fascination for Western, especially American lifestyle icons and exports carried the day. Twentieth-century U.S. poetry from Imagism to the Beats and subsequent trends, as well as British and American rock, which captured the imagination of the 1980s Romanian poets as never before in the country's cultural history, ranked very high among these exports. At the time, Manolescu had already referred to the Beat Generation as a source of inspiration for the young writers, but he did so strategically, downplaying the subversive thrust of their work with respect to Communist modernity.[21] This subversion, however, we can say today, did exist. But we should also note that it did not go far enough, and that Romania's 1980s poets did not follow in the Beats' footsteps consistently. Had they done so, their critique of modernity should have been, implicitly, a critique of broader, Western modernity as well.

Otherwise, Cărtărescu, the most prominent writer of his generation as well as of the postcommunist period, has repeatedly revealed his passion for Beat literature both as a poet and as a historian of Romanian postmodernism. He has openly expressed his admiration for Ginsberg in a tribute poem, "am căpătat un exemplar din *Howl* semnat de Ginsberg" (I've received a copy of *Howl* signed by Ginsberg), included in the 1994 volume *Dragostea* (Love). This veneration is obvious throughout Cărtărescu's poetry, and also in Coșovei and Iaru, where the reader cannot miss the beatnik arrangement and enumerative accumulation of one line after another. It is Cărtărescu, though, who, creatively speaking, distances himself the most from Ginsberg. In Coșovei, the anti-war and anti-industrial strains of beatnik resistance are only slightly altered, while Iaru basks in the surreal aura of Lawrence Ferlinghetti's imagination. In Cărtărescu, however, the energy of Ginsberg's public revolt is channeled toward the erotic. This type of lyricism is steeped in a mundane that has little in common with the drabness of Communist Romania, for Cărtărescu's everyday is a flamboyant dreamworld for whose projection the author also draws from local masters such as Romantic poet Mihai Eminescu, the modernist Tudor Arghezi, and the playwright and prose author Ion Luca Caragiale, a satirist of the foibles of nineteenth-century Romanian society. Intertwined with the impact of American literature and of postmodernism broadly, this recycling of domestic tradition defines the interculturally and intertextually two-pronged aesthetic game played by the 1980s generation.

Cărtărescu terms the game's outcome "a coherent hybrid," and this is, indeed, what his oeuvre pursues throughout.[22] Take, for instance, "Regele Soare" (The Sun King), a 1985 poem that resembles the beatnik ethos in what might sound like a metaphoric condemnation of the sociopolitical freeze the Sun is called on to thaw: "oh, Sun,/I stand before you with bigger cavities in my teeth, with transfixed eyes,/my jeans more ragged and my chest barer than before./... I wish you were a cross between Ginsberg and Bertolucci,/... /I wish you burned us down as in Hiroshima or in Guernica and waged star wars/on our skin ..."[23] In the 1982 text "Femeie, femeie, femeie" (Woman, Woman, Woman), the Ginsberg prototype is reworked even more creatively. After opening with a wink at *Howl* ("in the howl of this December morning ..."), the poem unfolds a narrative divided into several segments featuring lengthy lines and rhyming refrains similar to Ginsberg's. In a nostalgic-vindictive move, the poet pretends to invoke his beloved by piling up hyperbolic references to the "uproar of objects" strewing Bucharest's cityscape[24]:

> who releases so much light, so much light from her fingers?/who sets off these cyclonic electric discharges, who makes lampshades crack/and cameras click out of the blue in their displays.../who paints so many clouds of liquid purple on the Muzica store's windows?/who pours a giant sparkling water glass on the exhaust-colored marble of the walls of the phone company building?/who strides wearing a blaze for lipstick into the frozen, transparent bucharest?[25]

The logic behind the escalating accumulation of these disparate details stems from European Surrealism in that not only does the object presumably described become gradually less recognizable as a woman, but the mystery of her identity also deepens. The "message" here is the climactic accumulation itself, which provides the best definition of woman and even of love itself insofar as they both embody the sheer tension, the avalanche of sensations and images seared into memory. These pieces, then, do adopt Ginsberg's style and meter, and yet one cannot help asking: to what end? What are the political consequences of the Romanian poet's distancing himself from his source? Is the American author's subversiveness watered down, perhaps even neutralized in Cărtărescu's love poems? Or, on the contrary, do the latter speak out, however obliquely, against the systemic pressure to toe the line? And, if so, do they allow a more political tone to piggyback on the expression of one's most personal feelings and thus interfere with eroticism's distinctly intimate voice?

A careful reading of these texts and of Cărtărescu's pre-1990 work more broadly would have to come to grips, I propose, with the ambiguity of this work's "subversion." That is, this corpus *is* "subversive" but in the equivocal way characteristically cultivated not only by the writers of the 1980s but also by the critics who, in the reviews they published during the decade, had to make sure neither their commentaries nor these commentaries' object raised too many red flags for censors.[26] In fact, both as a historian of his generation and as the author of a 1999 PhD dissertation, *Postmodernismul românesc* (Romanian Postmodernism), where he credits his peers with inventing a local variety of postmodernism, Cărtărescu himself has encouraged this ambiguous kind of response to the politics of the most innovative and cosmopolitan literature of the 1980s, a reaction that, given its political circumstances, had to be and was itself no less "political," that is to say, guarded. Thus, he has maintained that he and his friends were drawn not so much to the Beats' politics as they were to the beatnik aesthetic. The San Francisco poets' appeal to the Romanian postmoderns lay, he specifies, not in their political agenda but in a more "pragmatic" and engaged poetic language—in a "street poetry" conceivably at odds with modernist abstractions and escapism.[27] His colleagues, Cărtărescu says, absorbed many of the Beats' rhetorical elements but little if anything of the American writers' anticapitalist ideology, which the Romanian poets, we are told, mostly ignored or outright rejected.[28] Interestingly enough, his position is consistent with an older formalist doctrine known in Romanian literary criticism as "the autonomy of the aesthetic" and that gives weight to literature's independence from economic and sociopolitical forces. His explanations bear witness, at the end of the twentieth-century, to the resurgence of the post-Romantic debate between those who, like Titu Maiorescu, had opposed, as early as the 1860s, the introduction of Western "forms" into the country on the assumption that such forms were incompatible with local "substance" and those who, like modernist critic and ideologue Eugen Lovinescu, had endorsed such imports because, they had thought, these forms, once adopted, would eventually develop a substance of their own. During the 1980s, objections such as Maiorescu's were one more time raised by voices speaking on behalf of the regime, which was openly wary of cosmopolitanism and, more generally, of the threats outside influences posed to the nationalist–isolationist values of the culture fostered under Communism even when those external sources were critical of the capitalist world; after 1989, similar complaints have been raised about the 1980s poets' depoliticizing appropriation of Beat anti-status quo pathos, a critique that corroborates critic Mircea Martin's view of "a [Romanian] postmodernism without postmodernity."[29]

In Cărtărescu, the decoupling of the two harks back to Lovinescu, but it does so equivocally. On the one hand, the poet stresses that the external source is bound, once it has been transplanted into a new cultural environment, to turn into something else. The conduit of this transformation, he adds, is not ideological but formal; what we should be looking for in the 1980s Romanian poets is, then, not how they carry the ideological torch of the American model but how "poetic form" morphs according to its own "logic," given that the only "reality" poetry ought to serve is that of art and the artist's true freedom and measure of agency lie inside him or her, beyond space, time, and extra-artistic causalities.[30] This aesthetic individualism makes the poet a "citizen of the cultural universe" and living proof of "the relative independence of culture from the economic and sociopolitical reality in [the world's] marginal zones."[31] On the other hand, Cărtărescu argues in the same history of Romanian postmodernism *against* the autonomy thesis, contending that the 1980s writers purposefully assimilated and adapted Beat political views and postmodern thought in general. Thus, as advocates of a "neoliberal" and even "libertarian or anarchist" politics, the Romanian poets "took up" and "carried forward," says Cărtărescu, the "message of [radical] Western movements," forming an ideologically coherent group whose well-defined "target" was a kind of mirror image of the Beats' own adversary: the *establishment* embodied by "the Communist regime, officially left-wing but de facto peddling an extreme form of right-wing politics."[32] Alongside another important poet, critic, and theorist of Romanian postmodernism, Ion Bogdan Lefter (1957–), Cărtărescu also claims that the young 1980s writers' sociopolitical commitment shaped not only their response to outside literature but also their insurgent self-positioning within national culture's history. For, he insists, they started a "canonical battle [that is] still in full swing today" and in which "postmodernity" has designated "a theoretically advanced stance," has nurtured "*the* literature of our times," has been synonymous with "civilization" and "progress," and, as such, has brought contemporary Romania into "sync with the spiritual pulse of the democratic and liberal Western world."[33]

3. The Post-1989 Era: New Critical Perspectives

During the decades since the Cold War's end, Romanian critics have emphasized the oppositional élan of the 1980s poets. In the dramatically changed cultural climate, however, new reactions—critical and literary, to Cărtărescu's generation as well as to its American models—become unavoidable. Thus, in the early 2000s, Marius Ianuș, an author born in 1975 but representative of the first postcommunist generation of Romanian poets, leans on Ginsberg's "America" for inspiration in *România*, a segment of a two-part poem, "Manifest anarhist" (Anarchist Manifesto), dedicated to Ginsberg and Jack Kerouac. Ianuș's title refers to a country that has just embarked on the bumpy road of transition to capitalism. Here, the rhetorical sophistication and the playfully creative inventiveness of Cărtărescu, Iaru, and others are all but discarded. Ianuș is not interested in flaunting the "inner world" and its freedom nor the erudite imagination that transcends the destitute mundane. He borrows the voice of an abandoned child who takes his country to task in no uncertain terms: "I feel like I am going crazy, Romania/I get the inner world /and the outside world all mixed up, Romania/I would have been a poet of the inner world/had I eaten something,/Romania/I am hungry, Romania ..."[34] The poem marks a return to Ginsberg's originary, anti-capitalist ethos and by the same movement a departure from the abstract, potentially anti-system or anti-Communist "protest" of Cărtărescu's generation. As Ianuș puts it sarcastically in an article, the Romanian postmoderns were "making cartoons in the country of frozen radiators."[35] He appreciates neither the presumed authenticity of "street poetry" nor the intertextual mechanics of postmodern poetics, which he ridicules and whose political effectiveness he questions head-on. To him, the new literature of the 1980s was less an attempt to bring Romanian letters in line with developments under way in the world's cultural capitals and more a gratuitous exercise in "ludic" bookishness whose perverse effect was to draw attention *away* from the trials of the country under Communism. A direct challenge to the professed and implied goals of the Romanian postmodern project, this reading has been lying at the heart of the critique of the 1980s writers by their feisty successors, the poets and critics of the "2000s Generation."

Most authors who had already made a name for themselves during the years before the fall of the Berlin Wall, however, have been largely stucking to their guns. A case in point is Christian Moraru's recent series of articles and book chapters. A member of the 1980s generation himself, Moraru has remained a staunch promoter of Cărtărescu's work and an advocate for the generational ethos driving it. Expounding on this ethos, the critic has pointed up its twin cosmopolitan impetus, which renders the writer a citizen of the planet rather than a mouthpiece of a closed-off social, political, or ethnic group while striving to open up national tradition and mores to the West, particularly to U.S. culture. Cărtărescu, Moraru further explains, fully encapsulates the postmodern 1980s' aesthetics and politics, which stand at loggerheads with the anti-European and reactionary ideologies professed by National-Communism's quasi-official successors— the neo-Communist establishment of the 1990s as well as the intensely mediatized, twenty-first-century progeny of pre–Second World War right-wing intelligentsia. Unlike either, we are told, Cărtărescu's work stages "worldly" values such as cultural alterity, "relatedness," and "planetarity," which are located in and presented as intrinsic to national culture. The Cărtărescu chapter in Moraru's 2015 book *Reading for the Planet* treats the writer's Communist-era fiction and the 1996–2007 *Orbitor* (Blinding) trilogy as the blueprint of an entire "cosm*allogy*," as a "spectacle of the planetary All,"[36] and this reading is consistent with other analyses Moraru has devoted to Cărtărescu in Romanian[37] and American publications.[38] Whether latent or manifest, "planetarity" speaks, in Cărtărescu and other 1980s poets, to the world-systemic scope of their work, an aspect at which the remainder of my essay takes a closer look.

4. Subversion through "Co-Option"?

If one approaches this literature as a "superstructure" of a Socialist type of economic basis, then one way to describe the relationship of this corpus with American poetry is by recourse to a world-systems lexicon that includes not only the "core" and "periphery" dyad but also "semi-periphery," "ex[-]centricity," and other, more nuanced terms, which are important in Wallerstein and Casanova and do justice to Romania's particular circumstances at the end of the twentieth century. Employed by Steven Tötösy de Zepetnek to capture the distinctiveness of Central and Eastern Europe, "inbetween peripherality" also applies to the geocultural terrain under scrutiny here, for, indeed, it would help to imagine Romania's 1980s authors as staking out their space somewhere inside a triangle whose corners roughly coincided with three economic and political centers: Marxist–Communist, deployed around, and practically enforced as, Soviet colonialism; local or domestic, administered by the Romanian state; and Western.[39] Thus, besides the two geopolitical polar opposites, the USSR and the United States, there was a third hub of power, namely, the country's own authoritarian regime, which, over the course of its history, had been evolving away from Moscow and toward the "alternate" models of Asian Communism provided by the Chinese and North Koreans, finally settling for a "homegrown," nationalist variety. The Romanian zone was therefore underpinned by a set of dovetailing antagonisms between the Americans and the Soviets, then between these two external hegemons and a government apparatus basically identical with the Communist Party structure, and also between the latter and the majority of a population for whom quickly deteriorating living standards were making it easier to see through Ceaușescu's late 1970s self-aggrandizing independence ambitions. It was within this triad that the young Romanian writers sought to position themselves, but this was no simple task. For they could not fail to notice that this triangular geography of political and aesthetic authority was not only increasingly tensioned but also shifty. Thus, after the Romanian Communist Party had decided to stop doing Moscow's bidding and all but ditched Marxist internationalism in favor of an operatic sort of nationalism, the triangle turned into an antipodal structure organized, at one end, outside Romania, around the "free world"—aspirational in essence, American in reality, and largely capitalist—and, at the other end, inside the country, around the repressive, National–Communist regime.

The poets of the 1980s were eager, as we have seen, to borrow from the literary production of what was gradually emerging as the quasi-undisputed center of the late-global world-system, but whether their "peripheral" condition automatically follows from this overt cultural mimesis is an entirely different matter altogether. Besides, it is not clear at all if the economic "unequal trade" concept, which is so prominent in the Braudel–Wallerstein line of inquiry and undergirds the Marxist emphasis Casanova and Moretti lay on the "inequality" ingrained in world literature, truly helps us get a handle on the fairly one-directional flows of aesthetic material and inspiration from San Francisco and New York to Romania's burgeoning poetry groups.[40] It is therefore worth asking: How mimetic and thus how dependent on their "sources" were the Romanian authors thematically, formally, and otherwise? Moreover, how much creative freedom with respect to those influences could their work accrue *and* display? How lopsided was the exchange system they joined, and how do they talk back to the putatively "universal" language in which the center spoke to them from across the world?

To answer, one should first recognize that their writings do present some of the hallmarks of a geoculturally peripheral practice, including the anxiety—typical of Romanian artists and literati throughout modernity—that they come "late," perhaps "too late," and inevitably *after* their Western forebearers. To compensate for this fated "belatedness," the young poets of the 1980s set out to step outside national, "slow" time and compete internationally in the contemporary arena, like "genuine moderns"— and possibly as *post*moderns—even though in that broader, transnational context, their "revolutionizing" of Romanian literature signified basically an "update."[41] This synchronizing move pursued a "trade deficit" in which literary imports by far outweighed the exports and was perfectly in line with domestic tradition, whose main objective had been all along the building up of a literary patrimony through the tailoring of outside prototypes to "national specificity." The contrast with the regime's participation in international commerce is quite striking: unlike the Romanian economy of the 1980s, which was relying, bizarre as it may sound, mainly on exports, the rising writers of the decade imported feverishly. In so doing, they seemed particularly aware neither of the "unbalanced" exchange of which they were partaking nor of what their place in the wider scheme of things effectively involved, a worldview "blind spot" otherwise characteristic, observes Casanova, of actors from the planet's cultural peripheries, who take in the globe's fashion, masterpieces, and trends but are less curious about the political configuration of global structures.[42] Accordingly, Romanian poets' interest in post–Second World War U.S. authors did not also presuppose an interest in how and why the American writers developed a certain political consciousness, viz., a critical awareness and oftentimes a vocal criticism of their society. Not much of this critical attitude transpares in how the Beats' overseas fans see this society. In fact, their West is a depoliticized and, to a notable extent, idealistic construct quasi-synonymous with freedom, political pluralism, prosperity, and opportunity, while the less bright side of things gets little attention. This one-sided assessment of Western and especially American sociocultural space and its consolidating centrality in the world-system may well account for the Romanian authors' fascination with U.S. poetry and, more significantly still, for the strikingly *asymmetrical* fashion in which they harness its radical political thrust to a critique of Communist rather than capitalist modernity, largely ignoring the broader world picture in which the mutual imbrication of the two are hard to miss.

Historically, similar—and similarly asymmetrical—overlaps, parallelisms, and continuities organize, within modernity, its oppositional narrative, and they too force us to rethink the marginal condition of the new literature coming out in 1980s Romania. There is little doubt, for instance, that the ethos of this literature grew to no negligible degree out of the so-called "world revolution of the 1968," which marked the decline of liberalism's hegemony, as Wallerstein claims, but also the quickly deepening crisis of the Eastern Bloc.[43] Echoing chiefly, and metaphorically, the economic symptoms of this defining post–Second World War juncture, the poets of the generation were, however, less sensitive to sociopolitical issues such as the rights of groups constituted around identitarian formations and practices of ethnicity, race, gender, and sexuality, which were all, and have remained, critical flashpoints in post-1968 Western public discourse and reforms. Thus, the crisis they were confronting was certainly neither of liberalism nor of U.S. hegemony. True, they did share with artists and other social categories in the West the frustrating feeling of being politically underrepresented, but what mattered to them was how unrepresentative and abusive the Communist regime was.[44] The anti-Americanism of the 1968 upheavals, the failure of the Old Left to deliver, the putative "convergence" of world ideologies, the tacit "agreement" between the USSR and the United States, and the resulting containment of "revolutionary" ideals by capitalism, which are all milestones in Wallerstein's version of the post–Second World War world-system story, did not preoccupy, at least publicly, the Romanian writers. Historically, they were living in a quasi-mythical time in which the heroes and villains could be easily told apart; skepticism, disillusion, and possibly opposition to the broader context to which Romania willy-nilly belonged were still distant prospects, and there was hardly any indication that, if they were to arise eventually, they would convey the poets' dissatisfaction with the regime's "betrayal" of the Marxist–Leninist revolution's "principles." Geographically, the scope of their politics rarely transcended the nation-state, and, its substantial, American and world literature intertextuality notwithstanding, their work lacks a truly global perspective, let alone a critical one.

Inside the country, however, this politics—more precisely, the writers' relationship with the omnipotent Party-State apparatus—did replay, on a smaller scale, the tensions and constitutive dealings between the Wallersteinian world-system and the anti-systemic movements spawned by it. Yet again, if the 1980s poets did turn on the Communist subsystem, that did not index a critique from the leftist position typical of Western counterculture, but, more likely, an optimistic look ahead to the benefits of free-market societies. Further compounding this game across and with geocultural and aesthetic-political systems is the multiply ambivalent position this critique paradoxically entails insofar as its voicing was a public act. For they seemed "co-opted" twice: externally, as "Americanophiles," by the United States-led "free world" and internally, as they were seeking and accepting publication inside a national and political system by which they appeared "legitimized" and which they in turn seemingly "authorized." A defining mechanism of systemic containment of dissent, according to Wallerstein, the officially sanctioned production and distribution of books by the 1980s poets *under* Communist censorship resonated with audiences with an intensity that, with the exception of Cărtărescu's work, has remained unmatched after the regime's demise, when, intriguingly enough, it has become increasingly clear that the writers have lost much of their readership. This suggests that their "subversiveness" actually *depended* on, and in certain cases was arguably a function or byproduct of, a range of governmental structures and policies, from the Communist state-controlled publishing industry and media to censorship, surveillance, and the like. Speaking to the odd logic of opposition under totalitarianism, the synergetic dynamic of transformative critique and systemic co-option in the Romanian 1980s demonstrates, as Bruce Robbins has observed, that "you can't blame without system, which teaches you what must and what can be changed."[45]

5. "Repurposing" the Beats: Poetry as Double Discourse

Furthermore, the ambiguities of the domestic politics of change only played up the complexities of cross-cultural exchange. For this reason, the "unequal exchange" theory of discourse formation does not pan out as one might expect. Granted, the late Cold War Romanian literary "periphery's" taste for the American center's symbolic production is conspicuous. However, the Beat output was not "imported" as such; it was neither read nor emulated for what it was and was designed to do sociopolitically in its initial form and context. Instead, it was transformed and *de*contextualized, "delinked" from the specific oppositional philosophy of its sociohistorical environment. Thus disjoined from its circumstances and aims, beatnik anti-capitalist critique was redirected at Communist modernity by Cărtărescu, Coșovei, and Iaru. They adopted the cynicism, prosaism, realism, biographism, "microhistoricism," "micropolitics," and other fixtures of the antiestablishment—and sometimes anti-U.S. hegemony—playbook of the last century's counterculture but either altered or ignored the characters and props of the political and historical "plot" in which such techniques and foci had been originally featured. In following Fredric Jameson, Moretti talks about cultural centers' pressure on peripheries to accept a "compromise" between foreign (central) form and autochthonous (peripheral) material, more exactly, between "foreign *plot*" and "local *characters* [and] *narrative voice*,"[46] but this is not the center–margin scenario we are witnessing here.[47] Narrative or not, the 1980s Romanian poets' "voice"—and their entire "form," in effect—is not "local," for it ventriloquized the Beats' left-wing rhetoric. Rather, their political plot is, because it adjusted and got "localized" as they scrambled to retrofit the anti-systemic discourse of the American writers with an anti-Communist agenda, no matter how effectively oppositional this procedure would prove. In the process, the actors of the literary commerce drama swapped roles. As the poetic "commodity" exported by the center was assigned a completely new function and changed accordingly, so did the center itself as *model*, undergoing the ontological transformation one usually assumes would affect the replica or the imitating agent. For, once it got recycled by its Romanian "imitators," the prototype lost its identity, serving as a sort of supplier of raw poetic material and spare rhetorical parts.

The repurposing or polemical rewriting of the original in a culturally heterogeneous, "marginal" context has been addressed extensively by World Literature scholars. Wai Chee Dimock, for example, notes that, from Henry David Thoreau to Mahatma Gandhi, *Bhagavad Gita* was repeatedly rewritten so as to routinely lay out a philosophical vision fitting a cultural–historical setting markedly distinct from that in which the great poem had been composed,[48] while David Damrosch points, apropos of The Book of Job, to the mobilization of "elements derived from the foreign works in order to create an alternative discourse *within* their own traditions" as well as a "polemical reworking of foreign traditions."[49] For the Romanian poets, the scope of the polemic was national, at most coextensive with the Soviet world. The alternative they strove to work out by retooling Beat literature was, then, largely internal: it was Romanian nationalist-Communism that they tried to challenge, to associate with, if critically, without being politically "domesticated" by their association and losing the edge of their "subversiveness." Simply put, their goal was a double discourse, in a sense that itself was double layered: formally or textually, within their country's system, they decided to "play along" just enough to get themselves published and, despite all the ambiguities of publication itself, hopefully educate their readers in the rhetoric of subversion and thereby gesture, at least, toward a way out the totalitarian status quo; cross-culturally or intertextually, their poetry was oriented toward two centers, for, besides the internal one, which horrified and repelled, there was an external hub of culture and prestige, which fascinated, authorized culturally and politically, and supplied "technical assistance" for undermining the former. This tactical, multifaceted way of engaging with systems, small and big, political and literary, allowed Romanian writers a modicum of "autonomy" or maneuvering freedom with respect to said systems and their centers, although, because they could not travel nor publish abroad during Ceaușescu's rule, their success was circumscribed to the national market and territory.

Hardly "international" as far as their readership went, they *were* transnational in their writing praxis. As such, they exemplified a situation exactly opposite to what Moretti has in mind when he refers to "the difficulty of saying in an European language experiences which are European no longer,"[50] for the poets couched fundamentally East European experiences in the language of radical American poetry. Most obviously, the Beat poems did not circulate and, once arrived at destination, were not processed the way consumer goods would be on the world market. Their "consumption"—a reception and rewriting practice that "repurposed" them—altered them to the point that, back at the center, where they had been produced, they may have become unrecognizable, possibly something new and unique. With a final but also apparent paradox, then, the peripheral mechanisms of literary *re*production could and can produce, within a planetary framework of exchange, something original and, by the same token, affirm their own standards and cultural independence. What seems to act one-directionally, tilt the world playing field, and push these mechanisms to imitate and acquiesce to their derived, secondary status becomes a source of creativity instead. It is this empowering creativity, itself a political reality, that forces us to revisit the political paradigm traditionally employed to work out the minutiae of the core–margins interactions of modern world-systems.

Notes

1   Immanuel Wallerstein, *World-Systems Analysis: An Introduction* (Durham, NC: Duke University Press, 2004), 16–17.

2   Immanuel Wallerstein, *Geopolitics and Geoculture: Essays on the Changing World-System* (Cambridge: Cambridge University Press, 1991), 198. This problem has been taken up, among others, by Alexander Beecroft. See his article "World Literature without a Hyphen: Towards a Typology of Literary Systems," in *World Literature in Theory*, ed. David Damrosch (Chichester: Wiley Blackwell, 2014), 180–181. On this subject, also see Pascale Casanova, who thinks the term "world-structure" is better suited to literary studies than "world-system." On this issue, see Pascale Casanova, "Literature as a World," in *World Literature in Theory*, ed. David Damrosch, 199–200.

3   See, in this respect, the contributions of Richard E. Lee ("The Modern World-System: Its Structures, Its Geoculture, Its Crisis and Transformation") and Bruce Robbins ("Blaming the System") in *Immanuel Wallerstein and the Problem of the World*, ed. David Palumbo-Liu et al. (Durham, NC: Duke University Press, 2011), 27–40 and 41–63, respectively.

4   See Casanova, "Literature as a World," 202, and Franco Moretti, *Distant Reading* (London: Verso, 2013), 115.

5 For an overview of such objections raised by Jêrome David, Efraín Kristal, Jonathan Arac, and Jale Parla, see Moretti, *Distant Reading*, 107–119.

6 Following Fernand Braudel and Wallerstein, Wai Chee Dimock has advanced the concept of "deep time," but she also challenges Wallerstein's economic model by turning to fractal geometry and relativity theory in *Through Other Continents: American Literature across Deep Time* (Princeton, NJ: Princeton University Press, 2006), 4–5.

7 See Wallerstein, *Geopolitics and Geoculture*, 109–114; for an extensive discussion of the anti-systemic nature of Socialist and nationalist movements over the last two centuries, see Giovanni Arrighi, Terence K. Hopkins, and Immanuel Wallerstein, *Antisystemic Movements* (London: Verso, 1989).

8 See Christian Moraru, *Reading for the Planet: Toward a Geomethodology* (Ann Arbor, MI: University of Michigan Press, 2015), 26, where the author refers to the Cold War and its "conglomerate of nation-states and national subsystems ('blocs')."

9 See Andrei Terian, "Is There an East-Central European Postcolonialism? Towards a Unified Theory of (Inter)Literary Dependency," *World Literature Studies* 4, no. 3 (2012): 21–36.

10 See Bogdan Murgescu, *România și Europa. Acumularea decalajelor economice (1500–2010)* (Iași: Polirom, 2010), 325–407.

11 See Katherine Verdery, *National Ideology under Socialism: Identity and Cultural Politics in Ceaușescu's Romania* (Berkeley, CA: University of California Press, 1991).

12 If in 1950, 6.7 percent of the state budget had been allocated to cultural institutions, the amount dropped to 0.6 percent in 1989. See Ioana Macrea-Toma, *Privilighenția. Instituții literare în comunismul românesc* (Cluj-Napoca: Casa Cărții de Știință, 2009), 163.

13 On the connection between the concept of "transitivity" and the young poetry of the 1980s, see Gheorghe Crăciun, *Aisbergul poeziei moderne* (Pitești: Paralela 45, 2002).

14 Florin Iaru, *Poeme alese 1975–1990* (Brașov: Aula, 2002), 69.

15 Traian T. Coșovei, *Ninsoarea electrică* (Bucharest: Liter-net [no year]), 85.

16 Mariana Marin, *Un război de o sută de ani* (Botoșani: Axa, 2001), 53.

17 For a discussion of Coșovei's poetry in relation to its American sources, see Teodora Dumitru, "Traian T. Coșovei și avatarurile modernității," *Caiete critice* 7 (2014): 32–42.

18 The 1980s Generation also includes several "neoexpressivist" poets. The most important is Ion Mureșan (1955–). The role U.S. poetry's influence plays in their work is less significant than in their colleagues' poems.

19 Mircea Cărtărescu, *Poezia* (Bucharest: Humanitas, 2015), 128.

20 Coșovei, *Ninsoarea electrică*, 104.

21 Nicolae Manolescu, *Literatura română postbelică*, vol. 1 (Brașov: Aula, 2001), 343.

22 Mircea Cărtărescu, *Postmodernismul românesc* (București: Humanitas, 2010), 121.

23 Cărtărescu, *Poezii*, 322–323.

24 Eugen Simion, *Scriitori români de azi*, vol. 4 (Bucharest: Cartea Românească, 1989), 485.

25 Cărtărescu, *Poezii*, 181.

26 The subversion in the poetry of the 1980s Generation also contributed to a broader cultural politics of "resistance," "oppositional discourse," or "critical innovation" along the lines of a *Glasnost* phenomenon." For this argument, see Marcel Cornis-Pope, *The Unfinished Battles: Romanian Postmodernism before and after 1989* (Iași:

Polirom, 1996), 7–35. The turn to postmodernism in East European literatures, coupled with the revisitation of their own literary traditions, is interpreted by Cornis-Pope as resistance. "The new literatures of Eastern Europe," he maintains, "adopted Western postmodern strategies as part of their aesthetics of 'resistance'" (10).

27 Cărtărescu, *Postmodernismul românesc*, 154–155.

28 Cărtărescu, *Postmodernismul românesc*, 152.

29 Mircea Martin, "D'un postmodernisme sans rivages et d'un postmodernisme sans postmodernité," *Euresis* 1–4 (2009): 11–22.

30 Cărtărescu, *Postmodernismul românesc*, 374.

31 Cărtărescu, *Postmodernismul românesc*, 367.

32 Cărtărescu, *Postmodernismul românesc*, 365.

33 Cărtărescu, *Postmodernismul românesc*, 155, 156, 480.

34 Marius Ianuș, *Manifest anarhist și alte poeme* (Anarchist Manifesto and Other Poems) (Bucharest: Vinea, 2000), 11.

35 Marius Ianuș, "Iubirea subterană," *Fracturi* 2 (2002): 1.

36 Moraru, *Reading for the Planet*, 114.

37 Christian Moraru, "'Modelul Cărtărescu' *versus* 'modelul Patapievici,'" *Observator cultural* 177 (2003): 32. In Moraru's view, Cărtărescu illustrates here the antithesis of the neo-conservative disciples of philosopher Constantin Noica (1909–1987).

38 Christian Moraru, "Beyond the Nation: Mircea Cărtărescu's Europeanism and Cosmopolitanism," *World Literature Today* 4 (July–August 2006): 41–45. "Romanian Postmodernism," notes Moraru, was a "political movement" that, by showing a predilection for foreign and especially Western sources, declined to heed the official directives to "reflect" local, that is, national–Communist values.

39 Steven Tötösy de Zepetnek, *Comparative Literature: Theory, Method, Application.* (Amsterdam: Rodopi, 1998), 132–147.

40 "One, and unequal:… one world literary system… but a system which is different from what Goethe and Marx had hoped for, because it's profoundly unequal," writes Franco Moretti in his article "Conjectures on World Literature," reproduced in Moretti, *Distant Reading*, 46–47.

41 Pascale Casanova, *The World Republic of Letters*, trans. M. B. DeBevoise (Cambridge, MA: Harvard University Press, 2004), 94, 99.

42 Casanova, *The World Republic of Letters*, 44. Casanova's position has been critiqued and charged with Eurocentrism and nationalism ("Gallocentrism"). For an overview of this criticism, see *Literature for Our Times: Postcolonial Studies in the Twenty-First Century*, ed. Bill Ashcroft et al. (Amsterdam: Rodopi, 2012), especially the contributions by Frank Schulze-Engler and Debjani Ganguly.

43 Wallerstein, *World-Systems Analysis*, 77.

44 See Wallerstein, *Geopolitics and Geoculture*, 114.

45 Robbins, "Blaming the System," in *Immanuel Wallerstein*, 58.

46 Moretti, *Distant Reading*, 50–52.

47 Moretti, *Distant Reading*, 116–117. For a critical look at the ways in which Moretti's concept of "compromise" has been used in the study of Central and Southeast European literatures, see Marko Juvan, "Worlding Literatures between Dialogue and Hegemony," *CLCWeb: Comparative Literature and Culture* 15, no. 5 (2013), available at http://docs.lib.purdue.edu/clcweb/vol15/iss5/10. In her contribution to this issue, Carmen Mușat provides further examples that support

her critique of Moretti's approach to centers and peripheries in "Conjectures on World Literature."

48 Dimock, *Through Other Continents*, 20.
49 David Damrosch, "World Literature as Alternative Discourse," *Neohelicon* 38 (2011): 308, 310.
50 Moretti, *Distant Reading*, 40.

14

How Does Exile Make Space?
Contemporary Romanian Émigré Literature and the Worldedness of Place: Herta Müller, Andrei Codrescu, Norman Manea

Doris Mironescu

What scholars are discovering after the "spatial turn" in the humanities is that the critical deployment of space-derived categories and tropes has become both urgent and tricky. The intensely debated crisis of what Neil Brenner calls "state-centric epistemology," on one side, and the ethically motivated apprehensions toward the globalist paradigm, on the other, have prompted a shift to spatiality at the same time that they have rendered the unqualified use of space-related categories, figures, and references a risky proposition.[1] Routinely pressed into the service of transnational and, of late, World Literature arguments about connectivity, border-crossing, "deep-space" interchanges, inclusion, and cosmopolitan community, notions as basic as "inside" and "outside," for instance, remain charged ideologically as their associations, old and new, with the paradigms of exclusionary nationalism and homogenizing globalism, respectively, still have to be renegotiated.[2] Exile, expatriate, and émigré literature is, I maintain, one steadily broadening world cultural domain where this renegotiation is currently dramatized, and this dramatization provides us with a template for upgrading our spatial concepts and tools for the twenty-first century. For not only is the connection to space paramount within this body of work, whether we talk about confining, protective, exclusionary, out-of-bounds, or longed-for areas or territories, but driving this flourishing literature is a complex topological, cultural, and political mechanics of *displacement* that inherently and emphatically undoes, amends, and reworks spatiality and associated ideas and representations while maneuvering identity into new positions and meanings. Here, strange, uncomfortable, improbable, evasive, forbidden, or open spaces are never given. Instead, they are constructed or, better still, continuously reconstructed, quintessentially shape-changing, and what happens to them—how space is made and remade under the auspices of exile, migration, and the like—illuminates and largely parallels the situation and *re*situation of selfhood in the world.

Following Thomas Bender's call on critics to reframe their spatial approaches for a transnational but not necessarily "globalist" age, as well as Wai Chee Dimock's "scales of aggregation" analytic model, my intervention focuses on recent exile and emigrant fiction as an identity-repositioning project that stakes out the worlded place of the human.[3] As I argue, the topo-tropology characteristic of this prose articulates what I determine as *worlded spatiality*. That is, these tropes unfold a *worldedness* or a heterogeneous topology where personal and collective, familiar and foreign, national, regional, and planetary zones, vicinities, and boundaries thereof intersect to relocate and redefine the exile, the outcast, and the displaced. Specifically, I will be concentrating on works by German-Romanian Nobel Prize winner Herta Müller, currently residing in Germany, and by Jewish-Romanian writers Andrei Codrescu, who is an American author too, and Norman Manea, who, like Codrescu, has also been living in the United States for many years. Notably, all of them have experienced Romanian totalitarianism, with Manea also a survivor of Romania's infamous Second World War Transnistria concentration camps; they were all by and large forced to leave their native country at various points during Communism; and all three have published widely acclaimed books that set out to upend discourses keyed to naturalizing worldviews centered on nationalist–territorialist understandings of political commitment, community loyalty, and group affiliation. Instrumental to this critique are de- and re-spatializing tactics geared toward projecting alternatives to narrowly conceived perimeters of identity membership. These alternatives are *world spaces* in whose fictional production local lore, minority history, personal experience, recovered literary traditions, and unofficial, affective, sensorial, subjective, and imaginary geographies serve as sub-, supra-, and transnational coordinates and building blocks. But, weary as they are of essentializing-prone modalities of belonging of the ethnicist-statal kind, expatriate writers are not sold on the uncritical utopia of internationalism either. As Codrescu explains in his tellingly titled 1990 book *The Disappearance of the Outside: A Manifesto for Escape*, exile is not simply a matter of trading in the ambiguous "protection" of the inside—of a certain citizenship and association with kinship and its turf—for the oftentimes theoretical, gossamer "freedoms" of the outside. This is because, as doctrine and structure, the state or, in Codrescu's topo-political terminology, the "Center" has the power to replicate itself globally given that nationalism and globalism are not always incompatible. To be sure, the global offers no escape if what one "escapes" to is the world market. For here the writers often find themselves trapped once more "inside" spatiality systems crystalized around power, influence, and prestige masquerading as "universal" values and equal cultural opportunity, and this is exactly what Manea suggests in *The Hooligan's Return* when he repurposes Zbigniew Herbert's anti-communist poem "Report from Paradise" as an anti-consumerist manifesto directed at happy-go-lucky capitalist America.[4]

But, it goes without saying, the well-known disillusions and trials of exile have not prevented writers from choosing it throughout history either. On the other hand, whether they are treated in more general terms, as "philosophical" issues, or bear witness to actual experiences, exile, abandoned home, defection, migration, and so on have always been central themes of literature. Paradoxically or not, this centrality has been given a boost in modern literature, which views the "exilic condition" as ontologically defining for human existence.[5] In James Joyce, Samuel Beckett, and other modernists, exile lies, of course, in the heart of an entire, quasi-religious doctrine of literary autonomy seen as a moral imperative and ultimately leading to language games and other forms of aestheticism. With contemporary exile and émigré writers and intellectuals coming from Romania, other countries of the former Eastern Bloc, as well as Germany, India, Sri Lanka, and elsewhere, exilic discourse ups, however, the political ante as these artists, much like other socio-professional categories of defectors, refugees, and expatriates, are deeply and sometimes violently affected by state apparatuses of control, surveillance, exclusion, and uprooting. Because such apparatuses and their institutions and rhetorics are situated and operate territorially, these authors are characteristically keen on the space-power nexus and on the "politicization" of spatiality, of "being-in-space," of belonging (or not) and on its spatial structures, and in particular on how these structures do the bidding of ethnicism, chauvinistic narrow-mindedness, or politically convenient oblivion, as the case may be. Consequently, these writers make use of metaphor, irony, intertextuality, and certain narrative techniques to deflate membership rhetorics that dissimulate the exclusionary and monistic workings of nation-state space management. What is more, in critiquing this spatial politics, their narratives of exile foster another, counter-spatiality, in which cloistered, isolated, and carceral places open out toward a multifarious world of many worlds, toward a worldedness whose geographies of light and darkness, hope and grief alternate, dovetail, or overlap. Paving the way to a closer look at this spatial poiesis in Müller, Codrescu, and Manea is, in my essay's next section, a quick review of recent scholarship on space and the planetary dimension of world literature. Turning to the authors at hand, the segment after that zeroes in on displaced identity, its territory, and this space's "defamiliarization" in the writers' fiction, while the third section takes up the allegorical telescoping of culture, country, home, and of their sometimes haunting loss into material yet densely symbolic spatial "containers." I close with a couple of considerations on the "wording" of world space in exile and émigré literature.

1. Space, Otherness, Worldedness

Modern literary-cultural theorists and, in particular, narratologists have admittedly attended to issues of temporality more than they have to the problematics of space. Nonetheless, there is a long line of critics and theorists, from Mikhail M. Bakhtin, Erich Auerbach, and Georg Lukács to Gaston Bachelard, Henri Lefebvre, Edward Said, and Fredric Jameson, who have explored the dynamics of space and culture and have laid the groundwork for a full-blown, spatial reorientation across the humanities. The imminence of such a reorientation was already clear to Michel Foucault, who famously proclaimed in the 1960s that "We are in the epoch of simultaneity: we are in the epoch of juxtaposition, the epoch of the near and far, of the side-by-side, of the dispersed."[6] "Simultaneity" may be a temporal notion, but, as one can see, Foucault and others after him approach it as a geographical attribute harder and harder to ignore. It is in this context that geography gained momentum as a pivotal discipline in the 1970s and 1980s. On the other hand, increasingly aware of the importance of social meaning-making in space measuring, geographers themselves began, around the same time, to pay more attention to culture and politics. In this vein, Yi-Fu Tuan has highlighted the differences between "space" and "place," with the former described as "abstract" and "undifferentiated" and the latter as "space endowed with value."[7] Further echoing the spectacular upgrade and diffusion of communication technologies, data exchange, commerce, and travel, the new forms of human experience brought into play by such global networks, as well as the ethical and political ramifications of the transnational domains and environs arising in our growingly webbed world, space studies is both descriptive and critical. A case in point is David Harvey's "time–space compression" analysis, which entails spatial critique in a classical, Marxist-culturalist sense.[8] Similarly, Edward Soja has drawn on Lefebvre to advocate "a distinct mode of critical spatial awareness" and theorize his influential "Thirdspace" while attempting to tackle the imaginary dimension of "real-and-imagined" spaces.[9] Taking his cue from Soja, "geocriticism" founder Bertrand Westphal has maintained that, by virtue of their capacity to play off reality against fiction, literature and the mimetic arts can "bring out the hidden potentialities of space-time without reducing them to stasis."[10]

Where Soja canvases "postmodern geographies," Gayatri Chakravorty Spivak reacts in her later work to the globalization of formerly discrete postcolonial sites and regions, a development of which, like Harvey and others, she is quite apprehensive. Thus, she proposes "planetarity" as a counter to globality's homogenizing assault on alterity. In *Death of a Discipline*, she endorses a planetary world literature that embraces cultural openness and irreducible otherness. As opposed to the "global," she specifies, "planetary" thought and the human concept built into it are "intended toward [an] other" who is neither a variety of the selfsame, of "being here," nor "our dialectical negation."[11] Adamant about that which, in the world forum, must remain singular, immeasurable, and unrationalized, this distinction has resonated with other critics, especially comparatists, who have gone on to ground it more firmly in literary studies. At the advancing front of this trend, Emily Apter has posited untranslatability as a telling example of the "otherness" that needs to be brought to the fore of world literature studies so as to counteract the tendency of globalist hegemonies to reduce the idiosyncratic, the particular, and the local to sameness. Her attention to the untranslatable, as opposed to the "entrepreneurial, bulimic drive to anthologize and curricularize the world's cultural resources," follows in the footsteps of Spivak's reading of otherness and informs, accordingly, an intellectually nuanced and ethically driven understanding of our complex and diverse planet.[12]

Concerns for the spatial and cultural complexity of the world as planet—rather than "totalizing" globe—are also paramount in Christian Moraru's work. Moraru has coined the term "cosmodernism" to account for a shift in recent American literature and culture, a transitional moment that parallels, chronicles, and engages ethically with the sweeping transformations the world has been going through under the pressure of post–Cold War webs of cultural and material interaction.[13] Expanding his inquiry beyond U.S. fiction, the critic looks in his recent book *Reading for the Planet* at the contemporary literary imaginary as a form of "planetarity" and calls for "a new way of approaching late global literature ... as a dramatization of world withness."[14] Along similar lines, Pheng Cheah discerns a planetary vocation in literature's ability to forge human copresence and intellectual exchanges, insisting that such connections are foregrounded in narration, which sets up a temporality under whose auspices future-rich, world-making and world-remaking scenarios become possible. For Cheah, "time itself is the force of transcendence that opens a world" and by the same token sets in motion narrative mechanisms of worlding that bring closer together geographically, culturally, and emotionally distinct experiences, audiences, and *Weltanschauungen*, all of which are, as we will see momentarily, crucial to the literature under scrutiny here and, more specifically still, to its space-engendering thrust.[15] Calling to mind Moraru's cosmodernism, Cheah embraces "a modality of cosmopolitanism that is responsible and responsive to the need to remake the world as a hospitable place, that is, a place that is *open* to the emergence of peoples that globalization deprives of world."[16] This modality unfolds, again, along a twofold, "deep" spatiotemporal axis, as does in critics like Wai Chee Dimock, for whom "planetary" designates an attribute of cultural time as well as the scope of the intertextual commerce she has studied throughout her work and which has allowed her to map out the planet through literature.[17] By adapting traditional theories of literary influence to a geocultural and materialist reconceptualization of fictional textuality, Dimock has shown that the bridges thrown across ages and continents by planetary writers and readers facilitate encounters of the mind and body whose interpersonal, space-fostering—*topo-poietic*—fervor translates, as we will also notice below, into a whole range of worlding territorial games, spatial formations, and community venues.

2. Streets Full of Rhinos: Defamiliarizing Territory

Exile writers often reclaim their place in the world and, in a way, carve out spaces for themselves in it by relativizing and sometimes twisting the meaning and shape of a native or formerly native territory. Thus, they take a familiar geocultural perimeter and "defamiliarize" it. That is, they make it "unfamiliar," an other to itself via a narrative cartography poised to replace official geographies, charts, and histories with representations and descriptions not yet settled in collective memory, to flaunt the many fashions in which space is constructed rather than a natural given since times immemorial, and to uncover the variety of ethnic-religious and linguistic groups, cultural traditions, polities, and types of belonging the same terrain can and should accommodate.[18] Underpinning this receptiveness to the many worlds nested in one is Soja's "critical spatial awareness" or, more simply put, the castaway and expatriate's painfully acquired knack for experiencing space differently and *as* different, in its many-sidedness and strangeness, whether it is the home left behind or new residences and landscapes. Retrospectively, exiles develop, indeed, a particular perception of their birthplaces, one that can be colored by nostalgia, fantasy, and pining, but also by disaffection, resentment, and criticism. An expatriate himself, Salman Rushdie has in fact observed that people like him "are haunted by some sense of loss, some urge to reclaim, to look back, even at the risk of being mutated into pillars of salt. But if we do look back, we also do so in the knowledge—which gives rise to profound uncertainties—that our physical alienation from India almost inevitably means that we will not be capable of reclaiming precisely the thing that was lost: that we will, in short, create fictions, not actual cities or villages, but invisible ones, imaginary homelands. Indias of the mind."[19] Like Rushdie, countless exile writers deploy their fantasy-imbued recreations of their homelands to stimulate historical introspection and open their countries up to discrepant, interior and surrounding spaces, vicinities, and possibilities of life and culture previously less visible or acknowledged, imagined or real—or, as Soja would insist, at once real and imagined. In effect, both Soja's postmodern geography and Westphal's geocriticism dwell on this ambiguity extensively, with the French critic studying in particular its manifestations and procedures such as "multifocalization," "polysensoriality," "stratigraphic vision," and intertextuality.[20] These all are or can be conducive to as many forms of deterritorialization or territorial defamiliarization, where the historical, the topological, and the sensorial are worked over—and reworked together—to remake a certain spatial domain into a space of many spaces, memories, and traditions.

This remaking, this breaking open of a familiar landscape so that geocultural and historical multitudes can spring forth, is the very project of Norman Manea's 2003 memoir, *The Hooligan's Return*.[21] In his book, Manea appeals to the region's memory—much as he does to his own—to revisit critically the shopworn descriptions of the area. An important part of Romania's culture and history, his native Bukovina also occupies a special place on the map of the Holocaust, for it is here and in neighboring Bessarabia that the Romanian authorities committed unspeakable crimes against the Jewish population. The writer was only five years old when he was deported with his family to Transnistria, and the traumatic event gives a uniquely personal dimension to his account of Bukovina's official history, a version both symbolically reinforced and ominously compounded by Manea's recollection of how the former province of the Austro-Hungarian Empire had rediscovered in May 1986, one year before he left Romania, its East European identity as the radioactive plume blown into the atmosphere by Ukraine's Chernobyl disaster traveled, in its path across Northern Europe, over Northeastern Romania as well. Manea's remembrance conjures up a poignantly unconventional image of Bukovina, and it does so to no negligible degree by declining to pander to nationalist–territorialist sensitivities. To the contrary, from afar, authorial memory *misplaces* Bukovina by placing it on other maps of this European corner, maps that have existed but have been variously erased by geopolitics and contending nationalisms or maps that nobody has ever drawn but are possible. In *The Hooligan's Return* and elsewhere in his work, temporal embodiments—in this case, tragic historical occurrences such as the Holocaust and Cold War nuclear catastrophes—enable spatial reshufflings and their narrative corollary, fictional maps. Here, Manea is in distinguished company, for exile literature has often played with extant political maps and ingeniously so, especially when it has dealt with geographies with complicated and contested histories and identities. In the 1955 novel *The Issa Valley*, for instance, Czeslaw Milosz draws on his childhood memories of Polish Lithuania at a time the country was a Soviet republic and its pre-USSR history unmentionable in print. Thus, he challenges the geography of totalitarianism, that is, of a certain place, formerly a country (Lithuania), under a totalitarian regime, and also of a totalitarian geography, of a violent, defacing, and incarcerating way of drawing, "picturing," and representing a world and the bigger world within and around it, hence the worlding mixes of real and imagined settings and mainstream and minority histories. These combinations are both disorienting and potentially liberatory. The "mongrel," alternate geographies they limn jocularly test a reader's sense of space and direction, as well as his or her knowledge of or fondness for a certain place, and so they can convey a whole array of emotional responses to native lands, from irony to nostalgia and from the disappointment of return to the pathos of homecoming. In Vladimir Nabokov's 1969 novel *Ada, or Ardor*, for example, amid fictitious countries such as "Estoty" or "Canady," one comes across "Amerussia," an onomastic collage transparently combining the names of Russia, where the writer was born, and America (the United States), his home between 1940 and 1961.[22] In his 1980 book *Midnight's Children*, Rushdie, too, paints a similar cultural-political entity, "India of the mind," and also with a magical-realist brush, which allows him to survey various corners of the country and assign them metaphorical significations. Undoubtedly, it is not by chance that the mock-messianic protagonist's face resembles a map of India, for his travels endow places on the subcontinent with new—some might say, "out-of-place"—meanings, and intertextually so, as it happens with the Dantesque Inferno-like mangrove forests of Bangladesh.[23]

A different experience of homeland and different kinds of space-making shape Müller's work. Caught throughout her life "between myths of belonging" that sanction arrogance and oppression, the Romanian-born German writer does not, overall, go out of her way to express attachment, yearning, and other feelings of this sort for a given region or political–administrative entity.[24] Her narratives typically trudge across a *vague* space, for they do seem deliberately sketchy about where they are set as the particular countries, zones, and locales featured in Müller are often left unnamed or equivocally pinpointed. Frequently, her world's topography is not so much realistically described as it is suggested through images that capture the feel of a street, the fleeting impression given by the sound of toponyms, by a scent, by a taste, and other perceptions and representations whose spectacle helps Müller make known lands unrecognizable and dislocate political geography. Thus, her 2009 novel *The Hunger Angel* depicts a Soviet labor camp without placing it on the Gulag's map, as if its exact location did not matter or was impossible to ascertain. But images from back home are also blurred beyond recognition. The main hero, a young German from Transylvania's Hermannstadt (Sibiu), fails to recognize Romania's geographical contour when he summons it in a dream—"Who switched my country?" he asks.[25] A homesick detainee in a Ukrainian prison, the boy finds solace in the fairytale-sounding names of places from his native city. Not only do Bridge of Lies, Thimble Stairway, and Treasure Chest pawnshop remind him of the comfort of home, but, in kindling the imagination, they also provide temporary escapes from the bleak reality of deportation and detention. Home recollections also bring back to life the smell of roasted chestnuts bought for him by his grandfather, former Austro-Hungarian sailor on a ship fittingly named *Donau* (the Danube).[26] As the old man comes from a time when Transylvania was part of another political entity, the "dual monarchy" of Austria-Hungary, the apparently insignificant olfactory detail works here as a "hook" into another world, a historical-spatial relay of sorts linking up this episode and its location with others, explicitly evoked or solely hinted at. Famously pioneered by Marcel Proust in *In Search of Lost Time*, the intricate and deep-running interplay of places, their names, remembrance, effect, and fantasy subtends Müller's novel, and, just as in Manea's memoir, unsettles established political spaces, boundaries, and narrative accounts thereof. Revoked and then one more time reevoked, remade through sensations and poetic-imaginative projections, the once familiar place or place-name latches onto and spreads out before the reader a greater world across the borders enforced by one despotic regime after another.

In *The Hooligan's Return*, too, toponymy is a powerful "geo-affective" driver, but nostalgia is not the only feeling it stirs. Bucharest's street names trigger in one of Manea's heroes, a longtime Romanian émigré, a strong but contradictory response, at once enthusiastic and irritated. "I can hear his melodious voice," the narrator tells us,

> as he recites the archaic names: "Palas Street, Rahovei, Antim, Rinocerului, Labirint, Gentilă Street. Concordiei and right next to it, Discordiei! Here we have Trofeelor, Olimpului, Emancipată. Listen to this, Emancipată! Isn't it wonderful? And Rinocerului, Labirint, Gentilă, Gentle Street! And Cuțitul de Argint, Puțul cu apă and Cuțitul de argint—the Water Well and the Silver Knife!"[27]

This onomastics is real, and Manea calls up, via its unique musicality and allusive semantics, old Bucharest, to which the narrator abandons himself wistfully. The names have an innocent, naïve, carefree ring to them, connoting bourgeois gentleness and an emphatically if somewhat oddly reiterated distaste for violence (Gentle Street, Concord Street, "and, right next to it, Discord"), a penchant for references at once classical and kitschy (Palas Street, Olympus Street), and an ingenuous fondness for the decorative and the exotic (Silver Knife Street, Rhinoceros Street). At first blush, the irony these references pack may not have a lot of bite to it. On closer inspection, though, much of this nomenclature serves as an intertextual echo chamber for the topography known to Romanian audiences from the short stories of nineteenth-century classic Ion Luca Caragiale (1852–1912), who exiled himself to Berlin during the last years of his life and who figures prominently in *The Hooligan's Return*. Interestingly enough, Caragiale's social critique of early Romanian modernity was partly inspired by the capital's clumsy toponymy, which, to him, smacked of hasty, over-the-top attempts to suggest, if not to forge "nominally"—through appellations, street name placards, and pompous labels of all kinds—a modernity whose effectiveness was otherwise a matter of debate. For Caragiale, the city was rather a laid-back and tranquil place where happy-go-lucky drunkards would shoot the breeze late into the night, quarrelling about politics passionately but vacuously and ineffectively. Accordingly, in his work designations such as Emancipation Street or Fidelity Street gesture ironically to the young Romanian Kingdom's striking disconnect between pretentious, largely inane public rhetoric and the reality of democratic and moral life. This is, in Caragiale, precisely the contrast allegorized by the gypsy women living in dire poverty on Emancipation Street, who are all victims of hurried and ill-conceived "modernizing" reforms, and the young nouveau riche who resides on Fidelity Street and turns out to be a philanderer. Following in Caragiale's footsteps, Manea is, then, hardly longing for a peaceful, olden-days Bucharest. In fact, such stark disjuncture, alongside the broader crisis, of linguistic and social rationality, which Caragiale pursued more memorably than any other Romanian author, takes Manea to "Rhinoceros Street" and thus to another exile writer from Bucharest, Eugène Ionesco (1909–1994), who, a few decades after Caragiale and under the powerful influence of his style and themes, reached back into his own Romanian past to build the world-famous absurdist allegory of *Rhinoceros* (1960). Commenting on the play, Ionesco pointed, in fact, to Romanian politics, specifically to the 1930s Fascist radicalization of his fellow Romanians, whose irrational and frenzied advocacy of brutal behavior would prompt him to liken them to large, aggressive wild beasts. On Bucharest's map, the street marks, underneath the homesickness-inducing melancholy cityscape awash in the fatuous pontifications of Caragiale's dramatis personae, another, darker and dehumanizing geography of prejudice and anti-Semitic violence. In Manea's survey, Bucharest is no longer a world but many in one, a multilayered, puzzling, and sometimes disquieting urban space in which histories, cultures, and discourses clash and confound the observer.

Intertextuality plays a similarly "topogenetic" role in Manea's 1992 text "Proust's Tea." In the short story, a small boy, on his way back home from a Transnistria extermination camp, gets a cup of tea and sugar from a Red Cross worker. The bewildering taste of the tea automatically reminds him of the playful ritual invented by his grandfather back in the camp, who would tie the last cube of sugar with a piece of string to the ceiling and have the family drink their tea staring at the sugar and trying to imagine the sweet taste in their mouths. For the child, however, the little game was entirely meaningless at the time. Besides, he had been too young to remember how sugar tasted. And yet he manages, in hindsight, to make sense of his relative's actions.[28] The sweetness of the drink, which the boy fully registers only now, as something "new," from "around here," and in that "real," connects him with his late grandfather, as if "the souls of those we've lost indeed take refuge in inanimate objects."[29] The title's Proustian reference is, then, scarcely ironic, nor is it made by a character. It represents a comment, as well as a clue, offered by the mature author who is telling a quasi-autobiographical story and is glossing on its implications. Reliving his childhood of pain and horror and discovering that time lost and remote places can indeed be "regained," Manea reenacts in another, far more traumatic context the Madeleine episode along with Proust's broader intuition about the past, those passed with it, the faraway, and their recovery. The literary nexus joining the Romanian writer and his French precursor resembles and, in a sense, performs a personal interaction, for Manea, as Proust's reader, suddenly finds himself going through the same mental processes and reflecting on the same insights as the great modernist decades ahead of him in another place and under completely different circumstances. The interpersonal affords a continuum that is both spatial and historical, a worldedness bodied forth in translocal, "planetary" space and time, as Dimock would point out. The American critic would probably also insist that the intercultural is, and must be, the steppingstone of this "chronotopic" undertaking, as she does in her discussion of Osip Mandelstam, and it can be argued actually, still following Dimock, that Manea's relation with Proust in the short story works analogously to the Jewish-Russian poet's passion for Dante in the Gulag.[30] Distant yet close, intensely personal and *inter*personal, located and far-reaching at once, such readings draw voices, moments, and places together and set up this togetherness as a spatiality without ontological precedent.

3. Packing Oneself into Silence: Allegorizing Exile

Insofar as it has effects on the reader and writer—and on the writer *qua* reader—and to the extent that it is built mentally, this space is as real, as rooted in geography and history, as it is imagined. But space-imagining hardly starts out from a clean slate culturally speaking. This is why, as we have learned, in Manea topo-imagination works intertextually. Sometimes, however, allegorization takes over by way of elaborate metaphors suggestive of exile and its multiple transgressions, exilic identity and its troubles, and old and new countries, abodes, and localities. Literary allusions frequently work in Manea as analytic prisms through which he scans an erstwhile intimate and homely stomping ground, breaking up past sites, incidents, and representations thereof into less habitual, less "homey," and even *unheimilich*, "uncanny" and unsightly zones of physical expanse, meaning, power, and responsibility. There are situations, though, in Manea and other writers, when a similarly prismatic, decomposing flashlight is focused on the character and on exiled, dislocated subjectivity more broadly. In this case, it is not the territory, the familiar land, that is defamiliarized to and distanced from the character but, quite the other way around, in certain geo-historical situations it is the heroes and heroines who become less familiar, less close, or less comprehensible, and more estranged intellectually, affectively, and spatially to their environment itself, past and present, to others, and even to themselves. The rhetorical vehicle of this existential isolation and self-isolation is a cluster of recurring and frustrating images of a world across whose emotional topography of adversity, solitude, and confusion the protagonist treks over and over again only to confront insubstantial and illusory, desert mirage-like specters, symbols, and reminders of scenes and places from back home. In Michael Ondaatje's 1992 novel *The English Patient*, for example, the characters take refuge in a derelict, postwar Italian villa whose walls are full of holes that let in the wind, smells, and noises of the natural surroundings, a fitting metaphor of the shattered identity that, cast into the violent and wide world, can heal only by opening itself up to it.[31] The Sri Lankan-Canadian author does imagine selfhood as a "patient," as a structure gelling around a drama of suffering, pain, and loss, but loss, the wholeness one neither is nor shares in any more as a healthy body, member of the body politic, and otherwise, entails both a traumatic experience and an opportunity for healing, for a "recompletion" that acknowledges the bigger universe outside the injured and sick body. This acknowledgment alone does not suffice either, as in W. G. Sebald's 2001 novel *Austerlitz*, for instance. The German writer's narrating hero, a former beneficiary of a 1939 *Kindertransport* from Nazi Germany to England, is fascinated by the building of a Parisian railway station that, for some reason, shares its name with his. Sebald explains this attraction by means of an allegory—as we find out, his character walks into the station one Sunday afternoon, but the place is deserted and covered in pigeon feathers, "like the site of an unpunished crime."[32] This is, in fact, just one place of this sort in Sebald. Teeming with train halts and railroad terminals, fortresses, concentration camps, and libraries, his world is a space fractured and multiplied by wars and their horrors but oddly held together by mementos thereof, archives, memories, commemorations, and repentance no less than by their cynically unrepentant absence and tokenism. It is the latter that Sebald's empty and desolate sites reference, as does the French building. Evoking the haunting image of the Austerlitz railroad station as a symbol of tragedy, forgetfulness, and cavalier attitude toward history and its dehumanizing precincts, the Parisian place foregrounds the author and the hero's strained relationship with home, homeland, and native and communal spaces.

A similar theme is the tenor of allegorical language in *The Hooligan's Return*. Oftentimes, the book illuminates insistently the darkly ambiguous geometry of the spatiality of belonging through a complex symbolism of life and death, traumatic birth, embodiment, struggle, and survival. In one scene, the hero has just been born in pain, after protracted labor, and is still caught between life and death, but his grandfather welcomes him into the world with a stern and prophetic remark. If he has got fingernails, the old man proclaims, the child would live.[33] It turns out that the newborn does have them, and, metaphorically speaking, they will serve him later as he will have to fight—tooth and nail, of course—for his life in Transnistria. The incident is brought back one more time later on, when the boy is on his way back home, after four years spent in detention:

> A melodrama as sweet and delicate as the placenta of the newly born swelled the concertina bag's rainbow in honor of the victors—us.

> I watched them cry, embrace, recognize each other. I hung back on the platform of the truck, biting my fingernails. The street was the stage and I was a bewildered spectator. Finally, they came back for the one left behind, left behind in the past.

> Before I allowed myself to be lowered back into the world again, I managed to bite my fingernails deeply once more. I had acquired this nasty habit, I bit my fingernails.[34]

Manea stages the homecoming scene as a parody of the reconciliation between the formerly deported and the country that sent them to their death, for the boy's return is anything but a rebirth into the loving arms of his brethren—hence the invocation of an accordion song "as sweet and delicate as the placenta of the newborn." What looks like a celebration is no more than a grotesque masquerade or, better still, is *also* a sinister travesty since, in the event as such, truth and its hypocritical mystification bleed into one another as the child's actual birth nearly killed both him and his mother, and the figurative return to life back in Bukovina was preceded by and predicated on a long struggle with annihilation in Transnistria's death factories.

The many-faceted allegory sets off the quintessential ambiguity of homeland, native territory, and autochthonism. This ambiguity is sometimes couched in slippery symbolism, as in Andrei Codrescu's own, post-Cold War "return" saga, the 1991 *Hole in the Flag: A Romanian Exile's Story of Return and Revolution*.[35] In his travel narrative, the Romanian-American poet and novelist dwells on a much-publicized iconic image of Romania's 1989 uprising, namely, the flag with a hole in its center, out of which the Communist emblem had been cut. For Codrescu, that gap is not only the symbol of his country's problematic break with its past but also the window through which the exile steps back into the world he had left as a child. "It's through that hole, I thought," he writes, "that I am returning to my birthplace."[36] It is an unsettling picture, as it should be, since his return, one more time equated to a rebirth, is likened to a very physical birth and so is as bloody and traumatizing as the chaotic, murderous, and vengeful 1989 coup-cum-upheaval. Furthermore, similarly to the "revolution" that is not one, for it does not bring about an immediate departure from totalitarianism and therefore does not mark a return to democracy, Codrescu finds himself stuck in the flag's missing center, as it were, in a political and topo-cultural interregnum—the "void" or "vacancy" of power touted at the time by the newly emerged Romanian authorities—because the place he means to go back to does not exist anymore.

Yet again, the place can be reconstituted allegorically, if critically, as it happens in Manea, in *The Hole in the Flag*, or in Dubravka Ugrešić's 2005 exile novel *The Ministry of Pain*. The book is an exercise in "Yugonostalgia" as a group of students from former Yugoslavia, now refugees in Amsterdam, tries to conjure up their old country by recalling its emblematic brands, pop culture, and collective celebrations. True, Yugoslavia's territorial body has been dismembered, but literature has the power to *re-member* it, to put it back together and reembody it affectively rather than effectively, by dint of memory and the imagination. In Ugrešić's novel, Codrescu's absent, "voided" body is hauled around in a metaphorical container stuffed with recollections, memorabilia, and assorted signifiers of Yugoslavia. This receptacle of emotional cultural space is a migrant's traveling bag sporting the national colors red, white, and blue. The carryall allegorizes a complex metamorphosis affecting subjectivity and its native space, viz., the violent, post-1990s transformation of countless Yugoslav nationals into immigrants, as Ugrešić takes the idea of belonging to and within a nation-state's territory and turns it on its head. What the former citizens are left with, she implies in an insightful parallel to Codrescu's "revolutionary" glosses, is a mock national flag, a banner that is hardly one. For its colors shine in a medium or on an object that does not stand for a stable space, polity, territory, and identity but for their very dissolution and supplanting by contrasting realities and notions such as exodus, flight, migration, vagrancy, and the world spaces in which former natives become transients, newcomers, and guests in other people's homes and countries.

Just as the flag is more of an anti-flag, Yugonostalgia's practical effects are essentially its opposite. The Yugoslavia Ugrešić paints may feel like a homeland from afar, but it does not exist anymore. And if it did, it does not seem that it would manage to pull the Bosnian, Croatian, and Serbian asylum seekers back into its fold because the bad memories outweigh the good, and in them tormenting zones outnumber the homey and cozy spaces. This is the imbalance that also characterizes Müller's spatial poetics and, more broadly, accounts for her preoccupation with trauma, harassment, threat, loss, and their sites in Cold War Romania. The heroes and heroines of her novels live in shabby apartment complexes and student dorms and are interrogated by secret police officers in nondescript buildings. However, Müller does not spend too much time on realistic descriptions of inhabited, residential, and domestic spatial units either big or small, be they countries, cities, neighborhoods, homes, or rooms. Forced to live—quite literally—in places of isolation and terror inside an aggressive world, her characters try to shut out this world along with the myriad of details that make it both real and threatening, and so they take symbolic refuge in smaller spaces of identity, that is, in *objectual* spaces— expanses and whole worlds metaphorically packed or morphed into things. The title of her 2009 novel *Atemschaukel*, translated into English as *The Hunger Angel*, is a clever metaphor for such a space. The German word means "breath swing" and signifies the up-and-down movement of the gasping lungs in their rib cage in moments of panic or exhaustion. Thus, similarly to the mechanics of our breathing organs, Müller's narrative is not straightforward but back and forth, indirect, and oblique, as it is twisted stylistically by allusion, poetic language, and wordplay. The story and its meaning move, then, one can say, not unlike the lungs, the air in them, and the vulnerable soul breath symbolizes, all of them trapped together inside the body. Exile and internment, she implies, are hard to couch in the traditional story with a beginning, a smoothly linear plot development, an ending, and a moral lesson. Deportation occasions extreme experiences whose multiple, simultaneous, and conflicting meanings call, accordingly, for a synthetic, concentrated, and thus inevitably elusive expression comparable to poetry, which is why the book reads at times like a prose poem.

A tool of choice in Müller's poetic tool kit, allegory is wielded from the outset to convey people's material sense of space. Thus, on *The Hunger Angel*'s very first page, a seventeen-year-old German boy, getting ready for the journey to a Soviet labor camp, packs his things in a gramophone case for, unlike Ugrešić's characters, he has no travel bag. He is certainly not prepared for what awaits him. He has neither warm clothes of his own nor enough time to think about what to take along. All the same, he must somehow figure out a way to make sure the items he does carry with him will help him survive in more ways than one. In this regard, the box is quite fitting, if not for its physical qualities, for what the musical device is literally, then for what it epitomizes and, in a sense, preserves: the intimate, protective space of home complete with the family's musical afternoons. For the teenager, those precious hours still resonate inside the case, but they cannot but compete for room against the boy's "silent baggage"— the homosexuality he had never mentioned to his parents. His secret forces him to "pack himself" into a silence "whose" meaning no words will "unpack."[37] This other identitarian space, his sexual identity hideout, cancels out the comforting place metaphorically folded in and indexed—showed off, "unwrapped"—by the makeshift suitcase, for, no doubt, his world's homophobia prevents him from fully expressing himself. A little later, the object returns, this time around to symbolize the burden of memories haunting the hero at night:

> For sixty years now, I try to recall the objects from the camp: the things I carry in
> my night-suitcase. Ever since I came back, the sleepless night is a suitcase made
> of black leather. And the suitcase is lodged in my forehead. For sixty years now
> I don't know if I can't sleep because I'm trying to recall the objects, or whether
> I struggle to recall them because I can't sleep. One way or the other, the night
> always packs its black suitcase against my will. And it's against my will that I have
> to remember. And even if I didn't have to, but wanted to, I'd rather not have to
> want to.[38]

Back from the USSR, the former inmate has not "unpacked." The past, which now
includes the detention years, is even bulkier and tormenting. The hero's baggage has
meanwhile gotten heavier. The suitcase, still unopen, is the objectualized hetero-space
inside which the bygone and present days, the Russian wastelands and the German
village in Romania, the outside or milieu ("the sleepless night") and the inside (the dark
thoughts and recollections bumping against his "forehead"), the collective history of an
ethnic group and the private drama of a closeted gay man frame and signify each other
and serve as each other's container, guise, and vehicle. Away from the family, repressed
sexuality, tightly packed in the metaphorical case, makes faraway home less homey;
back into Romanian native space, the remembrance of hard labor and deprivations
only compounds the predicament as recollections, emotions, and the places carved
into them interleave with one another or comprise each other as so many Chinese
boxes.

The ambivalent structure of this topo-allegory queries our notions of
departure, exile, dislodgement, on one side, and, on the other, the concepts of
return, homecoming, along with the very possibility of home—to have one
originally as well as to regain one. Codrescu's 1993 poem "Not a Pot to Piss In"
speaks precisely to this spatial and cultural-affective conundrum. Intertwining
fictional and nonfictional narrative, "true stories," cultural myths, and richly
suggestive geocultural tropes, this autobiography in verse shuttles back and forth
between his Romanian adolescence and the mature American years to track his
large Whitmanian self across decades and meridians. The author strings out
a series of metaphors of pots and pottery along his lyrical life story to retrieve
memorable experiences and to flesh out his dynamic vision of a world culture
in which identity is nomadic, mobile, and unfixed, and where, by the same
movement quite literally, exile does not designate an exception, an "unusual"
human condition anymore.[39] The poem presents us with three sets of symbolic
receptacles and vessels hinting at the "pottification" of space—of spaces preserved,
contained, "poured" into a hollow utensil, taken along across other territories, and
thus interspersed with other spaces and worlds. The first brings before the reader
actual containers designed for all kinds of purposes, from drinking to urinating to
enjoying aesthetically, and ranging from wine jugs to chamber pots to the exquisite
porcelain bowls on display in Codrescu's hometown art museum. Foregrounding
a more problematic relationship with the domestic, emotional, and cultural spaces
concentrating in or into such objects, the second set marks a crisis of belonging

and community as it institutes a cultural semiotics of separation and alienation. Peasants who have relocated to city apartments keep pottery from back home in their glass cupboards; ancient amphorae make us think of their ancient users, of the grain trade and shipping routes across the Mediterranean, but also of the thriving cultural commerce with the Middle East and of the prodigious "Oriental" imaginary—"those huge Arabian Nights pots where Ali Baba and the forty thieves hid;" the small Balkan nations at war with each other in the early 1990s are compared to pots under pressure, ready to explode, which should be handled gently so as to diffuse, without damaging them, the rage boiling over inside.[40] Once again, around and in all these jugs and dishes neighbors and neighboring worlds, indigenous and transient domains, adjoining cultures and cultures far apart come together, peacefully or less so. Further adding to this worldly richness is the third class of symbolic objects, where the focus is actually on those objects' parts, rather, which are themselves symbolic and, as such, heighten spatial incorporation at the intersection of the immaterial, the physical, and the cultural. Here, Codrescu is drawn not only to potters' language—"shoulders," "lips," "neck," "leg," etc.—which is replete with sensuous, bodily metaphors that in turn hint at how deeply the corporeal and, on another level, the erotic and the sexual are bound up with the aesthetic, but also to a fantastic connection of sorts between past and present moments and places. The poet suggests that, if one listens carefully, one can hear in the museums' antique vases, when silence is complete, the voices of their makers or of whoever happened to be around thousands of years ago, when the items were crafted:

> My friends, potters digging up the earth,
> leaving holes in it until the whole mass of it
> becomes artefact or art
> you must divine the vectors of its new order—
> that's the price for not keeping still in paradise.
> After words ceramics are the most legible writing
> and words themselves are written mostly upon the dishes
> to which I keep my ear,
> and what they say is,
> it's a long story of mud & of hands
> and the hands that fashion the mud refashion the world.[41]

The objects in their cases, the author ventures, allow different ages, people, humans, and things to communicate across the chasms of time, space, and ontology, and so pottery and art in general emerge as a world-making activity that brings into contact separate and apparently incompatible zones and facets of existence. Clay molding transforms the earth itself—earth as dirt, substance, as well as extension and nurturing ground, soil bed of culture—into a "world-heavy" artifact, changes "mud" into a world and by the same token the world as we know it into a new one.

4. Worlding, Wording

Pottery is not only poetry's anagram but also a kindred craft. Like pottery, poetry is a multifaceted art of fashioning—word molding and world making at the same time. This is surely the case of Codrescu's art, which is more than a form of world representation. It is, to be sure, a worlding activity, too, an ontologizing project in its own right insofar as it enables diverse audiences to participate in one and the same planetary condition by experiencing the poet's re-spatialization of historically, geographically, and culturally spaced-out locales, occurrences, and emotions into unifying symbolic sites, objects, and artifacts. A concern of literature at large, this worldly minded making of space is a task most exiled and émigré writers eagerly assume thematically as well as stylistically and linguistically. To institute spaces in which places, communities, and symbolic objects act as windows onto the bigger world, they rework language into a new body, for, indeed, worlding happens through wording. As we have seen, the three authors favor wording and other textual modalities ranging from irony and intertextuality that render cloistered, little, familiar and sometimes familial precincts larger, strange, and full or strangers to allegory that abbreviate, synthesize, and integrate, in small objects and other "containing" sites and symbols, whole worlds, forcing us to rethink how we orient ourselves in culturally and politically marked territories, more broadly, how we engage with space and its basic coordinates and categories such as "here" and "there," "within" and "without," and the like. In *The Disappearance of the Outside*, which narrates his story as an expatriate, rising poet wrestling with tradition, and post–Cold War-era intellectual, Codrescu tackles precisely this fast-spreading, world-scale indistinctiveness. Specifically, he worries that the non-West "out there" is becoming fast a Western "in here" in disguise, which he also acknowledges, is likely to affect us all no matter who and where we are because both social progress and the literary imagination depend on an "outside" or "beyond" external or posterior to our habits, customs, comfort zones, and inertias.[42] Differently put, endemic or highly private developments of certain places and individuals, from collective traditions to poetic innovation occurring within a culture or a poet's mind, presuppose the greater "outside" and the effectiveness with which this space works as a portal to other communal and personal "interiors." He embraces, then, the "outside," or what is left of it, while knowing full well that it is defined, made possible, and variously enabled—in ways both heartening and troubling—by other spaces, their insides, and insiders, real or so perceived. This is why he also insists that, much as he remains weary of unqualified enthusiasms for the "outer world," literature's job is to help us evade the multiple "interiors" we are part of without even noticing it and to safeguard those inner sanctums, cultural zones, and existential possibilities we may not be aware of because they lie beyond our horizons. Acquitting itself of this task, literature asserts, as Cheah observes, its "world-making power as a structure of address that announces a subject and a process that imparts meaning."[43] This process, this meaning-making, is in émigré and exile literature frequently thematized as space-making and carried out by individualizing protocols of worlding and wording in which the world and their representations clash and crash, break up, and comingle.

Notes

1　Neil Brenner, "The Space of the World: Beyond State-Centrism?" in *Immanuel Wallerstein and the Problem of the World: System, Scale, Culture*, ed. David Palumbo-Liu, Bruce Robbins, and Nirvana Tanoukhi (Durham, NC: Duke University Press, 2011), 109.

2　On the spatial turn and world literature, also see Andrei Terian's book *Critica de export. Teorii, contexte, ideologii* (Bucharest: Editura Muzeul Literaturii Române, 2013), 75–88.

3　Thomas Bender, "Historians, the Nation, and the Plenitude of Narratives," in *Rethinking American History in a Global Age*, ed. Thomas Bender (Berkeley, CA: University of California Press, 2002), 1–21; Wai Chee Dimock, "Scales of Aggregation: Prenational, Subnational, Transnational," *American Literary History* 18, no. 2 (Summer 2006): 219–228.

4　Pascale Casanova, *The World Republic of Letters*, trans. M. B. DeBevoise (Cambridge, MA: Harvard University Press, 2004), 172.

5　John Durham Peters, "Exile, Nomadism, and Diaspora: The Stakes of Mobility in the Western Canon," in *Visual Culture: Critical Concepts in Media and Cultural Studies*, ed. Joanne Morra and Marquard Smith (New York: Routledge, 2006), 141.

6　Michel Foucault, "Of Other Spaces," *Diacritics* 16, no. 1 (Spring 1986): 22.

7　Yi-Fu Tuan, *Space and Place: The Perspective of Experience* (Minneapolis, MN: University of Minnesota Press, 1977), 6.

8　David Harvey, *The Condition of Postmodernity: An Enquiry into the Origins of Cultural Change* (Oxford: Blackwell, 1990), 22.

9　Edward W. Soja, *Thirdspace: Journeys to Los Angeles and Other Real-and-Imagined Places* (Cambridge: Blackwell, 1996), 11.

10　Bertrand Westphal, *Geocriticism: Real and Fictional Spaces*, trans. Robert T. Tally Jr. (New York: Palgrave Macmillan, 2011), 73.

11　Gayatri Chakravorty Spivak, *Death of a Discipline* (New York: Columbia University Press, 2003), 73.

12　Emily Apter, *Against World Literature: On the Politics of Untranslatability* (New York: Verso, 2013), 3.

13　Christian Moraru, *Cosmodernism: American Narrative, Late Globalization, and the New Cultural Imaginary* (Ann Arbor, MI: University of Michigan Press, 2011), 66.

14　See, on this subject, Christian Moraru's book *Reading for the Planet: Toward a Geomethodology* (Ann Arbor, MI: University of Michigan Press, 2015).

15　Pheng Cheah, "World against Globe: Toward a Normative Conception of World Literature," *New Literary History* 45, no. 3 (Summer 2014): 323.

16　Cheah, "World against Globe," 326.

17　Wai Chee Dimock, "Planetary Time and Global Translation: 'Context' in Literary Studies," *Common Knowledge* 9, no. 3 (Fall 2003): 490.

18　My use of "defamiliarization" differs from Viktor Shklovsky's. In my essay, the term designates all forms of representing alternatives to geographical spaces close or familiar to characters. For Shklovsky's concept, see "Art as Technique," in *Russian Formalist Criticism: Four Essays*, ed. Lee T. Lemon and Marion J. Reiss (Lincoln, NE: University of Nebraska Press, 1965), 3–24.

19　Salman Rushdie, *Imaginary Homelands: Essays and Criticism 1981–1991* (London: Granta, 1991), 10.

20　Westphal, *Geocriticism*, 111–147.

21   The English-language scholarship on Norman Manea deals mostly with exile and identity. See, for instance, Mihai Mîndra, "Inescapable Colonization: Norman Manea's Eternal Exile," in *Literature in Exile of East and Central Europe*, ed. Agnieszka Gutthy (New York: Peter Lang, 2009), 193–210; Oana Elena Strugaru, "Choosing to Be a Stranger: Romanian Intellectuals in Exile," in *Negotiating Identities: Constructed Selves and Others*, ed. Helen Vella Bonavita (Amsterdam: Rodopi, 2011), 111–134; and Anamaria Falaus, *Imagining Home: Exilic Reconstructions in Norman Manea and Andrei Codrescu's Diasporic Narratives* (Tyne: Cambridge Scholars, 2014). On Manea's 2003 memoir, see Robert Boyers, *The Dictator's Dictation: The Politics of Novels and Novelists* (New York: Columbia University Press, 2005), 79–90; Matei Calinescu, "On Norman Manea's *The Hooligan's Return*," in *The Writer Uprooted: Contemporary Jewish Exile Literature*, ed. Alvin H. Rosenfeld (Bloomington, IN: Indiana University Press, 2008), 27–50; and Jeanine Teodorescu, "Norman Manea: 'I Am Not a Writer of the Holocaust,'" in *Local History, Transnational Memory in the Romanian Holocaust*, ed. Valentina Glajar and Jeanine Teodorescu (New York: MacMillan, 2011), 175–194. Two monographs on Manea's work should be mentioned here: Donato Cerbasi, *Norman Manea e la lingua romena* (Roma: Nova Cultura, 2014); Claudiu Turcuş, *Norman Manea: Aesthetics as East Ethics* (New York: Peter Lang, 2016).

22   Rachel Trousdale, *Nabokov, Rushdie, and the Transnational Imagination: Novels of Exile and Alternate Worlds* (New York: Palgrave Macmillan, 2010), 60.

23   Norbert Schürer, *Midnight's Children: A Reader's Guide* (New York: Continuum, 2004), 36.

24   Thomas Cooper, "Herta Müller: Between Myths of Belonging," in *The Exile and Return of Writers from East-Central Europe: A Compendium*, ed. John Neubauer and Borbála Zsuzsanna Török (New York: Walter de Gruyter, 2009), 474. Other discussions of Müller's cultural background include Valentina Glajar, *The German Legacy in East-Central Europe* (New York: Rochester, 2004), 115–160, and Doris Mironescu, "Uncomfortable Spaces: Language and Identity in Herta Müller's Work," *World Literature Studies* 7, no. 2 (2015): 60–70. For an analysis of trauma in Müller, see Lyn Marven, *Body and Narrative in Contemporary Literatures in German* (Oxford: Oxford University Press, 2005), 53–114. Wide-ranging essays on the political and poetical dimensions of Müller's writing can be found in Bettina Brandt and Valentina Glajar, eds., *Herta Müller: Politics and Aesthetics* (Lincoln, NE: University of Nebraska Press, 2013), and Brigid Haines and Lyn Marven, eds., *Herta Müller* (Oxford: Oxford University Press, 2013). Also, Pavlo Shopin works out a narrative analysis of *The Hunger Angel* in his article "Unpacking the Suitcases: Autofiction and Metaphor in Herta Müller's *Atemschaukel*," *Seminar: A Journal of Germanic Studies* 50, no. 2 (May 2014): 197–215.

25   Herta Müller, *The Hunger Angel*, trans. Philip Boehm (New York: Metropolitan Books, 2012), 157.

26   Müller, *The Hunger Angel*, 158.

27   Norman Manea, *The Hooligan's Return*, trans. Angela Jianu (New York: Farrar, Straus and Giroux, 2003), 319.

28   Dana Mihăilescu, "Being without Pleasurable Memories: On the Predicament of the Shoah Child's Survival in 'Proust's Tea' and Kindred Narratives," *American Imago* 70, no. 1 (2013): 117.

29   Norman Manea, "Proust's Tea," *Partisan Review* 56, no. 1 (1992): 84–85.

30   Wai Chee Dimock, "Literature for the Planet," *PMLA* 116, no. 1 (January 2001): 174.

31   Sonja Lehmann, "Transnational Identities in Michael Ondaatje's Fiction," in *Stranger, Migrant, Exiles: Negotiating Identity in Literature*, ed. Franke Reitemeier (Göttingen: Universitätsverlag Göttingen, 2012), 332. Allegorizing within the same physical and textual space both the real devastations of war and the traumatized self of the novel's protagonist, Ondaatje's damaged building image is a "chronotope," and in that it sets off, according to Mikhail M. Bakhtin, "a literary work's artistic unity in relationship with an actual reality." For this definition, see M.M. Bakhtin, *The Dialogic Imagination: Four Essays*, trans. Caryl Emerson and Michael Holquist (Austin, TX: University of Texas Press, 1981), 243.

32   W.G. Sebald, *Austerlitz*, trans. Anthea Bell (New York: Random House, 2011), 406.

33   Manea, *The Hooligan's Return*, 65.

34   Manea, *The Hooligan's Return*, 66.

35   For interpretations of Codrescu's "return from exile" narrative, see Noemi Marin, *After the Fall: Rhetoric in the Aftermath of Dissent in Post-Communist Times* (New York: Peter Lang, 2007), 73–107; Bogdan Ştefănescu, "Voices of the Void: Andrei Codrescu's Tropical Rediscovery of Romanian Culture in *The Hole in the Flag*," *University of Bucharest Review* X, no. 2 (2008): 11–21; Ioana Luca, "Between Two Worlds: Andrei Codrescu's *The Hole in the Flag*," in *Autobiography and Mediation*, ed. Alfred Hornung (Heidelberg: Winter, 2010), 271–286. For discussions of exile, memory, and language in Codrescu, see Noemi Marin, "The Rhetoric of Andrei Codrescu: A Reading in Exilic Fragmentation," in *Realms of Exile: Nomadism, Diasporas, and Eastern European Voices*, ed. Domnica Radulescu (Lanham, KY: Lexington Books, 2002), 87–103. Notable monographs on Codrescu's work include Kirby Olson's *Andrei Codrescu and the Myth of America* (Jefferson, NC: McFarland, 2005); Oana Strugaru, *Exilul ca mod de existenţă: Andrei Codrescu în spaţiul textual al dezrădăcinării* (Bucharest: Editura Muzeul Literaturii Române, 2013).

36   Andrei Codrescu, *The Hole in the Flag: A Romanian Exile's Story of Return and Revolution* (New York: W. Morrow & Co., 1991), 67.

37   Müller, *The Hunger Angel*, 9.

38   Müller, *The Hunger Angel*, 28.

39   John Durham Peters, "Exile, Nomadism, and Diaspora: The Stakes of Mobility in the Western Canon," in *Visual Culture: Critical Concepts in Media and Cultural Studies*, ed. Joanne Morra and Marquard Smith (New York: Routledge, 2006), 143.

40   Andrei Codrescu, *Selected Poetry/Poezii alese*, trans. Ioana Ieronim (Piteşti: Paralela 45, 2000), 316.

41   Codrescu, *Selected Poetry*, 320–322.

42   Codrescu, *The Disappearance of the Outside: A Manifesto for Escape* (Lebanon, IN: Addison-Wesley, 1990), 199.

43   Cheah, "World against Globe," 325–326.

15

Made in Translation: A National Poetics for the Transnational World

Mihaela Ursa

The geopolitical imaginary undergirding the theory, practice, and reception of translation in Romania and its neighbors has registered a major change in the post–Cold War era. Until 1990, translating into Romanian as well as into other Central and East European languages had been, with some notable exceptions, part and parcel of the national project. Guided by concerns and discourses of nationhood and national identity as they had been since the mid-nineteenth century, modern translational cultures arising in the region essentially enacted a dualistic, self–other and here–there dynamic whose actors and places were often seen as neatly and sometimes rigidly separated spatially, culturally, and otherwise. As I contend in my essay, this antinomianism has subsided since the Cold War. More to the point, after the early 1990s flare-up of nationalist conflicts, the national project fell by the wayside as the authoritarian regimes sponsoring it collapsed and, consequently, translation initiatives and policies were shaped, in and around Romania, less and less by the nation-state and increasingly by book markets, major publishers, and their transnational extensions and partners. Accordingly, the translation industry's focus has shifted over the last three decades or so away from particular and discrete national identities and their officially sponsored reinforcement to the planetary spectacle of ever-more interconnected places, communities, and literatures. In Romania, I further propose, the previously monolithic, nation-state oriented, often nationalist translation program has yielded to a range of uncoordinated "microprograms" in which the translational, alongside other domains, discourses, and practices of *national* culture, characteristically does the bidding of the *trans*national. Largely paralleled by the treatment renditions of Romanian authors into foreign languages receive in the world arena, this situation goes to show that, as I also suggest in conversation with a number of critics, translations literally do make a literature, whether this making plays into how this literature comes about domestically, in the national context of its formation and reception, or into what it means among other literatures of the ever-morphing literary world-system.

1. "A Mirror of World Literature"

As is well known, translation and collective identity have been intimately bound up with one another in the post-Romantic era. The assumption has been that when one translates from a foreign literature one does so from a corpus that encapsulates certain defining values of a group, and that, conversely, one translates into and adds to the body of work already existing in a language of a literary culture thought to couch some characteristics of a community, usually one understood ethnically or nationally. In modern translational traditions such as Romania's, said characteristics fall into two categories. One is more emphatically ethnographic when the object of translation belongs to presumably "minor" or Central-East European cultures, and when the original, once rendered into Romanian, satisfies a sort of anthropological curiosity and desire to discover "the other," "the neighbor." In this case, the Romanian public is offered an opportunity to take notice of "typical" forms of nationhood or of "national specificity" and compare them to its own. The other class of features are or, more likely, are thought to be less anthropological, that is, less idiomatic, less geoculturally circumscribed or historically constructed. Such traits are considered to describe "major" literatures, those who enjoy a wide, sometimes planetary circulation. On this assumption, French, German, or English works' Romanian versions have been billed ordinarily not as windows into local customs and ethnoculturally "specific" rites but as Romanian-language reincarnations of "universal" cultural models and, relatedly, as elements of an exclusive world canon. For more than 200 years, these items have been presented to the national audience as pinnacles of literary craftsmanship, and, indeed, a so-called theory of peaks guided Romanian translation efforts and policies since the 1930s until the 1990s. Implying and at times explicitly laying out the structure of a world literary canon in a sense similar to Harold Bloom's 1995 *The Western Canon: The Books and School of the Ages*, the theory and the translation programs undergirded by it urged translators to privilege the "most important" works of the literatures to which above I referred to as "major." It was Romanian comparatist Adrian Marino (1921–2005) who, in developing his "comparative poetics" project, offered that, when introducing a "major," world literature to a national literature, one should focus on the aesthetic "peaks" of the former.[1] Marino went on to argue that, after identifying those acmes of aesthetic accomplishment, the comparatist should be able to extrapolate from them so as to draw conclusions about the entire tradition of that foreign literature. If a neighboring or similarly "marginal," peer literature presents interest and is translated into Romanian because it is "different," a literature whose enviable topography features world summits is worth translating insofar as it embodies "universal" standards of achievement—in short, because it is *superior*, and because its central presence on the world map of values charts a progress Romanian authors still have to make, that is, a process of taking in and working over the influence, the stylistic-thematic majesty of the "peak." Remarkably enough, if a comparative poetics is possible among peers situated at indeed "comparable" altitudes, the influence-influenced model leaves little room for it. Or, to put it another way, comparison *can* take place, but it does so along a vertical axis with most literatures looking up to the peaks and aspiring to meet some day their standards of "universality." This hierarchy can be and has been projected horizontally, in which case axiology translates into geography, with a system of cultures distributed into centers of symbolic capital such as Paris and peripheries like Buenos Aires and Bucharest. This is, of course, what Pascale Casanova's Gallocentric world republic of letters looks like. What interests me here, however, is that, when translation comes into play, the critic acknowledges a dynamic somewhat different from this centripetal hegemony, making allowances for a revitalization of France's literature through French versions of works coming from "marginal" or "minor" cultures like Romania. As Romanian postcolonial critic Bogdan Ștefănescu has observed, in this translation-driven process, reallocations of cultural capital and prestige obtain that pressure "European literature [to] find a new distribution for its old asymmetrical coherence."[2]

Whether or not peripheral status—real or so deemed—has indeed turned into an advantage under late globalization, and whether or not this change has occurred under the aegis of translation, geocultural marginality hardly gave one an edge in the age of nations. Likewise, as Casanova suggests, if valleys and peripheries have also become object of translations in peak locations over the past half-century or so, translation traffics were going almost exclusively in the other direction before that, feeding all along into the broader undertaking of national formation. In countries like Romania, the development of a translational corpus was part and parcel of nation building. In that, translation's cultural-political work was no different from the work done by other genres, fictional and nonfictional, or from how literary history and other humanist disciplines functioned throughout modernity, as Alex Goldiș and other critics insistently point out in *Romanian Literature as World Literature*. Reiterating this reality in a recent essay on translation and national literatures,[3] David Damrosch acknowledges that, although imported works have rarely been *considered* a core, original part of a national literature, their renditions into that literature's idiom have, in reality, always played a crucial role within the respective tradition, where their presence, impact, and overall behavior in the nation's cultural system have been almost "indistinguishable from that of home-grown works."[4] Otherwise put, while some Romanian cultural ideologues and politicians may have been publicly apprehensive of the influence of outside literatures—and of "influences" and "outside" broadly—on "national specificity" and the nation generally, translations did get through this nationalist resistance, were quite abundant, and, not at all paradoxically, were mostly geared to the fostering of the very nation whose building translation-weary critics feared Romanian versions of foreign writers might jeopardize. A clear understanding of the intertwining of the national and translational dates back to at least 1894, when Romanian critic Constantin Dobrogeanu-Gherea (1855–1920) recommended translation as a tool of cultural advancement, and a translated poem's impact, he thought, was comparable to that of poetry written in the national idiom. To him, both were creative acts. "Translating," he actually believed, "is creating."[5] For this reason, he added, "the translator must be an artist."[6] Moreover, a lack of translations from other literatures, Dobrogeanu-Gherea contended, hurts "our intellectual development."[7] "A *well-translated* literary work," he argued, "becomes part of the literature of our country, influencing it, if not to the same degree, at least in the same direction as an artistic work written in the language of our country."[8]

Dobrogeanu-Gherea and others like him already had a sense of the copresence of the nation and the world via renditions into Romanian of the likes of Jean Racine and William Shakespeare. While not changing automatically the "minor" status of a nation, translation may and does participate in the making of the nation; the translational can be, and has been, a bulwark and a definitional vector of the nation, affording the latter not only an ontological modality—"being-in-translation"—but also a different, less hierarchical engagement with the world and its major cultural players. As American critic and translator Sean Cotter posits, a minor nation "designates a lack of political agency and cultural significance, when compared to a major nation. A minor nation thus shares the same categories of definition as the major nation and participates in the same fantasies of power and significance; it simply fails where the major succeeds .... The minor is not a failed state or a potentially great one, but a translated nation."[9]

Nor does a "translated nation" imply subordination and derivation, even though, for a while, translations were suspected to bring about a second-order literary culture and more largely influences prone to stifling local originality. Beginning with the second half of the nineteenth century, influence actually takes center stage in translation and other cultural debates, whether as a positive and encouraged phenomenon or, again, as something threatening the bourgeoning culture and its nation. Thus, a leading critic, ideologue, and politician of the Romantic era, Mihail Kogălniceanu (1817–1891), famously declared that "translations do not make a literature" and "longing for imitation" is "a dangerous mania, for it kills the national spirit in us."[10] The more cosmopolite Ion Heliade Rădulescu (1802–1872) gets off the ground, around the same time, a genuine translation program and is personally behind a real translation boom. The two authors have been seen as ideological adversaries as far as the place of translation in the greater national scheme goes, but their main objective is the same, namely, the modernization—that is, Europenization—of Romanian literature, culture, and society, and with it an "accelerat[ion of] the integration process of the Romanian nation in the sphere of ideas, aspirations, and interests of modern civilization."[11] Translation- and influence-skeptics such as pro-German conservative critic Titu Maiorescu (1840–1917) took up sometimes more radical stances, as he did in 1868, when he spoke peremptorily against the "direction" in which Romanian culture had been going as a result of the Romantics' enthusiastically imitative turn to Europe, its institutions, and writers. Maiorescu's influential argument would get one of its most significant pushbacks from modernist critic Eugen Lovinescu (1881–1943), for whom imitation—and by the same token translation as an original's "imitation" in another language—is not the whole story culturally speaking, allowing, after French sociologist Gabriel Tarde, for a quantum leap of sorts from "simulation" and its ensuing "contentless" forms to "stimulation," cognate creativity, and the creation of the nation complete with its "national identity" in the bargain. As other critics also comment in this book, according to Lovinescu, translations, adaptations, borrowings, and the like ultimately gave Romanian literature a chance not only to make itself but also to make itself coeval with other literatures inside the cultural Eurosystem and even to make itself distinct from them—to operate, that is, not only as a tool of identity formation but also as instrument of identity differentiation.[12]

Largely advancing on the trail blazed by Lovinescu, twentieth-century translation and cultural theory cast aside the imitation (derivation)-originality (creativity) antinomy and, with it, the theoretical–ideological prevalence of the influence model. Instead, translation began to be viewed as a productive act in and of itself, connected to the original work but reinventing or, better yet, making it over and for a different ethnolinguistic environment. In this vein, translation was seen as a particular, transformative form of adaptation, or, to reiterate Lawrence Venuti's term, as "domestication." In his analysis of the "victimology of translation,"[13] Venuti observes that translations set in train various domesticating protocols to "engage readers in domestic terms that have been defamiliarized to some extent, made fascinating by a revisionary encounter with a foreign text."[14] The critic also writes that, on one side, "fluency is assimilationist,"[15] and, on the other side, "good translation is minoritizing."[16] Triggering both processes, authentic, creative translation "open[s] up the standard dialect and literary canons to what is foreign to themselves" by deploying new idioms to produce renditions that make the alien domestic, accessible to local audiences, and the familiar national language "foreign" and by the same token ready to carry a national literature. The apparent paradox was largely shared by Romanian poet, philosopher, and translator Lucian Blaga (1895–1961), who placed translation "halfway between the interpretive arts and the creative ones."[17] Thus, Blaga urged a recreation through a translation art that would resort to "local or regional words" sparingly[18] so as to ensure national literature's chances of becoming a reflection of the universal or, in his own words, "a mirror of world literature."[19]

2. The World at Home, at Home in the World

As Romanian critic Paul Cornea has insisted, at the turn of the twentieth century "national interest" provided, for the first time in the country's history, a major "criterion" fully and self-consciously employed to assess initiatives and developments in the public arena.[20] Rather than judged aesthetically, translations were measured with this political or, more exactly, nationalist yardstick. But, with another paradox that is not one, the more actively involved the translational was in the production of the national, and the more the nation—still in the spirit of Lovinescu's prompts—was "catching up" with Western Europe, the more Romanian translators were making the world, its histories, cultural forms, and traditions a home and at home inside Romanian literature, and, with that, the more that literature started looking, being, and feeling of the world. This shift was slow in coming, however, and for almost the entire rest of the century the "translational" national interest largely prevailed. This does not mean that either the "world literature" concept or, more specifically yet, world literature as a counterweight to national literature and nationalism was unknown. Quite the contrary. As elsewhere in Europe, *Weltliteratur* had already made an impact at Romanian universities. However, it had been understood and taught not as such, namely, as World Literature as we know it today, but "translated," filtered through the Sorbonne as *literatură universală* (*littérature universelle*), to wit, as "universal literature" complete with its geosymbolic peaks and valley and therefore marked by nationalist pecking orders and imperial prerogatives barely coated in "universalist" claims. For the entire duration of modernity in Romania and elsewhere, this contradiction, or at least tension, had been in play with various degrees of obviousness, as the discipline of universal literature, in building on the Goethean pronouncements, has been hewing, if not always in so many words, to a nationalist agenda Goethe himself had seen fit to scrap as early as in 1827, when he had told his secretary Johann Peter Eckermann that "national literature no longer makes much sense: the time has come now for world literature."[21] Much less quoted is another declaration by Goethe, who talked to Eckermann about his pleasure of reading *Faust* in French, where it sounded "again fresh, new, and spirited."[22] Full benefits, thought Goethe, are, then, enjoyed not only by the author of the translated text but also by the artist at the translation's end, in whom the original sets off creative protocols, whereas, even though the reader stands to profit perhaps most substantially from the translation process, he or she is expected to stay connected to the energizing power grid of the national language.[23]

By the time Romanian philosopher Constantin Noica (1909–1987) wrote his "anti-Goethe" book, which was published in 1964 as *Despărțirea de Goethe* (Parting Company with Goethe), and where, in "disagreeing" with the German thinker, Noica toyed with the grand idea of Romania as "Europe's translator," things had taken a turn for the worse in the country. In the 1950s, when Noica was completing his Goethe manuscript under house arrest, Social Realism was in full swing in Romania. Because Mircea Martin dwells at length on the phenomenon in his essay featured in this collection, worth reiterating here is only that, during that time, "the literal practice of translation was essential to the metaphorical translation of the country into Soviet control during the beginnings of Communist Party control of Romania," with both kinds of translation keyed to a wholesale, imperialist "self-alienation" or "estrangement" of Romania from itself.[24] Taking stock of this situation, Cotter also points to "a massive project of translation, both technical and literary ... coupled ... with a politics of language and an ideology of reading, all of which was meant to bring the new Romania into line with the Soviet Union." "The translation project," the critic concludes, "was the cultural counterpart of power consolidation and national modernization, a golden age meant to usher in the luminous dawn of communism."[25] This explains why, against the ideological odds on which Martin focuses in such painstaking detail, the 1961–1970 interval witnessed real progress in both the range and quality of translations into Romanian. Great care began to be given to the literary criticism forming around these translations, which appeared with prefatory texts, authors' biographical sketches, glosses, comments, and an entire philological apparatus. Prominent in this epoch became the notion that translations are first and foremost a major act and duty of culture, and fulfilling such obligation with panache was, more than any other press, Univers Publishing House, which, between 1961 and 1980 alone, managed to put out 2007 Romanian translations of foreign titles.

In 1971, however, after a "liberalization" that had lasted about half a decade, things began to deteriorate. Recently returned from North Korea, where he had been quite taken with the country's Maoist cultural revolution and extravagant personality cult,

Communist ruler Nicolae Ceaușescu issued the infamous "July Theses," which steered official cultural policies in neo-Stalinist directions.[26] Past this point, translations became politicized or, better yet, repoliticized in new forms, but writers and translators also began to resist in new ways the rising pressures of Ceaușescu's bizarre Socialist-Nationalism. Opposition to translation censors and their *Index of Banned Books* grew among publishers such as Univers or Meridiane, where Soviet translations were issued alongside modern or contemporary writers and thinkers of "the free world," as it did through translations of banned contemporary Romanian poets such as Ana Blandiana and Ștefan Augustin Doinaș. Much like Romanian writers in general, the translators, editors, and critics associated with venues where translations appeared and were commented on developed a whole range of tactics designed to disguise what they were doing or what the meaning of what they were doing was and otherwise to deflect the pressures of the surveillance, propaganda, and censorship apparatus. Moreover, new and highly successful series were set up at publishing houses, with "theory" as one of the fields that was deeply shaped by the flurry of translations. Univers once again led the way with a new and highly reputable series such as "Studii" (Studies) and "Eseuri" (Essays), in which Romanian authors such as Romul Munteanu, Radu Toma, Mihai Gramatopol, Nina Ivanciu, and Christian Moraru appeared alongside translations from foreign theorists from the Russian Formalists to the French poststructuralists and from Northrop Frye and René Wellek to Paul Ricoeur, Jean Starobinski, and Hans Robert Jauss. I might also note that the infusion of such Western authorities was absolutely massive and came at a time when a large and influential segment of Romanian criticism, sold as it was on the virtues of close reading and "aesthetic taste," was still ambivalent about theory. Let us also recall too that, at a time Wellek was banned in his own country of origin despite Czechoslovakia's more "liberal" brand of Socialism, his monumental multivolume *History of Modern Criticism: 1750–1950* was, among other works by him, available in Romanian and thus, in this form at least, to scholars of all Central-Eastern Europe.

Some of the most voracious readers of the Univers series would come along in the 1980s. They would be the poets, prose authors, critics, and theorists who would get their name as a group from the decade, the last one of Romanian Communism: the "1980s Generation." They were the Romanian postmoderns for whom, as Teodora Dumitru shows in her essay in this book, other national literatures proved paramount. The leader of this generation is Mircea Cărtărescu, poet, fiction writer, and essayist who has often acknowledged being influenced more by the American novel than by Romanian prose. It is quite tenable, actually, that William Faulkner, Gabriel García Márquez, Thomas Pynchon, and John Salinger are more present in the literature of the 1980s than earlier Romanian authors. But, as mentioned above, Cărtărescu and his friends were well read not only in the great canon of American poetry and fiction but also in criticism and theory, and this background shows in their works, in which the theoretical, philosophical, intertextual, metalinguistic, and self-reflective elements characteristically abound. Coming on the heels of this largely translational, cultural-theoretical oversaturation of the 1980s writers' poems, short stories, and criticism is thus an entire mutation that took place around this time in contemporary Romanian literature. This major turn had been impossible before, in a sociocultural context more emphatically dominated by issues, priorities, entries, and related items from the national "dictionary." With Cărtărescu's Generation, a whole frame of reference changed, paving the way to a Romanian literature better attuned to the world, more intimately inscribed into its literary and cultural scripts, and overall more firmly positioned at its noisy intersections. To be sure, with the Romanian writers of the 1980s, "comparison without interaction," as Goldiș calls one of the cultural dialogue models he analyzes in his essay from *Romanian Literature as World Literature*, is the opposite of what went on in the translation-driven poetics of the young 1980s writers.

Highly monitored and planned, officially vetted and controlled throughout their production and distribution circuitries as they were, pre-1990s translations, along with other cultural forms and entire disciplines, were roughly following the lead of politics, which, in Romania, had been, with the exception of the two decades after the Second World War, one of a marked national and even nationalist bent. With the new series of authors of the 1980s, the world's cultural interchanges, terminals, and high-traffic spots are the cool places to be. Was the decade a harbinger of things to come? To some, it may appear so because anything seems to be going in post–Cold War Romania. Indeed, it only appears so, because the patient critic is bound to notice sooner or later an important shift, one away from the national and to the transnational. The worn-out pun is probably one last time serviceable: the translational all but becomes the transnational—or, at any rate, becomes one of its cultural-linguistic operators and, as such, a barometer of world markets and an index of the integration of the domestic and the international. This momentous change occurs under auspicious geopolitical circumstances right after the so-called Romanian Revolution of December 1989, when West Europeans and the West generally start paying special attention to Romania as well as to other recently freed Communist countries, and this suddenly aroused curiosity literally translates into an increased number of Romanian works made available in many other languages. On the Romanian side, which is the one that interests me most here, things do not quite take off with any sense of decision or direction amid the sociopolitical confusion and economic chaos of the years immediately after the big upheaval, and the engine of the new translation industry sputters along, one step forward and two steps back. Accordingly, translation policies—transnational or not— are not reviewed and redrawn until after the dawn of the third millennium. At the same time, in Romania and elsewhere in the former East, an unprecedented translational frenzy is underway. Foreign contemporary authors are translated into Romanian, sometimes from languages other than that of the original and almost simultaneously with its publication, which does not prevent the writers, many of them celebrities, to show up at Romanian international literary fairs. Unlike in previous years, local translators risk deeper forays into "minor" and "marginal" cultures such as Hungarian, Czech, Bulgarian, Swedish, and Norwegian.

The "state of the art" in translation studies, on the other hand, tells another story. The field has remained something of an oddity in Romanian scholarship, and yet, as in other pockets of the mixed-bag situation characterizing said industry, one comes across notable exceptions as well. They include a few chapters by a literary theorists like

Cornea,[27] a few volumes of notes on World Literature such as Traian Herseni's *Sociologia literaturii*,[28] Gelu Ionescu's earlier book on the subject, *Orizontul traducerii*,[29] and the more recent *Totul trebuie tradus: Noua paradigmă (un manifest)* by Bogdan Ghiu.[30] Also, one can find a quite large but unsystematically organized body of comments on translation theory and practice in the more important Romanian academic journals whose foci are comparative literature and literary theory, especially in *Secolul 20*, which has set aside repeatedly whole issues for questions of translation and has published a large amount of excellent translations from modern and contemporary literatures alongside competent and comprehensive critical commentaries. Also, the Sextil Pușcariu Institute of the Romanian Academy brought out in 2005 *Dicționar cronologic al romanului tradus în România* (Chronological Dictionary of Novels Translated in Romania), which makes for a "big data" gold mine.[31] Lacking an adequately theorized interpretation of its rich information as it does, this reference instrument speaks, nonetheless, to broader and older problems in the field. Before 1989, prefaces, introductions, afterwords, and other criticism accompanying works translated into Romanian usually served descriptive-analytic rather than theoretical purposes as critics and translators were spending time mostly talking about translated texts rather than about translation theory and methodology. In his book, Ionescu deplores the situation, and he also speaks against national literature "protectionism." In a vein similar to the writers of the 1980s, he finds a French writer like André Gide more important to the history of the Romanian novel than local prose authors such as Duiliu Zamfirescu, in an equation where the towering giant of modernist fiction is visible from afar and spares us the trouble of getting into the down and dirty of effective comparatism.[32] In Ionescu, world literature is still a universalist paradigm and presupposes a one-directional, culturally and geopolitically predetermined stream of influences, summit to bottom and center to margin, and one should be mindful that opening up the national theoretically and methodologically so as to rethink national literature around its "genetic" outside falls short of its task if this operation does not go both ways and any number of ways, itineraries, and circuits for that matter. If, as Franco Moretti contends, "there is no other justification for the study of world literature (and for the existence of departments of comparative literature) but this: to be a thorn in the side, a permanent intellectual challenge to national literatures—especially … local literature," and so, as he claims, "if comparative literature is not this, it's nothing," then all literatures must feel this fruitful discomfort within a truly World Literature framework.[33]

3. Thorny Issues: Big Data as History and Map

The post–Cold war situation is thorny in a way most Romanian translators, publishers, and critics find too close for comfort, intellectually and otherwise. The transnational makeover of the translational has taken place, but problems and ambiguities, old and new, remain. To tackle them *en masse* would be a daunting job here, but a quick look at some available "big data" might help uncover a few of the meaningful patterns and trends shaping this planetary moment in the long history of Romanian translations.

Bibliografia generală a studiilor critice despre arta traducerii (General Bibliography of Critical Studies on the Art of Translation) would be a good place to start given this instrument's content.[34] The book lists a series of essays on "the art of translation," that is, on both translations and translation theory. The articles appeared in Romanian periodicals from 1838 to 1995. It seems—and this is somewhat significant—that Romanians were busiest writing on these issues during the Second World War, between 1940 and 1944, when they published an average of ten such pieces a year (sixteen in 1944), then between 1967 and 1970, the brief "liberalization" interval prior to the "July Theses," with an average of eleven texts each year, and between 1978 and 1985, when, with the exception of 1981, fifteen articles on the subject came out yearly. For the same period, lows are registered between 1945 and 1960, with a feeble increase of two articles per year after 1955, but no translation scholarship whatsoever appeared between 1948 and 1954. Oddly enough, after 1989, when translation really takes off, data becomes, like other elements and resources of the society, unavailable, unsystematically gathered, unreported, or decentered logistically, building up in new places. In any event, only one or two articles on translation are listed for each year since the fall of Communism. Now, if one correlates all this information to the corresponding social and cultural contexts, it becomes clear why translation into Romanian had been less debated than simply done before 1940. The war brought about radical and brutal change through which the world seemed to rush in, and such transitional and tempestuous ages usually witness, as one might expect, a surge in translations into one's own idiom, which activity slows down once national culture has resettled. As for the theoretical aspect of Romanian translational culture, things look, again, different. Basic as it may sound, a true theoretical debate and sometimes a debate pure and simple require a modicum of freedom of expression and critical thinking. These had certainly existed before 1945, and they had been applied to the problematics of cultural exchange, literary and fashion "imports," and the like, as we have seen. But framing the whole conversation on the subject had been, as I have also noted, priorities clustered around the national narrative, with national ideology as a kind of default theory that could easily dispense with additional and comparatively "academic" theoretical concerns. During the years of aggressive Socialist propaganda, translation itself—namely, the business of translating into Romanian the kind of texts Martin refers to in his essay—was in good shape financially insofar as it fulfilled its "educational" role. Precisely for the same ideological and "instructive" reason, looking into what translational work and theory meant from a broader, cultural-philosophical perspective was not encouraged. The same is true again for the immediate aftermath of Ceaușescu's 1971 guidelines, which dearth of material is made up for by the post-1978 comeback of relevant scholarship. This goes to show that translational activity in Romania, steadily substantial ever since its early medieval beginnings and impactful culture- and nation-wise, does not necessarily come with a theoretical or "metatranslational" package, and that, when one takes into account the Second World War years, the most auspicious periods for translation studies appear to be those enjoying a certain ideological—rather than purely political—relaxation and a measure of freedom of speech and research, which, by contrast to the previous decades, made themselves felt in the 1980s.

If the data of *Bibliografia generală* is organized and becomes meaningful along a temporal axis, and so what a translation scholar might be able to put together by mining the volume is something like a *history*, then the *Index Translationum*, UNESCO's database of book translations, might help one draw a *map*—a map, one map possible of Romanian literature as world literature.[35] Similar to the succinct translational historiography attempted above, the cartography I am sketching out below pursues the transnational metamorphosis of the translational. To that effect, I will also have to factor in, this time around, renditions of Romanian writers into the world's languages. The *Index* was established in 1932, and since 1979, the records have been computerized and are updated regularly with tallies of translations of individual books from countries that are members of the United Nations. While digging into this resource does have its shortcomings, sifting through the data and rankings available for the 1979–2014 interval would be worth the mapmaker's while. In line with most upshots of the transnational turn in Romania's translational culture, the map is another mixed bag—a mixed map, really. For starters, no Romanian author makes it in the top fifty of most translated authors, although Romania is ranked twenty-seventh among countries with most translated works, after Hungary (thirteenth), the Czech Republic (eleventh), and Bulgaria (twenty-fourth), but before Croatia (twenty-ninth), Slovenia (thirty-second), and the Slovak Republic (thirty-third). Similarly, Romanian ranks twenty-fifth among the original languages of translated literature worldwide, after Hungarian (nineteenth), Serbian (twenty-fourth), Czech (thirteenth), and Polish (fourteenth), but before Estonian (twenty-sixth), Bulgarian (thirty-second), Croatian (thirty-third), and Slovenian (thirty-eighth). As for the number of translations into a certain target language, the same rankings include Romanian in twenty-third place, before Croatian (twenty-fourth), Slovak (twenty-fifth), and Slovenian (twenty-sixth), but after Czech (eleventh), Hungarian (fifteenth), Bulgarian (twentieth), and Serbian (twenty-first).

A most interesting and at the same time most baffling piece of statistics, a combined ranking, in fact, is buried partly in the top ten most translated authors in Romania, with the rest of it—and of the resulting map—hidden in a symmetrical dataset, the top ten most translated authors from Romanian into other languages. The first place in both rankings is held by Ceaușescu, the former dictator, who was executed in 1989. The obvious explanation is that, after the early 1970s, Ceaușescu's personal cult was orchestrated by the Communist Party so as to emulate Mao Zedong's glory, and so, just as Mao's works come in second after the *Holy Bible* in various rankings, Ceaușescu tops most translated books in the world because his propaganda apparatus took great care in hawking them inside and outside the country. In the top ten most translated authors in Romania, Ceaușescu is oddly followed by Jules Verne and Alexandre Dumas, and, with the exception of the tenth place, which went to Shakespeare, the rest of the list is either adventure fiction (Karl May, Mark Twain) or romance (Sandra Brown, who was extensively translated in the early 1990s). As for other rankings where Ceaușescu came on top, he is followed by Mircea Eliade and Mihai Eminescu in second and third place, respectively, with Mircea Cărtărescu and Emil Cioran barely making the ninth and tenth. The oddity of these lists makes perfect sense once we understand that, for the deeply fractured historical period between 1979 and 2014, obsessively coordinated propaganda and, more broadly, planned-economy publishing during Communist times are, in terms of promotional focus, no match to the multitude of possibilities, choices, and avenues the post-1990 translation industry can pursue in a market economy environment in which fluctuating but otherwise dependable mass interest in translations of popular genres compounds a situation already hard to figure out.

On the list of top countries that have published translated Romanian literature, now, France has 290 titles, pre-1991 USSR 234, Germany 219, Hungary 164, the United States 157, and the United Kingdom 118, while the languages most translated into Romanian are, according to the same statistics for 1979–2014, English (9,243 titles), French (4,601), German (1,681), Russian (964), Italian (766), and Spanish (529). Yet, one more time, it would have been helpful to know, too, how translation interests and trends shift, who is in, and who is out, and in and out of where, as well as who gets translated, and who does not, and generally how things evolve not only across political borders but also when they get past temporal milestones such as the all-important collapse of Communism. That is to say, it would have been nice if we could use the map to orient ourselves in the translational territory historically. We can, however, turn to another big data trove of translations into Romanian and discover that, from 23,800 in 1990, European literature translations show a 60 percent increase by 2005. Not unexpectedly, the English language is in the lead. In fact, almost 50 percent of all translations into Romanian after 1990 are from English, a situation comparable to that of the neighboring countries, among which Hungary is at almost 65 percent.[36] There is a drop in translational activity in the early 1990s, but soon, in the mid-1990s, it goes back up spectacularly, a change of course that has a sheer quantitative, indiscriminate dimension to it and is part of the abovementioned "anything goes" translational agenda at a time practically anything gets rendered into Romanian. Erotica and crime, fiction and nonfiction, as well as cheap editions of humanity's "great books" saturate the Romanian market. Also, the country has the highest share of French-language translations (almost 23 percent) of all Central and Eastern Europe, compared to Hungary, which has less than 8 percent, the Czech Republic, which cannot boast more than 6 percent, and Bulgaria with slightly over 10 percent. This is because French culture still exerts its historically strong and wide influence in Romania, because French is still largely spoken and read by many Romanian readers, because France is still viewing Romania as a Francophone country worth investing in culturally, and also because free access to the French works of Cioran or Eugène Ionesco is whetting Romanians' appetite for France's culture and literature. The market branding coming on the heels of the "postcommunist" vogue proves lucrative translation-wise in the early 1990s too, contributing to an upsurge in Romanian translations from the literatures of the former Eastern Bloc. But, in Romania and elsewhere in the world, they go out of fashion once the event gets smaller and smaller in history's rearview mirror. In places like the United States, the event's exotic cache wears out fast. As the authors of the PEN report *To Be Translated or Not To Be* point out, most East European books translated in the United States—and included, I might add, in the meager 3 percent of the country's book industry—"speak of the victims of communism, censorship and repression, and the economic slump in Eastern Europe that followed the Soviet withdrawal."[37] Andrej Blatnik, the Slovenian PEN Center Secretary, quips that the dominant feeling among American publishers is now that "there's no point in importing love stories or other frivolous fare from far-off lands no matter how well they are written because we've got plenty of that stuff here."[38]

No such restrictions hold sway in Romania, whose post-1990 book market forces us to visualize a map—of cultures, authors, and genres—totally different from the one suggested to so many commentators by the infamous 3 percent. The yearly number of new translated titles skyrockets during this time from 2,200 in 1990 to 10,000 in 2000, with little slumps in 1994 and between 1997 and 1998. Initially, fiction and poetry make up about 30 percent of all new titles. About 11–18 percent of the entire amount of new titles coming out during the last decade of the twentieth century are translations.[39] Since 1990, the total number of translations has increased 7.5 times, another indicator of the strict and largely self-defeating translational policies in place before 1990 and of the dramatic, cultural as well as political change that occurred at that point. The amount of translated fiction and poetry shrinks sharply from 80 to 50 percent by 2005, however, and this *is* a trend with respect to which Romanian and world charts seem to agree. Generally, fiction makes for the bulk (40–50 percent) of translated books for the 1998–2005 period. As for literary translations, they peak in 1995, when they constitute 66.6 percent of all translations, before starting sinking steadily after 1998. Furthermore, when we add in the number of translations per capita in Romania between 1990 and 2005, we learn, with J. Heilbron, that

> English is the most commonly translated source language (1.00), followed by French (0.48) and German (0.15). Compared to European translation practices, these numbers somewhat fell behind the continental average, the high amount of translated French titles notwithstanding. Romania's GDP per capita can be compared to that of Turkey, Russia, Bulgaria, and Serbia .... In that circle, the share of translated French literary originals only exceeded that of Bulgaria, even though Romanian is a Latin language, with over 30% of its words coming from Italian or French. Regarding literature translations in the region ..., the number of translated English titles can be described as lower than average; it was only higher than in Slovenia and Slovakia. In terms of French translations, on the other hand, Romania's numbers are outstanding, as the number of translated French originals was higher only in Poland.[40]

One must, one more time, factor the operating constraints, formats, and gathering protocols into such data. It does matter, I think, that the information is coming from the national libraries of countries that are UNESCO members, for this appears to suggest that coverage is neither exhaustive nor entirely systematic. More significant yet is the Venutian "scandal of translation," the hierarchy or translational order one can discern on our map, with "dominant," translated cultures in central locations still directing literary flows out of Casanova's capitals toward eagerly importing, "dominated" peripheral cultures, whose translating endeavors, in turn, tend to skip these countries' neighbors and gravitate toward American, British, overall Anglophone, and other "well-capitalized" hubs of fame and authority.[41]

4. Do You Speak Translatese?

If not all hope is lost, that may also be because, in a way, as critics from Damrosch to Rebecca L. Walkowitz variously reassure us, everything has already been lost—already lost *and* found, already made, unmade, and remade in translation, in "impurifying" exchanges and adulterating swaps, in trades, deals, and barterings, in imports and exports, in adoptions, recyclings, cominglings, and redistributions that have prevented both nations and national literatures from being the "chthonic self-creations" politicians, ideologues, and philosophers intended them to be.[42] In this sense, nations *and* literatures have never been immutable but always made in transition and in translation, as they were changing places and undergoing changes into other idioms and possibility of being. When he told his audience that "translations do not make a literature," Kogălniceanu failed to mention that the "original creations" available to Romanian readers at the time and which they were asked to keep "making" were, to no negligible degree, either translations or shoddy imitations of French works. His own nationalist—anti-translationalist—theory is largely inspired by French thinkers. He thought that translation could be somehow cut off from other cross-cultural operations into which it was built, with which it dovetailed, and which in turn fashioned it, whereas "translation does not happen in a vacuum, but in a continuum; it is not an isolated act[;] it is part of an ongoing process of intercultural transfer, ... [it] is a highly manipulative activity that involves all kinds of stages in that process of transfer across linguistic and cultural boundaries."[43] Because such processes are both inevitable and requisite in the formation of a nation and nation-state, translation is not a hindrance but a steppingstone in any nation building. It was so when, one way or the other, appreciatively or not, it was tied into the national project, and it is so today, when translations are taking national writers into the world. The planet's longstanding translational dynamic is getting into high gear.

Not all is swell in our republic of letters, though. Between 2000 and 2006, an average of one Romanian title was translated in the United States every *other* year, which makes you wonder if such a republic really exists. Assuming it does, even when more and more writers from Romania and other less-known literatures are granted citizenship in it, the price paid sometimes in and to adoptive culture is appropriation and a kind of reception that has been called commodifying. "Adoption" or identity transfer— another kind of translation—seems to be necessary or rolled in said price, and the whole transaction speaks of a certain implicit and outmoded pressure to affix a national identity label to each writer, or to accept such a tag if you are the writer, a procedure that appears to involve a premise similar to the presumption that every person should have, publicly own up to, and somehow "abide by" one of the gender identities listed in government forms. Romanian *and* world literature authors such as Cărtărescu or Dan Lungu embody different kinds of identities and relate differently to different locations and communities. With them—and with their characters, too—a new human type comes along in Romanian fiction. This individual is Aihwa Ong's "flexible citizen,"[44] not necessarily a world traveler, and certainly not a jet-setter, but surely a twenty-first-century cosmopolite, a "translatese" speaker "born in translation," as Walkowitz says, thriving in and through it, and running our shared earth through his or her planetary imaginaries, translating it through his or her minds and vocabularies and letting himself or herself be translated by its translators and readers.[45] Writers like him or her dare us to imagine new and exciting ways to bridge the divides between original and translated works, national and transnational; to realize that *"the national language itself is,"* as Damrosch puts it, "the medium through which original and translated work circulate together to form our ineluctably international national literatures";[46] and to think what it would take to persuade publishing houses that, even though they are no longer beholden to obsolete nationalisms and do have the right to do their own planning and watch their bottom-line, they can still do a lot for the public good. I am, in closing, only restating the obvious: in what they do, in the business they conduct, an entire sociocultural *poiesis* is at stake, for neither private nor collective identities would stand a chance of fully forming without translations, other than in translation.

Notes

1 Adrian Marino, "Din istoria teoriei 'formă fără fond,'" *Anuar de lingvistică și istorie literară* 19 (1968): 185.

2 Bogdan Ștefănescu, "Why Compare? What's to Compare? The Practice of Comparative Literature in a Postcolonial/Postcommunist Context. A Response to David Damrosch," *University of Bucharest Review: Literary & Cultural Studies Series* 1, no. 1 (2011): 27.

3 David Damrosch, "Translation and National Literature," in *A Companion to Translation Studies,* ed. Sandra Bermann and Catherine Porter (Chichester: John Wiley & Sons, 2014), 347–360.

4 Damrosch, "Translation and National Literature, 351.

5 Damrosch, "Translation and National Literature, 402.

6 Constantin Dobrogeanu-Gherea, "Greutățile traducerii," in *Opere complete*, vol. 7 (Bucharest: Editura Politică, 1980), 412.

7 Dobrogeanu-Gherea, "Înrâurirea traducerilor," 399.

8 Constantin Dobrogeanu-Gherea, "Înrâurirea traducerilor," in *Opere complete*, vol. 7 (Bucharest: Editura Politică, 1980), 399–404.

9 Sean Cotter, *Literary Translation and the Idea of a Minor Romania* (Rochester, NY: University of Rochester Press, 2014), 1–2.

10 Mihail Kogălniceanu, "Introducție la *Dacia literară*," in *Despre frumos și artă. Tradițiile gândirii estetice românești*, anthology, chronology, and introductory notes by Vasile Morar, foreword by Ion Ianoși (Bucharest: Editura Minerva, 1984), 12–13.

11 Paul Cornea, "*Cerere* și *ofertă* în determinarea profilului traducerilor de la jumătatea veacului trecut (O contribuție de sociologie a literaturii la rezolvarea unei probleme de literatură comparată)," in *Probleme de literatură comparată și sociologie literară*, ed. Al. Dima et al. (Bucharest: Editura Academiei R.S.R., 1970), 109.

12 See Eugen Lovinescu, *Istoria civilizatiei române moderne*, 3 vols. (Bucharest: Editura Ancora, 1924).

13 Lawrence Venuti, *The Scandals of Translation: Towards an Ethics of Difference* (London: Routledge, 1998), 5.

14 Venuti, *The Scandals of Translation*, 5.

15 Venuti, *The Scandals of Translation*, 12.

16 Venuti, *The Scandals of Translation*, 11.

17 Lucian Blaga, "Arta de a traduce," *Secolul 20* 259–261, no. 7–9 (1982): 187–192.

18 Blaga, "Arta de a traduce," 188.

19 Blaga, "Arta de a traduce," 187.

20 Cornea, *"Cerere și ofertă,"* 115.

21 Fritz Strich, *Goethe and World Literature*, trans. C.A.M. Sym (New York: Greenwood Press, 1949), 349.

22 Hans-Joachim Schulz and Phillip H. Rhein, eds., *Comparative Literature: The Early Years; an Anthology of Essays* (Chapel Hill, NC: University of North Carolina Press, 1973), 8.

23 Hans-Joachim Schulz and Phillip H. Rhein, *Comparative Literature: The Early Years; an Anthology of Essays*, 8.

24 Sean Cotter, "The Soviet Translation: Romanian Literary Translators after World War Two," *Meta: Journal des traducteurs/Meta:Translators' Journal* 53, no. 4 (2008): 841. The process of "foreignization" goes through the following stages: "Soviet military presence (1944 to 1958), the Petru Groza government (1945 to 1947), and 'the internationalist' Gheorghe Gheorghiu-Dej period (1948 to 1965) that preceded the nationalist, 'maverick' period of better-known Nicolae Ceaușescu" (Cotter, "The Soviet Translation, 841). Also see Sean Cotter, "Romania as Europe's Translator: Translation in Constantin Noica's National Imagination," in *Contexts, Subtexts and Pretexts: Literary Translation in Eastern Europe and Russia*, vol. 89, ed. Brian James Baer (Amsterdam: John Benjamins Publishing, 2011), 79–96.

25 Cotter, "The Soviet Translation, 842.

26 This is the abbreviated title given to Nicolae Ceaușescu's absurdly verbose "Presentation Regarding the RCP Program for the Improvement of Political-Ideological Activity and for Raising the General Knowledge Level and the Socialist Education of the Masses in Order to Set Relations in Our Society on the Basis of Principles of Socialist and Communist Ethics and Equity."

27 In Cornea, *"Cerere și ofertă,"* 109–116, but I also refer the reader here to Paul Cornea's 1966 book *De la Alexandrescu la Eminescu: Aspecte, figuri, idei.*

28 Traian Herseni, *Sociologia literaturii* (Bucharest: Editura Univers, 1973).

29 Gelu Ionescu, *Orizontul traducerii* (Bucharest: Editura Institutului Cultural Român, 2004).

30 Bogdan Ghiu, *Totul trebuie tradus: Noua paradigmă (un manifest)* (Bucharest: Cartea Românească, 2015).

31 Doru Burlacu et al., *Dictionarul cronologic al romanului tradus în Romania de la origini până în 1989* (Bucharest: Editura Academiei Romane, 2005).

32 Ionescu, *Orizontul traducerii*, 5–15.

33 Franco Moretti, "Conjectures on World Literature," *New Left Review* 1 (2000): 68.

34 Archives of the University Library of Bucharest University, http://cachescan.bcub. ro/Scriitori_romani_traducatori/GHID_BIBLIOGRAFIC-v3_Literatura%20 Romana_Biblio_P867-889.pdf. Accessed February 1, 2016. Also here: *Bibliografia*

relațiilor literaturii române cu literaturile străine în periodice (1859–1918).
Volumes I-III, ed. Ioan Lupu and Cornelia Ştefănescu, foreword by Zoe Dumitrescu-Buşulenga (Bucharest: Editura Academiei RSR, 1980–1985), vol. 1: *Literatura universală. Literaturi germanice*, 1980; vol. 2: *Literaturi romanice*, 1982; vol. 3: *Literaturi clasice, slave, orientale şi alte literaturi. Ecouri ale literaturii române în literaturi străine*, 1985.

35 This is available at http://portal.unesco.org/culture/en/ev.php-URL_ID=7810&URL_DO=DO_TOPIC&URL_SECTION=201.html. Accessed January 25, 2016.

36 See the report by *The Budapest Observatory—Regional Observatory on Financing Culture in East-Central Europe for Making Literature Travel* entitled "Publishing Translations in Europe: Trends 1990–2005." Based on analysis of the Index Translationum Database, Literature Across Frontiers, Mercator Institute for Media, Languages and Culture, Aberystwyth University, Wales, UK. Report prepared by *Literature Across Frontiers* and available at http://portal.unesco.org/culture/en/files/41748/13390726483Translation_trends_1990_2005_Dec_2010.pdf/Translation%2Btrends%2B1990_2005_Dec%2B2010.pdf. Accessed January 25, 2016.

37 Simona Škrabec, in Esther Allen, ed., *To Be Translated or Not to Be, PEN/IRL Report of the International Situation of Literary Translation*, foreword by Paul Auster, afterwords by Narcis Comadira and Ngugi wa Thiong'o (Barcelona: Institut Ramon Llull, 2007), available at http://www.pen-international.org/wp-content/uploads/2011/04/Translation-report_OK-2.pdf. Accessed February 2, 2016.

38 Allen, ed., *To Be Translated or Not to Be.*

39 *The Budapest Observatory*, "Publishing Translations in Europe," 123.

40 *The Budapest Observatory*, "Publishing Translations in Europe," 126.

41 See J. Heilbron, "Towards a Sociology of Translation: Book Translation as a Cultural World-System," *European Journal of Social Theory* 2, no. 4 (1999): 429–444.

42 Damrosch, "Translation and National," 349.

43 Susan Bassnett and Harish Trivedi, "Introduction: Of Colonies, Cannibals and Vernaculars," in *Post-Colonial Translation: Theory and Practice*, ed. Susan Bassnett and Harish Trivedi (New York: Routledge, 2012), 12.

44 See Aihwa Ong, *Flexible Citizenship: The Cultural Logics of Transnationality* (Durham, NC: Duke University Press, 1999).

45 Rebecca L. Walkowitz, *Born in Translation: The Contemporary Novel in an Age of World Literature* (New York: Columbia University Press, 2015), 175–178.

46 Damrosch, "Translation and National," 359.

Bibliography

Adamovsky, Ezequiel. *Euro-Orientalism: Liberal Ideology and the Image of Russia in France*. Bern: Peter Lang, 2006.

Adams, Rachel. "The Worlding of American Studies." *American Quarterly* 53, no. 4 (December 2001): 720–732.

Agache, Catinca. *Literatura română în țările vecine*. Iași: Princeps Edit, 2005.

Alecsandri, Vasile. *Soldații noștri: ediție pentru soldați*. Bucharest: Socec & Co., 1878.

Alexander, Jeffrey C., and Piotr Sztompka, eds. *Rethinking Progress: Movements, Forces, and Ideas at the End of the 20th Century*. Boston, MA: Unwin Hyman, 1990.

Alexandrescu, Sorin. *Privind înapoi, modernitatea*. Translated by Mirela Adăscăliței, Șerban Anghelescu, Mara Chirițescu, and Ramona Jugureanu. Bucharest: Univers, 1999.

Allen, Esther, ed. *To Be Translated or Not to Be*. PEN/IRL Report of the International Situation of Literary Translation. Foreword by Paul Auster. Afterwords by Narcis Comadira and Ngugi wa Thiong'o. Barcelona: Institut Ramon Llull, 2007, http://www.pen-international.org/wp-content/uploads/2011/04/Translation-report_OK-2.pdf. Accessed January 25, 2016.

Almăjan, Slavco. *Rigoarea și fascinația extremelor*. Panciova: Libertatea, 2007.

Amador de los Ríos, José. *Historia crítica de la literatura Española*. 7 vols. Madrid: José Rodriguez, 1861–1865.

Ames, Roger T., Thomas S. Kasulis, and Wimal Dissanayake, eds. *Self as Image in Asian Theory and Practice*. Albany: State University of New York Press, 1998.

Anderson, Benedict. *Imagined Communities: Reflections on the Origin and Spread of Nationalism*. London and New York: Verso, 2006.

Anghelescu, Mircea. *Lâna de aur. Călătorii și călătoriile în literatura română*. Bucharest: Cartea Românească, 2015.

Anghelescu, Mircea. *Literatura română și Orientul*. Bucharest: Minerva, 1975.

Antohi, Sorin. "Cuvânt-înainte: Modernism și antimodernism." In *Modernism și antimodernism*, edited by Sorin Antohi, 7–8. Bucharest: Cuvântul and Muzeul Literaturii Române, 2008.

Antohi, Sorin, ed. *Modernism și antimodernism. Noi perspective interdisciplinare*. Bucharest: Cuvântul and Muzeul Literaturii Române, 2008.

Appadurai, Arjun. *Modernity at Large: Cultural Dimensions of Globalization*. Minneapolis: University of Minnesota Press, 1999.

Appiah, Kwame Anthony. "Myth, Literature, and the African World." In *Perspectives on Wole Soyinka: Freedom and Complexity*, edited by Biodun Jeyifo, 157–171. University Press of Mississippi, 2001.

Apter, Emily. *Against World Literature: On the Politics of Untranslatability*. London: Verso, 2013.

Arghezi, Tudor. "Artă pentru." *Adevărul*, 27 October 1946, p. 2.

Ascari, Maurizio. *Literature of the Global Age: A Critical Study of Transcultural Narratives*. Jefferson, NC: McFarland, 2011.

Bakhtin, Mikhail. *The Dialogic Imagination: Four Essays*. Translated by Caryl Emerson and Michael Holquist. Austin: University of Texas Press, 1981.

Balázs, Imre József. "Creating the 'New Man': Propaganda and Its Alternatives in Hungarian Literature from Romania, 1948–65." In *War of Words: Culture and the Mass Media in the Making of the Cold War in Europe*, edited by Judith Devlin and Christoph Hendrik Müller, 180–191. Dublin: University College Dublin Press, 2013.

Balázs, Imre József. "Histories of "Transylvanian Hungarian Literature." *Transylvanian Review* 4 (2004): 52–59.

Balázs, Imre József. "Hungarian Literature from Romania between the Minor and Majority Language Usage." In *Identité nationale: réalité, histoire, littérature*, ed. Ioana Bot, Adrian Tudurachi, 245–257. Bucharest: Institutul Cultural Român, 2008.

Balotă, Nicolae. *Scriitori maghiari din România*. Bucharest: Editura Kriterion, 1981.

Bartov, Omer. *Erased: Vanishing Traces of Jewish Galicia in Present-Day Ukraine*. Princeton, NJ, and Oxford: Princeton University Press, 2007.

Bassnett, Susan, and Harish Trivedi, eds. *Postcolonial Translation: Theory and Practice*. New York: Routledge, 2012.

Bauman, Zygmunt. *Culture in a Liquid Modern World*. Translated by Lydia Bauman. Cambridge, UK: Polity Press, 2011.

Bauman, Zygmunt. *The Illusion of an End*. Cambridge, UK: Polity Press, 1994.

Bauman, Zygmunt. *Intimations of Postmodernity*. London and New York: Routledge, 1992.

Beck, Ulrich. "Cosmopolitan Sociology: Outline of a Paradigm Shift." In *The Ashgate Research Companion to Cosmopolitanism*, edited by Maria Rovisco and Magdalena Nowicka, 17–32. Farnham: Ashgate, 2011.

Beebee, Thomas Oliver, ed. *German Literature as World Literature*. New York: Bloomsbury Academic, 2014.

Beebee, Thomas Oliver. "The World Literary Network of Lessing." Presentation on the "Lessing and World Literature" Panel. Modern Language Association Convention, Philadelphia, PA, January 6, 2017.

Bender, Thomas, ed. "Historians, the Nation, and the Plenitude of Narratives," in *Rethinking American History in a Global Age*. Berkeley: University of California Press, 2002.

Benga, Grațiela. *Rețeaua. Poezia românească a anilor 2000*. Timișoara: Editura Universității de Vest, 2016.

Benvenuti, Giuliana, and Remo Ceserani. *La letteratura nell'età globale*. Bologna: Il Mulino, 2012.

Bereschi, Mihaela. "Sub ochiul 'broaștei germane' prin *Niederungen* ale Hertei Müller." *Vatra* 1 (2012): 40–46.

Bhabha, Homi K. "DissemiNation: Time, Narrative, and the Margins of the modern nation." In *Nation and Narration*, edited by Homi K. Bhabha, 291–322. London and New York: Routledge, 1990.

Bhabha, Homi K. *The Location of Culture*. London and New York: Routledge, 1994.

Bhabha, Homi K. "Making Emptiness." http://anishkapoor.com/185/Making-Emptiness-by-Homi-K.-Bhabha.html. Accessed August 27, 2016.

Bhose, Amita. *Eminescu și India*. Iași: Junimea, 1978.

Bican, Bianca. "O controversă nu doar literară. Ce este *rumäniendeutsche Literatur*." *Vatra* 1 (2012): 25–26.

Blaga, Lucian. "Arta de a traduce." *Secolul 20* 259–261, no. 7–9 (1982): 187–192.

Blaga, Lucian. "Getica." In *Dreptul la memorie*, vol. IV, edited by Iordan Chimet, 23–40. Cluj-Napoca: Dacia, 1993.

Blaga, Lucian. *Spațiul mioritic*. Bucharest: Humanitas, 1994.

Blecher, Max. *Adventures in Immediate Unreality*. Translated by Michael Henry Heim. New York: Directions, 2015.

Bodor, Ádám. *Az érsek látogatása*. Budapest: Magvető, 1999.

Bodor, Ádám. *Sinistra körzet*. Budapest: Magvető, 1992.

Bodor, Ádám. *Verhovina madarai*. Budapest: Magvető, 2011.

Boldrini, Lucia. "Comparative Literature in the Twenty-First Century: A View from Europe and the UK." *Comparative Critical Studies* 3 (2006): 13–23.

Bölöni, Domokos. "Fără prispă." *Vatra* 8 (1999): 8.

Book Institute, The. "Dawid Bieńkowski." http://www.bookinstitute.pl/autorzy-detal,literatura-polska,3700,bienkowski-dawid.html

Boyers, Robert. *The Dictator's Dictation. The Politics of Novels and Novelists*. New York: Columbia University Press, 2005.

Brandt, Bettina, and Valentina Glajar, eds. *Herta Müller: Politics and Aesthetics*. Lincoln: University of Nebraska Press, 2013.

Brătianu, Gheorghe I. *An Enigma and a Miracle of History: The Romanian People*. Translated by Patricia H. Georgescu. Bucharest: Editura Enciclopedică, 1996.

Brenner, Neil. "The Space of the World: Beyond State-Centrism?" In *Immanuel Wallerstein and the Problem of the World: System, Scale, Culture*, edited by David Palumbo-Liu, Bruce Robbins, and Nirvana Tanoukhi, 101–137. Durham, NC: Duke University Press, 2011.

Breton, André. *Les vases communicantes*. Paris: Gallimard, 1970.

Brown, Garrett Wallace, and David Held, eds. *The Cosmopolitanism Reader*. Cambridge: Polity, 2010.

Budai-Deleanu, Ion. *Țiganiada sau Tabăra țiganilor*. Edited by Florea Fugaru. Timișoara: Amarcord, 1999.

Budai-Deleanu, Ion. *Tsiganiada ou Le Campement des Tsiganes*. Translated into French by Romanița Aurélia and Valeriu Rusu. Put into verse by Françoise Mingot-Tauran. Port-de-Bouc: Wallâda 5; Bucharest: Biblioteca Bucureștilor, 2003.

Budai-Deleanu, Ion. *Zingareide o l'accampamento degli zingari*. Translated into Italian by A. Senatore. Bari: Carucci, 2015.

Buden, Boris. "Ce este postcolonial în postcomunism?" Translated by Cristian Cercel. *Suplimentul de cultură* 144, no. 2 (September 2007): 8–14.

Buduca, Ioan. "Putem fi naționaliști și prin ceea ce *nu* facem." *Vatra* 8 (1999): 53.

Burlacu, Doru, et al. *Dicționarul cronologic al romanului tradus în România de la origini până în 1989*. Bucharest: Editura Academiei Romane, 2005.

Burton, Richard. *Prague: A Cultural and Literary History*. Oxford: Signal Books, 2003.

Byron, George Gordon. *Don Juan*. London: Hodgson & Co., 1823.

Călinescu, George. *Istoria literaturii române de la origini pînă în prezent*. 2nd, revised ed., prefaced and edited by Alexandru Piru. Bucharest: Minerva, 1982.

Călinescu, George. *Opere*. 3 vols. Edited by Nicolae Mecu, Ileana Mihăilă, and Daciana Vlădoiu. Foreword by Eugen Simion. Bucharest: Fundația Națională pentru Știință și Artă, 2016.

Călinescu, George. *Principii de estetică*. Bucharest: Editura Fundației pentru Literatură și Artă, 1939.

Calinescu, Matei. "On Norman Manea's *The Hooligan's Return*." In *The Writer Uprooted. Contemporary Jewish Exile Literature*, edited by Alvin H. Rosenfeld, 27–50. Bloomington: Indiana University Press, 2008.

Călinescu, Matei. *Cinci feţe ale modernităţii. Modernism, avangardă, decadenţă, kitsch, postmodernism.* 2nd ed., revised and expanded. Translated by Tatiana Pătrulescu şi Radu Ţurcanu. Iaşi: Polirom, 2005.

Camus, Albert. "L'artist et son temps." *Essais*, NRF. Gallimard: Paris, 1965.

Cândea, Virgil. "Les intellectuels du Sud-est européen au XVIIe siècle." *Revue des études sud-est européennes* 2 (1970): 181–230.

Cantemir, Dimitrie. *Istoria ieroglifică.* Edited by P.P. Panaitescu and I. Verdeş. Bucharest: Minerva, 1997.

Cantemir, Dimitrie. "The Hieroglyphic History: Glossary." Translated by Florin Bican. In *Plural 3/2000: The Seductive Discourse: Romanian Philosophical Literature.* Bucharest: The Romanian Cultural Foundation, 2000.

Cantemir, Dimitrie. "The Hieroglyphic History." Fragment translated by Alastair Ian Blyth. 2009. http://dialognaporoge.blogspot.ro/2009/04/hieroglyphic-history.html. Accessed March 31, 2017.

Cantemir, Dimitrie. *The History of the Growth and Decay of the Othman Empire.* Translated from Latin by Nicolas Tindal. London: James, John and Paul Knapton, 1734.

Cantemir, Dimitrie. *Opere complete, I. Divanul.* Edited by Virgil Cândea. Bucharest: Editura Academiei Republicii Socialiste România, 1974.

Cantemir, Dimitrie. *The Salvation of the Wise Man and the Ruin of the Sinful World.* Edited and Translated by Ioana Feodorov. Bucharest: Editura Academiei Române, 2006.

Caraion, Ion. "Criza culturii româneşti." *Jurnalul de Dimineaţă*, 17 October 1946: 2.

Cărtărescu, Mircea. "Situaţia mi se pare anormală." *Vatra*, 8 (1999): 58.

Cărtărescu, Mircea. *Visul chimeric.* Bucharest: Litera, 1992.

Cârdu, Petru. "Despre literatură, poezie şi condiţia poetului." *Secolul 21*, 7–12 (2013): 87–90.

Cârdu, Petru. "Fac ce vreau în cultura sârbă." *Secolul 21*, 7–12 (2013): 83.

Cartojan, Nicolae. *Istoria literaturii române vechi.* Revised edition and Preface by Dan Horia Mazilu. Edited by Rodica Rotaru and Andrei Rusu. Bucharest: Editura Fundaţiei Culturale Române, 1996.

Cartwright, David E. *Schopenhauer: A Biography.* New York: Cambridge University Press, 2010.

Caruth, Cathy, ed. *Trauma: Explorations in Memory.* Baltimore, MD: Johns Hopkins University Press, 1995.

Casanova, Pascale. "La guerre de l'ancienneté," In *Des littératures combatives. L' internationale des nationalismes littéraires*, edited by Pascale Casanova, 9–32. Paris: Éditions Raison d' agir, 2011.

Casanova, Pascale. *Republica Mondială a Literelor.* Translated from the French by Cristina Bîzu. Bucharest: Curtea Veche, 2007.

Casanova, Pascale. *The World Republic of Letters.* Translated by M.B. DeBevoise. Cambridge, MA: Harvard University Press, 2004.

Cerbasi, Donato. *Norman Manea e la lingua romena.* Roma: Nova Cultura, 2014.

Cernat, Paul. *Avangarda românească şi complexul periferiei. Primul „val."* Bucharest: Cartea Românească, 2007.

Cernătescu, Radu. *Literatura luciferică. O istorie ocultă a literaturii române.* Bucharest: Cartea Românească, 2010.

Cernovodeanu, Paul I., and Alexandru Duţu, eds. *Dimitrie Cantemir. Historian of South East European and Oriental civilizations: Extracts from the History of the Ottoman Empire.* Bucharest: Association internationale d'études du sud-est européen, 1973.

Cheah, Pheng. "What Is a World? On World Literature as World-Making Activity." *Daedalus* 137, no. 3 (Summer 2008): 26–38.

Cheah, Pheng. "World against Globe: Toward a Normative Conception of World Literature." *New Literary History* 45, no. 3 (Summer 2014): 303–329.

Chinezu, Ion. *Aspects of Transylvanian Hungarian Literature (1919–1929)*. Translated by Liviu Bleoca. Cluj-Napoca: Centrul de Studii Transilvane—Fundaţia Culturală Română, 1997.

Chiper, Grigore. "Proza scurtă între diletantism şi profesionalism." In *O istorie critică a literaturii din Basarabia*, edited by Mihai Cimpoi, 121–164. Chişinău: Ştiinţa - Arc, 2004.

Chitnis, Rajendra A. *Literature in Post-Communist Russia and Eastern Europe*. London and New York: Routledge, 2005.

Cimpoeşu, Petru. "Dacă aş fi scriitor maghiar în România." *Vatra* 8 (1999): 55–56.

Cimpoi, Mihai, ed. *O istorie deschisă a literaturii române din Basarabia*. 3rd revised and augmented ed. Bucharest: Editura Fundaţiei Culturale Române, 2002.

Ciobanu, Mircea V. *Deziluziile necesare*. Chişinău: Arc, 2014.

Cioran, Emil. *Istorie şi utopie*. Bucharest: Humanitas, 1992.

Cioran, Emil. *Opere*. Volume 1. Edited by Marin Diaconu. Bucharest: Academia Română, Fundaţia Naţională pentru Ştiinţă şi Artă, 2012.

Cioran, Emil. *Schimbarea la faţă a României*. Bucharest: Humanitas, 1990.

Cistelecan, Al. "O anchetă cu două feţe (despre literatura maghiară din România)." *Vatra* 8 (1999): 3.

Codrescu, Andrei. *The Hole in the Flag: A Romanian Exile's Story of Return and Revolution*. New York: W. Morrow & Co., Inc., 1991.

Codrescu, Andrei. *Selected Poetry/Poezii alese*. Translated by Ioana Ieronim. Piteşti: Paralela 45, 2000.

Compagnon, Antoine. *Antimodernii. De la Joseph de Maistre la Roland Barthes*. Translated into Romanian by Irina Mavrodin and Adina Diniţoiu. Bucharest: Art, 2008.

Compagnon, Antoine. *Les cinq paradoxes de la modernité*. Paris: Seuil, 1990.

Cooper, Thomas. "Herta Müller: Between Myths of Belonging." In *The Exile and Return of Writers from East-Central Europe. A Compendium*, edited by John Neubauer and Borbála Zsuzsanna Török, 475–496. Berlin and New York: Walter de Gruyter, 2009.

Cooppan, Vilashini. "World Literature between History and Theory." In *The Routledge Companion to World Literature*, edited by Theo D'haen, David Damrosch, and Djelal Kadir, 194–203. London and New York: Routledge, 2011.

Cordoş, Sandra. *Literatura între revoluţie şi reacţiune*. Apostrof: Cluj-Napoca, 1999.

Cornea, Paul. "*Cerere şi ofertă* în determinarea profilului traducerilor de la jumătatea veacului trecut (O contribuţie de sociologie a literaturii la rezolvarea unei probleme de literatură comparată)." In *Probleme de literatură comparată şi sociologie literară*, edited by Al. Dima et al., 109–116. Bucharest: Editura Academiei R.S.R., 1970.

Cornea, Paul. "Conceptul de «influenţă» şi paradigmele sale." In *Regula jocului. Versantul colectiv al literaturii: concepte, convenţii, modele*, 102–118. Bucharest: Editura Eminescu, 1980.

Cornea, Paul. *De la Alexandrescu la Eminescu. Aspecte, figuri, idei*. Bucharest: Editura Pentru Literatură, 1966.

Cornea, Paul. *Oamenii începutului de drum*. Bucharest: Editura Cartea Românească, 1974.

Cornea, Paul. *Originile romantismului românesc: spiritul public, dinamica ideilor şi literatura, 1780–1840*. Bucharest: Minerva, 1972.

Cornea, Paul. "Romantismul sud-est european: Schiță de caracterizare zonală." In *Regula jocului. Versantul colectiv al literaturii: concepte, convenții, modele*, 198–207. Bucharest: Editura Eminescu, 1980.

Cornis-Pope, Marcel. "On Writing Multicultural Literary History Focused on the Novel and Other Genres." *Euphorion* 27, no. 1 (2016): 28–34.

Cornis-Pope, Marcel. "The Search for a Modern, Problematizing Historical Consciousness: Romanian Historical Fiction and Family Cycles." In *History of the Literary Cultures of East-Central Europe: Junctures and Disjunctures in the 19th and 20th Centuries*, vol. I, edited by Marcel Cornis-Pope, John Neubauer, 499–504. Amsterdam and Philadelphia: John Benjamins B.V./Association Internationale de Littérature Comparée, 2004.

Cornis-Pope, Marcel. "Shifting Paradigms: East European Literatures at the Turn of the Millennium." In *Postcommunism, Postmodernism, and the Global Imagination*, edited by Christian Moraru. Introduction by Aaron Chandler, 25–45. Boulder, CO: East European Monographs/Columbia University Press, 2009.

Cornis-Pope, Marcel, and John Neubauer, eds. *History of the Literary Cultures of East-Central Europe: Junctures and Disjunctures in the 19th and 20th Centuries*. 4 vols. Amsterdam: John Benjamins, 2004–2010.

Cosma, Mihail. "Binomul cu exponentul de argint." *Punct* 2 (November 1924): 3.

Cotter, Sean. *Literary Translation and the Idea of a Minor Romania*. Rochester: University of Rochester Press, 2014.

Cotter, Sean. "Romania as Europe's Translator: Translation in Constantin Noica's National Imagination." In *Contexts, Subtexts and Pretexts: Literary Translation in Eastern Europe and Russia*, vol. 89, edited by Brian James Baer, 79–96. Amsterdam: John Benjamins Publishing, 2011.

Cotter, Sean. "The Soviet Translation: Romanian Literary Translators after World War Two." *Meta: Journal des traducteurs Meta:/Translators' Journal* 53, no. 4 (2008): 841–859.

Crețu, Bogdan. *Inorogul la porțile Orientului*. Iași: Institutul European, 2013.

Crohmălniceanu, Ovid S. *Literatura romană și expresionismul*. Bucharest: Eminescu, 1971.

Csejka, Gerhardt. "Utopia mijlocitorului." *Transilvania*, no. 12 (1983): 34–36.

Cunningham, Mary B., and Elizabeth Theokritoff. "Who Are the Orthodox Christians? A Historical Introduction." In *The Cambridge Companion to Orthodox Christian Theology*, edited by Mary B. Cunningham and Elizabeth Theokritoff, 1–20. Cambridge, UK: Cambridge University Press, 2008.

Curtius, Ernst Robert. *European Literature and the Latin Middle Ages*. Translated by Willard R. Trask. With a new introduction by Colin Burrow. Princeton, NJ: Princeton University Press, 1952.

Dainotto, R. M. "'All the Regions Do Smilingly Revolt': The Literature of Place and Region." *Critical Inquiry* 22, no. 3 (Spring 1996): 486–505.

Damrosch, David. "Translation and National Literature." In *A Companion to Translation Studies*, edited by Sandra Bermann and Catherine Porter, 347–360. Chichester: John Wiley & Sons, 2014.

Damrosch, David. *What Is World Literature?* Princeton, NJ: Princeton University Press, 2003.

David, Jérôme. *Spectres de Goethe. Les métamorphoses de la "littérature mondiale."* Paris: Les Prairies Ordinaires, 2011.

Delanty, Gerard. "The Idea of Critical Cosmopolitanism." In *Routledge Handbook of Cosmopolitanism Studies*, edited by Gerard Delanty, 38–46. Abingdon: Routledge, 2012.

Delanty, Gerard, ed. *Routledge Handbook of Cosmopolitanism Studies*. Abingdon: Routledge, 2012.

Deleuze, Gilles. *Dialogues*. Paris: Flammarion, 1996.

Deleuze, Gilles, and Claire Parnet. *Dialogues II*. Translated by Hugh Tomlinson and Barbara Habberjam. New York: Columbia University Press, 2002.

Deleuze, Gilles, and Félix Guattari. *Kafka. Pentru o literatură minoră*. Translated from the French and Afterword by Bogdan Ghiu. Bucharest: Art, 2007.

Deleuze, Gilles, and Félix Guattari. *Kafka: Toward a Minor Literature*. Translated by Dana Polan. Minnesota: University of Minnesota Press, 1986.

Deleuze, Gilles, and Félix Guattari. *Mii de platouri*. Translated from the French by Bogdan Ghiu. Bucharest: Art, 2013.

Demény, Péter. "Înseamnă a te teme." *Vatra* 8 (1999): 4.

Derrida, Jacques. *Sovereignties in Question: The Poetics of Paul Celan*. Edited by Thomas Dutoit and Outi Pasanen. New York: Fordham University Press, 2005.

D'haen, Theo. *The Routledge Concise History of World Literature*. London and New York: Routledge, 2011.

Dharwadker, Vinay. "Late Colonial and Postcolonial Selves in Hindu and Marathi Poetry." In *Self as Image in Asian Theory and Practice*, edited by Roger T. Ames, Thomas S. Kasulis, and Wimal Dissanayake, 241–259 (Albany, NY: State University of New York Press, 1998).

Dimić, Milan V. "Romantic Irony and the Southern Slavs." In *Romantic Irony*, edited by Frederick Garber, 250–266. Amsterdam: John Benjamins, 1988.

Dimock, Wai Chee. "Genre as World System: Epic and Novel on Four Continents." *Narrative* 14, no. 1 (January 2006): 85–101.

Dimock, Wai Chee. "Literature for the Planet." *PMLA* 116, no. 1 (January 2001): 173–188.

Dimock, Wai Chee. "Planetary Time and Global Translation: 'Context' in Literary Studies." *Common Knowledge* 9, no. 3 (Fall 2003): 488–507.

Dimock, Wai Chee. "Scales of Aggregation: Prenational, Subnational, Transnational." *American Literary History* 18, no. 2 (Summer 2006): 219–228.

Dimock, Wai Chee. *Through Other Continents: American Literature across Deep Time*. Princeton, NJ: Princeton University Press, 2008.

Dimock, Wai Chee, and Lawrence Buell, eds. *Shades of the Planet: American Literature as World Literature*. Princeton, NJ: Princeton University Press, 2007.

Dinu, Tudor. *Dimitrie Cantemir și Nicolae Mavrocordat, rivalități politice și literare la începutul secolului XVIII*. Bucharest: Humanitas, 2011.

Dixon, Robert, and Brigid Rooney, eds. *Scenes of Reading: Is Australian Literature a World Literature?* Melbourne: Australian Scholarly Publishing, 2014.

Dobrenko, Evgheny, and Galin Tihanov. *A History of Russian Literary Theory and Criticism: The Soviet Age and Beyond*. Pittsburg, PA: University of Pittsburg Press, 2011.

Dobrescu, Caius. *Mihai Eminescu: Imaginarul spațiului privat. Imaginarul spațiului public*. Brașov: Aula, 2004.

Dobrescu, Caius. "World Literature and Romanian Literary Criticism." *CLCWeb: Comparative Literature and Culture* 15, no. 2 (2014): http://dx.doi.org/10.7771/1481.4374.2368.

Dobrogeanu-Gherea, Constantin. *Opere complete*, vol. 7. Bucharest: Editura Politică, 1980.

Dović, Marjan, and Jón Karl Helgason. *National Poets, Cultural Saints: Canonization and Commemorative Cults of Writers in Europe.* Leiden: Brill, 2017.

Dumitru, Teodora. *Rețeaua modernității. Paul de Man—Matei Călinescu—Antoine Compagnon.* Bucharest: Editura Muzeului Literaturii Române, 2016.

Durišin, Dionýz. *Theory of Literary Comparatistics.* Translation by Jessie Kocmanová. Bratislava: Veda, 1984.

Duțu, Alexandru. *Political Models and National Identities in "Orthodox" Europe.* Bucharest: Babel, 1998.

Eaglestone, Robert. "'You Would Not Add to My Suffering If You Knew What I Have Seen': Holocaust Testimony and Contemporary African Trauma Literature." *Studies in the Novel* 40, no. 1–2 (2008): 72–85.

Eco, Umberto. *Art and Beauty in the Middle Ages.* Translated by Hugh Bredlin. New Haven and London: Yale University Press, 1986.

Eliade, Mircea. *The Fate of Romanian Culture.* Translated by Bogdan Ștefănescu. Bucharest: Athena, 1995.

Eliade, Mircea. *Fragments d'un journal.* Paris: Gallimard, 1973.

Eliade, Mircea. *The Romanians: A Concise History.* Translated by Rodica Mihaela Scafeș. Bucharest: Roza vînturilor, 1992.

Elias, Amy J., and Christian Moraru, eds. *The Planetary Turn: Relationality and Geoaesthetics in the 21st Century.* Evanston, IL: Northwestern University Press, 2015.

Emilian, Constantin I. *Anarhismul românesc.* Bucharest: Institutul de arte grafice "Bucovina"—I. E. Torouțiu, 1932.

Eminescu, Mihai. *Opere.* 17 vols. Edited by Perpessicius, Dumitru Vatamaniuc, and Petru Creția. Bucharest: Fundația Regală pentru Literatură și Artă/Editura Academiei, 1939–1999.

Eminescu, Mihai. *Poezii—Poems.* Translated by Roy MacGregor-Hastie. Cluj-Napoca: Dacia, 1980.

Eminescu, Mihai. *Poezii—Poems.* Translated by Corneliu M. Popescu. Bucharest: Editura Fundației Culturale Române, 1999.

Eminescu, Mihai. *Poezii—Poems.* Translated by Leon Levițchi and Andrei Bantaș. Bucharest: Teora, 2000.

Eminescu, Mihai. *Poezii alese—Selected Poems.* Translated by Adrian George Sahlean. Foreword by Dumitru Radu Popa. Bucharest: Univers, 2000.

Erizanu, Gheorghe. "Incomodul Druță." http://erizanu.cartier.md/incomodul-druta-6402. html. Accessed December 15, 2016.

Faifer, Florin. *Semnele lui Hermes. Memorialistica de călătorie (până la 1900) între real și imaginar.* Bucharest: Minerva, 1993.

Falaus, Anamaria. *Imagining Home: Exilic Reconstructions in Norman Manea and Andrei Codrescu's Diasporic Narratives.* Tyne: Cambridge Scholars, 2014.

Farrell, Kirby. *Posttraumatic Culture: Injury and Interpretation in the Nineties.* Baltimore, MD: Johns Hopkins University Press, 1998.

Fassel, Horst. "Două vechi istorii literare românești în limba germană: Wilhelm Rudow (1892) și Gheorghe Alexici (1906) și literatura și cultura română." *Philologica Jassyensia* 22 (2015): 147–164.

Feodorov, Ioana. "The Arabic Version of Dimitrie Cantemir's *Divan.* A Supplement to the Editor's Note." *Revue des études sud-est européennes* 1–4 (2008): 195–212.

Fine, Robert. *Cosmopolitanism.* New York: Routledge, 2007.

Focşineanu, Alina-Georgiana. *Kalīla wa Dimna şi Istoria ieroglifică. O posibilă filiaţie*. Iaşi: Ars Longa, 2015.

Foucault, Michel. "Of Other Spaces." *Diacritics* 16, no. 1 (Spring 1986): 22–27.

Foucault, Michel. *The Order of Things: An Archaeology of the Human Sciences*. London: Routledge, 2002.

Franklin, Michael J. "Orientalism: Literature and Scholarship." In *Encyclopedia of the Romantic Era, 1760–1850*, vol. 2, edited by Christopher John Murray, 832–835. New York: Fitzroy Dearborn, 2004.

Fundoianu, B. *Imagini şi cărţi din Franţa*. Bucharest: Editura Socec, 1922.

Ghiu, Bogdan. *Totul trebuie tradus: Noua paradigmă (un manifest)*. Bucharest: Cartea Românească, 2015.

Giles, Paul. *The Global Remapping of American Literature*. Princeton, NJ, and Oxford: Princeton University Press, 2011.

Gille, Klaus F. "*Germanistik* and Nation in the 19th Century." In *Nation Building and Writing Literary History*, edited by Menno Spiering, 27–57. Amsterdam and Atlanta: Rodopi, 1999.

Gillman, Susan, Kirsten Silva Greusz, and Rob Wilson. "Worlding American Studies." *Comparative American Studies* 2, no. 3 (2004): 259–270.

Glajar, Valentina. *The German Legacy in East-Central Europe*. New York: Rochester, 2004.

Goldiş, Alex. "'Alegoria naţională' în discursul identitar românesc." *Transilvania* 44, no. 12 (2015): 1–5.

Gregori, Ilina. *Ştim noi cine a fost Eminescu? Fapte, enigme, ipoteze*. Bucharest: Art, 2008.

Griffin, Roger. *Modernism and Fascism: The Sense of a Beginning under Mussolini and Hitler*. London: Palgrave Macmillan, 2007.

Griffin, Roger. "Modernitate, modernism şi fascism: O 're-sintetizare a viziunii.'" In *Modernism şi antimodernism. Noi perspective interdisciplinare*, edited by Sorin Antohi, 45–79. Bucharest: Cuvântul and Muzeul Literaturii Române, 2008.

Griffin, Roger. "Modernity, Modernism, and Fascism: A 'mazeway resynthesis.'" *Modernism/Modernity* 15, no. 1 (2008): 9–24.

Groys, Boris. "Situaţia postcomunistă." Translated by Maria Magdalena Anghelescu. *Ideea* 21 (2005). http://idea.ro/revista/?q=ro/node/40&articol=318. Accessed November 15, 2016.

Günther, Hans. "Post-Soviet Emptiness (Vladimir Makanin and Viktor Pelevin)." *Journal of Eurasian Studies* 4, no. 1 (2013): 100–106.

Haines, Brigid. "'The Unforgettable Forgotten': The Traces of Trauma in Herta Müller's *Reisende auf einem Bein*. In *German Life and Letters* 55, no. 3 (July 2002): 266–281.

Haines, Brigid, and Lyn Marven, eds. *Herta Müller*. Oxford: Oxford University Press, 2013.

Hall, Richard C. *The Balkan Wars 1912–1913: Prelude to the First World War*. London and New York: Routledge, 2000.

Harris, Wilson. *Tradition, the Writer and Society*. London and Port of Spain: New Beacon, 1973.

Harvey, David. *The Condition of Postmodernity: An Enquiry into the Origins of Cultural Change*. Oxford: Blackwell, 1990.

Hazzlit, William. "The Spirit of the Age: Or, Contemporary Portraits." In *The Complete Works of William Hazzlit*, Centenary ed., edited by P.P. Howe, 21 vols. London: Dent, 1930–1934.

Heilbron, J. "Towards a Sociology of Translation: Book Translation as a Cultural World-System." *European Journal of Social Theory* 2, no. 4 (1999): 429–444.

Heise, Ursula K. *Sense of Place and Sense of Planet: The Environmental Imagination of the Global.* New York: Oxford University Press, 2008.

Henseler, Christine. *Generation X Goes Global: Mapping a Youth Culture in Motion.* New York and Abingdon: Routledge, 2013.

Herder, Johann Gottfried von. *Philosophical Writings.* Translated and edited by Michael N. Forster. Cambridge, UK: Cambridge University Press, 2002.

Herf, Jeffrey. *Reactionary Modernism: Technology, Culture, and Politics in Weimar and the Third Reich.* Cambridge, UK: Cambridge University Press, 1984.

Herseni, Traian. *Sociologia literaturii.* Bucharest: Editura Univers. 1973.

Hitchins, Keith. *A Concise History of Romania.* Cambridge, UK: Cambridge University Press, 2014.

Hitchins, Keith. "Religion and Rumanian National Consciousness in Eighteenth-Century Transylvania." *The Slavonic and East European Review*, 57, no. 2 (1979): 214–239.

Hitchins, Keith. *Rumania: 1866–1947.* Oxford: Oxford University Press/Clarendon Press, 1994.

Hopkin, James. "On the Road to Babadag by Andrzej Stasiuk—Review. A Eulogy for the Peripheral Corners of Eastern Europe." *The Guardian*, July 8, 2011.

Hutcheon, Linda. *A Poetics of Postmodernism.* New York and London: Routledge, 1988.

Hutcheon, Linda, and Mario J. Valdés, eds. *Rethinking Literary History: A Dialogue on Theory.* Oxford: Oxford University Press, 2002.

The Hymns of the Rigveda. Translated by R.T.H. Griffith. New Delhi: Motilal Banarsidass, 1995.

Idel, Moshe. *Kabbalah and Eros.* New Haven, CT: Yale University Press, 2005.

Ioanid, Radu. *The Holocaust in Romania: The Destruction of Jews and Gypsies under the Antonescu Regime, 1940–1944.* With a foreword by Elie Wiesel. Chicago: Ivan R. Dee, 2000.

Ionesco, Eugène. *Notes et contre-notes.* Paris: Gallimard, 1998.

Ionescu, Gelu. *Orizontul traducerii.* Bucharest: Editura Institutului Cultural Român, 2004.

Ionescu, Nae. *Roza vânturilor. 1926–1933.* Edited by Mircea Eliade. Bucharest: Cultura națională, 1937.

Iorga, Nicolae. *Byzance après Byzance: continuation de "l'Histoire de la vie byzantine."* Bucharest: Institute for Byzantine Studies, 1935.

Iorga, Nicolae. *Istoria literaturii române în secolul al XVIII-lea (1688–1821)*, vol. I. Edited by Barbu Theodorescu. Bucharest: Editura Didactică și Pedagogică, 1969.

Iovănel, Mihai. *Evreul improbabil. Mihail Sebastian: o monografie ideologică.* Bucharest: Cartea Românească, 2012.

Iovănel, Mihai. *Ideologiile literaturii în postcomunismul românesc.* Bucharest: Editura Muzeului Literaturii Române, 2017.

Irr, Caren. *Toward the Geopolitical Novel: U.S. Fiction in the Twenty-First Century.* New York: Columbia University Press, 2014.

Ivașcu, George. *Istoria literaturii române*, vol. I. Bucharest: Editura Științifică, 1969.

Jagoda, Patrick. *Network Aesthetics.* Chicago: The University of Chicago Press, 2016.

Jameson, Fredric. *Fables of Aggression: Wyndham Lewis, the Modernist as Fascist.* Berkeley: University of California Press, 1979.

Jánosházy, György. "Dezavantajele de a fi scriitor și de a fi maghiar." *Vatra* 8 (1999): 10.

Jay, Paul. *Global Matters: The Transnational Turn in Literary Studies.* Ithaca, NY: Cornell University Press, 2010.

Jianu, Angela. *A Circle of Friends: Romanian Revolutionaries and Political Exile, 1840–1859.* Leiden and New York: Brill, 2011.

Kaufmann, Vincent. "L'arrière-garde vue de l'avant." In *Les arrières-gardes du XX-esiècle*, edited by William Marx, 27–34. Paris: PUF, 2004.

Kellman, Steven G. *The Translingual Imagination*. Lincoln and London: University of Nebraska Press, 2000.

Keyserling, Graf Hermann. *Das Spektrum Europas*. Heidelberg: Niels Kampmann Verlag, 1927.

Kiossev, Alexander. "Notes on Self-Colonising Cultures." In *Art and Culture in Postcommunist Europe*, edited by Bojana Pejić and David Elliott, 114–118. Stockholm: Moderna Museet, 1999.

Kogălniceanu, Mihail. "Introducție la *Dacia literară*." In *Despre frumos și artă. Tradiţiile gândirii estetice românești*. Anthology, chronology, and presentations by Vasile Morar, foreword by Ion Ianoşi. Bucharest: Editura Minerva, 1984.

Kohn, Marek. "On the Road to Babadag: Travels in the Other Europe, by Andrzej Stasiuk, trans. Michael Kandel." *The Independent*, October 23, 2011. http://www.independent. co.uk/arts-entertainment/books/reviews/on-the-road-to-babadag-travels-in-the-other-europe-by-andrzej-stasiuk-trans-michael-kandel-2327564.html. Accessed November 15, 2016.

Kristeva, Julia. *Nations without Nationalism*. Translated by Leon S. Roudiez. New York: Columbia University Press, 1993.

Kurasawa, Fuyuki. "Critical Cosmopolitanism." In *The Ashgate Research Companion to Cosmopolitanism*, edited by Maria Rovisco and Magdalena Nowicka, 279–293. Farnham: Ashgate, 2011.

LaCapra, Dominick. *History and Memory after Auschwitz*. Ithaca, NY: Cornell University Press, 1998.

LaCapra, Dominick. *Representing the Holocaust: History, Theory, Trauma*. Ithaca, NY: Cornell University Press, 1994.

LaCapra, Dominick. *Writing History, Writing Trauma*. Baltimore, MD: Johns Hopkins University Press, 2001.

Láng, Gusztáv. "Plimbare în jurul unei definiţii." In *Travers. O antologie a literaturii maghiare din Transilvania*, edited by Balázs Imre József and Ciprian Vălcan, 13–26. Iaşi: Polirom, 2002.

Láng, Zsolt. *Bestiárium Transylvaniae. A föld állatai*. Pozsony: Kalligram, 2011.

Láng, Zsolt. *Bestiárium Transylvaniae. A tűz és a víz állatai*. Pécs: Jelenkor, 2003.

Láng, Zsolt. *Bestiárium Transylvaniae. Az ég madarai*. Pécs: Jelenkor, 1997.

Lanson, Gustave. *Histoire Illustrée de la Littérature Française*. 2 vols. Paris: Hachette, 1923.

Leerssen, Joep. *National Thought in Europe: A Cultural History*. Amsterdam: Amsterdam University Press, 2006.

Leezenberg, Michiel. "The Oriental Origins of Orientalism: The Case of Dimitrie Cantemir." In *The Making of Humanities*, vol. II: *From Early Modern to Modern Disciplines*, edited by Raens Bod, Jaap Mat, and Thijs Westeijn, 243–263. Amsterdam: Amsterdam University Press, 2012.

Lefter, Ion Bogdan. "Prefață. Vântul potrivit bate tot mai tare … Despre poezia germană din România." In *Vânt potrivit pînă la tare. Tineri poeţi germani din România*, edited by Peter Motzan, 2nd ed., and preface by Ion Bogdan Lefter, 5–25. Bucharest: Editura TracusArte, 2012.

Lehmann, Sonja. "Transnational Identities in Michael Ondaatje's Fiction." In *Stranger, Migrant, Exiles. Negociating Identity in Literature*, edited by Franke Reitemeier, 281–352. Göttingen: Universitätsverlag Göttingen, 2012.

Lemny, Stefan. "Die rumänische Aufklärung. Mit einer Grundlagenbibliographie." In *Aufklärung(en) im Osten*, edited by Carsten Zelle, 36–57. Gröningen: Wallstein, 1995.

Lemny, Stefan. *Les Cantemir. L'aventure européenne d'une famille princière au XVIIIe siècle.* Paris: Editions Complexe, 2009.

Leonard, Philip. *Literature after Globalization: Textuality, Technology and the Nation-State.* London: Bloomsbury, 2013.

Lindfors, Bernth, ed. *Conversations with Chinua Achebe.* Jackson, MS: University Press of Mississippi, 1997.

Lovinescu, Eugen. *Istoria civilizatiei române moderne*, 3 vols. Bucharest: Editura Ancora, 1924.

Lovinescu, Eugen. *Istoria literaturii române contemporane*, vols. 1–6. Bucharest: Ancora, 1926–1929.

Luca, Gherasim. "Denaturarea poeziei." *Cuvântul liber* 27 (11 May 1935): 5.

Luca, Gherasim. "Femeia Domenica d'Aguistti." *Alge* 6 (1931): 1.

Luca, Gherasim, and Serge Bricianier. "Le poeme s'éclipse devant ses conséquences." *Oiseau-tempête* 2, no. 4 (Hiver, 1998): 32–33.

Luca, Gherasim. *Niciodată destul.* Bucharest: Negația negației, 1947.

Luca, Gherasim. "Poem cu un domn in frac." *Algae* 2 (April 1933): 3.

Luca, Gherasim. "Poem de dragoste." *Algae* 2 (April 1933): 2.

Luca, Gherasim. "Poemul oamenilor blânzi." *Cuvântul liber* 43 (September 1, 1933): 3.

Luca, Gherasim. "Prezența poeziei." *Cuvântul liber* 17, no. 2 (March 1935): 5.

Luca, Gherasim. *Roman de dragoste.* In *Inventatorul iubirii*, edited by Ion Pop. Cluj-Napoca: Dacia, 2003.

Luca, Gherasim. "Sfânta împărtășanie." *Meridian* 11 (1937): 9.

Luca, Gherasim. "Tragedii cari trebuie să se întâmple." *Viața imediată* (December 1933): 3.

Luca, Ioana. "Between Two Worlds: Andrei Codrescu's *The Hole in the Flag*." In *Autobiography and Mediation*, edited by Alfred Hornung, 271–286. Heidelberg: Winter, 2010.

Lungu, Eugen. *Portret de grup. O altă imagine a poeziei basarabene.* Chișinău: Cartier, 2015.

Lungu, Eugen. "Spații și oglinzi." In *O istorie critică a literaturii din Basarabia*, edited by Mihai Cimpoi, 121–164. Chișinău: Editurile Știința - Arc, 2004.

Maiorescu, Titu. *Opere.* 4 vols. Edited by Dumitru Vatamaniuc. Foreword by Eugen Simion. Bucharest: Fundația Națională pentru Știință și Artă, 2005–2006.

Manea, Norman. "Proust's Tea." *Partisan Review* 56, no. 1 (1992): 82–86.

Manea, Norman. *The Hooligan's Return.* Translated by Angela Jianu. New Haven and London: Yale University Press, 2013.

Manolescu, Nicolae. *Istoria critică a literaturii române: 5 secole de literatură.* Pitești: Paralela 45, 2008.

Mareș, Gabriel. *Literatura română în spațiul ceh sub comunism.* Foreword by Mihai Mitu. Bucharest: Editura ALL, 2012.

Marin, Irina. *Contested Frontiers in the Balkans: Habsburg and Ottoman Rivalries in Eastern Europe.* London and New York: I.B. Tauris, 2013.

Marin, Noemi. "The Rhetoric of Andrei Codrescu: A Reading in Exilic Fragmentation." In *Realms of Exile: Nomadism, Diasporas, and Eastern European Voices*, edited by Domnica Radulescu, 87–103. Lanham: Lexington Books, 2002.

Marin, Noemi. *After the Fall. Rhetoric in the Aftermath of Dissent in Post-Communist Times.* New York: Peter Lang, 2007.

Marino, Adrian. "Din istoria teoriei 'formă fără fond." *Anuar de lingvistică și istorie literară*, no. 19 (1968): 185–188.

Martin, Mircea. "Cosmopolitism: scurt istoric și implicații actuale." *Observator cultural* 851, December 8, 2016, http://www.observatorcultural.ro

Martin, Mircea. "D'un postmodernisme sans rivages et d'un postmodernisme sans postmodernité." *Euresis: Cahiers Roumains d'Études Littéraires et Culturelles*, no. 1–4 (2009): 11–22.

Martin, Mircea. "Europe from an Eastern Perspective. Some Notes on European Cultural Identity." In *From the World of Borders to the World of Horizons*, edited by Jacek Purchla, 214–230. Cracow: International Cultural Centre, 2001.

Martin, Mircea. *Exil et littérature: écrivains roumains d'expression française*. Bucharest: Univers, 1993.

Martin, Mircea. *G. Călinescu și "complexele" literaturii române*. Bucharest: Editura Albatros, 1981.

Martin, Mircea. *G. Călinescu și "complexele" literaturii române*. Pitești: Paralela 45, 2002.

Martin, Mircea. "Le communisme comme colonialism." *Euresis* 1 (2005): 3–26.

Martin, Mircea. *Radicalitate și nuanță*. Bucharest: TracusArte, 2015.

Marven, Lyn. *Body and Narrative in Contemporary Literatures in German*. Oxford: Oxford University Press, 2005.

Marx, William, ed. *Les arrières-gardes du XX-e siècle. L'autre face de la modernité esthétique*. Paris: PUF, 2004.

Matei, Alexandru. "Introducere în noua ecologie a criticii literare." *Observator cultural* 722, May 30, 2014, http://www.observatorcultural.ro

Mazilu, Dan Horia. *Barocul în literatura română din secolul al XVII-lea*. Bucharest: Editura Minerva, 1976.

Mbembe, Achille. *On the Postcolony*. Berkeley, Los Angeles, and London: University of California Press, 2001.

McDonald, Christie, and Susan Rubin Suleiman, eds. *French Global: A New Approach to Literary History*. New York: Columbia University Press, 2010.

McHale, Brian. *Postmodernist Fiction*. London: Routledge, 1991.

Mihăilescu, Dana. "Being without Pleasurable Memories: On the Predicament of the Shoah Child's Survival in 'Proust's Tea' and Kindred Narratives." *American Imago* 70, no. 1 (2013): 107–124.

Mihăilescu, Gabriel. *Universul baroc al Istoriei ieroglifice: între retorică și imaginar*. Bucharest: National Foundation for Science and Arts & The Institute of Literary History and Theory "G. Călinescu" of the Romanian Academy, 2002.

Miller, J. Hillis. "Globalization and World Literature." *Neohelicon* 38, no. 2 (December 2011): 251–265.

Milosz, Czeslaw. *Histoire de la littérature polonaise*. Fayard: Paris, 1996.

Mîndra, Mihai. "Inescapable Colonization: Norman Manea's Eternal Exile." In *Literature in Exile of East and Central Europe*, edited by Agnieszka Gutthy, 193–210. New York: Peter Lang, 2009.

Mironescu, Doris. "Uncomfortable Spaces: Language and Identity in Herta Müller's Work." *World Literature Studies* 7, no. 2 (2015): 60–70.

Miyoshi, Masao. "Turn to the Planet: Literature, Diversity, and Totality." *Comparative Literature* 53, no. 4 (Fall 2001): 283–297.

Morar, Ovidiu. *Literatura în slujba Revoluției*. Iași: Al. I Cuza University Press, 2016.

Morar, Ovidiu. *Scriitori evrei din România*. Bucharest: Hasefer, 2014.

Morar, Ovidiu. *Suprarealismul românesc*. Bucharest: TracusArte, 2014.

Moraru, Christian. "Către o nouă poetică." In *Competiția continuă. Generația 80 în texte teoretice*, edited by Gheorghe Crăciun, 25–29. Pitești: Paralela 45, 1999.

Moraru, Christian. *Cosmodernism: American Narrative, Late Globalization, and the New Cultural Imaginary*. Ann Arbor: University of Michigan Press, 2011.

Moraru, Christian. "Geocriticism and the 'Reinstating' of Literature." Essay-review on Robert T. Tally, ed. *American Book Review* 37, no. 6 (September–October 2016), 6–7.

Moraru, Christian. *Reading for the Planet: Toward a Geomethodology*. Ann Arbor: University of Michigan Press, 2015.

Moraru, Christian. "'World,' 'Globe,' 'Planet': Comparative Literature, Planetary Studies, and Cultural Debt after the Global Turn." *American Comparative Literature Association*. The 2014–2015 Report on the State of the Discipline of Comparative Literature website—Paradigms. http://stateofthediscipline.acla.org. Accessed December 8, 2014.

Moraru, Nicolae. "Criza culturii române?" *Contemporanul* (October 11, 1946): 8.

Moretti, Franco. "Conjectures on World Literature." *New Left Review* 1 (January–February 2000): 54–68.

Moretti, Franco. *Distant Reading*. New York: Verso, 2013.

Moretti, Franco. *Graphs, Maps, Trees: Abstract Models for a Literary History*. London: Verso, 2005.

Motzan, Peter, ed. *Vânt potrivit pînă la tare. Zece tineri poeți germani din România*. Bucharest: Kriterion, 1982.

Motzan, Peter, ed. *Vînt potrivit pînă la tare. Tineri poeți germani din România*. 2nd ed. Preface by Ion Bogdan Lefter. Bucharest: TracusArte, 2012.

Mușat, Carmen. "Is There a Romanian Postmodernism?" *Euresis: Cahiers Roumains d'Études Littéraires et Culturelles*, no. 1–4 (2009): 305–320.

Müller, Herta. *The Appointment*. Translated by Michael Hulse and Philip Boehm. New York: St. Martin's Press, 2002.

Müller, Herta. *The Hunger Angel*. Translated by Philip Boehm. New York: Metropolitan Books, 2012.

Müller, Péter P. "Hungarian Drama Available in English Translation." In *Babel Guide to Hungarian Literature in English Translation*, edited by Ray Keenoy, Vivienne Menkes Ivry, and Zsuzsanna Varga, 99–104. Oxford: Boulevard Books, 2001.

Muthu, Mircea. *Balcanismul literar românesc*, 3 vols. Cluj-Napoca: Dacia, 2002.

Muthu, Mircea. *Strategiile subversiunii: Incursiuni în proza postmodernă*. Bucharest: Cartea Românească, 2008.

Naum, Gellu, Paul Păun, and Virgil Teodorescu. *Critica mizeriei*. Bucharest: Colecția Suprarealistă, 1945.

Neef, Sonja A.J. *Der babylonische Planet. Kultur, Übersetzung, Dekonstruktion under den Bedingungen der Globalisierung*. Heidelberg, Germany: Universitätsverlag, 2013.

Neubauer, John. "Introduction" to "Part IV. Literary Histories: Itineraries of National Self-Images." In *History of the Literary Cultures of East-Central Europe: Junctures and Disjunctures in the 19th and 20th Centuries*, vol. III, edited by Marcel Cornis-Pope and John Neubauer, 345–354. Amsterdam: John Benjamins, 2007.

Neubauer, John, and Borbála Zsuzsanna Török, eds. *The Exile and Return of Writers from East-Central Europe. A Compendium*. Berlin and New York: Walter de Gruyter, 2009.

Neuberger, Benyamin. "The African Concept of Balkanisation." *The Journal of Modern African Studies* 14, no. 3 (1976): 523–529.

Nisard, Désiré. *Histoire de la littérature française* 3 vols. 2nd ed. Paris: Firmin Didot, 1854.

Nixon, Rob. "Of Balkans and Bantustans: 'Ethnic Cleansing' and the Crisis in National Legitimation." *Transition* 60 (1993): 4–26.

Noica, Constantin. *Istoricitate și modernitate.* Bucharest: Capricorn, 1990.

Obecny, Edmund. "Translator's Note [to Juliusz Słowacki's *In the Tomb of Agamemnon*]." *Free Poland*, no. 4 (April 1, 1918): 208.

Oișteanu, Andrei. *Inventing the Jew: Antisemitic Stereotypes in Romanian and Other Central-East European Cultures.* Translated from Romanian by Mirela Adăscăliței. Lincoln and London: University of Nebraska Press, 2009.

Olson, Kirby. *Andrei Codrescu and the Myth of America.* Jefferson, NC: McFarland, 2005.

Omăt, Gabriela, ed. *Modernismul literar românesc în date (1880–2000) și texte (1880–1949)*, vols. 1–2. Bucharest: Institutul Cultural Român, 2010.

Ong, Aihwa. *Flexible Citizenship: The Cultural Logics of Transnationality.* Durham, NC: Duke University Press, 1999.

Ornea, Zigu. *Tradiționalism și modernitate în deceniul al treilea.* Bucharest: Editura Minerva, 1980.

Papadima, Ovidiu. *Ipostaze ale iluminismului românesc.* Bucharest: Editura Minerva, 1975.

Papastergiadis, Nikos. "Spatial Aesthetics: Rethinking the Contemporary." In *Antinomies of Art and Culture: Modernity, Postmodernity, Contemporaneity*, edited by Terry Smith, Okwui Enwezor, Nancy Condee, 363–381. Durham, NC: Duke University Press, 2009.

Papu, Edgar. *Poezia lui Eminescu.* Iași: Junimea, 1979.

Patapievici, Horia-Roman. *Cerul văzut prin lentilă.* Bucharest: Nemira, 1995.

Perloff, Marjorie. *Unoriginal Genius: Poetry by Other Means in the New Century.* Chicago: University of Chicago Press, 2010.

Peters, John Durham. "Exile, Nomadism, and Diaspora. The Stakes of Mobility in the Western Canon." In *Visual Culture. Critical Concepts in Media and Cultural Studies*, edited by Joanne Morra and Marquard Smith, 141–160. London and New York, Routledge, 2006.

Petrescu, Ioana Em. *Ion Budai-Deleanu și epopeea comică.* Cluj-Napoca: Dacia, 1974.

Petreu, Marta. *De la Junimea la Noica. Studii de cultură românească.* Iași: Polirom, 2011.

Pippidi, Andrei. *Tradiția politică bizantină în Principatele Române în secolele XVI–XVIII.* Bucharest: Publishing House of the Academy of the Socialist Republic of Romania, 1983.

Pogge, Thomas. "Cosmopolitanism and Sovereignty." In *The Cosmopolitanism Reader*, edited by Garrett Wallace Brown and David Held, 114–133. Cambridge: Polity, 2010.

Pop, Ion. *Din avangardă spre ariergardă.* Bucharest: Vinea, 2010.

Popovici, Dimitrie. *La Littérature roumaine à l'époque des Lumières.* Sibiu: Center for Transylvanian Studies and Research, 1945.

Pradeau, Christophe, and Tiphaine Samoyault, eds. *Où est la littérature mondiale?* Saint-Denis: Presses Universitaires de Vincennes, 2005.

Prickett, Stephen, and Simon Haines, eds. *European Romanticism: A Reader.* London: Bloomsbury, 2014.

Ramazani, Jahan. "Poetry, Modernity, and Globalization." In *The Oxford Handbook of Global Modernisms*, edited by Mark Wollaeger and Matt Eatough, 288–309. New York: Oxford University Press, 2012.

Ramazani, Jahan. *A Transnational Poetics.* Chicago: The University of Chicago Press, 2009.

Rothberg, Michael. "Decolonizing Trauma Studies: A Response." *Studies in the Novel* 40, no. 1–2 (2008): 224–234.

Rothman, E. Natalie. *Brokering Empire: Trans-Imperial Subjects between Venice and Istanbul*. Ithaca, NY and London: Cornell University Press, 2015.

Rushdie, Salman. *Imaginary Homelands. Essays and Criticism 1981–1991*. London: Granta, 1991.

Sanders, Karin. "A Man of the World: Hans Christian Andersen." In *Danish Literature as World Literature*, edited by Dan Ringgaard and Mads Rosendahl Thomsen, 91–114. New York: Bloomsbury Academic, 2017.

Sandqvist, Tom. *Dada East: The Romanians of Cabaret Voltaire*. Boston, MA: MIT Press, 2006.

Sánta-Jakabházi, Réka. "Cenzura literară și consecințele ei pentru lirica lui Franz Hodjak." *Vatra*, 1 (2012): 21.

Sassen, Saskia. "Neither Global Nor National: Novel Assemblages of Territory, Authority and Rights." *Ethics & Global Politics* 1, no. 1–2 (2008): 61–79.

Scarpetta, Guy. *Elogiu cosmopolitismului*. Translated into Romanian by Petruța Spânu. Iași: Polirom, 1997.

Schopenhauer, Arthur. *The World as Will and Representation*. 2 vols. Translated by E.F.J. Payne. New York: Dover Publications, 1969.

Schulz, Hans-Joachim, and Phillip H. Rhein, eds. *Comparative Literature: The Early Years; an Anthology of Essays*. No. 55. Chapel Hill: University of North Carolina Press, 1973.

Schürer, Norbert. *Midnight's Children: A Reader's Guide*. New York: Continuum, 2004.

Scridon, Gavril. *Istoria literaturii maghiare din România*. Cluj Napoca: Promedia Plus, 1996.

Sebald, W.G. *Austerlitz*. Translated by Anthea Bell. New York: Random House, 2011.

Segel, Harold B. *The Columbia Literary History of Eastern Europe since 1945*. New York: Columbia University Press, 2008.

Seyhan, Azade. *Writing Outside the Nation*. Princeton, NY: Princeton University Press, 2001.

Shafir, Michael. *Romania: Politics, Economics and Society: Political Stagnation and Simulated Change*. London: Frances Pinter & Boulder: Lynne, 1985.

Shklovsky, Viktor. "Art as Technique." In *Russian Formalist Criticism: Four Essays*, edited by Lee T. Lemon and Marion J. Reiss, 3–24. Lincoln: University of Nebraska Press, 1965.

Shopin, Pavlo. "Unpacking the Suitcases: Autofiction and Metaphor in Herta Müller's *Atemschaukel*." *Seminar: A Journal of Germanic Studies* 50, no. 2 (May 2014): 197–215.

Soja, Edward W. *Thirdspace: Journeys to Los Angeles and Other Real-and-Imagined Places*. Cambridge: Blackwell, 1996.

Song, Min Hyoung. "Becoming Planetary." *American Literary History* 23, no. 3 (2011): 555–573.

Spiridon, Monica. "On the Borders of Mighty Empires: Bucharest, City of Merging Paradigms." In *History of the Literary Cultures of East-Central Europe: Junctures and Disjunctures in the 19th and 20th Centuries*, vol. 2, edited by Marcel Cornis-Pope and John Neubauer, 93–104. Amsterdam: John Benjamins, 2006.

Spivak, Gayatri Chakravorty. *An Aesthetic Education in the Era of Globalization*. Cambridge, MA: Harvard University Press, 2011.

Spivak, Gayatri Chakravorty. *Death of a Discipline*. New York: Columbia University Press, 2003.

Spivak, Gayatri Chakravorty. "World Systems and the Creole." *Narrative* 14, no. 1 (January 2006): 102–112.

Spyra, Ania. "Between Theory and Reality: Cosmopolitanism of Nodal Cities in Paweł Huelle's *Castorp*." *Comparative Literature* 63, no. 4 (2012): 286–299.

Starr, Deborah. *Remembering Cosmopolitan Egypt: Literature, Culture, and Empire.* Oxford and New York: Routledge, 2009.

Ştefănescu, Bogdan. "Constantin Noica." *The Literary Encyclopedia.* First published 13 January 2014, http://www.litencyc.com/php/speople.php?rec=true&UID=13291. Accessed November 15, 2016.

Ştefănescu, Bogdan. "Filling in the Historical Blanks: A Tropology of the Void in Postcommunist and Postcolonial Reconstructions of Identity." In *Postcolonial Europe? Essays on Post-Communist Literatures and Cultures,* edited by Dobrota Pucherova and Robert Gafrik, 107–120. Amsterdam: Brill/Rodopi, 2015.

Ştefănescu, Bogdan. "Marginal Romanian Meets European Model: Noica and Modernity as Colonial Trauma." In *European Integration/National Identity; Plurilingualism/ Multiculturality—Romanian Language and Culture: Evaluation, Perspectives,* edited by Ofelia Ichim, 289–302. Roma: Aracne Editrice, 2014.

Ştefănescu, Bogdan. *Postcommunism/Postcolonialism: Siblings of Subalternity.* Bucharest: Bucharest University Press, 2013.

Ştefănescu, Bogdan. "Voices of the Void: Andrei Codrescu's Tropical Rediscovery of Romanian Culture in *The Hole in the Flag.*" *University of Bucharest Review* X, no. 2 (2008): 11–21.

Ştefănescu, Bogdan. "Why Compare? What's to Compare? The Practice of Comparative Literature in a Postcolonial/Postcommunist Context. A Response to David Damrosch." *University of Bucharest Review: Literary & Cultural Studies Series* 1, no. 1 (2011): 25–37.

Steiner, George. *The Poetry of Thought: From Hellenism to Celan.* New York: New Directions, 2011.

Stoiciu, Liviu Ioan. "Există un ferment al autodistrugerii la scriitorii maghiari din România." *Vatra* 8 (1999): 59–60.

Strich, Fritz. *Goethe and World Literature.* Translated by C.A.M. Sym. Greenwood Press, 1949.

Strugaru, Oana Elena. "Globalization and Literature: What Is Left of Literary History?" *Euresis* (2013): 140–146.

Strugaru, Oana. "Choosing to Be a Stranger. Romanian Intelectuals in Exile." In *Negociating Identities: Constructed Selves and Others,* edited by Helen Vella Bonavita, 111–134. Amsterdam: Rodopi, 2011.

Strugaru, Oana. *Exilul ca mod de existenţă. Andrei Codrescu în spaţiul textual al dezrădăcinării.* Bucharest: Editura Muzeul Literaturii Române, 2013.

Styvendale, Nancy Van. "The Trans/Historicity of Trauma in Jeannette Armstrong's *Slash* and Sherman Alexie's *Indian Killer.*" *Studies in the Novel* 40, no. 1–2 (2008): 203–223.

Suciu, Adrian. "Prăpastia care ne desparte." *Vatra,* 8 (1999): 55–56.

Sztompka, Piotr. "Cultural Trauma: The Other Face of Social Change." *European Journal of Social Theory* 3, no. 4 (2000): 449–466.

Tally, Robert T., Jr. "World Literature and Its Discontents." *English Language and Literature* 60, no. 3 (2014): 401–419.

Tănase, Stelian. *Avangarda românească în arhivele Siguranţei.* Iaşi: Polirom, 2008.

Ţăranu, Dan. *Toposul marginalităţii în romanul romanesc: Dimensiuni ale marginalităţii.* Bucharest: Muzeul Literaturii Romane, 2013.

Teodorescu, Jeanine. "Norman Manea: 'I Am Not a Writer of the Holocaust.'" In *Local History, Transnational Memory in the Romanian Holocaust,* edited by Valentina Glajar and Jeanine Teodorescu, 175–194. New York: MacMillan, 2011.

Terian, Andrei. *Critica de export. Teorii, contexte, ideologii.* Bucharest: Muzeul Literaturii Române, 2013.

Terian, Andrei. *G. Călinescu. A cincea esență*. Bucharest: Cartea Românească, 2009.

Terian, Andrei. "National Literature, World Literatures, and Universality in Romanian Cultural Criticism, 1867–1947." *CLCWeb: Comparative Literature and Culture* 15, no. 5 (2013), http://-dx.doi.org/10.7771/1481-4374.2344.

Terian, Andrei. "Romanian Literature for the World: A Matter of Property." *World Literature Studies* 7, no. 2 (2015): 3–14.

Teverson, Andrew. "Salman Rushdie's Post-Nationalist Fairy-Tales." In *Salman Rushdie*, edited by Robert Eagleston and Martin McQuillan, 72–138. London, New Delhi, New York and Sidney: Bloomsbury, 2013.

Thomsen, Mads Rosendahl. *Mapping World Literature: International Canonization and Transnational Literature*. London: Continuum, 2010.

Todorova, Maria. "The Trap of Backwardness: Modernity, Temporality, and the Study of Eastern European Nationalism." *Slavic Review* 64, no. 1 (Spring 2005): 140–164.

Toma, Iulian. *Gherasim Luca ou l' intransigeante passion d' être*. Paris: Honoré Champion, 2012.

Tomlinson, John. *Globalizare și cultură*. Translated by Cristina Gyurcsik. Timișoara: Amarcord, 2002.

Trencsényi, Balázs, and Michal Kopeček Russo, eds. *Discourses of Collective Identity in Central and Southeast Europe (1770–1945). Texts and Commentaries. Volume I: Late Enlightenment—Emergence of the Modern "National Idea."* Budapest: Central European University Press, 2006.

Trencsényi, Balázs, and Michal Kopeček Russo, eds. *Discourses of Collective Identity in Central and Southeast Europe (1770–1945). Texts and Commentaries. Volume II: National Romanticism—The Formation of National Movements*. Budapest and New York: Central European University Press, 2014.

Trevor-Roper, Hugh. *History and the Enlightenment*, 54–70. New Haven, CT: Yale University Press, 2010.

Trousdale, Rachel. *Nabokov, Rushdie, and the Transnational Imagination: Novels of Exile and Alternate Worlds*. New York: Palgrave Macmillan, 2010.

Tsu, Jing. "World Literature and National Literature(s)." In *The Routledge Companion to World Literature*, edited by Theo D'haen, David Damrosch, and Djelal Kadir, 158–168. London and New York: Routledge, 2011.

Tuan, Yi-Fu. *Space and Place: The Perspective of Experience*. Minneapolis and London: University of Minnesota Press, 1977.

Tuan, Yi-Fu. *Cosmos and Hearth: A Cosmopolite's Viewpoint*. Minneapolis: University of Minnesota Press, 1996.

Turcuș, Claudiu. *Norman Manea: Aesthetics as East Ethics*. New York: Peter Lang, 2016.

Tzara, Tristan. "Furtuna și cântecul dezertorului." *Chemarea* no. 2 (October 11, 1915): 26–27.

Tzara, Tristan. "Vacanță în provincie." *Chemarea* no. 1 (October 4, 1915): 12.

Ungureanu, Cornel. *Geografia literaturii române, azi*, vol. 1 and 4. Pitești: Paralela 45, 2003, 2005.

Ungureanu, Cornel. *Mitteleuropa periferiilor*. Iași: Polirom, 2002.

Valdés, Mario J., and Linda Hutcheon. "Rethinking Literary History—Comparatively." American Council of Learned Societies, occasional paper no. 27, 1995.

Vancu, Radu. *Eminescu. Trei Eseuri*. Sibiu and Cluj-Napoca: InfoArtMedia-Argonaut, 2011.

Venuti, Lawrence. *The Scandals of Translation: Towards an Ethics of Difference*. London: Routledge, 1998.

Verdery, Katherine. *National Ideology under Socialism: Identity and Cultural Politics in Ceaușescu's Romania*. Berkeley, CA, Los Angeles, and Oxford: University of California Press, 1991.

Verona, Roxana M. "The Intercultural Corridor of the 'Other' Danube." In *History of the Literary Cultures of East-Central Europe: Junctures and Disjunctures in the 19th and 20th Centuries*, vol. 2. edited by Marcel Cornis-Pope and John Neubauer, 232–243. Amsterdam, Philadelphia: John Benjamins B.V./Association Internationale de Littérature Comparée, 2004.

Vianu, Tudor. "Asupra caracterelor specifice ale literaturii române." *Studii de literatură română*, 545–559. Bucharest: Editura Didactică și Pedagogică, 1965.

Vianu, Tudor. "Goethe și ideea de literatură universală." *Studii de literatură universală și comparată*. Bucharest: Editura Academiei Republicii Populare Române, 1963.

Vinea, Ion. "Modernism și tradiție." *Cuvântul liber* 1 (1924): 101–102.

Vinea, Ion. "Pentru contimporani." *Contimporanul* 34 (1923): 1.

Voisine-Jechova, Hana. *Histoire de la littérature tchèque*. Fayard: Paris, 2001.

Volovici, Leon. *Nationalist Ideology and Antisemitism: The Case of Romanian Intellectuals in the 1930s*. Oxford: Pergamon Press, 1991.

Vulcănescu, Mircea. *Tânăra generație*. Edited by Marin Diaconu. Bucharest: Editura Compania, 2004.

Walkowitz, Rebecca L. *Born Translated: The Contemporary Novel in an Age of World Literature*. New York: Columbia University Press, 2015.

Walkowitz, Rebecca L. "The Location of Literature: The Transnational Book and the Migrant Writer." *Contemporary Literature* 47, no. 4 (2006): 527–545.

Wei, Su. *The School and the Hospital: On the Logic of Socialist Realism in Chinese Literature in the Second Half of a Modern Century. A Critical Survey*. Edited by Pang-yuan Chi and David Der-wei Wang. Bloomington: Indiana University Press, 2000.

Werner, Michael, and Bénédicte Zimmermann. "Beyond Comparison: *Histoire croisée* and the Challenge of Reflexivity." *History and Theory* 45 (February 2006): 30–50.

Westphal, Bertrand. *Geocriticism: Real and Fictional Spaces*. Translated by Robert T. Tally, Jr. New York: Palgrave Macmillan, 2011.

White, Hayden. "Modernism și primitivism." In *Modernism și antimodernism. Noi perspective interdisciplinare*, edited by Sorin Antohi, 17–32. Bucharest: Cuvântul and Muzeul Literaturii Române, 2008.

Wittgenstein, Ludwig. *Tractatus logico-philosophicus*. Translated by Mircea Dumitriu and Mircea Flonta. Bucharest: Humanitas, 2012.

Wolff, Larry. *Inventing Eastern Europe: The Map of Civilization on the Mind of the Enlightenment*. Stanford, CA: Stanford University Press, 1994.

Wollaeger, Mark, and Matt Eatough. *The Oxford Handbook of Global Modernisms*. New York: Oxford University Press, 2012.

Zarycki, Tomasz. *Ideologies of Eastness in Central and Eastern Europe*. Abingdon and New York: Routledge, 2014.

Zielinski, Anthony J. *Poland in the World of Democracy*. St. Louis: Laclede, 1918.

Zivancevic, Nina. *With Sarane Alexandrian in Paris*, http://nyartsmagazine-.com/67/nina.htm. Accessed December 31, 2002.

Žižek, Slavoj. *Tarrying with the Negative: Kant, Hegel, and the Critique of Ideology*. Durham, NC: Duke University Press, 1993.

Zub, Al., ed. *La Revolution française et les Roumains: impact, images, interprétations: études à l'occasion du bicentenaire*. Iași: Al. I. Cuza University Press, 1989.

Index

Lightning Source UK Ltd.
Milton Keynes UK
UKHW020106030221
378152UK00009B/102

9 781501 354649